PRINCIPLES OF INTERACTIVE COMPUTER GRAPHICS

WILLIAM M. NEWMAN

Professor of Information and Computer Science,
University of California at Irvine

ROBERT F. SPROULL

Stanford University

McGRAW-HILL BOOK COMPANY

New York   St. Louis   San Francisco   Düsseldorf   Johannesburg
Kuala Lumpur   London   Mexico   Montreal   New Delhi   Panama
Rio de Janeiro   Singapore   Sydney   Toronto

Library of Congress Cataloging in Publication Data

Newman, William M   1939–
    Principles of interactive computer graphics.

    (McGraw-Hill computer science series)
    Bibliography: p.
    1. Computer graphics. 2. Computer input-output
equipment. 3. Information display systems. 4. Programming (Electronic computers) I. Sproull, Robert F.,
joint author. II. Title. III. Title. Interactive
computer graphics.
T385.N48   001.55   72-5574
ISBN 0–07–046337–9

PRINCIPLES OF INTERACTIVE COMPUTER GRAPHICS

23456789–MAMM–76543

This book was set in IBM Baskerville. The editor
was Richard F. Dojny; and the production supervisors
were Alan Chapman and Sally Ellyson.

PRINCIPLES OF INTERACTIVE COMPUTER GRAPHICS

McGraw-Hill computer science series

RICHARD W. HAMMING
Bell Telephone Laboratories

EDWARD A. FEIGENBAUM
Stanford University

CONTENTS

To Ivan E. Sutherland

PREFACE

Computer graphics is one of the most extensive branches of computer technology that has until now been without a proper text. Why this is so is not clear; there has certainly been a serious need for such a text for some years. We present this book as a belated attempt to supply this need.

The lack of a text has affected many who work and study in this area. It has made it difficult for instructors to teach the subject to students; it has impeded the efforts of graduate students and research workers; and it has been a particular problem to graphics system designers in industry. We have not aimed this book at any specific one of these three groups: instead we have attempted to provide a book that, with judicious reading, will suit anyone who wishes to learn about computer graphics.

The reader will see from the table of contents that the book consists of an introduction and five parts. The introduction we recommend to anyone to whom the subject is a new one, or who is uncertain where to begin reading. In this introduction we try to explain what interactive computer graphics is, what problems it presents, and briefly how they can be solved.

The remaining five parts effectively discuss display hardware, graphic output, graphic input, three-dimensional graphics and graphics systems. Each of these is a nicely cohesive topic, somewhat dependent on what precedes it but in a manner that permits some choice in the order of reading. More important, however, the five parts deal with successively more advanced and less well-established topics, and this hopefully makes the book suitable for teaching computer graphics at a variety of levels.

A short undergraduate course may for example be planned around the introduction and Parts I and II. This course might typically run for eight weeks. It will not cover graphical input, but will on the other hand require the use of only the very simplest graphics equipment for exercises. Students of such a course should be conversant with high-level and assembly-level programming, and will benefit from some knowledge of data structures. They should also have some experience of using trigonometry and matrices.

A longer undergraduate course may be formed by adding Part III. This course should also involve the student in a certain amount of direct use of the display. It will leave him competent in all the basic techniques of computer graphics.

A graduate course can cover all five parts in two quarters or a semester. The last two parts are particularly relevant to graduate study, for they cover areas in which there is still research to be done.

Exercises have been included at the end of every chapter of Parts I to IV. They are designed to test the reader's comprehension of the text and to lead him into more detailed investigation of selected topics. In some cases these investigations will involve the use of simple graphics equipment. The exercises are arranged in approximate order of ascending difficulty.

We have tried throughout the book to avoid excessively detailed descriptions of any of the techniques mentioned. In some cases we have referred the reader to a work listed in the bibliography, but some of the techniques we wished to cover have never been adequately documented: specific examples are the Warnock hidden-line algorithm and the Ledeen character recognizer. We have therefore added appendices containing detailed descriptions of these techniques for those who wish to implement them or develop them further.

The many programming examples that appear in the text presented problems to us, for there was no one language that could serve to illustrate every example. We eventually decided to try to standardize on two languages, one a simple assembly language and the other the language SAIL, an Algol-like language developed for general purposes including system building. The essential features of each language are described in the appendices.

This book has, like many texts, grown out of notes prepared for use in class, and we would like to acknowledge the contributions made to the book's development by students of various courses — AM252 at Harvard, CS200 and CS551 at the University of Utah, and ICS180 at

the University of California, Irvine. We would also like to thank the many people who have read the text and offered helpful comments, including R. S. Barton, E. Feigenbaum, R. M. Baecker, and D. Romein. Many thanks are also due Lee Sproull for her help with the manuscript. We are grateful to M. I. Bernstein for the information he provided on character recognizers. Karmen Curtis gave invaluable service in typing the original manuscript, of which the final version was prepared only by means of hours of editing at terminals to the PDP-10: we are most grateful to our respective computer facilities for making this service available. We would also like to thank the many people who assisted us in preparing typesetting tapes directly from our PDP-10 files.

Our greatest debt, however, is to Ivan Sutherland. Ivan was not only the original source of inspiration for the book but the strongest voice of encouragement during the long period during which the book progressed towards completion. He has spent so much time discussing the manuscript with us, and has provided so much in the way of concepts, simplifications and written notes, that he has been like a third author. We owe him a deep debt of gratitude for all this, and indeed for much of our education in computer graphics. We hope we can pass on a little of what we have learned from him by means of this book.

Acknowledgments for illustrations

We wish to thank the following who provided illustrations for inclusion in this book: Dr R. J. Feldmann, National Institutes of Health, Figure I-1; University of Utah, Computer Science, Figures I-3, I-6, 14-2, 14-40, 14-45; Applicon Inc., Figure I-4; Dr A. P. Armit, British Aircraft Corp. and Cambridge University C.A.D. Project, Figure I-4; Princeton Electronic Products Inc., Figure 1-19; Owens Illinois Inc., Figures 1-20 and 1-21; AFIPS Press, Figure 4-9. The computer-generated objects shown in Figures I-3, I-6, 14-2, 14-40 and 14-45 were created by M. Archuleta, H. Gouraud, I. E. Sutherland, J. E. Warnock and G. S. Watkins, Computer Science, University of Utah, during research supported by the Advanced Research Projects Agency of the Department of Defense, monitored by Rome ADC, GAFB, New York under contract F30602-70-C-0300.

INTRODUCTION

The graphical display is without a doubt one of the most fascinating devices that computer technology has produced. To see one in action for the first time can be an unforgettable experience; it is difficult to come away without a greatly increased awareness of the computer's potentialities. The graphical display increases these potentialities in several different ways. We can use the display as an exceptionally fast and versatile computer output device; or we can equip the computer with a graphical input device such as a graphic tablet, and use the system as a drafting device with unique properties.

Figures I-1 to I-9 illustrate a few of the large number of applications to which we can put the graphical display. We can display pictures of molecules (Figure I-1) and by rotating them gain insight into their structure. We can design buildings (Figure I-2) and see them displayed in true perspective (Figure I-3). A variety of other objects can be designed with the aid of the display; these include integrated circuits (Figure I-4), aircraft (Figures I-5 and I-6), even political boundaries (Figure I-7). The speed of the display in responding to signals from the computer, coupled with man's quickness of visual perception, makes the display capable of giving us insight into high-speed processes such as the inner workings of the computer during execution of a program (Figure I-8). We can use graphical input devices in novel ways: for example, we can program the computer to recognize input messages written by the user with the aid of a tablet (Figure I-9). These are just a few examples; graphical displays have been used in many other areas of design, simulation, information retrieval and control.

The technology of using a computer-driven display in this way is

FIGURE I-1

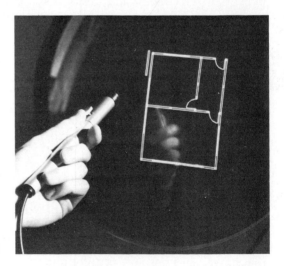

FIGURE I-2

called *interactive computer graphics*. The word *interactive* distinguishes this subject from other branches of computer graphics in which digital plotters, film recorders and other similiar devices are used to generate pictures. These 'hard copy' devices are extremely useful, both in their own right and as adjuncts to a display. However, they generate pictures

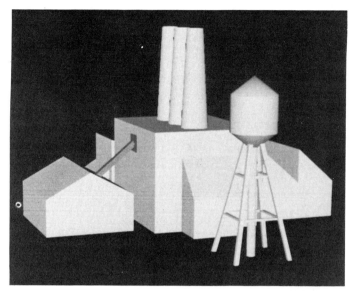

FIGURE I-3

so slowly that they cannot really be used to conduct a 'conversation' between the user and the computer. Equipped with a display, on the other hand, the computer can respond to the user as fast as he can respond to it. User and computer can *interact* with each other in a fashion that is particularly effective compared with other methods of using a computer. Many applications, such as the molecule display program mentioned above, cannot function without this facility for rapid interaction.

It is difficult to define the scope of the term *interactive computer graphics*. The problem is that there are extremely few topics that belong exclusively to computer graphics. Most of the topics that we discuss under the heading of interactive graphics are in fact applications of other branches of computer technology, such as information structures, operating systems, programming languages and hardware design. If we were to disqualify these topics, interactive graphics would be a very exclusive subject. On the other hand, if we let these topics in, we are in danger of letting in all sorts of other subjects that have only a passing relevance to interactive graphics — subjects like artificial intelligence, computer-aided design, information retrieval. These latter subjects are really areas in which interactive graphics can be applied; we must be careful to distinguish them from topics that can be applied to computer graphics.

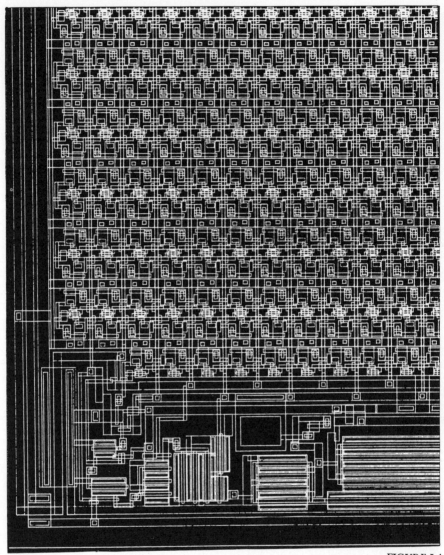

FIGURE I-4

In this book, *interactive computer graphics* is interpreted as including all branches of computer technology that contribute directly to the design of interactive graphics systems, i.e. of systems that allow us to interact with a computer process by means of pictures. Because of the scarcity of problems that belong exclusively to computer graphics, this might appear to be a rather narrow and uninteresting field. In fact it is

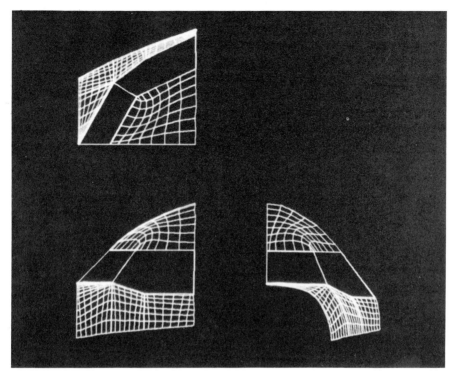

FIGURE I-5

altogether fascinating, partly because of the engaging quality of computer-generated pictures, and partly because the design of an interactive graphics system is an unusually challenging task, that brings us in contact with many other sciences and technologies, and that tests our ability to apply them in the proper fashion. The next few pages briefly describe some of the issues involved in interactive computer graphics.

HOW PICTURES ARE PRODUCED

Interactive graphics started as an attempt to use the cathode ray tube as a computer output device. It was inevitable that this should happen, for cathode ray tubes were always to be found around even the earliest digital computer installations, where they were employed both in the oscilloscopes used for testing circuits and, in the case of the Williams Tube [308], for actual storage of information. The first machine with which the CRT was used as an output device appears to have been

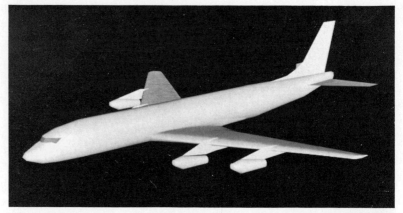

FIGURE I-6

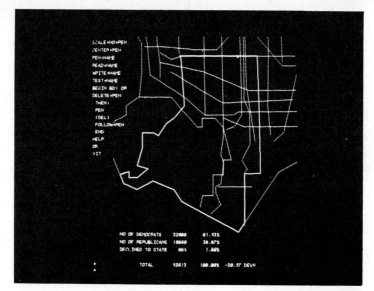

FIGURE I-7

Whirlwind I [85], which became operational in 1950. Ever since then, the CRT has maintained its place as virtually the only device suitable for generating graphical output at high speeds. The various properties and limitations of the CRT have had a profound effect on the development of computer graphics.

The principal failing of the CRT is its inability to maintain a picture on the screen. If a line is displayed once, it quickly fades out of sight.

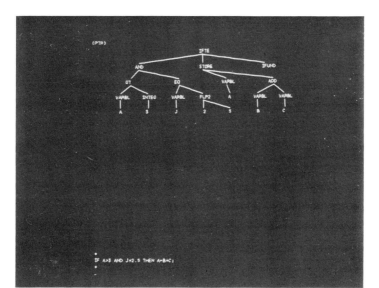

FIGURE I-8

FIGURE I-9

This problem can be remedied by *refreshing* the CRT from data stored in the computer's memory. However, this technique places a premium on the speed at which lines can be drawn, since the display will *flicker* if too many lines are being displayed. Recently, special direct-view *storage tubes* have been invented that avoid the need for refreshing; they are in some respects less versatile than the conventional CRT, however. Another recent invention has been the *plasma panel* [22], an alternative to the CRT that stores and displays pictures by means of tiny gas discharge cells.

The process of refreshing a CRT may be controlled directly by the computer. For this purpose, the picture is broken down into individual points, and the x and y coordinates of each point in turn are issued to the display. The picture is refreshed by repeating this process thirty or more times a second. Only a limited number of points can be refreshed in this way; nowadays a more popular technique is to build a separate *display processor* whose task is to read data from memory and use this data to generate both points and lines on the CRT screen.

In recent years, extremely powerful display processors have been built, capable of applying a wide variety of *transformations* such as rotation, scaling etc., to the picture definition. At the other end of the scale, progress has recently been made towards building extremely inexpensive display processors and terminals, some of which have made use of direct view storage tubes. These low-cost terminals, used with time-shared systems, have made it possible for many more people to afford to use interactive graphics.

Part I of this book is devoted to display terminals and their design. It covers the basic features of cathode ray tubes in Chapter 1, and discusses simple methods of using them in Chapter 2. Chapter 3 describes various techniques for displaying straight lines; Chapter 4 covers display processors and terminals, and discusses their desirable features.

PROGRAMMING THE DISPLAY

We write an interactive graphical program by specifying a sequence of operations that produces a list of instructions for the display processor. This list of display instructions is called the *display file*, and a great many ingenious techniques have been proposed for display file construction and manipulation.

One of the most basic requirements of an interactive graphics system is that it should be possible to change the picture in a dynamic fashion. Often we would like to remove one part of the picture, or change its position: this can be done by regenerating the entire display file, or we can *segment* the display file and just regenerate the part that is to change. In order to simplify the use of repeated symbols in the picture, we often use *display subroutines*, shared segments of display code somewhat analogous to conventional subroutines. The notion of using symbols can be extended to allow these symbols to be individually scaled and rotated by different amounts.

A set of functions for building and manipulating a segmented display file can generally be written without much difficulty: we call such a set of functions a *display file compiler*. The problem becomes more difficult, however, if we wish to specify scaling and rotation of parts of the picture. We need a simple notation for defining such transformations, and we need a means of detecting and removing parts of the picture that when transformed lie off the screen. The first problem is solved by using *matrices* to define transformations; the second involves the use of *clipping* programs.

The transformation of pictures with matrices represents an interesting application of the techniques of algebra and trigonometry. Clipping, on the other hand, is a technique found only in computer graphics. Various techniques, some based on hardware and others on software, have been proposed for performing these transformations as rapidly as possible.

All these techniques are described in Part II. Chapter 5 discusses the principal features of display file compilers. Matrix transformations are introduced in Chapter 6, and clipping in Chapter 7. Chapter 7 also discusses the *windowing* transformation, in which the scaling of a picture is defined by specifying the size of the visible region before and after scaling. Chapter 8 discusses some of the problems involved in building the software to perform these transformations.

INTERACTING WITH THE PROGRAM

A number of devices such as tablets, joysticks and light pens have been invented for the input of graphical information to a computer. Used with a display, these devices make it possible to interact extremely effectively with the program. It is possible to draw lines and position symbols on the screen, or to point at items in order to change them or delete them. Some very ingenious techniques have been developed that use these devices for a variety of types of interaction. Extensive use has been made of visual *feedback*, an effect that permits the use of relatively inaccurate input devices that need not write directly on the screen surface.

Programming these devices is a slightly unconventional task, because many of them communicate with the computer in non-standard ways. Furthermore the user frequently makes use of two or more input devices at once. Generally the simplest way to handle inputs from these devices is by means of *interrupt routines* which receive the input data, and which pass this data on to the main program in the form of an *attention*.

Part III of this book discusses graphical input devices and their usage. Chapter 9 describes their construction, and Chapter 10 the design of interrupt routines that enable them to be used easily. Chapter 11 presents a compendium of interactive techniques by which these devices may be used to input data and to control an interactive program.

DRAWING THREE-DIMENSIONAL OBJECTS

One of the most intriguing branches of computer graphics is the subject of drawing pictures of solid objects. In order to generate a realistic picture, such as the one shown in Figure I-3, we must first apply a *perspective transformation* to the object, and then remove hidden lines and surfaces. The latter task can be extremely time-consuming, for it may be necessary to apply repeated tests to each edge of the object before we can be sure it is unobscured.

Like clipping, hidden line and hidden surface removal are topics that belong exclusively to computer graphics. They are also topics of great fascination: many people have become deeply involved in the search for fast hidden line and hidden surface algorithms. Some pioneering work was done on the problem by Roberts at MIT's Lincoln Laboratory [234]. His solution was an elegant one, but was rather extravagant in its use of computing power. Since then, some particularly important advances towards a better solution have been made at the University of Utah: these include John Warnock's subdivision algorithm [300], and the work of Watkins and Gouraud on the design of an algorithm suitable for building into hardware [301, 104].

Part IV describes all this work: it covers perspective transformations in Chapters 12 and 13, the latter covering specifically those transformations required by hidden-line and hidden-surface algorithms. Chapter 14 describes each of the hidden-line and hidden-surface algorithms mentioned above, and further details of them are given in Appendices VI and VII.

BUILDING A SYSTEM

We have reviewed some of the major topics in interactive graphics. One other interesting set of problems remains: these are the problems that arise when we try to put all the techniques together into a useful system. We would like such a system to provide the maximum capability for solving problems with the aid of interactive graphics, and at the same time to be as simple to program and as inexpensive as possible.

During the gradual development of computer graphics technology, there have been various shifts of interest among those involved in graphics system design. Originally the system designer's principal concern was to develop the system's capability to the point at which it could perform a useful task. This point was reached in the mid-1960's, when a few large, expensive graphics systems were introduced into the automobile and aircraft industries for use in computer-aided design [127, 41]. Once these systems had demonstrated that interactive graphics was indeed useful, interest shifted towards reducing the cost of graphics systems. A lot of effort was put into the design of operating systems to allow displays to be used as terminals to time-shared computer systems; this led to the development of some highly ingenious *satellite* graphics systems [44, 58]. Up to this time, however, graphics systems tended to be very complex, and therefore depended on expert programmers to write the application programs. The obvious disadvantages of this situation led to the development of simpler, cheaper display terminals and better, more convenient programming languages for graphics.

Interactive graphics, after ten years of research and development effort, is now entering a phase in which it promises to become very widely used. The chance for this to happen has been created by a combination of the recent work on languages and system design, and of the simultaneous precipitous drop in the cost of computing hardware. Although graphical displays are still relatively expensive devices, the processors to support them are becoming extremely inexpensive. This turns out to be essential for the widespread use of computer graphics, since interactive displays require large amounts of cheap processing power to perform picture transformations. The implications of these recent advances are discussed further in Part V, under three headings: command languages, programming languages and graphics system design.

Viewed as a whole, interactive graphics may appear to the reader to be dominated by software techniques. This is not true, however. Interactive graphics is essentially a matter of finding the best way to provide certain capabilities. Until recently the high cost of hardware and the relatively small demand for graphics equipment has meant that most graphics systems relied heavily on software. Now it is becoming much easier to justify investment in hardware. This makes it feasible to propose, in Chapter 17, the use of a small, single-user computer for graphics in place of a time-shared system serving several terminals. In the future we can expect to see more and more use of specialized hardware to provide faster and cheaper graphics systems, relying far less on software than they do at present. Hopefully the principles presented in this book will remain relevant even then.

Display Devices

PART ONE

Display Devices

1
CATHODE RAY TUBES

1.1 CATHODE RAY TUBES

The modern digital computer transmits information by means of electrical signals. These signals fluctuate extremely rapidly, and by very small amounts; they are completely unintelligible to human beings. The only way to make them intelligible is to convert them to another form. Generally we convert them into either visible or audible signals. For example, we can generate legible text by connecting the computer to an electric typewriter; however, we must slow down the computer's rate of transmission by a huge factor. Audible information can be produced by connecting the computer to a loud-speaker, but it takes either a highly-trained ear or an intricate program to make any sense of the results.

To generate pictorial output from the computer, we must connect it to a device capable of generating pictures from electrical signals. A well-known device with this capability is the *cathode ray tube* or CRT. The CRT has been used for many years in a number of applications, many of them unrelated to computers. It forms an essential part of the radar display used for aircraft control and navigation. It is also used in the oscilloscopes with which electrical engineers test circuits and other equipment. By far the commonest use of the cathode ray tube is of course in the home television set. Because of the importance of these three applications, cathode ray tube technology has been developed to an extremely advanced level. This has made it possible to use the CRT as a computer output device.

The cathode ray tube depends for its operation on two distinct phenomena. One of these is the *phosphorescent* behaviour of certain substances: if they are bombarded with electrons they emit a visible glow for quite a perceptible period after the bombardment has ceased. The other is the effect of electric fields on the movement of electrons. This effect permits a stream of electrons to be accelerated to high speed, to be focused into a fine beam, and to be moved over a phosphorescent surface. In this way a visible trace is produced. It is important to understand these two effects, and how they limit the CRT's performance, for on the CRT's performance depends the effectiveness of most interactive graphics systems.

1.2   THE MOTION OF ELECTRONS

The two kinds of electric field used in a CRT are the *electrostatic field* and the *electromagnetic field*. Not only are these fields generated by different techniques, but their effect on electrons is quite dissimilar.

An *electrostatic field* is created between two plates or *electrodes* which are raised to different potentials. If the plates are parallel, then the lines of force of the field are approximately perpendicular to the plates, as shown in Figure 1-1. An electron placed in this field will be accelerated towards the positive electrode along one of the lines of force. We can determine the electron's change in velocity from its energy equation:

$$eV = \tfrac{1}{2}m\left(v_1{}^2 - v_0{}^2\right)$$

where m = electron mass
e = electron charge
v_0 = initial velocity, perpendicular to field
v_1 = final velocity
V = field potential difference

The electrostatic field is well suited to the task of accelerating a beam of electrons to high speed. It can also be used to focus or deflect a

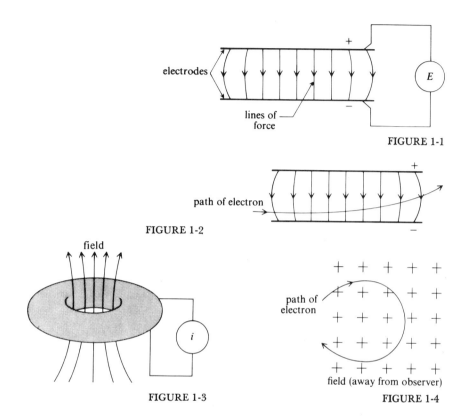

FIGURE 1-1

FIGURE 1-2

FIGURE 1-3

field (away from observer)

FIGURE 1-4

beam, since an electron not moving parallel to the lines of force will change direction, as shown in Figure 1-2.

An *electromagnetic field* is created when current flows through a conductor, such as the coil shown in Figure 1-3. An electron moving through such a field is deflected at right angles both to its direction of motion and to the lines of force. Thus it will tend to spin in a circle, as shown in Figure 1-4. This property makes the electromagnetic field particularly suitable for beam deflection. The angular velocity ω of the electron is proportional to the field strength B:

$$\omega = \frac{Be}{m}$$

1.3   ELEMENTS OF A CATHODE RAY TUBE

The CRT uses electric fields to generate a finely focused, high speed beam of electrons, and to deflect the beam to various parts of the screen surface so as to generate a visible trace. The basic components

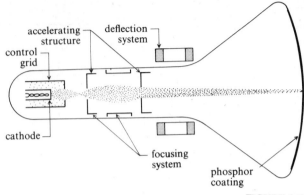

accelerating — structure   deflection — system
control grid
cathode —
focusing system
phosphor coating

FIGURE 1-5

that make up the CRT are shown in the simplified diagram of Figure 1-5. They include:

1. a *cathode* which when heated emits electrons;
2. a *control grid* which controls both the direction and rate of emission of electrons;
3. an *accelerating structure* which produces a high-velocity beam of electrons;
4. a *focusing system* which makes sure that the beam is focused to a fine spot when it hits the screen;
5. a *deflection system* for moving the beam around on the screen;
6. a *phosphor coating* which glows when the beam strikes it.

These components are all enclosed in an evacuated conical glass bottle.

1.3.1   CATIIODE

The cathode is a small metal cylinder which is heated by an enclosed filament to a temperature at which it emits electrons.

1.3.2   CONTROL GRID

Electrons leave the cathode in random directions, and are brought to order by the control grid, a second metal cylinder surrounding the cathode. This cylinder is at a lower potential than the cathode, so it repels the electrons, most of which remain within the control grid

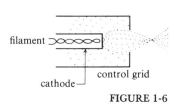

filament

cathode

control grid

FIGURE 1-6

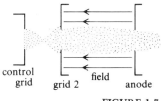

control
grid   grid 2   field   anode

FIGURE 1-7

except for a few that escape through a hole in the end. Careful design of the control grid produces a flow of the form shown in Figure 1-6, in which all the electrons pass through a point; this *point source* simplifies the later problems of focusing the electron beam.

The lower the potential of the control grid relative to the cathode, the fewer electrons escape through the hole. Therefore by changing this potential we can alter the number of electrons bombarding the screen, and so control the picture's brightness. If the negative potential is decreased far enough, the flow of electrons, or *beam current*, becomes zero. The potential at which this occurs is called the *cut-off voltage*, and is generally in the range -20 to -100 volts.

1.3.3   ACCELERATING STRUCTURE

The purpose of the accelerating structure is to raise the electrons' velocity so that the beam strikes the phosphor with sufficient energy to produce a visible spot. After the electrons leave the control grid they pass through a small hole in a second grid (grid 2) and are accelerated by a powerful electrostatic field between this grid and a positive electrode or *anode*. This anode also has a small hole in it, out of which the now fast-moving beam passes (Figure 1-7). As mentioned earlier, the speed reached by the beam is proportional to the square root of the accelerating potential: some actual values are given in Table 1-1. High-performance cathode ray tubes usually use potentials of 10 000 to 20 000 volts.

1.3.4   FOCUSING SYSTEMS

The glow produced by the beam striking the phosphor should be confined to a very small spot. When the spot size is small, points and lines drawn close together can be resolved more easily by the eye, and

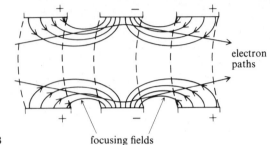

+   −   +

electron
paths

FIGURE 1-8   focusing fields

+   −   +

text is more legible. Good-quality focusing systems can generally confine the spot size to 1/100 inch diameter or less.

Contrary to popular belief, the electron beam is not uniformly thin during its passage down the tube. Instead it narrows to a point source shortly after leaving the control grid, then widens again up to the point where focusing is applied, and from there onwards converges to meet the screen in a fine point.

Either electrostatic or magnetic fields may be used for focusing the beam. When electrostatic focusing is used, the general aim is to produce a field of the form shown in Figure 1-8 by using three cylindrical electrodes. These three electrodes form a field which acts on the electron beam rather like a lens on a beam of light. The drop in potential between the first and second electrode makes the beam diverge, while the second and third electrodes have the opposite effect and bring the beam to a finely focused point. The arrangement shown

Table 1-1: Relationship between beam velocity and accelerating potential

Potential (volts)	Beam velocity ($m/s \times 10^6$)
1 000	18
2 000	25
5 000	42
10 000	60
20 000	84

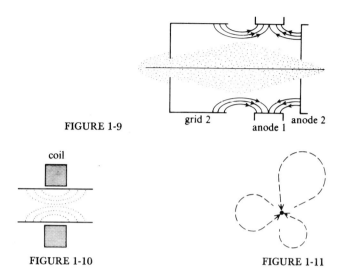

FIGURE 1-9   grid 2   anode 2
                                  anode 1

coil

FIGURE 1-10   FIGURE 1-11

in Figure 1-9 employs grid 2 and the accelerating anode (anode 2) as part of the focusing system, with an additional anode in between.

Magnetic focusing is done by means of a coil wrapped around the neck of the tube; this produces a field of the form shown in Figure 1-10. The axial component of this field, like the field shown in Figure 1-4, tends to add a circular motion to any electron that is not moving exactly parallel to the axis. This, combined with the electron's velocity along the axis, turns the electron's path into a helix. Focusing is achieved by making sure that every such helix passes through the point where the axis meets the screen. Figure 1-11 shows a number of these helical electron paths, viewed along the CRT's axis. Magnetic focusing is usually more effective than electrostatic, and is therefore used when spot size is critical. For most interactive graphic displays the simpler electrostatic method is adequate.

1.3.5 DEFLECTION SYSTEMS

Either electrostatic or magnetic fields may be used for deflection. For electrostatic deflection, two pairs of electrodes are mounted as shown in Figure 1-12 so that one pair controls the beam's movement in the x-direction, the other in the y-direction.

Magnetic deflection requires two pairs of coils mounted outside the tube so that they produce perpendicular fields (Figure 1-13). The pair

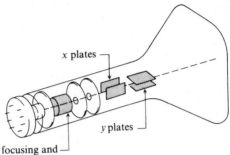

FIGURE 1-12   focusing and accelerating structure

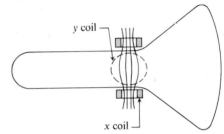

FIGURE 1-13

of coils on either side of the CRT are used to deflect the beam up and down, and the pair above and below deflect it from side to side.

An important attribute of any deflection technique is its *sensitivity*, by which we mean its ability to produce large angles of deflection from small signals. Without good sensitivity, the only way to achieve large deflections is to lengthen the tube, which results in a bulky display.

The sensitivity of the *electrostatic* deflection technique is given by the following equation:

$$\tan \alpha = \frac{L V_d}{2 D V_a}$$

where α = angle of deflection (see Figure 1-14)
V_a = accelerating voltage
V_d = deflection voltage
L = length of deflection plates
D = separation of plates

Thus a high-speed beam, for which V_a is large, requires high deflection voltages. The equation for *magnetic* deflection is as follows:

$$\tan \alpha = \frac{B L}{\sqrt{2 k V_a}}$$

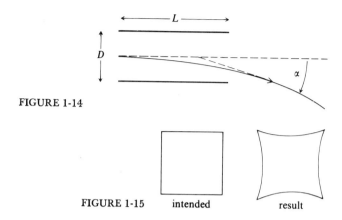

FIGURE 1-14

FIGURE 1-15   intended   result

where B = magnetic field strength
L = effective length of deflection field
k is a constant (= $\frac{1}{2}$ (mass/charge) of electron)

Once again, fast beams require stronger fields and therefore larger currents. However, the current requirement is proportional to $\sqrt{V_a}$ instead of V_a. It follows that the magnetic method generally allows the use of higher-speed beams which produce brighter pictures.

There are many other factors that influence the choice between magnetic and electrostatic deflection. An important factor is power requirement. Electrostatic deflection, although it uses relatively little power, calls for high voltages, and this may increase the cost of the power supplies. Magnetic deflection generally requires only modest currents, and the power used is low unless the beam is swung very rapidly.

Deflection coils are often wound on iron *cores* to concentrate and increase the magnetic field. The core tends to retain its magnetism, causing a form of distortion in the picture called *hysteresis:* when a deflecting current is applied and removed, the beam fails to return exactly to its original position. Electrostatic deflection also creates distortion, because the two sets of plates are mounted at different points on the axis. If the beam is deflected by the first set of plates its trajectory through the second is longer, and the effect of the second set is altered. This produces the 'pin-cushion' distortion effect shown in Figure 1-15.

Some of the arguments for and against the two methods of deflection are summarized in Table 1-2. For the types of picture used in

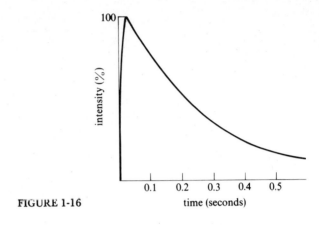

FIGURE 1-16

interactive graphics, magnetic deflection has a number of advantages and is therefore more commonly used.

1.3.6   PHOSPHORS

Under normal circumstances, the glow produced by the electron beam dies away soon after the beam moves away from the spot. Figure 1-16 shows a typical curve of brightness against time. After 1/5 second over

Table 1-2: Comparison of magnetic and electrostatic deflection

MAGNETIC		ELECTROSTATIC	
Good points	*Bad points*	*Good points*	*Bad points*
Produces smaller spot size	High energy field means slower response	Fast response	Produces larger spot size
More sensitive on fast, high-brightness beams	Hysteresis distortion	Low power requirements	Pin-cushion distortion
Low voltage requirement			High voltage requirement

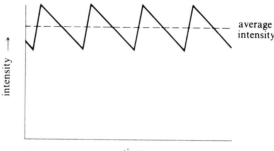

average intensity

intensity →

FIGURE 1-17

time →

half the brightness has disappeared. A single sweep of the beam therefore produces a trace that is only momentarily visible. This lack of *persistence* in phosphors is a fundamental flaw of the CRT: it means that the same pattern must be *refreshed*, or traced out repeatedly by the beam, in order to produce a steady picture. As shown in Figure 1-17, if this is done frequently enough, the average intensity of the displayed trace can be maintained at quite a high level. Moreover, because of the rapid rate of refreshing, the intensity of the picture appears constant to the observer.

In general it is desirable to use phosphors that do not have to be refreshed very frequently, for a long *refresh cycle* gives the CRT time to display more information. This can be achieved by using a phosphor with a fairly long persistence. There are a number of additional features that a phosphor should possess: small grain size, high contrast, resistance to burning and so forth. Many different phosphors have been produced in attempts to improve performance in one or other of these respects. They are made from compounds of calcium, cadmium and zinc. Before the neck of the CRT is sealed a suspension of the phosphor is poured into the tube, which is left face-downwards until a deposit of phosphor has settled out onto the screen.

Different phosphors are identified by numbers — P1, P2, P3 on up to P40 or so. The dominant colors with which phosphors glow vary a great deal. Some are colorless, like the P4 phosphor used in televison tubes. The ones most frequently used in graphics displays are P7, which is blue, and P31, which is green.

P7 is a phosphor with medium persistence, on the order of 30 milliseconds. There are phosphors with much longer persistence, up to several seconds in length, but they are rarely used in interactive computer graphics because they leave ugly 'smears' behind as the picture changes.

P31 has shorter persistence but has high efficiency and gives better-quality pictures as a result; however it is rather susceptible to *phosphor burns*. If we multiply the beam's voltage (typically 10 000 volts) by its current (typically 10 microamps) we find that the beam's power is 0.1 watts. This is not a great deal, but when concentrated on a spot 1/100 inch in diameter it represents over 1000 watts per square inch, more than on the surface of an electric heater element. The only way to prevent the phosphor from burning up is to make sure the beam never dwells for more than a few microseconds on each spot. If either the program or the deflection system should fail, and leave the beam stationary for a second or two, the phosphor will be burnt away leaving a permanent dark spot on the screen. The stronger the phosphor's resistance to burning, the less likely this is to happen.

In Table 1-3 some of the properties of the more commonly used phosphors are summarized.

1.4   STORAGE TUBES

A variety of techniques have been developed for storing the data from which a CRT is refreshed. Most of these involve the use of a separate memory, and are described in later chapters. One technique, however, stores the information within the tube itself: this is the technique of the *storage* cathode ray tube. The most widely used form of storage tube is the Direct-view Storage Tube, sometimes abbreviated to DVST.

Table 1-3: Phosphor Characteristics

Phosphor	*Color*[1]	*Persistence*[2] *(ms)*	*Efficiency*[3] *(%)*
P1	Yellowish green	24.5	32
P4	White	.06	43
P7	White/green	400	43
P12	Orange	210	—
P28	Yellowish green	600	43
P31	Green	.038	100

Notes: 1. Where two colors are given, the first is the color of the florescence, the second of the phosphorescence.
2. Time taken to decay to 10 per cent of initial brightness.
3. Relative to P31.

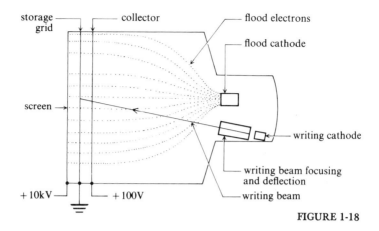

storage grid — collector — flood electrons

flood cathode

screen →

writing cathode

writing beam focusing and deflection

writing beam

+10kV — +100V

FIGURE 1-18

1.4.1   THE DIRECT-VIEW STORAGE TUBE

Outwardly the direct-view storage tube behaves like a CRT with an extremely long-persistence phosphor. A line written once on the screen will remain visible for up to an hour before it fades out of sight. Inwardly, too, the storage tube resembles the CRT, for it has similar focusing and deflection systems, and a somewhat similar phosphor-coated screen. The beam does not 'write' directly on the phosphor, however, but on a very fine-mesh wire grid, coated with dielectric and mounted just behind the screen. A pattern of positive charge is left on this grid and is 'copied' onto the screen by a continuous flood of electrons issuing from a separate cathode. The general arrangement of the direct-view storage tube is shown in Figure 1-18.

Just behind the storage grid is a second grid, the *collector*, whose main purpose is to smooth out the flow of the flooding electrons. These electrons pass through the collector at a low velocity, and are attracted to the positively-charged parts of the storage grid but repelled by the rest. Those electrons that are not repelled pass right through the storage grid and strike the phosphor. In order to raise the energy of these electrons and create a bright picture, the screen is maintained at a high positive potential by means of a thin aluminum coating on the back.

Because the electron flood is moving fairly slowly, it hardly affects the charge on the storage grid. In fact one of the problems of the storage tube is that this charge cannot be removed rapidly. The normal method of erasing the picture is to apply a positive pulse, lasting half a second or so, to the storage grid. This tends to produce a rather unpleasant flash covering the entire screen. Another problem is the

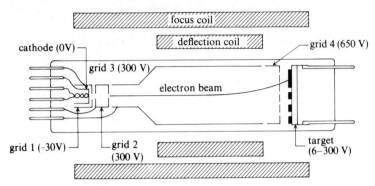

FIGURE 1-19

gradual build-up of background glow, caused by the flood electrons charging the storage grid. It is generally this, rather than a drop in the picture intensity, that renders the picture invisible after an hour or so.

These problems make the direct-view storage tube less satisfactory than the conventional CRT as a graphical output device. The DVST presents a further problem to the programmer since selective erasure is difficult, if not impossible, to perform. This somewhat restricts the degree of interaction possible with displays based on the direct-view storage tube.

1.4.2 ELECTRICAL OUTPUT STORAGE TUBES

The direct-view storage tube involves two separate principles:

1. the storage of an image as charges on a grid;
2. transfer of the image to a phosphor-coated surface by means of a flood of electrons.

There are other ways of making the image visible besides the use of a flood of electrons. One particularly promising technique is to *scan* the grid in a raster pattern, and so generate a signal that can be used to drive a TV set.

This is the basis of operation of the Silicon Target Tube [217]. The tube itself is very small, less than one inch in diameter, and is arranged as shown in Figure 1-19. A conventional electrostatic accelerating and focusing structure is used, and is supplemented by a magnetic focusing coil. Additional acceleration is provided by a pierced *mesh electrode* close to the target. The target itself is a disk coated with silicon dioxide. If held at a relatively high potential, the target retains a charge when the electron beam strikes it. The pattern of charges stored on the target can be 'read' by lowering the potential of the target and scanning it with an electron beam in a raster fashion, thus generating a fluctuating current at the target that can be amplified and used to drive a TV monitor. Because of the beam's relatively low velocity during the 'read' operation, no additional charge is deposited on the target. However, the charge deposited during the 'write' operation gradually drains away as the target is scanned, and the picture quality therefore slowly deteriorates.

One of the advantages of the silicon target tube is that a variable charge may be stored at each point on the target. In this way a shaded picture of varying tone density is generated. Also it is possible to vary the field of view of the scanning process, and hence vary the scale of the picture dynamically in a manner that is very difficult to mimic on a conventional display. The problems with the electrical storage tube are just those that we encountered with the direct-view version: the picture deteriorates in quality when it is being scanned; it can be selectively erased only by retracing all the points that are to be blanked out; and complete screen erasure takes an appreciable time.

1.5   OTHER DISPLAY DEVICES

Display designers have for years been searching for an alternative to the cathode ray tube — for a device that retains the image indefinitely without loss of quality, that can be accommodated in a small space, and that requires only low-voltage power supplies. No such device has yet been discovered that retains the high performance and quality of the CRT. One promising alternative to the CRT has been proposed, however: it is the *plasma panel*, and it meets almost all the display designer's needs.

1.5.1   THE PLASMA PANEL

The plasma panel's construction is shown in Figure 1-20. It consists of two sheets of glass with thin, closely spaced gold *electrodes* attached to the inner faces and covered with a dielectric material. The two sheets of glass are spaced a few thousandths of an inch apart, and the intervening

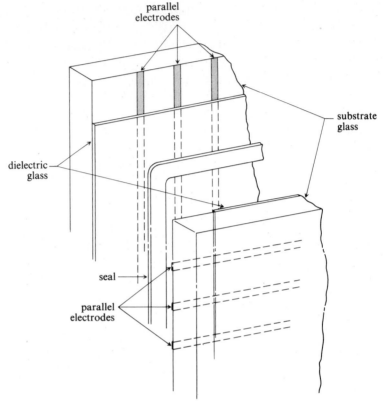

FIGURE 1-20

space is filled with a neon-based gas and sealed. By applying voltages between the electrodes, the gas within the panel is made to behave as if it were divided into tiny cells,* each one independent of its neighbors. By an ingenious mechanism, certain cells can be made to glow, and thus a picture is generated. A cell is made to glow by placing a 'firing' voltage across it by means of the electrodes. The gas within the cell begins to discharge, and this develops very rapidly into a glow. The glow can be sustained by maintaining a high-frequency alternating voltage across the cell; the shape of this *sustaining signal* is shown in Figure 1-21. Furthermore, if the signal amplitude is chosen correctly, cells that have not been 'fired' will not be affected. In other words, each cell is bistable.

---

* Early versions of the panel [22] separated the cells by means of an inner sheet of glass drilled with tiny holes. Later it was found possible to dispense with this sheet.

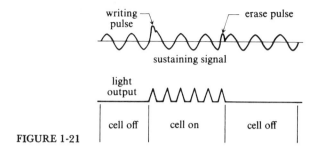

FIGURE 1-21

Cells can be switched on by momentarily increasing the sustaining voltage; this can be done selectively by modifying the signal only in the two conductors that intersect at the desired cell. Similarly, if the sustaining voltage is lowered, the glow is removed. Thus the plasma panel allows both selective writing and selective erasure, at speeds of about 20 microseconds per cell. This speed can be increased by writing or erasing several cells in parallel.

The simplicity of construction of the plasma panel suggests that it can potentially replace the CRT for many computer graphics applications. In its current state of development it compares very favorably with the direct-view storage tube: it presents a sharper image that does not deteriorate with time, it has a reliable selective erase mechanism, its power requirements are less stringent, it has a longer life, and it occupies less space. Although it currently offers only a single brightness level, recent research [214] has shown that a cell may be maintained in one of several different stable states, representing several different intensities. It also appears that a color display based on the panel is feasible [34]. The largest currently available panel is only $8\frac{1}{2}$ inches square, but larger panels are under development.

The only obvious weaknesses of the plasma panel are the relatively wide spacing of the cells (60 points per inch), and the panel's slow write and erase rates. With parallel addressing techniques it is clear that lines and points can be written onto the panel almost as fast as they can be transmitted to a CRT display. However, it is not so obvious how to achieve rapid erasure of large segments of the picture at the speeds possible with a conventional CRT.

2
POINT-PLOTTING DISPLAYS

2.1 DIGITAL CONTROL OF THE CATHODE RAY TUBE

The cathode ray tube is an awkward device to attach to a digital
computer. As the previous chapter has shown, it requires continuously
varying signals to deflect the beam. An analog computer could generate
this kind of output signal quite easily; a digital computer is limited to
producing outputs that change by discrete amounts at discrete intervals.
Moreover the digital computer's outputs are coded in a binary format.
This binary coded information must be turned into the appropriate
voltages by means of a *digital-to-analog converter* (D/A converter).

The control of a cathode ray tube also requires very accurate timing.
The CRT's usefulness as an output device depends on the use of very
high deflection speeds, at which any inaccuracy in controlling the
intensity or in synchronizing the x and y deflection systems is obvious
to the user. Inaccuracies are avoided only by careful design of the
controller that contains the conversion and synchronizing circuitry for
the CRT.

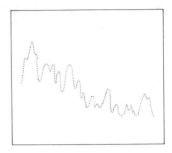

FIGURE 2-1

2.2   THE POINT-PLOTTING DISPLAY

The simplest form of visible output that a display can generate in response to a computer is a point. All that is required is that the deflection signals be set to the right levels, and the beam current be pulsed once to generate a spot on the screen. A controller for this purpose, together with a cathode ray tube and deflection system, form what is known as a *point-plotting display*.

Point-plotting displays have been used for years in simple graphical output applications such as displaying curves of experimental data (Figure 2-1). Pictures of this kind are made by issuing the coordinates of each point in turn to the controller, which in each case sets the deflection signals accordingly and pulses the beam current. The process must be repeated in order to maintain a picture on the screen. This repetitive process is called *refreshing* the display; it must generally be carried out at least 30 times a second to avoid flicker.

It is possible to display points so close together that they appear to merge into a continuous line. Thus geometric figures can be drawn on the screen; by a similar technique text can also be displayed.

2.2.1   NUMBERING CONVENTIONS

The programmer who wishes to use a point-plotting display cannot do so unless he knows something about the *coordinate system* of the display. Suppose for example he wishes to display a point at the center of the screen: what binary numbers must his program issue to the display controller?

Coordinate systems vary a good deal from one display to the next. The one property that they share is that they are all *Cartesian:* the programmer specifies a point's position by an x-coordinate and a y-coordinate. However there is some variation in the *precision* that

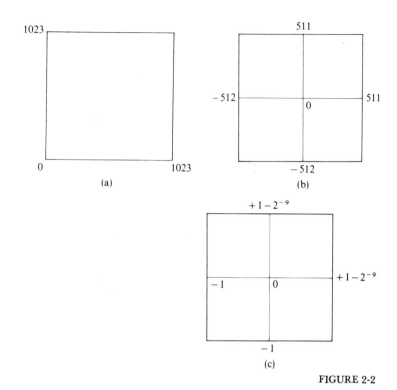

FIGURE 2-2

displays offer, i.e. the number of different points that may be specified along each axis. In some displays this is as small as 256; in others it is as large as 4096. The limiting factor is normally the *resolution* of the CRT, i.e. the distance apart at which two displayed points become distinguishable from a single point. Nothing is gained by offering more precision than this, for the observer will not be able to tell the difference. On the other hand, if the precision is much less than this, a gap appears between adjacent points and it becomes impossible to form smooth lines and legible text. The CRT used in the average graphical display has a resolution of about 1/100 inch, and a deflection system that performs linearly over an area about 10 inches square. It therefore uses ten binary digits of precision, giving an addressable area of 1024 x 1024 points.

Most displays treat the binary coordinate data they receive as unsigned integer information. Thus a conventional ten-bit display controller assigns the origin to the lower left-hand corner of the screen and the point (1023,1023) to the upper right-hand corner (Figure 2-2a). An alternative convention is to treat coordinates as *signed* integers. Figure 2-2b shows the result of using ten-bit, twos-complement, signed integers. The bottom left-hand corner is the point $(-512,-512)$ and the top is $(511,511)$; the origin is almost exactly at the center of the screen. This is a very convenient arrangement for displaying simple perspective pictures. However it is rarely used because it involves non-standard digital-to-analog conversion techniques.

An alternative to integers is the use of *fractional* coordinates. For example, we could treat coordinates as signed, twos-complement fractions. This would place opposite edges of the screen at -1 and at approximately $+1$, instead of at -512 and $+511$ (Figure 2-2c). Use of this notation does not affect the controller mechanism, because any given point on the screen is specified by the same sequence of 0's and 1's whether signed integer or signed fractional coordinates are in use. It does however affect the way the display is programmed. Fractional screen coordinates are particularly convenient for dealing with scaled pictures and perspectives, and are therefore adopted in the later chapters of this book that discuss these topics. In simple programming problems, however, integer coordinates are easier to use. In this chapter coordinates are assumed to be ten-bit unsigned integers in the range 0 to 1023.

2.2.2   CONVERSION TECHNIQUES

Whenever a point is to be displayed, the computer passes two digital coordinates to the display controller. These two numbers are then converted to analog voltages for use by the CRT's deflection system. A simple D/A converter is shown in Figure 2-3. Each bit of the binary number controls a switch, through which a regulated current I flows when the switch is closed. The network of resistors reduces the output voltage e_o in proportion to the value of the bit. For example, if the most significant bit is set, its switch will close and a current $I/2$ will flow through the top resistor in the network, resulting in a value of e_o equal to IR. If instead the next most significant bit is set, the current in this resistor is $I/4$, and e_o is $IR/2$. If more than one bit is set, the effect on e_o is additive.

It is possible to use a single voltage source in place of the multiple current sources: this simplifies the design of the converter, but results in longer *conversion delays*. Therefore current-switching D/A converters are more frequently used in high-speed displays.

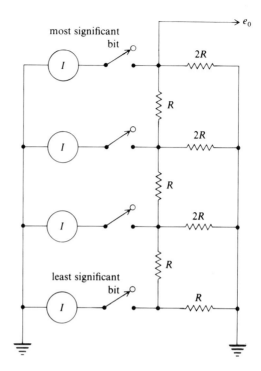

most significant bit

least significant bit

FIGURE 2-3

To the conversion delay must be added an additional *settling delay* inherent in the CRT's deflection system. Settling delays are a particular problem in magnetic deflection systems and may be as high as 30 microseconds for full screen width changes in beam position. It is essential that the controller should delay intensifying the point until the beam has settled; otherwise ugly streaks will be displayed in place of precise dots. Settling delays are much shorter (about 5 microseconds maximum) if electrostatic deflection is used instead of electromagnetic. However, this form of deflection is usually so expensive that the main advantage of the point-plotting display, namely its low cost, is lost.

Delays in both conversion and settling are shorter if beam movement is less between consecutive points. If the movement is only one coordinate unit the delay is likely to be less than one microsecond. A line or character constructed from a sequence of adjacent points can therefore be plotted very rapidly — speeds faster than one point per microsecond are easily attained.

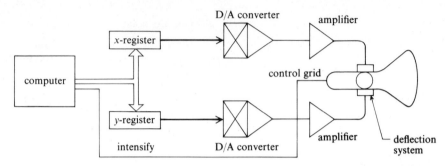

FIGURE 2-4

2.2.3   POINT INTENSIFICATION

The controller contains two ten-bit *coordinate registers* in which the coordinate values are held during D/A conversion. When the signal to display a point is received, the beam current is pulsed to generate a spot on the screen.

The general arrangement of a simple point-plotting display is shown in Figure 2-4. Some displays are more elaborate than this. For example, a third register is often provided for *brightness control* (sometimes called *z-axis modulation*). The value in this register is converted in the same fashion as the others, and is used to control the beam current. Three or four bits of brightness precision are usually adequate for most applications.

2.3   COMPUTER CONTROL OF POINT-PLOTTING DISPLAYS

The two stages in the process of displaying a point are:

1. Loading the x- and y-registers and D/A conversion;
2. Point intensification.

The simplest way in which a computer can control the process is by means of a separate *explicit instruction* to perform each operation. This is not the most efficient method, for it prevents the computer from performing any other tasks while points are being displayed. However it greatly reduces the complexity, and hence the cost, of the controller. Chapter 4 describes some more efficient techniques using channels and processors.

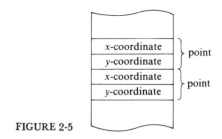

FIGURE 2-5

2.3.1   CONTROL BY EXPLICIT INSTRUCTION

A computer with an accumulator greater than 20 bits in width can control a point-plotting display by means of a single instruction. This instruction copies one half of the accumulator's contents into the display's x-register, copies the other half into the y-register, and intensifies the point.

If the computer's accumulator is too small to hold both coordinates, the solution is less simple. The x and y coordinates must be transmitted to the display by separate instructions, with a third to start the intensifying process. The following is a typical set of instructions for a single-accumulator computer controlling a point-plotting display:

DXL   Load x-register from accumulator
DYL   Load y-register from accumulator
DIP   Intensity point

The user of these instructions will frequently wish to intensify the point as soon as one or other of the coordinate registers has been loaded. It is therefore convenient if two extra instructions are provided, so that intensification can be included as part of the loading instruction:

DXI   Load x-register from accumulator and intensify
DYI   Load y-register from accumulator and intensify

2.3.2   REFRESHING THE DISPLAY

With the aid of these five instructions, a computer display may easily be programmed to present any simple pattern on the screen. Suppose, for example, we wish to display a graph of points representing experimental data, as shown in Figure 2-1. The data is broken down into points whose coordinates are stored in memory as shown in Figure 2-5. Then a program traverses this array of coordinates, sending them alternately to the x-register and to the y-register. Only a very simple program is required:*

```
OUTER:    LAW  PTS          set up P to point to start of
          DAC  P            coordinate array
          LAC  MCOUNT       set up C to contain
          DAC  C            negative count of points
INNER:    LAC  I P          fetch x value into accumulator
          DXL               load x-register
          ISZ  P            increment P
          LAC  I P          fetch y value into accumulator
          DYI               load y-register and intensify point
          ISZ  P            increment pointer P
          ISZ  C            increment count C, skip if zero
          JMP  INNER        if not last point,
                            return to INNER for next
          JMP  OUTER        if last, return to OUTER
                            and start again
```

The inner loop of this piece of code contains eight instructions, and may take 15 to 20 microseconds to execute each time. Furthermore it may be necessary to refresh the picture at least 30 times a second in order to prevent flicker. This would mean that only 1500 to 2000 points could be displayed flicker-free by this display. A display with such a small capacity is almost useless in applications that involve line-drawing. However some faster line-drawing techniques have been developed; these are described in the next chapter.

2.3.3   TEXT DISPLAY BY POINT PLOTTING

By displaying dots in a pattern such as the one in Figure 2-6 it is possible to produce a display of text. The dot positions for a whole string of text may be held in a simple list as described in Section 2.3.2. However there are more efficient techniques that save space and make it easier to add characters to the list and to remove them.

For example, each character may be defined by a list of the coordinates of its constituent points, measured relative to one corner of the character. Such a list is shown in Figure 2-7. To display the

* The instruction set used in these examples is described in Appendix III.

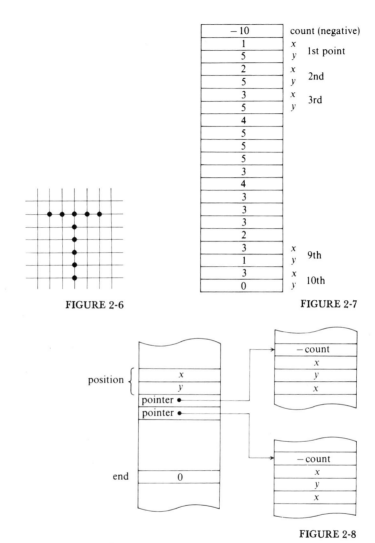

FIGURE 2-6   FIGURE 2-7

FIGURE 2-8

character in any position, we simply add the coordinates of this position to each of the relative coordinates in turn. The list of data for display need then contain only the coordinates of the first character in the string of text, followed by a pointer for each of the characters in the string (Figure 2-8). Each pointer provides the address where the list of relative coordinates for the character is to be found.

The following program will refresh a list of characters stored in this way. It performs the addition of relative coordinates to character positions during the refresh process; after each character has been displayed, the position of the next character is computed by adding to the current character position a fixed horizontal displacement equal to the character width. The end of the text string is indicated by a zero pointer.

OUTMOST:	LAW	CHLIST	set up *CP* to point to
	DAC	CP	start of text string
	LAC	I CP	fetch first word
	DAC	X	= *x* coordinate
	ISZ	CP	increment *CP*
	LAC	I CP	fetch second word
	DAC	Y	= *y* coordinate
OUTER:	ISZ	CP	increment to next character pointer
	LAC	I CP	fetch pointer
	SNA		test for zero = last
	JMP	OUTMOST	last so start again
	DAC	P	set list pointer *P*
	LAC	I P	first word of list is word count
	DAC	C	set up count (negative)
INNER:	ISZ	P	increment to next word
	LAC	I P	fetch *x* coordinate
	ADD	X	add character position
	DXL		load *x*-register
	ISZ	P	increment to next word
	LAC	I P	fetch *y* coordinate
	ADD	Y	add position
	DYI		load *y*-register and intensify
	ISZ	C	increment count, skip if zero
	JMP	INNER	not done
	LAC	X	done, so add width to *x*
	ADD	WIDTH	
	DAC	X	
	JMP	OUTER	and display next character

This program can refresh almost as many points flicker-free as the previous one of Section 2.3.2, i.e. 1500 or thereabouts. Thus if the average character is made up of 15 dots, the program can refresh about 100 characters without flicker.

Notice the similarity between the two programs for displaying points

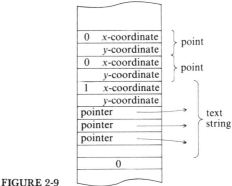

FIGURE 2-9

and for displaying text. It would obviously be possible to write a program that combined the functions of both, and could process a list containing both point and text data. It would be necessary to mark entries in the list to distinguish points from text. This could be done by using one bit in the first word of each entry, as shown in Figure 2-9. Using the techniques described in the next chapter, the program could also be extended to handle entries defining straight line segments.

EXERCISES

2-1. Mention was made of problems in converting from signed coordinate information to analog voltages. What specific problems would arise in converting from (a) twos-complement integer information; (b) ones-complement integers?

2-2. If the computer word is 20 or more bits wide, we can load both the x- and the y-registers and intensify, all in a single operation. How much faster does this allow us to display points?

2-3. The format shown in Figure 2-7 for storing character definitions is very inefficient. Suggest a more efficient one, and write the program to refresh the display.

2-4. Expand the program of Section 2.3.3 or of Exercise 2-3 to display both points and text, by marking entries in the display list as suggested.

3
VECTOR GENERATION

3.1 DOTS AND LINES

Straight lines occur frequently in pictures generated on CRT displays. As shown in Chapter 2, such lines may be displayed on point-plotting displays as a sequence of points. This process permits only about 1500 points to be displayed without flicker. The display can be equipped with special *vector generation* hardware which will draw lines much more rapidly.

There are two basic approaches to vector generation: either points on a straight line are computed digitally and the line is drawn as a series of dots, or an analog circuit is used to move the CRT beam continuously from the starting point to the ending point of the line. Digital line-drawing algorithms can be implemented in software, using point-plotting techniques to produce each dot on the line, or they may be performed with digital hardware. Analog generators are of necessity implemented with electronic circuits.

Digital generators compute the locations of points on the screen coordinate grid which lie near the desired line, and then pass these

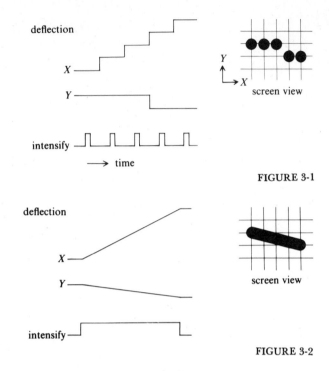

FIGURE 3-1

FIGURE 3-2

points to the deflection circuitry for intensification. The deflection of the CRT beam changes in a sequence of discrete steps in which each step represents a new dot being displayed (Figure 3-1).

Analog generators produce continuous signals instead of discrete step functions. As the deflection of the beam follows these signals, the beam current is left on, thus intensifying any spot struck by the moving beam (Figure 3-2). The endpoints of an analog line are measured in the coordinate system of the screen, a discrete grid resulting from the fixed resolution of the conversion from digital numbers to analog deflection signals. However, the deflection signals generated when a line is traced can cause the beam to intensify spots other than grid points.

Both kinds of vector generators aspire to similar goals:

1. The line should be straight.
2. The visible line should begin and end where the programmer requested.
3. The intensity of a line should be independent of the length and slope of the line and should be uniform along the length of the line.

4. The generation of the line should be performed very rapidly in order to permit many lines to be displayed without objectionable flicker.

The wide variety of vector generators marketed is indicative of the difficulties in attaining these goals and in striking an acceptable balance between performance and cost.

3.2   EQUATIONS OF A LINE

The various vector generators make use of different formulations of the equation of a straight line. Throughout the discussion, we will denote the two endpoints of a line as (X_a, Y_a) and (X_b, Y_b). Further, $\Delta X = X_b - X_a$ and $\Delta Y = Y_b - Y_a$.

The formulations are:

1. Differential form

$$\frac{dY}{dX} = \frac{\Delta Y}{\Delta X} \qquad (3\text{-}1)$$

with boundary conditions such that (X_a, Y_a) and (X_b, Y_b) are endpoints of the line.

2. Integral form

$$X = X_a + \int \frac{\Delta X}{T} \, dt$$

$$Y = Y_a + \int \frac{\Delta Y}{T} \, dt \qquad (3\text{-}2)$$

The range of $0 \leqslant t \leqslant T$ will trace out the line.

3. Exponential Parametric form

$$X = X_a + \Delta X(1 - e^{-t/T})$$

$$Y = Y_a + \Delta Y(1 - e^{-t/T}) \qquad (3\text{-}3)$$

The range of $0 \leqslant t \leqslant \infty$ will trace out the line.

4. Linear Parametric form

$$X = (1 - \alpha) X_a + \alpha X_b$$

$$Y = (1 - \alpha) Y_a + \alpha Y_b \qquad (3\text{-}4)$$

The range of $0 \leqslant \alpha \leqslant 1$ will trace out the line.

3.3   LINE LENGTH ESTIMATES

All vector generation algorithms estimate the length of each vector they draw. The estimate is not always needed for the same purpose: for digital generation, it is used to terminate the line after an appropriate number of dots has been displayed. The analog generators use the estimate to insure that the intensity of all lines is constant.

The exact form of the line-length estimate depends on the particular vector generator. For various reasons, the estimate need not always be very precise. The exact length of a line is:

$$\sqrt{(X_b - X_a)^2 + (Y_b - Y_a)^2} \qquad (3\text{-}5)$$

The computation of the exact length requires multiplication and square root extraction, and is therefore quite complicated and time-consuming. Various simpler *estimates* of the length are:

The larger of the two deltas:

$$\text{MAX}\,(|\Delta X|, |\Delta Y|) \qquad (3\text{-}6)$$

The larger of the deltas plus one-half of the smaller:

$$\text{MAX}\,(|\Delta X|, |\Delta Y|) + (\text{MIN}\,(|\Delta X|, |\Delta Y|))/2 \qquad (3\text{-}7)$$

The sum of the deltas:

$$|\Delta X| + |\Delta Y| \qquad (3\text{-}8)$$

The smallest power of two exceeding the largest delta:

$$2^i \text{ such that } 2^{i-1} \leqslant \text{MAX}\,(|\Delta X|, |\Delta Y|) < 2^i \qquad (3\text{-}9)$$

The intensity corrections for analog lines are needed because the CRT beam does not always trace out the line at the same rate for all lines. If the rate varies, so does the intensity of the line, unless the beam current is controlled so that the visual intensity of the line remains constant. The intensity correction problem for digital vector generators is not dependent on line length, but rather on point spacing. If each dot is displayed with the same brightness, then lines drawn at a slope of 45 degrees will be only 70% as bright as horizontal lines (see Figure 3-3). Estimating the line length to be N, we can summarize as follows:

Digital Techniques: The algorithm generates points to represent the line, taking N steps in the computation (i.e. the count N is used to

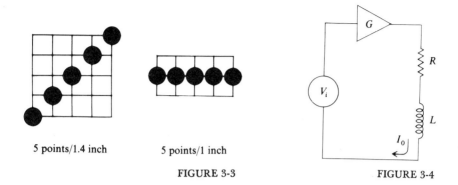

5 points/1.4 inch   5 points/1 inch

FIGURE 3-3   FIGURE 3-4

terminate the computation). Some algorithms will display fewer than N points.

Analog Techniques: N is used to control intensity correction so that lines of different lengths will have identical intensities.

3.4   HIGH SPEED LINE DRAWING

Analog and digital vector generators create positioning signals for the CRT beam very rapidly, and it is essential that the electronics that drive the beam deflection system respond rapidly and accurately to the signals. Digital algorithms generate binary numbers for the coordinates of each successive dot displayed; the speed at which points can be plotted depends on the response of the digital-to-analog converter, on the deflection amplifiers, and on the beam-control electronics. Analog generators produce voltages or currents which vary continuously as a line is traced; the deflection circuitry must respond rapidly to the variations.

The response of a typical deflection system affects design of vector generators. For simplicity, we shall assume that a deflection system is constructed as shown in Figure 3-4. An input voltage V_i is fed to an amplifier of gain $G = 1$; the amplifier drives a magnetic deflection yoke with inductance L; R is a lumped resistance representing impedances in the yoke and in the amplifier circuitry. The deflection of the beam is proportional to the magnetic field in the yoke, i.e. proportional to the current I_o.

Suppose we are generating the line digitally, by using a step function such as Figure 3-1. The response of the circuit to the step function is

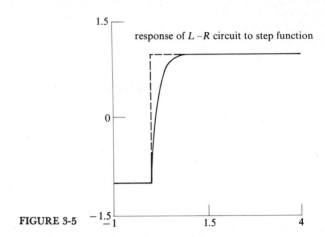

FIGURE 3-5

shown in Figure 3-5. The dashed line represents V_i, the step function input to the deflection system, and the solid line represents I_o, the deflection current which results. The time-constant L/R is 0.1.

If the beam position is to settle to within 1/2 grid unit of the correct new position before the beam is turned on to produce a dot, we must wait

$$\frac{L}{R}\log_e(2\beta) \qquad (3\text{-}10)$$

seconds, where β is the number of grid units the beam was moved. Although this time is fairly long for large β, β is usually 1 for steps of the staircase function generated by a vector generator. Thus, we need only wait about one time-constant (L/R seconds) between points.

An analog generator creates continuous voltage ramps as shown in Figure 3-2. For example:

$$V_{ix} = X_a + \gamma(\Delta X)t$$

and

$$V_{iy} = Y_a + \gamma(\Delta Y)t$$

As t ranges from 0 to $1/\gamma$, the voltages (V_{ix}, V_{iy}) will trace out the line. The reponse of the L-R circuit to such a ramp is shown in Figure 3-6. The dashed line represents the input ramp V_i, and the solid line represents the resultant deflection current I_o. The time-constant L/R is 0.1.

The deflection current eventually reaches the same slope as the driving signal, but never 'catches up' with it. Just as the ramp begins,

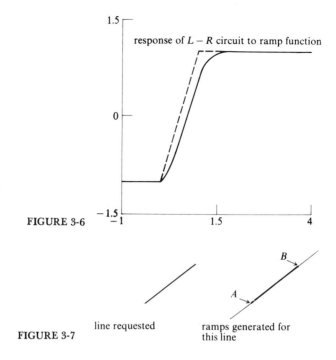

FIGURE 3-6

FIGURE 3-7

the beam deflection is moving much more slowly than the ramp has specified. The rate at which the slope of the deflection current approaches the slope of the ramp depends on the *slope of the ramp*. This means that, in general, the X and Y deflection currents will approach their correct ramps at different rates. Thus the beam will depart from a straight line during this initial period of time.

Many analog generators use a 'running start' to avoid crooked lines due to deflection lags. The ramps are generated for a line somewhat longer than the line requested, as shown in Figure 3-7. The initial lags in the deflection electronics will be finished by the time the beam reaches point A. At this instant, the beam current is turned on. When the line reaches point B, the beam current is turned off.

3.5 DIGITAL TECHNIQUES

It is not possible to draw a continuous line with a point-plotting display; the discrete grid permits intensification only of points lying on intersections of the coordinate grid. We can, however, display a

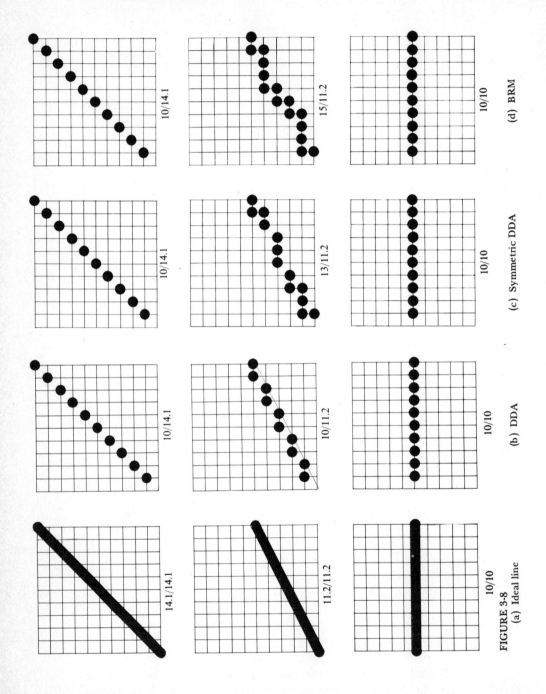

10/14.1

15/11.2

10/10

(d) BRM

10/14.1

13/11.2

10/10

(c) Symmetric DDA

10/14.1

10/11.2

10/10

(b) DDA

14.1/14.1

11.2/11.2

10/10

FIGURE 3-8
(a) Ideal line

sequence of dots which approximates the desired straight line. A good approximation is one which displays dots (a) of approximately the same spatial density regardless of the slope of the line, and (b) with an unbiased selection of approximate points. The first criterion insures that lines of all slopes will be equally bright; the second that the approximated line will not appear crooked. Figure 3-8 shows the results of three digital vector generators on three different lines (The ratio shown with each illustration is the point density, the number of points displayed divided by the Euclidean length of the vector). The generators differ in the point density and in the precision of the approximation to the ideal line.

The digital vector generation algorithms calculate a sequence of points (X_i, Y_i) to be intensified. These algorithms are incremental: the calculation of a point (X_n, Y_n) depends on the coordinates of the previous point (X_{n-1}, Y_{n-1}). The incremental approach often saves considerable complexity in the hardware or software required for the calculations. Multiplication operations, which are costly in time and hardware, can often be reduced to incremental additions, a much cheaper computation.

3.5.1   DIGITAL DIFFERENTIAL ANALYZER

The approximation of Figure 3-8b is generated with a device called a Digital Differential Analyzer (DDA), which gets its name from its use in solving linear differential equations. The differential equation of a straight line is simply equation 3-1, which is readily solved by a DDA.

$$\frac{dY}{dX} = \frac{\Delta Y}{\Delta X} \qquad (3\text{-}1)$$

The DDA produces only a discrete *approximation* to the continuous solution of the differential equation, but this approximation provides us directly with digital positioning commands for a point-plotting CRT.

The particular DDA of Figure 3-8b generates points that are spaced one grid unit apart along the axis of greater delta (the X axis in the figure). The line length estimate is thus the absolute value of the largest delta (equation 3-6). The spacing in the Y direction is merely the best approximation to $\Delta Y/\Delta X$ units. The absolute value of the ratio $\Delta Y/\Delta X$ is always less than or equal to 1, because we have chosen a line whose direction of largest delta is along the X axis.

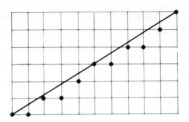

FIGURE 3-9

The computation of the X coordinate of successive points is very simple — we merely add one grid unit each time, or:

$$X_0 = X_a$$
$$X_n = X_{n-1} + 1 \qquad (3\text{-}11)$$

which we repeat N times (N is the line-length estimate).

The fraction $\Delta Y/\Delta X$ is used to compute an approximate Y value to accompany each X value. The immediate suggestion is to let:

$$Y_0 = Y_a$$
$$Y_n = Y_{n-1} + (\Delta Y/\Delta X) \qquad (3\text{-}12)$$

but then Y_n would have a fractional part which could not be displayed. We can use the integer part of Y_n as the Y value to send to the display hardware:

$$Y_0 = Y_a$$
$$Y_n = Y_{n-1} + (\Delta Y/\Delta X)$$
$$Y_{\text{display}} = \lfloor Y_n \rfloor \qquad (3\text{-}13)$$

However, all points generated in this fashion are biased to lie entirely on one side of the ideal line, as shown in Figure 3-9. Clearly we should *round* the value of Y_n to the nearest integer, not *truncate* it as above. Rounding is equivalent to adding 1/2 and truncating, or

$$Y_{\text{display}} = \lfloor Y_n + 1/2 \rfloor$$

Or, moving the addition outside the loop:

$$Y_0 = Y_a + 1/2$$
$$Y_n = Y_{n-1} + (\Delta Y/\Delta X)$$
$$Y_{\text{display}} = \lfloor Y_n \rfloor \qquad (3\text{-}14)$$

To Deflection System

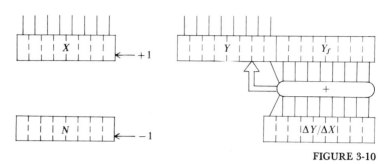

FIGURE 3-10

This is the method used to generate the points of Figure 3-8b.

Although the computation for X_i is a simple counting procedure, the computation for Y_i must be performed with adequate fractional significance. Equation 3-14 can be realized in hardware, as shown in Figure 3-10. The registers labeled X and Y are connected directly to the digital-to-analog converters of the point-plotting display. Initially, X and Y are loaded with X_a and Y_a. The N register is loaded with the line length estimate, in this case ΔX. Y_f (the fractional part of Y) is initialized to 1/2. Each time a new point is to be generated, the X register is incremented, the $Y.Y_f$ register is loaded with $Y.Y_f + (\Delta Y/\Delta X)$, and N is counted down. Now X and Y have the coordinates of a new point. The process is repeated until N reaches zero.

The number of bits provided for the N, $\Delta Y/\Delta X$, and Y_f registers determines the maximum length of the vectors that the DDA will draw. If vectors are to be drawn between any two points on a 10-bit coordinate grid, N must be capable of holding 10-bit numbers, as must Y_f (consider the vector from (0,0) to (1023,1) in a 10-bit display). The high order bit of the $\Delta Y/\Delta X$ register must coincide with the low order bit of the Y register because the maximum value of $\Delta Y/\Delta X$ is 1.

The division required to compute $\Delta Y/\Delta X$ is a disadvantage of the unit-increment DDA. The computation may be performed by the computer controlling the display or by special hardware in the vector generator. In any case, the division is expensive in either time or circuitry.

In practice, the control for the DDA is somewhat more complicated than demonstrated in our example, because we must handle cases where X is not the direction of greater movement, or where X is decremented with each step rather than incremented. The details should be immediately apparent and are reflected in a short software implementation of the algorithm:

```
PROCEDURE DDA (INTEGER XA,YA,XB,YB);
BEGIN    INTEGER DELTAX,DELTAY,STEPS,XCHANGE,YCHANGE;
         REAL REM,SLOPE;

         DELTAX  ←  XB ← XA; DELTAY  ←  YB ← YA;
         REM  ←  .5;  "PRELOAD WITH 1/2"

         XCHANGE  ←  IF DELTAX>0 THEN +1 ELSE -1;
         YCHANGE  ←  IF DELTAY>0 THEN +1 ELSE -1;

         IF ABS(DELTAX) > ABS(DELTAY) THEN BEGIN "X IS GREATER"
                 SLOPE  ←  ABS(DELTAY) / ABS(DELTAX);
                 FOR STEPS  ←  1 STEP 1 UNTIL ABS(DELTAX) DO BEGIN
                         REM  ←  REM+SLOPE;
                         IF REM GEQ 1 THEN BEGIN
                                 YA  ←  YA+YCHANGE;
                                 REM  ←  REM-1;
                         END;
                         XA  ←  XA+XCHANGE;

                         PLOT (XA,YA);  "PUT POINT ON DISPLAY"
                 END;
         END ELSE BEGIN "Y IS GREATER"
                 SLOPE  ←  ABS(DELTAX) / ABS(DELTAY);
                 FOR STEPS  ←  1 STEP 1 UNTIL ABS(DELTAY) DO BEGIN
                         REM  ←  REM+SLOPE;
                         IF REM GEQ 1 THEN BEGIN
                                 XA  ←  XA+XCHANGE;
                                 REM  ←  REM-1;
                         END;
                         YA  ←  YA+YCHANGE;

                         PLOT (XA,YA);
                 END;
         END;
END "DDA";
```

If the program is coded in machine language, the two separate loops can often be merged into one.

A program of this sort accepts two pairs of coordinates as input and generates a list of coordinate pairs as output. The treatment of the generated coordinate pairs varies: they may be recorded in an array, as shown in Figure 3-11, and used to refresh the display. Alternatively, the DDA itself can be used to refresh the display, as shown in Figure 3-12. In order to maintain the picture, the DDA must run continuously, circulating through all lines which are to appear on the screen. The second technique can be used only if the DDA can generate points rapidly enough to avoid flicker. Fortunately, the DDA is such a simple program that it is capable of refreshing the display almost as fast as the point-list technique.

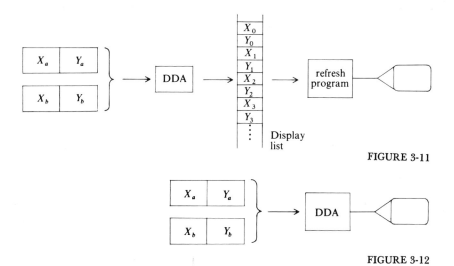

FIGURE 3-11

FIGURE 3-12

3.5.1.1   Symmetrical DDA

The DDA described above is really a very special one which uses a unit increment for the coordinate of maximum excursion. Ordinarily, a DDA operates identically on each variable:

$$\frac{dX}{dn} = \frac{\Delta X}{N} \qquad \frac{dY}{dn} = \frac{\Delta Y}{N} \qquad (3\text{-}15)$$

where N is the line length estimate. The difference equations are thus:

$$X_0 = X_a + 1/2; \; Y_0 = Y_a + 1/2$$
$$X_n = X_{n-1} + (\Delta X/N)$$
$$Y_n = Y_{n-1} + (\Delta Y/N)$$
$$X_{display} = \lfloor X_n \rfloor$$
$$Y_{display} = \lfloor Y_n \rfloor \qquad (3\text{-}16)$$

If we choose the line length estimate N to be MAX $(|\Delta X|, |\Delta Y|)$, these equations are precisely the algorithm for the unit-increment DDA given above. However, this choice requires a division to compute $\Delta X/N$ or $\Delta Y/N$, which is undesirable. Many hardware DDA's choose N to be some power of 2; this means that neither $\Delta X/N$ nor $\Delta Y/N$ is likely to be a unit increment. As a result, some points will be displayed twice, and some extraneous points will be generated. This is demonstrated in Figure 3-8c.

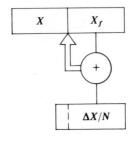 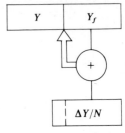

FIGURE 3-13

In practice, these unwelcome effects are minimized by choosing a line-length estimate which forces one of the increments to be near unity, i.e. either

$$1/2 \leqslant \left|\frac{\Delta X}{N}\right| < 1$$

or

$$1/2 \leqslant \left|\frac{\Delta Y}{N}\right| < 1 \qquad (3\text{-}17)$$

The line-length estimate used to achieve these results is called 'normalization' (equation 3-9). Since neither increment is ±1, it is still possible to display some points twice; the algorithm can be augmented to check for this condition and hence to avoid displaying the second point.

The hardware used to implement the symmetrical DDA is identical for the X and Y calculations, as shown in Figure 3.13. The symmetrical DDA requires values of X_a, Y_a, ΔX and ΔY as input quantities. No division is required prior to starting the DDA. The line-length estimate N and the ratios $\Delta X/N$ and $\Delta Y/N$ can be computed by shifting binary numbers.

3.5.2   BINARY RATE MULTIPLIER

The last and least satisfactory straight line approximation is produced with a binary rate multiplier (BRM). The BRM is based on a clever observation: as a binary counter counts up, bits change from 0 to 1 at varying frequencies: the low order bit of the counter changes from 0 to 1 at 1/2 the counting frequency, the next bit at 1/4, the next at 1/8, etc. Consider the 4-bit binary counting sequence shown in Figure 3-14. Suppose we consider ΔX and ΔY values which are also 4 bits long. We

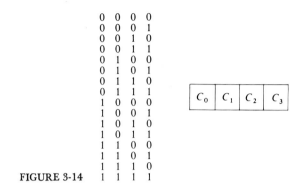

FIGURE 3-14

shall draw a line by loading the X and Y registers with the initial endpoint and then incrementing or decrementing these registers as required to trace out the approximate line. We shall let the 4-bit counter run as this process proceeds: the object is to add ΔX increments to X and ΔY increments to Y, evenly spaced in time. Let us rewrite the value of ΔX as a 4-bit quantity:

$$\Delta X = 8\, X_0 + 4\, X_1 + 2\, X_2 + X_3$$

where the X_i represent the bits of the ΔX value. If the X_0 bit is on in ΔX, we should plan to count up X by 8 counts at equal intervals during the generation of the line. But C_3 makes exactly 8 transitions from 0 to 1 during the counting cycle. Let T_i represent the assertion that 'on the next count of the counter, C_i will make a transition from 0 to 1.' Notice that for any count, only one T_i is true. The logic function to specify that the X register be counted is therefore:

count $X = (T_0 \lor X_3) \land (T_1 \land X_2) \lor (T_2 \land X_1) \lor (T_3 \land X_0)$

If ΔX is actually negative, we put $|\Delta X|$ in X_0, X_1, X_2, X_3 and use the above condition to determine when to decrement the X register. A similar process occurs concurrently for the Y coordinate.

The BRM should generate a straight line, because both X and Y are being counted at appropriate intervals as the counter goes from 0 0 0 0 to 1 1 1 1. But the count pulses are not evenly spaced in time, and the line appears quite ragged. A bad case occurs when $\Delta X = \neg \Delta Y$ (the bits of the deltas are complements), as is the case in the middle line of Figure 3-8d. The BRM generates far from pleasant lines; its low cost is the only reason for its use.

Counter (x indicates 0−1 transition)	Count X $\Delta X = 1010$	Count Y $\Delta Y = 0101$
0 0 0 0		
x	x	
0 0 0 1		
x		x
0 0 1 0		
x	x	
0 0 1 1		
x	x	
0 1 0 0		
x	x	
0 1 0 1		
x		x
0 1 1 0		
x	x	
0 1 1 1		x
x		
1 0 0 0		
x	x	
1 0 0 1		
x		x
1 0 1 0		
x	x	
1 0 1 1		
x	x	
1 1 0 0		
x	x	
1 1 0 1		
x		x
1 1 1 0		
x	x	
1 1 1 1		
	10 counts	5 counts

FIGURE 3-15

3.6   ANALOG METHODS

Analog vector generators are capable of drawing lines at much higher rates than digital generators: whereas deflection lags are encountered each time a new digital dot is displayed, they affect only the beginning and end of an analog line. In addition, analog lines are discernably smoother than point sequences. The drawbacks of analog schemes are their greater cost and sensitive alignment difficulties. However, both of these disadvantages are diminishing as new semiconductor technology emerges.

3.6.1   INTEGRATION METHODS

The integral equation for a line (equation 3-2) suggests that an analog integrator can be used to generate the X and Y ramps. A simple

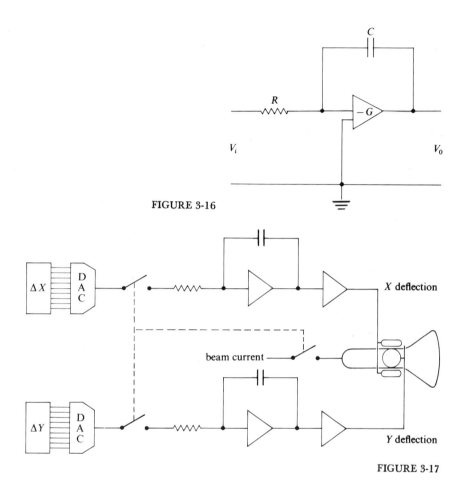

FIGURE 3-16

FIGURE 3-17

integrator is shown in Figure 3-16. The ideal integrator of this form obeys the following equation:

$$V_o = \frac{-1}{RC} \int V_i \, dt \qquad (3\text{-}18)$$

Notice that the integration is always with respect to time.

A simple system can now be constructed as shown in Figure 3-17. Two registers hold the desired changes in X and Y as digital values. These are converted to analog voltages by two digital-to-analog converters and are fed to the two integrators. Initially all switches are open. Because the inputs to both integrators are 0 volts, the outputs remain constant at voltages which cause the deflection system to address, for example, the point (X_a, Y_a). This corresponds to the initial conditions of our integral equation. When the switches are closed, the beam is turned on and the integrators produce continuous ramps for X and Y deflection. After a fixed period of time T, the point (X_b, Y_b) is reached, and the switches are opened. Once again, the integrators have inputs of 0 and the deflection remains at (X_b, Y_b). The integration circuits are fast enough that high deflection speeds, about 1 inch per microsecond, can be attained.

The high speed of the integrators requires fast response from the deflection amplifiers and switching circuits. If the deflections of the beam lag the ramps and the intensification of the beam, the resultant line will appear to have a bright spot at (X_a, Y_a) where the beam was intensified but not yet moving. Similarly, a small section of the other end of the line will be unintensified. The line will appear quite crooked unless the X and Y integrators, amplifiers, and switches have identical lags.

A more fundamental problem is fluctuating line intensity. If all lines are drawn in a fixed time interval T, long lines will be fainter than short ones. By increasing the beam current when drawing long lines we can compensate for these variations. However, the range of control is large: line lengths on a 10 inch screen vary from 0.01 inch to 14.14 inches or 1 to 1414, a range beyond beam control methods. Another method is to vary T so that $\sqrt{(\Delta X)^2 + (\Delta Y)^2} / T$ is constant for all lines, but this requires continuous variation of R or C in the integrator circuit, a very difficult process. An unsatisfactory but popular method is to restrict the magnitudes of ΔX and ΔY.

The intensity problem is usually solved with a combination of methods, for example use $|\Delta X| + |\Delta Y|$ to select one of several time intervals T (e.g. 2, 4, 6, 8, 12, 16, 28, 36 microseconds), then adjust the beam power proportional to $\sqrt{(\Delta X)^2 + (\Delta Y)^2} / T$. This is a particularly accommodating solution: T can be changed by selecting from among several resistances R for the integrators; the range of beam currents is now only 2:1 because the changes in T accomplish most of the required correction. A great deal of ingenious design is used to control all these parameters with simple circuits.

The circuit of Figure 3-17 is wholly unacceptable because of drift and other cumulative errors of the integrators. The circuit can be improved remarkably by introducing *feedback* to compute ΔX. The circuitry for X deflection is shown in Figure 3-18 just prior to starting the line from (X_a, Y_a) to (X_b, Y_b). The difference between the target

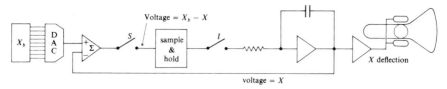

FIGURE 3-18

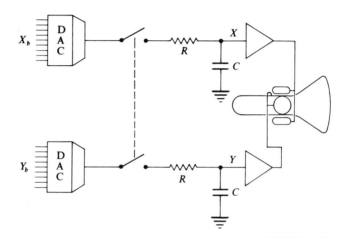

FIGURE 3-19

position and the present position is computed. Switch S is closed momentarily to 'remember' this $X_b - X_a$ voltage in a sample-and-hold circuit. Then I is closed to start the integration. During this time, the output of the sample-and-hold remains fixed at $X_b - X_a$, even though the input to the sample-and-hold circuit is changing. Identical circuitry is included to generate Y deflection signals.

3.6.2   EXPONENTIAL METHODS

The parametric exponential form of the line equation (Equation 3-3) has a particularly simple hardware implementation. Figure 3-19 shows how the charging of capacitors is used to provide the exponential. Suppose the switches are open and $X = X_a$, $Y = Y_a$. When the switches are closed, the voltages X and Y begin to change:

$$X = X_a + (X_b - X_a)(1 - e^{-t/RC})$$

$$Y = Y_a + (Y_b - Y_a)(1 - e^{-t/RC}) \qquad (3\text{-}19)$$

The X and Y voltages therefore trace out a straight line. Equation 3-19 suggests that X becomes equal to X_b only when $t = \infty$. In practice, R is decreased as the generation process proceeds, thus decreasing the time constant RC, and hastening the approach of X to X_b.

The RC time-constants for the X and Y deflection generators must be closely matched. If they differ slightly, the linearity of the line will suffer. No feedback is needed in this circuit: the switches remain closed (except for a brief interval when the D/A converters are given new coordinates) and thus the X and Y voltages will not drift from the output voltages of the D/A converters.

This vector generator is interesting because it requires varying intensity corrections as the line is being drawn. We can compute the drawing rate:

$$\frac{\mathrm{d}(\sqrt{(X - X_a)^2 + (Y - Y_a)^2}}{\mathrm{d}t} = \sqrt{(\Delta X)^2 + (\Delta Y)^2}\left(\frac{1}{RC}\, e^{-t/RC}\right) \qquad (3\text{-}20)$$

If the beam current is made proportional to this drawing rate, the brightness of the line will appear constant. A simple parallel RC circuit can generate the requisite $e^{-t/RC}$ time-varying function. There are several methods of including the line-length term: one is to provide several discrete values for R.

3.6.3 α, $1 - \alpha$ METHODS

An excellent compromise between the accuracy of digitally generated lines and the elegance of sweep-generated lines can be found in a group of 'α, $1 - \alpha$' methods. The name is derived from the form of the equation for a straight line given in equation 3-4:

$$X = (1 - \alpha)X_a + \alpha X_b$$
$$Y = (1 - \alpha)Y_a + \alpha Y_b \qquad (3\text{-}4)$$

This formulation is impractical for digital systems because of the multiplications involved. If, however, we provide α and $1 - \alpha$ as analog voltages and X_a, Y_a, X_b and Y_b as digital numbers, these equations can be realized in analog hardware. The key element is the *multiplying digital-to-analog converter* (MDAC) which multiplies an analog voltage by a digital fraction to yield a new voltage. The MDAC is slow to respond to changes in its digital inputs (about 2 microseconds) but this does not hinder rapid variations of the analog input. A schematic

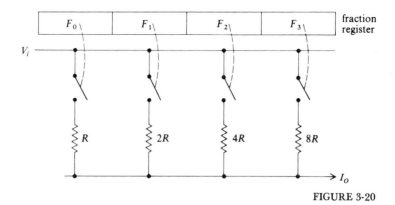

FIGURE 3-20

version of an MDAC might be as shown in Figure 3-20. A switch is closed if the corresponding bit of the fraction F is a 1. The current I_o is clearly proportional to the digital fraction F:

$$I_o = \frac{2FV_i}{R} \qquad (3\text{-}21)$$

A typical display using these converters is shown in Figure 3-21. To operate this device, we load X_a, Y_a, X_b, and Y_b, and set the voltage α to 0. Then we start α on a linear rise to $\alpha = 1$ by closing switch I, and we turn the CRT beam on. When $\alpha = 1$, we turn the beam off and open I. The output will have traced the desired line. A line-length estimate is used to control beam current when the beam is on, thus insuring that all lines are equally bright.

Several features of this circuit make it particularly free from traditional analog difficulties. The ramp α need not be particularly linear since the multipliers for both X_a and X_b are derived from the same signal α. We can avoid resetting α to 0 at the beginning of each line by passing the new endpoints alternately to each set of multiplying digital-to-analog converters. This is demonstrated in the following sequence:

Initially, $\alpha = 0; A \leftarrow X_a, Y_a$

$B \leftarrow X_b, Y_b$
$0 \rightarrow \alpha \rightarrow 1$ (display line)
$A \leftarrow X_c, Y_c$
$1 \rightarrow \alpha \rightarrow 0$ (display line)
$B \leftarrow X_d, Y_d$
   . . .

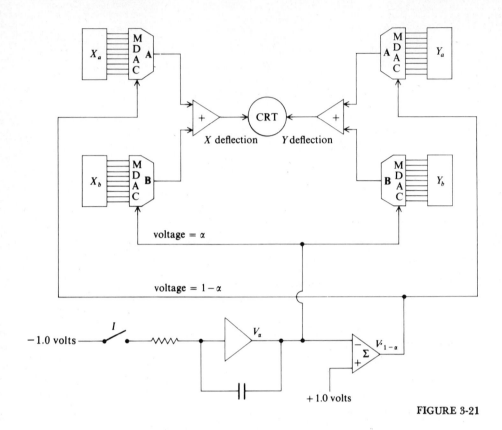

FIGURE 3-21

The circuit can be arranged to provide a 'running start' to combat the deflection lag problem. Rather than running α from 0 to 1, we run it from -0.1 to 1.1. Suppose $X_a = 100$ and $X_b = 400$. The deflection system will start $(\alpha = -0.1)$ at $X = 70$ and finish $(\alpha = 1.1)$ at $X = 430$. Because the deflection system starts with $X = 70$, by the time $X = 100$ $(\alpha = 0)$, the real starting point of the line, the initial lag period is over and the deflection system is responding smoothly. We need only turn the beam on exactly when $\alpha = 0$, and turn it off when $\alpha = 1.0$ (see Figure 3-22). The rate of rise of α can be matched to the speed of any deflection system.

This method has one serious shortcoming. Although the linearity of α is unimportant, the identity

$$V_\alpha + V_{1-\alpha} = 1 \qquad (3\text{-}22)$$

must always be true to better than 1 part in 1024. Consider the case where $X_a = X_b = 1000$. If, when $V_\alpha = 0.5$, $V_{1-\alpha} = 0.495$ (1% error),

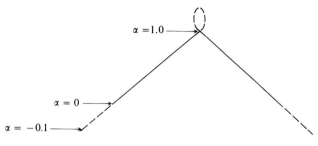

$\alpha = 1.0$

$\alpha = 0$

$\alpha = -0.1$

FIGURE 3-22

then X will be 995, not 1000. This error is particularly noticeable when the X's are very close to each other and very large (for example in a character drawn in the upper right corner of the CRT screen). In addition, the two multiplying digital-to-analog converters for each deflection system must be extremely closely matched. A mismatch yielding a 1% error in the output will have the same effect as an error of 1% in the $V_\alpha + V_{1-\alpha}$ identity.

The difficulties can be solved by replacing the four multiplying digital-to-analog converters by two of a different design. If X_a and X_b are close together (say 1005 and 1010), we might say: 'The 1000 part is constant. Only the 5 and 10 need be multiplied by $(1-\alpha)$ and α respectively.' We compare the numbers X_a and X_b bit-by-bit to see which bits are the same, and which bits differ. Those that are identical are used to form a new number X_o. Then we have:

$$X = X_o + (1 - \alpha)(X_a - X_o) + \alpha(X_b - X_o) \qquad (3\text{-}23)$$

The three binary numbers X_o, $X_a - X_o$, and $X_b - X_o$ never have bits in common. Thus, one MDAC, modified slightly, can be used to provide a current proportional to the sum of the three terms of equation 3-23, as shown in Figure 3-23.

A vector generator based on this generation principle is marketed by the Evans and Sutherland Computer Corp. The precision of this technique is superior to other analog generators because the digital values for the vector endpoints are involved directly in the generation of the deflection signals. The 'running start' technique permits this kind of vector generator to be matched to almost any deflection system, magnetic or electrostatic, and to drive the deflection at maximum speeds.

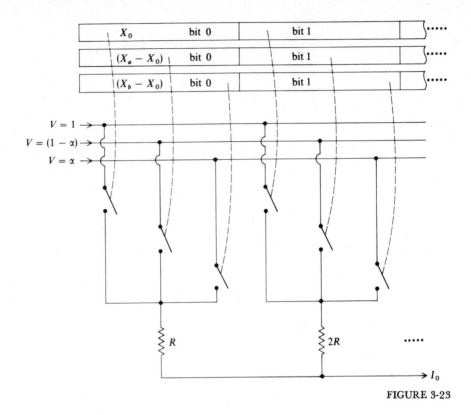

FIGURE 3-23

EXERCISES

3-1. We can easily compute the density of points for a DDA with unit increment as the number of points plotted divided by the true length of the line plotted:

$$\frac{\Delta X}{\sqrt{\Delta X^2 + \Delta Y^2}} = \frac{1}{\sqrt{1 + s^2}}$$

where s is the slope of the line. For $0 \leqslant s \leqslant 1$, this has a minimum at $s = 1$ and a maximum at $s = 0$. Make similar computations for the symmetric DDA and BRM.

3-2. The DDA designs can be simplified slightly if the Y and Y_f registers are kept separate. Whenever the addition of Y_f and $\Delta Y/\Delta X$ overflows, a 'carry' is generated which counts the Y register by ± 1 (see software program). Complete the details of this design. What about the case when $|\Delta Y/\Delta X| = 1$?

FIGURE 3-24

3-3. If a line is drawn from (0,0) to (10,5) with a symmetrical DDA, how many iterations are performed? How many distinct points are shown? How many points did the DDA generate twice in a row? Will it ever generate the same point three times in a row? How does the line-length estimate affect the answers to these questions?

3-4. Write a program to implement the BRM vector generator.

3-5. Find the worst case of a BRM line, i.e. under what conditions does a displayed point depart farthest from the ideal line?

3-6. Notice that neither of the two digital vector generators does any multiplications, although either might, if they took Equation 3-4 as a model for their computations. This is the *incremental* aspect of their operation. Can you characterize incremental techniques, and find other purposes to which they may be put?

3-7. Show the effect of non-linearities in the α ramp. Do they affect the straightness of the line? The brightness?

3-8. Solve the differential equations for the *L-R* circuit of Figure 3-4, and show:

　1. The deflection current *always* lags the ramp input, but the lag becomes constant after several time-constants have elapsed.
　2. Suppose we wish to have the deflection current I_o have *exactly* the ramp behavior shown in Figure 3-24. What should V_i look like to make this happen?
　3. The time constant of the *L-R* circuit is L/R seconds. This suggests that the time constant can be reduced to a very small value simply by increasing R. Why is this impractical?

3-9. The DDA is an excellent example of an incremental method for drawing a straight line. A DDA can be arranged to solve other kinds of differential equations. The differential equation of a circle is:

$$\frac{dY}{dX} = -\frac{X - X_0}{Y - Y_0}$$

if the center of the circle is at (X_0, Y_0). In this case, the increments used for each iteration of the DDA are not constant, but depend on X and Y. The circle about the origin can easily be generated with a DDA. Show how this is done. How many points will be generated?

The DDA implementation calculates the following function:

$$[X_i \ Y_i] = [X_{i-1} \ Y_{i-1}] \begin{bmatrix} 1 & -\epsilon \\ \epsilon & 1 \end{bmatrix}$$

This does not really generate a circle, but an expanding spiral. Demonstrate this. How does the spiral aspect depend on the value of ϵ?

The determinant of the matrix above is not 1, but $1 + \epsilon^2$, which causes the points to spiral out. How can the matrix be modified to correct this problem? What figure is then generated? For further reading, see Reference [48].

3-10. What does Figure 3-3 suggest about optimal spot-sizes for digital vector generation? Is the variation of intensity with slope dependent on spot size?

4
DISPLAY PROCESSORS

4.1 CONTROLLING A VECTOR-DRAWING DISPLAY

A vector-drawing display is potentially several orders of magnitude faster than a point-plotting display. Sequences of connected vectors can be drawn without any intervening settling delay, in as little as one or two microseconds each. This means that a refresh program of the type described in Section 2.3 is totally inadequate, for it takes 20 microseconds or longer to process each pair of data words. It would thus reduce the capacity of the display by a factor of five or ten.

4.2 CHANNELS

Fortunately there is a simple hardware substitute for the refresh program, called a *channel*. The channel is a device that can pass words or characters repeatedly between the computer and one of its peripheral devices at speeds up to one word per microsecond. A channel can therefore read any number of sequential words from memory and pass them, one by one, to a display controller. It does this with the aid of two registers, an *address register* that tells it where to find the next word, and a *word count register* that indicates how many words are to be transferred. After each word has been transferred, both the address and the word count (which is kept in negative form) are incremented. When the word count reaches zero, transfer ceases and the computer is interrupted. The computer may then reset the channel's registers and start another transfer.

A display channel can thus read a list of points such as the one described in Section 2.3.2, and send them to a point-plotting display as fast as the display can handle them. Alternatively it can pass a list of vector parameters to a vector-drawing display. Ideally it should be able to do both; however the list must in this case be marked with *codes* to distinguish points from vectors, and the channel must include logic to *decode* the words it receives so that they are sent to the appropriate registers. A two-bit code might be used as follows:

Code	Meaning	Action
00	point	load two words into x-register and y-register, and intensify
01	position	load two words into x- and y-registers, no intensification
10	vector	load two words into Δx- and Δy-registers and draw vector from previously specified point.

Data words identified by codes in this fashion are usually called *display instructions* since they closely resemble machine instructions for a simple computer. A list of display instructions is generally called a *display file*.

4.3   DISPLAY PROCESSORS

One of the more inconvenient features of a display channel is its word count register. This register must always be initialized to the correct value, and determination of this value is an extra step that the program must perform whenever the display file is altered. It is often more convenient to insert a special code at the end of the display file. This word may have the effect of interrupting the computer, so that the latter can reset the address register to point to the start of the display

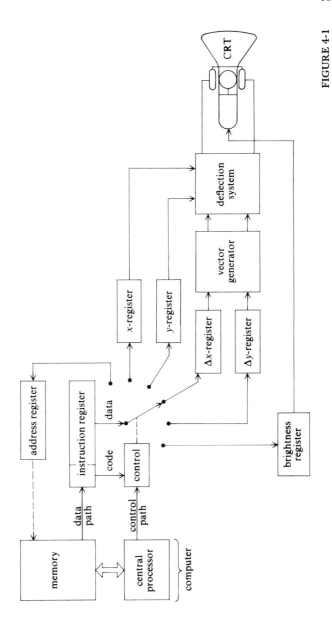

FIGURE 4-1

file. Better still, the word can include the address of the start of the display file, which the channel can use to reset its own address register. This gives the effect of a 'jump' instruction in the display file:

11   jump   reset address register to specified address

The channel is now capable of operating continuously, completely independently of the computer, and therefore deserves the status of a *display processor*. The simple ability to operate in this independent fashion, and hence to reduce the load on the central processor, is the main advantage that display processors have over display channels. As we shall see, the processor's ability to take data from non-sequential memory locations also leads to much more efficient display files.

The general arrangement of a simple display processor is shown in Figure 4-1. Instructions are brought from memory into an *instruction register* where they are decoded. The data content of the instruction is then loaded into the appropriate register.

Figure 4-1 also shows a *control path* from the computer to the display processor. This is essential so that the computer can maintain overall control over the display processor. In particular the computer must be able to reset the address register, to start transfer of data, and to *stop* transfers. For certain styles of programming it is also convenient if the computer can read the contents of registers such as the address register and the x- and y-registers.

4.4   AN INSTRUCTION SET FOR A DISPLAY PROCESSOR

The instruction set described above could be used without difficulty to construct simple pictures. However it has some drawbacks and limitations. There is no means of altering the brightness of points and vectors; and it is impossible to display characters or other symbols in a manner analogous to the technique of Section 2.3.3. A number of additional features are desirable in a display that is to be used for general-purpose interactive graphics. In the following pages, instruction set design is discussed by means of a specific, hypothetical example. We shall assume in this example that the display instructions are stored in a memory constructed from 16-bit words, and that the display screen has a coordinate system running from 0 to 1023 in each direction.

There are of course innumerable ways of arranging instruction formats within 16 bits. The choice is somewhat reduced, however, if we take two factors into account:

1. The processor hardware is simplified if all instructions have a similar format.
2. Most display files are not hand-coded, but are generated by an interactive program; the instruction set should facilitate the design of this program.

Out of consideration for the these factors, it is best to use a single standard format for all instructions:

0	2	3	4	15
op. code		I	data	

This allows 12 bits of data, and leaves three bits to specify the data type. The bit marked I is used for intensification control. Operation codes are numbered from 0 to 7. We shall discuss first those instructions that control the CRT, i.e. those that draw lines and points.

4.4.1   CRT CONTROL INSTRUCTIONS

4.4.1.1   Positioning

Two instructions are required for setting the x- and y-registers, and for intensifying points:

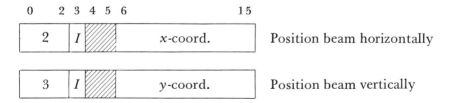

The I bit is used to intensify the point if necessary. These instructions are the equivalents of the DXL, DYL, DXI and DYI instructions of the point-plotting display. They load the x- and y-registers from the lower 10 bits of the instruction and deflect the beam, bypassing the line-generating hardware.

4.4.1.2   Vectors

A line may be specified either by its two endpoints, or by one of its endpoints and its length. The second method is generally just as convenient as the first, and has the great advantage that entire pictures can be defined relative to a single point in the picture. This is essential if subroutines are to be used (see Section 4.4.2.2). The use of relative vector instructions also means that the Δx and Δy values can be fed straight into the line generator's registers.

A full-length vector obviously cannot be specified in 16 bits of data, so we must use two words:

0	2 3	4	5 6	15	
4	1	D	±	Δx	x-vector

| 5 | 1 | D | ± | Δy | y-vector |

In these instructions the intensify bit is set to one, indicating a visible line. The D or *display* bit is essential, for it allows the Δx or Δy register to be loaded without immediately drawing the vector. Thus to draw a vector we set the starting point with a pair of *position* instructions, load Δx with the D bit cleared, and load Δy with the D bit set so as to draw the line (see Figure 4-2). One of the great advantages of this instruction format is that it permits the two instructions specifying a vector to be separated; this greatly simplifies the task of creating display files in small blocks of memory.

Notice that a sign bit is included in the vector instructions. Most displays use sign-magnitude notation in vector-drawing instructions, even though they are designed to work with computers that have ones- or twos-complement arithmetic. This is done so that the magnitude of the line can be fed straight to the vector generator. For ease of programming it is best if the computer's notation is used. Twos-complement creates a problem, however, for it is possible to represent the number -1024 in ten bits. The magnitude of this number cannot be converted by a ten-bit D/A converter. As a result, sign-magnitude notation is normally used in displays attached to twos-complement computers.

Besides drawing relative vectors, the display should be capable of

2	0		x_1	set x
3	0		y_1	set y
4	1	0	$x_2 - x_1$	set Δx
5	1	1	$y_2 - y_1$	set Δy, draw

FIGURE 4-2

relative beam movements, so that complete pictures can be specified in relative form:

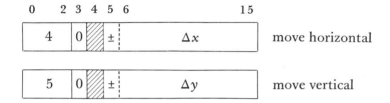

These do not always use the vector generator hardware. Instead a digital adder is often used to compute the new x or y value and load it into the x- or y-register. There is no need for a D bit in these instructions — they take immediate effect.

4.4.1.3   Short vectors

It is wasteful to use two words to specify very short vectors, i.e. those less than 32 grid units in length. Both the Δx and Δy components of such a vector can be accommodated in a single word, forming a 'short vector' instruction:

```
  0    2 3 4 5      9 10 11     15
┌───┬──┬─┬──────┬─┬──────┐
│ 1 │ 1│±│  Δx  │±│  Δy  │      draw vector
└───┴──┴─┴──────┴─┴──────┘
```

Δx and Δy may be up to six bits each in size including sign.* Short

---

* The shorter we make our maximum short vector, the fewer bits are needed to specify it. If the maximum change in x or y is 3 units, for example, both Δx and Δy can be specified in 6 bits, and several such vectors can be specified in a single instruction. This is generally called an *increment* instruction.

vectors are very useful for coding small symbols and characters. A corresponding instruction is the 'short move:'

4.4.1.4 Brightness control

If the display permits control of brightness, an instruction will be needed for setting the brightness register:

This instruction permits eight different levels of brightness to be specified.

4.4.2 PROCESSOR CONTROL INSTRUCTIONS

So far we have created an instruction set that can cope quite efficiently with the majority of rectilinear pictures. Now we should consider the non-graphical or *control* instructions.

4.4.2.1 Jump instruction

As mentioned earlier, one very important instruction is the *jump* instruction, which gives the display processor independence from the computer:

The 12-bit address field provided by this instruction allows the display to address 4096 words directly. This is normally adequate in a processor that is refreshing a single display — it permits pictures containing up to 2000 long vectors or 4000 short ones. For greater addressing capability the *I* bit may be used, either to extend the address field to 13 bits or to provide indirect addressing. Some displays permit memory to be addressed as a number of banks of 4K words, with the aid of special instructions for switching banks.

4.4.2.2   Subroutines

One of the most powerful control instructions in a display is the *subroutine jump*. It is of particular value in displaying symbols that appear repeatedly in a picture. Without a subroutine feature, all these identical symbols must be represented by repeating the same instructions, perhaps many times. This is shown in Figure 4-3a. With the inclusion of the subroutine feature, it becomes feasible to represent all the appearances of such symbols by calls to subroutines, as shown in Figure 4-3b. The subroutine, like its counterpart in a computer program, is terminated by an instruction that resets the address register to point to the instruction following the call.

Subroutines are useful only if the symbols that they define may be placed anywhere on the screen. It is for this reason that relative drawing capability is so important in a display. A subroutine defined by absolute positioning commands cannot be drawn in more than one position on the screen.

Return from a subroutine can be effected in a number of ways. Some displays provide a *return address register* in which are placed the contents of the address register whenever a subroutine jump takes place. A special instruction is required to reset the address register from the return address register so as to effect the return. This technique has the disadvantage that subroutine calls cannot be 'nested,' i.e. no subroutine calls may be included in subroutines themselves. For example, we could not use a subroutine representing the letter *R* in a subroutine depicting a resistor, because a call to the *R* subroutine would destroy the first return address and prevent return from the resistor subroutine.

The ability to nest subroutines to a number of levels is a feature almost as useful as the subroutine itself. It is most conveniently provided by means of a *push-down stack*. The stack consists of a number of core memory locations or hardware registers. An additional *stack pointer* register is needed to indicate the position of the 'top' of the stack, i.e. the most recently used location. When a subroutine jump takes place, the return address is 'pushed' into the stack: the stack

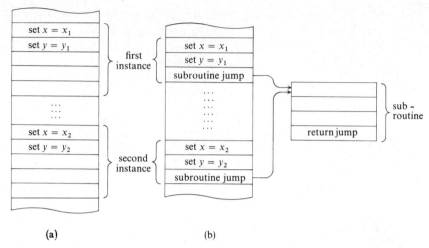

FIGURE 4-3

pointer is 'raised' to point to the next location, in which is deposited the return address. To effect a return, the return address is 'popped' off the stack: the contents of the top location are transferred to the address register, and the stack pointer is lowered. Figure 4-4 shows the state of the stack at various points during the display of a set of nested subroutines.

To provide a push-down stack subroutine capability, two further instructions are required:

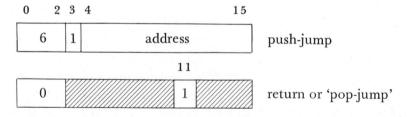

In addition the computer must be able to set the stack pointer. In certain applications it is also useful if the computer can read the stack pointer and the contents of the stack. If so, it is more convenient to keep the stack in core memory. On the other hand, the use of special registers avoids some of the problems that arise when a display processor is allowed to write into the computer's memory; for example, it prevents the stack from overflowing into areas occupied by programs or display files.

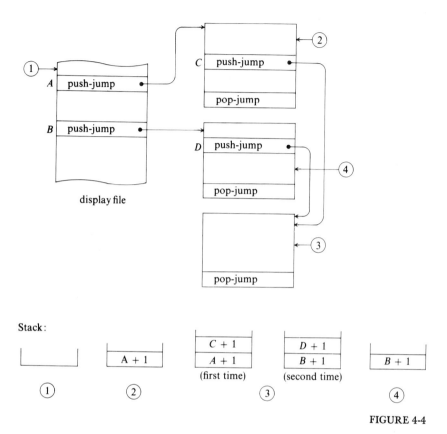

FIGURE 4-4

4.4.2.3 Timing and interrupt control

It is essential to provide some means of maintaining a constant refresh rate. If we simply place a jump at the end of the display file, pointing back to the start, the display will vary in brightness according to the length of the display file. If the display file is very short, the picture may be so bright that the phosphor is burned.

The computer may have an interval timer or *clock*, that it can use to start the display at regular intervals. A simpler method is to provide a timer in the display, together with a synchronizing instruction that causes the display processor to wait until the start of the next interval:

wait until next interval

This instruction need be included at only one point in each display file in order to synchronize it and maintain the display at constant brightness.

It is often useful if the display can *interrupt* the computer. For example, if the computer is interrupted at the end of the refresh cycle, it can make whatever changes are necessary to the display file before the start of the next cycle. The interrupt instruction normally halts the display:

```
0    2              9
┌──────┬─────────┬───┬─────────┐
│  0   │/////////│ 1 │/////////│    halt and interrupt
└──────┴─────────┴───┴─────────┘
```

4.5   CHARACTER GENERATORS

4.5.1   CHARACTER SUBROUTINES

One reason why the subroutine feature is so important in a display processor is that it allows text to be included in the display file in a compact fashion. Each character may be represented by a subroutine that starts at the left-hand side of the symbol and finishes at the right, as shown in the letter *A* in Figure 4-5. Then a string of characters may be represented by a single pair of positioning commands, followed by a series of subroutine calls.

4.5.2   HARDWARE CHARACTER GENERATORS

Text is displayed more efficiently, however, if a *character generator* is used. In the first place, the character generator permits text to be packed more compactly in the display file. We may use a special instruction code to indicate text, and follow the instruction with character codes packed two per word:

```
0    2        7 8              15
┌──────┬────────┬──────────────┐
│  7   │////////│   1st char    │
├──────┴────────┼──────────────┤
│   2nd char    │   3rd char    │
├───────────────┼──────────────┤
│   4th char    │   5th char    │
└───────────────┴──────────────┘
```

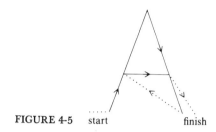

FIGURE 4-5   start   finish

The display will continue to interpret instructions as packed characters until it encounters an 'escape' character such as zero, which returns it to normal execution.

A preferable technique is to include the *address* of the text in the initial instruction:

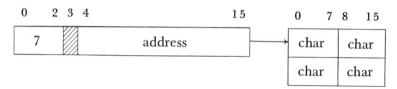

This simplifies the task of adding to the string while the display is running. It also reduces the danger that the processor will try to execute text as normal instructions. This could happen in the first scheme if a 'jump' to the start of the text were miscalculated by one place. The usual result of such an error is that the display 'runs wild,' particularly if some of the character pairs are identical to 'jump' instructions. In the second scheme this is less likely to happen. The second scheme also makes it easier to include text messages that are part of a data structure and cannot therefore be embedded in the display file.

As the display processor unpacks the characters in the text string, the appropriate symbols must be traced out by the beam. In effect, therefore, our hardware character generator must provide the same functions as the subroutine method for text display, with a six- to eight-bit code in place of each subroutine call.

Some character generators simply interpret the text string as a list of subroutine calls [70, 84]. Each byte in the string is used as an index into a table of subroutine addresses, and the appropriate subroutine is called (see Figure 4-6). Since the subroutines and the table are stored in core, the character set can be changed at will. This is a great advantage.

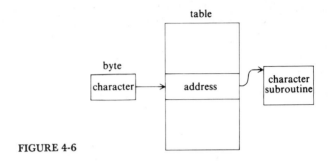

FIGURE 4-6

On the other hand, the programmable character generator is not a particularly fast method of displaying text: typically characters take 20 to 30 microseconds each to display. Speeds of five microseconds per character can be achieved by some of the hardware character generators now available.

These usually use a separate memory, either diode matrix or integrated circuit, to store the character shapes. When a character is displayed, the appropriate section of memory is read out in the form of pulses that drive either a *stroke generator* or a *dot generator*. The stroke generator is somewhat similar to the analog vector generator described in Chapter 3, but is generally much simpler since there are far less stringent performance requirements. It produces very legible characters but tends to require more frequent adjustment than the dot generator. The dot generator uses x and y counters to control the beam's movement, rather in the fashion of the DDA and BRM. Pulses stored in memory step the counters up and down, and also control intensity as the character is traced out.

4.6   DISPLAY TERMINAL DESIGN

The instruction set discussed in this chapter is summarized in Table 4-1. During this discussion we have made the assumption that the display is refreshed out of the computer's memory: the control instructions shown in Table 4-1 are designed with this in mind. There are however a number of reasons why we may not wish to refresh the display directly from computer memory: the computer may not permit the *direct memory access* (DMA) that this involves; or its performance may be affected by the numerous memory accesses that the display makes. This becomes a particularly severe problem if the computer is time-shared;

Table 4-1: Summary of display instruction set

0	2	3	5	7	9	11	13	15	
0				0					null operation
0							1	level	set brightness
0						1			pop-jump (return jump)
0					1				wait for interval timer
0				1					halt and interrupt
1	0	±	Δx		±	Δy			short move
1	1	±	Δx		±	Δy			short vector
2	I		x-coordinate						position x
3	I		y-coordinate						position y
4	I	D	±	Δx					x-vector
5	I	D	±	Δy					y-vector
6	0		address						jump
6	1		address						push-jump
7			address						display text

Computer instructions for display control:

Set address register
Set stack pointer
Start display
Stop display
Read address register
Read x register
Read y register
Read stack pointer
Read brightness register
Read run status, i.e. whether display is running

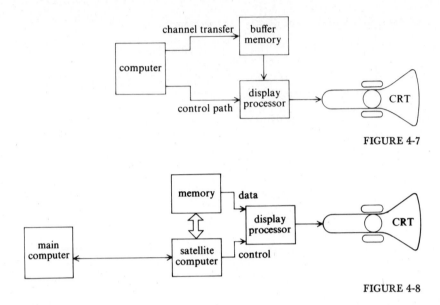

FIGURE 4-7

FIGURE 4-8

furthermore, it is desirable in this case to be able to place the display at some distance from the computer. A number of different designs have been proposed for *display terminals*, i.e. displays that are physically separate from the computer and that can be placed at an appreciable distance away from it.

The earliest display terminals simply used a separate core memory, known as a *buffer* (Figure 4-7). The buffer could be loaded by channel transfer from the computer. However, there were severe problems in programming these devices: it was generally impossible to change the contents of the buffer without stopping the display, which would therefore go blank for long periods; reorganization of the buffer's contents was even more time-consuming, and often could be done only by keeping an exact copy of the buffer's contents in the computer's memory; transmission errors were a problem, for the display rarely contained anything very elaborate in the way of error-checking apparatus. Added to all this, buffered displays were generally very expensive.

One solution to the buffered display's deficiencies has been to add a small, general-purpose processor to the terminal, creating the *satellite display terminal* shown in Figure 4-8. This is potentially a very powerful arrangement, for the satellite computer can not only handle buffer memory management, but can also execute user programs that require rapid response. The programming problems involved in this sort of system are still quite severe; they are discussed in some detail in Chapter 17. An alternative approach has been to use low-cost storage media for refresh purposes, and to simplify the display's functions so as to avoid programming problems. This leads to what is known as the *low-cost display terminal*.

4.6.1   LOW-COST DISPLAY TERMINALS

One of the earliest successful attempts to build a low-cost graphics terminal was the GLANCE terminal, designed and built at Bell Telephone Laboratories [44]. The general arrangement of the system is as shown in Figure 4-9: several terminals are clustered around a disk, on which the picture is stored as very short vectors. The display is refreshed from the disk via a high band-width transmission line, whose maximum permitted length is about 1000 feet.

4.6.1.1   Direct-view storage tube terminals

The development of the direct-view storage tube has revolutionized the design of low-cost graphics terminals. Use of this tube avoids the need for conventional memory to store the display file. Several manufacturers have developed terminals using this storage tube: their general arrangement is as shown in Figure 4-10.

An important difference between these terminals and the GLANCE terminal is the use of serial character transmission, both for text and for graphics. For example, a vector is transmitted to the terminal as a special control character, followed by two or more characters specifying the length of the vector. This use of character transmission greatly simplifies the task of integrating these terminals into an existing time-shared system.

The chief drawbacks of the direct-view storage tube are its small size, poor erase characteristics and low picture quality. The lack of selective erase capability in these terminals makes it impossible to program highly interactive graphical techniques. The picture can be erased in its entirety, but this takes half a second or so, during which the screen is flooded with a distracting flash. The use of serial character transmission generally imposes a fairly severe limit on the speed at which pictures can be transmitted, for speeds above 2400 bits/second are often beyond the capacity of the transmission line.

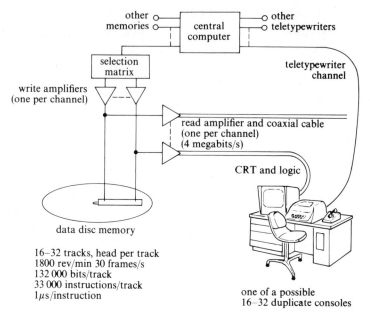

write amplifiers
(one per channel)

FIGURE 4-9

16–32 tracks, head per track
1800 rev/min 30 frames/s
132 000 bits/track
33 000 instructions/track
1μs/instruction

one of a possible
16–32 duplicate consoles

4.6.1.2   Video terminals and systems

A number of terminals and systems have been designed to use standard television monitors as displays. The TV monitor itself is, as we all know, a very inexpensive device; however the signal used to drive the monitor is completely different from the signals we have learned how to generate from the computer. It is an analog signal, representing by its modulation the intensity of spots on the screen. These spots are traced out in a *raster* fashion, as a succession of horizontal lines. To reduce flicker, two successive rasters are displayed, each one generating alternate lines as shown in Figure 4-11.

The design of a video terminal presents its own set of problems, generally rather different from the problems we have encountered in designing conventional line-drawing displays. In the first place, line and text information received from the computer must be converted to raster information: this involves a difficult process called *scan-conversion*. Once converted, there is the problem of where to store the raster definition. It can be stored in digital form, but the quantity of data is rather large — one million bits of information for a raster of 512 x 512 points, allowing for 16 different brightness levels. All this

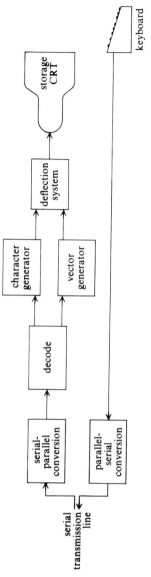

FIGURE 4-10

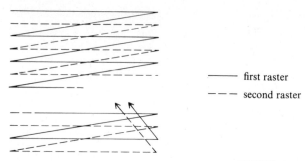

first raster

second raster

FIGURE 4-11

information must be converted to analog form and passed to the TV monitor 30 times a second. Alternatively the information may be stored in analog form. Once stored, the information is difficult to change selectively: whichever method is used, the bits of information representing a line are scattered around in the stored data.

Rose [239] has described a video graphics system in which scan conversion is performed by placing a line-drawing CRT and a television camera face-to-face as shown in Figure 4-12. A similar technique has been used in the RAND Video-graphics System [293]. The converted picture is then stored on a disk in analog form. The digital storage technique has only recently become economically feasible: a low-cost terminal that uses integrated-circuit shift registers for picture storage is now being marketed [250]. Only one brightness level, however, is permitted.

The silicon target tube described in Chapter 1 has also been used as a basis for a very simple video terminal [218]. Lines and text are drawn on the tube's target area in the normal fashion, and the picture is scanned to generate the TV signal. This terminal is operationally very similar to the direct-view storage tube terminals described above, with the advantages of variable brightness and better picture quality.

4.6.1.3   Low-cost terminals with processing power

The recent decline in the cost of integrated circuits has made it possible to produce small, general-purpose processors very inexpensively. At least one low-cost terminal has been produced equipped with such a processor in addition to a full-fledged display processor [124]. The functional arrangement of such a terminal is identical to that of the satellite terminal shown in Figure 4-8; however, the low cost of the

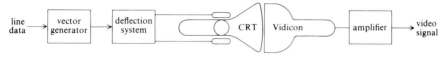

line data → vector generator → deflection system → CRT | Vidicon → amplifier → video signal

FIGURE 4-12

terminal allows it to be used without concern for wasting the power of the terminal's processor. Generally these terminals are connected by serial transmission lines to time-shared terminals, and are operated in much the same fashion as other low-cost terminals.

4.6.2   EXTENDING THE TERMINAL'S POWER

During the last few years, display designers have been interested principally in ways of simplifying the display so as to make it less expensive. An alternative approach is to add features to the display so as to augment its capabilities and hence its range of uses. These additional features in turn require additions to the instruction set.

Care is needed in attempting to extend the instruction set beyond the level of Table 4-1. As Myer and Sutherland have pointed out [193], it is possible to become trapped in a 'wheel of reincarnation' in which the display processor is developed to the point at which it turns into a general-purpose computer, and requires a separate channel to refresh the display. This paradoxical situation can be avoided by careful consideration of the way in which the display is to be used.

If we make such a careful study, we will often find that the display processor does not need an elaborate instruction set in order to do its job well. Its primary responsibility is to maintain a picture on the screen without flicker and with as sparing use as possible of memory. A lesser but still important requirement is that the display should not make excessive demands on the computer to which it is attached. What is not often realized is that the best way to aid the computer is to simplify its task of generating display files. This is done, not by extending the instruction set to the ultimate in complexity, but by keeping it simple and consistent.

Thus although the display's instruction set can be extended in a variety of ways, it is by no means true that any form of extension will improve the display. Many categories of display instruction, such as arithmetic operations and skip instructions, complicate the task of display file generation and take up valuable time in the refresh cycle.

The simplest and surest way to improve a display is to add to its ability to control the CRT, for example with the aid of instructions to draw dotted or broken lines, or to generate colored pictures. Instructions can be added for drawing circles and arcs of circles, but the range of application of these instructions is rather small.

There have been many exercises in building displays with the ability to *transform* pictures, i.e. to change the scale of the picture, rotate it and so forth. This is a legitimate way of trying to reduce the load on the computer. However it involves more than just the addition of a few instructions. Careful attention must be paid to the problem of *clipping* the picture (removing lines that are off the screen), and to the concatenation of transformations. These operations can all be performed by the display processor but, as is shown in Chapters 6, 7 and 8, they are not simple. A display processor that performs them properly is likely to be expensive.

EXERCISES

4-1. Section 4.4.2.2 mentions the problems that can occur if we keep the return stack in core. How can these problems be avoided?

4-2. Some displays provide only a short vector instruction for line-drawing. Assume that the long vector instructions (operation codes 4 and 5) are omitted from the instruction set of Table 4-1. Write or flow-chart a routine to generate the short vector instructions to represent lines of any length. Note that some of the techniques described in Chapter 3 are applicable.

4.3. In reference [302], Watson *et al.* suggest using a *marked* return address stack: return addresses are marked by adding the 'jump' operation code, so that the top word in the stack can be *executed* to effect the return. They also suggest adding instructions to push the contents of other registers into the stack. Suppose the following instructions were added:

push x	push contents of x-register into stack, marked as 'position x' instruction;
push y	push contents of y-register;
push x and y	push both;
peel	execute stack until a 'jump' is encountered and executed.

In what ways would you expect these instructions to be useful? Which way up would you design the stack to operate?

4-4. Why does the second form of the 'display text' instruction, described in Section 4.5.2, simplify the task of adding text to a string while the display is running?

4-5. The position and vector instructions we have considered use immediate data, i.e. the data is in the instruction itself. What would be the advantages and disadvantages of designing these instructions to *address* the data instead?

4-6. Table 4-2 shows the instruction sets of three hypothetical displays, representative of displays that are or have been marketed by various manufacturers. Discuss their good and bad points.

4-7. Design an instruction set, along the lines of Section 4.4, (a) for a 12-bit display, (b) for a 24-bit display.

Table 4-2

DISPLAY A

In control mode (mode 0):

```
 0    2  3  4  5        8  9   10   11   12          15
┌──────┬──────┬////////┬──┬────────┬───┬──────────┐
│mode¹ │ l.p.²│////////│S │ scale³ │ B │intensity⁴│
└──────┴──────┴////////┴──┴────────┴───┴──────────┘
```

In point mode (mode 1):

```
 0    2  3  4  5 6                             15
┌──────┬──────┬──┬────────────────────────────┐
│ mode │ l.p.²│I⁵│     x- or y-coordinate      │
└──────┴──────┴──┴────────────────────────────┘
```

In vector mode (mode 2):

```
 0 1 2  3          8  9   10                   15
┌──┬──┬──┬───────────┬──┬────────────────────────┐
│E⁶│I⁷│± │ Δx-value⁸ │± │      Δy-value⁸          │
└──┴──┴──┴───────────┴──┴────────────────────────┘
```

In jump mode (mode 3):

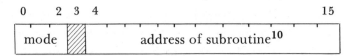

0		2	3	4											15
mode			I^9	address											

In subroutine mode (mode 4):

0		2	3	4											15
mode			▨	address of subroutine[10]											

In character mode (mode 5):

0	1	2						8	9						15
E^6	▨	first character						second character							

Notes

1. The 'mode' bits determine how the *next* instruction will be interpreted; the display always starts in mode 0.
2. In modes 0 and 1, the light pen is enabled if bits 3 and 4 contain 11, and is disabled if they contain 10. If bit 3 is 0, the light pen status is unaffected.
3. If bit 9 is set, bits 10 and 11 are interpreted as a scale setting: $00 = x1$, $01 = x2$, $10 = x4$, $11 = x8$.
4. If bit 12 is set, bits 13 to 15 determine the brightness level, 0 to 7.
5. If bit 5 is set, the point is intensified.
6. During vector and character modes, the mode remains unchanged until an instruction is encountered in which bit 0 is set: this causes the next instruction to be interpreted in control mode.
7. If bit 1 is set, a line is drawn; otherwise the beam is moved without drawing a line.
8. Sign-magnitude notation is used.
9. If bit 3 is set, and indirect jump takes place, using the contents of the addressed location as the jump address.
10. When a subroutine jump is performed, the return address is deposited in the specified location, and execution of the subroutine commences at the instruction following this location.

DISPLAY B

0		2	3						9	10	11	12	13	14	15	
0			▨						W^1	R^2	I^3	S	scale^4			set parameters[5]

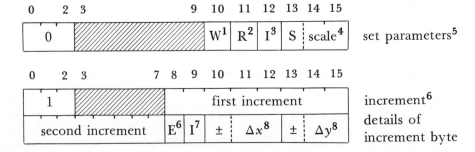

0		2	3				7	8	9	10	11	12	13	14	15	
1			▨				first increment									increment[6]
second increment					E^6	I^7	±	Δx^8		±	Δy^8					details of increment byte

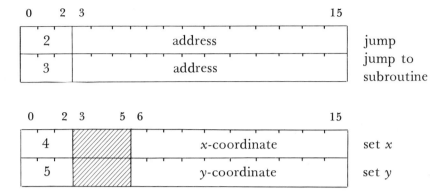

Notes
1. Setting bit 10 causes the display to wait until the next 60 Hz pulse.
2. Setting bit 11 causes a subroutine return jump.
3. Setting bit 13 causes a point to be intensified at the previously specified x and y.
4. See Display A, note 3.
5. If all bits in this instruction are zero, the display halts.
6. Ensuing words are interpreted as pairs of increment bytes, until a byte is encountered with the E bit set.
7. If this bit is set, a line is drawn; otherwise the beam is moved.
8. Sign-magnitude notation is used.

DISPLAY C

In text mode:

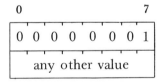

In graphics mode:

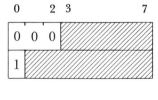

```
 0  1  2  3  4        7  8                          15
┌──┬──┬──┬──┬──────────────────────────────────────┐ ⎫
│ 0│ 1│I²│L³│          x-coordinate⁴                │ ⎪
└──┴──┴──┴──┴──────────────────────────────────────┘ ⎪
 16          19 20     23 24                       31 ⎬ set point⁵
┌────────────┬───────────────────────────────────┐   ⎪
│////////////│          y-coordinate⁴             │   ⎪
└────────────┴───────────────────────────────────┘   ⎭
```

Notes
1. Byte contents are interpreted as character codes.
2. If bit 2 is set, point is intensified.
3. If bit 3 is set, line is drawn from previous position.
4. Integer in range 0 to 4095.
5. This instruction must start at a byte address that is an exact multiple of four.

## PART TWO

Display Files

5

DISPLAY FILE COMPILERS

5.1 DISPLAY CODE GENERATION

A display file is effectively a *program* for execution by the display processor. It exhibits many of the features of a conventional computer program — it includes jump instructions, subroutines and instructions to load registers with immediate data; and it is executed in much the same fashion as a computer program, with the aid of a program counter. Display files can even be created in the same manner as computer programs, by writing down the instructions to represent the desired picture, and then assembling them into binary data.

Display files are rarely created in this way, for this would mean that the program could only display pre-defined pictures. Instead a computer program is written, one of whose functions is to generate the display file. For example, a printed-circuit layout program may be designed to generate display files from the data that it computes or that the user of the program supplies. This process, the generation by a program running in one processor of a program for execution by another, is very similar to the operation of a *compiler*. We can

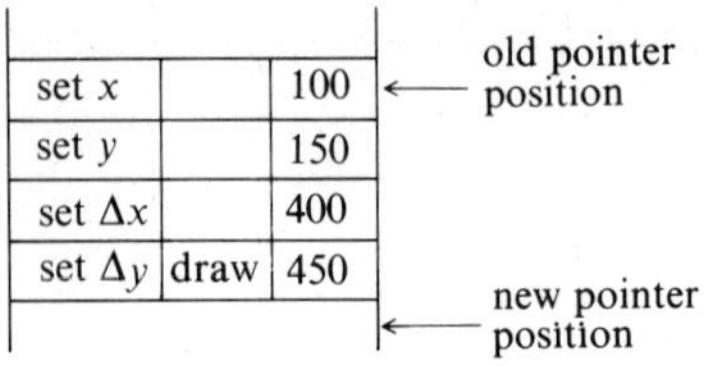

set x		100	← old pointer position
set y		150	
set Δx		400	
set Δy	draw	450	← new pointer position

FIGURE 5-1

conveniently call the process *display file compilation*. In this chapter we shall discuss display file compilers, i.e. those programs whose task is to generate display files.

5.2   GRAPHICAL FUNCTIONS

It is important to understand just what tasks the display file compiler performs. It receives *graphical function calls* from elsewhere in the program; typically each of these function calls will be a request to the compiler to add to the display file a graphical entity such as a line or a point. The coordinates of the line or point are passed as the parameters of the call. Using these parameters, the compiler constructs the appropriate sequence of display instructions and adds them to the display file.

To illustrate this process, let us follow through the action of a typical graphical function:

LINE(100,150,500,600);

This represents a command to add to the display file a straight line from the point (100,150) to the point (500,600). Figure 5-1 shows the resultant addition to the display file for a typical line-drawing display. Four more instructions have been added, and the pointer marking the end of the display file has been moved forward four places. This is a particularly simple example; the line-drawing function is one that may be termed a *primitive function* of the display file compiler. Other primitive functions are required to plot points, to display text and to clear the screen. As this chapter proceeds it will also present some of the more complex functions that the display file compiler may provide.

The set of functions that constitute the display file compiler may be used with a variety of different application programs. They may be grouped as a package of subroutines* that the applications programmer loads with his program. Better still, they may be included in the system library so that they are loaded automatically.

5.3   THE VIEWING ALGORITHM

Where do the parameters of the function calls originate? In some cases they originate with the user of the program: he types in two pairs of coordinates, for example, and the application program calls the LINE function with these coordinates as parameters. One can imagine a number of line definitions being typed in (or alternatively being drawn in with a graphical input device), so that a complete circuit diagram or building layout is assembled on the screen.

A program of this sort can be put to very little use if the incoming data is used only to create display file instructions, and is not retained for future use by the program. For example, if we were to draw the plan of a house in this way, it would be useful if the program could compute the areas of the rooms and so forth. This means that some sort of data structure must be built as the plan is drawn, so that the program can trace through it to determine the shape of each room. Notice that as long as this data structure exists it is possible to re-create the original picture definition; thus pictures erased from the screen are not permanently lost. The process that re-creates pictures is similar to the one that computes areas, for it too traces through the data structure. However, the *algorithm* for this process is quite different: it involves different calculations, and makes extensive use of graphical output functions. We will call it the *viewing algorithm*.

The program gains considerably in simplicity and ease of development if all graphical output is generated by means of viewing algorithms, i.e. by output procedures that make no direct communication with input devices but use the program's data base as a source of parameters. More than one such procedure may be included in a single program, in order to generate several different kinds of picture from the same data. An advantage of separating the input and output routines is that it is easier to change the program's mode of input or output; and the modular concept of program construction leads to greatly simplified program design. The separation of input and output is a concept that is used throughout this text.

---

* For this reason, a display file compiler is often called a *graphics package*.

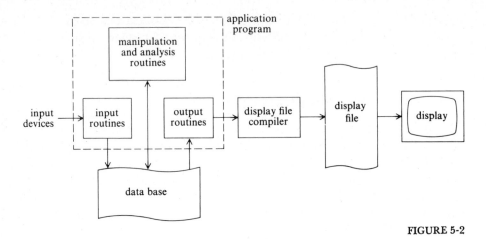

FIGURE 5-2

Figure 5-2 shows the general structure of the process of generating a display file. The application program is on the left. It includes routines for reading information from input devices and storing it in the program's data base; it includes routines like the area computation routine, for manipulating and analyzing the data base; and it includes output routines based on viewing algorithms. The function calls made by the output routines are handled by the display file compiler, generating a display file that is refreshed by the display processor.

5.4   SEGMENTED DISPLAY FILES

An important attribute of any display file compiler, particularly if it is part of an interactive program, is the speed at which it compiles. Consider the example of a program to display a three-dimensional object, such as a machined component, by showing a two-dimensional view of it on the screen and allowing the operator to rotate it with the aid of a tracker-ball. Unless the display processor includes hardware for rotation, then each time the ball is moved the program must compile a fresh display file. Before compilation is complete the ball may be moved again, so that a fresh request for compilation is generated and is waiting for the compiler when it completes each new display file. In this sort of application the compiler is running almost continuously, and its speed is vitally important. Unless new display files can be generated at the rate of ten or more per second, the motion of the

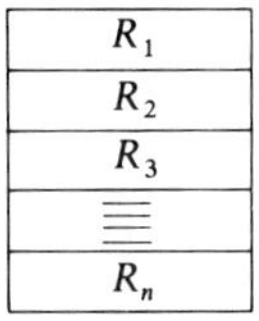

FIGURE 5-3

component will appear jerky; if the frequency drops to one new frame per second or less, the operator may lose all control over the program.

Fortunately in many cases only part of the picture changes dynamically and it is therefore possible to avoid re-compiling the whole diplay file. For example, if our machined component is only one of several on the screen and the others are unaffected by moving the tracker-ball then it may be unnecessary to re-compile their images. In order to re-compile pictures selectively they must be presented to the compiler in distinct segments. These must in turn be compiled into separate segments of the display file, so that when the picture changes the compiler can leave the static segments unaltered. Nowadays almost all interactive graphical programs use segmented display files.

5.4.1   DOUBLE BUFFERING

Suppose we have constructed a segmented display file whose structure is as shown in Figure 5-3. R_1, R_2, etc. are the separate segments, or *records* as they are better called to avoid confusion with program segments. The display processor refreshes the picture by periodically starting at the beginning of R_1 and executing all the instructions it encounters until it reaches the end of R_n.

Now suppose we wish to change the contents of R_2. This record may for example depict an object that is being continuously rotated. There is a good reason why we cannot simply overwrite the contents of R_2 with fresh display instructions. If we do this there is a distinct possibility that the display processor may attempt to execute R_2 while it is in course of reconstruction. Generally an operation of this sort, in which one processor is writing a record while another is reading it, produces indeterminate results unless extreme care is taken in constructing the record. In display file compiling, 'extreme care' means making sure the record is readable every time an instruction is added to it. A compiler that does this is usually large and slow.

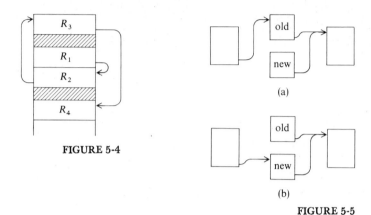

FIGURE 5-4

(a)

(b)

FIGURE 5-5

Some programs set a 'flag' to identify a record that is being modified, so that the display processor will omit this record and pass on to the next. This means that the record is not refreshed as often as the rest of the display file, and it therefore flickers or appears rather faint. In the worst case, where it is being recompiled at the maximum possible rate, it will vanish completely. When we consider the effect of this on the user, whose attention is probably focused on this part of the picture, we realize how undesirable it is.

The correct way to modify a segmented display file is to use *double buffering*. We reconstruct the record in an unused area of memory, meanwhile leaving the existing version in the display file. When the new record is complete it takes the place of the old version, and the vacated space becomes free for future use. Double buffering obviously creates discontinuities in the display file, which may eventually look something like Figure 5-4. Each record in this display file is followed either by the next consecutive record or by a jump instruction pointing to it. For the sake of generality it is best to assume that all records terminate with a jump instruction that may simply address the following location in memory.

There is a critical moment in the double-buffering operation when the new record is exchanged for the old. This must be done in the right sequence, shown in Figure 5-5. The new record should be completely compiled and should include a final jump instruction pointing to the next record in the display file, as shown in Figure 5-5a. Then the jump instruction in the previous record can be switched to point to the new record as in Figure 5-5b. In this way a smooth transition is achieved.

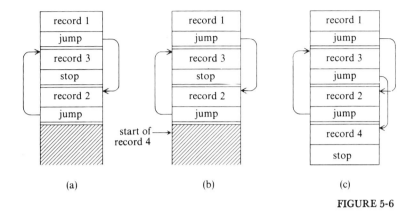

FIGURE 5-6

5.4.2   FUNCTIONS FOR SEGMENTING THE DISPLAY FILE

If we add to the display file compiler the ability to segment the display file into records, then we must add functions to permit the programmer to define individual records. At the very least these functions must allow him to create records, to redefine them and to delete them. As well as adding these functions we must enable the programmer to identify the record he wishes to modify or delete. This implies adding some form of *naming* capability.

The most straightforward naming technique gives each record a *unique integer name*. Suppose we have three records in the display file, with names 1, 2 and 3 (Figure 5-6a). We can create a new record by means of a function call:

OPEN(4);

This function *opens* a new record with name 4. It sets up a pointer to the start of a free area in the display buffer (Figure 5-6b) so that ensuing graphical function calls will add display instructions in this area. Finally when the record has been completely defined it is *closed*:

CLOSE;

The CLOSE function terminates the record and adds a pointer from the previous record so that the new record is included in the refresh cycle (Figure 5-6c). No argument is required, provided only one record may

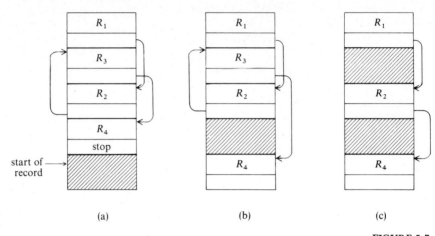

(a)   (b)   (c)

FIGURE 5-7

be open at one time, for the name of the record to which the **CLOSE** applies is then obvious.

When a record is to be redefined a slightly different operation must be carried out, since the old version of the record is to be discarded. However we begin the process exactly as before, by setting the pointer to the start of a free area (Figure 5-7a). This means we can use the same function:

OPEN(4);

When the new definition is complete we must close it and replace the old one in the manner described earlier. We can make use of the same **CLOSE** function, since this function can check whether there is an existing record to be replaced. The final result is as shown in Figure 5-7b.

Records can be removed from the display file very easily. We need a single **DELETE** function, called as follows:

DELETE(3);

which has the effect of bypassing the record as shown in Figure 5-7c. Thus the three functions **OPEN**, **CLOSE** and **DELETE** permit all the basic display file manipulations.

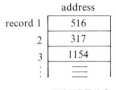

FIGURE 5-8

<table>
<tr><td></td><td>name</td><td>address</td></tr>
<tr><td></td><td>1237</td><td>1036</td></tr>
<tr><td></td><td>715</td><td>334</td></tr>
<tr><td></td><td>331</td><td>710</td></tr>
</table>

FIGURE 5-9

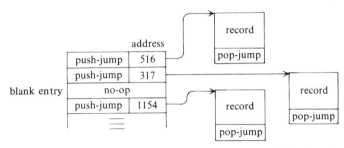

FIGURE 5-10

5.4.3   NAMING MECHANISMS

In order for these functions to succeed in deleting or redefining an existing record, they must be able to determine the physical position of the record in the display file. This information can be provided by a *table*. The simplest form of table, shown in Figure 5-8, uses the integer name as an *index* and contains the starting address of each record. This sort of table restricts the programmer to a range of names equal to the size of the table. It is more convenient if he is allowed to use any integer; this can be arranged by adding a lookup table of the type shown in Figure 5-9. The use of a lookup table does however add to the overhead involved in opening and deleting records.

A more elegant linkage mechanism may be used with displays that have push-jump subroutine instructions. The table of addresses may then be replaced by a table of push-jumps to the various records, each of which is terminated by a return jump (Figure 5-10). Blank table entries contain a null instruction. An extension of this technique that avoids the inconveniences of the fixed-size table has been suggested in the Computer Display Review [139]; it is shown in Figure 5-11. Records are linked together by jump instructions located in the second word of each record. Following this instruction is the name, around which the display is directed by means of a push-jump instruction. Thus

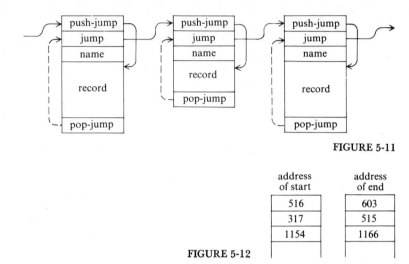

FIGURE 5-11

address of start	address of end
516	603
317	515
1154	1166

FIGURE 5-12

in order to look up a name we scan down the linked list of records examining the third word of each one. It is to simplify this scanning process that the pointers are placed in the second word of each record.

5.4.4   APPENDING TO RECORDS

It is often convenient if additional data can be added to an existing record without redefining it completely. This APPEND function can be included in the display file compiler, but only at the expense of some extra complexity.

In the first place, it becomes necessary to know not only where a record starts but where it ends, so that the extra instructions can be added in the right place. This necessitates an additional table, as shown in Figure 5-12. A more severe problem is that double buffering is no longer feasible, except by going to the extreme of making a copy of the entire record every time something is appended to it. So it may prove necessary to remove the record from the refresh cycle while additions are made to it. This is very undesirable, for it means that during a rapid succession of appending operations the record will practically disappear.

The only elegant solution to this problem is to make additions to the record in such a way that it need not be removed from the refresh cycle. Figure 5-13 illustrates what this implies, using the same example

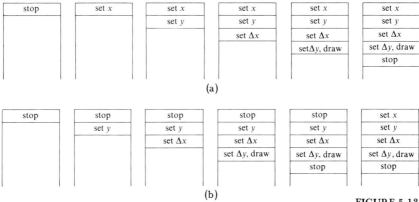

(a)

(b)

FIGURE 5-13

of a LINE function call as earlier. In Figure 5-13a we see the standard method of adding instructions in a double-buffered environment. Figure 5-13b shows the same instructions being added to a record that is simultaneously being refreshed. Thus the inclusion of an APPEND function in the display file compiler has implications on the design of all the compiler's graphical functions. Not all displays permit as simple a solution as the one shown in Figure 5-13b.

5.5   FREE STORAGE ALLOCATION

When a record is deleted or redefined, the vacated area of memory must be made available for re-use. This means that the display file compiler must be supported by some form of *free storage system* which allocates blocks of memory and to which blocks are returned when no longer in use.

Although there are many different approaches to the design of a free storage system, only a few of them are applicable to display files. The reason for this is that it is generally impossible to tell how big a record will be at the time it is opened, so there is no way of choosing a free block of the right size. In these circumstances it is best to allocate free storage in one of the following ways:

1. allocate a large block of free storage whenever a record is opened, and return the remainder when it is closed; or
2. construct all records out of blocks of the same size.

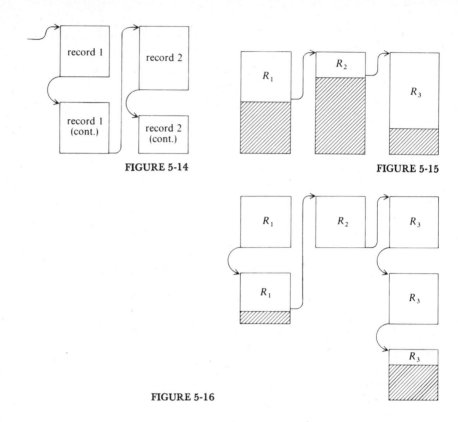

FIGURE 5-14

FIGURE 5-15

FIGURE 5-16

The first technique makes the more efficient use of memory. Provided a large enough block is allocated, display file compiling is very simple, for instructions are always generated sequentially. Occasionally a very large record is generated, however, and a second block must be allocated to take the overflow. This generates *fractured* records which must be connected by jump instructions (Figure 5-14). A more severe problem with this method is that small, unusable free blocks gradually accumulate and can only be eradicated by *garbage collection*, i.e. by shifting records around in memory so that free space can be amalgamated. It is generally impossible to do this without stopping the display processor.

We can avoid garbage collection by using fixed size blocks. This is wasteful of memory, as we can see from Figure 5-15. However, wastage can be reduced if relatively small blocks are used. Many records will then be fractured (Figure 5-16) but the wasted space at the end of each record is quite small.

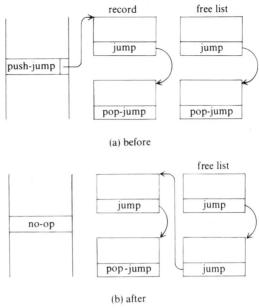

(a) before

(b) after

FIGURE 5-17

The advantages of this method are its simplicity and speed of operation, plus its ability to do without garbage collection. Return of free storage is particularly simple if we use one of the push-jump techniques described above for linking records; we can then append the returned blocks to the free list without disturbing the linkages. This is illustrated in Figure 5-17.

Many other types of free storage system may be used in display file compilers; space does not permit a thorough description of each one. The reader in search of more information on this subject is referred to Knuth [147].

5.5.1   DELAYED RE-USE

Whatever free storage allocation technique is used, there is a danger that when a block is returned to free storage the display may still be executing instructions within the block. Although the block is no longer in use by the central processor, it is still in use by the display processor. If the block is re-used while the display processor is still tracing through it, the display file will be overwritten and the display

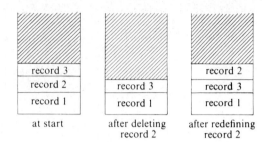

FIGURE 5-18

will run wild. One way to avoid this problem is to stop the display when the record is removed and restart it on the next record. However this produces an annoying discontinuity in refreshing if the same record is redefined at a rapid rate. A better solution is to delay re-using the free storage until it is safe to do so. This can be achieved by placing the blocks in a reserve free list which is amalgamated with the main list at the end of the refresh cycle.

5.5.2   COMPACTING

It is possible to avoid all the problems of free storage allocation by adopting the following simple strategy: all new records are added at the end of the display file, which is compacted to fill gaps created by deletions and redefinitions (Figure 5-18). The display processor must generally be stopped as this is done, which means that even if double buffering is used there will be short periods when the screen goes blank. Nevertheless the extreme simplicity of the compacting technique makes it ideal for unpretentious graphics systems.

5.6   DISPLAY SUBROUTINES

Many displayed pictures include repeated symbols such as logic circuit elements, architects' symbols, chemical pipework symbols and so forth. It is convenient to define each such symbol once only and to be able to refer to this definition whenever a reference to the symbol occurs in the display file. This is made possible by the use of *display subroutines*. A display subroutine is a single segment of display code that can be used several times in the display file. Its implementation in an efficient

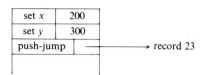

FIGURE 5-19

manner relies on the use of some sort of subroutine jump instruction, such as the one described in Section 4.4.2.2.

The simplest way to handle subroutines in a display file compiler is to treat them as a special variety of record. After such a record has been defined, a reference to it can be inserted with the aid of a CALL function:

CALL(23);

Normally the call is preceded by a statement specifying the position at which the symbol is to appear, as in the following example:

POSITION(200,300);
CALL(23);

This might add to the display file the instructions shown in Figure 5-19.

The OPEN-CLOSE sequence described earlier cannot be used for defining subroutine records, since it adds the record to the refresh cycle. One solution to this problem is to employ a special function to open definitions of subroutine records:

OPENSUB(23);

Another solution is to treat all records as subroutines. To add a record to the main refresh cycle we simply make a call to the record from a special 'base record.' This technique is implicit in the use of *groups* and *items* as described below in Section 5.6.2.

Within a subroutine record all graphical data must be defined *relative* to the starting point of the subroutine: absolute coordinate data will prevent the subroutine from being located at different points on the screen. Thus a relative line-drawing function is required in addition to the LINE function described in Section 5.2.

The table in which subroutine addresses are stored may be organized in much the same fashion as the table for ordinary records. However if

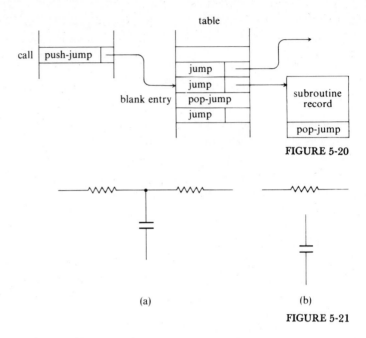

FIGURE 5-20

(a)   (b)

FIGURE 5-21

the push-jump technique of Section 5.4.3 is used, it is best to lay out the subroutine address table as shown in Figure 5-20. In this case, blank entries should contain return jump instructions. This arrangement allows subroutines to be redefined very easily.

5.6.1   STRUCTURED DISPLAY FILES

It is possible to include in subroutines not only graphical data but calls to other subroutines. For example we could define a record to represent the circuit shown in Figure 5-21a, making use of the two symbols shown in Figure 5-21b. The first record could then be used as a subroutine several times in a circuit layout (see Figure 5-22). This technique of building *structured display files* is often used to generate displays of circuit diagrams and of other pictures with a similarly clearly evident structure.[*]

The use of structured display files demands a display processor with the ability to call subroutines to several levels of depth, such as is

---

[*] Structured display files are particularly popular as a basis for light pen interaction. This is discussed further in Chapter 10.

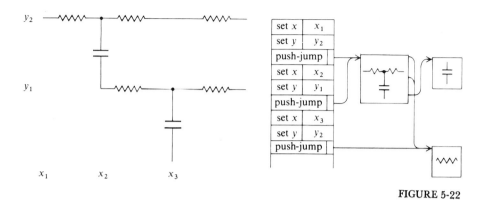

FIGURE 5-22

possible with the aid of a push-down stack. If this is not the case, we can employ a technique used in various systems including Graphic-2 [44, 206]. Subroutine jumps are not used; instead a local computer is interrupted when the subroutine call is encountered, and the call is *interpreted* by the computer. This approach enables highly complex display file structures to be used without the need for a correspondingly complex display processor.

5.6.2   GROUPS AND ITEMS

The set of functions described so far has one serious limitation: it is impossible to delete or modify a single call within a record. For example, a record defining a logic circuit might be created from a large number of calls to various subroutines representing logic symbols. It would be impossible to modify the position of one symbol except by re-creating the entire record.

The LEAP language [247, 91] has been used as the basis for a set of functions that avoids this limitation. Two types of display record are used. One of these is an *item*; it resembles a normal record, but can contain no calls, only graphical information. It is defined by a normal OPEN-CLOSE sequence.* The other type of record is called a *group*, and can contain only calls to items and to other groups. There is no need to open or close a group; instead a call is added to the group simply by naming the group and the called entity, at the same time

---

* To conform with the set of functions used in this chapter, the function names used in this description differ from those used in the original LEAP implementation of groups and items.

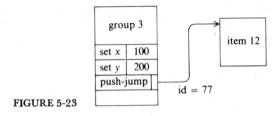

FIGURE 5-23

specifying the position of the called entity and an *identifier* for the call. This operation acts like an APPEND. For example, if we wish to add to group 3 a call to item 12, to be positioned at (100,200), we write:

CALLITEM(12,3,77,100,200)

The number 77 is the identifier of the call. Figure 5-23 shows the effect of this function. If at a later point we wish to move the symbol, say to (200,300), we use the same function:

CALLITEM(12,3,77,200,300)

To remove the symbol, we delete the call, giving its identifier and the name of the group it is in:

DELETECALL(3,77)

A CALLGROUP function is required so that calls can be made to groups as well as to items. For example, to add a group to the refresh cycle, we include a call to it in a special group 0, equivalent to a base record. Here the position may not matter, and can be omitted:

CALLGROUP(3,0,888)

Groups are best implemented as linked lists of blocks, rather than as single blocks of memory. Figure 5-24 shows a suitable arrangement. Here the identifier of the call is included in the block to avoid the need for a separate table.

The execution of a CALLITEM or CALLGROUP involves checking whether the group to which the call is to be added is already in existence; if it is not, a new group must be created. If it exists, then a search must be made for an existing call with the given identifier. If

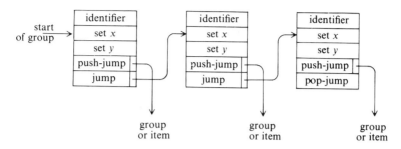

FIGURE 5-24

such a call is found, its position is altered as indicated by the call; otherwise a new call is added to the group.

The provision of groups and items adds an extra degree of flexibility to the display file compiler; this flexibility may be invaluable in certain areas of application. Compared with the scheme suggested earlier in this chapter, groups and items make slightly heavier use of memory, because of the linked-list group structure. The extra links also slightly reduce the speed of refreshing. However, these overheads are often amply justified by increased program efficiency.

5.7   GRAPHICAL DATA STRUCTURES

Two processes are involved in producing a display file from a data structure: firstly the data structure is scanned by a viewing algorithm, i.e. by an output routine that generates graphical function calls; secondly the display file compiler in response to these function calls creates a display file. The cumulative effect of these two processes is to generate a second data structure from the first. Often the original data will be changed out of all recognition by this process. On the other hand it is easy to think of cases where the display file might be almost indistinguishable from the original data. An example is an 'inking' program that reads coordinates from a graphical input device and displays its path as a trail of dots.

Suppose we store the points as they are received from the device, each one as a relative displacement from the previous point (Figure 5-25). The output routine passes each of these displacements to the display file compiler, with the command to compile a line of this length. The final display file will consist largely of a string of vector

−11	5
−3	2
5	4
—	—
—	—

FIGURE 5-25

vector	−11	5
vector	−3	2
vector	5	4
	—	
	—	

FIGURE 5-26

commands to the display processor, as shown in Figure 5-26. The only difference between one of the original data words and the corresponding display file instruction is the 'vector' operation code that has been added. Both of these lists of data may reside in the memory of the same computer, and memory may be a scarce commodity. So it may be worthwhile to try to make one set of data serve both purposes.

In the case of the 'inking' program this takes very little effort. As fresh positions are received from the input device they are compiled directly into display commands, producing the format shown in Figure 5-26; this display file can then be used by the program as data. This technique can also be applied to more complex applications. A circuit diagram could be defined entirely by the display subroutines representing the circuit symbols and by the lines joining them.

The use of display subroutines in this manner creates a shared data base that is commonly known as a *graphical data structure*.* Figure 5-27 illustrates a typical graphical data structure representing a simple modular building layout. As can be seen in Figure 5-27a, the building is constructed from five units: two windows, two walls, and a door. Figure 5-27b shows the building as it might conceptually be represented, using a structure containing five elements; each element represents one modular unit and designates the type of unit and its position. Figure 5-27c shows an equivalent graphical data structure, with the units' coordinates represented by suitably scaled positioning commands, and the identity of each unit represented by a jump to the subroutine that draws the unit.

The structure shown in Figure 5-27c could conceivably both generate a satisfactory picture and provide a convenient data base for the application program. However the application program is likely to need

---

* The name *graphical data structure* has also been taken by some to mean any structured display file and by others to mean any data structure used in a graphical program. Neither of these deserves the use of the term, for structured display files cannot normally be used for storage and retrieval of data, and general purpose data structures do not become graphical simply by virtue of being used in a graphical program.

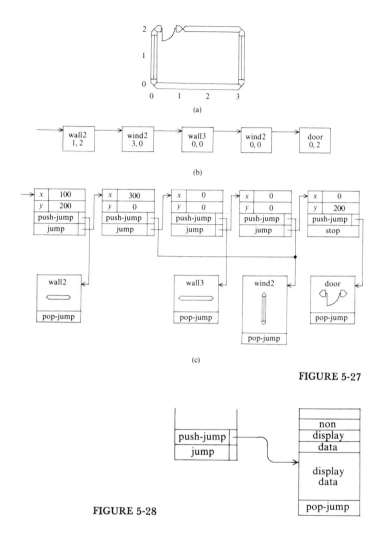

(a)

(b)

(c)

FIGURE 5-27

FIGURE 5-28

extra information about each unit — cost, overall dimensions and so forth. This data cannot be included in the refresh cycle, but may be attached to the head of the subroutine record as shown in Figure 5-28, where it is accessible to the application program but inaccessible to the display processor. By means of further extensions of this sort, the structure can be built up into a comprehensive data base.

An early example of the use of graphical data structures can be found in Sutherland's SKETCHPAD [277], where objects and diagrams were modeled in a ring structure similar to Figure 5-27c. These

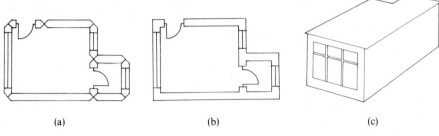

(a)   (b)   (c)

FIGURE 5-29

structures led to the development of CORAL [232, 281], a macro-language for building and manipulating general-purpose ring structures, that could be used to store graphical information. Further extensions of this technique can be found in Graphic-2 [44] and other related systems. All of these systems use list or ring structures, for these are the only structures that a conventional display processor can handle. An interesting alternative has been proposed by Guedj in his processor with its symbolically-addressed subroutine mechanism [110].

Compared with the conventional approach of generating the display file by using a viewing algorithm to scan the data base, graphical data structures have two conspicuous advantages: they save space, and they ensure that the displayed picture is an up-to-date representation of the data base. They also have a number of disadvantages. In the first place, they are much less convenient to use than non-graphical data structures like arrays and lists. Much of the data is buried in the display instructions themselves, and the operators to retrieve this information are generally quite different from the operators that create the data in the first place. This makes the use of these structures quite a skilled art.

Another problem with graphical data structures is their lack of flexibility. Once a structure has been defined it is very difficult to alter the fashion in which it is represented on the screen. For example, it would be difficult to alter the style of display from that of Figure 5-29a to that of Figure 5-29b, and even more difficult to generate Figure 5-29c. If this degree of versatility is required then the viewing algorithm approach is the best.

EXERCISES

5-1. Make a list of a convenient set of primitive graphical functions for inclusion in a display file compiler.

5-2. Take one or more of your primitive functions, and write programs or flow charts showing how the display file compiler generates display code. Use the display instruction set of Table 4-1; or alternatively use one of the sets of Table 4-2, and see how this modifies your answer to Exercise 4-6. A particularly difficult exercise is to write the LINE function for the display A of Table 4-2, suitable for use during an APPEND operation.

5-3. Reference [123] is an interesting example of a display file compiler for use with the FORTRAN language and the IBM 2250 display. Read it, and then try to figure out how the display file compiler was implemented, using only the information given in the paper. Pay particular attention to the mechanics of the PLOT and UNPLOT functions, and to the implications of the statement $A = A + B$.

5-4. Although the first set of functions described in Section 5.6 does not provide the same flexibility as the use of groups and items, this flexibility can be added by writing functions in a language such as SAIL, to carry out the CALLITEM, CALLGROUP and DELETECALL operations. Write these functions, and estimate their space usage compared with the implementation of Figure 5-24.

5-5. Devise a data structure from which the two displays of Figures 5-29a and 5-29b can be generated by two different viewing algorithms. Design these two algorithms.

5-6. Find an expression for the approximate wastage of space caused by using fixed size blocks to construct display file records. Let the block size be B, and assume that record sizes are evenly distributed over a range greater than B, with the average record size being R. Show that the optimum block size is independent of the number of words N allocated to the display file, and is proportional to $\sqrt{R}$. What other factors would influence your choice of block size?

6

TWO-DIMENSIONAL TRANSFORMATIONS

6.1   THE NEED FOR TRANSFORMATIONS

A graphics system should allow the programmer to define pictures that include a variety of transformations. For example, he should be able to scale a picture up so that detail appears more clearly, or down so that more of the picture is visible. It should also be possible to apply transformations to subpictures and symbols. We have already discussed positioning of subpictures: this amounts to applying a *translation* to the subpicture information. It is also useful to be able to change the *scale* of a subpicture, and to *rotate* it through some angle.

Two aspects of the formulation of transformations should be emphasized: first, a transformation is a single mathematical entity, and as such can be denoted by a single name or symbol. Second, two transformations can be combined, or *concatenated*, to yield a single transformation which has the same effect as the sequential application of the original two. For example, transformation A might be a translation and transformation B a scaling. The concatenation property allows us to determine a transformation $C = A\ B$ which has the effect of

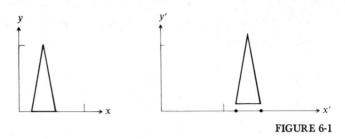

FIGURE 6-1

translating and then scaling. The principles of concatenation and denotation will pertain to all transformations described in this book: clipping, windowing, three-dimensional, and perspective transformations.

Each of these transformations is used to generate a new point (x', y') from the coordinates of a point (x, y) in the original picture description. If the original definition includes a line, it suffices to apply the transformation to the endpoints of the line and display the line between the two transformed endpoints.

6.1.1   TRANSLATION

The form of the translation transformation is:

$$x' = x + T_x$$
$$y' = y + T_y \qquad (6\text{-}1)$$

As an example, consider a triangle defined by its three vertices (20,0), (60,0), (40,100) being translated 100 units to the right and 10 units up $(T_x = 100, \ T_y = 10)$. The new vertices are (120,10), (160,10), and (140,110) (see Figure 6-1).

6.1.2   ROTATION

To rotate a point (x, y) through a clockwise angle θ about the origin of the coordinate system, we write:

$$x' = x \cos \theta + y \sin \theta$$
$$y' = -x \sin \theta + y \cos \theta \qquad (6\text{-}2)$$

The triangle (20,0), (60,0), (40,100) rotated 45° clockwise about the origin is $(10\sqrt{2}, -10\sqrt{2})$, $(30\sqrt{2}, -30\sqrt{2})$, $(70\sqrt{2}, 30\sqrt{2})$ (see Figure

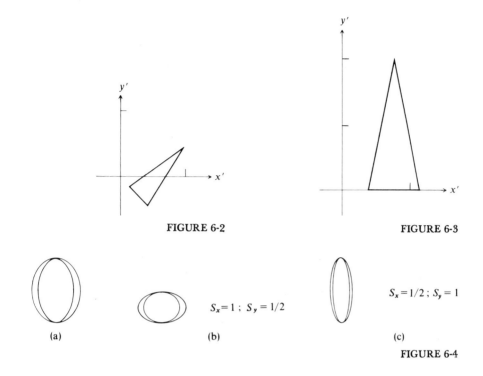

FIGURE 6-2   FIGURE 6-3

$S_x = 1 ; S_y = 1/2$

$S_x = 1/2 ; S_y = 1$

(a)   (b)   (c)

FIGURE 6-4

6-2). These equations can only be used if rotation is about the origin of the coordinate system.

6.1.3   SCALING

The scaling transformations:

$$x' = xS_x$$
$$y' = yS_y \qquad (6\text{-}3)$$

can be used for a variety of purposes. If the picture is to be enlarged to twice its original size, we might choose $S_x = S_y = 2$. Notice that the enlargement is relative to the origin of the coordinate system. The triangle (20,0), (60,0), (40,100) becomes (40,0), (120,0), (80,200), as shown in Figure 6-3.

If S_x and S_y are not equal, they have the effect of distorting pictures by elongating or shrinking them along the directions parallel to the coordinate axes. For instance, Figure 6-4a can be distorted as shown in Figure 6-4b or 6-4c.

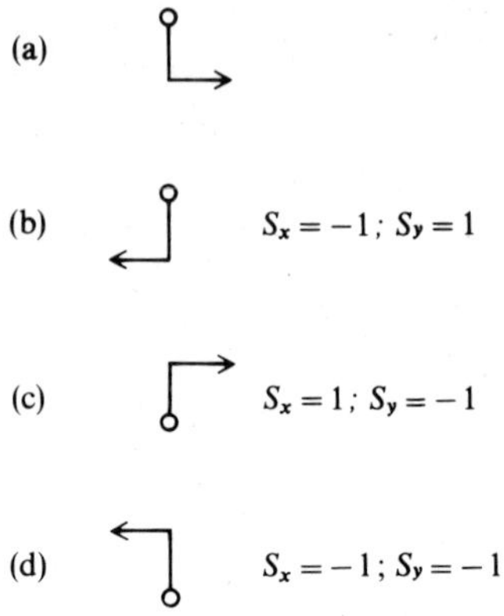

(a)

(b) $S_x = -1; S_y = 1$

(c) $S_x = 1; S_y = -1$

(d) $S_x = -1; S_y = -1$

FIGURE 6-5

The mirror image of an object can be generated by using negative values of S_x or S_y. Mirror images of Figure 6-5a can be generated as shown in Figure 6-5b, 6-5c or 6-5d.

6.2   CONCATENATION

Sequences of transformations can be combined into one transformation by the *concatenation* process. These sequences occur very frequently in picture definitions.

It is fairly rare that we want to apply a simple transformation such as rotation about the origin or scaling relative to the origin. In general, we need to perform more complex transformations like rotations about arbitrary points. Rotation about an arbitrary point can be performed by applying a sequence of three simple transformations: a translation, followed by a rotation, followed by another translation.

Sequences of transformations also arise when subroutine calls are nested, as in a structured display file. If each call has a relative transformation associated with it, a graphic item specified in a subroutine may have to undergo several transformations before the item can be displayed.

The ordering of a sequence of transformations must not be destroyed by the concatenation. Consider the sequence: rotate a point 90 degrees, then translate it with $T_x = -80$, $T_y = 0$. The resulting triangle is shown in Figure 6-6. If the order of application of the two transformations is reversed, the new figure is as shown in Figure 6-7.

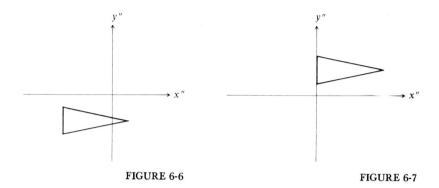

FIGURE 6-6   FIGURE 6-7

The main aim of concatenation is to represent a sequence of transformations as one transformation. The sequence above is:

$$x' = y$$
$$y' = -x \qquad (6\text{-}4)$$

followed by

$$x'' = x' - 80$$
$$y'' = y' \qquad (6\text{-}5)$$

The concatenation is simply:

$$x'' = y - 80$$
$$y'' = -x \qquad (6\text{-}6)$$

Use of the concatenated transformation has several advantages. We can represent it more compactly than a sequence, and we can generally compute the transformation with fewer arithmetic operations than if we were to apply each of the transformations in the sequence one after the other. However the rules for concatenating transformation equations are quite complex. They are much simpler if we use *matrices* to define transformations.

6.3   MATRIX REPRESENTATIONS

Two-dimensional transformations can be represented in a uniform way by a 3 x 3 matrix (see Appendix I for a discussion of matrix techniques). The transformation of a point (x, y) to a new point (x', y')

by means of any sequence of translations, rotations and scalings is then represented as

$$[\,x'\,y'\,1\,] = [\,x\,y\,1\,] \begin{bmatrix} a & d & 0 \\ b & e & 0 \\ c & f & 1 \end{bmatrix} \quad (6\text{-}7)$$

where the 3 x 3 matrix completely specifies the transformation. The matrix, a single entity, represents the transformation. We can give this matrix a name, and hence gain the ability to denote the entire transformation by a single name.

The addition of the third element of unity to the $[\,x\,y\,]$ vector enables it to be transformed by the 3 x 3 matrix. The point vector and matrix must be in the form given above in order to specify all simple transformations and concatenations of simple transformations with one notation (see Appendix II for a complete discussion of the three-element vectors).

6.3.1   MATRIX FORMULATION OF TRANSFORMATIONS

The parameters of the 3 x 3 transformation matrix can be arranged to make the matrix represent the simple transformations of translation, rotation, and scaling:

Translation:

$$[\,x'\,y'\,1\,] = [\,x\,y\,1\,] \begin{bmatrix} 1 & 0 & 0 \\ 0 & 1 & 0 \\ T_x & T_y & 1 \end{bmatrix} \quad (6\text{-}8)$$

Rotation:

$$[\,x'\,y'\,1\,] = [\,x\,y\,1\,] \begin{bmatrix} \cos\theta & -\sin\theta & 0 \\ \sin\theta & \cos\theta & 0 \\ 0 & 0 & 1 \end{bmatrix} \quad (6\text{-}9)$$

Scaling:

$$[\,x'\,y'\,1\,] = [\,x\,y\,1\,] \begin{bmatrix} S_x & 0 & 0 \\ 0 & S_y & 0 \\ 0 & 0 & 1 \end{bmatrix} \quad (6\text{-}10)$$

The reader can easily verify that these formulations are equivalent to Equations 6-1, 6-2, and 6-3.

6.3.2   CONCATENATION OF MATRIX TRANSFORMATIONS

The virtue of the matrix formulation is that concatenation of transformation sequences is particularly straightforward. Consider the sequence: scale a point with $S_x = S_y = 2$, then translate it with $T_x = 10$, $T_y = 0$. We have:

$$[\, x'\, y'\, 1\,] = [\, x\; y\; 1\,] \begin{bmatrix} 2 & 0 & 0 \\ 0 & 2 & 0 \\ 0 & 0 & 1 \end{bmatrix} \qquad (6\text{-}11)$$

$$[\, x''\, y''\, 1\,] = [\, x'\, y'\, 1\,] \begin{bmatrix} 1 & 0 & 0 \\ 0 & 1 & 0 \\ 10 & 0 & 1 \end{bmatrix} \qquad (6\text{-}12)$$

The result $[\, x'\, y'\, 1\,]$ is merely an intermediate one; we can eliminate it by substituting the first equation into the second:

$$[\, x''\, y''\, 1\,] = \left([\, x\; y\; 1\,] \begin{bmatrix} 2 & 0 & 0 \\ 0 & 2 & 0 \\ 0 & 0 & 1 \end{bmatrix} \right) \begin{bmatrix} 1 & 0 & 0 \\ 0 & 1 & 0 \\ 10 & 0 & 1 \end{bmatrix}$$

$$= [\, x\; y\; 1\,] \left(\begin{bmatrix} 2 & 0 & 0 \\ 0 & 2 & 0 \\ 0 & 0 & 1 \end{bmatrix} \begin{bmatrix} 1 & 0 & 0 \\ 0 & 1 & 0 \\ 10 & 0 & 1 \end{bmatrix} \right) \qquad (6\text{-}13)$$

The two 3 x 3 matrices are independent of the (x, y) points being transformed, and are derived only from the parameters specified in the transformation sequence (S_x, S_y, T_x, T_y). We can therefore simplify the equation by multiplying the two 3 x 3 matrices to yield a new 3 x 3 matrix:

$$[\, x''\, y''\, 1\,] = [\, x\; y\; 1\,] \begin{bmatrix} 2 & 0 & 0 \\ 0 & 2 & 0 \\ 10 & 0 & 1 \end{bmatrix} \qquad (6\text{-}14)$$

Thus the product of two matrix transformations represents the concatenation of those transforms. Irrespective of the number of transformations in a sequence, we can always concatenate so that *one* 3 x 3 matrix represents the entire sequence.

Complex transformations can be described as concatenations of simple ones. Suppose we wish to derive a transformation which will rotate a point through a clockwise angle θ about the point (R_x, R_y). The rotation transformation (Equation 6-2 or 6-9) can only be applied to rotate points about the origin. Therefore we must first translate points so that (R_x, R_y) becomes the origin:

$$[\, x'\, y'\, 1 \,] = [\, x\, y\, 1 \,] \begin{bmatrix} 1 & 0 & 0 \\ 0 & 1 & 0 \\ -R_x & -R_y & 1 \end{bmatrix} \quad (6\text{-}15)$$

Then the rotation can be applied:

$$[\, x''\, y''\, 1 \,] = [\, x'\, y'\, 1 \,] \begin{bmatrix} \cos\theta & -\sin\theta & 0 \\ \sin\theta & \cos\theta & 0 \\ 0 & 0 & 1 \end{bmatrix} \quad (6\text{-}16)$$

And finally, we translate the point so that the origin is returned to (R_x, R_y):

$$[\, x'''\, y'''\, 1 \,] = [\, x''\, y''\, 1 \,] \begin{bmatrix} 1 & 0 & 0 \\ 0 & 1 & 0 \\ R_x & R_y & 1 \end{bmatrix} \quad (6\text{-}17)$$

These may be concatenated:

$$[\, x'''\, y'''\, 1 \,] =$$

$$[\, x\, y\, 1 \,] \begin{bmatrix} 1 & 0 & 0 \\ 0 & 1 & 0 \\ -R_x & -R_y & 1 \end{bmatrix} \begin{bmatrix} \cos\theta & -\sin\theta & 0 \\ \sin\theta & \cos\theta & 0 \\ 0 & 0 & 1 \end{bmatrix} \begin{bmatrix} 1 & 0 & 0 \\ 0 & 1 & 0 \\ R_x & R_y & 1 \end{bmatrix} \quad (6\text{-}18)$$

If values for R_x, R_y and θ are known, the three matrices may be multiplied to yield one transformation matrix.

6.3.3 EFFICIENCY

When generating a picture for display, we may need to apply a transformation to a large number of points. This application must be as efficient as possible. The computation

$$[\, x\, y\, 1 \,] \begin{bmatrix} a & d & 0 \\ b & e & 0 \\ c & f & 1 \end{bmatrix} \quad (6\text{-}19)$$

seems at first glance to require 9 multiplications and 6 additions. However, in the formulation given here, the third column of the 3 x 3 matrix will always be:

$$0$$
$$0$$
$$1 \qquad (6\text{-}20)$$

even if the matrix is the result of many concatenations. The computations for x' and y' thus reduce to:

$$x' = ax + by + c$$
$$y' = dx + ey + f \qquad (6\text{-}21)$$

which requires fewer arithmetic operations (four multiplications and four additions) than the full vector multiplication. A matrix notation for this abbreviated computation is:

$$[\, x'\, y'\,] = [\, x\ y\ 1\,] \begin{bmatrix} a & d \\ b & e \\ c & f \end{bmatrix} \qquad (6\text{-}22)$$

The transformation matrix is now a 3 x 2 matrix. In the transformation systems discussed in Chapter 8 we use this 3 x 2 matrix to define two-dimensional transformations. Note however that we cannot concatenate two 3 x 2 matrices by multiplying them together: before we multiply them we must first return them to 3 x 3 form by attaching a third column.

EXERCISES

6-1. Prove the assertion: the transformation of a line between two points A and B is equivalent to the line between the transform of A and the transform of B. Consider only the translation, rotation and scaling transformations.

6-2. The matrix formulation suggests other transformations that we have not considered, e.g.

$$x' = x + ay$$

$$y' = y$$

Can you characterize these transformations?

6-3. Suppose we know a point (x', y') and the fact that it was transformed from an unknown point (x, y) by a known matrix Q. Describe a mechanism for finding the original point (x, y). Is this mechanism likely to be useful in graphics?

CLIPPING AND WINDOWING

7.1   CLIPPING

If a picture is defined in the coordinate system of the screen and then scaled, rotated or translated, it is very likely that some of the picture will be transformed off the screen. For example, if the picture is rotated clockwise by 45 degrees about its center, a point in the top right-hand corner of the screen will be transformed into a point some way to the right of the right-hand edge of the screen; a line joining this point to the point at the screen center will lie partly on the screen and partly off (Figure 7-1).

Some displays can cope with this problem by a process called *scissoring*. They provide what is conceptually a larger definition space than the screen, and intensify points and lines only when they lie within the screen boundary (Figure 7-2). Unfortunately they still continue to devote time to tracing through the invisible parts of the picture, so even if the visible portion is very simple it may flicker intolerably. Ideally the information that is passed to the display should be *clipped*, i.e. restricted to just those parts that lie on the screen. What

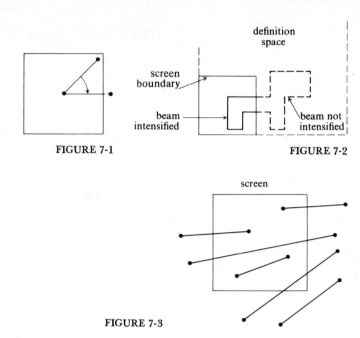

FIGURE 7-1   FIGURE 7-2

FIGURE 7-3

is needed is a *clipping algorithm* to determine which parts of the picture lie within the screen boundary.

If the entire picture were to be defined as a list of points, clipping would be a trivial problem: each point could be accepted for display or rejected by comparing its coordinates with those of the edges of the screen. There is no such simple test that indicates whether a *line* lies within the screen boundary, and if so, how much of the line should be drawn. Even if both endpoints are outside, the line may be partly visible: for example, the endpoints may lie on opposite sides of the screen. Figure 7-3 shows a number of different attitudes that a line may take with respect to the screen. Notice that because the screen has a convex shape, clipping a line never generates more than one visible segment. Nevertheless the only case that is easy to deal with is the one with both endpoints on the screen. Lines in this class are visible in their entirety.

If we were to generate the line in a point-by-point fashion by means of a DDA or BRM, we could create a list of all the visible points on the line. However this method would be appallingly slow. Moreover we do not need to generate and test each point. The visible segment of a line can be defined by its two endpoints, and all that the clipping algorithm need do is compute the coordinates of these two points. The following algorithm, invented by Dan Cohen and Ivan Sutherland, is designed not only to find these endpoints very rapidly, but also to reject even more rapidly any line that is clearly invisible. This makes it a very good algorithm for clipping pictures that are much larger than the screen.

7.1.1   A CLIPPING ALGORITHM

The algorithm has two parts. The first determines whether the line lies entirely on the screen, and if not, whether it can be trivially rejected as lying entirely off the screen. If it satisfies neither of these tests, then it is divided into two parts, and these two tests are applied to each part. The algorithm depends on the fact that every line either is entirely on the screen, or can be divided so that one part can be trivially rejected.

The rejection test is implemented by extending the edges of the screen so that they divide the space occupied by the unclipped picture into nine regions, as shown in Figure 7-4. Each of these regions has a four-bit code, and the two end-points of the line are assigned codes appropriate to the regions they are in. The four bits in the code mean the following if set:

first bit: point is above top edge of screen
second bit: point is below bottom edge
third bit: point is to right of right-hand edge
fourth bit: point is to left of left-hand edge

Clearly if the four-bit codes for both endpoints are zero, the line lies entirely on the screen. What is less obvious is that if the logical

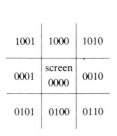

FIGURE 7-4

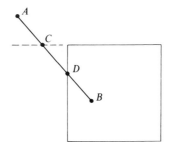

FIGURE 7-5

intersection of the two codes is not zero, the line must lie entirely off-screen.

If the line cannot be eliminated by either of these tests, then it must be subdivided. A simple method of subdivision is to find the line's point of intersection with one of the screen's edges and to throw away the part that lies off-screen. For example, the line AB in Figure 7-5 could be subdivided at C, and the portion AC thrown away. We now have a new line BC, to which the trivial rejection tests are applied. The line still cannot be trivially rejected, so we subdivide again at D. The resulting line BD is found to lie entirely inside. It is not always easy to determine whether subdivision should be made first at C or at D, but if we apply the rejection test in a repeated fashion, the order in which subdivisions are made does not affect the final result.

The inherent simplicity of this algorithm is demonstrated by the following implementation of it in SAIL:

```
REAL XL,XR,YB,YT;

PROCEDURE CLIP (REAL X1,Y1,X2,Y2);            T B R L
BEGIN INTEGER C1,C2;                           | |

        INTEGER PROCEDURE CODE (REAL X,Y);
        RETURN ((IF X<XL THEN '01 ELSE (IF X>XR THEN '10 ELSE 0)) +
                (IF Y<YB THEN '100 ELSE (IF Y>YT THEN '1000 ELSE 0))));

        C1 ← CODE (X1,Y1);
        C2 ← CODE (X2,Y2);

        WHILE NOT (C1=C2=0) DO BEGIN "COMPUTE"

        IF C1 LAND C2 THEN RETURN;   "NO PART OF THE LINE VISIBLE"
        IF C1=0 THEN BEGIN "EXCHANGE POINTS 1 AND 2"
            C1 SWAP C2; X1 SWAP X2; Y1 SWAP Y2
        END;

        IF C1 LAND '1 THEN BEGIN "PUSH TOWARD LEFT EDGE"
                Y1 ← Y1+(Y2-Y1)*(XL-X1)/(X2-X1);
                X1 ← XL
            END ELSE
        IF C1 LAND '10 THEN BEGIN "PUSH TOWARD RIGHT EDGE"
                Y1 ← Y1+(Y2-Y1)*(XR-X1)/(X2-X1);
                X1 ← XR
            END ELSE
        IF C1 LAND '100 THEN BEGIN "PUSH TOWARD BOTTOM EDGE"
                X1 ← X1+(X2-X1)*(YB-Y1)/(Y2-Y1);
                Y1 ← YB
            END ELSE
        IF C1 LAND '1000 THEN BEGIN "PUSH TOWARD TOP EDGE"
                X1 ← X1+(X2-X1)*(YT-Y1)/(Y2-Y1);
                Y1 ← YT
            END;

        C1 ← CODE(X1,Y1);   "RECOMPUTE THE CODE"
        END "COMPUTE";

"IF WE REACH HERE, THE LINE FROM (X1,Y1) TO (X2,Y2) IS VISIBLE"
        DRAWLINE (X1,Y1,X2,Y2)
END;
```

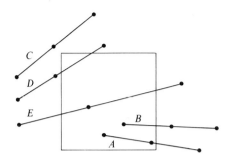

FIGURE 7-6

7.1.2   MIDPOINT SUBDIVISION

We can subdivide the line at its midpoint, and in this way avoid direct computation of the line's points of intersection with the edges of the screen. This modification makes the algorithm more suitable for machines without hardware for multiplication and division. The midpoint variation of the algorithm has been implemented in hardware, in the Clipping Divider [267].

The first part of the algorithm, in which the line is tested for trivial rejection, is unchanged. In the second part, the line is divided in two at its midpoint, yielding two line segments. The algorithm is then applied to each of these segments, with the following restrictions:

1. One endpoint of the original line may have been visible (see Figure 7-6, lines *A* and *B*). If so, one of its halves must either be entirely visible (line *A*), or else a trivial reject (line *B*). This half is discarded, and the algorithm is applied to the other half.
2. If both endpoints of the original line were invisible (Figure 7-6, lines *C, D* and *E*), each of the two halves is treated on its merits. Both halves may be trivial rejects (line *C*) in which case the entire line is invisible; only one segment may be trivially rejected (line *D*); or the midpoint may be visible, in which case neither half can be rejected (line *E*). In this last case the algorithm is applied to both halves.

The effect of this subdivision process is to perform a *logarithmic search* for the endpoints of the visible segment of the line. The search for an endpoint stops either when both halves of the line are rejected or when the midpoint coincides with one of the edges of the screen. The number of subdivisions that must be performed before this happens is at most equal to the number of bits of precision in the representation of *x* and *y*.

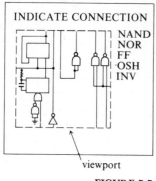

INDICATE CONNECTION

NAND
NOR
FF
OSH
INV

viewport

FIGURE 7-7

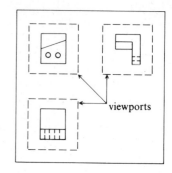

viewports

FIGURE 7-8

7.2   VIEWPORTS

The clipping algorithm permits the boundaries of the clipping region to be set anywhere on the screen. This is a very useful feature. It allows us to display the picture in a rectangle smaller than the screen, thus leaving blank areas in which to display messages, command menus and so forth (Figure 7-7). A rectangular region such as this is called a *viewport*. It is possible to clip several different pictures to different viewports and display them simultaneously on the screen (Figure 7-8).

7.3   WINDOWS

As we have described it, the process of preparing a transformed picture for display takes place in two steps: transformation into screen coordinates; and clipping to the viewport boundary. There is an element of wastefulness about performing the process in this order. We may transform a great many lines, only to find that most of them lie entirely off the screen. It would be far better if we could distinguish invisible lines *before* transforming them, and hence avoid unnecessary and time-consuming transformations.

This can be done by clipping to the *window*, which is the image of the viewport in the coordinates of the picture before transformation. As Figure 7-9 demonstrates, the window is always another four-sided region; it is always the same shape as the viewport provided the picture is scaled by the same amount in x and y (Figure 7-9a); and if no rotation is applied the window, like the viewport, has its edges parallel

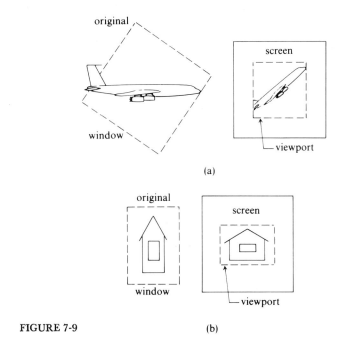

FIGURE 7-9   (b)

to the axes (Figure 7-9b). If we can clip to this window before transforming we can save time by not transforming invisible lines.

Unfortunately the clipping algorithm described above does not work efficiently with tilted clipping regions. Therefore when rotated information has to be clipped we apply clipping *after* transformation, using the viewport as the clipping region. Unrotated pictures, on the other hand, are clipped before transformation, using the window. The programs to perform these two clipping operations are virtually identical.

In the latter case, after each line has been clipped it must be scaled and translated as desired before being displayed. This transformation may be specified in the form of a matrix as discussed in Chapter 6; alternatively it may be defined entirely in terms of the dimensions of the window and viewport. In this way the entire transformation of the picture may be considered as a single *windowing transformation* from the original definition space to the screen. In the following description we shall use the term *page coordinates* for the original definition space, and continue to talk of *screen coordinates* as the final definition space.

7.3.1   THE WINDOWING TRANSFORMATION

Window and viewport are often more convenient to use than scale and translation in defining the transformation from page to screen. For example, if we wish to examine a large picture, we keep the viewport and the window size fixed, and move the window position; this allows us to scan the picture at a fixed magnification. Fixing the window center and varying its size changes the magnification.

The windowing transformation is very simple. Let us first assume that we have chosen the entire screen to be our viewport. Let us choose the window shown in Figure 7-10, whose center is at (W_{cx}, W_{cy}) in the page coordinate system. Its size, measured from the center, is W_{sx} by W_{sy} in the x and y directions. The equations defining the transformation of a point (X_p, Y_p) in the page to a point (X_s, Y_s) on the screen are:

$$X_s = \frac{X_p - W_{cx}}{W_{sx}} \qquad (7\text{-}1)$$

$$Y_s = \frac{Y_p - W_{cy}}{W_{sy}} \qquad (7\text{-}2)$$

Notice that all the symbols used in the right-hand expressions are measured in page coordinates. This means that X_s and Y_s are unitless and represent the deflection of the point from the center of the screen, assuming screen coordinates to run from -1 to $+1$.

Alternatively we can introduce a viewport covering less than the full screen. Suppose this has its center at (V_{cx}, V_{cy}) and is of size $V_{sx} \times V_{sy}$, measuring the size from the center and expressing all in screen coordinates. Then the point (X_p, Y_p) in page coordinates maps into the following point in screen coordinates:

$$X_s = \frac{X_p - W_{cx}}{W_{sx}} V_{sx} + V_{cx} \qquad (7\text{-}3)$$

$$Y_s = \frac{Y_p - W_{cy}}{W_{sy}} V_{sy} + V_{cy} \qquad (7\text{-}4)$$

If we continue to use the same window shown in Figure 7-10, then the resulting transformed point is (X_s, Y_s) shown in Figure 7-11. Effectively we take the dimensionless values of Equations 7-1 and 7-2 and interpret them as fractions of full-scale deflection within the

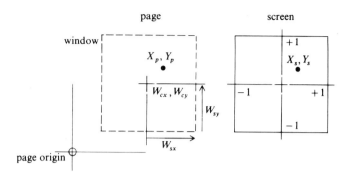

FIGURE 7-10

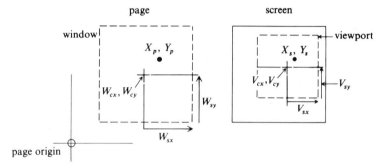

FIGURE 7-11

viewport. Adding the offset of the viewport from the origin gives the position on the screen.

Clearly it is possible, and often convenient, to specify the window and viewport by their edge positions rather than by center and size. This slightly modifies the equations governing the windowing transformation.

7.3.2 PAGE COORDINATE SYSTEMS

One of the convenient features of the page coordinate system is that it lets us choose any units of measurement we like. We can define a building layout in inches, a printed circuit board in millimeters, a map of the United States in miles. Or we can simply leave our units anonymous: this is what we would do if we were defining a flow chart or a circuit diagram.

We also have some freedom in our choice of numbering system in which to define page coordinates: we can use integers, fractions or floating point numbers. Floating point is by far the most convenient, for it lets us choose our page units without worrying about possible overflow or lack of precision. However we must choose a numbering system in which it is feasible to perform the entire windowing transformation. Thus if the choice is floating point it implies that clipping will be done in floating point, as will the transformation from page to screen coordinates; only then will coordinates be converted to integer or fractional form for inclusion in display instructions.

If the computer we are using does not possess floating point hardware, it is best to use integers or fractions. It is then important that sufficient *precision* be allowed in specifying page information. This precision should be adequate to provide a useful range of magnifications between page and screen; however high this magnification, there should be no apparent 'grain' in the picture due to insufficient precision in the page definition. Thus if the screen measures 1023 x 1023 units and the highest possible magnification is 256 times the lowest, we shall require a page that measures 2^{18} x 2^{18} units. The inconvenience of using integers like 2^{18} as coordinates is avoided if floating point page coordinates are used.

7.4   INSTANCES

The page is a coordinate space in which we can define a picture in whatever units are most convenient; having defined it, we then specify, by means of a window, the part of the picture that we would like displayed. This approach to picture definition can be extended to pictures containing repeated symbols. The symbols can themselves be defined in some arbitrary coordinate system, and then included in the picture by specifying where, and at what magnification, they are to appear.

When we indicate the use of a symbol in this manner, we are creating an *instance* of the symbol: this is the name we give to a subroutine that is transformed by the windowing transformation. The symbol must itself be defined elsewhere in what is called the *master copy* of the symbol. When we include the symbol in the picture, we specify not only the name of the symbol but the *transformation* that is to be applied to it. This is called the *instance transformation*.

7.4.1   INSTANCE TRANSFORMATIONS

The master copy of a symbol is defined in its own *master coordinate system*, relative to its own local origin. It is often convenient to use different units in the master and in the page. For example, a plan of a housing development might be defined in units of six inches. Each of the houses appearing on the plan might be derived from master copies defined in 1/8 inch units. In applications of this sort we would like always to use units of the appropriate size. We can do so if we transform each instance by a form of the windowing transformation described above.

Consider the example shown in Figure 7-12. Here a point in the master definition has position (X_m, Y_m), measured in *master coordinates*. An instance of it appears in the page at a position (I_{cx}, I_{cy}), and at a size $I_{sx} \times I_{sy}$, all measured in *page coordinates*. The point (X_m, Y_m) transforms into a point (X_p, Y_p) in the page where:

$$X_p = X_m I_{sx} + I_{cx} \qquad (7\text{-}5)$$

$$Y_p = Y_m I_{sy} + I_{cy} \qquad (7\text{-}6)$$

These equations assume that master coordinates run from -1 to $+1$, and that the whole of the master space is mapped into the instance. This may not be the case. We may choose part of a symbol, such as an arc of a circle, and reproduce it on the page (see Figure 7-13). In this case we choose a 'window' on the master, which we will suppose to be positioned at (M_{cx}, M_{cy}) and to be $M_{sx} \times M_{sy}$ in size, all measured in *master coordinates*. Then the transformation becomes:

$$X_p = \frac{X_m - M_{cx}}{M_{sx}} I_{sx} + I_{cx} \qquad (7\text{-}7)$$

$$Y_p = \frac{Y_m - M_{cy}}{M_{sy}} I_{sy} + I_{cy} \qquad (7\text{-}8)$$

Notice the similarity between these two equations and the earlier equations 7-3 and 7-4 for the page-to-screen transformation. Obviously the same transformation routine can be used for each operation. However, immediately after transforming the symbol to page coordinates we shall want to apply the second transformation from

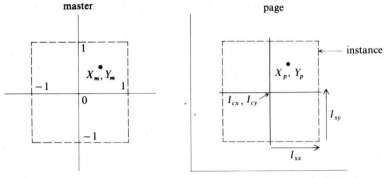

FIGURE 7-12

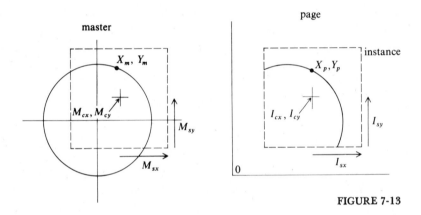

FIGURE 7-13

page to screen coordinates. The concatenation of these two linear transformations is another linear transformation:

$$X_s = \frac{X_m I_{sx} - (M_{cx} I_{sx} - M_{sx} I_{cx} + M_{sx} W_{cx})}{M_{sx} W_{sx}} V_{sx} + V_{cx} \qquad (7\text{-}9)$$

$$Y_s = \frac{Y_m I_{sy} - (M_{cy} I_{sy} - M_{sy} I_{cy} + M_{sy} W_{cy})}{M_{sy} W_{sy}} V_{sy} + V_{cy} \qquad (7\text{-}10)$$

This again can be handled by the program that handles Equations 7-3 and 7-4. We can thus transform directly from master to screen coordinates, omitting the unnecessary and time-consuming master-to-page transformation. However, we must take care to clip the instance correctly.

7.4.2   BOXING

Concatenation of windowing transformations is not always as simple as indicated by equations 7-9 and 7-10, for the relationship between the window and instance may vary. This is illustrated in Figure 7-14. In each case the region in the master space that is visible on the screen, and the rectangle that it occupies there, are shaded. These two areas can be treated exactly like a window and a viewport — they determine which portions of the master symbol are visible and where on the screen the picture is to appear. Each line of the symbol is clipped against the shaded 'window' on the symbol, and is then mapped onto the display screen using equations 7-9 and 7-10.

The operation of computing the size and location of the window on the symbol is called *boxing*. A convenient way to perform it is to transform the edges of the current window into the master coordinate system, using the *inverse* of the transformation specified in equations 7-7 and 7-8. We then compare the edges of the window with the corresponding edges of the master, and compute the region of intersection.

Another way of detecting the case of no overlap is to clip one of the diagonals of the instance rectangle against the window. If the line can immediately be *trivially rejected*, using the clipping algorithm described above, then the instance lies entirely outside the window. If it cannot, then they overlap (see Figure 7-15). This may or may not be the quickest software technique; the Clipping Divider uses it to economize on hardware.

We can gain great advantages in speed by the intelligent use of boxing. Imagine, for example, a very large picture made up of many instances, that we are examining through a relatively small window. Almost all the instances will lie entirely outside the window, as in Figure 7-14d. We need not even bother to clip any of the lines representing these instances, but can pass directly on to the next instance. The number of lines which must in the end be clipped will be a very small fraction of the total number in the master picture. Moreover this process can be carried to many levels; symbol definitions may include instances of other symbols. These two aspects of the boxing operation — concatenation of windowing regions and rapid rejection of invisible subpictures — make boxing a valuable part of any graphics system.

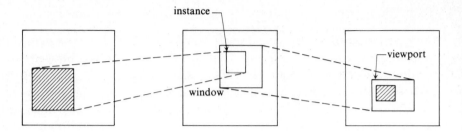

(a) instance entirely within window

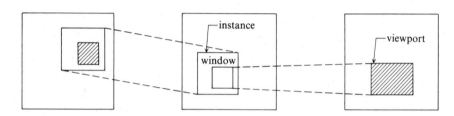

(b) window entirely within instance

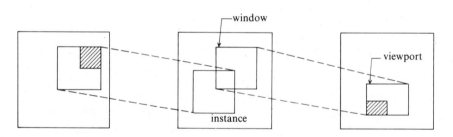

(c) instance and window partly overlap

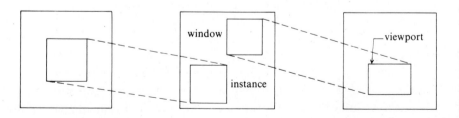

(d) no overlap between instance and window

FIGURE 7-14

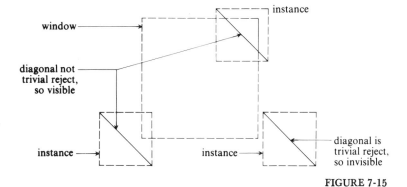

FIGURE 7-15

EXERCISES

7-1. Code the midpoint clipping algorithm, either in SAIL or in any other language of your choice.

7-2. The clipping algorithm given in Section 7.1 is optimized in favor of pictures much larger than the window. What features would you look for in an algorithm suitable for pictures only slightly larger than the window? Devise such an algorithm.

7-3. Write down the equations corresponding to equations 7-3 and 7-4 that define the windowing transformation in terms of the window and viewport *edges*, rather than their centers and sizes. Under what circumstances might it be more convenient to use these equations rather than equations 7-3 and 7-4?

7-4. Devise a clipping algorithm capable of clipping to an arbitrary convex polygonal window.

TRANSFORMATION SYSTEMS

8.1 ADDING TRANSFORMATIONS TO THE DISPLAY FILE COMPILER

In Chapters 6 and 7 we have encountered a number of different two-dimensional transformations applicable to pictures. These include clipping, scaling, rotation, translation, and general homogeneous matrix transformations. In this chapter we shall discuss how a display file compiler of the type described in Chapter 5 is extended to handle these transformations.

We can use either hardware or software to apply transformations. There are displays in existence today that can carry out all of the above transformations by hardware. We specify transformations to these displays by means of instructions in the display file: in effect these instructions say such things as 'rotate the following object clockwise by 45°,' or 'scale down this data by a factor of 4.' Provision of this full transformation capability is expensive and therefore somewhat uncommon. Most displays instead offer a *partial* transformation capability: some for example can clip and scale but not rotate; a few can do all three but cannot perform general 3 x 3 matrix transformations. Because display hardware to perform transformations is so rare, we shall assume in this chapter that transformations are to be carried out by software.

In the design of transformation systems, i.e. the software to perform picture transformation, a crucial issue is *speed* of transformation. The reason is just the same as the reason given in Chapter 5 to justify building fast display file compilers: without speed, highly dynamic computer graphics becomes impossible. Unfortunately even very fast transformation routines may take several seconds to transform a fairly complex picture: thus however fast a transformation system we build, it will probably introduce sizable delays into the process of generating display files. Effectively the transformation system is the bottleneck in the process. The faster we can perform transformation, the less noticeable this bottleneck becomes. So we are justified in devoting a lot of attention to speed of transformation.

A second important point, which itself affects the speed of transformation, is that it must be possible to *concatenate* two or more of the transformations we use into one transformation. Without this, transformation of highly structured pictures will involve applying several transformations to each point. All the transformations we have discussed in Chapters 6 and 7 can be concatenated into single transformations, provided we avoid certain transformation sequences. One of the tasks of this chapter is to identify those sequences.

8.2   THE TRANSFORMATION OF SUBPICTURES

Although hardware with full transformation capability is rare, the majority of vector displays can in fact perform one class of transformation, namely translation. They allow a subpicture or symbol, defined by means of relative vector commands, to be positioned anywhere on the screen. If we define a display subroutine in this fashion, then every call effectively implies translating the subroutine to the beam position immediately preceding the call. Generally we ensure correct translation by including a pair of beam-positioning commands before each subroutine call. This simple example of picture transformation illustrates two important points:

1. We almost always apply transformations to subpictures and symbols, i.e. to those parts of the picture that are most naturally represented

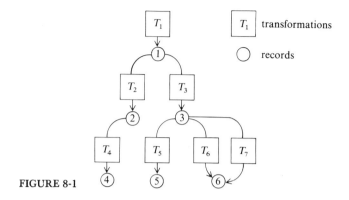

FIGURE 8-1

by subroutines. The only exception occurs when we transform the whole picture.

2. Each time we use a symbol in a picture we apply a different transformation to it. We therefore cannot consider the transformation to be part of the definition of the symbol to which it applies; instead we must treat it as part of the call itself.

Thus if we apply transformations within a typical structured display file we create a structure such as the one shown in Figure 8-1. Each subpicture or *record* is defined relative to its own local coordinates, and each call specifies the transformations $(T_1, T_2, T_3, \text{etc.})$ that are to apply to the subpicture. Notice that the topmost node in the structure is itself transformed: it is here that the windowing transformation is applied to the whole picture.

8.2.1   TRANSFORMATION CONCATENATION

When we define the transformation that we wish to be applied to a subpicture, we define it relative to the record that calls the subpicture. To transform the subpicture, we could apply in turn each of the transformations that apply to it and to the elements above it in the picture structure. For example, we could transform element 4 by applying to it first T_1, then T_2, then T_4.

If the picture is highly structured, this will be very time-consuming. Fortunately it is rarely necessary. We can instead *concatenate* all the transformations into one transformation, and apply this transformation to the information in the element. Thus we can transform element 4 by concatenating T_1, T_2 and T_4, and applying the combined transformation.

Concatenation of transformations is one of the more complex tasks that a general-purpose graphics system must handle. It is a particularly difficult task for a display processor to perform, for it involves reading the contents of the registers that hold the transformation coefficients, multiplying them by the new coefficients and replacing the registers' contents with the result. Effectively we need a processor with the same arithmetic capability as a general-purpose computer. This is one of the reasons why transformation by hardware is so expensive.

8.3   PSEUDO-DISPLAY FILES

Transformation by software is an operation that cannot be done during the display refresh cycle, for the calculations take far too long. Instead we must generate a fresh set of display instructions to represent each transformed element of the display file. For example, the picture definition might include an instance of the symbol shown in Figure 8-2a, translated and rotated into the position shown in Figure 8-2b. This would mean generating the display code shown in Figure 8-2d from a symbol definition such as the one in Figure 8-2c.

It might seem sensible to generate transformed display code only for those parts of the picture that demand it, and in this way reduce the amount of computation to be done. However the savings that we gain in this way are not dramatic. In order for the transformation software to determine just what transformation it should apply to a certain picture element, it must trace through the picture structure, concatenating all the transformations that apply to the picture element (Figure 8-3). This operation can be quite time-consuming.

The main factor in favor of transforming the display file in its entirety rather than piecemeal is simplicity, however. Figures 8-2c and 8-2d illustrate one problem posed by the piecemeal approach; the information to be transformed is in the form of display instructions, so the transformation software has to decode these instructions before it can transform the data they contain. On the other hand, if the entire picture is to be transformed it can be stored in a format that suits the transformation routines. The structure representing the picture is then constructed, not as a display file, but as a special-purpose data structure

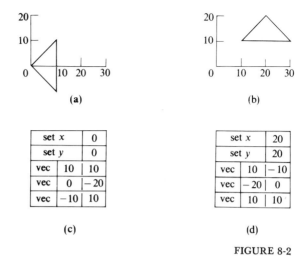

set x	0
set y	0
vec	10	10
vec	0	−20
vec	−10	10

(c)

set x	20
set y	20
vec	10	−10
vec	−20	0
vec	10	10

(d)

FIGURE 8-2

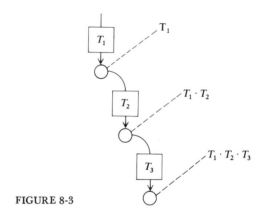

FIGURE 8-3

that is scanned by the transformation routines in order to produce the display file proper. We cannot call this special-purpose structure a display file since it is no longer used to refresh the display; instead we use the term *pseudo-display file*. The output of the transformation process we call the *transformed display file*.

In the following discussion we shall adopt the terminology of Chapter 7 to refer to elements of the pseudo-display file. Thus we shall refer to the definition of a symbol as the *master copy*, and to each use of the symbol as an *instance* of it.

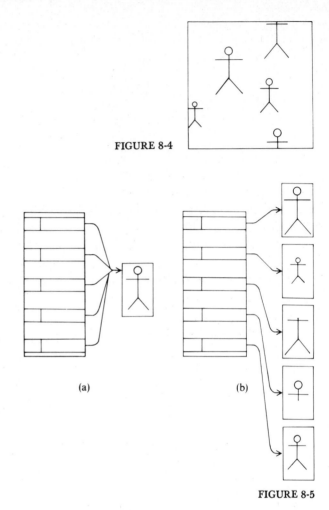

FIGURE 8-4

(a)   (b)

FIGURE 8-5

8.3.1   THE STRUCTURE OF THE TRANSFORMED DISPLAY FILE

Each time we apply a different transformation to an element of the pseudo-display file, we may generate a completely different sequence of display instructions. Consider, for example, the picture shown in Figure 8-4. Only one symbol is used here, but because of the use of different scales, and because of the effect of clipping, all five instances that appear on the screen are modified in different ways. Thus five different code sequences are required.

We could generate five separate subroutines to represent these five instances, producing the transformed display file structure shown in

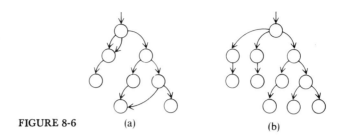

FIGURE 8-6   (a)   (b)

Figure 8-5b from the original structure shown in Figure 8-5a. Similarly, a more complex picture definition (Figure 8-6a) would generate an equivalent* but no longer cross-connected structure (Figure 8-6b).

It is sometimes desirable to retain this degree of structure in the transformed display file. The existence of the structure makes it easier to replace individual parts of the display file that correspond to modified sections of the pseudo-display file. Also it is possible to use the traditional method of light pen hit detection. However it is a fallacy to suppose that the entire structure of the pseudo-display file must always be retained. Often we use instances in the pseudo-display file to save space rather than to define the structure of the picture. There is no need for instances of this sort to be represented in the structure of the transformed display file. As we shall see, a very simple arrangement of the transformed display file will often suffice.

8.4   TRANSFORMED DISPLAY FILE COMPILATION

We can think of the process of transforming a pseudo-display file as four subprocesses. The first of these, the *trace routine*, threads its way through the pseudo-display file structure, passing on to the appropriate subprocess the information it encounters. Transformation information is passed to the *concatenation routine*, which combines the new parameters with those currently in effect. Graphical information is passed to the *transformation and clipping routine*, which takes the graphical information contained in the pseudo-display file and transforms it into screen coordinates. The fourth subprocess, the *display code generator*, compiles each transformed graphical entity into the appropriate display file instructions. These four processes are shown

---

* The structures of Figure 8-6 are equivalent in the sense that each instance in the pseudo-display file generates a call to a unique subroutine in the transformed display file.

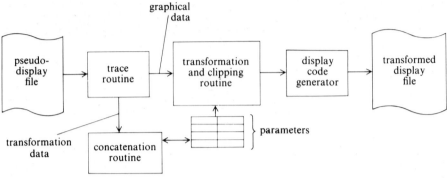

FIGURE 8-7

in Figure 8-7. Notice that the concatenation routine, in order to generate new parameters, must have access to the parameters currently in effect.

Figure 8-8 shows how these four processes may be interfaced to the various display file compiling processes discussed in Chapter 5. If the display processor itself can handle all the transformations involved, then the four extra processes are unnecessary; we need only the output routine and the display file compiler, as shown in Figure 8-8a. If more complex transformations are required then we replace the display file by a pseudo-display file, and add the four processes as shown in Figure 8-8b.

We may combine the data base and pseudo-display file into a single graphical data structure. However it is still necessary in most cases to transform this data by software in the manner of Figure 8-8c. In the exceptional case where the display processor can handle all the transformations specified in the graphical data structure, display file compilation reduces to the process shown in Figure 8-8d. A fifth and rather different approach using *display procedures* is discussed in Section 8.8 of this chapter.

Whether we use a separate data base as shown in Figure 8-8b or a graphical data structure as in Figure 8-8c, the software transformation process is more or less unchanged; the only differences are those caused by variations in the type of structure that the trace routine must interpret. The reader may therefore assume that the following discussion applies equally well to all forms of transformation by software.

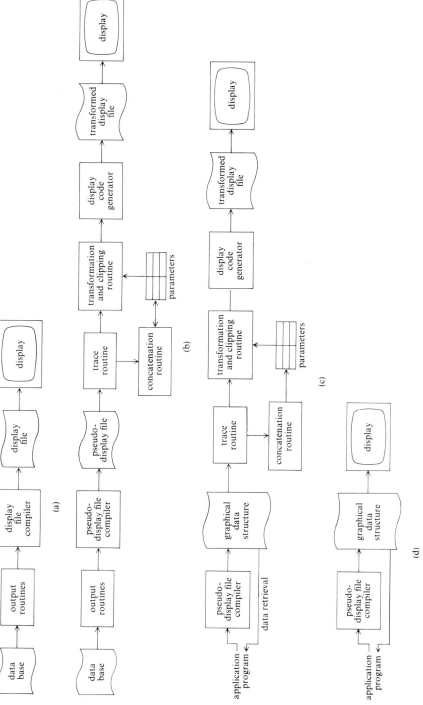

FIGURE 8-8

8.5   TRANSFORMATION CAPABILITY

The first task we face in setting out to design a transformation system is to decide on the range of transformations that the system must handle. This *transformation capability* may be so limited as to include only translation, or may extend as far as handling all the transformations listed at the start of this chapter — clipping, scaling, rotation, translation and general 3 x 3 matrix transformations. Each of these transformations has its uses, but each one involves an additional overhead in terms of the complexity and speed of the transformation process. When we set out to design a graphics system we must decide what applications to cater for and what transformation capability they will require. Two particularly commonly used sets of transformations are:

1. Clipping, scaling and translation.
2. Clipping, scaling, translation and rotation.

In the following sections we shall discuss the design of graphics systems with these two capabilities. For convenience, we shall refer to them as *systems without rotation* and *systems with rotation*.

8.6   THE SEQUENCING OF TRANSFORMATIONS

8.6.1   ADAPTIVE TRANSFORMATION SYSTEMS

Chapters 6 and 7 discussed two different approaches two-dimensional transformations. Chapter 6 used a 3 x 2 matrix to define a variety of transformations including scaling, rotation and translation. Chapter 7 presented the alternative *windowing transformation* which combines scaling and translation, and also includes clipping. It is not always easy to decide which method to use. Matrix transformation of a single point involves carrying out six multiplications and four additions, whereas only two multiplications and two additions are required for scaling and translation. It is therefore fairly clear that if we want to gain speed we should use the latter method in a system without rotation, but does this mean that we should always use matrix transformation in a system with rotation? To do so would clearly be extravagant in cases where very few parts of the picture are being rotated. What is needed is an *adaptive* transformation and clipping routine, that chooses the technique appropriate to the transformations currently in effect.

One example of the adaptability that we should like to achieve concerns the choice of when to apply clipping. As shown in Chapter 7, we can apply clipping before the windowing transformation, since no rotation is involved. However, we cannot do so if the picture definition includes rotation: then clipping must be performed after the rotation. A system with rotation should be capable of switching between these two different transformation sequences.

8.6.2   BOXING

The full windowing transformation described in Chapter 7 permits the *dimensions* of the master to be specified, by center and size or by some other equivalent notation. Different dimensions may be specified for each instance of a subpicture. This use of master dimensions has two advantages: firstly it allows part of the subpicture to be used instead of all of it; secondly, during transformation we can test whether any of an instance is visible, by comparing its boundary with the edges of the window. This test is performed during the *boxing* operation which determines the overlap of instance and window, and computes the position on the screen of the corresponding viewport.

If full advantage is to be taken of boxing, the master dimensions must be specified among the transformations applied to each *instance* of the symbol in question. However, it is possible instead to specify center and size in defining the *master copy*. These dimensions are equally suitable for use in the boxing test. They cannot, however, be used to choose different parts of the master to appear in each instance. Instead they indicate the *extent* of the master copy, and their sole purpose is to speed up transformation by permitting the clipping and transformation of many instances to be avoided.

Figures 8-9 and 8-10 illustrate these two alternative methods of defining master dimensions; we shall call these two methods *dimensioning in the instance* and *dimensioning in the master*. In Figure 8-9, dimensioning in the instance is used to draw two different logic symbols, making use of clipped segments of a circle. Figure 8-10 shows a number of such symbols, whose dimensions are defined in the master, being boxed to determine whether or not they are visible.

The provision of one or other of these forms of boxing is an asset to any transformation system. However, the use in a system with rotation of dimensioning in the instance has very serious implications. This is

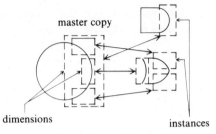

master copy

dimensions

instances

FIGURE 8-9   dimensioning in the instance

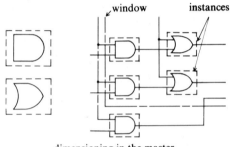

window   instances

FIGURE 8-10   dimensioning in the master

because it violates the rule that transformations should lend themselves to concatenation. If we specify dimensions in the instance, together with instance rotation, we generate a tilted instance as shown in Figure 8-11a. This tilted instance boundary cannot be concatenated with an orthogonal window by the standard boxing technique, and in the case shown in Figure 8-11b a clipping region is generated that is not rectangular and cannot therefore be used by the clipping routine. The only practical solution is to apply clipping in two stages, with rotation applied in between. Thus we have identified a transformation sequence, clip-rotate-clip, that cannot be concatenated into a single transformation and a single clipping operation.

If we dimension the master in the master copy itself, the problem disappears. After rotation has been applied it is possible to compute new, *approximate* dimensions as shown in Figure 8-12. These dimensions can be used equally well to eliminate invisible instances; only in certain cases, such as the one shown in Figure 8-13, will instances be transformed and clipped that would have been discarded if the exact extent were used. The reason why this eradicates the problem

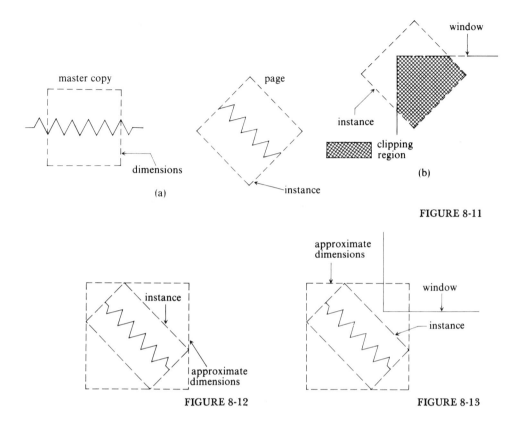

FIGURE 8-11

FIGURE 8-12   FIGURE 8-13

is that we are no longer using dimensions as a means of *clipping* the master, only as an indication of its approximate *extent*.

Thus although we are free to implement boxing in either fashion, using dimensions defined in the master or in the instance, we should impose one restriction: we should not permit dimensioning in the instance in a system with rotation. If this type of dimensioning is allowed in such a system, it will occasionally be necessary to combine transformations, not by concatenating them, but by applying them one after the other. Not only is this very slow, but it adds a great deal of extra complexity to the system.

8.7   THE DESIGN OF A TRANSFORMATION SYSTEM

The previous sections have introduced several major problems that are posed during the design of a transformation system, and have suggested some solutions. In this section we take each stage of the system and

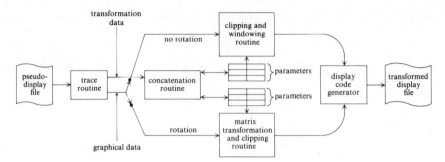

FIGURE 8-14

discuss its design in greater detail. The system we shall discuss is the system with rotation: this is a more complex and more interesting case than the system without. However we shall also identify the parts of the system that may be removed in order to generate a system without rotation.

The main reason why the system with rotation is more complex is not that rotation is involved, but that an *adaptive* transformation and clipping routine is needed. This routine must process rotated lines by first multiplying them by the transformation matrix and then clipping the result. If the line is not to be rotated, however, the windowing transformation is used in order to save time. Thus we effectively require *two* transformation and clipping routines, as shown in Figure 8-14.

Figure 8-14 shows all the processes required in a system that performs rotation. The trace routine scans the pseudo-display file, passing all transformation data to the concatenation routine, and all graphical data to whichever of the two transformation and clipping routines is in use. If no rotation is in effect, the windowing routine receives the data; otherwise the data is passed to the matrix transformation and clipping routine. Both of these routines pass their output data to the same display code generator.

The concatenation routine, which receives transformation data from the trace routine, is the routine that determines which transformation and clipping routine should be used. Whenever rotation goes into effect, the concatenation routine switches the data path to the matrix transformation and clipping routine; when rotation is no longer in effect, the data path is switched back to the windowing routine.

8.7.1   BUILDING THE PSEUDO-DISPLAY FILE

The pseudo-display file is effectively a structured display file that is designed to be interpreted by the trace routine, rather than by the display processor. Most of the techniques discussed in Chapter 5 for building display files apply equally well to pseudo-display files; there are some minor differences that result from the use of software rather than hardware to interpret the structure, and from the inclusion of a richer variety of transformations.

Because the pseudo-display file is interpreted by software we have a good deal more freedom to design its structure as we wish. In particular we can choose between using integer and floating point numbers to define lines and points. Although the use of integers will generally lead to a more compact structure, the use of floating point is recommended since it gives the programmer a great deal more freedom in his choice of coordinate systems.

The main difference between the two types of structure lies in the way transformations are specified, both in the functions that generate the structure and within the structure itself. In Chapter 5 we showed how subroutine translations could be specified by preceding each call with a beam positioning command:

        POSITION(100,250);
        CALL(35);

We can use the same technique to define other transformations such as scaling and rotation:

        POSITION(100,250);
        SCALE(5);
        ROTATE(0.5);
        CALL(35);

Alternatively we can specify all transformations as additional parameters to the CALL function:

        CALL(35,100,250,5,.5);

The first method, although more pleasing to the eye, is slightly misleading, for it gives the impression that the transformations are

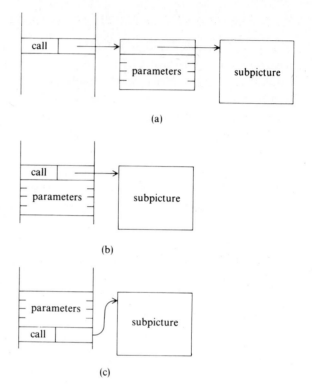

FIGURE 8-15

applied in the order specified. This is not so. The transformations have no effect until the trace routine reaches the 'call;' they are then applied to the data within the master copy. Ideally we would like to build a structure in which the parameters are linked to the call in the manner of Figure 8-15a. It may prove simpler to store them in locations following the call as shown in Figure 8-15b. Either of these arrangements can be generated by the second type of call given above; and they are both preferable, in terms of tracing efficiency, to the ordering of Figure 8-15c, which would be the natural result of using the first calling sequence.

A system that uses separate functions to specify each transformation must be capable of resolving the various ambiguities and inconsistencies that may arise. For example, a function must be provided for specifying viewports, but this will generally be meaningless if applied to any but the topmost call in the tree structure. We can avoid this problem by providing a special *call* function whose parameters include viewport and window dimensions. The effect of this call is analogous to including the called record in the refresh cycle.

In one respect pseudo-display file compilation is much simpler than compiling display instructions. Because the pseudo-display file is not being refreshed while it is being compiled, there is no need to worry about conflicts between the computer and the display processor; therefore such refinements as double-buffering and reserve free lists are no longer necessary.

8.7.2   THE TRACE ROUTINE

The trace routine is the simplest of the four subprocesses in the transformation system. It must be capable of following the structure of the pseudo-display file, and of distinguishing the different types of data that it encounters. Graphical information is passed to the appropriate transformation and clipping routine, while transformation parameters are passed to the concatenation routine to be combined with those currently in effect.

Whenever the pseudo-display file is changed, the transformed display file should be updated accordingly. This may be done by automatically tracing through the entire pseudo-display file after every change. This is a simple but rather wasteful solution. If the structure of the transformed display file parallels the pseudo-display file structure in the manner of Figure 8-6, it is possible to arrange to trace the appropriate part of the pseudo-display file automatically after every change. Otherwise the programmer must initiate the trace process by means of a special TRACE(n) function that traces the indicated portion of the pseudo-display file.

8.7.3   THE CONCATENATION ROUTINE

As it computes new parameters, the concatenation routine must save the old parameters on a *push-down stack*, so that they can be restored when the instance has been completely processed. The new parameters must be computed as rapidly as possible, and must be generated in a form convenient for use by the transformation and clipping routine. Clearly a completely different set of parameters is required by each of the two transformation and clipping routines.

8.7.3.1   Windowing parameters

In the case of the windowing routine, there are various ways in which the page-to-screen transformations may be defined: one obvious method is to specify window and viewport boundaries. However the transformation and clipping routine operates more efficiently if we provide it with the following parameters:

1. *Window edge positions* W_{lx}, W_{rx}, W_{by}, W_{ty}, defining in page coordinates the positions of the left-hand, right-hand, bottom and top edge respectively of the window.
2. *Scale* S_x, S_y of screen information relative to page information (the deformation that results from using different S_x and S_y is often useful).
3. *Translation* T_x, T_y. These terms represent the screen coordinates of the page origin. They enable us to perform transformations 7-3 and 7-4 given in Chapter 7 as follows:

$$X_s = X_p S_x + T_x$$
$$Y_s = Y_p S_y + T_y$$

where X_p, Y_p are the page coordinates of a point and X_s, Y_s are the screen coordinates into which it is transformed.

These, then, are the parameters used by the windowing routine. What new set of parameters should be passed to the concatenation routine so that it can most easily combine the two sets? In the absence of master dimensions, only the following are required:

1. *Instance position*, i.e. the position in page coordinates of the origin of the symbol's master coordinates.
2. *Scale factors* to be applied to the master copy to transform it into page coordinates. If omitted, default scale factors of unity should be used.

If dimensions are specified, they will be defined in master coordinates, either in the instance or in the master copy.

Often it is more convenient for the programmer if he has a choice of ways of specifying instance transformations. For example, he may wish to specify dimensions by edge positions instead of center and size. One particularly convenient notation for instances of symbols is the use of instance and master dimensions only: in other words, the programmer says, 'I want *this* much of the master to appear in *this* rectangle.' By using this notation he avoids having to use scale factors or even, in the case where he uses fixed master dimensions defined in the master copy, having to know what coordinate system is used in the master definition. All of these variations should be possible, and it is the task of the concatenation routine to extract the information it needs from the information passed to it by the trace routine.

When concatenation is complete, new values will have been computed for W_{lx}, W_{rx}, W_{by}, W_{ty}, S_x, S_y, T_x and T_y. However it is desirable to avoid all this computation in cases where the boxing test shows the instance to be completely invisible. The concatenation routine should establish visibility as rapidly as possible.

8.7.3.2   Matrix concatenation

The process described above is performed only in cases where neither the current transformation nor the new one involves rotation. In any other circumstance, the matrix transformation and clipping routine is the one that receives the new concatenated transformation. In the case where no rotation is currently in effect, but the new transformation specifies rotation, the transformation matrix must be set up as follows, using the current windowing parameters:

$$\begin{bmatrix} S_x & 0 \\ 0 & S_y \\ T_x & T_y \end{bmatrix}$$

Then the old transformation parameters may be combined with the new ones by matrix multiplication. At the same time that the matrix is constructed from the windowing parameters, viewport dimensions must be computed from those of the window.

Once the matrix is established, further concatenations are simply a matter of multiplying this matrix by the matrix representing the new instance transformation. However, a full multiplication of two 3 x 3 matrices is unnecessary. Instead we can multiply together the two 2 x 2 matrices formed by the upper two rows of the 3 x 2 transformation matrices. The new third row is found by transforming the new instance position with the old transformation matrix. The viewport, once determined, need not be altered except when master dimensions are specified.

In the case of the system without rotation, this part of the concatenation routine is omitted, as is the matrix transformation and clipping routine.

8.7.4   TRANSFORMATION AND CLIPPING ROUTINES

8.7.4.1   The windowing routine

Each line passed to the transformation and clipping routine is first clipped while it is still defined in page coordinates. Then each of the endpoints is transformed into screen coordinates. Finally the line in its new form is passed on to the display code generator. Often pictures are constructed from sequences of connected lines, as shown in Figure 8-16. It is very inefficient to transform each point in this sequence twice, as we would if we used the above technique. Therefore it is best to maintain a record of the endpoint of each clipped line, with which we can compare the starting point of the next in order to determine whether we need to transform it. The result of this comparison should be passed to the display code generator, for it may enable an unnecessary pair of beam-positioning commands to be omitted. Notice, however, that even if the lines are connected, their clipped versions may not be: this is why a comparison is always necessary.

Because of the large variety of page coordinate systems that may be used, clipping and transformation are best performed in floating-point arithmetic. Without the appropriate hardware this can be very slow, however, and fixed-point arithmetic may be used as an alternative. After each point has been transformed its coordinates should be converted to fractional form for use by the display code generator.

Besides lines and points, both of which are quite easily clipped and transformed, the pseudo-display file may include *text* information. This is a much more difficult problem. We generally use a fixed size of text on the screen instead of scaling the text in proportion to the surrounding graphical information. The reasons for this are twofold: the text must always be large enough to be legible; and we would like to be able to make use of whatever character-generating hardware the display possesses.

It is clearly possible to determine whether a character of a certain

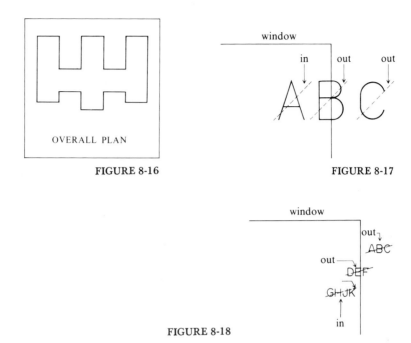

FIGURE 8-16   FIGURE 8-17

FIGURE 8-18

size positioned at a certain point on the screen lies entirely within a certain viewport. We can find out by clipping one of the diagonals of the character (see Figure 8-17). However the clipping region we use in a system without rotation is the window, not the viewport, so we must determine the size in page coordinates of the character whose size we know in screen coordinates. This involves an inverse transformation.

A lot of time can be spent in clipping the diagonals of every character in a displayed string. Therefore it may be best to apply some form of boxing test to the entire string, to find out if it crosses the window boundary and must therefore be clipped on a character-by-character basis. This can be done if we know the length of the string and if we can assume that it contains no carriage-control characters, i.e. that all characters are of the same width (see Figure 8-18).

8.7.4.2   The matrix transformation and clipping routine

The matrix transformation and clipping routine receives exactly the same types of graphical information as the windowing routine, namely lines, points and text. It must also generate an identical form of output

to the display code generator. In between, however, a completely
different process is performed. Information is transformed using the
matrix stored in the routine's parameter registers, and is then clipped
against the viewport.

We have talked in this chapter and in Chapter 6 about transforming
with a 3 x 2 matrix. In order to do so we must attach a third element of
unity to each vector representing a point:

$$[X_p \; Y_p \; 1]$$

We can then perform the matrix multiplication. However it is
unnecessary to carry out a complete multiplication of the 1 x 3 vector
by the 3 x 2 matrix, for we know that the third element of the vector
will always contain unity. We can avoid two unnecessary
multiplications by multiplying the two-element vector:

$$[X_p \; Y_p \;]$$

by the 2 x 2 matrix formed by the first and second rows of the 3 x 2
matrix; we must then *add* the coefficients in the bottom row. Thus if
the transformation matrix is:

$$\begin{bmatrix} a & b \\ c & d \\ e & f \end{bmatrix}$$

we can compute the screen coordinates of the transformed point as
follows:

$$X_s = a \, X_p + c \, Y_p + e$$
$$Y_s = b \, X_p + d \, Y_p + f$$

8.7.5   THE DISPLAY CODE GENERATOR

One advantage of the four-stage process for transforming pictures is
that the same first three stages may be used to generate output for a
variety of different displays. All that is needed is a different display
code generator for each type of display. In this way we can build a
graphics system that is largely device-independent.

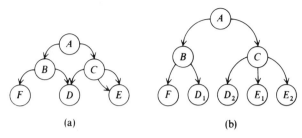

(a)   (b)

FIGURE 8-19

It is for this reason that we transform into fractional screen coordinates. We could instead use raster units, but this would mean adopting a specific screen range such as 1023 x 1023. If we should later wish to write a code generator for a range of 4095 x 4095, we could do so by multiplying every coordinate by 4095 / 1023, or 4.003. However, 12-bit precision cannot be reconstructed from the 10-bit information produced by the transformation and clipping routine. So it is best to use a universal screen coordinate system that provides enough precision for any output device we are likely to use. A 16-bit signed fraction offers this precision.

Once the line's endpoint coordinates have been converted to raster units, the rest of the code generation process is identical to display file compilation. It is, for example, possible to build a *segmented* transformed display file so that one segment may be replaced without having to transform the entire pseudo-display file. However the relationship between the resulting display file structure and the structure of the pseudo-display file must be thought out carefully.

As explained earlier, the cross-connected tree-structure of the pseudo-display file cannot be retained in its entirety after transformation, because a subroutine that is called several times will generally produce several different sequences of display code. If we start with a structure such as Figure 8-19a it is possible to generate the structure of Figure 8-19b. This degree of complexity in the display file may not be necessary, however: we may intend to use storage-tube displays that do not permit picture segmentation. In such a case it is best to generate a single unstructured list of display commands.

If we should decide to segment the display file, there are basically two ways to go about it. The first approach is to allow the pseudo-display file to be defined in the form of separate substructures, each with its own window and viewport specified at the top level. These

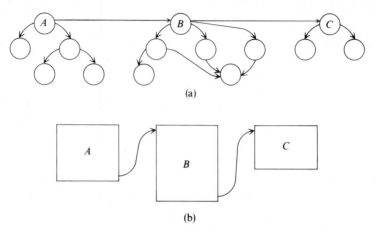

(a)

(b)

FIGURE 8-20

substructures, shown in Figure 8-20a, are analogous to the main records of a structured display file. In the transformed display file we create a separate segment for each substructure, as shown in Figure 8-20b. If we should change one element of a substructure we must regenerate the entire segment.

The other method is to retain as much of the picture structure as the programmer desires, up to the level shown in Figure 8-19b. If he wishes to create a separate segment in the display file, the programmer must indicate this when he builds the pseudo-display file. He may do so by adding a unique *name* to each branch of the structure that he wishes to correspond to a segment. Thus by specifying names as shown in Figure 8-21a we could generate the display file structure shown in Figure 8-21b. The names that the trace routine encounters in the pseudo-display file are passed unchanged to the display code generator to enable it to build this structure.

This technique allows the programmer to build enough structure into the display file for any minor modification to be made without extensive re-transformation. As we remarked earlier, it also permits hit detection to be carried out in the traditional manner with the aid of a light pen (see Chapter 11). However it relies on the use of display hardware that can interpret display file structures as complex as Figure 8-21b. It is possible to write display code generators that can produce simpler structures for simpler displays. However it is not generally possible to ensure that *programs* designed to use structured display files can be used successfully with low-powered displays, for these programs

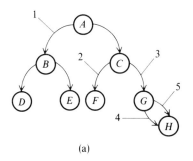

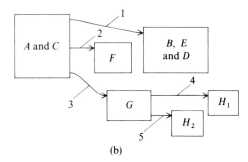

(a)   (b)

FIGURE 8-21

usually make extensive use of structured pictures. In systems that are likely to be used with a variety of types of display, it may be more prudent to use a single-level display file structure so as to discourage this sort of device-dependent programming.

8.8   DISPLAY PROCEDURES

Earlier in this chapter we discussed several different ways of organizing a graphics system. The most widely used is the one shown in Figure 8-8b: a pseudo-display file is generated from the program's data base, using a viewing algorithm; then this pseudo-display file data is transformed into displayable information.

   This system organization, although widely used, is far from ideal. In the first place it is very inefficient in its use of memory, for the information that appears on the screen is represented three times; once in the data base, once in the pseudo-display file and once in the transformed display file. The other system organizations shown in Figure 8-8 have been proposed as methods of avoiding this triplication by omitting the transformed display file (Figure 8-8a), the original data base (Figure 8-8c) or both (Figure 8-8d).

   Another drawback of the scheme of Figure 8-8b is its complexity. All that is achieved is a pictorial representation of the data base, yet six separate steps are required and an intermediate data structure must be built. It would obviously be worthwhile to reduce the number of steps in the process; and if we examine the process in detail we find that some of the steps are indeed redundant.

   Suppose we wish to use a certain symbol several times at various positions and with various rotations. For the sake of simplicity let us

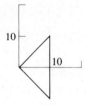

FIGURE 8-22

set	0	0
vec	10	10
vec	0	−20
vec	−10	10
end		

FIGURE 8-23

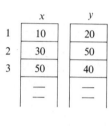

	x	y
1	10	20
2	30	50
3	50	40
	—	—

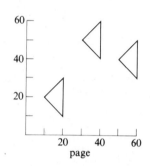

FIGURE 8-24

take as an example the inverter symbol shown in Figure 8-22. A record defining this symbol must appear in the pseudo-display file so that we can reference it several times. Therefore at an early point in the application program we must create this record:

```
OPEN(1);
POSITION(0,0);
VECTOR(10,10); VECTOR(0,−20); VECTOR(−10,10);
CLOSE;
```

These function calls create a pseudo-display file master copy of the form shown in Figure 8-23. We may add several instances of this master copy, each with its own transformations. The viewing algorithm to do this will normally scan the data base for the transformation parameters. For example, we might choose to store the coordinates of the symbols in a pair of arrays called X and Y (see Figure 8-24). Then we can generate the pseudo-display file by the following statement (N is the total number of symbols):

```
FOR I←1 STEP 1 UNTIL N DO
  BEGIN
    TRANSLATE (X(I), Y(I));
    CALL(1)
  END
```

When the trace routine interprets the pseudo-display file it encounters each of the instances, sets up the transformation parameters and then scans the master copy of the symbol. Since the information in the master copy is purely graphical it is passed directly to the transformation and clipping routine, which therefore receives the following data:

position at (0,0);
vector of length (10,10);
vector of length (0,−20);
vector of length (−10,10);

Notice that this is identical to the data supplied in the original function calls that created the master copy. The only difference is that we define the master copy just once, whereas the trace routine traverses it several times, once for each instance. We can 'fool' the transformation and clipping routine by rewriting the POSITION and VECTOR functions so that they pass the data directly to the routine instead of generating pseudo-display file. We will have to pass the data several times, but this can be achieved by defining a *procedure* which is called the appropriate number of times:

```
PROCEDURE INVERTER;
  BEGIN
    POSITION (0,0);
    VECTOR (10,10); VECTOR(0,−20); VECTOR(−10,10)
  END;
```

We can also modify the TRANSLATE function to pass its parameters directly to the transformation system. This leads to a very similar viewing algorithm:

```
FOR I←1 STEP 1 UNTIL N DO
  BEGIN
    TRANSLATE (X(I),Y(I)); COMBINE;
    INVERTER; RESTORE
  END;
```

The TRANSLATE function passes the symbol's coordinates to the transformation system; then the COMBINE function concatenates this translation with the current transformation. Next the call to the INVERTER procedure generates the graphical data, and finally we restore the original parameters. The effect is exactly as if we had traced through the pseudo-display file, but the need for the pseudo-display file has been eliminated.

The organization of the system we have described is shown in Figure 8-25. The viewing algorithm contains a number of procedures like INVERTER, and passes graphical data directly to the transformation and clipping routine. Transformation parameters are passed to a concatenating routine identical to the one discussed in Section 8.7.3. Transformed graphical elements are passed to the display code generator just as before.

What if we should wish to apply the boxing test to each instance of the inverter? This would imply that certain calls to the INVERTER procedure are to be bypassed if the symbol is found to be invisible. We can provide a function VISIBLE that checks for this:

```
FOR I←1 STEP 1 UNTIL N DO
  BEGIN
    TRANSLATE (X(I),Y(I)); COMBINE;
    IF VISIBLE THEN INVERTER; RESTORE
  END;
```

There are more concise ways of expressing the above algorithm. Chapter 16 will show how we can replace the whole statement by the following:

```
FOR I←1 STEP 1 UNTIL N DO INVERTER AT (X(I),Y(I));
```

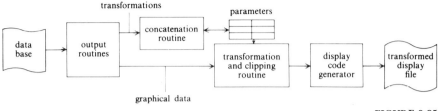

FIGURE 8-25

When we write 'inverter at $(X(I),Y(I))$' we are asking the following steps to be performed:

1. apply the boxing test to the symbol at $(X(I),Y(I))$;
2. if the symbol is invisible, ignore this call; otherwise:
3. save the current transformation on the stack;
4. combine the translation $(X(I),Y(I))$ with the current transformation;
5. call the INVERTER procedure;
6. restore the old transformation from the stack.

In order to achieve all these steps in one call we must arrange for the language compiler to generate the appropriate code. We must also allow the programmer to specify *overall dimensions** in a procedure definition:

> PROCEDURE INVERTER; DIMENSIONS (5,0,5,10);
> BEGIN
> . . . .

A procedure of this sort is clearly a very different entity from a normal procedure. It has dimensions associated with it, and it can be transformed in various ways when it is called. We therefore call it a *display procedure* [203]. It is possible to apply a variety of different transformations to such a procedure:

> INVERTER AT $(X(I),Y(I))$ ROTATION R(I) SCALE S(I);
> CIRCLE AT (1,0.5) DIMENSIONS (0.5,0,1,1);

---

* These may be defined as center and half-size, as used in Chapter 7.

It is also possible to call display procedures from other display procedures:

> PROCEDURE CIRCUIT; DIMENSIONS (0,0,100,100);
> FOR I←1 STEP 1 UNTIL N DO INVERTER AT (X(I),Y(I));

Thus we can achieve the same hierarchy in our procedure calls that we would have created in the pseudo-display file. However we can do a great deal more. A display procedure may contain any type of statement including conditional statements in particular; so we could write the following display procedure:

> PROCEDURE INVERTER; DIMENSIONS (5,0,5,10)
>   BEGIN
>   POSITION (0,0);
>   VECTOR (10,10); VECTOR (0,−20); VECTOR (−10,10);
>   IF LABELING THEN
>   BEGIN
>   POSITION (3, −2)
>   DISPLAY "INV"
>   END
>   END;

This procedure will generate the picture shown in Figure 8-26 if LABELING is true, and will otherwise output the unlabeled symbol of Figure 8-22. By introducing conditional statements into display procedures we can generate a great variety of different styles of output from the same data base. We can omit detail at small scales, or define several different representations of a symbol to be used under different circumstances. For example we could define a display procedure FLIPFLOP to generate any one of the three symbols shown in Figure 8-27, according to the state of a global variable. This flexibility is virtually impossible to achieve in a pseudo-display file.

In an interactive environment it is essential to be able to change one segment of the display file without having to regenerate the rest. We can create and modify segments by means of techniques such as we discussed in Chapter 5:

> OPEN(3);
> WINDOW(0,0,500,500); VIEWPORT(0,0,1,1);
> CIRCUIT;
> CLOSE;

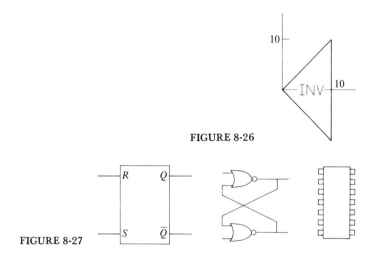

FIGURE 8-26

FIGURE 8-27

A more elegant construction analogous to the display procedure is the *frame procedure* which achieves the same as the above:

> FRAME F1;
> CIRCUIT WITHIN(0,0,500,500) ONTO (0,0,1,1);
> . . . . .
> . . . . .
> F1;

This again requires extension to the language compiler. Like the display procedure it gives us the ability to call picture elements by name rather than by number.

By using function calls we can incorporate the display procedure technique into more or less any language without having to modify the compiler. A graphics system of this sort is particularly easy to implement, for it involves only three processes: the concatenating routine, the transformation and clipping routine and the display code generator. However a language in which the functions are incorporated into the call is much easier to use. In Chapter 16 we shall discuss the design and implementation of such a language.

EXERCISES

8-1. Suppose the computer could for some reason perform clipping to an arbitrary window as rapidly as to a rectangular one. How would this modify the design of the transformation system?

8-2. Design a transformation system to perform scaling, translation and rotation by multiples of 90°.

8-3. The execution of a display procedure often closely parallels the operation of the trace routine on part of a pseudo-display file. However, the trace routine is normally written in machine code, whereas the display procedure is not. Try to evaluate the effect this will have on the speed of regeneration of the picture.

8-4. Investigate methods of using subroutines in the transformed display file to reduce the space it occupies and to reduce the amount of data that the display code generator must output.

8-5. Suppose you were using the display procedure technique with a storage-tube display. What methods might you use to avoid regenerating the entire picture after each modification?

## PART THREE

Interactive Graphics

9

GRAPHICAL INPUT DEVICES

9.1 POINTING AND POSITIONING DEVICES

Most display terminals provide the user with an alphanumeric keyboard with which to type commands and enter data for the program. For some applications, however, the keyboard is inconvenient or inadequate. The user may, for example, wish to indicate one of a number of symbols on the screen, in order to erase the symbol. If each symbol is labeled he can do so by typing the symbol's name; if he can *point* at the symbol, however, he may be able to erase it more rapidly, and the extra clutter of labels can be avoided.

Another problem arises if the user has to add lines or symbols to the picture on the screen. Although he can identify an item's position by typing coordinates, he can do so even better by pointing at the screen, particularly if what matters most is the item's position relative to the rest of the picture.

These two examples illustrate the two basic types of graphical interaction: *pointing* at items already on the screen, and *positioning* new items. The need to interact in these ways has stimulated the development of a number of different types of graphical input device, some of which are described in this chapter.

9.2   CHARACTERISTICS OF GRAPHICAL INPUT DEVICES

Ideally a graphical input device should lend itself both to pointing and to positioning. In reality there are no devices with this versatility. Most devices are much better at positioning than at pointing; one device, the light pen, is the exact opposite. Fortunately, however, we can supplement the deficiencies of these devices by software, and in this way produce a hardware-software system that has both capabilities. Nevertheless, the distinction between pointing and positioning capability is extremely important.

Another important distinction is between devices that may be used directly on the screen surface and devices that may not. The latter variety of device might appear to be less useful; however, this is far from being true. Radar operators and air traffic controllers have for years used devices like the *joystick* (Figure 9-1) and the *tracker ball* (Figure 9-2), neither of which can be pointed at the screen. Nevertheless they are effective input devices. They rely on the principle of visual *feedback:* the x and y outputs of the device control the movement of a small cross or *cursor* displayed on the screen (Figure 9-3). The user of the device 'steers' the cursor around the screen rather like a toy boat on the surface of a pond. Although this operation sounds as if it requires a lot of skill, it is in fact very easy.

The use of visual feedback has an additional advantage: just as in any control system, it compensates for any lack of *linearity* in the device. A linear input device is one that faithfully increases or decreases the input value in exact proportion to the user's hand movement. If the device is being used to trace a graph or a map, linearity is important. A cursor, however, can be controlled quite easily even if the device behaves in a fairly non-linear fashion. For example, the device may be much less sensitive near the left-hand region of its travel: a one-inch hand movement may change the x-value by only 50 units, whereas the same movement elsewhere may change x by 100 units. The user will simply change his hand movement to compensate, often without even noticing the non-linearity. This phenomenon has allowed simple, inexpensive devices like the SRI 'mouse' to be used very successfully for graphical input.

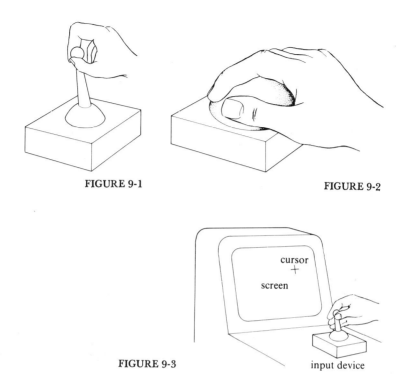

FIGURE 9-1   FIGURE 9-2

FIGURE 9-3   input device

9.3   THE STANFORD RESEARCH INSTITUTE 'MOUSE'

The SRI 'mouse' consists of a small plastic box resting on two metal wheels, whose axes are horizontal and at right angles [81, 79]. Each wheel is connected to a potentiometer, as shown in Figure 9-4. As the mouse is rolled around on a flat surface, its movement in two orthogonal directions is translated into rotation of the potentiometers. These rotations can be measured by applying a voltage across each potentiometer, and sampling the outputs through analog-to-digital converters. The converted values may be held in registers accessible to the computer, or written directly into core memory. Values are normally sampled thirty or sixty times a second, a rate which permits low-cost, low-performance analog-to-digital converters to be used. Every time the coordinate values are sampled, the cursor must be repositioned. Push-buttons may be mounted on top of the mouse, and the user can work them with his fingers as he moves the mouse. Ideally the computer should be able to read the position of these buttons whenever it reads the coordinates of the mouse.

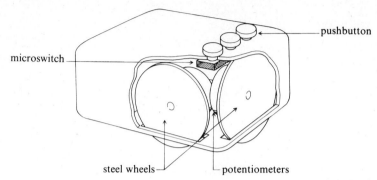

microswitch

pushbutton

steel wheels

potentiometers

FIGURE 9-4

In addition to its simplicity and low cost, the mouse has the advantage that the user need not pick it up in order to use it — it simply sits on the table surface until he needs it. The mouse has some unique properties that are liked by some and disliked by others. For example, if the mouse is picked up and put down somewhere else, the cursor will not move; if the cursor is moved right off one edge of the screen, it 'wraps around' and comes on the other side. This can be useful as a means of moving the cursor rapidly from one side of the screen to the other. The mouse has two real disadvantages: it cannot be used for tracing data from paper, since a small rotation of the mouse or a slight loss of contact will cause a cumulative error in all the readings; and it is very difficult to hand-print characters for recognition by the computer (see Section 11.12). For these types of application a tablet is essential.

9.4   TABLETS

The term *tablet* is used to describe a flat surface, generally separate from the display, on which the user draws with a *stylus* (see Figure 9-5). The likeness of the tablet and stylus to paper and pencil makes them a particularly natural combination for graphical input. However, progress towards building inexpensive tablets has been rather slow.

9.4.1   THE RAND TABLET

The RAND Tablet was developed at the RAND Corporation [64], and was developed further and marketed by Bolt, Beranek and Newman, Inc. It provides a flat drawing area ten inches square, and rests on a

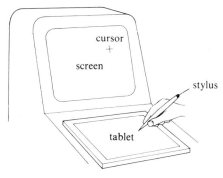

FIGURE 9-5

table top. In the surface of the tablet are 1024 lines parallel to the x-axis and 1024 lines parallel to the y-axis. Each line is made of copper about 3 thousandths of an inch wide, and each plane of lines is about one thousandth of an inch thick. The lines are spaced about one one-hundredth of an inch apart, and the two planes of lines are separated from each other by a thin sheet of Mylar. Each individual line carries a unique digitally coded signal that can be picked up by the stylus. The coding used is a 'Gray-code' scheme such that the sequence of pulses in each wire is unique, and the sequence of pulses in two adjacent wires differs only in one pulse position.

The purpose of the stylus is to pick up the coded signals from the tablet. It has a fine tip which is capacitively coupled to the wires to which it is closest. Within the stylus, a sensitive amplifier detects the pulses from these wires, amplifies them and delivers them via a coaxial cable to the decoding logic. The sequence of pulses picked up by the stylus is a unique representation of its position on the tablet, and can easily be converted from Gray-code to binary integer form for delivery to the tablet's buffer registers.

In addition to detecting the position of the stylus, the decoding logic can tell whether the pen is pressed down by means of a small switch in the tip. The status of this switch can therefore be kept in an extra bit in the buffer register. The logical arrangement of the RAND Tablet is shown in Figure 9-6.

The RAND Tablet is one of the most accurate and linear input devices available, and will accurately record a stylus movement of one-hundredth of an inch. The use of capacitive coupling between the stylus and the tablet allows the stylus to be separated from the tablet

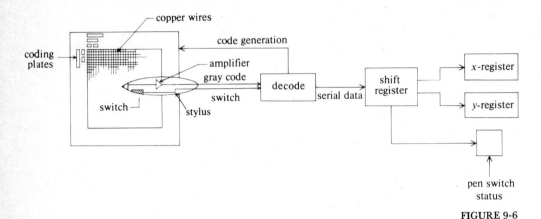

FIGURE 9-6

surface, and hence to be used to trace through a sheet of paper. The principal drawbacks of the tablet are its complexity and resultant high cost; furthermore the stylus is somewhat susceptible to wear and tear.

9.4.2   THE VOLTAGE-GRADIENT STYLUS

An alternative coordinate input technique uses voltage gradients within a resistive plate. In the simplest configuration, a sheet of partially conductive material is used as the tablet surface. During successive time intervals, a potential is applied first horizontally and then vertically across the sheet. Diodes may be used in the connections to the edges of the sheet, as shown in Figure 9-7, to prevent one set of connections from distorting the field generated by the other set. The stylus is kept in contact with the conductive sheet, and senses a potential corresponding to its position. The x and y coordinates of the pen can be determined by measuring the potential during the horizontal and vertical time periods. Absence of any potential indicates that the pen is not in contact with the surface.

The main difficulty in building a voltage-gradient tablet lies in obtaining a material suitable for the tablet surface. The material must be sufficiently tough to withstand the wear of constant contact with the moving stylus. If we intend to use the tablet for tracing charts and plans, then it must be fairly linear: this implies that the surface material must have uniform resistivity. The problem is made more difficult by the need for a surface of high resistivity across which a reasonable potential can be developed. Thus the conducting surface cannot be

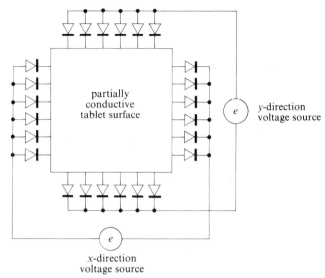

FIGURE 9-7

made of a copper plate, which would be ideal in other respects. Recent experiments have suggested that conductive rubber might make an ideal, low-cost tablet surface.

9.4.2.1   The Sylvania Tablet

The Sylvania Company has developed a tablet device similar to the voltage-gradient stylus [288], in which the resistive sheet is a layer of stannous-oxide fused into a glass plate and covered with another glass plate. Only seven contacts need be made to each edge of the plate in order to achieve one percent precision. Moreover, compensation for the non-linearities in the plate itself can be achieved by means of resistors connected to these seven contacts. This makes it possible to use relatively low quality conducting sheets, and to achieve the desired precision by individually compensating each tablet.

The signals in the plate are high-frequency alternating currents applied in such a way that the phase detected by the stylus varies for different positions on the sheet. Two different frequencies are used, one for horizontal sensing and one for vertical sensing. The received signal can be filtered into the two frequency components, whose phases correspond to the coordinates of the stylus on the plate. Because high-frequency signals are used, considerable separation can be introduced between the stylus and the conducting surface; in fact the Sylvania tablet works quite acceptably through a book. The magnitude of the received signal is measured and is used to indicate height information to the computer. Three height levels are provided, one indicating that the stylus is within about 1/32 inch of the surface, and one indicating that the stylus is actually touching the surface; the final indication is given by a mechanical switch.

9.4.3   THE ACOUSTIC TABLET

An ingenious tablet has been designed by the Science Accessories Corporation [255]; it works on an acoustic principle suggested by Brenner [33]. It is dependent on the use of *strip microphones*, which are mounted along two adjacent edges of the tablet as shown in Figure 9-8. The stylus has a small piece of ceramic mounted close to its tip, and at regular intervals a small spark is generated across the surface of the ceramic, between two electrodes. The microphones pick up the pulse of sound generated by the spark, and two counters record the delay between creating the spark and picking up the sound. These two delays are proportional to the stylus' distance from the two edges of the tablet where the microphones are mounted. They may therefore be used as x and y values.

The acoustic tablet continues to provide coordinate values even when the stylus is lifted from the tablet surface. However, the values are incorrect, as can be seen from Figure 9-9. Nevertheless, this property has an interesting side-effect, for it lets us determine the position of the stylus in *three dimensions*. All that is required is a second pair of microphones, mounted along the other two sides of the tablet, and a second pair of counters.

We then receive four distance measurements, shown in Figure 9-10 as d_1, d_2, d_3 and d_4. If the tablet dimensions are $2a \times 2a$, and x and y are measured from the tablet center, then we can show that:

$$
\begin{aligned}
4ax &= d_1{}^2 - d_2{}^2 \\
4ay &= d_3{}^2 - d_4{}^2 \\
z^2 &= d_1{}^2 - (x + a)^2 \\
&= d_2{}^2 - (x - a)^2 \\
&= d_3{}^2 - (y + a)^2 \\
&= d_4{}^2 - (y - a)^2
\end{aligned}
$$

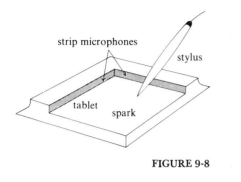

strip microphones

stylus

tablet

spark

FIGURE 9-8

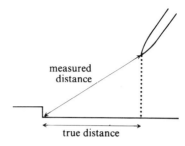

measured
distance

true distance

FIGURE 9-9

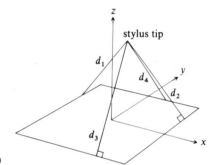

z

stylus tip

d_1

d_4

y

d_2

d_3

x

FIGURE 9-10

These yield the following values for x, y and z^2:

$$x = \frac{d_1^2 - d_2^2}{4a}$$

$$y = \frac{d_3^2 - d_4^2}{4a}$$

$$z^2 = \tfrac{1}{4}(d_1^2 + d_2^2 + d_3^2 + d_4^2) - \tfrac{1}{2}x^2 - \tfrac{1}{2}y^2 - a^2$$

The acoustic tablet was not the first device to rely on the speed of sound as a basis for positioning in three dimensions. In 1966 a device called the *Lincoln Wand* was developed at MIT's Lincoln Laboratory [235]. This device used a hand-held ultrasonic transmitter, emitting pulses of sound that were picked up by four microphones mounted at the four corners of the screen. The equations from which x, y and z were computed were almost identical to those given above.

The TX-2 computer to which the Lincoln Wand was attached used about half a millisecond of computation every 40 milliseconds to compute x, y and z. Clearly, many computers could take a lot longer than this, to the extent that overall system efficiency might be seriously affected.

9.4.4   SUPERIMPOSING THE TABLET ON THE DISPLAY

The Sylvania Tablet is a transparent device, since it is made mainly of glass and uses a transparent stannous-oxide coating. The acoustic tablet can use any writing surface. It would therefore be possible to mount these tablets directly in front of the display screen. It is not clear that this offers any advantages; instead it makes it likely that the user's hand will obscure part of the picture while he is drawing. Moreover there are problems in ensuring that the pen position corresponds with the position of the 'cursor' on the display screen: the two devices may use raster units of different sizes.

The RAND Tablet can also be used in this way, and a display system has been built around this concept at the System Development Corporation [101]. The RAND Tablet is not transparent, but because a space is left between adjacent wires in the tablet surface, the tablet is translucent and a projection CRT can be used to create a visible display on the tablet surface. The image is not as bright, however, as on the screen of a direct-view CRT.

9.5   THE LIGHT PEN

The devices we have discussed so far are all *positioning* devices: they possess hardware to track the stylus or otherwise ensure that the x and y values in the buffer registers represent the current position of the device. At fairly regular intervals, perhaps whenever the internal clock generates an interrupt, the x and y values are read from the buffer register. These values can be used to reposition the cursor and to modify the display file in any desired fashion. If the device incorporates a tip-operated switch or a push-button, this can be sampled at the same time, and used to control branching within the program.

In contrast, the light pen is a *pointing* device. If it is pointed at an item on the screen, it generates information from which the item can fairly easily be identified by the program. However, the light pen does not generally have any associated tracking hardware. Instead, tracking is performed by software, making use of the output function of the display.

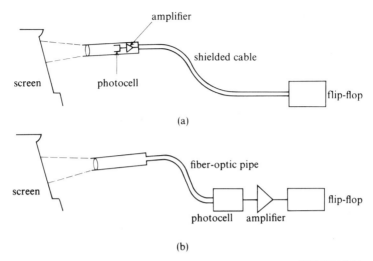

(a)

(b)

FIGURE 9-11

In concept the light pen is extremely simple. Two alternative arrangements are shown in Figure 9-11a and Figure 9-11b. In each case the two main elements of the light pen are a photocell and an optical system which focuses onto it any light in the pen's field of view. A pen-shaped housing permits the light pen to be held in the hand and pointed at the display screen. On this housing is either a finger-operated switch, or a shutter that must be depressed to allow light to reach the photocell. The output of the photocell is amplified and fed to a flip-flop which is set whenever the pen is pointed at a sufficiently bright source of light. This flip-flop can be read and cleared by the computer.

To make use of the light pen for positioning, some sort of *tracking program* must be running in the computer. Pointing is much simpler, however, particularly if we are refreshing the display with the aid of a program of the sort described in Chapter 2: we can test the light pen flip-flop after displaying each point, and in this way determine the exact spot at which the pen is pointing. Alternatively, we can use an *interrupt* feature, such as is described in the next chapter, to indicate when the flip-flop is set. The computer can read the contents of the display's address register when an interrupt occurs, and from this determine which item was 'seen' by the pen. Programs for pointing and positioning with the light pen are described in Chapter 10. As we shall see, they rely on the ability of the display processor to *enable* and *disable* the light pen during the refresh cycle, and in this way to prevent certain parts of the picture from being 'seen' by the pen.

All light pen programs depend on a rapid response from the pen when it is pointed at the screen. A particularly fast response is required if the light pen is to be used with high-speed displays. Suppose, for example, a display executes one instruction every two microseconds, but the delay between displaying a point or line and setting the light pen flip-flop is three microseconds. By the time this happens, the display will be processing either the next instruction or the one after that. The program may therefore identify the 'seen' item incorrectly.

Fast-response light pens can be built by using a highly sensitive photocell such as a photo-multiplier tube. However, this sort of device is too bulky to be held in the hand, so the light must be focused onto it by a fiber-optic pipe as shown in Figure 9-11b. Transistor-type photocells, such as the photodiode, are cheap and small enough to be hand-held; moreover, the self-contained light pen which results is less liable to be damaged than the fiber-optic pipe variety. However, photodiodes generally take one or more microseconds to respond and are therefore more suited to light pens for slower displays.

9.6   COMPARATORS

In this chapter we have encountered several different devices suitable for positioning and one device, the light pen, that is convenient for pointing. The next two chapters describe ways of programming each class of device to perform both functions.

It is possible to add extra hardware to compensate for the shortcomings of each class of device. We can add *tracking hardware* to permit the light pen to be used as a positioning device; however, this is rarely done, for the hardware is quite complex, and it also tends to interfere with the refreshing of the display. A positioning device can be used for pointing with the aid of a much simpler attachment called a *comparator*.

The comparator is a device that continuously compares the beam position with a pair of reference values. It may use *digital* reference values, and compare them with the values in the display's x and y registers. However, this technique is applicable only to point-plotting displays. A comparator for use with an analog vector-drawing display uses a pair of reference *voltages* which are continuously compared with the display's deflection signals. These reference voltages are derived by digital-to-analog conversion from a pair of registers set by the computer. When both pairs of signals agree, the comparator issues a pulse which sets a flip-flop. The computer can change the reference position by reloading the comparator's x and y registers; normally the program will do this after sampling the stylus position. The comparator issues a pulse when the signals agree to within a certain tolerance, perhaps equivalent to one tenth of an inch on the screen. This gives the effect of a small square 'region of interest' around the tip of the stylus. A third register may be provided to enable the tolerance of the comparator to be reset by the program.

Notice that the x and y registers of the comparator need not be loaded directly from the coordinate registers of the graphical input device. If these two sets of registers are permanently wired together, a great deal of flexibility is lost in the way the comparator can be used. It should in general be possible to load the comparator registers with any desired transformation of the pen coordinates. It is sometimes useful even to use coordinates that are completely unrelated to the pen's position. The comparator should be treated, not as an input device, but as an extension of the facilities offered by the display.

9.7   CONCLUSION

This last point regarding comparators is very relevant to input devices as a whole: we should make every effort to separate the input and output functions of a graphics system. Moreover, we should not relax this rule in special cases, even though we may be tempted to do so. For example, by clever programming we can create the effect of 'drawing' on the screen with the input device. It is as though the device were leaving behind a 'trail of light' as it moves. It is easy to form the mistaken impression that the device itself creates the picture on the screen, and from there to leap to the conclusion that a device with this ability is more valuable than one without. As we shall see in Chapter 11, most of the interactive graphical techniques we use depend on the fact that input devices *do not* leave behind such a 'trail of light'. It is mainly for this reason that these devices are so much more powerful than paper and pencil as drafting instruments.

The sole function of a graphical input device should therefore be to provide, by means of coordinate values or otherwise, an indication of its position. The computer may then use this information as input data, and may as a result generate or modify a picture. This process may involve the computer in many successive steps between receiving the input data and generating the output. However, the computer's speed is usually sufficient to make the picture changes appear to follow the hand's movement. Input devices that attempt to ease the computer's task in generating output data often succeed only in restricting their own usefulness.

EXERCISES

9-1. Find an expression that is symmetrical in d_1, d_2, d_3, d_4, a, x and y, that can be used to check the validity of the x, y and z values computed for the three-dimensional acoustic tablet.

9-2. Derive the expressions relating the coordinates of the Lincoln Wand to the distances d_1, d_2, d_3 and d_4 of the wand from the four corners of the screen where the microphones are mounted. Assume the screen measures $2a$ x $2b$ in size. Derive also an expression for a value E from which you could check the validity of the x, y and z values.

9-3. What instructions would be needed in addition to those shown in Table 4-1, Chapter 4, to enable a light pen to be used for pointing and tracking? Consider both display instructions and computer control instructions.

10

INTERRUPT HANDLING

10.1 DEVICE HANDLING

Graphical input devices have been attached to computers of all sizes.
Much of the original research on tracked input devices was carried out
on Lincoln Laboratories' TX-2 [282], a huge, powerful machine.
Nowadays it is more common to use a small minicomputer to control a
display and to handle its input devices; the task of designing a monitor
or device-handling program for such a system is a classic one in
computer graphics [119]. The following sections therefore describe
input device handling as it is commonly applied to small machines.
Examples are given in the assembly language described in Appendix III.

On-line input devices fall into two classes: those that provide *discrete*
inputs, and those that operate in a *continuous* fashion. The
alphanumeric keyboard and the push-button are examples of discrete
devices, whereas most coordinate input devices such as the tablet and

mouse provide continuous* inputs. The discrete input device is rather easier to program by conventional methods, and is used as the subject of our initial discussion.

10.1.1   POLLING

An on-line keyboard cannot be programmed simply by issuing a 'read' command whenever the program needs data. Such a command would bring the program to a halt, where it would remain until the user felt like typing something. This would prevent the program from attending to other inputs and outputs. Also we should have to make sure to issue 'read' commands often enough to capture every character typed. What is needed is a means by which the program can tell when a key has just been pressed.

Figure 10-1 illustrates a mechanism for doing this. The keyboard control logic contains a *buffer register* and a *flag*. The buffer register holds the *code* of the character just typed: this is a number, generally in the range 0 to 127, identifying the character. The flag is a one-bit register, i.e. a single flip-flop, indicating by its contents whether a key has been pressed. It can be cleared to zero by the program, which can also examine its contents. When a key is pressed, the character code is loaded into the buffer register and the flag is set to 1.

The keyboard is programmed in the manner shown in Figure 10-2. After the flag has been cleared the program sits in a loop, testing the flag repeatedly until it changes from 0 to 1. When this happens the computer reads the contents of the buffer register. In assembly code this would be written as follows:

```
          KCF              clear keyboard flag
LOOP:     KSF              test flag, skip if not set
          JMP   LOOP       if not set, jump back and test again
          KRB              read buffer contents into accumulator
```

What does this achieve that the single 'read' command did not? Nothing much, since the computer is effectively at a halt while it remains in the loop. The advantage of the flag is that it allows us to handle several

---

* Although these devices are often capable of generating continuously varying voltages, it is of course impossible to pass these signals in their analog form to a discrete, digital device like the computer. We shall use the term *continuous* to refer to devices that generate inputs at rapid and regular intervals, independent of the rate of user action.

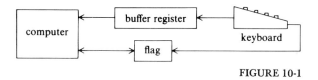

FIGURE 10-1

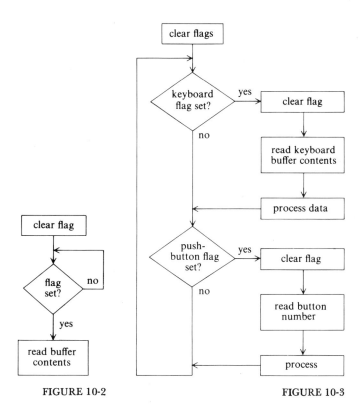

FIGURE 10-2   FIGURE 10-3

devices at once by means of a *polling loop,* in which each device's flag is tested in turn. Figure 10-3 shows such a polling loop, monitoring a keyboard and a set of push-buttons.

Notice that whenever a flag is found set, the program clears the flag, reads the contents of the device's buffer register and processes the data. Then the polling loop is resumed at the next test. It is dangerous to resume elsewhere, such as at the start of the loop, for this allows the first device in the loop to get all the attention and the rest none. A convenient way to code the flag-processing routine is as a subroutine: here is an example, written in assembly language:

```
LOOP:      KSN                   skip if keyboard flag not set
           JMS   KB              if set, call keyboard subroutine
           BSN                   skip if push-button flag not set
           JMS   BTN             if set, call push-button subroutine
           JMP   LOOP            return to start of loop


KB:        0                     return address saved here
           KCF                   clear keyboard flag
           CLA                   clear accumulator
           KRB                   inclusive-or keyboard buffer
                                   contents into AC

           DAC   I CHIX          store in table
           ISZ   CHIX            increment table pointer
           JMP   I  KB           return from subroutine
```

Only one of the two flag-processing subroutines is shown here: it reads the character code from the keyboard buffer and deposits it in a table, using the pointer CHIX.

10.1.2   THE POLLING OF OUTPUT AND TIMING DEVICES

Most output devices are provided with flags, and these too should be tested in the polling loop. For example, a teletypewriter controller normally contains two flags, one for the keyboard and one for the print mechanism. When a string of characters is to be printed it is stored in an *output buffer*, and the first character is sent to the printer. After each character has been printed, the printer flag is set, indicating to the computer that the printer is ready for another character from the buffer.

A device that is frequently useful in computer graphics is a *real-time clock* that sets a flag every sixtieth of a second or at some other fixed interval. The clock flag may be used to invoke various functions like light-pen tracking at regular intervals, or to permit devices that do not possess flags to be checked at the right frequency. If the display does not have a 60-cycle wait instruction, a clock is essential as a means of ensuring that a fixed refresh rate is maintained.

10.2   INTERRUPTS

Notice that Figure 10-3 includes a box labeled 'process data.' The 'process' involved may be as simple a matter as ignoring the data altogether, or as complex as carrying out a full-scale reorganization of the display file. If the process is a lengthy one there is a danger that input data may be lost during the process: the user may generate another input while the process is being executed. This is the main disadvantage of the polling technique — it works well with a few fairly slow devices but cannot cope with situations where many devices, some running at appreciable data rates, are competing with lengthy processing tasks. In such cases it is necessary to handle input and output by means of *interrupts*, as explained in the next section.

10.2.1   SINGLE-LEVEL INTERRUPT HANDLING

It would be convenient if the computer could automatically execute the appropriate subroutine whenever a flag is set; and this is just what interrupt-handling hardware can arrange for us. The simplest form of interrupt handling — single-location, single-level — has the computer transfer to a fixed location, the *trap location*, whenever a flag is set. Many small computers transfer to location 1; at the same time they store in location 0 the address of the instruction about to be executed. Thus the computer has only to execute the appropriate routine, and can then return to what it was doing previously by performing a jump indirectly via location 0.

Since setting *any* flag will cause a transfer to location 1, the computer must ascertain which flag caused the interrupt before it can call the appropriate routine. Accordingly it runs through a *skip chain*, testing each flag until it finds one set:

```
0:          0                  return address saved here
1:          DAC  SAVE          save accumulator
            KSN                skip if keyboard flag not set
            JMP  KBFLAG   ·    if set, jump to keyboard routine
            BSN                skip if push-button flag not set
            JMP  BTFLAG        etc.
            . . . .
            . . . .
```

We no longer code flag-processing routines (now called *interrupt routines*) as subroutines, for we do not wish the computer to resume flag-testing after the routine has been executed; instead it should return to the main program. Before it does so, it must perform two tasks:

1. *Restoration of the state of the machine.* The computer's active registers must be returned to the values they held when the interrupt occurred. This is why, in the example above, the first thing we do is save the contents of the accumulator. Any other active registers should be treated likewise, unless there is no possibility that they will be affected by the interrupt routine.
2. *Enabling further interrupts*, i.e. permitting further interrupts to be handled. During execution of an interrupt routine it is essential that no further interrupts be processed, for the return address in location 0 would then be overwritten. The interrupt hardware therefore *disables* further interrupts when it transfers to location 1; and the program must *enable* them.

Here, then, is the code that may be used to terminate an interrupt routine and transfer correctly back to the main program:

```
      . . .
      . . .
      LAC   SAVE            restore accumulator contents
      ION                   enable interrupts*
      JMP   I 0             jump via location 0
```

10.2.2   MORE EFFICIENT INTERRUPT SCHEMES

If many devices are in simultaneous use, the method of interrupt handling just described will involve the computer in a lot of flag-testing each time an interrupt is received. This may add 50 microseconds or more to the time taken to process an interrupt, an overhead that could seriously affect efficiency if interrupts should take place frequently. The problem is solved by using a computer with more than one trap location. Some computers provide each device with its own unique trap location: the total number may exceed one hundred. Others provide a smaller number, grouping a few devices around each trap location so that only a small amount of flag-testing is necessary.

---

* The ION instruction enabling interrupts in fact takes effect only after the JMP I 0 has been executed. This prevents an interrupt from occurring before the JMP has taken place.

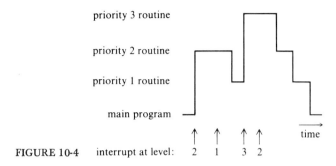

FIGURE 10-4   interrupt at level: 2   1   3   2

A more serious drawback of the interrupt-handling scheme described is that it still does not deal with the problem of lengthy processing tasks. It is possible for execution of an interrupt routine to take so long that two or more inputs have meanwhile been received from some other device. Normally this problem is solved by setting up an *attention queue:* requests for attention are added to the queue when interrupts are received, and these activate routines that are performed with interrupts enabled. This technique is described later in this chapter.

Instead of enabling and disabling interrupts, we can use a *priority interrupt system*. Hardware for this purpose is either standard or optional extra equipment on most of today's computers. Each device is assigned a *priority level*, and its interrupt routine may itself be interrupted by a device with higher priority. When the high-priority interrupt routine has been executed, the lower-priority one is resumed (see Figure 10-4). High priorities are normally assigned to devices that interrupt frequently, or that demand immediate service; devices that involve lengthy interrupt processing are assigned low priorities. It is possible for an interrupt routine running at one priority to initiate an interrupt at another level, by generating a *programmed interrupt;* the programmed interrupt feature is also frequently provided in modern computers.

10.3 THE GENERAL ORGANIZATION OF INTERRUPT ROUTINES

A set of interrupt routines is in effect a multiprogramming system. In a typical case, while a teletypewriter output routine is working its way through a buffer-full of characters, a clock routine is restarting the display every 16 milliseconds and a keyboard interrupt routine is activated every second or so to handle characters typed by the user. Each of these routines, whether it runs unmolested to completion or is occasionally interrupted by another, is executed asynchronously and independently from all the others.

Asynchrony is a result of the more or less random sequence in which inputs occur, and the different speeds of operation of output devices. It implies that each interrupt routine must be designed to function independently, since at no time can one routine assume that another is in a cooperative state. Direct communication between routines must be avoided for the same reason. Two or more routines may share the same data files, but care is needed to prevent interference between several routines modifying the same file.

Although interrupt routines are not allowed to communicate with each other directly, indirect communication is necessary, both between pairs of interrupt routines and between each routine and the main program. For example, the keyboard interrupt routine may wish to request the teleprinter output routine to echo the input character; it may also wish to inform the main program that a character has been received. In either case there is the danger that the recipient of the message may not be ready to receive it, so the the message must be put in a special form of shared data file, namely a *queue*. Periodically the recipient will examine the queue and remove a message.

Since interrupt routines communicate with the main program in much the same way that they communicate with each other, we may ask ourselves if there really exists a fundamental difference between interrupt routines and the main program. In fact the differences are not fundamental, but a matter of degree. The main program is simply a routine that has a lower priority than all the others, and that therefore runs when no other routine is active. It follows that we could permit the existence of several 'main programs,' communicating with each other by means of message queues. These programs or processes could share the use of data files and could, like interrupt routines, start up other processes. This is effectively how a time-shared computer system operates. It is a good way to organize any interactive program.

10.4   THE ATTENTION QUEUE

The attention queue can be thought of as a simple first-in, first-out queue (Figure 10-5). Interrupt routines add attention messages at one end, to be removed at the other so as to initiate processes. This

interrupt routines → attention no. 3 | attention no. 2 | attention no. 1 → processes

FIGURE 10-5

mechanism ensures that processes are initiated in the same order that the corresponding inputs occur.

The program that removes attentions from the queue is called the *task scheduler*. Besides removing attentions it must decide which processes to initiate. There are two reasons why this is so, and why the attention message hence cannot include a pointer to the process. In the first place, the choice of which process to run may depend not only on the input but on the outcome of the previous process, which may still be in progress when the input occurs. Secondly, a table look-up may be required in order to determine which process should be activated; it is unwise to make the interrupt routine responsible for this quite lengthy task. This second point suggests that, far from trying to identify the process within the interrupt routine, as little extra work as possible should be done at this stage and the attention message should be as simple as possible. Generally it is adequate to specify just the *device* causing the interrupt and the *data* received from it.

10.4.1   THE DESIGN OF AN ATTENTION QUEUE

The simplest way of constructing an attention queue is with a circular buffer of the type shown in Figure 10-6a. Fresh entries are added to the tail, and when these overflow the end of the buffer they are added at the start; meanwhile the task scheduler removes entries from the head of the queue. In Figure 10-6a each entry is of the same length; Figure 10-6b shows how easily the queue accommodates variable-length attention messages.

It is a simple matter to tell if a circular buffer is empty, for the head and tail then coincide. It is also easy to distinguish when the buffer is full: adding the word which fills the buffer causes the tail to overlap the head. It is important not to let this happen unless the program knows how to distinguish a full queue from an empty one, and how to cope with further inputs that occur while the queue is full.

The vexing problem of attention queue overflow can be solved in a number of ways, the best of which is to ensure that it never happens. If it does happen, the buffer must be enlarged, either by copying its

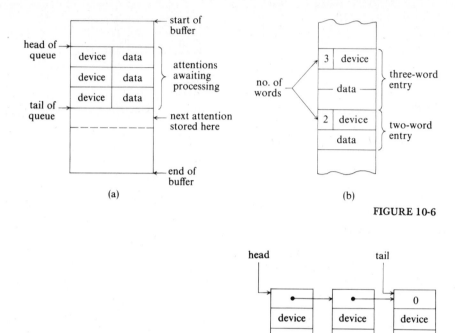

FIGURE 10-6

FIGURE 10-7

contents into a larger free area or by inserting a pointer to a reserve buffer. Both of these solutions involve access to free storage, and it may seem simpler to construct the entire queue out of blocks of free storage, as shown in Figure 10-7. Any use of free storage to build or extend the attention queue must be planned with care, however, for it means that the free storage subroutines must be both interruptable and sufficiently fast to be used within an interrupt routine. It is factors of this sort that make a non-overflowing circular buffer such an attractive solution.

10.4.2   THE USE OF LATCHES

The attention queue is particularly likely to overflow if inputs are being received frequently from a device like a stylus, and if the interval between these inputs is less than the time taken to run the appropriate process. This could happen if the stylus were being used to modify a complex picture in a 'rubber band' fashion (see Figure 10-8, and the discussion in Section 11.7). We may try to prevent overflow by using a

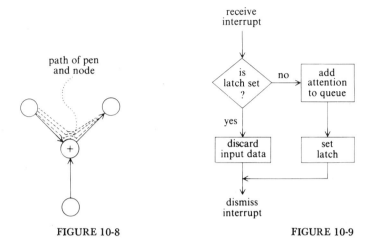

FIGURE 10-8   FIGURE 10-9

very large circular buffer, and hoping that users will not indulge in such operations for long enough to cause overflow. Imagine, however, what will happen: since attentions will arrive at the end of the queue faster than they can be removed, the process will lag further and further behind the user's hand, and he will eventually lose all control over the program.

In a situation of this sort it is essential to discard some inputs in order to slow down the flow of attentions. The easiest way of doing this is with a semaphore or *latch*. The latch is a software switch which is set when an attention enters the queue and is cleared when it leaves; while it is set all further inputs from this device are ignored. Figure 10-9 shows how the latch is added to the interrupt routine. The net effect of adding the latch is to make sure that there is never more than one attention from the device waiting in the attention queue.

The latch technique provides a basis for preventing overflow of the attention queue, for it regulates inputs of the continuous variety whose rate of flow cannot be controlled by the user. Discrete inputs from devices such as the keyboard or push-button are a different matter. Although the user can control their rate he is still liable to use them faster than the computer can process them, and if we use the latch technique we risk losing essential data. If we use a fixed-size circular buffer we are bound to have to discard data eventually if the user gets too far ahead of the program. A reasonable compromise solution is to set a latch when the queue is almost full; while it is set, further inputs are discarded and the user is signalled in some manner — perhaps by

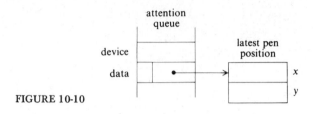

FIGURE 10-10

ringing a bell — to slow down. Although this solution is not very elegant, it is acceptable to most users.

The use of the latch with a coordinate input device has an interesting visible effect. The latch is cleared when each graphical attention is removed from the queue, so the next attention will enter the queue shortly after this event, i.e. shortly after the corresponding process is activated. By the time the process has finished, the coordinates of the attention in the queue may be quite out of date. The effect seen by the user is of the picture lagging some way behind the cursor or tracking cross, by a distance that depends on the speed of movement and on the time taken to execute the process. This is not a very annoying effect, but perfectionists may wish to prevent it by making sure that the coordinates in the attention represent the latest received from the input device. One way to do this is to include in the attention a pointer to the data, as shown in Figure 10-10.

10.5 TASK SCHEDULERS

Each attention added to the tail of the attention queue is eventually removed from the head of the queue by the task scheduler, which must then decide what process if any to invoke in response. In simpler varieties of task scheduler, this decision is based solely on the information contained in the attention message, i.e. input device and input data. In more complex systems, the input's *context* is also taken into account. For example, the same push-button may be used to start a process and to stop it; the task scheduler, on receiving two identical inputs in succession, must react in two different ways.

The simpler form of system is rather rare. It is sometimes possible to write an application program that responds to each individual input in only one way. Relatively few applications can be reduced to such a simple form, however. By far the majority of programs demand a more complex type of task scheduler, capable of responding to attentions not just as individual inputs but as members of a sequence. Examples of such sequences are the push-button sequence given above, or a sequence of keyboard inputs representing a character string; the sequence may be made up from a mixture of inputs from different devices. Each sequence effectively forms a *command*, and a complete set of commands defines the *command language* with which the user communicates his desires to the program. This notion has led to the use of the term *language processor* for any task scheduler that interprets a command language. The design of a language processor naturally depends very much on the sort of command language it has to handle. In Chapter 15, command languages and language processors are discussed in some detail.

10.6 INTERRUPTS FROM GRAPHICAL INPUT DEVICES

The ability of the stylus, mouse and light pen to follow continuous movements of the hand makes them extraordinarily useful as input devices. It also makes them somewhat awkward to program by traditional methods. This will be well known to anyone who has tried to persuade a conventional operating system to handle such a device.

It is of course hopeless from the start to expect a digital computer to adapt gracefully to a truly continuous input device. Digital computers operate in discrete steps and prefer discrete input devices like the keyboard. An analog computer could do a good job of following continuous hand movements, but a digital computer can at best sample these movements at discrete intervals. Provided it samples often enough, it can handle the device quite well.

The sampling rate of a coordinate input device is rarely an intrinsic function of the device. More often it is a function of the hardware interface between the device and the computer. We can classify these interfaces into three groups:

1. Those that impose a fixed sampling rate.
2. Those that allow the computer to sample at its own rate.
3. Those that may be sampled only on a signal from the user, e.g. pressing a switch or push-button.

The fixed rate interface is normally designed in an analogous manner to the keyboard interface, using a flag and a pair of coordinate buffer registers. The flag is set at a regular frequency, generally between 30 and 1000 times a second, and the computer reads the register contents when interrupted by the flag. The rate at which these interrupts occur can be rather overwhelming — the RAND Tablet [64], for example, is capable of interrupting every 250 microseconds. Special action may be necessary to prevent the computer from being swamped by the stream of interrupts.

The most convenient type of interface is generally class 2, the one that allows the computer to choose the sampling rate. The flag is then omitted, and the coordinates are sampled on every clock interrupt, or less frequently if so desired. Most clocks run at 50 or 60 Hz, which are more than adequate sampling rates: few applications require more than 10 samples per second.

The third class of interface, sampled by the computer only on a request by the user, is very different from the other two. It has a flag, but the flag only changes state when the switch is pressed or released. This effectively turns the stylus or mouse into a discrete input device. The computer can determine the device's coordinates only when interrupted, and hand movements that occur between interrupts are invisible to the computer. This type of interface is often used in remote display terminals, since it permits the use of low-speed transmission lines. In any other circumstances this technique reduces the usefulness of the input device, and is to be avoided.

10.6.1   CURSORS

Every time a fresh position is received from a coordinate input device it must be displayed on the screen in the form of a cursor (Figure 10-11); otherwise the device is unusable. This task, which is somewhat analogous to echoing input characters on a teletypewriter, is one of several that must be carried out by the interrupt routine responsible for the device. Generally it is a very simple matter: the x and y coordinates read from the buffer registers are converted into 'set x' and 'set y' display instructions that are placed just before the instructions for the cursor symbol. Figure 10-12 shows a scheme in which the cursor forms the first item in the display file. If the screen and input device use different coordinate systems, conversion will be necessary, but this generally involves little more than a simple shifting operation.

Interfaces are sometimes designed to reposition the cursor automatically. Interfaces belonging to class 3 above are required to do

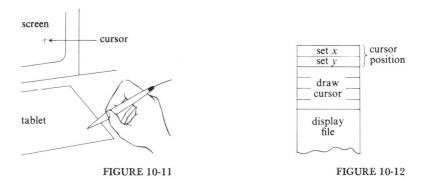

FIGURE 10-11   FIGURE 10-12

so, for the computer is told the device's position only at irregular intervals. Some low-cost displays use the actual analog voltages generated by the mouse or stylus as deflection signals to reposition the cursor; conversion to digital values then need only be done when the switch is pressed. Engelbart and English [80] have used an interface that automatically generates the 'set x' and 'set y' instructions and deposits them in the proper core locations, just before the cursor. This allows a single time-shared computer to track a large number of coordinate input devices without being swamped by the task.

10.6.2   LIGHT PEN INTERRUPTS

The light pen interface, with its single flag and absence of buffer registers, cannot really be placed in any of the three categories mentioned. It most closely resembles class 3, with the added restriction that the pen's position can be sampled only when the pen is pointed at an intensified spot on the screen. This action sets the flag and interrupts the computer; the display must be halted so that the contents of its various registers can be read by the computer.

As mentioned in the previous chapter, the light pen can be used in two modes, for tracking and for pointing. The light pen interrupt routine normally has to take care of both of these functions, for which reason it is often quite lengthy and complicated. The following factors must be taken into account:

1. Pointing the pen at an item on the screen produces a stream of interrupts which lasts as long as the item is 'visible' to the pen. Normally we would like the computer to ignore all but the first of these interrupts.

2. If the pen is pointed at a line drawn by an analog vector generator, the pen's position cannot be found since only the line's endpoints can be determined from the contents of the registers in the display.
3. This may mean that the only register containing information useful to the computer is the display address counter. Its contents will be of value only if a mechanism exists for linking the display address with an item in the data base.
4. Furthermore, even the display address counter cannot be relied upon to point to the right place once the display has stopped. Sometimes it will point to an address two or three words beyond the correct instruction. This is due to delayed pen response and is a particularly common problem with fast vector-drawing displays.

These problems, which might seem rather daunting to the systems programmer, have instead inspired programmers to heights of ingenuity that sometimes verge on the absurd. It is not the purpose of this chapter to chronicle all this ingenuity, or even to encourage the continued use of the light pen. For those who have no choice but to use it, the following two sections provide the essentials of light pen programming, and the bibliography gives further details [139, 271].

10.6.2.1   Light pen hits

When the light pen is pointed at a line or point on the screen, the pen flag is set and the display stops. The computer is interrupted, and transfers to an interrupt routine that performs the following tasks:

1. It determines as much information as necessary about the item 'seen' by the pen. This information is later passed to the main program in the form of an attention.
2. It makes the item 'invisible' to the pen, to prevent further interrupts.
3. It restarts the display.

Identification of the item normally requires the use of a segmented or structured display file. The structure shown in Figure 10-13 uses the push-jump technique described in Chapter 5. Note that it provides more than just the identity of the 'visible' items: all the ancestors of the item can be identified from the data in the return stack. As we shall see in

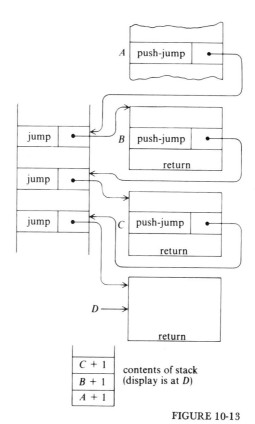

FIGURE 10-13

the next chapter, not all of this information need be passed back to the main program.

In the absence of push-jump hardware it may be necessary to use more complicated linkage mechanisms. The most complex of all is probably the one used in Graphic-2 [44, 206] in which the computer is interrupted at the end of every block of display file, so that in effect the computer *interprets* a structure that is otherwise similar to Figure 10-13.

Rendering the item invisible is usually easy, since most displays designed for use with light pens have instructions for enabling and disabling pen interrupts from within the display file. Therefore a 'disable pen' instruction placed before the call to the item will have the desired effect.

Restarting the display is also quite straightforward provided the state of the display is not disturbed by the interrupt routine; in fact some displays have a 'resume' instruction just for the purpose. Note that in one respect the state of the display must be changed: the light pen must be disabled for the rest of the current item, for it will otherwise immediately generate another interrupt.

10.6.2.2   Light pen tracking

Light pen tracking is essentially a feedback technique: the computer displays a *tracking pattern* in the region where it believes the pen is being pointed, the pen picks up part of the pattern, and the computer calculates a revised position and scans again. This simple process has been the basis for an incredible variety of programs employing an even more incredible variety of tracking patterns: rasters, circular blobs, converging spirals, diverging spirals, enclosing squares, crosses drawn inwards, crosses drawn outwards, crosses drawn logarithmically, twin crosses, eight-pointed stars. Many programs employ several different patterns for different situations. Some use predictive techniques in order to track rapid hand movements, while others have followed the SKETCHPAD convention of ceasing to track after a rapid flick of the hand. The simplest technique of all is to cover the screen with a fine mesh of dots (Figure 10-14b); unfortunately this tends to obscure the picture on the screen. The reader is advised to use a cross (Figure 10-14a): this gives the most accurate estimate of the pen's position, and is virtually unaffected by conical fields of view.

It is generally more convenient to draw the cross point-by-point inwards, starting at the extremity of each arm. The light pen will then interrupt as each arm of the cross emerges into the field of view. If the coordinates of the most recent point are read after each interrupt, four points p_1, p_2, p_3, p_4 will be found which lie on the circumference of the field of view (Figure 10-15). The center of the field of view is the point,

$$(\tfrac{1}{2}(x_1 + x_2), \tfrac{1}{2}(y_1 + y_2))$$

To ensure reliable and efficient tracking the following steps are recommended:

1. Draw each arm from one side of the cross to the other, in case the center of the cross is outside the field of view (Figure 10-16).

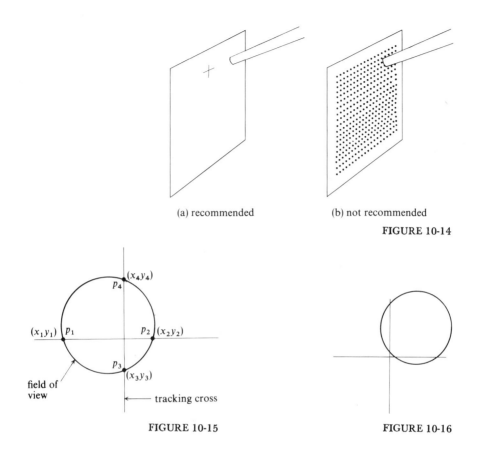

(a) recommended   (b) not recommended

FIGURE 10-14

FIGURE 10-15   **FIGURE 10-16**

2. Draw each arm of the cross several times if necessary, to increase the pen's chance of detecting it.
3. Disable pen interrupts, except within the tracking cross, while pen tracking is in progress.
4. Do not track too often, or both flicker and the efficiency of the main program will be badly affected.

Opinions differ on how to commence tracking, how often to display the cross and what to do if the pen fails to detect the cross. To the first and last of these questions the most popular answers are:

(a) do nothing — the user can point at the cross to start tracking, and can retrieve the cross if it gets left behind; or
(b) display dots all over the screen at the start and whenever tracking fails.

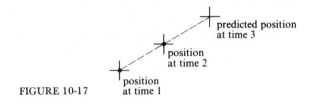

FIGURE 10-17

Neither of these can be guaranteed to keep all users happy all of the time.

As far as frequency is concerned, tracking is most easily carried out at the end of each refresh cycle. However, it is more likely to succeed if performed at a fixed frequency, using the clock. The latter technique is not always feasible, since the computer may not have the power to stop the display so as to insert the tracking cross. Even if it can stop the display, the computer must be able to read the complete state of the display so that it can restore the state and restart the display successfully after displaying the cross.

In an attempt to improve the performance of their tracking programs, many have used *predictive* schemes. Instead of displaying the cross at the latest pen position, these programs display it where the pen is *expected* to point, the next time tracking is performed (see Figure 10-17). Some complex schemes, taking account of second-order effects, have been developed.

10.7 PRACTICAL ASPECTS OF INTERRUPT AND ATTENTION HANDLING

The aim of this chapter has, as in earlier chapters, been to present a *general* approach to the subject matter, in this case interrupt and attention handling. In many branches of computer graphics it is to our advantage to adopt a general approach; for example, a general-purpose display file compiler is usually easier to use than one designed for a single application. In the case of interrupt and attention handling, however, we may be handicapped by trying to be too general. A system that attempts to handle all inputs in a completely general way is likely either to restrict the type of graphical interaction that it permits, or else to be so complex that none but expert programmers can make use of it.

A specific example of how input handling may suffer from too general an approach is in coordinate input handling. We have suggested passing stylus coordinates to the program via the attention queue in the standard manner, if necessary limiting the number of attentions by means of a latch. This works well when the inputs are used for positioning items or for drawing the endpoints of lines. However, the intermittent nature of the latch means that the points defined in the attentions may not be equally spaced in time. If we use these points for 'inking,' we may generate a rather irregular trace in place of the smooth path of the pen.

This is one of several applications that demand a specific solution, rather than a general one. Inking is best performed by a low-priority interrupt routine that builds a table of points out of those received from the stylus, meanwhile adding the appropriate vector or point commands to the display file. When the stylus is raised, indicating the end of the stroke, an attention is generated and the address of the table is passed to the program. Since we do not want all strokes of the stylus to be inked, it must be possible for the application program to activate and deactivate the inking routine, and to erase the trace that the inking routine creates.

Inking is an example of a case in which it is advisable for the interrupt routine to *buffer* the input data, rather than pass it on to the program as it is received. It may be convenient to treat keyboard inputs in the same fashion. In this way command strings can be assembled by the interrupt routine and passed on to the program only when the terminating character is received. This reduces the frequency at which attentions are generated, and avoids the need for special programs, running at the user level, to pack characters into strings and numbers. On the other hand, it is both difficult and wasteful to build into the interrupt routine all the different features we might conceivably like to use in character handling — variable terminators, no terminator (i.e. single character commands), number recognition, recognition of commands from the first few characters typed (command *anticipation*).

Problems like these make the design of input handlers a specialized task. Generally the system designer must make some compromises in order to produce a system that is both versatile and economical. These compromises will be of two kinds — those that involve the use of non-standard input-handling techniques, and those that restrict the range of interactive techniques available to the programmer. The system designer will be wise to study the list of techniques in Chapter 11 before deciding which of these his system should allow.

EXERCISES

10-1. The speed at which a light pen may be moved during tracking depends on the rate at which the tracking pattern is displayed, on the type of tracking pattern used, and in most cases on the pen's field of view. Calculate the effects on tracking speed and flicker of using different tracking patterns and frequencies. In particular, calculate the maximum hand speed if tracking is performed 30 times a second, the field of view is 1/4 inch diameter and a four-armed tracking cross is used.

10-2. Discuss the relationship between the rate at which interrupts are received from devices, the length of time taken to execute their interrupt routines, and the effect of interrupts on system performance.

10-3. Suppose coordinate positions are being received at regular intervals from a tablet stylus, representing points on a closed curve being drawn by the user. How would you establish an *accurate* estimate of (a) the circumference of the curve; (b) the enclosed area?

11

INTERACTIVE GRAPHICAL TECHNIQUES

11.1 A COMPENDIUM OF GRAPHICAL INPUT TECHNIQUES

A great deal of ingenuity has been devoted over the years to devising new ways of using graphical input devices. This activity, although it has produced some of the most original ideas in computer graphics, has been very poorly documented.* This chapter attempts to provide a list of some of the more successful and widely used graphical input techniques. These techniques are the basic ingredients that the programmer uses to construct the *command language* for a graphical program.

   The chapter is divided into sections, each section describing one technique or a closely related group of techniques. After a general description of the technique and a discussion of its advantages and drawbacks, each section provides the following information:

1. *Applications:* areas of application in which the technique may be found useful.

---

* The origins of many of these techniques are obscure. As a result, credits are often omitted.

2. *Hardware investment:* the computing and peripheral equipment required to support the technique.
3. *Software investment:* the amount of programming effort involved to implement the technique, including in some cases details of how the technique is programmed.
4. *Alternatives:* other techniques that may be used for the same purposes.

Under the heading 'Hardware investment,' reference is frequently made to *local processing power.* As mentioned in Chapter 4, some display terminals are not equipped with general-purpose processing power of their own, but use a remote processor, frequently time-shared. This greatly affects the degree of response that these terminals can offer.

11.2   POSITIONING

This is the most direct technique for adding symbols and pre-defined subpictures to the information on the screen. The pen or stylus is used to indicate the required position, and the symbol is added by pressing a button or pen switch (Figure 11-1).

Applications: Computer-aided design, and other applications in which the user, rather than the program, creates the data base.

Hardware and software investment: Minimal; within the capabilities of virtually any display system. Positioning can even be performed without using a graphical input device, by programming a keyboard-propelled cursor that can be stepped to the desired position.

Alternatives: Dragging (see Section 11.6) is sometimes more convenient but requires a greater investment in hardware and software; on-line character recognition (see Section 11.12) may also be used effectively.

FIGURE 11-1

FIGURE 11-2

11.3   SPECIFYING LINES BY ENDPOINT POSITIONING

The simplest way to define a line is to indicate its endpoints by the positioning technique. In the absence of any constraints (see Section 11.5), the program responds to the second input by drawing a straight line between the two points (Figure 11-2).

Applications: Layout of graphs, networks, flow diagrams etc; defining symbols and picture parts; many other uses.

Hardware and software investment: Minimal; similar to positioning.

Alternatives: Rubber-band line drawing (see Section 11.7) may be more convenient but requires a display with selective erase capability and local processing power.

11.4   SCALES   AND   GUIDELINES   FOR   DRAWING   AND POSITIONING

It is very difficult to draw or position accurately without assistance from the program. Since the user can rarely judge by eye to the accuracy of a stylus, he is liable to find that lines that he meant to draw vertical are slightly aslant, symbols that should be aligned are out of alignment and so forth.

This problem can be solved by displaying a *grid* on the screen (Figure 11-3); this provides the same assistance as a piece of squared paper. However the grid is liable to obscure important detail unless it be drawn at reduced brightness, and it may also tend to increase flicker. A more convenient method is the use of a *guideline* parallel to one of the axes (Figure 11-4); however, the guideline must be repositioned very

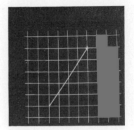

FIGURE 11-3

FIGURE 11-4

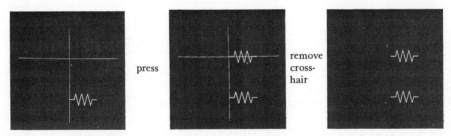

FIGURE 11-5

frequently, and this can be time-consuming. Simpler still is the full screen-width *cross-hair*, which moves as the stylus moves and which therefore makes alignment very simple (Figure 11-5). For accurate dimensioning without a grid, the user can draw a graduated *scale* in the appropriate position, and remove it later (Figure 11-6).

Applications: Any of those mentioned earlier, particularly where accurate layout is essential.

Hardware investment: Of these techniques, the grid is the only one applicable to displays that do not possess selective erase capability —

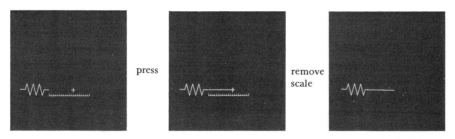

press   remove scale

FIGURE 11-6

guidelines and scales must be erased after they are no longer in use. Cross-hairs that move with the stylus require a small amount of local processing power.

Software investment: All are relatively simple to implement: cross-hairs may be programmed within the stylus interrupt routine.

Alternatives: Use of constraints (see Section 11.5), generally more convenient but involving more software.

11.5   CONSTRAINTS APPLIED TO DRAWING AND POSITIONING

In many applications, symbols and line endpoints are positioned on the intersections of a modular grid, rather than arbitrarily on the screen. Although displaying the grid helps the user to position on the intersections, it is even simpler if the program applies a *modular constraint*. The user then indicates the approximate position, and the program rounds to the nearest grid intersection (Figure 11-7). This technique works equally well with or without a displayed grid.

Another useful form of constraint is the *horizontal or vertical constraint* applied to lines. In many applications the majority of lines are drawn parallel to the axes. If the program knows the starting point and direction of the line, then only one of the coordinates of the endpoint is significant and the other may be discarded (Figure 11-8). There are two ways of applying this type of constraint: in one the user indicates beforehand whether the line is horizontal or vertical; in the other the program chooses the axis direction closest to the direction of the drawn line, e.g. horizontal if the drawn line is less than 45 degrees to the horizontal (Figure 11-9). The latter method is very economical

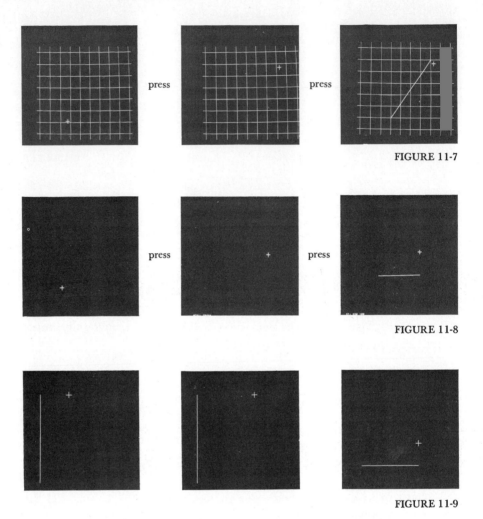

FIGURE 11-7

FIGURE 11-8

FIGURE 11-9

of user commands, but the former is more powerful, since the user can align the endpoint of the line with any other point on the screen.

A more sophisticated constraint is the *gravity field*, useful for connecting lines to existing lines. Around each existing line is defined an invisible region, either dumbell or sausage shaped (Figure 11-10); if the user points within this region, the new line will be attached to the old one (Figure 11-11). Thus less accuracy of aim is required. The dumbell-shaped gravity field makes it slightly easier to attach to endpoints than to the rest of the line.

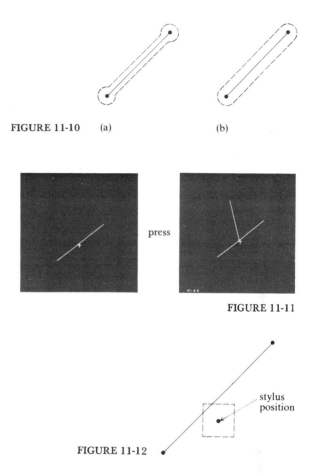

FIGURE 11-10   (a)   (b)

press

FIGURE 11-11

stylus
position

FIGURE 11-12

Applications: As in Sections 11.2 and 11.3 above. Horizontally and vertically constrained lines with gravity fields are particularly useful in drawing circuit diagrams.

Hardware investment: Minimal, since none of these requires the selective erase capability.

Software investment: Minor, except in the case of the gravity field. It is quite difficult to simulate a gravity field faithfully, so that in cases of conflict the closer line is chosen. Fortunately a fairly crude implementation will generally suffice. For example, the stylus position may be assumed to lie within the gravity field if a small square region inscribed around the stylus position is intersected by the line (Figure 11-12). To achieve the dumbell, we can check the endpoints first, using

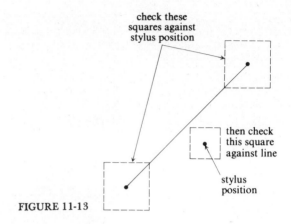

check these
squares against
stylus position

then check
this square
against line

stylus
position

FIGURE 11-13

a slightly larger square (Figure 11-13). This method is fairly easily programmed using the windowing method of hit-detection described below.

Alternatives: See 'scales and guidelines,' Section 11.4.

11.6   DRAGGING

A symbol or picture part may be positioned by fixing it relative to the stylus coordinates so that it appears to be attached to the stylus (Figure 11-14). This 'dragging' technique generally makes correct positioning much easier, for the item can be seen in position before the user, by pressing the stylus switch or push-button, 'fixes' it in place. Dragging is indispensable in situations where the correct position cannot be judged from the stylus position alone (see Figure 11-15). To achieve very accurate positioning, we can scale down the stylus movement, in effect simulating a second-order lever (see Figure 11-16). Other relationships between stylus and item position, both linear and non-linear, may be used.

Applications: General layout of symbols, etc.

Hardware investment: Requires selective erase capability and some local processing power.

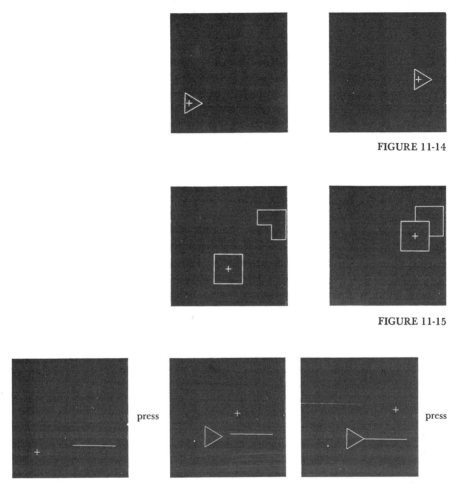

FIGURE 11-14

FIGURE 11-15

FIGURE 11-16

Software investment: Provided continuous stylus movements are passed to the program, dragging is quite simple to program. Under time-sharing, however, smooth dragging is difficult to achieve unless it can be programmed as a function of the graphics terminal.

Alternatives: Positioning (see Section 11.2), generally less convenient but more economical in hardware and software.

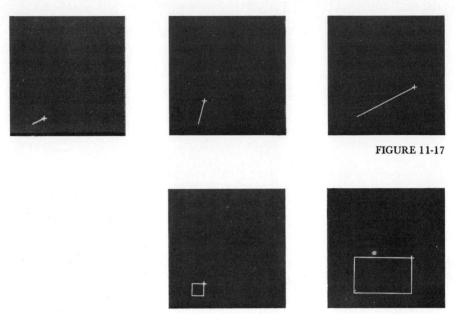

FIGURE 11-17

FIGURE 11-18

11.7   RUBBER-BAND LINES

The user defines a rubber-band line just as he does a conventional line, by specifying its two endpoints with the aid of the stylus and a push-button or switch. The difference is that the program, after the first point has been specified, repeatedly re-draws a line from this point to the current stylus position. The effect is of a line 'stretching' from the starting point to the stylus position: hence the name. When the line appears satisfactory to the user he presses the button or switch to indicate the endpoint (Figure 11-17).

The rubber-band technique may be applied to other constructs besides simple lines. For example, horizontally or vertically constrained lines, squares, circles, rectangles and many other shapes may be drawn in this fashion (Figure 11-18).

Applications: Suitable whenever the dimensions of the line or entity depend on its appearance or on its visual relationship to the rest of the picture. For example, the rubber-band technique is very useful in adjusting the layout of a complex or congested diagram.

Hardware investment: All rubber-band operations depend on the use of selectively erasable displays, and on having access to a certain amount of local processing power. Complex rubber-band operations may in fact require a large amount of processing power, since the picture will have to be re-drawn ten or more times a second.

Software investment: Rubber-band line drawing may be incorporated as a system function without much difficulty. A generalized rubber-band drawing capability is rather more difficult to provide, however, because it requires special language constructs, and because each different rubber-band drawing process requires a fresh program to be written for the display's local processor.

Alternatives: Endpoint positioning (see Section 11.3), rather less powerful but much simpler and less expensive.

11.8 DIMENSIONING   TECHNIQUES   AND   GRAPHICAL POTENTIOMETERS

Lines drawn in a rubber-band fashion may be positioned accurately with the aid of a grid or with one of the other positioning aids mentioned in Section 11.4. However the local processing power that we use in drawing the rubber-band line can also be used to display the dimensions of the line as it is changing (Figure 11-19). In this way the line may be drawn accurately without any additional aids. Dimensions may be displayed during any rubber-band drawing operation, such as rectangle drawing (Figure 11-20), and in a similar fashion the coordinates of a symbol may be displayed while it is being dragged around the screen (Figure 11-21). The dimensions should be displayed

FIGURE 11-19

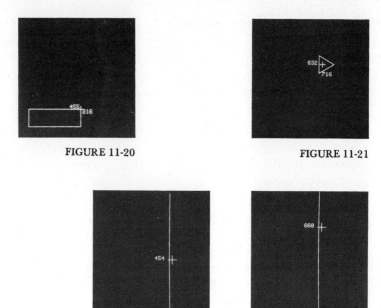

FIGURE 11-20   FIGURE 11-21

FIGURE 11-22

close to the pen or cursor, since this is where the user's attention is focused during drawing. After the line or symbol has been positioned the dimensions may be removed, but they should remain on the screen long enough for the user to verify that he has positioned accurately.

A similar technique may be used for the input of numerical data. Suppose we display the y-coordinate of the pen position as we move the pen around. We then have a mechanism similar to a *potentiometer,* which can be adjusted to any value we choose between 0 and 1023: this value may then be used by the program as an input parameter (Figure 11-22). Furthermore we are not restricted to the range 0 to 1023, since the pen coordinate may be scaled by any factor we choose. It may be convenient to scale logarithmically so as to achieve better accuracy at the lower end of the scale. Alternatively the output value may be changed at a rate proportional to the square or exponential of the pen velocity. This gives very fine control at low pen speeds.

Unless rate control is used, the linear potentiometer is limited in resolution to one part in one thousand or less. A device which does not suffer from this limitation is the *Light Handle* [199]. This is effectively eight potentiometers arranged side-by-side as shown in Figure 11-23. The rightmost potentiometer is for extremely accurate adjustment, and

FIGURE 11-23

each of the others has a scale factor of twice that of the potentiometer to the right of it. The displayed value remains constant as the pen is moved horizontally. Thus it can be adjusted coarsely by moving up and down one of the lefthand potentiometers and more accurately by one of the righthand ones. Circular pen motions 'wind' the value up or down.

Applications: Dimensions are useful whenever a grid or scale would obscure detail. Potentiometers offer the user a convenient means of entering numerical data without having to divert his attention from the screen. The potentiometer is of greatest value in applications where the user must exercise some form of continuous control over the program — for example, in controlling rotation of an object or in 'zooming' in on a picture.

Hardware investment: The same as is required for rubber-band drawing.

Software investment: Dimensions and potentiometers are simple to program, except in cases where the displayed numbers are liable to be obscured by the line or object being drawn; in such cases the program should be capable of choosing an unobscured position for the numbers. The Light Handle is not a complicated program, but its parameters require careful adjustment before it can be used with ease. All of these techniques are, like rubber-band drawing, dependent on a system organization and language that permit a user program to be run every time the pen moves. Rate control is even more demanding, for it requires inputs from the pen that represent points equally spaced in time.

Alternatives: Dimensioning can be done with the aid of a grid or scale (see Section 11.4) although these are sometimes less convenient.

Discrete values can of course be typed instead of being entered by means of a potentiometer; alternatively the keyboard may be simulated with light buttons (see Section 11.10). For continuous control the only real alternative to the potentiometer is some form of rotating control such as a tracker ball or a knob connected to a shaft encoder.

11.9   POINTING

All the techniques described so far have been methods of using graphical input devices to *add* information to a data base. Graphical input devices have another equally important use in applications where the user wishes to interact with an *existing* data base, by pointing at items on the screen. This is feasible both with devices like the light pen that react to the displayed image and with other devices that provide only coordinate input data.

The light pen was for obvious reasons the first device to be used in this way. It is still preferred by many for its ability to respond directly to pointing actions. In fact this ability is of dubious value. As we shall see in the software discussion, hit-detection is not always simplifed by the use of a light pen, and the light pen has so many other drawbacks — physical awkwardness, fixed field of view, incompatability with storage-tube displays — that its popularity appears unwarranted.

Applications: Whenever the interaction is with an existing data base or picture definition.

Hardware investment: The light pen works best with refreshed displays of the point-plotting and raster varieties. It may be used with most analog vector displays, but does not in this case report an exact coordinate position when pointed at a vector. The response of the light pen is generally too slow for it to be used with the fastest analog displays. It cannot normally be used with a storage tube display unless the picture is redrawn whenever the user wishes to point at an item; this is feasible only with high transmission rates. For easy hit-detection, the display with which the light pen is used should include a push-jump subroutine mechanism (see Chapter 4).

Most other graphical input devices require special software for hit-detection; they can then be used with any type of display. The same software may of course be used with a tracked light pen.

Software investment: Hit-detection cannot be implemented without a fair amount of software investment, whether the device to be used is a light pen or a non-interrupting device like a stylus. However the programming techniques used are so different in the two cases that they are best discussed separately.

Software investment for non-interrupting devices: Few input devices other than the light pen have any means of signaling explicitly to the computer that the user is trying to point at something. Occasionally such means is contrived: for example, one of the buttons on a mouse may be reserved for pointing. In general, however, the button will be used for other purposes, as of course will the switch on a tablet stylus. So in most cases there is nothing to distinguish an attention generated by a pointing operation from an attention for entering coordinate data. The job of telling them apart falls either to the task scheduler or to the application program.

For the task scheduler to know when to interpret such an input as a pointing operation, there must be some indication in the command language description. Typically this will specify that a certain key or button input is to invoke the hit-detection routine, using the most recently received cursor position. The same may be specified in the application program:

```
IF DEVICE=BUTTON3 THEN
    BEGIN
        HITDETECT (PENX,PENY);
        IF VISIBLE THEN . . .
```

Here the program calls a system procedure HITDETECT with the latest pen coordinates as parameters. The result is stored in a reserved boolean variable VISIBLE.

Whether hit-detection is carried out by the task scheduler or by the application program, the algorithm will be much the same. The crucial factor is the type of display file compiler used. Hit detection is most easily performed when the display file is generated with the aid of a transformation routine of the windowing variety. It is then possible to use the same windowing routine to perform hit-detection as follows:

1. A small square 'region of interest' is described around the pen position.

2. The coordinates of this square are transformed back from screen to page coordinates.
3. Using this square as a window, the display file is regenerated, omitting the final display code generation stage.
4. If any line or other entity is found to lie within the window, it represents a 'hit;' the regeneration process stops and the appropriate information is passed to the program.

This technique is costly in CPU time unless the boxing test is used to good effect in the picture definition, in which case very few lines reach the clipping stage. However this technique has two significant points in its favor:

(a) it can be implemented by means of a minor extension to any standard windowing routine;
(b) when the process encounters a 'hit' it will have traced the picture hierarchy to the exact point corresponding to the indicated item; therefore the required ancestry information is readily available.

This technique can also be used with display procedures (see Section 8.8). The picture is then regenerated by executing each frame procedure, until a 'hit' is detected. In this case, the process stops at the entry in the data base corresponding to the indicated item. In order to execute the frame procedures, a list must be kept of the frames that are currently being displayed. Note that this technique may fail if the data base is altered between generating the picture and processing the 'hit.' This is considered by some to be a disadvantage of the technique.

If this hit-detection technique cannot be used, then there are basically two alternatives: either to interpret the display file, or to trace through the data base looking for a 'hit.' The first technique may be assisted by compiling extra data into the display file. For example, we could include data at the start of each record or item indicating its overall dimensions (see Figure 11-24). The second technique uses what amounts to a viewing algorithm of the type mentioned in Chapter 5, and may in fact be implemented by suitably modifying the standard viewing algorithm along the lines described above, with reference to the windowing process.

Once a 'hit' has been detected the question arises of how much ancestry data should be passed to the program. System designers should avoid the 'ambiguity fallacy,' which postulates that since an item may have several levels of ancestry it is impossible to determine to which

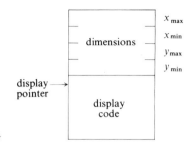

FIGURE 11-24

level the user is referring when he points at the item. This problem is often posed using a circuit as an example: if the user points at a resistor, is he trying to indicate the resistor, or the circuit of which the resistor forms a part, or just a certain line within the resistor? This situation should never occur in a well-constructed program, which should always either *know* the level in which the user is interested, or should *ask* him to state the level. It is an indication of serious deficiencies in the command language if the user is able to make an ambiguous pointing action.

Ideally the user should precede each pointing action with a command such as DELETE ITEM or DELETE LINE. It is then possible for the hit-detection process to restrict its search to the appropriate level. If the user is permitted to point first and indicate the level afterwards then the entire ancestry must be determined and passed to the program, which takes action only after the level information is received.

Software investment for light pens: In order for full advantage to be taken of the light pen's hit-detection capabilities, a structured display file must be used. Figure 10-13 shows a structure that makes use of push-jumps to determine the ancestry of the item in question. Displays that use other subroutine mechanisms make hit-detection more difficult. For example, the subroutine jump that stores the return address in the first word of the subroutine scatters the ancestry information in various places in the display file, and it is difficult even to determine the identity of the item itself.

Alternatives: There are few satisfactory alternatives to pointing as a means of interacting graphically with an existing data base. A solution for those deprived of a graphical input device is the use of labels which the user types in when he wants to identify an object. Another is the use of a keyboard-propelled cursor (see Section 11.2).

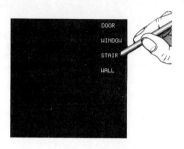

FIGURE 11-25

FIGURE 11-26

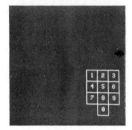

FIGURE 11-27

11.10   LIGHT BUTTONS AND MENUS

The light button is a small symbol, usually text, to which the user points with the pen or stylus in order to issue a command to the program (Figure 11-25). Typically several light buttons will be displayed at a time in what is sometimes called a *menu* of commands.

One of the advantages of using light buttons instead of typed commands is that the program need display only those commands that are valid at any given time. Thus the user can see what his choice of commands is, and is prevented from issuing an illegal command. In many cases, moreover, light buttons offer a faster means of control than the keyboard. However this advantage is lost if the menu is allowed to grow too large, for the user then spends a good deal of time searching the menu for the command he wants. A convenient technique, suggested by Wiseman [313], is to group a small set of light buttons around the cursor or tracking cross (Figure 11-26). This ensures that the light buttons are always close to hand during drawing operations.

Light buttons may be used for data input. A popular technique is the simulated numerical keyboard from which the user chooses digits to construct numbers (Figure 11-27). In this way he can input data

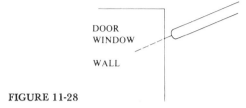

DOOR
WINDOW

WALL

FIGURE 11-28

without having to put down the pen and turn to the keyboard. This technique has sometimes been extended to give the user a complete simulated typewriter keyboard.

Applications: Light buttons are useful in all classes of application, particularly those with large and complex command languages.

Hardware investment: Minimal. The light button was first proposed as a technique using a light pen and refresh display, but can equally well be programmed for any other type of display or input device. Except in the case of movable light buttons, no local processing power is required.

Software investment: Light buttons may be programmed either as part of the stylus interrupt routine or by means of standard hit-detection software (see Section 11.9). In a general-purpose system it is often more efficient and more convenient to the programmer if the first approach is adopted.

Light button processing is quite simple if a stylus or mouse is in use. When a stylus switch or mouse button input is received a quick check is made to see if the device is positioned within the menu region; then the actual choice of light button is determined from the device coordinates. With a light pen, we must normally reserve a special area of the display file for light buttons. When a pen interrupt occurs the display address will tell us the identity of the light button chosen. It is often necessary to design the system so that the user does not accidentally point at one of the next set of light buttons, occupying the same position as the one he has just pointed at. A simple way to prevent this is to leave blank the position occupied by the chosen light button (see Figure 11-28).

Alternatives: Typed commands, or commands handprinted with the aid of a stylus (see Section 11.12).

FIGURE 11-29

11.11   INKING

If a line is drawn to each fresh stylus position from the previous one, a trail will be left behind the cursor in the manner of a pen drawing on paper (Figure 11-29). This technique is known as *inking*.

Applications: Inking is an essential component of on-line character recognition (see Section 11.12). Apart from curve tracing it has few other serious applications.

Hardware investment: Inking can be achieved on a storage-tube display by displaying the cursor in storage rather than write-through mode. Refresh displays require a small amount of local processing power to permit inking.

Although the path of any graphical input device may be inked, some are easier to use in this fashion than others. Pen-like devices such as the light pen and stylus are easy to handle, whereas it is quite difficult to trace accurately with a mouse or tracker ball. If it is essential to record an accurate inked path, a tablet must be used.

Software investment: Inking requires only a simple program that connects points received from the pen. Because points are usually very closely spaced it is sufficient just to display a dot at each point, but connected points are more attractive in appearance. It is important not to include in the display file successive points with the same coordinates, for this creates ugly bright spots. On the other hand it may be essential to record every point so that the program can compute writing speed. For reasons like these it may be necessary to keep two lists of points, one for display and the other for use by the program.

Alternatives: Curve-tracing may be carried out by pointing at successive points on the curve; this is slower than inking but is generally more accurate and requires no local processing.

FIGURE 11-30

11.12   ON-LINE CHARACTER RECOGNITION

We have left until last the input technique that is possibly the most powerful and general of all, and that certainly presents the most interesting issues to the programmer. This is the on-line character recognizer. It is possible to write a program that will take a symbol made up from a number of *strokes* drawn with a stylus, and to match the symbol to the alphanumeric character that it most closely resembles (Figure 11-30). Programs to do this have been in existence for several years. Recently some very successful recognizers have been developed that have been used extensively for a variety of purposes [108, 249, 227, 159].

In order to be successful, a recognizer must meet certain criteria. It must respond quickly with the recognized character; it must achieve a high rate of success in its recognition; it must tolerate a good deal of variation in the size, style and orientation of the drawn characters; and the program must be reasonably sparing in its use of computer resources. While no recognizers so far written can be claimed to meet all these criteria perfectly, in the last five years some significant advances have been made, particularly towards achieving reasonably economical recognizers that can tolerate widely varying writing styles.

One of the most interesting aspects of these recognizers is the fashion in which they accommodate variations in writing style, by 'learning' to recognize the style of each user. The user first 'teaches' the recognizer his own style by printing each character in the alphabet several times. Once this training phase is complete the recognizer is ready for use. The user's alphabet is retained in the form of a table and may be recalled on future occasions when he wishes to use the recognizer.

The first such *trainable* recognizer was developed by Teitelman [286]. Interest in character recognizers grew considerably after the development of the tablet as an input device: successful recognizers that used the RAND Tablet were developed by Groner [107] and Bernstein [21]. Groner's program is not trainable, however; the character set is fixed in the program and the user, instead of teaching the program his own style of writing, must learn to print in the style dictated by the program.

On-line character recognition has a number of advantages over the other techniques described in this chapter. In the first place, it permits the user to enter *all* of his data, whether graphics or text, with a single input device. This permits the use of a very simple command language. Furthermore each hand-drawn symbol embodies several items of information — its position on the screen, its size, its ratio of height to width as well as its identity. Thus by drawing a single symbol the user can input all the information contained in a complex typed command. The character drawn need not resemble the symbol displayed in response: for example, the user may draw a straight line, which on recognition is replaced by a resistor symbol.

Applications: Input of all forms of graphical and textual data, including non-standard characters and mathematical expressions.

Hardware investment: A tablet is essential. Some local processing power is necessary for inking and for recognizing the end of the character (normally done by waiting until the pen has been lifted for at least half a second). The recognizer itself need not be implemented in the local processor but must be capable of responding within half a second. This response can normally be supplied by a time-shared system provided it is not overloaded. Otherwise it is feasible to implement simple varieties of recognizer in a small, single-user machine, along the lines described below.

Software investment: Despite the widely differing techniques employed in character recognizers, almost all have employed the same sequence of basic processes. These are provided by the following routines:

1. The tablet routine, which reads points from the tablet at a fixed frequency, and applies any smoothing necessary.
2. The feature extraction routine: the shape of each stroke of the character is expressed in terms of a number of *properties* or *features*, such as curvature, relative end-point positions or number of inflexion points.

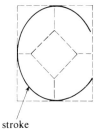

stroke

FIGURE 11-31

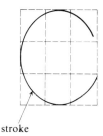

stroke

FIGURE 11-32

3. The dictionary lookup routine, which attempts to match the features of the strokes making up the character with one of the entries in a dictionary.
4. A training routine, for use in building the dictionary.

The dictionary lookup routine may fail to recognize the character, and must in this case notify the application program, which signals the user to try again. If it succeeds, the lookup routine will normally pass to the application program the identity of the recognized character, perhaps as an ASCII code, together with information about the character's size and position. It is then the responsibility of the application program to generate the appropriate 'echo,' i.e. to replace the inked trace by a replica of the recognized character, neatly drawn to the desired size and in the right position. Some recognizers provide a standard set of output symbols for this purpose.

As Teitelman has pointed out, the crucial part of the design of a recognizer lies in the choice of features to extract from the input strokes. These must be chosen so that the recognizer can discriminate effectively between different characters without discriminating between different examples of the same character. At the same time, the features must be chosen so as to minimize the space consumed by each entry in the dictionary, and so as to permit rapid lookup.

Most recognizers have based feature extraction on detecting the regions visited by the stroke. For this purpose the stroke is *normalized*, i.e. scaled in x and y so that it fits inside a standard rectangle. This rectangle is divided into a number of regions, and the program counts the number of times the stroke crosses each region boundary. Figure 11-31 shows the regions used in Bernstein's recognizer; Teitelman used nine regions (Figure 11-32), and devised a four-element code to indicate the region occupied by the stroke and hence to record, by changes in this code, the boundaries crossed by the stroke.

A common feature of most trainable recognizers is the use of a tree-structured dictionary. This simplifies the dictionary's construction, and also reduces the search time. Bernstein uses a tree to indicate the sequence of permissible strokes, while Teitelman includes region crossings in the tree.

A very simple recognizer was developed at Harvard University during 1967 by K. S. Ledeen; originally written for the DEC PDP-1, it has more recently been implemented on TX-2 [60] and on the DEC PDP-10. Ledeen uses a similar method of feature extraction to Teitelman, but adopts a different and much more compact dictionary organization. The features of each stroke are packed into 16 bits of data. This information is broken into four elements of four bits, each representing one property of the stroke. The program keeps lists of properties, each list indicating the various characters that it may match, and giving a frequency count or *weight* by which the recognizer makes the final choice.

The Ledeen recognizer is described in detail in Appendix VIII. Among the recognizers that have achieved extensive use by others besides their inventors, it appears to offer the best compromise between ability to recognize and demand on resources. Its only real shortcoming is that it finds certain pairs of characters, such as U and V, impossible to distinguish; this problem can only be solved by the user himself, who can for example write V as two strokes. The recognizer can be programmed in a few hundred instructions; the dictionary is similarly compact, and need not occupy much more than 1K 16-bit words for a full alphabet. Thus it is quite feasible to include such a recognizer as part of a single-user or time-shared graphics system.

EXERCISES

11-1. Devise a rapid technique for scanning a display file containing only lines, that determines whether a given point constitutes a 'hit.' Note that some techniques for doing this involve computing square roots of numbers, but these numbers lie in a fairly restricted range. How fast can such a square root be computed, and how does this affect your answer?

11-2. Program the Light Handle (Section 11.8), and experiment with it by modifying such parameters as the ratio of adjacent potentiometers, and by introducing velocity effects.

11-3. Program a Ledeen recognizer (see Section 11.12 and Appendix VIII).

11-4. Suppose inking (see Section 11.11) is to be performed in the terminal, and stroke descriptions are to be transmitted to the remote processor. Devise a compact format for stroke transmission.

11-5. Although some of the techniques described above are more costly than their alternatives in their use of processing power, they are often more convenient and effective. Program some experiments along the lines of those of English *et al* [81], to compare the effectiveness of some of these techniques, e.g. rubber-band versus endpoint positioning for line-drawing.

## PART FOUR

Three-Dimensional Computer Graphics

12

THREE-DIMENSIONAL TRANSFORMATIONS AND PERSPECTIVE

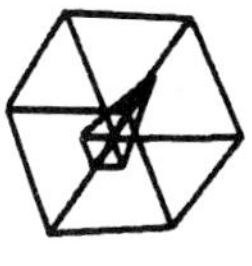

Fig. 12-10

12.1   THREE-DIMENSIONAL COMPUTER GRAPHICS

Many of the objects that we should like to show on a computer display are three-dimensional. There are a number of difficulties in displaying them effectively. First, a two-dimensional picture of the object will generally be inadequate unless we provide special depth information called *depth cues*; second, objects containing curved surfaces are difficult to display and we must generally approximate them as plane-surfaced polyhedra. Despite these difficulties, a number of effective techniques have been developed for displaying collections of three-dimensional objects. In the following description of the techniques, we shall call such a collection of objects a *scene*, and the two-dimensional picture generated, an *image*.

The objects in a scene are described in a three-dimensional Cartesian coordinate system called the *object coordinate system*. We can generate many images of the same scene depending on the position from which the scene is observed. In order to generate a particular image, we shall specify a *viewpoint* together with a viewing direction and aperture (see

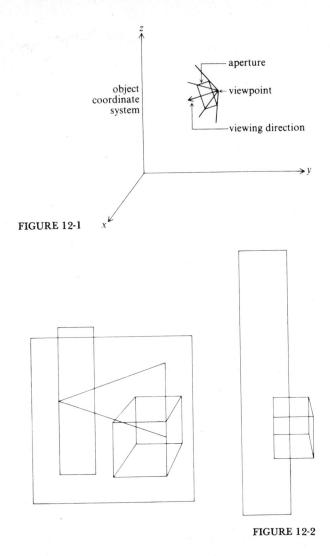

FIGURE 12-1

FIGURE 12-2

Figure 12-1). The selection of a viewpoint can be compared to locating and aiming a telescope in order to obtain a particular view.

A variety of techniques can be used for forming images of three-dimensional scenes. A very simple technique involves displaying several orthogonal views: a plan, two elevations, and possibly some sectional drawings. This technique depends on the viewer's ability to perceive the scene represented by the drawings; most people have difficulty reconstructing a complicated scene from such views.

Fig. 12-10

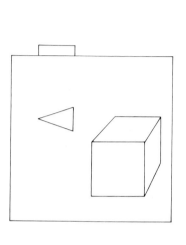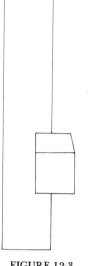

FIGURE 12-3

A better image is a *perspective* display of the scene. The following three chapters develop techniques for generating several kinds of perspective views: wire-frame, outline, and shaded views. The techniques differ in the display hardware needed for output, in the computation required to generate the display, and in the visual effect they create.

1. *Wire-frame drawing* of solid objects (Figure 12-2). The view is a perspective projection of the scene as viewed from an arbitrary position. The perspective effect helps to create the illusion of depth. This technique is reasonably simple and is probably the only one which can be used in interactive situations without the assistance of special-purpose hardware.

2. *Outline drawing* of objects with hidden lines removed (Figure 12-3). As in Figure 12-2, the view is a perspective projection from an arbitrary viewing position. However, lines or portions of lines hidden behind surfaces of the objects are not shown. This technique requires considerable computation, but is often justifiable for producing finished pictures of a design or scene.

FIGURE 12-4

3. *Shaded pictures* of the objects, with hidden surfaces omitted (Figure 12-4). The shading of a particular surface depends on, among other things, its reflectivity and its attitude with respect to the light source. This technique requires very little more computation than 2, but generates an array of dots of varying intensities which few displays can handle. Several display systems are available which use television monitors for output; some of these allow specification of separate intensities for each resolvable dot on the screen. A further refinement of this technique can be used to show shadows in the scene.

12.1.1   DEPTH CUES

Elimination of hidden lines or hidden surfaces is a very effective depth cue; accurate shading and shadowing also convey depth information. However, the perspective wire-frame drawing of Figure 12-2 often does not provide enough depth cues to eliminate possible ambiguities. An extreme example of such an ambiguity is shown in Figure 12-5a. Clearly the viewer needs more information about the depth (distance from the eye) of several lines in Figure 12-5a in order to resolve the

Fig. 12-10

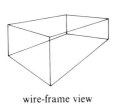

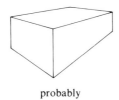

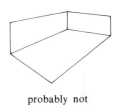

(a)   (b)   (c)

FIGURE 12-5

wire-frame view   probably   probably not

FIGURE 12-6

ambiguity. Figures 12-5b and 12-5c are certainly less ambiguous than Figure 12-5a, but these pictures rely on hidden-line elimination to convey the depth information.

A number of depth cueing techniques can be used on wire-frame pictures like Figure 12-5a. The methods of human depth perception are not yet understood, even though considerable psychophysical research has been devoted to this phenomenon. Evidence suggests that relevant cues are texture gradients (the apparent grain of a surface becomes finer as the surface recedes), shading of curved objects, extreme perspective effects, stereoscopy, and motion. The depth cueing techniques used in computer graphics have traditionally been chosen for their expediency and not for the accuracy of their effect [234].

12.1.1.1   Perspective

Perspective can help distinguish the ambiguous interpretations of a wire-frame drawing (Figure 12-6). In some cases it helps to exaggerate the perspective: this is equivalent to distorting the objects. The distortion may have undesirable side effects: when objects in the scene move, the distortions will change confusingly.

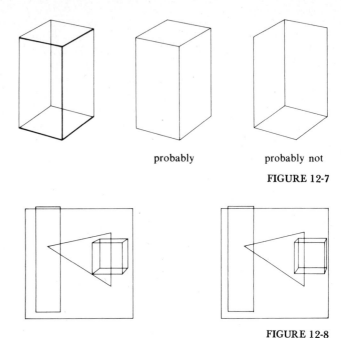

probably   probably not

FIGURE 12-7

FIGURE 12-8

12.1.1.2 Intensity Cues

One depth cue which is not expensive to implement in hardware is a modulation of the intensity of lines with depth: lines far away appear fainter than those near the viewer (Figure 12-7). As the complexity of the structure increases, the effectiveness of the intensity cue decreases. Also, if the range of the depths of the lines is very small, the line brightness does not vary enough to be noticeable.

12.1.1.3 Stereoscopic Views

A dramatic way to provide depth information is with two stereoscopic images, one shown to the left eye and generated from a view appropriate to the location of that eye, and the other generated analogously for the right eye (Figures 12-8, 12-9). Optical systems can be used to present the appropriate image to each eye. Alternatively, the left-eye and right-eye images can be alternately flashed on the screen about 20 times per second in synchrony with shutters in front of the eyes (this is a device marketed under the name Lorgnette). Many people

Fig. 12-10

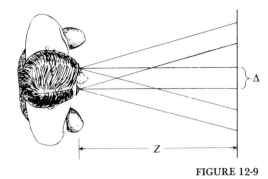

FIGURE 12-9

can fuse two separate images, such as the two shown in Figure 12-8, without mechanical or optical aid. The disadvantages of the stereo technique are that two completely independent pictures must be generated, and that tuning the parameters Δ and Z (Figure 12-9) is somewhat difficult.

12.1.1.4   Kinetic Depth Effect

A fourth technique to furnish depth cues relies on motion of the objects relative to the viewer's position. A very revealing motion is rotation about a vertical axis: lines close to the viewer move more rapidly than those far away; lines on opposite sides of the rotation axis appear to move in opposite directions, like a merry-go-round. Figure 12-10 shows this: flip the pages of the book and watch the cube rotate. If you stop flipping, the three-dimensional perception quickly vanishes and the ambiguity returns.

Generating successive images, each slightly rotated, consumes a good deal of computer time. Without specific hardware aids, the calculation of the motion may be so slow that the kinetic depth effect is not noticeable.

12.1.2   REPRESENTATION OF THREE-DIMENSIONAL OBJECTS

Two different representations can be used to describe polyhedra; each has its advantages and disadvantages for generating display images. One choice, a wire-frame description, is simply a list of edges of the polyhedron: each edge is a line defined by its endpoints in the object

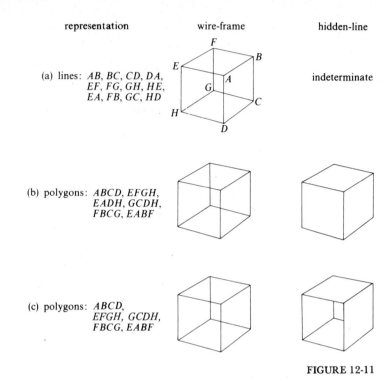

representation   wire-frame   hidden-line

(a) lines: *AB, BC, CD, DA,*
EF, FG, GH, HE,
EA, FB, GC, HD   indeterminate

(b) polygons: *ABCD, EFGH,*
EADH, GCDH,
FBCG, EABF

(c) polygons: *ABCD,*
EFGH, GCDH,
FBCG, EABF

FIGURE 12-11

coordinate system (Figure 12-11a). The disadvantage of the wire-frame description is that it does not contain sufficient information to generate an image with hidden lines eliminated.

The second representation, a surface description, records a polyhedron as a collection of polygons: each polygon is an ordered set of vertex points with coordinates measured in object space (Figure 12-11b, 12-11c). This description contains enough information for hidden-line computations, but is inconvenient for generating wire-frame images, because each edge of the polyhedron is listed twice (e.g. edge *AB* is part of polygons *EABF* and *ABCD* in Figure 12-11b).

Curved objects can be represented as mathematical objects (e.g. spheres) or approximated by polyhedra (Figure 14-2). Because many objects have no simple mathematical description, the polyhedron approximation is usually preferred. However, such polyhedra may have a more compact and useful representation than a collection of polygons: Coons patches [2, 55], Bezier patches [95], and quadric surface patches [233] are examples of such repesentations. The goals of

Fig. 12-10

these representations are: (1) compactness; (2) ease with which a display image of the approximating polyhedron can be generated; (3) ease with which the curved object represented can be deformed, moulded, faired, joined to other objects; and (4) mathematical convenience when performing computations related to the objects: volume, aerodynamic properties, surface area, etc. Such representations have been sought by builders of computer-aided design systems which aid development of aircraft, automobiles, ships, etc.*

The remainder of the chapter is concerned with useful transformations of three-dimensional objects: rotation, translation and perspective-viewing transformations. These transformations are applied to *points* in the three-dimensional Cartesian coordinate system (object space). In practice, it suffices to transform the vertex points of a polyhedron: all other points on the object are determined by the transforms of the vertex points.

12.2   THREE-DIMENSIONAL TRANSFORMATIONS

The matrix formulation of two-dimensional transformations can be extended easily to three-dimensional data. The two central features of transformations are retained in this formulation: the transformation is a single entity, a matrix; sequences of transformations can be *concatenated* to yield a single transformation which has the same effect as the application of the sequence.

12.2.1   TRANSLATION

The transformation which translates a point (x, y, z) to a new point (x', y', z') is:

$$[\, x'\, y'\, z'\, 1\,] = [\, x\, y\, z\, 1\,] \begin{bmatrix} 1 & 0 & 0 & 0 \\ 0 & 1 & 0 & 0 \\ 0 & 0 & 1 & 0 \\ T_x & T_y & T_z & 1 \end{bmatrix} \qquad (12\text{-}1)$$

where T_x, T_y, and T_z are the components of the translation in the x, y, and z directions respectively.

---

* Techniques for representing three-dimensional objects, and particularly curved surfaces, are still being developed. The bibliography lists several papers on current work in curve and surface description.

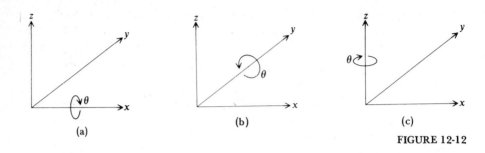

(a)

(b)

(c)

FIGURE 12-12

12.2.2 ROTATION

Three-dimensional rotation transformations have more complexity than two-dimensional rotation transformations: we must determine an *axis of rotation*. The specification of the axis includes its direction and location. In the two-dimensional situation we defined the rotations about the origin and showed how these rotations, together with translations, could be used to rotate a figure about any desired point. We proceed analogously here:

1. Rotation about x coordinate axis, through the point $(0,0,0)$, see Figure 12-12a.

$$[\, x'\, y'\, z'\, 1\,] = [\, x\, y\, z\, 1\,] \begin{bmatrix} 1 & 0 & 0 & 0 \\ 0 & \cos\theta & -\sin\theta & 0 \\ 0 & \sin\theta & \cos\theta & 0 \\ 0 & 0 & 0 & 1 \end{bmatrix} \qquad (12\text{-}2)$$

The rotation angle θ is measured clockwise about the origin when looking at the origin from a point on the $+x$ axis. Notice that the transformation matrix affects only the values of the y and z coordinates. The transformation is given for a *right-handed* Cartesian coordinate system.

2. Rotation about y coordinate axis, through the point $(0,0,0)$, see Figure 12-12b.

$$[\, x'\, y'\, z'\, 1\,] = [\, x\, y\, z\, 1\,] \begin{bmatrix} \cos\theta & 0 & \sin\theta & 0 \\ 0 & 1 & 0 & 0 \\ -\sin\theta & 0 & \cos\theta & 0 \\ 0 & 0 & 0 & 1 \end{bmatrix} \qquad (12\text{-}3)$$

3. Rotation about z coordinate axis, through the point $(0,0,0)$, see Figure 12-12c.

Fig. 12-10

$$[\,x'\,y'\,z'\,1\,] = [\,x\,y\,z\,1\,] \begin{bmatrix} \cos\theta & -\sin\theta & 0 & 0 \\ \sin\theta & \cos\theta & 0 & 0 \\ 0 & 0 & 1 & 0 \\ 0 & 0 & 0 & 1 \end{bmatrix} \qquad (12\text{-}4)$$

12.2.3   SCALING

The scaling transformation is:

$$[\,x'\,y'\,z'\,1\,] = [\,x\,y\,z\,1\,] \begin{bmatrix} S_x & 0 & 0 & 0 \\ 0 & S_y & 0 & 0 \\ 0 & 0 & S_z & 0 \\ 0 & 0 & 0 & 1 \end{bmatrix} \qquad (12\text{-}5)$$

12.2.4   INVERSE TRANSFORMATIONS

Each of the transformations given above has an inverse, which performs the symmetrically opposite transformation. The inverse of matrix 12-1 is:

$$\begin{bmatrix} 1 & 0 & 0 & 0 \\ 0 & 1 & 0 & 0 \\ 0 & 0 & 1 & 0 \\ -T_x & -T_y & -T_z & 1 \end{bmatrix} \qquad (12\text{-}6)$$

which undoes the effect of the translation of Equation 12-1. The inverse of 12-2 is simply:

$$\begin{bmatrix} 1 & 0 & 0 & 0 \\ 0 & \cos\theta & \sin\theta & 0 \\ 0 & -\sin\theta & \cos\theta & 0 \\ 0 & 0 & 0 & 1 \end{bmatrix} = \begin{bmatrix} 1 & 0 & 0 & 0 \\ 0 & \cos-\theta & -\sin-\theta & 0 \\ 0 & \sin-\theta & \cos-\theta & 0 \\ 0 & 0 & 0 & 1 \end{bmatrix} \qquad (12\text{-}7)$$

which is a rotation of the same magnitude and about the same axis as 12-2, but in the opposite direction.

We shall denote the inverse of transformation T by T^{-1}. The matrix which represents the inverse transformation T^{-1} is simply the matrix inverse of T (see Appendix I for a discussion of matrix inverses). The inverse of any transformation matrix can easily be determined by a computer program.

12.2.5   CONCATENATION

The successive application of two transformations T_1 and T_2 can be simplified to the application of one transformation T_3. The matrix T_3 is simply the product of the matrices T_1 and T_2. This can be easily demonstrated: the point (x, y, z) is transformed into (x', y', z') by T_1:

$$[\, x'\, y'\, z'\, 1\,] = [\, x\ y\ z\ 1\,]\ T_1 \qquad (12\text{-}8)$$

The point (x'', y'', z'') is generated by applying T_2:

$$[\, x''\, y''\, z''\, 1\,] = [\, x'\, y'\, z'\, 1\,]\ T_2 \qquad (12\text{-}9)$$

Substituting Equation 12-8 into Equation 12-9 gives:

$$[\, x''\ y''\ z''\ 1\,] = ([\, x\ y\ z\ 1\,]\ T_1)\ T_2$$

$$= [\, x\ y\ z\ 1\,]\ (T_1\ T_2) \qquad (12\text{-}10)$$

The *order* of application of the transformations must be preserved when the transformation matrices are multiplied together.

12.3   GENERATING A WIRE-FRAME PERSPECTIVE DISPLAY

12.3.1   THE EYE COORDINATE SYSTEM

In order to calculate the position of a point on the display screen which corresponds to a point on some object, we must first transform the point from object space into the *eye coordinate system*, which has its origin fixed at the viewpoint and its Z_e axis pointed in the direction of view (see Figure 12-13). The coordinate system is fixed to the viewpoint, the observer's eye: it moves and rotates as the eye moves and the head rotates.

A transformation called the *viewing transformation* V is used to convert points in object space (X, Y, Z) to points in the eye coordinate system (X_e, Y_e, Z_e).

$$[\, X_e\ Y_e\ Z_e\ 1\,] = [\, X\ Y\ Z\ 1\,]\ V \qquad (12\text{-}11)$$

Fig. 12-10

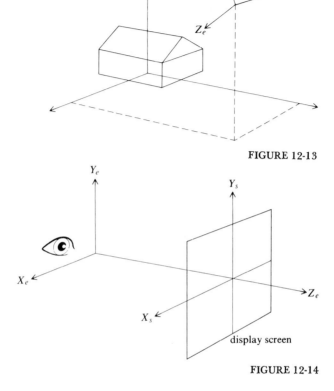

FIGURE 12-13

FIGURE 12-14

The parameters of this transformation completely determine the view: the transformation matrix itself may be derived by concatenating several rotations and translations.

The eye coordinate system is a *left-handed* Cartesian coordinate system: the Z_e axis points forward from the viewpoint, the X_e axis to the right, and the Y_e axis up. These conventions are chosen so that the X_e and Y_e axes will align with the X and Y axes of the display screen (see Figure 12-14).

12.3.2   SIMPLE PERSPECTIVE TRANSFORMATION

A perspective display can be generated by simply *projecting* each point of an object onto the plane of the display screen, as in Figure 12-15. The coordinates (X_s, Y_s) of the projected image of the point P measured in eye coordinates (X_e, Y_e, Z_e) are easily computed.

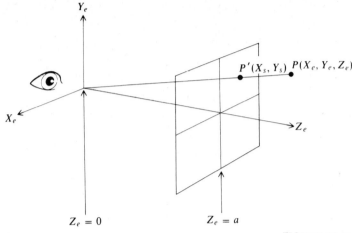

FIGURE 12-15

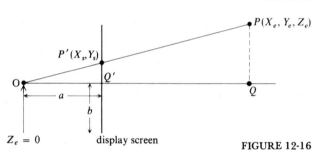

FIGURE 12-16

Consider the Y_e, Z_e plane drawn in Figure 12-16. The triangles $OQ'P'$ and OQP are similar, giving

$$\frac{Y_s}{a} = \frac{Y_e}{Z_e} \quad \text{and} \quad \frac{X_s}{a} = \frac{X_e}{Z_e} \quad (12\text{-}12)$$

The numbers X_s and Y_s can be converted to dimensionless fractions by dividing by the screen size:

$$X_s = \frac{aX_e}{bZ_e} \qquad Y_s = \frac{aY_e}{bZ_e} \quad (12\text{-}13)$$

or to screen coordinates by including a specification of the location of the image area (viewport):

$$X_s = \left(\frac{aX_e}{bZ_e}\right) V_{sx} + V_{cx}$$

$$Y_s = \left(\frac{aY_e}{bZ_e}\right) V_{sy} + V_{cy} \quad (12\text{-}14)$$

Fig. 12-10

This transformation is fundamentally different from those for rotation, translation, and scaling: it involves *dividing* by the Z_e coordinate value, whereas the others involve only multiplication and addition. *Generating a true perspective image requires dividing by the depth of each point.*

Luckily, however, a perspective image of a line can be generated easily by transforming only its endpoints and drawing the line between the two transformed endpoints. The process of generating a wire-frame perspective display thus involves retrieving the object-space coordinates of the endpoints of each line, using Equation 12-11 to obtain the eye coordinates of the endpoints, and then Equation 12-14 to obtain screen coordinates of each endpoint. A vector generator can then generate a line from the endpoint information.

Equation 12-14 reflects the independence of the eye coordinate system from the screen coordinate system. Values chosen for the viewport parameters are given in the same coordinate system that the display hardware uses to address locations on the screen. The values for the eye coordinate points, however, can be in a completely different form because a dimensionless ratio is formed in Equation 12-14. This independence is analogous to that of the two-dimensional screen and page coordinate systems described in Chapter 7.

The units of measurement of the parameters a and b are similarly independent of the other coordinate systems; only the ratio a/b is involved in Equation 12-14. If this ratio is small, the aperture will be broad, thus producing an image similar to that of a wide-angle lens. A large value of a/b specifies a narrow aperture, corresponding to a telephoto view. If the image is viewed from a distance a, the perspective effect will be exact; however the view from other distances is quite acceptable.

12.3.3   THREE-DIMENSIONAL CLIPPING

The simple application of Equations 12-11 and 12-14 to produce a perspective image has two undesirable effects: objects 'behind' the viewpoint may appear on the screen, and objects may exceed the prescribed limits of the viewport given in Equation 12-14. These effects can be eliminated by testing each point in eye coordinates against a *viewing pyramid*, which defines the portion of eye-coordinate space which the viewer can actually see (Figure 12-17).

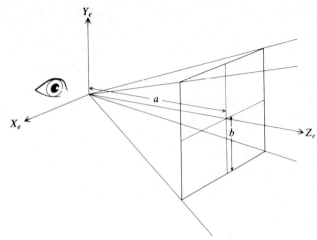

FIGURE 12-17

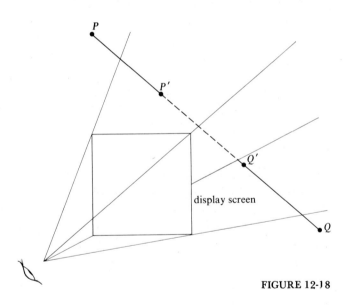

FIGURE 12-18

The conditions that a point be visible are:

$$-Z_e \leqslant (a/b)X_e \leqslant Z_e$$

and

$$-Z_e \leqslant (a/b)Y_e \leqslant Z_e \quad (12\text{-}15)$$

Note that these conditions exclude points behind the viewpoint $(Z_e \leqslant 0)$. If a point fails the test, it is not displayed. Otherwise,

Fig. 12-10

Equation 12-14 is applied to the eye coordinates to determine the position of the point on the display screen.

Lines cannot be processed as easily as points, and must be *clipped* against the limits of the viewing pyramid as defined in Equation 12-15. A line may be rejected as invisible if no part of it intersects the pyramid. Otherwise, the endpoints of the visible portion of the line are calculated in the three-dimensional eye coordinate system (Figure 12-18). Equation 12-14 is then applied to these endpoint coordinates, and the line is drawn on the screen. The clipping process must operate on three-dimensional lines, and generate three-dimensional lines as output (see Exercise 12-5).

The algorithm for clipping lines against the viewing pyramid is very similar to the two-dimensional algorithm given in Chapter 7. For the convenience of the algorithm, we define a new coordinate system (the clipping coordinate system, subscript c) in terms of the eye coordinate system:

$$[X_c \ Y_c \ Z_c \ 1] = [X_e \ Y_e \ Z_e \ 1] \ N$$

$$N = \begin{bmatrix} a/b & 0 & 0 & 0 \\ 0 & a/b & 0 & 0 \\ 0 & 0 & 1 & 0 \\ 0 & 0 & 0 & 1 \end{bmatrix} \quad (12\text{-}16)$$

The conditions of equation 12-15 become simply:

$$-Z_c \leqslant X_c \leqslant Z_c$$

and

$$-Z_c \leqslant Y_c \leqslant Z_c \quad (12\text{-}17)$$

The four-bit code of the Sutherland-Cohen clipping algorithm is then:

first bit: Y_c is above pyramid, i.e. $Y_c > Z_c$
second bit: Y_c is below pyramid, i.e. $Y_c < -Z_c$
third bit: X_c is to right of pyramid, i.e. $X_c > Z_c$
fourth bit: X_c is to left of pyramid, i.e. $X_c < -Z_c$

These codes are used to determine whether the line may be trivially rejected or accepted. If it cannot, it is passed to the second part of the algorithm. This part must intersect the three-dimensional line to be clipped with one of the *planes* $X_c = Z_c$, $X_c = -Z_c$, $Y_c = Z_c$, or $Y_c = -Z_c$. The intersection point divides the line into two pieces, each

of which may be tested with the acceptance and rejection tests, etc.
The full algorithm is:

```
COMMENT ****** THE 3-D CLIPPING ROUTINE ******

THE CODES GENERATED FOR EACH ENDPOINT ARE AS FOLLOWS:

                  \           \
           1001   \   1000    \   1010
                  \           \
           --------\--------\--------
                  \           \
           0001   \   0000    \   0010
                  \           \
           --------\--------\--------
                  \           \
           0101   \   0100    \   0110
                  \           \

THE CLIPPING PROCESS IS AS FOLLOWS:

1. COMPUTE CODES FOR BOTH ENDPOINTS.
2. IF THE "AND" OF THE CODES IS NOT ZERO THEN NO PART OF
        THE LINE IS VISIBLE.  IF BOTH CODES ARE ZERO, THE
        ENTIRE LINE IS VISIBLE -- DISPLAY IT.
3. IF POINT 1 IS ON THE SCREEN, EXCHANGE POINTS 1 AND 2.
4. "PUSH" POINT 1 TOWARD POINT 2 UNTIL IT INTERSECTS A LEGITIMATE
        BOUNDARY OF THE VIEWING PYRAMID.  WHICH BOUNDARY TO
        GO FOR IS DETERMINED BY THE BITS IN POINT 1'S CODE.
5. RECOMPUTE THE CODE FOR POINT 1.  THIS MUST BE DONE BECAUSE
        SOME COMPONENT MAY NOW BE ON THE SCREEN WHICH WAS NOT
        PREVIOUSLY, ETC.
6. GO TO STEP 2.

THE CALCULATION WHICH IS USED TO "PUSH" THE ENDPOINT 1
TOWARD THE OTHER ENDPOINT COMPUTES A VALUE OF THE PARAMETER
T, WHERE T=0 AT ENDPOINT 1, AND T=1 AT ENDPOINT 2,
THEN THE VALUES OF X,Y, AND Z ARE COMPUTED FROM THE
PARAMETER VALUE.

;

PROCEDURE CLIP (REAL X1,Y1,Z1,X2,Y2,Z2);
BEGIN INTEGER C1,C2; REAL T;

        INTEGER PROCEDURE CODE (REAL X,Y,Z);
        RETURN ((IF X<=-Z THEN '01 ELSE (IF X>Z THEN '10 ELSE 0))+
            (IF Y<=-Z THEN '100 ELSE (IF Y>Z THEN '1000 ELSE 0)));

        C1 + CODE (X1,Y1,Z1);
        C2 + CODE (X2,Y2,Z2);

        WHILE NOT (C1=C2=0) DO BEGIN "COMPUTE"
        IF C1 LAND C2 THEN RETURN; "NO PART OF THE LINE VISIBLE"
        IF C1=0 THEN BEGIN "EXCHANGE POINTS 1 AND 2"
                C1 SWAP C2; X1 SWAP X2;
                Y1 SWAP Y2; Z1 SWAP Z2;
        END;

        IF C1 LAND '1 THEN BEGIN "PUSH TOWARD X=-Z"
                T + (Z1+X1)/((X1-X2)-(Z2-Z1));
                Z1 + T*(Z2-Z1)+Z1;
                X1 + -Z1;
```

```
                    Y1 ← T*(Y2-Y1)+Y1;
                    END ELSE
        IF C1 LAND '10 THEN BEGIN "PUSH TOWARD X=Z"
                    T ← (Z1-X1)/((X2-X1)-(Z2-Z1));
                    Z1 ← T*(Z2-Z1)+Z1;
                    X1 ← Z1;
                    Y1 ← T*(Y2-Y1)+Y1;
                    END ELSE
        IF C1 LAND '100 THEN BEGIN "PUSH TOWARD Y=-Z"
                    T ← (Z1+Y1)/((Y1-Y2)-(Z2-Z1));
                    Z1 ← T*(Z2-Z1)+Z1;
                    X1 ← T*(X2-X1)+X1;
                    Y1 ← -Z1;
                    END ELSE
        IF C1 LAND '1000 THEN BEGIN "PUSH TOWARD Y=Z"
                    T ← (Z1-Y1)/((Y2-Y1)-(Z2-Z1));
                    Z1 ← T*(Z2-Z1)+Z1;
                    X1 ← T*(X2-X1)+X1;
                    Y1 ← Z1;
                    END;
        C1 ← CODE (X1,Y1,Z1);

        END "COMPUTE";

"THE LINE (X1,Y1,Z1;X2,Y2,Z2) LIES WITHIN THE VIEWING
PYRAMID.  WE MAY NOW PASS THIS LINE TO A PROCEDURE
TO GENERATE A PERSPECTIVE DISPLAY OF IT"

        SHOWLINE(X1,Y1,Z1,X2,Y2,Z2);

END;
```

Fig. 12-10

If the clipping process yields a visible line segment, we must still apply the inverse of transformation 12-16 followed by the perspective transformation (Equation 12-14) to calculate the screen coordinates of the endpoints of the line. Equation 12-14 can be rewritten to perform both operations:

$$X_s = \left(\frac{X_c}{Z_c}\right)V_{sx} + V_{cx}$$

$$Y_s = \left(\frac{Y_c}{Z_c}\right)V_{sy} + V_{cy} \qquad (12\text{-}18)$$

The transformations we have discussed so far form the basis for a transformation system for generating images of three-dimensional scenes. This process involves (1) a matrix multiplication, (2) a clipping process, (3) a proportional division as in Equation 12-18. A hardware device has been built which has implemented these three steps: the first is performed by a *matrix multiplier*, the second and third by a *clipping divider* [267]. This device performs the three operations extremely rapidly, at a rate of about 5 microseconds per line, and is a preprocessor for every line drawn, each frame. Thus, if the viewing transformation changes, the hardware-generated display will change immediately.

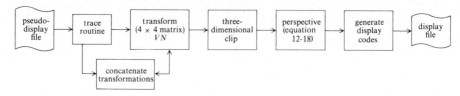

FIGURE 12-19

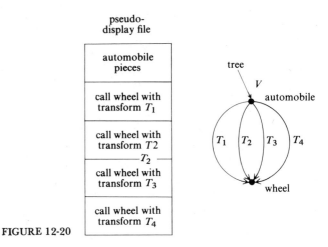

FIGURE 12-20

If hardware is not used, the same three processes can be implemented in a software transformation system as described in Chapter 8 (see Figure 12-19).

12.3.4 SUBROUTINES IN THREE DIMENSIONS

Common three-dimensional objects can be represented as subroutines in the same fashion that two-dimensional subroutines are embedded in a structured display file. Each subroutine call specifies a transformation to be applied to the items within the subroutine definition. For example, the four wheels of an automobile might be represented by one symbol. The display file might look like Figure 12-20.

The display items in the wheel symbol must be transformed by a concatenated transformation: $T_1 V$, $T_2 V$, $T_3 V$, $T_4 V$, etc. When the display file compiler encounters a subroutine call, the trace routine is responsible for saving the present transformation on a stack, concatenating the transformation specified in the subroutine call with

the present transformation, and then processing the display items in the
symbol definition with the newly formed transformation.

Fig. 12-10

The transformations T_i associated with the subroutine calls are
relative transformations: they convert points measured in the
coordinate system of the symbol definition to points measured in
object space. For example, the T_i might vary with time for the purpose
of showing the wheels rotating relative to the rest of the automobile. In
addition, V might vary with time so that the perspective drawing would
move to create a kinetic depth illusion. If the transformations vary with
time, then either hardware or software procedures must constantly
trace the structured display file to update the changing display.

12.4   EXAMPLES

12.4.1   ROTATION ABOUT AN ARBITRARY AXIS

The general rotation about an arbitrary axis through an arbitrary point
can be derived from combinations of the primitive transformations
(Equations 12-1 through 12-5). Let us define (X,Y,Z) as a point
through which the rotation axis passes, and (a,b,c) as the direction
cosines of the axis. (a,b,c) is simply a unit vector along the rotation
axis. The steps in the rotation through an angle θ about this axis are:

1. Translate the object into a new coordinate system where (X,Y,Z)
   maps into the origin $(0,0,0)$ (Matrix T). The object is described in a
   right-handed coordinate system.
2. Perform appropriate rotations about the X and Y axes of this
   coordinate system so the unit vector (a,b,c) is mapped into the unit
   vector along the Z axis $(0,0,1)$ (Matrices R_1, R_2).
3. Perform the desired rotation θ about the Z axis of the new
   coordinate system. The matrix 12-5 is the form of this
   transformation (Matrix R_θ).
4. Apply the inverse of step 2 (Matrices R_2^{-1}, R_1^{-1}).
5. Apply the inverse of step 1 (Matrix T^{-1}).

The purpose of steps 4 and 5 is to return the object to its original
coordinate system. The provisional coordinate systems created by steps
1 and 2 are only used as intermediate steps in the process.

The matrices are:

$$T = \begin{bmatrix} 1 & 0 & 0 & 0 \\ 0 & 1 & 0 & 0 \\ 0 & 0 & 1 & 0 \\ -X & -Y & -Z & 1 \end{bmatrix} \quad (12\text{-}19)$$

$$R_1 = \begin{bmatrix} 1 & 0 & 0 & 0 \\ 0 & c/v & b/v & 0 \\ 0 & -b/v & c/v & 0 \\ 0 & 0 & 0 & 1 \end{bmatrix} \quad (12\text{-}20)$$

where $v = \sqrt{b^2 + c^2}$

$$R_2 = \begin{bmatrix} v & 0 & a & 0 \\ 0 & 1 & 0 & 0 \\ -a & 0 & v & 0 \\ 0 & 0 & 0 & 1 \end{bmatrix} \quad (12\text{-}21)$$

where $v = \sqrt{b^2 + c^2}$

$$R_\theta = \begin{bmatrix} \cos\theta & -\sin\theta & 0 & 0 \\ \sin\theta & \cos\theta & 0 & 0 \\ 0 & 0 & 1 & 0 \\ 0 & 0 & 0 & 1 \end{bmatrix} \quad (12\text{-}22)$$

The complete transformation which includes the 5 steps is thus $T\,R_1\,R_2\,R_\theta\,R_2^{-1}\,R_1^{-1}\,T^{-1}$.

Notes on the derivation of Equations 12-19 to 12-22:

The direction cosines of the rotation axis have a very simple interpretation. Suppose one point on the rotation axis is (X,Y,Z) and another is (X',Y',Z') (see Figure 12-21). A vector along the axis is thus $(X'-X)\mathbf{i} + (Y'-Y)\mathbf{j} + (Z'-Z)\mathbf{k}$, where $\mathbf{i}$, $\mathbf{j}$, and $\mathbf{k}$ are unit vectors along the coordinate axes. If we normalize this vector:

$$\frac{(X'-X)}{\sqrt{(X'-X)^2 + (Y'-Y)^2 + (Z'-Z)^2}}\,\mathbf{i} +$$

$$\frac{(Y'-Y)}{\sqrt{(X'-X)^2 + (Y'-Y)^2 + (Z'-Z)^2}}\,\mathbf{j} +$$

$$\frac{(Z'-Z)}{\sqrt{(X'-X)^2 + (Y'-Y)^2 + (Z'-Z)^2}}\,\mathbf{k}$$

the coefficients are simply the direction cosines a, b, and c.

Fig. 12-10

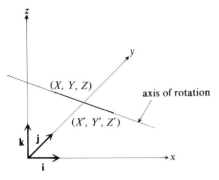

FIGURE 12-21

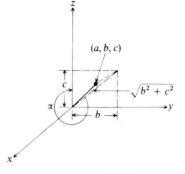

FIGURE 12-22

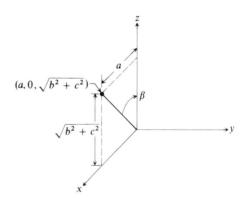

FIGURE 12-23

After the translation given by matrix T, we must align the (a,b,c) unit vector with the Z axis. This is done in two steps: a rotation about the X axis and a rotation about the Y axis (see Figure 12-22). The components of the axis vector in the yz plane are $b\mathbf{j}$ and $c\mathbf{k}$, i.e. $\cos \alpha = c\,/\sqrt{b^2 + c^2}$ and $\sin \alpha = -b\,/\sqrt{b^2 + c^2}$. These are precisely the parameters inserted into Equation 12-2 to yield the matrix of Equation 12-20.

The situation after the first rotation is shown in Figure 12-23. The rotation angle β is defined by $\cos \beta = \sqrt{b^2 + c^2}\,/\sqrt{a^2 + b^2 + c^2}$ and $\sin \beta = -a\,/\sqrt{a^2 + b^2 + c^2}$. These parameters used in Equation 12-3 yield Equation 12-21.

12.4.2   PERSPECTIVE VIEW OF A CUBE

Consider a cube centered at the origin of object space, and defined by points and lines:

Cube = lines: $AB, BC, CD, DA, EF, FG, GH, HE, AE, BF, CG, DH.$

points:	X	Y	Z
A	−1	1	−1
B	1	1	−1
C	1	−1	−1
D	−1	−1	−1
E	−1	1	1
F	1	1	1
G	1	−1	1
H	−1	−1	1

We will observe this cube from a point $(6, 8, 7.5)$, with the viewing axis Z_e pointed directly at the origin of the object coordinate system. There is still one degree of freedom left, namely an arbitrary rotation about the Z_e axis: we will assume that the X_e axis lies in the $Z = 7.5$ plane.

The viewing transformation can be established as follows:

1. Translate points so that the point $(6, 8, 7.5)$ maps into the origin (see Figure 12-24):

$$T_1 = \begin{bmatrix} 1 & 0 & 0 & 0 \\ 0 & 1 & 0 & 0 \\ 0 & 0 & 1 & 0 \\ -6 & -8 & -7.5 & 1 \end{bmatrix}$$

2. Rearrange the axes so that we have a left-handed coordinate system (see Figure 12-25):

$$T_2 = \begin{bmatrix} -1 & 0 & 0 & 0 \\ 0 & 0 & -1 & 0 \\ 0 & 1 & 0 & 0 \\ 0 & 0 & 0 & 1 \end{bmatrix}$$

Fig. 12-10

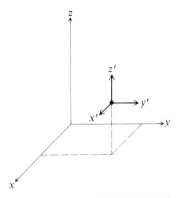

FIGURE 12-24

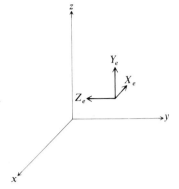

FIGURE 12-25

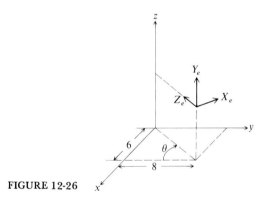

FIGURE 12-26

3. Rotate about the Y_e axis through an angle so that the Z_e axis points toward the point $(0, 0, 7.5)$. This will involve a rotation through an angle θ (see Figure 12-26):

$$\cos \theta = 8/10 \qquad \sin \theta = 6/10$$

$$T_3 = \begin{bmatrix} .8 & 0 & .6 & 0 \\ 0 & 1 & 0 & 0 \\ -.6 & 0 & .8 & 0 \\ 0 & 0 & 0 & 1 \end{bmatrix}$$

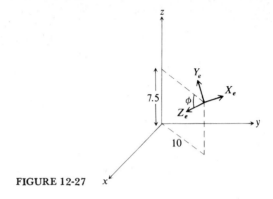

FIGURE 12-27 x

4. Rotate about the X_e axis so that the Z_e axis now points at the origin in object space. The rotation will be through an angle ϕ (see Figure 12-27):

$$\cos \phi = 4/5 \qquad \sin \phi = 3/5$$

$$T_4 = \begin{bmatrix} 1 & 0 & 0 & 0 \\ 0 & .8 & -.6 & 0 \\ 0 & .6 & .8 & 0 \\ 0 & 0 & 0 & 1 \end{bmatrix}$$

This completes the four simple transformations needed to establish the viewing transformation $V = T_1 \, T_2 \, T_3 \, T_4$.

Suppose that we wish to fill a 10 inch by 10 inch display screen, designed to be viewed from 10 inches away, and that the coordinate system of the screen runs from 0 to 1023. Hence:

$$a = 10 \text{ inch} \quad b = 5 \text{ inch}$$

$$V_{sx} = V_{cx} = V_{sy} = V_{cy} = 1023/2$$

The transformation 12-16 is therefore:

$$N = \begin{bmatrix} 2 & 0 & 0 & 0 \\ 0 & 2 & 0 & 0 \\ 0 & 0 & 1 & 0 \\ 0 & 0 & 0 & 1 \end{bmatrix}$$

Fig. 12-10

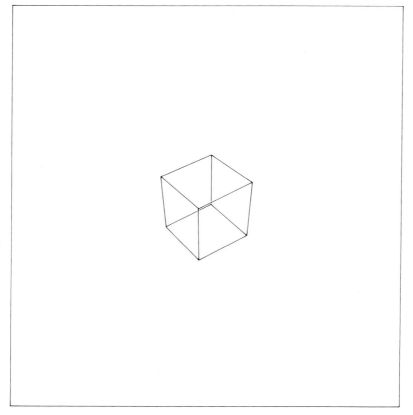

FIGURE 12-28

and Equation 12-18 becomes:

$$X_s = 511.5\,(X_c/Z_c) + 511.5$$

$$Y_s = 511.5\,(Y_c/Z_c) + 511.5 \quad (12\text{-}23)$$

All the details of the transformations have now been specified. A point of the cube $(A\text{-}H)$ is transformed by the matrix $V\,N$, then clipped, and then Equation 12-23 is applied.

$$T_1\,T_2\,T_3\,T_4\,N = \begin{bmatrix} -1.6 & -.72 & -.48 & 0 \\ 1.2 & -.96 & -.64 & 0 \\ 0 & 1.6 & -.6 & 0 \\ 0 & 0 & 12.5 & 1 \end{bmatrix}$$

We can now apply this transformation to the eight vertices of the cube:

	X_c	Y_c	Z_c
A	2.8	−1.84	12.94
B	−.4	−3.28	11.98
C	−2.8	−1.36	13.26
D	.4	.08	14.22
E	2.8	1.36	11.74
F	−.4	−.08	10.78
G	−2.8	1.84	12.06
H	.4	3.28	13.02

From this table, it is apparent that none of the lines of the cube need be clipped, i.e. all will be trivially accepted by the clipping algorithm. The screen coordinates of the line endpoints are calculated with Equation 12-23, and the lines are drawn as shown in Figure 12-28.

EXERCISES

12-1. Show that the perspective projection of a three-dimensional line is the same as the two-dimensional line between the perspective projections of its endpoints. If this were not true, the calculation of the perspective view of a line would be quite complicated. You are essentially asked to prove that the display formed by projecting endpoints and drawing two-dimensional lines (usually with display hardware) between them is an accurate perspective image.

12-2. In conventional photography, the image formed by the lens (focal length f) is on a small negative. Typical numbers (50 mm lens for 24 x 36 mm film) would give $a/b = 2$. Then an enlargement of the negative is made. The scaling is often by a factor of 5 to 50 and only affects the X and Y locations of points.

(a) You would suspect that a/b only controls the 'perspective' of the image, and viewport size the actual size of the screen. What is the relation between a/b and viewport size so that a particular three-dimensional point always appears on the same spot on the screen? Does the relation depend on the coordinates of the three-dimensional point? The results of your analysis are useful in implementing a facility to control the perspective of the picture: you may have to zoom in or out, but will want to keep the image size on the screen about constant.

Fig. 12-10

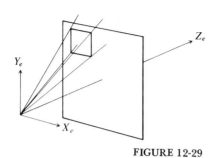

FIGURE 12-29

FIGURE 12-30

(b) We have assumed that the viewer desires a pyramid which is symmetric about the Z_e axis. Suppose he only wishes to see a smaller, off-axis view, placed appropriately on the display screen, as shown in Figure 12-29. How would you generate such an image? Is it equivalent to simple perspective generation as described in this chapter using (1) a smaller viewport, (2) a smaller ratio b/a and (3) a suitably rotated eye coordinate system?

12-3. Extend the discussion of three-dimensional instances to perform a function analogous to two-dimensional boxing, i.e. describe how we might be able to say 'no part of this three-dimensional instance will be visible inside the viewing pyramid' and thus avoid clipping any of the lines of the instance. We could pass over those instances which cannot appear, and thus save considerable processing time.

12-4. As an example of a rotation about an arbitrary axis, consider a representation for a chemical molecule shown in Figure 12-30.

Index	Name	X	Y	Z	M	bonds ...
1	A	—	—	—	5	
2	B	—	—	—	5 3 4	
3	C	—	—	—	2	
4	D	—	—	—	2	
5	E	—	—	—	1 2 6	
6	F	—	—	—	5 7 10	
7	G	—	—	—	6 8	
8	H	—	—	—	7 9 11 12	
9	I	—	—	—	8 10	
10	J	—	—	—	9 6	
11	K	—	—	—	8	
12	L	—	—	—	8	

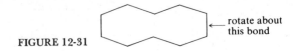

FIGURE 12-31

Suppose we wish to rotate the *ABCDE* part of the molecule about the axis determined by the *EF* bond, and leave the *FGHIJKL* part of the molecule unchanged. Notice we wish to alter the *X*, *Y* and *Z* coordinates of the points in the internal data structure; we are not yet concerned with generating a two-dimensional perspective display of the molecule.

Demonstrate that the coordinates of *E* and *F* remain invariant under your transformation.

Suppose the problem was rephrased: 'Rotate about the bond between atoms with index numbers 5 and 6 all the atoms on the same *side* of the bond as atom 5.' Give two algorithms to find all the atoms which need to have their coordinates transformed by the transform you derived above. Both algorithms must check for circularity: rotation about the bond indicated in Figure 12-31 is 'impossible' without some flexing of the molecule. You may make use of a 1-bit field *M* in the data structure for any purpose you like. One of the two algorithms should use recursion.

12-5. Why can we not project the three-dimensional lines onto a two-dimensional plane and then clip them against a two-dimensional window? (Hint: consider a line from (1,1,4) to (1,1,−4) as measured in eye coordinates in a viewing pyramid with $a/b = 1$).

12-6. How can the transformation system of Figure 12-19 be arranged to process two-dimensional lines as described in Chapters 7 and 8 as well as three-dimensional lines? Hint: consider the transformation:

$$[X\ Y\ 0\ 1] \begin{bmatrix} 1/W_{sx} & 0 & 0 & 0 \\ 0 & 1/W_{sy} & 0 & 0 \\ 0 & 0 & 0 & 0 \\ -W_{cx}/W_{sx} & -W_{cy}/W_{sy} & 1 & 1 \end{bmatrix}$$

12-7. How might you *exaggerate* the perspective of an object?

12-8. Write a midpoint-division version of the three-dimensional clipping algorithm.

Fig. 12-10

FIGURE 12-32

12-9. Art students are often taught to draw perspective pictures of city blocks and the like with a *vanishing point* method (see Figure 12-32). Under what conditions, if any, is the picture a true perspective drawing? What are the vanishing points of the perspective transformation (Equation 12-14)?

12-10. The derivation of Equation 12-14 assumes that the image on the screen plane is square (i.e. that V_{sx} would be the same as V_{sy}). Suppose this is not the case. What modifications to the procedure are required for generating a display?

12-11. A transformation of one three-dimensional space into another can be constructed if you know how four points transform:

$$A M = A'$$
$$B M = B'$$
$$C M = C'$$
$$D M = D'$$

How is the transformation matrix M actually computed? Is there any redundant information in the 8 vectors A, A', B, B', etc. That is, can the same transformation matrix be derived with less information?

12-12. Generalize the development of section 12.4.2 to compute a viewing transformation V given a viewpoint (X,Y,Z) and the viewing direction (a,b,c) as direction cosines. Suggest a good convention for the remaining degree of freedom.

PERSPECTIVE DEPTH

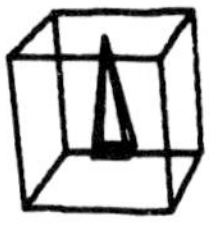

Fig. 12-10

13.1 PERSPECTIVE DEPTH

The operation of removing hidden lines or surfaces requires a perspective transformation with special properties. The image we wish to produce is a perspective view, but the *depth* of each point in the perspective image must be available for making decisions about which surfaces hide lines and other surfaces.

We shall augment the screen coordinate system to be a three-dimensional system: (X_s, Y_s, Z_s). The X_s and Y_s coordinates of a point in this system are precisely the coordinates required by the display hardware in order to show the point on the screen. The Z_s coordinate retains depth information about that point. Thus, the display of a point (X_s, Y_s, Z_s) is an *orthographic projection* of the point onto the display screen. An orthographic projection onto a plane is one in which the original point and its image lie on a line perpendicular to the plane, as shown in Figure 13-1. The Z_s value of a point is simply ignored when generating positioning commands for the display hardware.

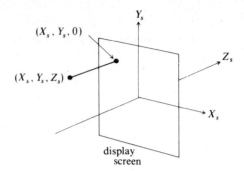

FIGURE 13-1

13.2   THE SCREEN COORDINATE SYSTEM

A photographic lens generates precisely the coordinate system we require. The *image* created by a lens is really a three-dimensional image: the image does not all lie in a plane. Focusing a camera is an adjustment required to position the film so that the film plane is *near* the location of the image.

The details of the image structure can be derived from elementary optics. Figure 13-2 shows a lens of focal length f positioned in the eye coordinate system, pointed in the viewing direction, along the Z_e axis. The image of point P is a point P', whose coordinates can be obtained by noting similar triangles:

$$\frac{Y_e}{f} = \frac{-Y_p}{-2f - Z_p}$$

$$\frac{-Y_p}{f} = \frac{Y_e}{Z_e} \qquad (13\text{-}1)$$

Solving, and including similar equations for X_p, we have

$$X_p = -f\,\frac{X_e}{Z_e}$$

$$Y_p = -f\,\frac{Y_e}{Z_e}$$

$$Z_p = -2f - \frac{f_2}{Z_e} \qquad (13\text{-}2)$$

This coordinate system appears to meet our needs: the values for X_p

Fig. 12-10

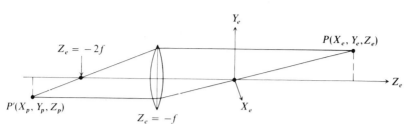

FIGURE 13-2

and Y_p represent a perspective projection (*cf.* Equation 12-13), and Z_p clearly contains information about the depth of the original point P.

We shall apply a slight transformation to Equation 13-2 to define the screen coordinate system. The X_p and Y_p values represent locations of the inverted image on the film; we wish to calculate the location on a display screen. We shall essentially make a photographic enlargement of the film image, and position the print in a viewport on the screen:

$$X_s = \left(S_x \frac{X_e}{Z_e}\right) V_{sx} + V_{cx}$$

$$Y_s = \left(S_y \frac{Y_e}{Z_e}\right) V_{sy} + V_{cy}$$

$$Z_s = \frac{-1}{Z_e} \tag{13-3}$$

The factors S_x and S_y correspond to the factor a/b of Equation 12-14; they will differ if the cross-section of the viewing pyramid is rectangular rather than square. The conditions that a point not exceed the viewport and not be behind the observer are:

$$-Z_e \leqslant S_x X_e \leqslant Z_e$$
$$-Z_e \leqslant S_y Y_e \leqslant Z_e \tag{13-4}$$

These equations define the *viewing pyramid*, as in Equation 12-15. The translation and scaling applied to the Z_p coordinate to yield Z_s are as innocuous as those used to establish X_s and Y_s (see Exercise 13-3).

13.3   PROPERTIES OF THE SCREEN COORDINATE SYSTEM

The properties of the screen coordinate system differ greatly from those of the eye coordinate system. The viewpoint, at $Z_e = 0$, is

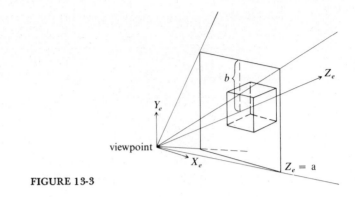

FIGURE 13-3

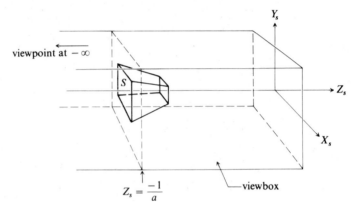

FIGURE 13-4

undefined in the screen coordinate system, but can be thought of as being infinitely far away along the $-Z_s$ direction. Thus 'rays' emanating from the eye are parallel to the Z_s axis. The viewing pyramid becomes a parallelepiped, called the *viewbox*.

Figure 13-3 is a perspective drawing of the eye coordinate system, the viewing pyramid, and a cube.

Figure 13-4 is a perspective drawing of the same scene converted into screen coordinates with Equation 13-3 ($V_{sx} = V_{sy} = 1$; $V_{cy} = V_{cx} = 0$; $S_x = S_y = a/b$). Examination of Figure 13-4 reveals the reasons why the screen coordinate system is used for hidden-line computations. Consider polygon S. Any point inside a box with S as cross-section will be hidden, as shown in Figure 13-5.

The box corresponds to the 'shadow' cast by surface S if a light source were placed at the viewpoint. We can show that point P is inside

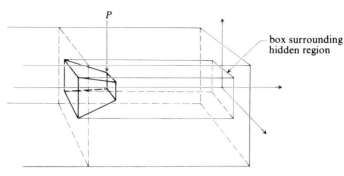

box surrounding
hidden region

Fig. 12-10

FIGURE 13-5

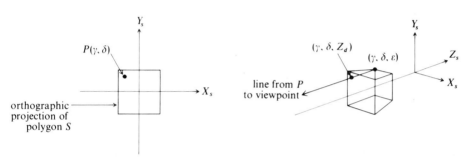

FIGURE 13-6

this box by only two calculations: the first calcuation shows that the orthographic projection of P is inside the orthographic projection of the boundaries of S, and the second shows that P is farther away from the viewpoint than S. These calculations are as follows (see Figure 13-6):

First Calculation: P is inside polygon S. The projection is very simple: we just use the X_s, Y_s values for P and the vertices of the polygon S.

Second Calculation: We compare the Z_s coordinates of P ($Z_s = \epsilon$) and the intersection of a line from P to the viewpoint with the plane S ($Z_s = Z_d$). Z_d can be calculated easily if the plane equation of S is known:

$$a\,X_s + b\,Y_s + c\,Z_s + d = 0$$

Substituting $X_s = \gamma$ and $Y_s = \delta$, we solve for Z_s, which is the desired Z_d.

The properties of the screen coordinate system aid these calculations. Computing the intersection of a ray from the viewpoint and a surface is simple because all rays from the viewpoint are parallel to the Z_s axis. The corresponding calculation in the eye coordinate system is complicated by the various angles at which rays emanate from the viewpoint.

13.3.1   STRAIGHT LINES TRANSFORM INTO STRAIGHT LINES

One of the most important properties of the screen coordinate transformation 13-3 is that straight lines in the eye coordinate system are converted to straight lines in the screen coordinate system. If this were not true, the screen coordinate system would be quite useless, because hidden-line algorithms need to compute the depth (Z_s values) of lines and planes at many points intermediate between endpoints and vertices. Because lines transform into lines, the depth of an intermediate point can be determined from a line or plane equation.

Equation 13-3 is not the only transformation which has this property (see Exercise 13-6). Any transformation of the three-dimensional eye coordinate space into a three-dimensional screen coordinate system will suffice for hidden-line elimination provided that the transformed X and Y values represent a perspective view of the eye coordinate system, and that the transformed Z value insures that lines in the eye coordinate system transform into lines in the screen coordinate system.

We shall represent a straight line in the eye coordinate system as

$$X_e = (1 - \alpha) X_{ea} + \alpha X_{eb}$$
$$Y_e = (1 - \alpha) Y_{ea} + \alpha Y_{eb}$$
$$Z_e = (1 - \alpha) Z_{ea} + \alpha Z_{eb} \qquad (13\text{-}5)$$

where (X_{ea}, Y_{ea}, Z_{ea}) and (X_{eb}, Y_{eb}, Z_{eb}) are the line endpoints, and $0 \leqslant \alpha \leqslant 1$. This line transforms into a line in the screen coordinate system:

$$X_s = (1 - \beta) X_{sa} + \beta X_{sb}$$
$$Y_s = (1 - \beta) Y_{sa} + \beta Y_{sb}$$
$$Z_s = (1 - \beta) Z_{sa} + \beta Z_{sb} \qquad (13\text{-}6)$$

where the points (X_{sa}, Y_{sa}, Z_{sa}) and (X_{sb}, Y_{sb}, Z_{sb}) are the transform

Fig. 12-10

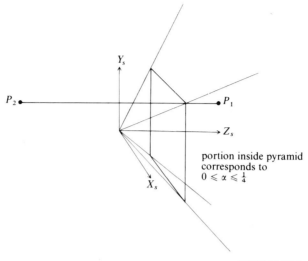

portion inside pyramid
corresponds to
$0 \leqslant \alpha \leqslant \frac{1}{4}$

FIGURE 13-7

of (X_{ea}, Y_{ea}, Z_{ea}) and (X_{eb}, Y_{eb}, Z_{eb}) respectively. The parameters α and β are not identical, but are related by:

$$\beta = \frac{Z_{eb}\,\alpha}{(1 - \alpha)\,Z_{ea} + \alpha Z_{eb}} \qquad (13\text{-}7)$$

This relation is derived from Equations 13-3, 13-5 and 13-6. When $\alpha = 0$, $\beta = 0$; when $\alpha = 1$, $\beta = 1$. If Z_{ea} and Z_{eb} are of the same sign, then as α ranges from 0 to 1, so does β although the ratio α/β is not constant. Thus, the line between eye coordinate points (X_{ea}, Y_{ea}, Z_{ea}) and (X_{eb}, Y_{eb}, Z_{eb}) maps into the line between (X_{sa}, Y_{sa}, Z_{sa}) and (X_{sb}, Y_{sb}, Z_{sb}).

However, this mapping fails for lines which pass through the $Z_e = 0$ plane because $Z_e = 0$ is a pole of the transformation in Equation 13-3. Equation 13-7 reflects this effect: the denominator will be zero for some value of α if the line passes through the $Z_e = 0$ plane. In this case values of α between 0 and 1 do not yield values of β in the range $0 \leqslant \beta \leqslant 1$, and hence do not represent points on a line *between* (X_{sa}, Y_{sa}, Z_{sa}) and (X_{sb}, Y_{sb}, Z_{sb}). Instead, the line maps into *all other* points on the infinite line determined by (X_{sa}, Y_{sa}, Z_{sa}) and (X_{sb}, Y_{sb}, Z_{sb}). For example, the line in eye coordinates from $(1, 1, 2)$ to $(1, 1, -2)$ has the aspect shown in Figure 13-7 to a viewing pyramid with $S_x = S_y = a/b = 1$.

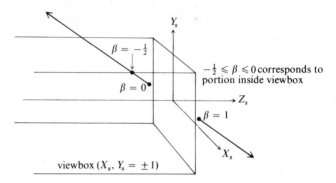

$-\frac{1}{2} \leqslant \beta \leqslant 0$ corresponds to portion inside viewbox

FIGURE 13-8

The *endpoints* of this line transform into the screen coordinate system as $(1/2, 1/2, -1/2)$ and $(-1/2, -1/2, 1/2)$, but the transform of the *line* looks like the diagram in Figure 13-8.

Thus, if a line passes through the $Z_e = 0$ plane, its image is two infinite rays in the screen coordinate system. In this case, the transformed line cannot be found by connecting the transformed endpoints.

This strange property occurs because the points $(X_e, Y_e, 0)$ in the eye coordinate system have all been mapped into points 'infinitely' far away in the screen coordinate system. Dually, a point infinitely far away in the eye coordinate system $(0, 0, \infty)$ has been mapped into a local point in the screen coordinate system $(0, 0, 0)$. These anomalies of projective transformations are relished by projective geometers, and are mathematically useful [175, 176].

13.3.2   CLIPPING IN SCREEN COORDINATES

The clipping procedure described in Section 12.3.3 must be applied to line endpoints before the screen coordinates can be computed with Equation 13-3. Line endpoints in the eye coordinate system are transformed into the clipping coordinate system:

$$[\, X_c \; Y_c \; Z_c \; 1 \,] = [\, X_e \; Y_e \; Z_e \; 1 \,] \, N$$

$$N = \begin{bmatrix} S_x & 0 & 0 & 0 \\ 0 & S_y & 0 & 0 \\ 0 & 0 & 1 & 0 \\ 0 & 0 & 0 & 1 \end{bmatrix} \qquad (13\text{-}8)$$

The limits of the pyramid in the clipping coordinate system are:

$$-Z_c \leqslant X_c \leqslant Z_c$$

$$-Z_c \leqslant Y_c \leqslant Z_c \qquad (13\text{-}9)$$

Fig. 12-10

After clipping, N^{-1} is applied to return clipped line endpoints to the eye coordinate system. Finally, Equation 13-3 is used to calculate the (X_s, Y_s, Z_s) coordinates of the line endpoints in the screen coordinate system.

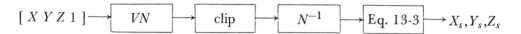

Clipping can be performed after the transformation into the screen coordinate system, but the clipping algorithm becomes extremely complicated.

The modified three-dimensional clipping operation would clip against the *viewbox*, which is the image of the viewing pyramid under the mapping of Equation 13-3. The limits of the viewbox are simply:

$$V_{cx} - V_{sx} \leqslant X_s \leqslant V_{cx} + V_{sx}$$

$$V_{cy} - V_{sy} \leqslant Y_s \leqslant V_{cy} + V_{sy}$$

$$Z_s \leqslant 0 \qquad (13\text{-}10)$$

The modified clipping algorithm is complicated by the special case of lines which pass through the $Z_e = 0$ plane, as shown in Section 13.3.1 (see Exercise 13-1).

13.4 HOMOGENEOUS COORDINATE REPRESENTATIONS OF PROJECTIVE TRANSFORMATIONS

A homogeneous coordinate system is a mathematical tool which aids describing projective transformations. The point (X, Y, Z) in three dimensions is represented by a vector of four numbers: $[\,a\ b\ c\ d\,]$. The four components of this vector are interpreted as coordinates in a four-dimensional space. In order to transform a point (X, Y, Z) in *ordinary* three-dimensional coordinates into a homogeneous representation, we merely choose some non-zero number W, and form the vector:

$$[\; WX \quad WY \quad WZ \quad W \;] \quad (13\text{-}11)$$

The number W is called a scale factor, or the homogeneous coordinate. For example, the point $(1, 2, 3)$ will become $[\; 1 \quad 2 \quad 3 \quad 1 \;]$ if we choose $W = 1$, or $[\; 2 \quad 4 \quad 6 \quad 2 \;]$ if we choose $W = 2$, etc. A point in three-dimensional space thus has an infinity of representations in homogeneous coordinates, each corresponding to a different value of W.

A homogeneous point $[\; a \quad b \quad c \quad d \;]$ can be converted to ordinary three-dimensional coordinates by dividing by the scale factor: the point is $(a/d, b/d, c/d)$. The two homogeneous vectors above clearly reduce to the same ordinary three-dimensional point.

The *division* required to compute the ordinary coordinates of a homogeneous point makes the homogeneous representation very useful. In particular, we shall see that the division of Equation 13-3 can be represented in this fashion. From a geometric standpoint, the division means that undefined points in three dimensions (the points at infinity) are well defined in the homogeneous coordinate system. For example, the homogeneous vector $[\; 0 \quad 0 \quad -1 \quad 0 \;]$ has no image in the three-dimensional system. However, we can get a feeling for such points by considering $[\; 0 \quad 0 \quad -1 \quad \epsilon \;]$ as ϵ approaches 0. The ordinary coordinates of the point are $(0, 0, -1/\epsilon)$: the point becomes infinitely far away along the $-Z$ axis as ϵ approaches 0.

The homogeneous representation can be viewed as a four-space which is related to three-space by the conversions described above:

$$(X, Y, Z) \Rightarrow [\; WX \quad WY \quad WZ \quad W \;]$$
$$[\; a \; b \; c \; d \;] \Rightarrow (a/d, b/d, c/d) \quad (13\text{-}12)$$

The division by the fourth coordinate suggests that the three-space is the projection onto the $W = 1$ hyperplane of the four-space.

Transformations such as translation, rotation, and scaling, which are defined as they apply to ordinary coordinates, can also be performed on the homogeneous representations of the points. In fact, the matrix notations outlined in Section 12.2 are precisely those for homogeneous representations: the introduction of the fourth vector element 1 simply

Fig. 12-10

represents a formation of the homogeneous vector for $W = 1$. The transformations will have the same effect regardless of the choice of W. For example, if we apply the translation:

$$\begin{bmatrix} 1 & 0 & 0 & 0 \\ 0 & 1 & 0 & 0 \\ 0 & 0 & 1 & 0 \\ 4 & 5 & -1 & 1 \end{bmatrix}$$

to two homogeneous representations of the point $(2, 3, 0)$: $[\,2\ 3\ 0\ 1\,]$ and $[\,4\ 6\ 0\ 2\,]$, we get $[\,6\ 8\ -1\ 1\,]$ and $[\,12\ 16\ -2\ 2\,]$ respectively, both of which represent the same point in three-space. Hence all the techniques of transformation, inverses, and concatenation developed in Section 12.2 can be applied directly to homogeneous representations of three-space.

The perspective transformation of Equation 13-3 can also be represented as a 4 x 4 matrix transformation of homogeneous vectors. We shall decompose Equation 13-3 into three steps, in order to correspond with the development of Section 12.3.

1. Scale the X_e, Y_e coordinates by S_x and S_y.

$$X_c = S_x X_e; \quad Y_c = S_y Y_e; \quad Z_c = Z_e \quad (13\text{-}13)$$

This transformation is accomplished with the matrix N:

$$[\,W_c X_c \ \ W_c Y_c \ \ W_c Z_c \ \ W_c\,] = [\,W_e X_e \ \ W_e Y_e \ \ W_e Z_e \ \ W_e\,]\ N$$

$$N = \begin{bmatrix} S_x & 0 & 0 & 0 \\ 0 & S_y & 0 & 0 \\ 0 & 0 & 1 & 0 \\ 0 & 0 & 0 & 1 \end{bmatrix}$$

$$(13\text{-}14)$$

2. Perform the perspective transformation:

$$X_p = X_c/Z_c; \quad Y_p = Y_c/Z_c; \quad Z_p = -1/Z_c \quad (13\text{-}15)$$

This transformation uses the division required to generate ordinary coordinates to accomplish the division by Z_c:

$$[\,W_p X_p \ \ W_p Y_p \ \ W_p Z_p \ \ W_p\,] = [\,W_c X_c \ \ W_c Y_c \ \ W_c Z_c \ \ W_c\,]\ P$$

$$P = \begin{bmatrix} 1 & 0 & 0 & 0 \\ 0 & 1 & 0 & 0 \\ 0 & 0 & 0 & 1 \\ 0 & 0 & -1 & 0 \end{bmatrix}$$

$$(13\text{-}16)$$

3. Apply the viewport transformation:

$$X_s = X_p V_{sx} + V_{cx}; \quad Y_s = Y_p V_{sy} + V_{cy}; \quad Z_s = Z_p \quad (13\text{-}17)$$

The matrix S accomplishes this:

$$[\ W_s X_s \ W_s Y_s \ W_s Z_s \ W_s \ ] = [\ W_p X_p \ W_p Y_p \ W_p Z_p \ W_p \ ]\ S$$

$$S = \begin{bmatrix} V_{sx} & 0 & 0 & 0 \\ 0 & V_{sy} & 0 & 0 \\ 0 & 0 & 1 & 0 \\ V_{cx} & V_{cy} & 0 & 1 \end{bmatrix}$$

$$(13\text{-}18)$$

The full perspective transformation sequence includes the viewing transformation V, the three steps given above, and the clipping procedure. It is therefore:

$$V N <\text{clip}> P S \quad (13\text{-}19)$$

If no clipping is required, we can concatenate this transformation into $V N P S$. To apply this transformation to a point (X, Y, Z), we choose a value of W, say 1, and form the homogeneous vector $[\ X \ Y \ Z \ 1\ ]$. Then we calculate $[\ a \ b \ c \ d\ ]$:

$$[\ a\ b\ c\ d\ ] = [\ X\ Y\ Z\ 1\ ]\ V N P S \quad (13\text{-}20)$$

Now the four-vector must be reduced to ordinary screen coordinates:

$$X_s = a/d$$
$$Y_s = b/d$$
$$Z_s = c/d \quad (13\text{-}21)$$

Notice that *division is still required to generate the perspective display*. The virtues of this new formulation are that all the transformations, excluding the division, are performed with *one* matrix, the concatenation of V, N, P and S.

If clipping is required, then the transformation $V N$ establishes the clipping coordinate system, and the clipping routine of Section 12.3.3 can be applied to each line.

$$[\ W_c X_c \ W_c Y_c \ W_c Z_c \ W_c \ ] = [\ WX \ WY \ WZ \ W\ ]\ V N$$

It appears that the calculation of values for X_c, Y_c, and Z_c might require a division by W_c. However, if we choose $W = 1$, and arrange V

Fig. 12-10

and N so that they always yield $W_c = W$, then the division can be omitted, because W_c will be 1. For this reason, the translation, rotation, and scaling transformations which form V and N never change the value of W.

EXERCISES

13-1. Give a clipping procedure for clipping lines in screen coordinates against the viewbox.

13-2. In Chapter 12, we clipped all lines before performing the division by Z_e to create a perspective display. If $Z_e = 0$, the only legal X_e and Y_e values are 0, and defining $0/0 = 0$ for the purposes of the perspective display is satisfactory. However, Exercise 13-1 proposes a method in which clipping can be performed *after* the division. This introduces the possibility of a division by 0 when calculating the screen coordinates of a line endpoint. Explain the circumstances in which this can occur and what to do so that the line is clipped correctly.

13-3. We said that Equations 13-2 and 13-3 are related by simple translations and scalings of the projective coordinate system. Characterize the viewboxes of each of these systems. Show that the observations of Section 13.3 are true for both representations.

13-4. The semi-infinite viewbox of Figure 13-4 presents some difficulties when defining a number system for the screen coordinate system. The values of X_s and Y_s resulting from Equation 13-3 are in the same coordinate measure used by the display hardware. These numbers need to be stored only to the precision that the CRT has, say 4096 units. (Is this really true?) However, resolution in Z_s has some difficulties. First, when Z_e is large, the resolution of the Z_s system may not be fine enough to show differences: if one object is at $Z_e = N$, and another at $Z_e = N - d$, then if these two objects are to be resolved in the Z_s system,

$$\frac{-1}{N} - \frac{-1}{N - d} > \epsilon$$

where ϵ is the grain of resolution of the Z_s system. Second, for Z_e small, $1/Z_e$ may grow so large that it exceeds the largest possible number which can be represented in the computer for Z_s.

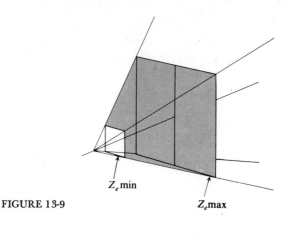

FIGURE 13-9

$Z_e\min$

$Z_e\max$

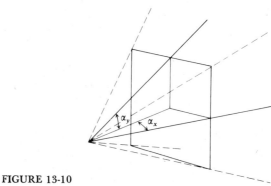

FIGURE 13-10

Analyze the precision problem. Propose some methods for guaranteeing adequate precision in Z_s to make depth calculations. (Hint: consider redefining the infinite viewing pyramid as a finite frustrum, as shown in Figure 13-9).

13-5. Equation 13-3 identifies S_x and S_y with the ratio a/b of Section 12.3. What is the significance of S_x and S_y? Suppose, rather than considering focal lengths, enlargement factors, screen sizes and the like, we are merely interested in the viewing angles α_x and α_y associated with the viewing pyramid shown in Figure 13-10. How are the α's related to a/b, S_x and S_y? Derive a perspective transformation which uses only the α's and a viewport description.

Fig. 12-10

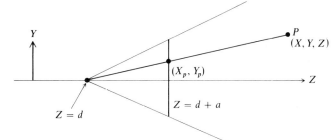

FIGURE 13-11

13-6. The screen coordinate system can be derived in another fashion. Consider the drawing of Figure 13-11. We project the point P onto the $Z = d+a$ plane:

$$X_p = \frac{aX}{Z - d}$$

$$Y_p = \frac{aY}{Z - d}$$

and perform a similar projection for Z:

$$Z_p = \frac{aZ}{Z - d}$$

Relate the (X, Y, Z) coordinate system to the eye coordinate system. Derive values for X_p, Y_p and Z_p in this system, and then augment them to include viewport information. How is your expression for Z_s related to that of Equation 13-3? Do lines transform into lines with your transformation? What is the class of transformations which yield (1) X and Y values that are perspective views of the eye coordinate system and (2) Z values so that lines transform into lines?

13-7. Equation 13-19 shows the mechanism for calculating screen coordinates of a point: the calculation involves homogeneous transformations, a clipping, and finally a division by the homogeneous coordinate. We observed that if V and N leave W unaltered, the clipping procedure of Section 12.3.3 can be used. Remove this restriction, and devise a clipping algorithm which operates on homogeneous vectors,

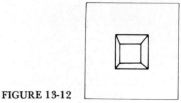

FIGURE 13-12

taking the value of W into account. Discuss the feasibility of altering Equation 13-9 to read

$$V N P < \text{clip}'> S$$

or

$$V N P S < \text{clip}''>$$

Why are we preoccupied with postponing the homogeneous division until the last moment? (Hint: see [267]).

13-8. Suppose we use a given viewing transformation V to make a full-screen display as shown in Figure 13-12. Then the user can define a portion of this view (i.e. viewport) which he wishes to see alone. The viewport can be anywhere on the screen. Describe the display-generation procedure required.

14

HIDDEN-LINE ELIMINATION AND SHADING

Fig. 12-10

14.1   HIDDEN-LINE AND HIDDEN-SURFACE ALGORITHMS

The algorithms available for elimination of hidden lines in three-dimensional scenes are among the most interesting in graphics. The resulting displays are very attractive views of the scene, particularly when continuous-tone pictures can be generated and displayed. The illusion of depth created by hidden-surface elimination and by shading surpasses the illusions created by other depth cueing techniques — kinetic depth effect, perspective, intensity, stereoscopy — described in Chapter 12.

The single disadvantage of hidden-line elimination is that considerable computation is required to decide which lines and surfaces are hidden. A great deal of effort and ingenuity has been applied to solving the hidden-line problem. The result is a sizeable collection of algorithms (see Bibliography listings).

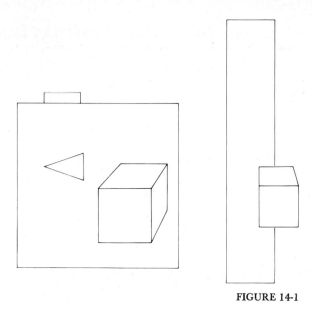

FIGURE 14-1

One reason for the wide variety of hidden-line algorithms is that one algorithm is not necessarily suitable for all kinds of display output. Two classes of output are:

1. Line drawing (Figure 14-1). This kind of image is suitable for line-drawing displays and for plotter equipment. The process of generating such an image is called hidden-*line* elimination.
2. Shaded picture (Figure 14-2). This image is suitable for display on raster-scan devices such as television monitors, or for generating photographic pictures with special-purpose hardware. The process of generating this image is called hidden-*surface* elimination.

We shall describe three algorithms in detail. The first, devised by Roberts, is the first practical solution to the hidden-line problem [234] and is noteworthy for its clever use of geometry and linear programming. The second, created by Warnock, is capable of generating either line drawings or shaded pictures [300]; we shall give the line-drawing form. This algorithm is interesting for its use of non-deterministic methods. The third algorithm is designed to produce shaded pictures on raster-scan displays [301]. It takes advantage of similarities between adjacent scan-lines to speed the computation.

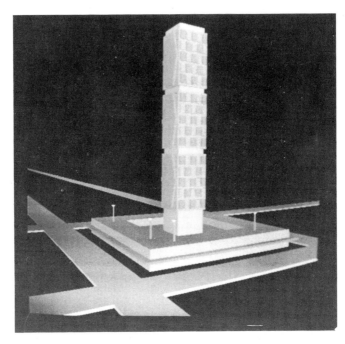

Fig. 12-10

FIGURE 14-2

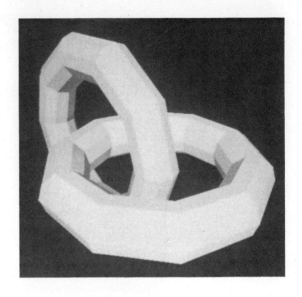

FIGURE 14-2

Fig. 12-10

FIGURE 14-2

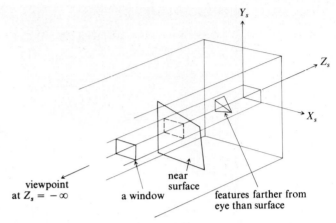

viewpoint
at $Z_s = -\infty$

a window

near
surface

features farther from
eye than surface

FIGURE 14-3

14.1.1   TWO APPROACHES

The most interesting technical aspect of the hidden-line elimination techniques we shall discuss is that they represent two entirely different approaches to generating the final picture. The first takes the view that each *line* in the three-dimensional scene should be examined to calculate which portions of it, if any, will not be hidden by some surface in the scene. Each line is tested against every opaque surface. The resulting line fragments are then displayed.

The second approach solves the hidden-line problem by asking, for various areas of the display screen, if any object is visible within that area. Each area is called a *window*. A window may be blank because no object appears there, or because some surface completely covers the window and is nearer the eye than other objects in the window. Figure 14-3 shows such a window and demonstrates a difference between the meaning of the term *window* as used here and the meaning used in Chapter 7: the window is a portion of the viewbox, bounded in X_s and Y_s, but boundless in Z_s.

An algorithm that uses the second approach must be sure to examine a set of windows which completely covers the display screen. The algorithm chooses windows in such a way that it is easy to decide what is visible within each window. The algorithm need never choose window sizes smaller than 1 x 1, because the resolution of the display hardware will be unable to show any details within such a window.

Fig. 12-10

14.2   ROBERTS' SOLUTION

Roberts solved the hidden-line problem for objects constructed from plane convex polyhedra. Any plane-surfaced solid object can be specified as a number of such polyhedra. Figure 14-4 shows an example. The advantage of specifying objects in this way is that a convex polyhedron can be completely defined by the planes making up its surfaces.

The data on which the program works are a set of polyhedra, each defined by the equations of its planes. Each plane P_o has the equation:

$$aX + bY + cZ + d = 0 \qquad (14\text{-}1)$$

where X, Y and Z are measured in the object coordinate system. The coefficients can be stored in a column vector:

$$\mathbf{P_o} = \begin{bmatrix} a \\ b \\ c \\ d \end{bmatrix}$$

Then if we represent a point S_o by the homogeneous coordinates:

$$\mathbf{S_o} = [\ WX\ WY\ WZ\ W\ ]$$

we can determine whether S_o lies on P_o by forming the dot product: if $\mathbf{S_o} \cdot \mathbf{P_o} = 0$, then S_o lies on P_o. Moreover, if $\mathbf{S_o} \cdot \mathbf{P_o} \neq 0$, then the *sign* of the product indicates on which side of the plane the point lies. Roberts chooses to represent planes of a polyhedron so that points *inside* the polyedron give positive products when multiplied by any of the plane vectors of the polyhedron.

In practice, the plane equations are transformed from object coordinates into screen coordinates and the hidden-line elimination is performed in that space. The transformation of a *point* is the familiar:

$$\mathbf{S_s} = \mathbf{S_o}\ V\,N\,P\,S \qquad (14\text{-}2)$$

Where V describes the viewing position, NP the perspective transformation, and S the viewport transformation. In the same way, the transformation $M = V\,N\,P\,S$ can be applied to plane equations:

$$\mathbf{P_s} = M^{-1}\mathbf{P_o} \qquad (14\text{-}3)$$

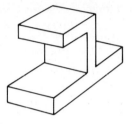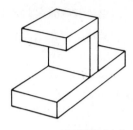

FIGURE 14-4

Notice that the matrix M^{-1} is used to *pre-multiply* $\mathbf{P_o}$. The list of planes defining a polyhedron is transformed by this equation into a new list of planes in screen coordinates.

The transformed plane vectors for each polyhedron are stored in a $4 \times n$ matrix called the *volume matrix*.

$$B = \begin{bmatrix} a_1 & a_2 & a_3 \ldots a_n \\ b_1 & b_2 & b_3 \ldots b_n \\ c_1 & c_2 & c_3 \ldots c_n \\ d_1 & d_2 & d_3 \ldots d_n \end{bmatrix}$$

where a_i, b_i, c_i, d_i are the coefficients of each transformed plane.

We can still apply the test mentioned above to determine whether a point transformed into screen coordinates lies within a transformed polyhedron: if the original point was inside, so will be the transformed point. If all the coefficients of the product of a point vector and the volume matrix are positive, the point must be inside the convex polyhedron defined by the volume matrix, or:

$$(\mathbf{S_s} \cdot B \geqslant 0) \text{ implies } \mathbf{S_s} \text{ is inside } B$$

The notation means that every element of $\mathbf{S_s} \cdot B$ is $\geqslant 0$.

14.2.1   STAGES IN LINE ELIMINATION

Roberts eliminates lines in three stages. Each line in turn is taken through the three stages, then the next line, and so on. The stages are:

1. Clipping against the screen boundary.
2. Rejection of back lines.
3. Testing the line against other volumes.

Fig. 12-10

The lines on which these operations are applied are the intersections of the planes of the polyhedron and are defined parametrically by their two endpoints:

$$v = s + t(r - s) \qquad (14\text{-}4)$$

$$0 \leqslant t \leqslant 1$$

where r and s are the two endpoints.

Some data must be carried with the volume matrix data to indicate which planes of a polyhedron intersect in vertices. The positions of these vertices can be determined from the plane equations: the vertex s at which the three planes P_1, P_2, P_3, meet is given by the bottom row of the inverse Q^{-1} of the following matrix Q:

$$Q = \begin{bmatrix} & & & 0 \\ P_1 & P_2 & P_3 & 0 \\ & & & 0 \\ & & & 1 \end{bmatrix} \qquad (14\text{-}5)$$

14.2.2   CLIPPING

Roberts uses the line equation (Equation 14-4) to carry out three-dimensional clipping on each line. This procedure eliminates all parts of lines which are off the edge of the screen, or which lie behind the observer ($Z_s > 0$). This is accomplished by checking points on the line against a special volume matrix B_o representing the edges of the viewbox in screen coordinates (see Chapter 13 for a discussion of the viewbox).

$$B_o = \begin{bmatrix} 1 & -1 & 0 & 0 & 0 \\ 0 & 0 & 1 & -1 & 0 \\ 0 & 0 & 0 & 0 & -1 \\ -V_{cx} + V_{sx} & V_{cx} + V_{sx} & -V_{cy} + V_{sy} & V_{cy} + V_{sy} & 0 \end{bmatrix}$$

The five columns of this volume matrix represent the left, right, bottom, top and $Z_s = 0$ planes of the viewbox respectively. The line v defined in Equation 14-4 must lie within this volume matrix for it to be visible. The extremities of the visible portion can be determined by multiplying the vector v by each of the columns of B_o in turn. We can represent the line by

$$v = s + td \quad \text{where } d = r - s, 0 \leqslant t \leqslant 1 \qquad (14\text{-}6)$$

Then we must have

$$s\,B_o + t\,\mathbf{d}\,B_o \geqslant 0$$

If $\mathbf{p} = s\,B_o$, $\mathbf{q} = \mathbf{d}\,B_o$, then for the jth column of B_o we have

$$p_j + tq_j \geqslant 0 \qquad (14\text{-}7)$$

This must be true for all j. We can determine the coefficients p_j and q_j, and from them find the maximum and minimum values of t. In fact for $q_j > 0$, $t \geqslant -p_j/q_j$; for $q_j < 0$, $t \leqslant -p_j/q_j$. The maximum and minimum values of t give the endpoints of the part of the line lying within the screen boundary.

14.2.3   REMOVING BACK LINES

The remainder of the program is concerned with rejecting lines that are partly or wholly invisible even though they are within the screen boundary. A particular case of an invisible line is one that is on the far side of the polyhedron of which it is an edge. Roberts applies a very simple test to determine whether these edges are visible: if one or both of the planes which meet at the edge have their face to the viewer, the edge is visible. If the plane coefficients $\mathbf{P}$ are formulated so that points $\mathbf{S}$ inside a polyhedron give positive values of $\mathbf{S} \cdot \mathbf{P}$, then planes which face away from the viewpoint will have a non-zero negative coefficient for Z_s (i.e. $\mathbf{P}_s \cdot [\,0\;\;0\;\;-1\;\;0\,] \geqslant 0$). In other words, the viewpoint is on the same side of the plane as is the inside of the polyhedron.

14.2.4   TESTING LINES AGAINST OTHER VOLUMES

Once the back lines have been removed, all the remaining lines are known to be unobstructed by the volumes of their polyhedra. By far the hardest part of the process still remains: testing each line for obstruction by other polyhedron volumes.

Suppose we take each point on a line: these points are represented by different values of t in the line equation:

$$\mathbf{v} = \mathbf{s} + t\,\mathbf{d}$$

For each such point, we can draw a line in the negative Z_s direction, i.e. toward the eye. If this line succeeds in reaching $-\infty$ without passing through any polyhedron, then we know that point is visible. If, on the

Fig. 12-10

other hand, the line drawn in the $-Z_s$ direction passes through a polyhedron, then that polyhedron must obstruct the point.

The line in the $-Z_s$ direction can again be represented parametrically:

$$\mathbf{u} = \mathbf{s} + t\mathbf{d} + \alpha\mathbf{z} \qquad (14\text{-}8)$$

where $\mathbf{z}$ is the vector $[\,0\ \ 0\ -1\ \ 0\,]$. The points on this line which interest us lie in the range $0 \leqslant t \leqslant 1$, $0 \leqslant \alpha$. To test for obstruction we multiply the line equation by the volume matrix of each of the polyhedra in turn, and look for all-positive coefficients which indicate that the line passes through the polyhedron:

or

$$\mathbf{u}\,B \geqslant 0$$

$$\mathbf{s}B + t\mathbf{d}B + \alpha\mathbf{z}B \geqslant 0 \qquad (14\text{-}9)$$

Notice that $\mathbf{z}\,B = -\mathbf{w}$ where $\mathbf{w}$ is the third row of B. If we keep the same definitions of $\mathbf{p}$ and $\mathbf{q}$, we have for all j:

$$p_j + tq_j - \alpha w_j \geqslant 0 \quad \text{where } 0 \leqslant t \leqslant 1 \quad \text{and} \quad 0 \leqslant \alpha \qquad (14\text{-}10)$$

These inequalities must be solved for maximum and minimum values of t for any positive value of α. Some ranges of p_j, q_j and w_j give obvious results. For example, $(q_j \geqslant 0)$ and $(p_j \geqslant 0)$ and $(w_j \leqslant 0)$ obviously satisfies the inequality for all values of t and α in the given ranges. This means that the line is entirely hidden by the volume. We can quickly recognize other combinations that indicate the line is completely unobstructed by the volume. In this way a large number of the lines in the picture can be tested very rapidly against each volume.

The non-trivial cases are solved by a method akin to linear programming. Each inequality can be thought of as representing a region of the t, α plane. This region is bounded by the lines

$$p_j + t\,q_j - \alpha\,w_j = 0$$

If all these boundary lines are drawn on the t, α plane, they, together with the lines $t = 0$, $t = 1$, and $\alpha = 0$, define a region that is the intersection of all the inequalities for that particular line and volume. This area of intersection, which contains values of t and α satisfying all the inequalities, may be non-existent. In such a case, none of the points on the line satisfies all the inequalities, so the entire line $\mathbf{v}$ is unobstructed. If the regions do intersect, then the maximum and minimum values of t can be calculated.

14.2.5 EXAMPLE

We shall demonstrate a brief example of the Roberts procedure. Consider the cube shown in Figure 14-5. In volume matrix form, the plane equations of the cube are:

$$B_c = \begin{bmatrix} 0 & 0 & 1 & -1 & 0 & 0 \\ 0 & 0 & 0 & 0 & 1 & -1 \\ 1 & -1 & 0 & 0 & 0 & 0 \\ 0 & 2 & 3 & -1 & 0 & 2 \end{bmatrix}$$

The signs of the coefficients have been chosen so that an interior point (e.g. $X = -2$, $Y = 1$, $Z = 1$ will yield all-positive coefficients when multiplied by B_c).

We establish a viewing position at $(0,0,-4)$, looking along the Z axis:

$$V = \begin{bmatrix} 1 & 0 & 0 & 0 \\ 0 & 1 & 0 & 0 \\ 0 & 0 & 1 & 0 \\ 0 & 0 & 4 & 1 \end{bmatrix}$$

and

$$NP = \begin{bmatrix} 1 & 0 & 0 & 0 \\ 0 & 1 & 0 & 0 \\ 0 & 0 & 0 & 1 \\ 0 & 0 & -1 & 0 \end{bmatrix}$$

(The ratio a/b is 1). The viewport transformation for X_s and Y_s values running from -1 to $+1$ is:

$$S = \begin{bmatrix} 1 & 0 & 0 & 0 \\ 0 & 1 & 0 & 0 \\ 0 & 0 & 1 & 0 \\ 0 & 0 & 0 & 1 \end{bmatrix}$$

Hence,

$$M = VNPS = \begin{bmatrix} 1 & 0 & 0 & 0 \\ 0 & 1 & 0 & 0 \\ 0 & 0 & 0 & 1 \\ 0 & 0 & -1 & 4 \end{bmatrix}$$

$$M^{-1} = \begin{bmatrix} 1 & 0 & 0 & 0 \\ 0 & 1 & 0 & 0 \\ 0 & 0 & 4 & -1 \\ 0 & 0 & 1 & 0 \end{bmatrix}$$

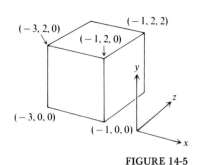

Fig. 12-10

FIGURE 14-5

Transforming the volume matrix for the cube into screen coordinates,

$$B = M^{-1}B_c = \begin{bmatrix} 0 & 0 & 1 & -1 & 0 & 0 \\ 0 & 0 & 0 & 0 & 1 & -1 \\ 4 & -6 & -3 & 1 & 0 & -2 \\ 1 & -1 & 0 & 0 & 0 & 0 \end{bmatrix}$$

The perspective view of the cube can be generated by multiplying each of the vertex vectors by M and displaying the resulting lines.

We shall now consider a new line from $s_o = (-3,4,5)$ to $r_o = (-3,-1,5)$ to see if it is hidden by the cube volume. The homogeneous coordinates for s and r are:

$$s_o = [\, -3 \quad 4 \quad 5 \quad 1 \,]$$
$$r_o = [\, -3 \quad -1 \quad 5 \quad 1 \,]$$

and

$$d_o = r_o - s_o = [\, 0 \quad -5 \quad 0 \quad 0 \,]$$

Transforming these points into screen coordinates, we get:

$$s = s_o M = [\, -3 \quad 4 \quad -1 \quad 9 \,]$$
$$d = d_o M = [\, 0 \quad -5 \quad 0 \quad 0 \,]$$

and

$$p = sB = [\, 5 \quad -3 \quad 0 \quad 2 \quad 4 \quad -2 \,]$$
$$q = dB = [\, 0 \quad 0 \quad 0 \quad 0 \quad -5 \quad 5 \,]$$
$$w = \quad [\, 4 \quad -6 \quad -3 \quad 1 \quad 0 \quad -2 \,]$$

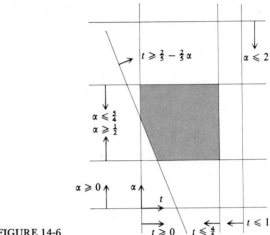

FIGURE 14-6

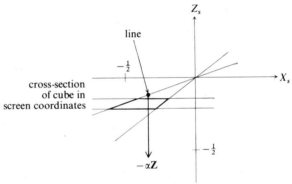

FIGURE 14-7

Equation 14-10 is now solved using these vectors. The solution is $0 \leqslant t \leqslant 4/5$, which gives the range of t for which the line is hidden. Hence, for $4/5 \leqslant t \leqslant 1$, the line is visible. This is the line from:

$$\mathbf{s} + \tfrac{4}{5}\mathbf{d} = [\,-3 \quad 0 \quad -1 \quad 9\,]$$

to

$$\mathbf{s} + \mathbf{d} = [\,-3 \quad -1 \quad -1 \quad 9\,]$$

The regions defined by the six inequalities from Equation 14-10 and by the inequalities $0 \leqslant t \leqslant 1$ and $0 \leqslant \alpha$ give a picture of the t, α plane as shown in Figure 14-6.

We can see the relationship of the line $(\mathbf{s}, \mathbf{r})$ and the cube by showing a picture in the $Y_s = 1/4$ plane (see Figure 14-7).

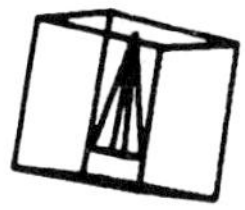

14.2.6   PERFORMANCE

The Roberts technique of removing hidden lines requires large quantities of computation. Roberts gives the figure of one second per object up to thirty objects. Above thirty, as one might expect, the time increases rapidly — 90 seconds for forty objects, 22 minutes for 200. Consequently, despite the elegance of the method, it is somewhat uneconomical as a means of presenting three-dimensional information.

Fig. 12-10

The computation for object-object comparisons grows as the square of the number of objects potentially visible. This behavior is a consequence of comparing each object to the plane faces of all other objects. If there are N objects, the number of such computations is proportional to

$$N(N-1) = N^2 - N$$

Thus the algorithm is extremely slow for complicated scenes.

14.3   WARNOCK ALGORITHM

John Warnock developed the idea of examining portions of the display screen for visible features rather than examining each feature to see if it is visible. This approach catalyzed further development of hidden-line and hidden-surface algorithms.

The key operation in the Warnock algorithm is determining, for a portion of the display screen, if anything interesting appears there. If nothing appears in this window area, then that portion of the screen need not be considered further: it is blank. If a feature (e.g. line, surface, vertex) appears in the window and is *simple enough* to display directly, the algorithm generates the display. However, the collection of features appearing within the window may be too complicated to analyze and display directly. In this case, the algorithm announces that it has *failed* to process the window. The examination of features in a window, then, has three possible results:

1. No features are visible in the window.
2. A display is generated because the feature or features in the window are classified as simple.
3. The algorithm fails because the features in the window are too complex to analyze.

Floyd calls such procedures *non-deterministic*, because they may announce failure if they cannot succeed in performing their given task [92].

The examination of windows is supervised by a *controller* that must (1) make sure that all possible windows on the display screen are examined and (2) cope with the *failure* of the procedure for examining a window.

If the procedure for examining a window fails, the controller divides the window into several smaller windows, and examines each of these in turn. This process is applied recursively until the window becomes smaller than a resolvable spot on the display screen. If the features within such a window are still too complicated for the algorithm to display directly, the controller calls for a dot to be displayed by default. Because the resolution of the screen is only 1024 by 1024 or less, 10 binary subdivisions of the window size will suffice to reach the finest level of resolution.

Figure 14-8a shows a scene with hidden-line elimination performed by the Warnock algorithm. Each small 'x' represents a dot displayed on the screen. Figure 14-8b shows the same scene, with no hidden lines removed. Figure 14-8c shows each of the square windows examined by the algorithm in the process of computing which dots to display. Notice that windows are subdivided only near visible features: the window marked *A* actually has an edge of a polygon passing through it (compare Figure 14-8b), but the algorithm has determined that nothing is visible in the window because a nearer surface completely fills the window.

The choice of criteria used to decide if information in a window is simple enough to display directly affects the number of subdivisions required to produce a display. Figure 14-8c is produced with a decision procedure which *never* finds information simple enough. The decision procedure used to produce Figure 14-8d, on the other hand, is able to detect certain cases in which only one polygon is visible in a window. For example, the line marked *B* was determined to be simple enough to display directly. The same line in Figure 14-8c was not found to be simple enough, the window was subdivided, and dots were eventually displayed when the window size reached the resolution of the screen.

The subdivision process can be viewed as a scheme for resolving the failure to examine large windows. Alternatively, it can be viewed as a process of selectively generating subgoals from the main goal of solving the hidden-line problem for the scene. If a goal proves too difficult to

Fig. 12-10

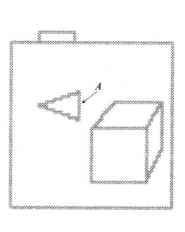

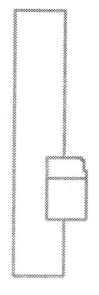

(a)

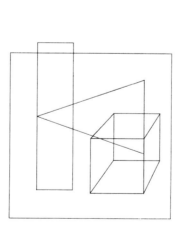

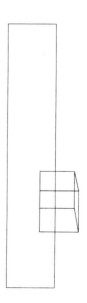

(b)

FIGURE 14-8

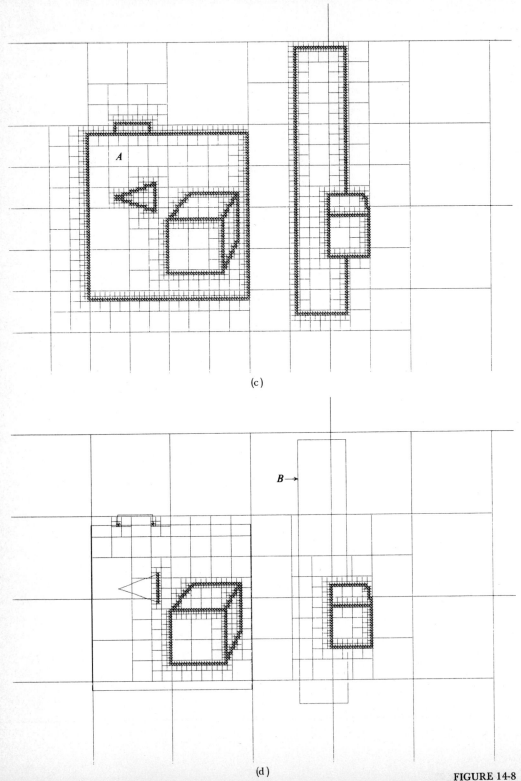

(c)

(d)

FIGURE 14-8

Fig. 12-10

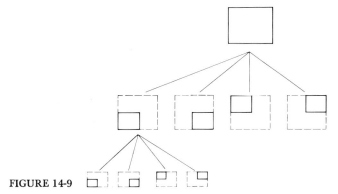

FIGURE 14-9

reach directly, the controller generates four subgoals whose solution is equivalent to the first goal (see Figure 14-9).

This view of the algorithm also suggests that whenever the attempt to achieve a goal fails, the algorithm calls itself recursively four times — once for each new subgoal. The tree picture of the subdivision process also suggests a terminology for describing the process. Subdivisions of a window are called *descendants* of the window and the larger window is called their *ancestor*.

We can characterize Warnock's algorithm by its five major components, discussed in subsequent sections: the Looker, the Thinker, Display by Computation, Display by Default, and the Controller. These five parts are shown in Figure 14-10. The Looker examines a particular window and determines what parts, if any, of the objects in the scene are visible in that portion of the screen. The Looker collects data about all potentially visible objects for subsequent use by the Thinker.

The Thinker uses the data collected by the Looker to determine if the features in this window can be displayed directly. If the Thinker is able to display the data presented to it by the Looker, it calls for Display by Computation. If the Thinker finds the situation described by the Looker too complicated, it will announce its failure, whereupon the Controller will subdivide the window or call for Display by Default.

The Controller system handles subdivisions of the windows examined by the Looker and maintains a list of unexamined windows. If the Thinker fails to provide answers and the window is so small that it covers only one resolution unit on the display, then Control will call for Display by Default which will result in a single dot on the screen.

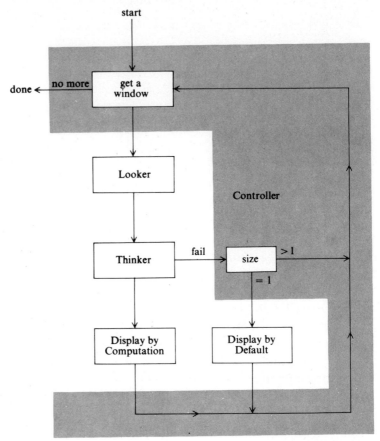

FIGURE 14-10

This processing technique is quite general. It could be applied to curved surfaces and to regions of the screen of any desired shape. The strategy of subdividing the window to produce simpler cases is sufficient to solve the hidden-line problem. The algorithm can be fitted with a trivial Looker and Thinker or with quite complicated ones; the simple versions make it quite easy to program the Warnock algorithm.

14.3.1 SPECIALIZATION OF THE ALGORITHM

We shall describe a particular algorithm within the general framework outlined above. The Controller, shown in Figure 14-11, is designed to process square windows. Subdivison, when it takes place, divides a

Fig. 12-10

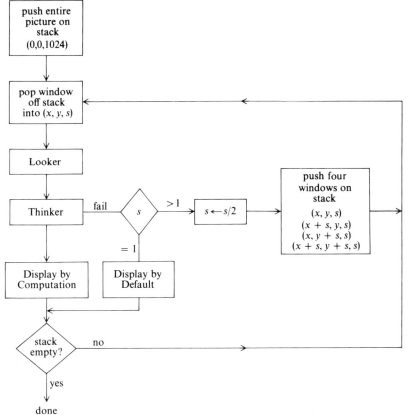

FIGURE 14-11

window into four square windows, each with one-half the length of the side of the original. This Controller does a prefix walk of the tree represented by the subdivided windows. The Controller keeps in a push-down stack the windows that have not yet been examined. If the Thinker fails on a window, the Controller subdivides the window into four and pushes these squares onto the stack. It repeatedly pops windows off the stack and processes them until the stack is empty.

We shall assume that objects are plane-faced polyhedra; each face of an object will be bounded by a polygon. There are many assumptions that we might make about the shape of this polygon. For instance, we could confine our attention to triangles or to polygons with four or fewer sides. We might insist that the polygons be convex, because it is relatively easy to determine if a convex polygon is outside a particular

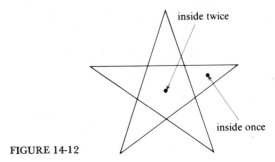

inside twice

inside once

FIGURE 14-12

window. We might allow non-convex polygons, or we might permit our polygons to overlap themselves in complicated ways as in Figure 14-12.

The version of the algorithm described here will assume that the polygons are planar, that they have an arbitrary number of sides, and that they may be represented as an ordered list of vertices. Coordinates of vertices are stored in screen coordinates, as in Equation 14-2.

14.3.2 THE LOOKER

The Looker compares a polygon taken from the data structure representing the scene with a window generated by the Controller. The size and position of the window are specified in screen coordinates, as are the X, Y and Z coordinates of the vertices of the polygon. The polygon may be spatially related to the window in the X-Y plane in one of several ways, as shown in Figure 14-13.

For each polygon, the Looker decides which of these cases pertains. It may suffice to detect three cases: surrounder (a), disjoint (b), and intersector (c,d,e).

The information calculated by the Looker is crucial to the elimination of hidden lines. A surrounding polygon clearly hides any features farther from the eye than the surrounding surface (Figure 14-14a).

The Looker considers all polygons of all objects. An essential part of the algorithm is that the list of polygons is sorted in an order such that the polygon whose nearest corner is closest to the eye appears first on the list, and the polygon with the farthest away nearest corner appears last. The value of Z_s at the nearest vertex of the polygon is called Z_{min}. Whenever the Looker encounters a surrounding polygon, it remembers the farthest away point of the polygon in the window as Z_{minmax}

Fig. 12-10

Name	*Drawing*	*Symbol*

 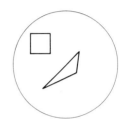

(a) Surrounder

 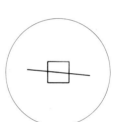

(b) Clean miss (disjoint)

 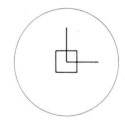

(c) Single line intersection

(d) Single vertex included

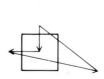 

(e) other, more complicated

FIGURE 14-13

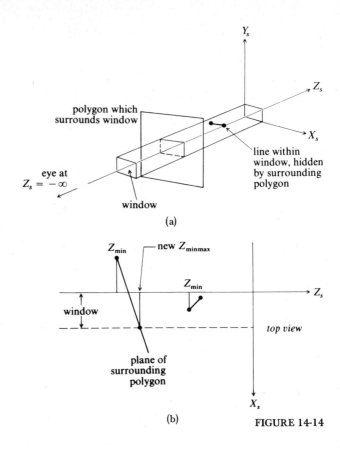

(a)

(b)

FIGURE 14-14

(Figure 14-14b). When considering another polygon in the list, if its Z_{min} is greater than Z_{minmax}, it is clearly hidden by the surrounder. Thus the search through the ordered list of polygons may be prematurely terminated by the discovery of a surrounder.

A great deal of computation can be avoided if the Looker retains *ancestral information* (Figure 14-15). For example, if a polygon surrounds a window, it clearly surrounds all subdivisons of that window. There is no point then in examining a polygon to see if it surrounds a window if it was known to surround some ancestor of that window. When the Looker decides that a polygon surrounds a window, the fact is recorded so that the computation need not be repeated for descendants of that window. It is also important to record the fact that a polygon is disjoint from a window, because it will be disjoint from all descendants of the window. Data is stored in the polygon table to

Fig. 12-10

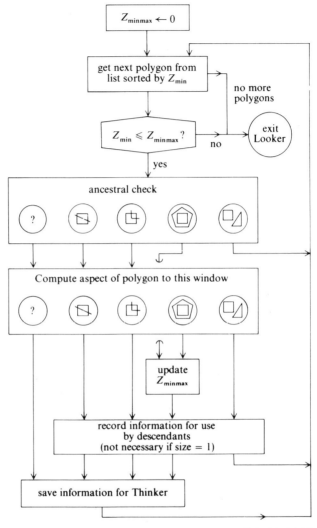

FIGURE 14-15

indicate whether polygons are known to be surrounders or known to be outside certain windows.

In addition, we might save data indicating that a polygon has only one edge in a window and no vertex, or that it has only one vertex in the window and no complete edges, or other data of a similar sort. Keeping records of such data can reduce the number of edges of the polygon which need to be considered in determining whether the polygon is of interest in subdivisions of the window.

The first thing the Looker does with a polygon is to make an ancestral check. The Looker retrieves any information known about that polygon, such as that the polygon was entirely outside some ancestor of the present window. In such a case, of course, the polygon need not be considered further. If the polygon surrounds an ancestor of the present window, it obviously surrounds the present window, and some computation can be avoided.

If the ancestral check fails to yield any information about the polygon, the Looker must compute the spatial relationship between the polygon and the present window. The Looker needs to know if any edge of the polygon passes through the window and if not, whether the polygon surrounds the window or is entirely outside the window, etc. The results of these computations are saved for ancestral checks in case the present window must be subdivided.

The results are also saved for use by the Thinker. In the particular form of Looker and Thinker we give here, the Looker keeps lists of all surrounding and intersecting polygons discovered

().

14.3.3 THE THINKER

The function of the Thinker is to solve the hidden-line problem. If the Looker has found no polygons which surround or intersect the window, clearly the window is blank. Otherwise, the question to be answered by

the Thinker is: does there exist a surrounder (⬚) which hides all

other surrounders and intersectors (⬚ ⬚ ⬚ ?) of the

window?

A simple way of answering this question is to compare the depths (Z_s values) of the planes of the polygons at the four corners of the window

Fig. 12.10

under consideration. If the depth of a surrounder polygon is less than the depths of all other polygons at the corners of the window, then that surrounder indeed hides all other possible features in the window. If we are producing a line-drawing (Figure 14-8a), the window is blank; if we are making a shaded image, we display a shade appropriate to the surrounder polygon surface.

The condition that the surrounder-polygon depth be less than the depths of other polygons at the corners of the window in order to hide the other polygons is sufficient but not necessary. The reason is that, for the purpose of the depth comparison, we are extending the planes of intersector polygons to cover the entire window. If the extended polygon is hidden, so will be the actual polygon. However, a surrounder might hide an intersector but not its extension.

If the depth tests fail to yield a surrounder nearer the eye than all other polygons, the Thinker announces that the situation is too complex to analyze, and the control will suitably subdivide the window.

This simple operation of the Thinker is adequate to solve the hidden-line problem (Figure 14-16). However, many subdivisions can be avoided if we design a slightly more complicated Thinker (compare Figure 14-8c and 14-8d). The more complex the Thinker, the fewer the subdivisions required. However, a complex Thinker might slow the algorithm more than might a few more subdivisions.

The first useful extension to the Thinker is one that enables it to detect the case of 0 surrounders of a window and exactly 1 intersector polygon. If we are generating an outline drawing, clearly every edge or portion of an edge of the intersector which falls within the window should be Displayed by Computation. In this case Display by Computation clips the edges of the intersector polygon against the window and displays any visible lines or portions of lines.

Another extension is detecting the case of a bonafide surrounder (the case where hider = 0 in Figure 14-16) and only one intersector which is not hidden and which lies entirely in front of the surrounder, as shown in Figure 14-17. The solid dots represent depth computations, used to establish that the plane of the intersector polygon lies closer to the eye than the surrounder polygon.

Another extension to the Thinker will process intersecting surfaces correctly. If two polygons intersect, we may desire to show the *implied edge* which appears at the intersection. The line labeled A in Figure 14-8a is such an edge; the tip of the triangle penetrates the square. The

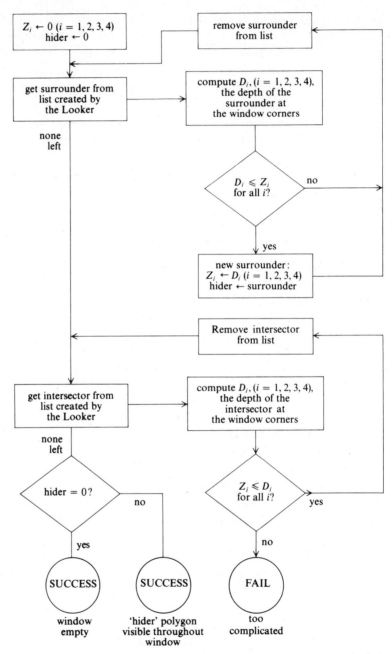

FIGURE 14-16

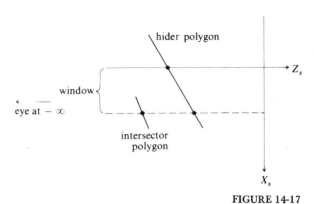

Fig. 12-10

FIGURE 14-17

Thinker of Figure 14-16 must be augmented to check for two surrounders which may *penetrate* each other within the window, as shown in Figure 14-18. The actual display of the implied edge results because windows with penetrating surrounders cause failure of the Thinker and hence cause subdivision. Eventually, the window size reaches 1, and a dot is Displayed by Default.

14.3.4   PERFORMANCE OF THE ALGORITHM

The computation time consumed by the Warnock algorithm is roughly proportional to the complexity of the final display and not proportional to the complexity of the scene. The amount of computation can be gauged by the number of subdivisions required. Subdivisions always result in a displayable feature somewhere within the window being subdivided; therefore computation time is proportional to *visible* complexity. The decision procedure used in the Looker and Thinker can speed processing of various classes of images: we have already shown that the Looker required to process penetrating polygons is more complex than the simple Looker. An evaluation of the performance of several decision procedures is given in [177].

If a shaded display is required, small modifications to the algorithm are necessary. When the Thinker finds a surrounder which hides all other features in the window, only one surface is visible throughout the window, namely the surface of the surrounder. This is enough information to determine the shading intensity for the entire window. Additional logic is needed to compute appropriate intensities for the dots generated when the window size is reduced to one resolution unit.

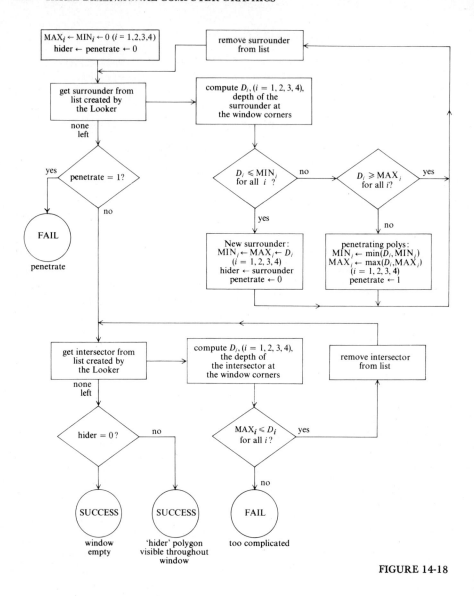

FIGURE 14-18

The output of the algorithm is not convenient for raster-scan displays, because windows are examined according to the goal-searching nature of the algorithm, and not according to ascending or descending Y_s coordinate. An interface between the Warnock algorithm and a raster display has been designed; it demonstrates ingenious use of hardware to drive video displays [47].

14.4   SCAN-LINE ALGORITHMS

Exceptionally realistic pictures of solid objects can be generated by Fig. 12-10 using a raster-scan display such as a television monitor. Generating these pictures requires techniques for removing hidden surfaces and for shading visible surfaces. The principal technique amongst these is the *scan-line algorithm* for hidden-surface elimination: an algorithm that generates a shaded picture on a line-by-line basis, ready for display on a television monitor. Several such algorithms have been developed, making use of some of the techniques used in the earlier hidden-line algorithms. In particular, they use the concept of generating a picture by treating each region of the screen in turn rather than each element of the object; and they use non-deterministic methods in a controlled fashion to resolve complex situations. In addition, two properties of raster-scan images are exploited to increase the efficiency of scan-line algorithms: *scan-line coherence* and geometrical simplification of the three-dimensional space into a two-dimensional space for making decisions about hidden surfaces.

Scan-line coherence is a property of scan-line displays of most scenes: that is, adjacent scan-lines appear very similar. The algorithm takes advantage of the similarities to reduce the computation required for each scan-line to an *incremental* calculation: information saved when processing one scan line is used to speed processing of the next one. The efficiency achieved by scan-line coherence is somewhat analogous to the ancestral checks of the Warnock algorithm and to the advantage the Warnock algorithm achieves from processing blank, uninteresting areas of the screen very rapidly, and concentrating only on those portions where detail is visible.

The geometrical simplification which aids the scan-line algorithms results from the particular choice of *windows* examined by the algorithm: the windows are one scan-line high and span the width of the screen (see Figure 14-19). As in the Warnock algorithm, the windows are positioned in the screen coordinate space. The windows are processed consecutively by ascending or descending Y_s coordinate, just as a raster-scan display might show the scan-lines represented by the windows. Furthermore, within each window the algorithms proceed in a strictly left-to-right manner. The use of a top-to-bottom, left-to-right window-processing strategy insures that display data are generated in the same order as required by the raster scanning hardware.

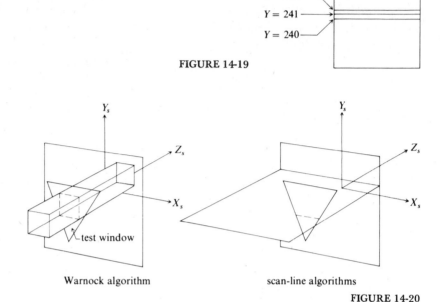

$Y = 242$

$Y = 241$

$Y = 240$

FIGURE 14-19

Warnock algorithm

scan-line algorithms

FIGURE 14-20

The geometrical simplification occurs when a planar polygon in the screen coordinate system is intersected with a scan-line window at Y_s as shown in Figure 14-20. The intersection is a *line* in the Y_s plane. The corresponding intersection with a window of the Warnock algorithm is a *polygon* in three-dimensional screen coordinate space.

The scan-line algorithm must decide what polygons are visible in a scan-line window, and these decisions are all made by comparing *line segments* in the X_s-Z_s plane. The decisions are substantially simpler than those of the Warnock algorithm, which requires comparisons of polygons.

The intersection of the scan-line window and a planar polygon is a collection of line segments. Figure 14-21 shows what segments might look like in the X_s-Y_s plane. On a given scan line, a polygon is described in terms of its segments. The polygon intersects the scan-line window at $Y_s = \alpha$ with one segment. The segment is described by the X_s coordinates of the edges of the polygon which bound the segment. For example, at $Y_s = \alpha$, the segment is bounded by the edges AD and AB. The X_s coordinates for the left and right edges of the segment are simple linear functions of Y_s, i.e. the edge equation is $X_s = a\,Y_s + b$.

Fig. 12-10

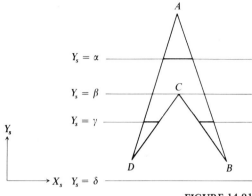

FIGURE 14-21

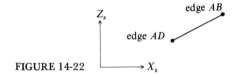

FIGURE 14-22

The polygon of Figure 14-21 viewed from above when $Y_s = \alpha$ is shown in Figure 14-22. The Z_s coordinates of the left and right ends of the segment are just the Z_s coordinates of the edges AD and AB at $Y_s = \alpha$. These coordinates are also simple linear functions of Y_s, i.e. $Z_s = c\,Y_s + d$.

At $Y_s = \beta$, the single segment becomes two segments because two new edges, CD and CB enter in the window at $Y_s = \beta$. Finally, at $Y_s = \delta$, no segments of this polygon remain.

14.4.1   PROCESSING A SCAN-LINE

The hidden-line problem is reduced to deciding, for each scan line, which segments or portions of segments should be displayed. In Figure 14-23, on scan line $Y_s = k$, there are two segments, as shown by the arrows.

This same scan line is drawn differently in Figure 14-24, using the plane of the paper to represent the $Y_s = k$ plane. We can see the depth relationships of the two segments, and also see which parts are hidden by other parts. But the situation could become quite complicated, as shown in Figure 14-25. In this case, the non-deterministic procedure

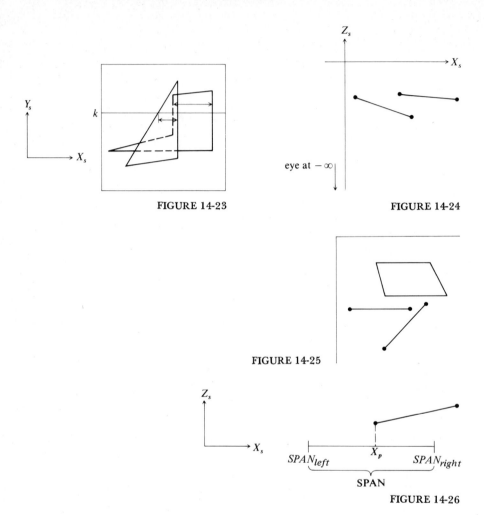

FIGURE 14-23

FIGURE 14-24

FIGURE 14-25

FIGURE 14-26

used to process scan lines announces *failure*. The width of the scan line is divided into smaller sections, or *sample spans*. Each span is defined by its left and right ends, in screen coordinates: $SPAN_{left}$ and $SPAN_{right}$. The same procedure is then applied to these spans.

We can detect several simple cases:

1. Only one segment is in the span (see Figure 14-26). This segment is clearly visible in the region $X_p \leqslant X_s \leqslant SPAN_{right}$. There are actually four similar cases, which are shown in Figure 14-27, and their handling is obvious.

Fig. 12-10

FIGURE 14-27

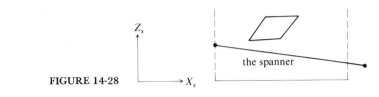

the spanner

FIGURE 14-28

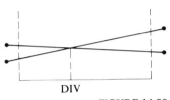

DIV

FIGURE 14-29

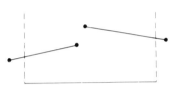

FIGURE 14-30

2. A *spanner* which hides all other segments. A spanner is defined as a segment which extends to or beyond the edges of the sample span (see Figure 14-28). The spanner segment is everywhere nearer the eye than any other segment. Hence it hides the other segments, and is visible in the region $SPAN_{left} \leq X_s \leq SPAN_{right}$.

3. Simple intersection. If only two segments fall inside the span, and they are both spanners, we may have the kind of intersection shown in Figure 14-29. In this case, we can compute the X_s coordinate of the point of intersection. One segment is visible for $SPAN_{left} \leq X_s \leq DIV$, the other for $DIV \leq X_s \leq SPAN_{right}$.

4. Complicated cases. The remainder of cases are considered complicated. Figure 14-30 shows an example. We must subdivide the sample span at some point and try the test procedures again. However, we do not recursively subdivide but instead ask: 'What is the left-most segment endpoint in the span?' and subdivide at that point. If there is no segment endpoint in the span, we divide the span at its midpoint by default.

The reason for dividing at the left-most endpoint is that this hastens our ability to resolve the complicated case. A simple

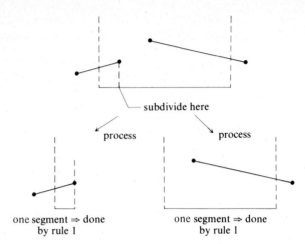

subdivide here

process   process

one segment ⇒ done   one segment ⇒ done
   by rule 1   by rule 1

FIGURE 14-31

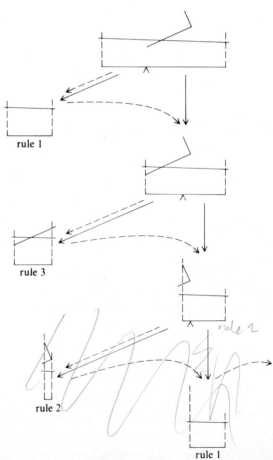

rule 1

rule 3

rule 2

rule 2

rule 1

FIGURE 14-32

Fig. 12-10

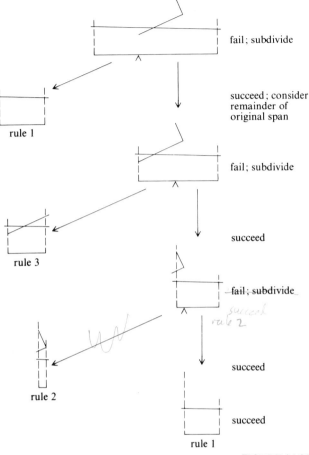

fail; subdivide

succeed; consider
remainder of
original span

rule 1

fail; subdivide

rule 3

succeed

fail; subdivide

succeed
rule 2

rule 2

succeed

succeed

rule 1

FIGURE 14-33

subdivision is shown in Figure 14-31. The example of Figure 14-32 is more complicated. This subdivision process gives a tree of divisions needed to decide on the shading for the original span.

Another subdivision scheme might find the division point, process the left sample-span and then try to process the entire remainder of the original span. The processing procedure is then non-recursive, as shown in Figure 14-33.

14.4.2   SCAN-LINE COHERENCE

The process we have detailed will generate the display for one scan-line from a description of segments on that scan-line. The process can be repeated for successive scan-lines. However, adjacent scan-lines often

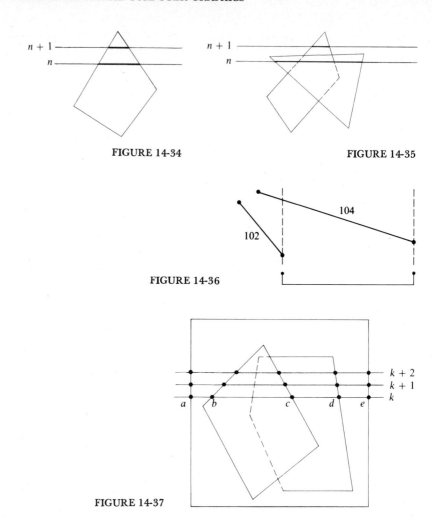

FIGURE 14-34

FIGURE 14-35

FIGURE 14-36

FIGURE 14-37

have very similar displays, as shown in Figure 14-34. Of course, this is not *always* the case, as demonstrated in Figure 14-35.

   Considerable savings in computation time can be made if the algorithm takes advantage of scan-line similarities. A reasonable guess is that if a certain span from one segment endpoint to another, as shown in Figure 14-36, is a simple case on scan line k, then it will also be simple on scan line $k+1$. The span will be a *predicted sample span* for scan-line $k+1$. Predicted sample spans are determined by positions of segment edges, and not by particular X_s values. As we move from scan

Fig. 12-10

line k to $k+1$, the X_s position of the edge will change, and our predicted sample span must change accordingly. Thus it is convenient to describe the predicted sample spans as 'from the right edge of segment 102 to the right edge of segment 104.' If, at any time, one of these edges exits or becomes hidden, we cease prediction of that span.

Stated differently, we use the record of subdivisions on scan line k to predict fruitful subdivisions for scan line $k+1$.

As an example, the heavy dots in Figure 14-37 divide each scan line into predicted sample spans. The dots are called *predicted sample points*. Thus the four sample spans *ab, bc, cd, de* will subdivide the entire scan line such that the decisions for each of the four spans are simple cases, i.e. they do not require further subdivision. With excellent scan-line to scan-line coherence, we should rarely need to subdivide a span.

14.4.3   IMPLEMENTATION AND PERFORMANCE

A variety of scan-line algorithms has been created; the discussion above is taken from the algorithm of Watkins [301], which was designed to be implemented in hardware and utilizes the non-determinism, windowing and screen-coordinate concepts of the Warnock algorithm. This algorithm was derived from earlier work by Wylie, Romney, *et al* [318, 238]. Another algorithm, designed by Bouknight [28, 29] uses explicit computation to avoid the non-deterministic behavior of the Warnock algorithm, but does not employ scan-line coherence speedups.

The scan-line algorithm described above is quite fast, although its dependence on complexity of the scene is difficult to analyze. Watkins tabulated the performance of the algorithm for a variety of scenes and discovered that the computation grows roughly as the *visible* complexity increases.

The algorithm can be implemented in software (Appendix VII) or hardware.* The hardware implementation is inexpensive compared to previous hardware techniques [246] and can generate images of quite complicated scenes in real time. By real time we mean that the calculations required to generate display information take no longer than the raster-scan of the frame.

---

* At the University of Utah, Watkins has built prototype equipment that implements his algorithm.

14.5   SHADING

The final step in a hidden-surface elimination must include calculating the *intensity* used to display the representation of a visible surface. The realism of the display depends on this calculation. We may wish to create certain visual effects:

1. Texture.
2. Specular reflection.
3. Shadows.
4. Reflection of scattered light from uniform surfaces.

In addition, the calculation might attempt to deal correctly with many of the variables affecting the viewed intensity:

1. Distance and angle of surfaces with respect to the light source.
2. Spectral components of the simulated or fictional light source.
3. Reflectance properties of surfaces (and color distribution).
4. Non-linearities in the display system.
5. Emission characteristics of the CRT phosphor.
6. Characteristics of any color filters placed over the screen.
7. Deficiencies in the human visual system (e.g. Mach band effect).

Accurate shading calculations based on all these effects are expensive. Fortunately, quite adequate pictures may be produced without considering many of the complicated visual and optical effects. The shading calculations described below are known to work, although they do not represent accurate models of physics and psychophysics.

Calculating the brightness of an object as seen by the eye is quite complicated unless some simplifying assumptions are made. First, we observe that the light energy density on a surface is proportional to $\cos \theta_i / r^2$ where θ_i is the angle between a normal to the surface and a vector to the light source, and r is the distance from the surface to the light source. Second, we make the approximation that light is *scattered* as a function of $\cos \theta_v$, where θ_v is the angle between the surface normal and a vector to the viewer. Specularly-reflected light energy can be assumed to vary as $(\cos (\theta_v + \theta_i))^n$. Large values of n (about 10) cause a surface to appear more shiny than do small values (about 0.5). Third, we observe that the perceived brightness of a surface is proportional to $1/ \cos \theta_v$. This arises because light from an oblique surface produces a higher energy density on the retina than that from a non-oblique surface (see Figure 14-38).

retinal image

Fig. 12-10

FIGURE 14-38

These three observations can be combined to yield an expression for the brightness of a surface resulting from scattered light:
$(\cos \theta_i / r^2) \cos \theta_v (1/ \cos \theta_v) = \cos \theta_i / r^2 .$

A simple shading rule to calculate an intensity s for a one-color display is:

$$s = a (\cos \theta_i) + b \quad (14\text{-}11)$$

where θ_i is the angle between a normal to the surface and a vector to the light source; a and b control the magnitude of numbers presented to the display hardware. The light source can be assumed to be in any position, but it is convenient to locate it at the same point as the eye. The parameter a may be a function of the surface being displayed; it corresponds roughly to the reflectance of the surface.

A somewhat better rule is:

$$s = \frac{a_1 (\cos \theta_i) + a_2 (\cos \theta_i)^n}{r + c} + b \quad (14\text{-}12)$$

where r is the distance from the light source to the surface, and n controls specular reflection, as described above. The equation only simulates specular reflection of a light source located at the eye, and not reflection of other *surfaces* in the scene. The denominator of the rule causes illumination to fall off as the reciprocal of the distance from the light source. Strictly speaking, illumination decreases as $1/r^2$. However, if the light source is located at the eye position, this produces very stark pictures. Normally, scenes are lit by scattered light or by point sources *very* far away.

The shading rule can be generalized for three-color displays:

$$s_{red} = \frac{R(\cos \theta_i) + W(\cos \theta_i)^n}{r + c} + b \quad (14\text{-}13)$$

$$s_{green} = \frac{G(\cos \theta_i) + W(\cos \theta_i)^n}{r + c} + b$$

$$s_{blue} = \frac{B(\cos \theta_i) + W(\cos \theta_i)^n}{r + c} + b$$

The parameters W and n controls the specular reflection component. Note that specular reflection is white, i.e. composed of equal parts of red, green and blue.

The triple (R,G,B) controls the hue and brightness of a surface. Let α be the minimum of R, G and B. Hue is determined by the *ratios* $(R-\alpha):(G-\alpha):(B-\alpha)$. Brightness can be thought of as being a function of $R+G+B$. Saturation of the color, or the purity of the color, is roughly inversely proportional to α. Roughly speaking, α is the amount of white in the reflected light from a surface; the more white light reflected, the less saturated the color. Hue is the ratio of color components, not counting the constant white component α. Brightness is a measure of the total amount of reflected light. These are rules of thumb and are not physically accurate.

The parameters R, G and B can be adjusted to yield any desired color. However, the human terminology for colors is misleading when adjusting these parameters. The values of R, G and B for saturated colors are:

```
'red'    = ( 0.20 , 0    , 0)
'green'  = ( 0    , 0.15 , 0)
'blue'   = ( 0    , 0    , 0.05)
'yellow' = ( 0.70 , 0.70 , 0)
```

Notice that 'yellow' requires a much higher reflectance than 'red' or 'blue.'

14.5.1   HARDWARE CONSIDERATIONS

The ability of the shading rules to reflect nuances of shading vastly exceeds the ability of most displays to present the nuances to the eye. Eight intensity levels are certainly insufficient. A television monitor with 40 MHz bandwidth offers about 32 intensity values for each dot. A method of displaying 256 levels is probably required for effective color displays and for high quality black and white pictures.

The intensity of a point is usually modulated by varying the energy used to excite the phosphor on the CRT screen. However, the response of the phosphor is non-linear and tends to saturate (see Figure 14-39). The low dynamic range of most phosphors makes them unsuitable for presenting a large number of intensity levels.

A very accurate method of controlling the intensity of a dot is

Fig. 12-10

FIGURE 14-39

dwell-time control: the exciting energy is constant and remains active for a length of time proportional to the desired intensity. This method is not suited to raster-scan systems which must operate at a fixed rate, but is usually quite easily implemented on a conventional computer display.

If an image is to be accurately recorded on film, the properties of the film must be included in the shading calculation. Film has a highly non-linear response to incident light; the process of developing and printing a negative involves variables which affect the contrast and brightness of the picture. Treatments of photometric properties of film and the eye can be found elsewhere (see Bibliography listings).

Careful display of images also requires accurate, noise-free deflection electronics. Figure 12-4 was created with a conventional CRT display with only 7 intensity levels. Many irregularities were caused by the deflection system. By contrast, Figures 14-2, 14-40 and 14-45 were all created with a precision CRT at the University of Utah.

14.5.2   CONTINUOUS SHADING

Curved surfaces are often represented by a series of nearly-planar polygons (see Figure 14-2). Gouraud has developed a remarkably simple technique for restoring the smooth appearance of these surfaces (Figure 14-40, [104]). The method depends on a simple linear interpolation of intensity values, based on intensities calculated for the vertices of the approximating polygons (see Figure 14-41). The intensity I_a is a linear interpolation between intensities I_1 and I_2; similarly I_b lies between I_3 and I_2. A dot on the visible segment has an intensity which is interpolated between I_a and I_b.

Linear interpolation is extremely easily implemented, although it does not, of course, really represent the correct intensity variation inside the polygonal approximation to the surface; calculations of the angle between the light source and the normal to the surface at every

FIGURE 14-40

Fig. 12-10

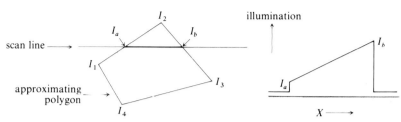

FIGURE 14-41

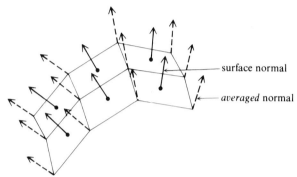

FIGURE 14-42

point would be required for precisely correct shading. Gouraud investigated more complicated interpolation techniques, and concluded that they consumed much more computer time than linear interpolation but added little to the realism of the picture.

The key to realistic shading is in determining values for I_1, I_2, I_3, and I_4, the intensities at the vertices of the polygon. A shading equation such as Equation 14-11 can be used to calculate an intensity, provided we have calculated a vector normal to the surface at the polygon vertex. A simple method to compute a normal at a vertex is to average the normals of all surrounding polygons, as shown in Figure 14-42.

This method becomes more accurate as smaller polygons are used to describe a curved surface. However, a large number of polygons slows the hidden-surface elimination procedure. As a result, it is preferable to limit the number of polygons used to describe a surface and rely on the shading interpolation to create a good visual impression of the surface.

There are, however, several cases which require that polygons be added in order to make the shading appear reasonable. Consider the surface shown in Figure 14-43a, represented by the polygons of Figure

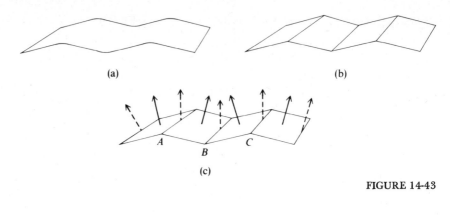

(a)

(b)

(c)

FIGURE 14-43

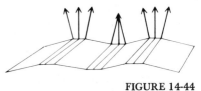

FIGURE 14-44

FIGURE 14-45

14-43b. The normals are computed as shown in Figure 14-43c. The normals at A, B and C are identical because of the averaging; thus the intensity between A and C will be constant and incorrect.

If we add several polygons to the representation of the surface, correct shading is generated, as shown in Figure 14-44. Using normals computed by averaging these polygon normals, the interpolated display looks like Figure 14-45. (The shading rule used to generate Figure 14-45 causes intensity to vary as $\cos^5 \theta_i$, giving the surface a shiny metallic appearance).

The facility for linear shading interpolation can be added quite simply to the Watkins scan-line algorithm: each segment description is

Fig. 12-10

expanded to specify the intensities I_a and I_b of the left and right edges. These have associated incremental values which specify the interpolation along an edge of the polygon. Whenever a portion of the segment is visible on a scan line, the values of I_a and I_b are used to calculate intensity values for visible points.

14.6   CONCLUSION

The hidden-surface techniques presented in this chapter are not yet sufficient to produce images of all possible scenes. In particular, the shading algorithms must be more accurate and more complex to produce realistic pictures. No techniques exist for dealing with specular reflections, translucence, or diffuse light sources; however, Bouknight and Kelley have developed a scan-line algorithm which shows shadows from single or multiple light sources [30].

Techniques for representing three-dimensional objects are also primitive. Much work is currently underway to find methods of describing curves and surfaces so that mathematical and display operations may be performed easily (see the Bibliography listings). Good representations may also yield techniques for manipulating objects interactively.

The hidden-line and hidden-surface algorithms themselves are not yet optimal: each has disadvantages, inefficiencies, and mistakes. However, the basic properties of these algorithms may one day be unified into an understanding of the nature of the process of hidden-surface elimination. Consider, for example, the sorting processes involved in the Warnock and Watkins algorithms. These algorithms both examine windows on the screen — the objects are sorted into these windows and then objects within each window are sorted by depth to determine which object is visible. The algorithms use different techniques for sorting: the Watkins algorithm sorts objects by Y into one of 1024 buckets, then uses a bubble sort to sort segments by X, and finally uses a one-to-one comparison of the depth of every object within a span to establish which object is visible. The Warnock algorithm sorts objects on X and Y coordinate values into windows using the Looker, a very complex comparison of objects to windows; objects within a window are sorted by depth with a one-to-one comparison. The algorithm uses a radix 4 sort in X and Y: if a window is subdivided, the objects which intersected that window are sorted into one or more of four smaller windows. The Watkins sort is faster, sorting X and Y with a radix 1024 bucket sort and a bubble sort of any segments on a scan-line. These observations suggest that hidden-line elimination may *inherently* involve sorting objects by X, Y and Z coordinates; the design of an efficient algorithm will require study of various sorting strategies and methods.

Further research on half-tone computer graphics will doubtless yield very realistic pictures, and may produce algorithms for hidden-surface elimination which are as elegant and natural as clipping and windowing are for two-dimensional graphics. This work may culminate in hidden-surface elimination and shading algorithms fast enough to support truly interactive half-tone graphics.

EXERCISES

14-1. Suggest modifications to the output of the scan-line algorithm which would yield *lines* for the visible *edges*, so that an outline drawing could be generated.

14-2. Suggest modifications to the Warnock algorithm so each visible line fragment is described by a single line rather than by a series of dots (see Figure 14-46).

14-3. How would you represent an open box, such as that shown in Figure 14-47, for the purposes of the Roberts algorithm? The clumsiness of the method suggests that a surface costs as much as a volume in computation. This also suggests a basic difference in philosophy between Roberts' technique and the other two algorithms. What is it?

14-4. Compare the Lookers and Thinkers of the Warnock and scan-line algorithms.

14-5. The three algorithms make various provisions for clipping. Roberts includes an explicit clipping step which correctly clips all lines. The Warnock algorithm will clip against the edges of the viewbox, simply because windows examined never venture outside the box, but the clipping fails for lines through the $Z_e = 0$ plane. The Watkins algorithm only clips against the left and right edges of the screen; if

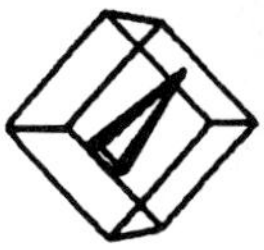

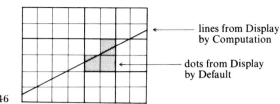

Fig. 12-10

FIGURE 14-46

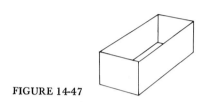

FIGURE 14-47

objects extend off the top and bottom, the algorithm will not produce a correct display. It also handles lines through the $Z_e = 0$ plane incorrectly.

1. How does Roberts avoid the problem of objects which pass through the $Z_e = 0$ plane, demonstrated in Section 13.4?
2. Can you suggest changes to the Watkins and Warnock algorithms which will deal correctly with objects off the screen?
3. Design a *polygon clipper* which takes as input polygons in eye coordinates (specified as an ordered list of vertices) and yields clipped polygons in eye coordinates (see Figure 14-48). Then the clipped polygons can safely be transformed into screen coordinates and passed to any of the three hidden-line algorithms. (Better still, design the polygon clipper to operate on homogeneous coordinate vectors describing points already in screen space).

14-6. Can you suggest a mechanism for automatically introducing new polygons to a surface description in order to avoid the mistaken shading (e.g. Figure 14-44)?

14-7. Describe in detail how the Roberts algorithm depends on *convexity* of polyhedra.

14-8. Demonstrate that the procedure outlined in Equation 14-5 has the right effect.

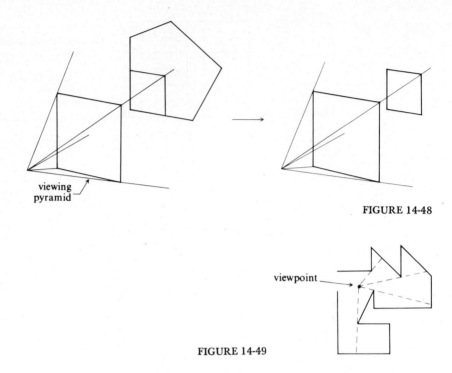

viewing
pyramid

FIGURE 14-48

viewpoint

FIGURE 14-49

14-9. Prove that both X_s and Z_s are linear functions of Y_s in screen coordinates (Section 14.4).

14-10. Write an algorithm for solving the hidden-line problem on a plane. You might choose to visualize this as a maze problem: a person is located in a two-dimensional maze. What walls or portions of walls can he see? See Figure 14-49.

PART FIVE

Graphics Systems

COMMAND LANGUAGES

15.1   COMMAND LANGUAGES AND DIALOGUES

The user of an interactive program must be provided with a set of *commands* by which to control the program. These commands fulfil two functions: they control which processes are activated; and they contain the data that is to be passed to these processes. For example, the user may create a picture, and then type the following in order to save a copy of the picture he has drawn:

SAVE PIC23

SAVE tells the program which process is to be invoked (the picture-saving process). PIC23 is the data for this process — the name under which the picture is to be filed.

It is generally advisable to define with some precision the range of commands that the program will accept, and to define the form or *syntax* of each command. There are two reasons for doing this. Firstly, the user then knows what commands he may use, and what form they should take; secondly, the program knows what commands to expect and how to separate the data from the control information. By defining the range of commands and their syntax, we define a *command language*, the language 'spoken' by the user as he operates the program. As he addresses the computer in this way, the computer addresses him, by means of displayed pictures and printed messages. In this way a *dialogue* is maintained.

These are familiar issues to a graphics application programmer: every time he writes an interactive program, he must provide a command language for its control. His choice of command language will often play a significant part in determining the success or failure of the program. It is therefore surprising to find that, despite the importance of command languages, relatively little has been done to make these languages easier to design and implement. In this chapter we shall discuss command languages and their characteristics, and shall look at some methods for defining them.

15.2 THE FEATURES OF A COMMAND LANGUAGE

Command languages tend to be quite different from the procedural languages used for writing programs. They differ both in their appearance and in their implementation. In appearance they are usually a great deal simpler, without any of the complex constructions for defining iterative or conditional operations. They differ in implementation because there is generally no need to compile commands into object code or to create a stored program of commands. In fact to do so would delay execution of each command, and this is rarely acceptable to the user. Instead the command is interpreted as it is received from the user, either by the application program or by a special task scheduler. Once the command has been interpreted, it is discarded by the program.

15.2.1 COMMAND LANGUAGE SYNTAX

We can learn a great deal about command language implementation by looking at the sorts of command language syntax that are used in graphics programs. We find that most commands[*] consist of a number

---

[*] For the purposes of this discussion, a *command* is defined to be any input or sequence of inputs that activates a process within the user program or modifies the user data base.

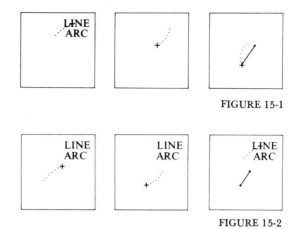

FIGURE 15-1

FIGURE 15-2

of elements, each specified by a separate user action. Examples of typical command elements are points and strokes specified with the stylus, light-button inputs, typed numbers and strings, function-key and push-button inputs. Each element serves one or more of the following functions:

1. It may act as the *verb* of the command, i.e. it may define what process is to be performed. An example of a verb element is the word SAVE in the command SAVE PIC23.
2. It may specify *data* for the program, as in PIC23.
3. It may act as the *delimiter* for a verb or data element. For example, SAVE is delimited by a space, PIC23 by a carriage-return.

Commands generally contain all three types of element. It is possible for one element to serve two functions: a push-button, for example, may act both as a verb and as the delimiter to a stroke of the stylus.

Most command languages place the verb either at the beginning or at the end of the command. For example, a stylus command to draw a line could take either of the following forms:

<point at LINE light button> <input point> <input point>
<input point> <input point> <point at LINE light button>

These two forms of the command are illustrated by the sequences of Figures 15-1 and 15-2. The first form, with the verb leading, is the most common, for it is easy to process and permits a wide variety of syntax following the verb. The trailing verb must generally be preceded by data

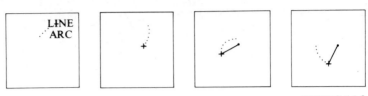

FIGURE 15-3

elements in a fairly rigidly defined sequence. The elements that follow a leading verb may include *subsidiary verbs* that control special subprocesses.

Use of the leading verb has a second advantage: it permits the program to respond in the appropriate way to *each* succeeding element of the command. For example, it could respond to the second element of the LINE command by starting a rubber-band line (see the sequence of Figure 15-3). This *feedback* effect is often essential in complex graphical operations, and cannot be provided if the verb is at the end of the command.

15.2.2   OTHER FEATURES OF COMMAND LANGUAGES

When we set out to design a command language, it is vital to consider how many different input devices are to be used. Some command languages make use of a wide variety of devices. For example, graphical data may be specified by a stylus, frequently-used verbs by function keys, less common verbs by strings of text on the keyboard, and so on. Other languages are based on the use of a single device, generally either the keyboard or a coordinate input device. While each approach can claim to be more efficient in one sense or another, the single-device approach often leads to simpler, more easily learned command languages. We shall see later that single-device command languages are also somewhat easier to implement.

It is desirable to be able to change the command language of a program easily, so that additional commands may be added, and so that concise commands may be provided for frequently performed operations. This can be provided at two different levels, one involving the programmer, the other the user. It should always be possible for the programmer to modify the command language with the minimum of effort and recompilation. A rather more sophisticated concept is introduced in the case of *user-extensible* command languages. They generally provide the user with special commands for defining *macros,* i.e. shorthand notations that the language processor will expand into full commands. He can in this way tailor the command language to his own personal needs. However, this idea is often rather difficult to explain to the user who has had little contact with computer programming.

15.3   COMMAND LANGUAGE DEFINITION

Within every interactive program there must be a definition of the program's command language. The command language may be defined explicitly by means of some form of table, or it may be implicit in the sequencing of input statements. In this section we shall discuss both methods of definition. To illustrate the methods we shall take a very simple example of a command language. It consists of four commands:

RIGHT n
LEFT n
FORWARD n
BACK n

Initially we shall assume that these commands are to be typed at a keyboard (n is any numerical value). The first two commands activate a procedure ROTATE, passing it and n and $-n$ respectively as argument; the second two activate the procedure MOVE, again with argument n and $-n$.

15.3.1   USE OF CONVENTIONAL PROGRAMMING LANGUAGES

We can program this example in any language that contains rudimentary string-processing facilities. For example, it can be programmed as follows in SAIL:

```
WHILE TRUE DO
 BEGIN REAL N; STRING S;
  S←INTEXT; N←INVAL;
  IF EQU(S,"RIGHT") THEN ROTATE(N) ELSE
  IF EQU(S,"LEFT") THEN ROTATE(−N) ELSE
  IF EQU(S,"FORWARD") THEN MOVE(N) ELSE
  IF EQU(S,"BACK") THEN MOVE(−N) ELSE ERROR
 END
```

This program is obviously a rather cumbersome and indirect expression of a very simple command language. The main reason for this is that the program is effectively not only a command language definition but a task scheduler: it receives inputs from the keyboard and activates the appropriate procedures. Every time we implement a command language in this fashion we must write all the input statements, all the statements that test the inputs and check for errors, and all the procedure calls. It is easy to make mistakes in doing this, and the program is difficult to modify.

A more serious problem with most conventional programming languages is that they do not permit more than one input device to be polled at a time. Input functions like INTEXT incorporate the *dynamic stop* at which the program pauses until input is received; in this way they prevent any other device from being polled. Thus it would not be possible to modify our SAIL program to accept either a light button input or a keyboard command. If we intend to use multiple-device command languages, it is highly desirable to separate the dynamic stop from the input function and thus allow more than one device to be polled at a time. Very few conventional programming languages allow this to be done.

15.3.2   LANGUAGE EXTENSIONS FOR COMMAND PROCESSING

It is relatively easy to add polling facilities to a programming language, giving it the ability to deal with multiple input devices. For example, the SAIL program could be extended to permit light button commands by adding to the language a WAIT function to wait for the next input, and a DEVICE function that returns the identity of the device causing the input:

```
WHILE TRUE DO
  BEGIN REAL N; STRING S;
    "DISPLAY FOUR LIGHT BUTTONS"
    LIGHTBUTTONS("RIGHT","LEFT","FORWARD","BACK");
    WAIT;
    "DEVICE 1=KEYBOARD, 2=LIGHT-BUTTON"
    IF DEVICE=1
      THEN S←INTEXT ELSE
    IF DEVICE=2
      THEN S←LBTEXT
```

```
        ELSE ERROR; "STORE LIGHT BUTTON TEXT IN S"
        N←INVAL;
        IF EQU(S,"RIGHT") THEN ROTATE(N) ELSE
        IF EQU(S,"LEFT") THEN ROTATE(−N) ELSE
        IF EQU(S,"FORWARD") THEN MOVE(N) ELSE
        IF EQU(S,"BACK") THEN MOVE(−N) ELSE ERROR
    END
```

Notice that the introduction of a choice of input device has lengthened the program considerably. This is one of the problems with defining command languages implicitly by means of conventional programming methods.

15.3.3   LANGUAGE PROCESSORS

As command languages become more complex, the use of conventional procedural languages in the fashion described above becomes more and more impractical. Moreover it is very difficult to accommodate the natural tendency for command languages to *evolve* — to acquire new commands, to discard others. Adding new commands to a program written in the above manner is a tiresome job.

These problems can be avoided by using a separate, *table-driven* task scheduler. The table contains a description of each command in the language, together with the name of the process to be activated by the command. Whenever a command is received, the task scheduler searches through the table until it finds a matching command description, and then activates the procedure. Figure 15-4 shows a typical table, which will match any of the commands in our earlier four-command example.

A task scheduler that is table-driven in this manner can handle a number of different command languages: to implement a new language, or modify an existing one, it is necessary only to generate a new table. Such a task scheduler is generally called a *language processor*.

15.3.4   THE MULTIPATCH SYSTEM

The basic issues involved in language processor design are well illustrated by the following example. This is the *Multipatch* system for designing curved-surface objects, developed by Andrew Armit at Cambridge University [8]. The system is designed to run in an 8K

RIGHT	1	ROTATE (n)
LEFT	1	ROTATE (−n)
FORWARD	1	MOVE (n)
BACK	1	MOVE (−n)

FIGURE 15-4

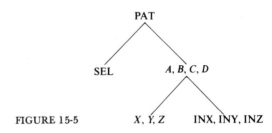

FIGURE 15-5

PDP-7 with display, and includes a table-driven language processor with interesting properties.

Although Multipatch is intrinsically a graphical system, it uses a non-graphical command language. Armit prefers the use of the keyboard over the light pen on the grounds of efficiency and convenience. A great deal of ingenuity has gone into making it possible to type powerful commands made up of as few characters as possible.

The system uses a leading-verb command syntax, and defines command syntax in the form of a *tree*. For example, Figure 15-5 shows part of the syntax of the PATCH command. Examples of commands that fit into this syntax are:

PAT SEL 3	select patch no. 3
PAT A X 30	set the x-coordinate of corner A of the patch to 30
PAT A INY 10	add 10 to the y-coordinate of corner A
PAT C INY −20	subtract 20 from the y-coordinate of corner C
PAT C INY 20	add 20 to the y-coordinate of corner C

Each of these commands can be traced through the tree structure, starting at the top. The language processor does not begin its search at the top, however, but at the last node of the previous command. If this does not lead to a match, the node one level higher is used, and so on

```
XK1: PAT
      XK2            /transfer to table XK2 on 'PAT'
      −1             /end of table
XK2: SEL
      JMP ADR1 /jump to ADR1 to select given patch
      A
      XK3
      B
      XK3
      C
      XK3
      D
      XK3
      −1
XK3: X
      JMP ADR2
      Y
      JMP ADR2
      Z
      JMP ADR2
      INX
      JMP ADR3
      INY
      JMP ADR3
      INZ
      JMP ADR3
      −1
```

FIGURE 15-6

until the top of the tree is reached. The processor allows other kinds of abbreviations: for example, the most recent command may be retracted by typing a minus sign. Thus the command sequence given above could be shortened to:

```
PAT SEL 3
A X 30
INY 10
C INY −20
−
```

The tables for Multipatch are defined as simple lists of alternating commands and addresses. For example, Figure 15-6 shows the table corresponding to the tree of Figure 15-5. As each command is processed, pointers are set up, indicating which symbol was encountered at each level. These pointers are used when the command is obeyed to determine the command parameters; they also provide historical data for use in parsing the next command. This together with a small set of string- and number-processing subroutines, is all that is required to construct the Multipatch language processor.

Armit introduced a number of restrictions into the Multipatch language processor in order to accommodate the entire design system in such a small machine. For example, each command may include only one numerical item. A more recent system by Armit, called *Multiobject* [9], removes many of these restrictions. It contains various extensions such as methods of defining iterative operations, and *macros* to enable frequently used commands to be shortened. The Multiobject system uses the PDP-7 as a satellite to a larger machine called Titan.

15.4   CONTROL ORIENTED LANGUAGES

Command languages more complex than the ones just described are generally best defined by using some form of table-definition language. In some cases, a single language is used to code both the table and the procedures to which it refers. This was done in the DIAL language (see Section 15.4.3). However, a more popular approach is to use a separate language for defining the table. This approach treats the task scheduler as a separate processor, for which the table is in effect an interpretive program. This is conceptually a rather more elegant strategy, and it also has practical advantages: a standard programming language may be used, without modification, for writing the procedures; and it is possible to link a variety of such languages with the table-definition language. We shall adopt the term *control-oriented language* to describe those languages that are used to define a command language in this way. We shall distinguish them from conventional programming languages by calling the latter *procedure-oriented languages*.

Much of the difficulty in devising control-oriented languages for computer graphics stems from the the need to use multiple input devices. Adding this additional factor means that before the language processor can examine the *data* content of a command it must determine from which *device* or *devices* the command originated. The second SAIL program (see Section 15.3.2) demonstrates how this can complicate input programming; and this is a particularly simple example. Complex graphical command languages demand a special type of control-oriented language if they are to be specified with any ease.

15.4.1   THE FINITE-STATE ANALOGY

Suppose we were to monitor a typical interactive program, by taking regular samples of its activity. We might sometimes find it engaged in display file compilation, sometimes manipulating the data base,

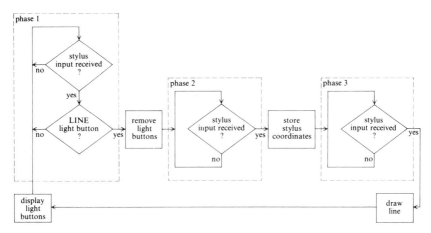

FIGURE 15-7

sometimes generating output files. In the great majority of cases, however, we would find it waiting for input. An interactive program generally obeys the user's requests very rapidly, and can therefore respond to the user much more rapidly than he can respond to it. While it waits for the next command, the program can do little more than poll the input devices; effectively it becomes completely inactive.

These periods of inactivity occur not only after each command has been processed, but after each *element* of a command has been received. Suppose the user defines a line on the screen as suggested in Section 15.2.1:

<point at LINE light button> <input point> <input point>

After receiving the light-button input, the program removes the light button, for it is no longer of use, and removal of it provides the user with valuable feedback. The program then waits for the first point to be received from the stylus. After it has received the point and stored it away, the program must then wait for the second point. Only when it has received the second point can the program draw the line; it then restores the menu and returns to wait for a fresh light-button input.

Thus the program passes through three waiting phases before it draws the line: these three phases are shown in Figure 15-7. During each phase the program is in fact waiting for a stylus input; however its *response* to stylus inputs is different in each case. If the user provides a stylus input during the first phase, the program tests to see if the stylus position is

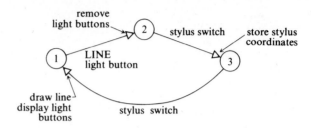

FIGURE 15-8

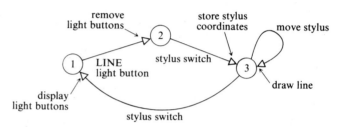

FIGURE 15-9

close to a light button. It it is, it removes the light button menu. In the second phase, the program responds to a stylus input by storing the input coordinates; in the third it responds by drawing a line. So although the program appears to be waiting in the same fashion in each case, it is in fact in a completely different *state*.

We can redraw the flow chart of Figure 15-7 much more compactly, as shown in Figure 15-8. Here we have borrowed the symbology of finite state machines, and have collapsed each of the phases of the flow diagram into a single circular *state* symbol. The *processes* that the program performs between states are shown as triangular arrowheads. The edges or *branches* in the diagram denote the command elements.

A very large variety of command languages can be represented by diagrams of this sort. For example, suppose we were to rewrite the program to draw a rubber-band line between receiving the first stylus input and receiving the second. This program could be represented as shown in Figure 15-9, by adding an extra branch to state 3 denoting the *action* of moving the pen, and the corresponding *reaction* by the program of redrawing the line. Our earlier four-command example is shown in Figure 15-10.

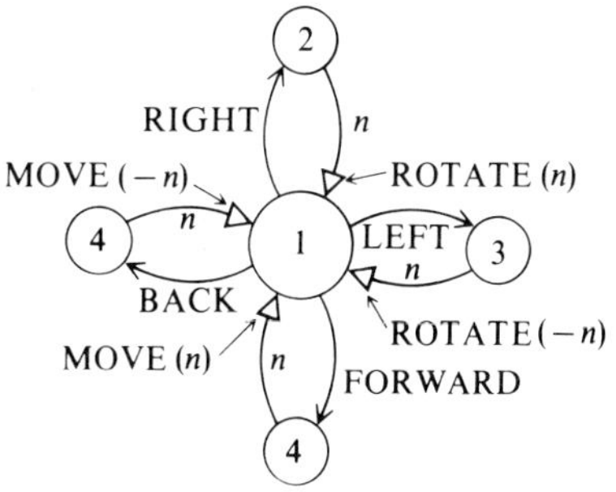

FIGURE 15-10

15.4.2 THE REACTION HANDLER

If we can provide the language processor with a description of the state diagram, together with a means of linking to the right procedures, we can use the state diagram as our definition of the command language. This has been done in a number of systems that used the term *Reaction Handler* to refer to this state-diagram-driven language processor.

The first implementation of the Reaction Handler was on a PDP-7 computer at Imperial College, London [200]. The state diagram was defined by means of a simple assembly language, which used some rather obscure terminology such as SE to denote the state entered by a branch, IEX (or 'instruction for execution') to name the process to be executed. From this state diagram description a ring-structured table was generated for use by the Reaction Handler. Processes were defined separately in assembly language.

A second version was implemented at Harvard University on a PDP-1 computer [198]. In this case the choice was provided of defining the state diagram either in an assembly language, similar to the earlier one but with some of the obscurities removed, or graphically using the display and RAND Tablet. Figure 15-11 shows a state diagram drawn in this way, representing a rubber-band line drawing program. Figure 15-12 shows the text definition of the same command language. State diagrams defined in either fashion were compiled incrementally into tables, and since the compiler included a Reaction Handler, the command language could be tested during definition. It was possible to convert graphical definitions into text, and by means of special positioning statements to convert text into graphics. The graphical version of the compiler, together with the DECAL language [180] in which processes were written, formed a very powerful system for defining interactive programs.

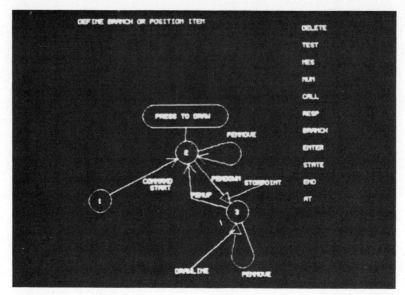

FIGURE 15-11

state 1
  branch command
  mes start
  enter 2

state 2
  branch penmove
  branch pendown
  call storpoint
  enter 3

state 3
  branch penmove
  call drawline
  branch pendown
  enter 2

FIGURE 15-12

15.4.3   THE DIAL LANGUAGE

The two early implementations of the Reaction Handler both adopted the approach of using separate languages, one *control-oriented* and the other *procedure-oriented*, to define the program. This was to some extent a matter of expediency — it avoided the need to implement or modify a procedure-oriented language. It also enabled the control-oriented language to be optimized in favor of its specific task. However, it created systems that were fairly complex and difficult to use.

The DIAL language [201], developed at the University of Utah, represents an attempt to provide both the state-diagram facility and the procedure-definition facility in a single high-level language. The language chosen was a subset of Algol 60; it was implemented on the PDP-10 computer with the aid of the Tree-Meta compiler-compiler [40]. DIAL includes the facility to generate graphical output by means of display procedures (see Chapter 8), and contains four extra statement types for defining the command language. These are the DURING statement, the ENTERING statement, the ON statement and the ENTER statement.

State N of a DIAL program is defined by writing:

DURING N DO <statement>

The subsidiary statement may be either a single ON statement defining a single branch, or a group of ON statements forming a compound statement. Change of state is specified by means of the ENTER statement. For example, the line-drawing routine could be written as follows:

```
DURING 1 DO
  ON LBUT "LINE" DO ENTER 2;
DURING 2 DO
  ON PENDOWN DO BEGIN
    X←PENX; Y←PENY;
    ENTER 3
  END;
DURING 3 DO
  ON PENDOWN DO BEGIN
    DRAWLINE(X,Y,PENX,PENY);
    ENTER 1
  END;
```

The ENTERING statement allows procedures to be executed every time a certain state is entered. For example, if the system were not to create light-button menus automatically, they could be added as follows:

ENTERING 1 DO LB("LINE","ARC");

It is also possible to use the DURING ALL statement to define commands that take effect whatever the state of the program. This provides a simple means of restarting any program no matter what state it is in.

15.4.4   USING THE STATE-DIAGRAM TECHNIQUE

For many types of command language, a state-diagram based definition language is very convenient; in some cases it provides the only simple means of defining the language. For other styles of command language the technique creates problems. For example, if we were to extend our earlier four-command language to 40 commands, we should require 41 states. If each of the 40 commands required two data elements instead of one, the number of states would rise to 81. Thus the state diagram technique may produce very complex programs defining quite simple command languages.

It is also possible to produce unsatisfactory command languages in this way, because of the freedom with which program states may be added. Since the program responds differently in each state, the user is likely to become confused unless he is very clearly guided by means of directions from the program.

The first of these problems could be solved by providing an alternative form of input besides the implicit polling loop. For example, the four-command language could be as follows, using an INVAL function to read a number from the keyboard:

```
DURING 1 DO
  BEGIN
    ON COMMAND "RIGHT" DO ROTATE(INVAL);
    ON COMMAND "LEFT" DO ROTATE(−INVAL);
    ON COMMAND "FORWARD" DO MOVE(INVAL);
    ON COMMAND "BACK" DO MOVE(−INVAL);
  END;
```

Another way to reduce the complexity of the diagram might be to break it down into a *hierarchy* of state diagrams. For example, we could reduce the diagram shown in Figure 15-13 to the simpler form of Figure 15-14a by representing certain groups of states as single states. The commands effective within such a 'super-state' could then be defined by subsidiary diagrams, as shown in Figure 15-14b. This

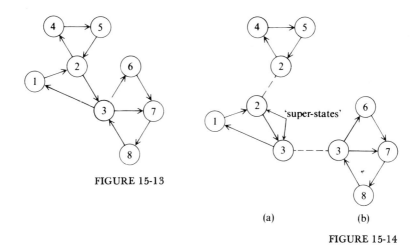

FIGURE 15-13

'super-states'

(a)   (b)

FIGURE 15-14

approach has the advantage of encouraging the programmer to design well-formed command languages.

The tendency of programmers to write programs with large numbers of states is less easy to control. It is analogous to the use by inexperienced programmers of the GOTO statement: if used to excess it creates incomprehensible programs. The best solution is for the programmer to give adequate thought to the design of his command language before he defines the state diagram. The design of interactive dialogues is discussed further in Section 15.6.

15.5   LANGUAGE PROCESSOR DESIGN

The design of a language processor involves the consideration of a number of issues. These fall under three headings: task scheduling, compiling the tables, and passing data to the program.

15.5.1   TASK SCHEDULER DESIGN

The general structure of a task scheduler is shown in Figure 15-15. This flow chart includes the idle loop or *dynamic stop* in which the program sits waiting for attentions. Sometimes the idle loop is kept separate from the rest of the task scheduler, which is written as a low-priority interrupt routine; the effect however is much the same. Whenever an

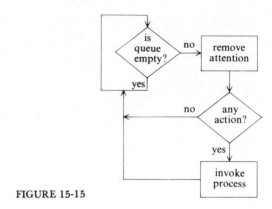

FIGURE 15-15

attention is found in the queue it is removed, the appropriate action is determined, and the scheduler either invokes the appropriate process or returns immediately to the idle loop.

The table used by the task scheduler should be designed to provide the best combination of compactness and ease of scanning by the task scheduler. Figure 15-16 shows the layout of the tables used in the graphical version of the Reaction Handler. Each set of branch descriptions defining a state is grouped separately; each of these descriptions specifies the *action* capable of causing the branch, and the *reaction* that results. Actions are defined in terms of input source and data; *source* effectively means the input device, although a single source may permit a choice of devices — light-button inputs and typed commands are considered to be a single source, for example; *data* can be defined as a single word, or as a pointer to a multi-word entry. Reactions are defined by the address of a subroutine and the number of the next state. Certain actions will inherently match the table entry regardless of data content — arbitrary text strings, stylus inputs and so forth. A flag must be set in the data entry if this is the case.

Notice that the sequential fashion in which the table is searched imposes a priority ordering on the branches; this priority is not apparent in the state diagram itself. In the text definition of the diagram it is possible to make use of the priority: for example, the Reaction Handler can check for specific text strings first, and if they do not match the input can take the last branch in the list. Unmatched actions may be treated as errors: in the Reaction Handler, however, they were ignored.

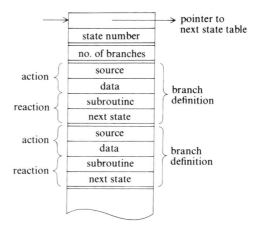

FIGURE 15-16

15.5.2   COMPILING THE TABLES

There are many ways of compiling the command language description. In the DIAL language, for example, there is no task scheduler table: instead the command language description is compiled as part of the program. This is best illustrated by the following example:

```
DURING 3 DO BEGIN
   ON COMMAND "GO" DO ENTER 4;
   ON COMMAND "RESTART" DO RESTRT;
   ON PENDOWN DO ENTER 5
END
```

This group of statements is translated by the DIAL compiler into PDP-10 assembly code; however it would be meaningless to many readers to quote the exact instructions generated. Instead let us look at what might be produced if the compiler translated into SAIL:

```
ST3:  WAIT;
      IF DEVICE=KEYBOARD AND
      CHAR=CARRIAGERETURN
      AND INPUTSTRING="GO" THEN GOTO ST4
        ELSE
      IF DEVICE=KEYBOARD AND
        CHAR=CARRIAGERETURN
        AND EQU(INPUTSTRING,"RESTART") THEN RESTRT
```

ELSE
IF DEVICE=PENSWITCH AND
SWITCHON THEN GOTO ST5
ELSE GOTO ST3;

The WAIT procedure effectively waits for an attention to be received on the attention queue. It then removes the attention and stores the device identity in DEVICE and the input character in CHAR. Characters are packed into a reserved string variable called INPUTSTRING. If a carriage-return is received, this string is tested with the two specified in the DURING statement. If it matches neither of them, the program checks whether the attention was from the pen.

In DIAL, then, the task scheduler is compiled into the object code. There is a certain degree of duplication involved in this approach, which we may wish to avoid by using a separate Reaction Handler program; in this case we must compile tables for its use. If we use a simple table layout, such as the one shown in Figure 15-16, then table compilation is quite easy. In the systems described in Section 15.4.2, the Reaction Handler was itself used to generate the table compiler. Figure 15-17 shows the diagram defining the syntax of the state-diagram definition language; this diagram was used to generate the state-diagram compiler. The process of generating this form of compiler naturally involves an initial 'bootstrapping' operation, which may be laborious. However, it is otherwise a very straightforward method of generating the compiler, and furthermore provides a good test of the compiler itself.

15.5.3   PASSING DATA TO THE PROGRAM

One of the simplest methods of passing data from the task scheduler to the program is by the usc of *reserved variables*. Each device is provided with a certain number of variables that are accessible to the program and in which the data from the device is placed after each input. For example, the coordinates from a stylus might be placed in two variables called PENX and PENY, so that a line could be drawn to the stylus position from some other point (X0,Y0):

SETPOINT(X0,Y0);
LINE(PENX,PENY);

Reserved variables may also be used to pass keyboard characters, identities of push-buttons and so forth. They provide a simple

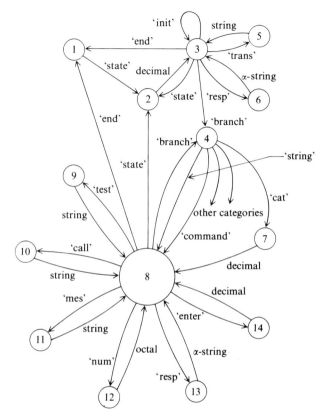

FIGURE 15-17

mechanism for passing items of input data not received directly from the device — for example, strings and numbers received from the keyboard. However, reserved variables have some drawbacks, of which the principal one is that modifications must be made to the compiler for the language in which the processes are written, so that references to reserved variables are compiled correctly. Another problem with reserved variables is that they make a program device-dependent: it is difficult to switch input devices since each reference to a reserved variable implies the use of a specific device.

These problems are avoided if a single *stack* is used for passing data. For example, the command *TRANSLATE 200 350* would place 200 and then 350 on the stack, so the process could remove them in the reverse order. The stack method allows a variable number of items of data to be passed in a command, and is particularly convenient for passing information about the hierarchy of a light-pen 'hit.'

A third method is the use of *dummy variables* in the definition of the command language. For example, we could specify the syntax and the semantics of the *TRANSLATE* command in a single definition:

$$\text{TRANSLATE X Y} \Rightarrow \text{TR(X,Y)}$$

meaning 'if you encounter the word **TRANSLATE** followed by two numbers representing X and Y, call procedure TR with X and Y as parameters.' This method of defining a language is called the *production* technique; it has been used very widely in generating compilers for procedure-oriented languages.

15.6   THE DESIGN OF INTERACTIVE DIALOGUES

Chapter 11 will have given the reader an idea of the proliferation of graphical input techniques available to him when he sets out to design an interactive program. Making the right choice from this proliferation is one of the most difficult tasks he has to face. It is particularly difficult because it involves knowledge of human factors, generally a subject unknown to most programmers. The ability to construct a good dialogue between the user and the program can generally be gained only with experience, both of writing interactive programs and of working with the people who will eventually use the program. It is particularly important to keep the user in mind when designing an interactive dialogue.

The three main qualities that the programmer should attempt to optimize are:

simplicity without which the user will never succeed in learning to operate the program;

consistency, i.e. a clear overall structure to the command language, an essential if the user is to avoid making mistakes; and

economy from both the user's and the program's standpoint.

Simplicity and consistency are most easily achieved if a single style of command is chosen and used throughout the program. For example, typed commands could be used throughout, or pointing and positioning, or character recognition. By making such a choice and holding to it the designer may sacrifice economy of action: for example, a single pointing operation might spare the user a large amount of typing. However, economy in use is also affected by how many times the user must switch from one device to another.

Economy in processing is generally attained only by using techniques such as pointing, positioning and typing, in which the information content of each action is relatively low. Often the decision about the choice of style will have to be made partly on economic grounds, for techniques like character recognition and rubber-band drawing are expensive to provide and their use may only be justified if the user's time is valuable, or if console usage must be kept to a minimum.

As well as aiming to satisfy these three requirements, the programmer should provide certain other features in every interactive program he writes:

Error recovery. The user should never be penalized unduly for an erroneous input. Many users are nervous when they first use an interactive program and make mistakes that the programmer probably never contemplated. It is therefore essential to adopt a general strategy of error recovery, rather than try to anticipate all forms that the user's errors will take; this strategy should make itself evident to the user. The program should respond to illegal or incorrect commands with a helpful message. If the user inputs incorrect data as part of a command, he should be allowed to re-enter the incorrect element without having to retype the entire command.

Explanatory messages. Whenever possible, the display should be used to help the user to operate the program. One of the simplest ways of doing this is to display messages explaining what he should do next.

Concise commands for experts. One problem in designing a command language is that the user gradually gains experience and therefore has less and less need for easily-remembered commands, explanatory text displays and error messages. He should be allowed to tailor the degree of assistance he receives to suit his level of competence. Examples of non-graphical programs that provide this feature are Deutsch and Lampson's QED editor [69], with its Quick and Verbose modes of operation, and BBN's TENEX operating system [25, 192] which allows the user to type as much or as little of each command as he wishes.

To conclude, this chapter can do no better than recommend the reader to study some of the better interactive graphical programs written, and try to analyze just what it is that makes them easy to use. Amongst those recommended for study are the following, all of which are documented on film:

The SKETCHPAD program of Ivan E. Sutherland [277, 188]. The development of this program on the TX-2 computer inaugurated interactive computer graphics. The film remains a remarkable demonstration of the smoothness and careful design of this early system.

The Augmented Human Intellect Project at Stanford Research Institute, directed by D. C. Engelbart [269, 80]. Here the accent is on text manipulation, using a display, mouse, keyset and keyboard. A very simple and consistent command language is used throughout.

The GRAIL System [222, 77, 78], a tablet-based programming system developed at the RAND Corporation by T. O. Ellis and W. L. Sibley. The user draws his flow chart and then writes the program by handprinting on the tablet.

The interactive circuit mask design program of F. K. Richardson and D. R. Oestreicher of MIT's Lincoln Laboratory [189, 227]. Controlled entirely by means of the tablet, this program demonstrates the use of a very simple command language to operate a very powerful program.

The BIOMOD program developed at the RAND corporation [108]. The program combines an elaborate graphical front-end and a differential equation solver. The system is intended for use in solving models of chemical and biological systems.

16

PROGRAMMING LANGUAGES FOR COMPUTER GRAPHICS

16.1 THE NEED FOR HIGH-LEVEL LANGUAGES

The importance of programming languages is often forgotten when a graphics system is designed. System designers become absorbed by such fascinating issues as display file structure and graphical interaction, and leave the provision of a convenient programming language until later. In the end no such language is implemented, and the unfortunate programmer is forced to write in assembly language.

This lack of interest in the development of programming languages has been one of the major obstacles preventing the widespread use of graphics. A great many worthwhile applications have been ignored or abandoned, or have turned into huge-scale programming efforts, because of the lack of programming systems other than assembly languages or crude graphics packages. To ensure that interactive graphics is used where it is needed, it is essential to make graphics systems not only inexpensive but simple to program. The programmer, whether novice or expert, should find it as easy to write a graphical program as a non-graphical one. All this can be achieved only if we develop *high-level* languages for computer graphics — languages that permit the programmer to express algorithms as he conceives them, that protect him from the peculiarities of the computer, and that enable him to trace and correct errors in his program with the minimum of trouble.

This chapter explores the subject of high-level languages for computer graphics. It looks in particular at facilities for generating graphical output and for building data structures. First, however, it takes a careful look at the features of general-purpose high-level languages, for these are the languages from which we must choose the foundation for our graphics language.*

16.2   FEATURES OF HIGH-LEVEL LANGUAGES

There are a number of features that a good language should possess. These features may be grouped broadly into two categories: those for defining program structure, and those for manipulating data.

16.2.1   PROGRAM STRUCTURE

Program structure facilities are extremely important, particularly those that define the overall structure of the program. We must be able to segment the program into procedures in a clear and simple fashion, for it is otherwise extremely difficult to develop large programs. It should be possible to call procedures *recursively*. At the more detailed level, it is advantageous if we can use *block structure* to define the separate parts of procedures, and to limit the scope of variables. We should also be able to express *conditional* operations conveniently, as well as repeated or *iterative* operations.

16.2.2   DATA MANIPULATION

Data manipulation in computer graphics generally means the manipulation of numbers; however, it is rare to find applications that do not also involve the use of strings of text or of logical expressions.

---

* It is possible to base a graphics language on a set of input and output functions, to which non-graphical functions are added as desired. This approach is rarely successful, for it makes it difficult to provide good facilities for defining algorithms and complex non-graphical procedures.

Facilities to handle these should also be provided. A more complex issue is that of *data structures*. Interactive programs generally call for extremely *dynamic* data structures that expand and contract during the program's execution. A language that is to be used for interactive applications must of course allow a wide range of *input-output* operations; it must also possess powerful *file-handling* facilities, for without files it is impossible to maintain continuity between sessions at the display.

All these features should be provided in the framework of a syntax that combines clarity with conciseness. The source description of a program can serve the valuable second function of providing documentation, as long as the syntax is readable and makes as little use as possible of obscure symbols.

An issue that is in some respects separate from the language itself is the *environment* in which the language is implemented. It should be easy to create programs, easy to trace and correct errors in them, and easy to make alterations. We should be able to change source statements at the console, without having to recompile the whole program. For debugging purposes we need clear, informative diagnostic messages, and we should be able to trace execution and set breakpoints. The language should permit direct execution of statements: for example, if the user types PRINT A, the program should print out the contents of variable A. Provision of this sort of *conversational* environment is not an entirely separate issue, for some languages are easier to implement in this way than others.

Taken as a whole, this is a stringent set of requirements. We shall discover this in the next section, which contrasts these requirements with the capabilities of some of the better-known high-level languages.

16.3   A SURVEY OF HIGH-LEVEL LANGUAGES

The languages that present themselves as candidates for use in interactive graphics fall into two groups: those developed for use in large scientific applications, and those designed from the outset to be used conversationally for more informal problems.

In the first category, one of the earliest and most respected languages is ALGOL 60 [72, 194]. This language, which dates from 1960 and earlier, is strongest in its program structure facilities: these have since been copied in many other languages. In data manipulation, however, ALGOL is rather weak. It contains no string-handling facilities, and offers only arrays as a means of building data structures. No input-output or file-handling facilities were defined in the original definition of ALGOL, so these must be added on an *ad hoc* basis.

A more recent language whose design was extensively influenced by ALGOL and which tries to avoid some of ALGOL's weaknesses is PL/I [262, 125]. It offers much more comprehensive data manipulation facilities, including more powerful data structures and quite comprehensive input-output facilities. These are provided somewhat at the expense of the syntax, which is neither as clear nor as elegant as that of ALGOL 60.

Both ALGOL 60 and PL/I place on the programmer the burden of declaring the *type* of each variable used. This should not be necessary in a high-level language. For example, we may declare a variable x and then assign a value to it as follows:

$$x \leftarrow 3.5$$

The meaning of this statement is clear, whether or not x has been declared to have type **real**. As we shall see in the description of the EULER language in Section 16.4, it is possible to define a very powerful language that is entirely free of type declarations.

ALGOL and PL/I are rarely implemented in conversational, incremental fashions, although subsets of PL/I exist in this form. The languages that have been implemented extensively in this way form a completely separate set, with entirely different characteristics. There exist, for example, a number of conversational languages based on the RAND Corporation's JOSS language [15, 261]. These languages are better suited to simple, informal problem-solving than to large, interactive applications: their program and data structure facilities are quite limited. The same can be said of BASIC [260], a language that is nevertheless very widely favored for interactive use. The only well-known conversational language suitable for complex problem-solving is APL [126]: this language has an unusual syntax that permits very powerful number- and vector-handling operations to be defined with extreme conciseness. Its syntactic structure is somewhat marred by dependence on branching to effect conditional and iterative operations; however, this has not prevented the formation of a large and growing body of APL enthusiasts.

Of these languages, only APL and to a lesser extent ALGOL and PL/I have inspired the development of graphics languages. One language which has been used time and time again as a graphics system basis is

FORTRAN. If it were not for this, there would be little need to mention FORTRAN at all, for its performance in meeting our criteria is abysmal. FORTRAN offers no program structure facilities of any worth: its subroutines and functions are non-recursive, and impose strange conventions regarding parameter-passing; the IF statement is clumsy and lacks an ELSE clause. The iterative DO loop is limited in its usefulness; and there is no block structure. In the data manipulation area, FORTRAN is about as weak as ALGOL 60, with the added liability of some notoriously obscure input-output facilities, designed in the 1950's to handle punched cards and scarcely modified since then. FORTRAN demands type declarations, although some types are implicit in the choice of variable names; it contains numerous syntactic oddities and obscurities; and it is rarely implemented in a convenient, conversational form.

Why does the use of FORTRAN persist? There are many reasons. It is widely known, and is available on virtually every computer. It has hence assumed the position of a more or less universal language, even though it is rarely possible to transfer FORTRAN programs between machines without conversion problems. The FORTRAN programmer can draw on a vast library of programs covering virtually every area of scientific computing; finally, FORTRAN is held to be efficient.

What is really meant here by *efficiency* is that a program written in FORTRAN will, if run on a conventional computer, complete its task more rapidly than an equivalent program written, say, in ALGOL 60. What is rarely taken into account is the sheer *inefficiency* of writing programs in FORTRAN, of debugging them, and of trying to understand those written by others. There must have been many cases in which the use of FORTRAN for an application has cost more in unnecessary development expense than it has saved in running costs. When eventually computers are properly designed to perform type-checking and procedure calls as they should, the arguments in favor of FORTRAN may disappear; until then the efficiency issue will undoubtedly continue to be raised, particularly by users of over-priced time-shared systems. Hopefully the enlightened graphics system designer will consider both sides to this issue.

16.4 THE EULER LANGUAGE

In any survey of general-purpose languages, EULER deserves to be mentioned as a language of particular merit. Other languages of similar elegance have been proposed: LISP [306, 178, 287] and CPL [18] are particularly important examples, for they have influenced language design extensively. EULER has had a lesser influence, but it remains one of the few examples of a language that is at once elegant, powerful and convenient. This section presents a brief description of EULER's more important features: the assumption is made that the reader is familiar either with ALGOL 60 or with SAIL.

EULER was designed by N. Wirth as a generalization of ALGOL 60 [310]. It is a language free of type declarations. This does not mean that there are no data types: data may consist of numbers, logical values, text strings, lists, even procedures. However, when we declare variables, we do not specify the type of information they are to contain:

>   begin new *a, b, p;*
>   *a* ← *"abc"; b* ← *3.5; p* ← *10;*
>   . . .

Lists provide a simple, dynamic data structure facility. They have the attractive property that they may contain mixed types of data — for example, a list *l* may be created to contain a real number, an integer, a logical value and a string, as follows:

>   *l* ← *(12.5, 10,* **true,** *"tom")*

By defining lists within lists, and by the use of references (see Section 16.7.2.1), we can create quite complex list structures.

EULER is particularly powerful in its ability to define program structure. Its facilities are similar to ALGOL's, but are somewhat simpler. As mentioned earlier, one of the types of information that we may assign to a variable is a procedure:

>   *p* ← *'a* ← *5; p* ← *(2,3)'*

The statements within the quotation marks form the procedure body, and are executed when p is referenced. If we wish to pass parameters to a procedure, we declare *formal* arguments within the procedure:

>   *istwo* ← *'***formal** *x;* **if** *x=2* **then** *out("yes")* **else** *out("no")';*
>   *istwo(3);*

This example, which would result in the output "no," also illustrates the conditional **if** statement. EULER includes ALGOL-like block structure, and the addition of **for** statements, as suggested by Wirth and Weber [311], make its program structure facilities extremely powerful and general. EULER has a number of other useful features: for example, procedures may be called by value or by name in a much simpler fashion than in ALGOL. Also, because each statement has a value, we can use statements in the following ways:

$a[k{\leftarrow}k+1] \leftarrow 10;$

i.e. add one to k, then store 10 in the kth element of the list $a;$

$b \leftarrow p(\textbf{if } a{>}b \textbf{ then}$
$\qquad \textbf{begin } d{\leftarrow}5; \ 35 \textbf{ end else begin } d{\leftarrow}2; \ 27 \textbf{ end});$

i.e. call p with parameter whose value is the result (either 35 or 27) of executing the enclosed **if** statement; store the result in b.

EULER has been implemented on a number of machines, including the DEC PDP-10 [204] and the IBM System/360 [303]; the latter is an interesting microprogrammed version. EULER's unusual type-checking and procedure-handling features generally demand that it be implemented in an interpretive fashion. However, it is clear that a computer with the ability to perform type-checking and procedure-handling by hardware can be built without much difficulty or expense.

16.5 EXTENDING LANGUAGES FOR GRAPHICS

It is much easier to choose the language on which to base a graphics system than to decide just how to add to it the necessary graphics features. However insignificant these additions may be, if they are poorly designed they will prevent the graphics system from being properly used, and will instead hamper the programmer. It is a familiar experience for the language designer to discover that the facilities that he provided, and considered so simple and straightforward, are incomprehensible to many of the language's users.

If we are considering adding certain features to the language, we should first ask ourselves a few questions:

1. Can they be misused or misunderstood?
2. Will they lead to reasonably concise programs?
3. Are we making as few additions as possible to the syntax?
4. Is the meaning of each construction fairly obvious from its written form?

Generally the only way to answer all these questions is to test out each construction very thoroughly by means of a variety of programs.

Graphical additions to a language fall neatly into two categories: features for input and features for output. Not all system designers have adopted this attitude, however. Some have tended to draw a rather vague dividing line between the two categories. For example, there have been systems which insisted that any input routines requiring periodic execution be included in the refresh cycle. It has also been popular to create strong links between between graphical output facilities and light pen interaction facilities. Techniques of this sort can be relied upon to confuse most novice users.

16.6   OUTPUT FACILITIES*

Graphical output facilities may be added to a language either in the form of graphical functions or by means of the *display procedure* technique described in Chapter 8. The reader should have gained from Chapters 5 and 8 an appreciation of the differeneces between the two approaches. It remains in this chapter to point out some of the differences in the way the two techniques are introduced to a programming language.

These differences may be summarized as follows: the display procedure approach requires minor modifications to the syntax of the language and therefore to its compiler; it also requires transformation, clipping and concatenation routines, together with a display code generator. To provide the same capability by means of functions, we must write a pseudo-display file compiler and a trace routine as well as all the other elements of the transformation system, and must ensure that the free storage system can satisfy the pseudo-display file compiler's needs; however, no modifications need be made to the language. If no transformations are to be permitted, a somewhat

* The reader is referred to Chapter 15 for a discussion of input facilities.

simpler display file compiler can be used. Simpler still, the graphics functions may be restricted to a set of graphical primitives, in which case implementation is a trivial task. Since the subject of functions for display file generation has been discussed previously at some length, this chapter merely summarizes the issues involved in choosing the functions. The display procedure technique is discussed in more detail, with hints on methods of implementation.

16.6.1   GRAPHICAL PRIMITIVES

The main criteria in choosing a set of primitive graphical functions are as follows:

1. *Clarity*. The functions will often be used by relatively inexperienced programmers, and should be as simple and comprehensible as possible. They should not be unduly influenced by the display's instruction set.
2. *Convenience*. The functions should permit all forms of point- and line-plotting and positioning, both by relative and by absolute coordinates.
3. *Compactness*. The set of functions should not be too large, for this will enlarge the software system and will increase the problems of conversion to other display devices. Circles and other more complex constructions should be provided by library functions.

A reasonable set of primitive functions for line- and point-plotting is therefore the following:

```
MOVE(DX,DY);      move beam through distance (DX,DY)
MOVETO(X,Y);      move beam position to (X,Y)
LINE(DX,DY);      draw line of length (DX,DY)
LINETO(X,Y);      draw line to (X,Y)
POINT(X,Y);       display point at (X,Y)
```

Text display may be provided by means of a string display function:

```
DISPLAY(S);       display string S at current beam position
```

This function can be used to display numerical values, if functions exist for converting numbers to string form. Alternatively we may extend the language syntax to include the following statement, analogous to the PRINT statement:

DISPLAY "ANSWER IS", N, "FT/SEC" IN F;

where F is some sort of format string. The only other requirement in the set of primitives is a CLEAR function to clear the screen.

16.6.2 FUNCTIONS FOR BUILDING STRUCTURED DISPLAY FILES

As mentioned in Chapter 5, there are two approaches to the design of a set of functions for building structured display files. One is to permit unnamed calls to subroutine records; the other is to allow named calls by means of *groups* and *items*. The second method is more powerful but requires a slightly larger set of functions.

Unnamed calls may be implemented by supplementing the graphical primitives listed above with the following functions:

OPEN(N);	open record N
CLOSE;	close the opened record (not added to the refresh cycle)
DELETE(N);	delete record N
APPEND(N);	open record N and add to its current contents
CALL(N);	call record N

The CALL function adds to the currently open record a call to the named record; if none is open, it adds the call to a 'base record,' so that the named record is included in the refresh cycle. *Names* may be integers, but it is often convenient if string names are allowed as an alternative:

OPEN("RESISTOR");

This requires a more complex name table.

In implementing *groups* and *items*, we may use the same set of functions — OPEN, CLOSE, DELETE and APPEND — to define items, i.e. the terminal nodes of the display file structure. Instead of the CALL function, we use the following structure-definition functions:

CALLITEM(n,g,i,x,y);

> add to group g a call to item n, with identifier i, translated by x and y.

CALLGROUP(n,g,i,x,y);

> add to group g a call to group n; i, x and y have the same meaning as before.

DELETECALL(g,i);

> delete from group g the call with identifier i.

The CALLITEM and CALLGROUP functions may be used to reposition existing calls by quoting their identifiers. To include a group in the refresh cycle, we add a call to it to group 0. Where translation is immaterial, as it will be in this case, x and y parameters may be omitted.

16.6.3   FUNCTIONS FOR PICTURE TRANSFORMATION

Transformation parameters are most conveniently defined in calls to subpictures, using the group and item technique. For example, we can specify scale and rotation as follows:

CALLITEM(n,g,i,x,y,r,s);

> add to group g a call to item n with identifier i, translation x and y, rotation r and scale s.

It is convenient to permit rotation and scale values to be omitted, and default values of 0 and 1 to be assumed.

Dimensions for clipping and boxing purposes may be specified by adding more parameters to the CALL function. Since this may generate function calls with inconveniently large numbers of parameters, it is best to store the dimensions in a list or array whose name is included in the call:

CALLITEM(n,g,i,x,y,s,d)

where d is a four-element array specifying the master dimensions.

This technique may be extended to permit all transformation parameters to be specified by a single array representing the transformation matrix:

CALLITEM(n,g,i,m)

where m is a 3 x 3 array.

This is particularly convenient if the program uses matrix manipulation functions to compute transformations in the form of arrays.

16.6.4 DISPLAY PROCEDURE IMPLEMENTATION

The implementation of display procedures involves the provision of a set of primitive functions; it also calls for four language extensions: frame procedures, frame deletion, display procedure calls and, in most cases, display procedures themselves.

The reason why *display procedures* are an optional extension is that they may be written using the standard procedure syntax; for example, using SAIL we could define the resistor symbol of Figure 16-1 as follows:

```
PROCEDURE RESISTOR;
  BEGIN INTEGER I;
    LINE(10,0); LINE(5,10);
    FOR I←1 STEP 1 UNTIL 4 DO
     BEGIN LINE(10,−20); LINE(10,20) END;
    LINE(5,−10); LINE(10,0)
  END
```

Display procedures defined in this way may be transformed in various ways when they are called: they may be translated, rotated and scaled, and they may be clipped by defining master dimensions in the call:

DRAW RESISTOR AT (100,200) SCALE 0.5 WITHIN (10,-20,100,20)

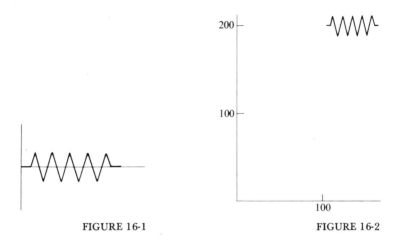

FIGURE 16-1   FIGURE 16-2

The parameters of WITHIN specify the coordinates of two opposite corners of the clipping rectangle. The result of this call is shown in Figure 16-2.

To specify master dimensions in the master itself, we should extend the syntax to treat display procedures separately; in this way, dimensions may be specified in the procedure head, again by the positions of two rectangle corners:

```
DISPLAY PROCEDURE RESISTOR;
DIMENSIONS(0,−20,110,20);
  BEGIN
   . . .
   . . .
  END
```

The DIMENSIONS declaration should be compiled so that the boxing test is applied before the procedure body is executed: effectively we should compile the procedure as if it read:

```
PROCEDURE RESISTOR;
  IF VISIBLE(0,−20,110,20) THEN
  BEGIN
   . . .
   . . .
  END
```

The VISIBLE function tests whether the symbol, drawn at the position and scale specified in the call, overlaps the window whose corners are given. If it does, the rest of the procedure is executed.

Frame procedures are also implemented as a special form of procedure:

>   FRAME F;
>   DRAW PIC3 WITHIN (0,0,100,100) ONTO (−1,−1,1,1);

These procedures are again very similar to normal ones, but have the added responsibility of opening and closing segments of the transformed display file:

>   PROCEDURE F;
>   BEGIN
>   OPENF(n);
>   DRAW PIC3 WITHIN (0,0,100,100) ONTO (−1,−1,1,1);
>   CLOSEF
>   END

OPENF and CLOSEF perform the opening and closing operations. The name n is assigned a unique integer value by the compiler, which must also assign the same integer value to any *frame deletion* commands:

>   DELETE F;

This operation must therefore be compiled as follows:

>   DELETEF(n);

If hit-detection is to be included among the system's functions, the compilation process is slightly more complex. Hit-detection involves re-executing every frame procedure that corresponds to a currently visible frame. Therefore a list is maintained of all such frames, in the form of a table of entry points to the appropriate procedures (Figure 16-3). When the hit-detection function is called, a small window is set and the frame procedures are executed until a visible element is detected (Figure 16-4). A simple addition to the compiled code of the frame procedure adds the appropriate address to the list when the frame is called, and a similar addition to the deletion process removes the address.

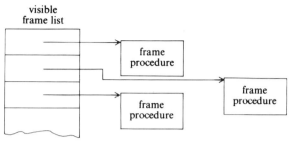

FIGURE 16-3

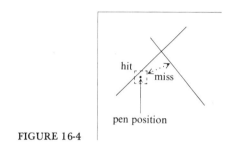

FIGURE 16-4

The syntax of the *display procedure call* is illustrated by the following examples:

        DRAW RESISTOR AT (100,100);
        DRAW RESISTOR AT (50,60) SCALE .5;
        DRAW RESISTOR AT (100,200) ROT PI/2 SCALE 2;
        DRAW RESISTOR IN (100,100,300,300);

Many combinations of transformations are possible, specifying translations, scales, rotations, instance and master dimensions, or complete transformations with matrices. The compiled code varies according to whether the transformations indicate that the boxing test should be performed. For example, the first case given above compiles as follows:

        SAVE;   save the current parameters
        SETPOS(100,100);   set translation (100,100)
        CONCAT;   concatenate transformations
        RESISTOR;   call RESISTOR
        RESTORE;   restore parameters

In contrast, the fourth example above compiles into the following steps:

```
IF VISIBLE (100,100,300,300) THEN
  BEGIN
    SAVE;
    SETSIZE(100,100,300,300);
    CONCAT;
    RESISTOR;
    RESTORE
  END;
```

In compiling this last example into machine code, it is of course possible to use the boxing parameters as transformation parameters without repetition.

One other parameter of interest may be added to the display procedure call: this is the *name* by which the hit-detection process identifies items:

```
DRAW RESISTOR AT (100,100) AS 123;
```

This adds an additional operation to the compiled code:

```
SAVE;
SETPOS(100,100);
SETNAME(123);
CONCAT;
RESISTOR;
RESTORE;
```

The SETNAME function is ignored during normal execution of the call. When the hit-detection process is invoked to search for picture elements close to the specified position, all the frames listed as visible are executed. During this operation a *name stack* is maintained, containing the names of all the calls being executed at any one time. The contents of this stack may be accessed by the application program when a hit is detected.

16.7   DATA STRUCTURES

The final topic we shall discuss in this chapter is the subject of data structures. This topic has often been held to be of particular relevance to computer graphics. In fact, data structures are important in computer graphics for two reasons. Firstly, we make use of various kinds of tree structures and linked lists when we build a display file; secondly, any interactive graphics program must be capable of building and manipulating a data base. Except in the special case when a dual-purpose graphical data structure is used, the display file and the data base remain two virtually separate issues.

The subject of display file structures has been discussed at some length in Chapter 5. The structures we talked about were relatively simple, as they must be if a display processor is to be able to trace through them. In this section we shall not discuss these structures, since they are manipulated by the output statements of the programming language. Instead we shall briefly review the topic of facilities for data base construction and manipulation.

16.7.1   THE BASIC REQUIREMENTS

Conventional arrays and vectors, although they are simple to implement and easy to use, do not perform well in interactive situations. The reason for this is that they are essentially *static* data structures, and do not expand or contract during a program's execution. We must define the dimensions of these structures, either at the start of execution or, worse still, before we compile the program. Then we must be careful that the program does not trespass beyond these dimensions. These are very inconvenient restrictions in any interactive program, for at the start of execution we rarely have any idea how much data will be stored in the data base. Therefore we must generally set large dimensions to prevent array overflow.

From this we can see that one of the most important qualities that we look for in a data structure for interactive use is its ability to expand and contract during execution: we call such a structure a *dynamic* structure. What are the other features we should look for?

To answer this question we must consider in more detail the types of operation we expect to perform on a data base. There are four particularly important ones:

1. We often want to create *sets* of things, for example all the vertices of a polygon.
2. We like to be able to define *attributes* of things such as the coordinates of points.
3. The sets of things that we create may be *ordered* according to some attribute; for example, we might like to order our points according to their z-coordinate values.

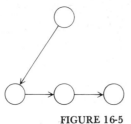

FIGURE 16-5

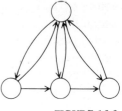

FIGURE 16-6

4. We like to define *relationships* between one thing and another: we might like to specify that one point is the nearest point to a certain other one.

A number of different techniques have been invented for modeling these operations. They can be classified broadly as techniques that model structures in the form of trees, and associative data structure techniques. We shall discuss both types of structure.

16.7.2   TREE STRUCTURES

Tree structures are normally built with the aid of *pointers:* cells in the data structure contain the addresses of other cells. By linking a group of cells we create a simple tree as shown in Figure 16-5.

There are many other ways to construct a tree besides the arrangement of Figure 16-5: these other methods generally use additional pointers to achieve greater speed of access. For example, we could use the structure shown in Figure 16-6 to build the same tree as is represented by the structure of Figure 16-5. It is important to note that the addition of pointers in this manner rarely alters the *range* of operations we can perform on the tree: it simply increases speed of access by eliminating some costly searching operations. Thus by adding all the pointers shown in Figure 16-6 we gain the ability to move in a single step between the top element and any other element in the tree; in the case of Figure 16-5 we can still reach all the elements, but some of them are accessible only after a succession of steps.

By increasing the number of pointers we also increase the amount of space that the structure occupies. This is not the only disadvantage of using multiple pointers, however: the task of modifying the structure becomes more involved, and therefore more time-consuming, unless the

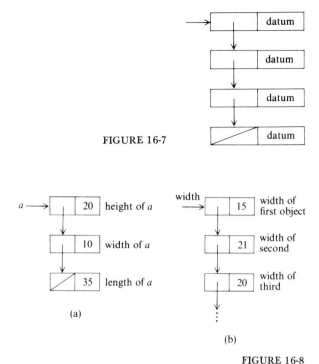

FIGURE 16-7

(a)

(b)

FIGURE 16-8

pointers are added in a careful manner. Highly interconnected tree-structures create problems as they grow larger, for it is very difficult to page them onto backing store in an efficient manner. These are some of the issues that must be considered when designing a tree-structured data base.

16.7.2.1   Simple tree structures

A simple tree structure, which provides most of the functions we have discussed in Section 16.7.1, is the linked list structure shown in Figure 16-7 [178, 196]. Each element of the list consists of a *datum* and a *pointer* to the next element. The final pointer in the list is set to zero or some null value.

Lists can very easily be modified. They are also very suitable for defining attributes of things. We can define attributes in two essentially equivalent ways: we can use a single list to define either all the attributes of a single thing (Figure 16-8a) or a single attribute of all

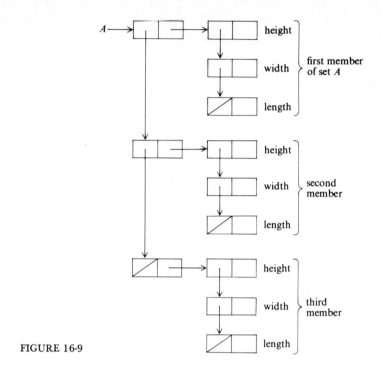

FIGURE 16-9

things (Figure 16-8b). We can store and retrieve this information by *indexing* the list:

    A←WIDTH[I]
    HEIGHT[I] ←300;

If we wish to use the technique of Figure 16-8a to define the attributes of more than one thing, then we need more than one list. If we wish to form a *set* of these things, we can use a list of lists, as shown in Figure 16-9. To access a particular attribute of a particular thing, we must use *double indexing;* thus we can find the width of the Ith thing of A as follows:

    A[I] [2]

16.7.2.2   Interconnected trees

A list such as the one in Figure 16-9 can clearly be *ordered* on any attribute. Thus we have achieved three of four objectives. How do we implement the fourth, namely relationships?

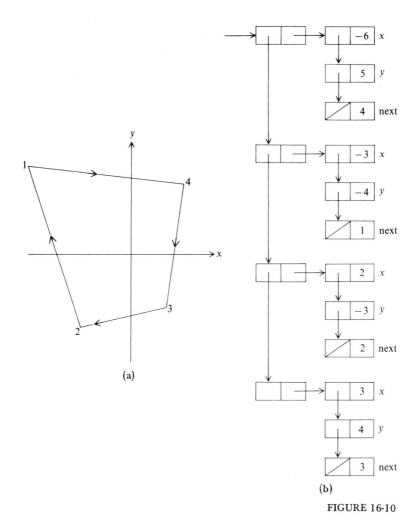

(a)

(b)

FIGURE 16-10

A simple method of introducing relationships is by defining indices referring to other things. Thus we could define the connected figure shown in Figure 16-10a by the list structure of Figure 16-10b. The list is ordered on values of x, and each subsidiary list defines x, y and the index of the next point in the figure. However, this method is inefficient, for it involves a lot of indexing to draw the figure; moreover, if we should add a point to the figure, some of the indices will be wrong, and will have to be changed. Both of these problems can be avoided by using *pointers* to indicate references, as shown in Figure 16-11.

The use of pointer references cannot be introduced casually, for it

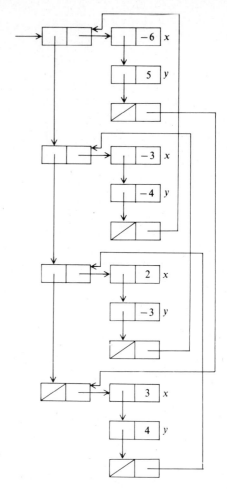

FIGURE 16-11

brings with it a great many undesirable side-effects. In the first place, it creates problems in the management of free storage. When a simple list structure, containing no references, is to be returned to free storage, all the suspended lists may be returned too. This cannot be done if references are permitted, for there may be references to the suspended lists from elsewhere in the data base. Therefore these suspended lists must be left intact, and *garbage collection* must occasionally be performed to retrieve disconnected list elements. Weizenbaum's SLIP system [307] contains an ingenious solution to this problem, involving the use of reference counts.

A second problem with references is that we need a means of tracing

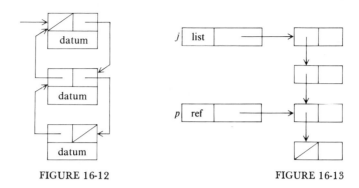

FIGURE 16-12   FIGURE 16-13

both ways along a list, so that we can delete an element of it. This need arises if we reach the element via a reference, rather than via an indexing operation which can always remember the address of the previous element. Two-way pointers may be used for this purpose (Figure 16-12).

A third problem is the need for operators in the language for defining references. EULER uses the @ operator:

@*j*[3]   is a reference to the third element of *j*; thus *p*←@*j*[3] has the effect shown in Figure 16-13.

We also need a way of accessing the referenced element; this is done by a dot in EULER:

p.   is the element addressed by the reference in *p*; in Figure 16-13 it would be equivalent to the third element of the list stored in *j*.

The one operation that the above scheme does not permit is the *reverse reference*, i.e. the ability to trace from a referred element to the referencing element. This again can be provided by two-way pointers, but the structure becomes very large. This is illustrated by Figure 16-14a. Here a single element is being referenced by a number of other elements. We can replace this structure by a *ring*, as shown in Figure 16-14b. The ring effectively defines as a set all the elements containing these references, and links them to the referenced element. A special bit

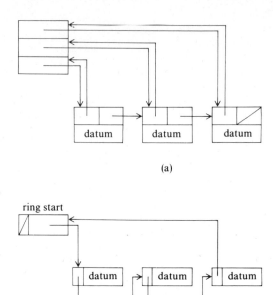

(a)

(b)

FIGURE 16-14

indicates the *ring start*, i.e. the first pointer in the ring. This technique is preferable to the technique of Figure 16-14a, for it allows elements to be added to the ring without increasing the size of the element at the start. As mentioned earlier, the number of pointers may be varied to achieve the desired balance between speed of access and economy of storage.

Ring structures can be used to perform all the four types of operation we suggested earlier. They tend to consume a lot of space because of the large number of pointers. However, space consumption can be reduced by eliminating the pointers within a ring defining an object. Thus if a certain class of object is always defined by four elements as shown in Figure 16-15a, there is no need to represent the object as a linked list: we can use four consecutive words as shown in in Figure 16-15b. Structures made up of such interconnected, multi-word blocks have been used in SKETCHPAD [277], AED [241], CORAL [281, 232] and ASP [155].

Although ring structures are extremely versatile, they are difficult to use because of their extreme generality. We can perform many different types of modification and access to structures of this sort, and therefore need a profusion of operators in the programming language.

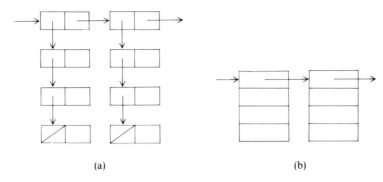

(a)   (b)

FIGURE 16-15

This will generally confuse a novice programmer. Furthermore, the searching operations that we perform on rings can become very time-consuming if the rings are large.

16.7.3   ASSOCIATIVE STRUCTURES

The real fault of ring structures is that they try to be *general* rather than *specific*. What the programmer needs is specific operations for defining sets, attributes, orders and relationships. The fact that rings can provide all of these is not enough, for the programmer must still write his own functions to perform specific operations. It is possible, however, to provide these specific operations in place of the general ones: in effect we hide the ring structure's implementation behind the syntactic expression of these specific operators.

Such a structure is called an *associative* structure. We define certain operators for manipulating the structure, such as operators to put objects in sets, to assign attributes to objects, to delete objects and so forth. We must also devise a way of *implementing* the structure. We can do this with rings but, as we pointed out, this is often inefficient. An alternative is to use *hash-coding*, i.e. storing and accessing data according to some function (the *hashing function*) of its data content.

The best known structure of this sort is Feldman and Rovner's LEAP system [91, 248]. This allows attributes to be assigned to objects by means of *associations:*

$$\textbf{make } \textit{next} \cdot x \equiv y$$

Here x is the object, *next* is the attribute, and y is called the *value* of the association. It is possible to retrieve information by means of the **foreach** statement:

foreach *next·q* $\equiv r$ **do make** *previous·r* $\equiv q$

LEAP also includes operations for defining sets. Objects, or *items* as they are called in general, may be put in sets and removed from sets:

put *pt1* **in** *points;*
remove *x* **from** *xlist;*

We can operate on all the items in a set:

foreach *p* **in** *points* **do put** *p* **in** *xpoints;*

We can form unions and intersections of sets:

upts $\leftarrow$ *points* $\cup$ *xpoints;*
inlns $\leftarrow$ *above* $\cap$ *left;*

The full capability of LEAP and its implementation are well worth detailed study, and are described further in Appendix V.

From the linguistic point of view, the strength of LEAP lies in the clarity and directness with which it allows complex data manipulations to be defined. The contrast in this respect between LEAP and a typical ring-structure language such as CORAL is quite striking. The other important feature of the LEAP structures is that they need not reside in fast, random-access memory. Instead they may be stored on a disk or drum, from which they are *paged* into core on a demand basis. The original LEAP implementation used a highly redundant storage technique, in which each association was stored three times in three separate pages; this enabled commonly-used retrieval operations to be performed with the minimum of drum accesses. This represents one of the few successful solutions of the problem of providing rapid access to large data structures.

17

GRAPHICS SYSTEM DESIGN

17.1 GRAPHICS SYSTEMS

In the course of the preceding sixteen chapters we have discussed, one by one, the various issues and problems involved in using interactive graphical displays. A number of principles and techniques have emerged from our discussions; taken as a whole, these represent the technology of interactive computer graphics. There is one final topic that must concern anyone wishing to employ these techniques in a chosen application. This is the issue of designing interactive graphics *systems:* of choosing the right hardware and software components to suit the application, and of making sure that they function properly together.

Graphics system design is by nature a rather different subject from the ones discussed in earlier chapters. In the first place, it is much less an analytical subject, and much more a matter of *synthesizing* a system design out of judiciously chosen hardware and software techniques. Secondly, graphics system design involves paying careful attention to the *application* for which the system is intended. It may be possible, at the time the system is designed, to determine a great deal about the application, and hence to design the system to fit very closely. In other cases we may know very little about the potential applications of the system, and must therefore make the system more general and flexible, producing what is usually called a *general-purpose* graphics system.

17.1.1   TYPES OF GRAPHICS SYSTEM

Systems designed for specific applications can often be understood and used by people without any prior computer experience. The same can rarely be said for systems of a more general nature. The majority of general-purpose graphics systems are in fact *programming* systems, designed to make it easier for programmers to generate application programs; they are virtually incomprehensible to the layman. The only way to maintain comprehensibility and at the same time to introduce some generality is to restrict the system to operating on *pictures*, so that the display effectively becomes a computer-controlled drawing board.

Thus we can identify three different types of graphics system, each designed to meet the needs of a different class of user:

1. *The picture-editing system.* The user may, as suggested above, wish to use the display simply as a powerful drawing board, perhaps to lay out an electrical circuit diagram or a flow chart. He may alternatively wish to generate sequences of pictures for use in psychological experiments or in film-making; or he may be an artist, interested in the displayed pictures for their aesthetic content. This class of system permits the user to manipulate the picture on the screen in a very direct manner, creating symbols and sub-pictures on-line for later use, and making extensive use of the stylus or light pen. The system rarely, however, permits non-graphical manipulation of the picture: for example, a circuit cannot be analyzed after it has been drawn. Many systems of this kind have been built, most of them based on SKETCHPAD [277]. Recent examples are Notley's GPDL [209] for static pictures, and Baecker's animation system GENESYS [13].

2. *The specialized application.* The user will typically be an engineer or scientist, interested in using the display for design or for the analysis of data. Some very spectacular and elaborate programs have been

written for applications such as aircraft design [216] and integrated circuit layout [227]. These are in some ways misleading examples: many applications of computer graphics involve relatively mundane problems, for which the bulk of the programming is non-graphical and the display serves merely to present the results clearly and quickly. An example is the RAND BIOMOD system [108]. Because graphics forms such a small part of these programs, it is more accurate to term them 'systems that use interactive graphics' rather than true 'graphics systems.'

3. *The general-purpose graphics system*. The user is an application programmer, and the purpose of the system is to make his task as easy as possible. To do so, the system must provide not only graphics facilities, but also a good high-level language, powerful data structure facilities, and aids to debugging and editing. The first system to meet these criteria was Feldman and Rovner's LEAP [247]; EULER-G [204] and GINO [315] are more recent attempts to provide similarly comprehensive programming facilities.

During this chapter we shall be concerned almost entirely with the third variety of system, the general-purpose graphics system. One of the reasons for this emphasis is that a good general-purpose system provides the best basis for application programming. It minimizes the effort involved in designing data structures and in writing routines to handle graphical input and output, and it frees the programmer to concentrate on the more intricate processes specific to the application. In the end, a graphical program written with the aid of such a system may be no more difficult to write than a non-graphical program. Thus the key to designing specialized systems lies in the provision of good general-purpose systems.

Nevertheless, application programs are often written without the aid of general-purpose systems or high-level languages. The justification is usually the lack of resources — limited processing power or lack of memory. A typical example is Armit's *Multipatch* system for designing with curved surface patches [8]. Here it was necessary to accommodate the entire system in an 8K, 18-bit memory: the system was therefore coded in assembly language, and a very compact data structure was used to store the surface patches. It is noteworthy, however, that even in such restricted circumstances, Armit found it worthwhile to develop a fairly general language processor to handle user commands. Typically the designer of such an application program will make use of many of

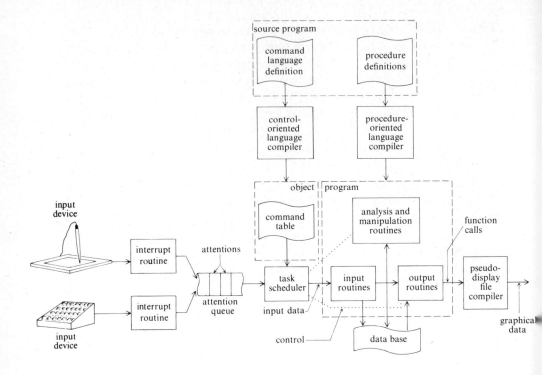

the more general techniques described in this and earlier chapters, although he may implement them very carefully to suit the application and the environment. Nowadays such an extreme lack of resources as Armit's is becomming rare, and it is increasingly difficult to justify building application systems without general-purpose facilities.

Picture-editing systems are an entirely separate issue. In the first place, they are generally much easier to implement than the other varieties of system. A simple picture-editing system need be little more than a conversational version of one of the display-file compilers described in Chapters 5 and 8. The user types a function name and some parameters, and the appropriate alteration is made to the display file. It may be advantageous to modify the calling sequences slightly — for example, the user will generally find it more convenient to specify the name of a new record when opening it rather than when closing it. Some picture-editing systems have been designed for control by the light pen or stylus in addition to the keyboard, but it is not at all clear that this makes the system easier to use. It is sometimes useful if the

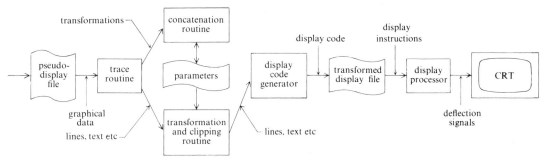

FIGURE 17-1

command language is extended to permit the definition of iterative operations and procedures.

Besides being easily built, picture-editing systems are rather entertaining to use. This perhaps explains why they exist in such profusion. Their actual value tends to be rather limited. Much more valuable are the systems adapted for special uses, such as animation and computer generation of movies; there is particular need for systems that allow editing of both pictures and text, and that can therefore be used for the preparation of illustrated documents. These are application areas in which work is still being done.

17.2   THE COMPONENTS OF A GRAPHICS SYSTEM

Earlier chapters have talked about the various *components* of a graphics system — the display file compiler, the transformation system, the interrupt routines and so forth. In Figure 17-1 the complete graphics system is shown for the first time, broken down into its components.

Apart from the specific devices shown at either end, Figure 17-1 is made up of three types of component: *processes*, represented by rectangular boxes; *data files*, shown as boxes with curly ends; and arrows representing *information transfers*. This is an important classification for it raises the following questions:

1. What species of *processors* should we use to execute the processes?
2. How should we store the data files?
3. How should we transfer information from one process to the next, and between processes and data files?

We shall try in this chapter to find answers to these three questions.

17.2.1   BALANCING THE SYSTEM

Our aim in trying to resolve these three questions should be to produce a *balanced* system. We should try to match the speeds of the various processors with each other and with the speeds of the transfer paths; and we should try to provide the right media for storing the data files, in the right amounts. If we should fail, the result will be an unbalanced system, containing bottlenecks which reduce the system's speed of response, or over-designed components whose capabilities are wasted. Imbalance can also result from inattention to the design of the programming and operating systems: for example, the system may be difficult to program because no high-level language is supplied, or because the system is overly complex.

A second objective must be to keep the *cost* of the system as low as possible. One of the major impediments to the wide use of computer graphics has been the excessive cost of graphics systems, both in hardware and in software. It is not easy, however, to produce a system that is both balanced and inexpensive. The inherent speed of the display encourages us to match it with similarly high-speed processors and transmission lines, but these are inevitably more expensive than low-speed components. If we try to use low-speed components, the money we save may in the end be absorbed in writing software to compensate for the hardware's shortcomings.

17.2.2   LOCATING THE COMPONENTS

Underlying the three questions posed above is a fourth: where should we *locate* the various components that make up the system? Should we group them all in a single processor, or distribute them among several?

The location or distribution of the system's components has for many years been a favorite subject for debate amongst system designers. A great many different solutions have been proposed. Many of these have become obsolete with the advance of technology, but there still remains a large and seemingly disorganized array of alternatives. Most of these involve some physical separation of the components of the system.

Figure 17-1 provides us with a framework within which we can evaluate most of these *distributed* graphics systems. Every graphics system contains two basic elements: the *terminal* which provides the user with a displayed image and with input devices so that he can interact with the program; and a *central processor* that controls, and in most cases executes, the application program. Each of the processes and data files must reside either in the terminal or in the central processor, and we can classify systems according to the placement of the dividing line.

The use of Figure 17-1 means that we must draw *two* dividing lines, for the two components that indisputably belong in the terminal — the CRT and the input devices — are at opposite ends of the diagram. Wherever we draw these two lines, the components between them reside in the central processor, and the terminal must accommodate the components that remain. This is shown in the simplified diagram of Figure 17-2. Not all positions for the lines make sense, however, and only a few have actually been suggested in the form of system designs. They include the following:

1. *Minimum-cost terminal.* The dividing lines are drawn to the right of the input devices and to the left of the transformed display file (Figure 17-3). This arrangement is exemplified by the low-cost graphics terminal attached to a time-shared system. The need for a display file may be avoided by using a storage CRT.
2. *Low-cost terminal with some processing power.* The dividing lines are drawn to the right of the interrupt routines and to the left of the display code generator (Figure 17-4). This is made possible by adding a small amount of processing power to the terminal so that it can handle interrupts, can convert the central processor's output to display instructions, and can perform simple display file manipulations.
3. *Programmable graphics satellite.* Some of the input and output routines reside in the terminal: the dividing lines are moved so that they overlap the application program itself (Figure 17-5).

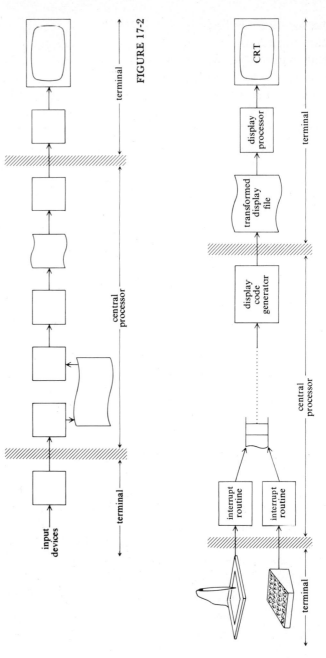

FIGURE 17-2

FIGURE 17-3

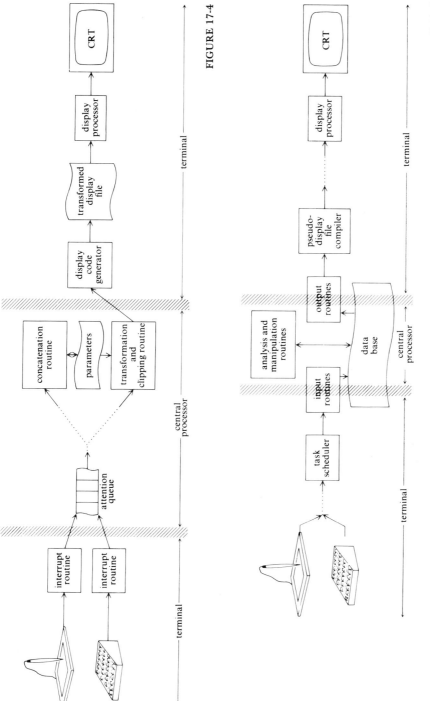

FIGURE 17-4

FIGURE 17-5

It is interesting to study the effect of locating the dividing lines in these and other positions. Foley [93] has published a detailed study of this problem, and of the problem of choosing the bandwidth of the transmission path between the central processor and the terminal. His approach is to devise a mathematical model for a time-shared graphics system, and to use this model to optimize the system's cost and speed of response. In choosing to optimize these parameters it is easy to overlook several important issues. One of these is the following: however we divide the system, we must keep the division as clean and simple as possible, so as to minimize software complexity. It is hopeless to place two components in the terminal if the component between them is in the central processor. For example, we cannot use the central processor to transform a pseudo-display file that is kept in the terminal. Similarly, we must be extremely circumspect about using graphical data structures, i.e. dual purpose structures, in a system that separates the terminal from the central processor. If we do so, we are faced with the conflicting desires both to place this structure in the central processor, so that the application program can use it, and to place it in the terminal, so that it can be used to refresh the display. This point has been ignored by several designers of satellite systems [43, 58].

An even more fundamental flaw in this entire approach to graphics system design is that there is no real need to *separate* the central processor from the terminal. It is quite feasible to take all the essential components shown in Figure 17-1, and group them in a single, inexpensive processor. In Section 17.4 we explore this approach to graphics system design; and in Section 17.5 an actual system design is presented in some detail. However, we should first look at the time-sharing approach to computer graphics and see what problems we encounter.

17.3   TIME-SHARED GRAPHICS SYSTEMS

Time-sharing was introduced in the mid-1960's as a means of providing interactive computing at a reasonable cost. The basic principle is to place as much as possible of the system's resources in a central facility, and to allocate these resources to the terminal users on demand. When one user demands resources that are allocated to another, the system must resolve the conflict. In the case of multiple demands on the processor, the system adopts a time-slicing solution: it cycles rapidly among all the users who require service. For other resources, such as peripherals, a queue of requests is normally maintained.

The more of the system's resources we place in the central facility, the fewer are left in the user's terminal. This is one of the main justifications for time-sharing. Any resources that we leave in the terminal are active only when the user makes a demand on them, and this happens very infrequently by computing standards. If the resources are centralized, then while one user has no need for them, the resources can be allocated to others. This has led to the development of very simple, inexpensive teletypewriter terminals.

The success of time-sharing has been partly due to the use of teletypewriters as terminals. Since the user must *type* his commands to the system, he is prevented from making demands at a very rapid rate; and because the computer's output is typed too, it can be transmitted over very low-speed transmission lines. The limited speed of the terminal, although it is often irritating to the user, provides a necessary control over his rate of interaction with the system. A second reason for time-sharing's success is one that the early system designers did not anticipate: this is the tremendous value of large, centralized file systems in both individual and group computer projects.

All this may appear to have rather little to do with computer graphics. It is very relevant, however, for two reasons in particular. In the first place, there is wide acceptance of the notion that time-sharing offers the cheapest basis for interactive computing. Many graphics systems designers accept this notion too, and their approach to systems design is to build *time-shared graphics systems.* However, the demand for interactive graphics is rarely enough to justify building a complete time-shared system specifically for graphics. Instead, use is made of a system designed originally for teletypewriter terminals. This second point is an important one, for it is the main reason why so few really successful time-shared graphics systems have been built. We shall look briefly at the two principal classes of time-shared graphics system.

17.3.1   SATELLITE GRAPHICS SYSTEMS

The satellite approach to computer graphics originated as an attempt to design a time-shared graphics system that could provide the responsiveness of a single-user graphics system. As was made clear in Chapter 11, many of the techniques we use in computer graphics depend on the use of local processing power: an example is the rubber-band line. Moreover, if the programmer is to use a wide range of techniques, he must be able to write procedures to be executed by the local processor. The satellite provides this capability by means of a small, general-purpose computer incorporated in the terminal.

A number of systems have been built around this concept, starting with the famous 'Kludge' at MIT [291]. Most have been basically experimental systems, but there have been a few attempts to build systems specifically for use by applications programmers; examples of the latter class of system include Bell Laboratories' GRAPHIC-2 [44, 206], Univac's 1108-1557/58 system [58] and the IBM software for the System/360 and the 2250 Model IV display [223]. Some of the experimental systems have been very successful in enabling pioneering applications work to be done: examples are the early GRAPHIC-1 system at Bell Laboratories [207], and the Titan/PDP-7 system at Cambridge University [154]. Systems designed from the outset to be used in applications work have, in contrast, been rather unsuccessful.

If any one reason can be found for this lack of success, it is that the extensive software with which these satellite systems have been equipped is excessively complex. Often this complexity results from making the mistake of using a graphical data structure: we have already discussed this in Section 17.2.2. Even if this mistake can be avoided, however, it is still necessary to split the program's *data base* between the two machines. This is clear from Figure 17-5: the data base is used both by the procedures in the central processor, and by the input and output procedures that reside in the satellite. In order for the two sets of procedures to communicate properly, at least a small subset of the data base must be accessible to both processors. Two of the biggest problems in designing a satellite system are to limit the amount of data stored in the satellite, and to provide a simple but efficient means of passing data between the processors.

Most designers of satellite systems have neglected to provide a convenient language for programming the satellite. This is understandable in view of the many problems in choosing a suitable language. On the one hand it is desirable to use the same language, or at least similar languages, in the two processors; on the other hand a conventional language, such as is likely to be used in the central processor, is quite unsuited to the tasks that the satellite must perform, and must in any case generally be redesigned to fit into such a small processor. Most satellite system designers have taken the simplest solution of all, and have provided only a low-level assembly language for programming the satellite. This to some extent explains these systems' lack of success.

17.3.2 LOW-COST TERMINAL SYSTEMS

A number of low-cost terminals were described in Chapter 4. These have all been designed for use with conventional time-shared systems. They vary considerably in their design and in their display capability; however they are generally similar to each other in cost and in their reliance on medium-speed, serial character transmission between the central processor and the terminal.

It is not difficult to build a system to make use of terminals of this sort. All that is required is a set of functions to transmit line and text information to the terminal in response to function calls generated by the application program. Several manufacturers of these terminals have in fact marketed software written in FORTRAN that performs basic scaling and clipping functions, and that can be used with FORTRAN application programs. The terminals are often equipped with graphical input devices that provide discrete inputs and can therefore be programmed analogously to a keyboard.

The real difficulty in using these terminals lies in compensating for their poor performance. As mentioned in Chapter 4, these terminals suffer from several deficiencies: poor picture quality, unsatisfactory transmission rates and, in most cases, lack of selective erase capability. This last problem is in many ways the most severe, for it combines with the problems of low transmission speed and poor time-shared response to make dynamic graphics almost impossible.

There are two ways to provide selective erase capability in the terminal. One is to allow parts of the picture to be *blanked out* by retracing them in a special mode; the plasma panel permits this, and it is also theoretically feasible on most storage tubes. The other approach is to provide a local memory and a small local processor: a complete segment of the picture can then be erased in response to a single command from the central processor.

This second technique has two very marked advantages. In the first place, the central processor need not keep a copy of the display file, whereas it must if retracing is required. Second, if a line is erased by retracing, gaps will be left in any lines crossed in the process (see Figure

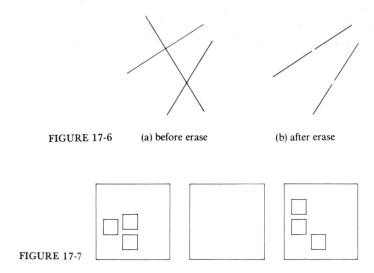

FIGURE 17-6   (a) before erase   (b) after erase

FIGURE 17-7

17-6); this is not a problem with refresh displays. The third advantage is best explained by taking as an example the problem of moving a segment of the picture. If we use each type of selective erase terminal and the non-selective erase display, we notice that the following steps are involved:

Non-selective erase: Erase entire picture;
                       Redraw entire picture with segment re-
                       positioned (Figure 17-7).
Selective erase by retrace: Retrace segment to erase it;
                       Redraw segment in new position (Figure
                       17-8)
Local memory and processor: Erase segment by command;
                       Redraw segment in new position (Figure
                       17-9)

The terminal with local processing power takes approximately half the time taken by the selective erase terminal, and very much less than the non-selective erase display. The slower the transmission speed, the more noticeable is this advantage. These are the main arguments in favor of terminals with processing power and memory: they are sufficient under many circumstances to justify these terminals' extra cost.

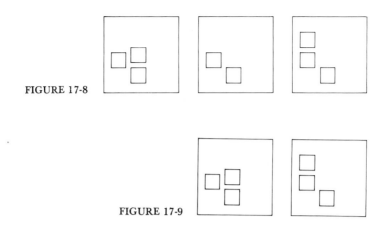

FIGURE 17-8

FIGURE 17-9

17.3.3   THE FUTURE OF TIME-SHARED COMPUTER GRAPHICS

Those who have for years proposed the construction of satellite graphics systems, and those who more recently have suggested the use of low-cost terminals, have essentially the same goal: to provide a highly interactive graphics system at the lowest possible cost. Their opinions differ on the correct interpretation of 'highly interactive:' this is one reason why two widely different solutions can be proposed to the same problem. Another reason is that the strategies adopted are quite different. One system designer starts with a set of performance requirements and builds the most inexpensive system that he believes will meet them: this produces the satellite. The other seizes on a new invention, the low-cost terminal, and finds the cheapest source of computing power with which he can use it: this results in the low-cost terminal system.

Thus only the satellite system can be deemed a deliberate attempt to keep to the original standards of what constitute a highly interactive system. The designer of the low-cost system in effect sets his own standards, in accordance with the capabilities of the terminal. This is a more realistic approach, and has in recent years been more successful in producing systems that are cost-effective, reliable and easy to implement and use.

Nevertheless it is important to point out that low-cost terminal systems represent a *lowering* of the standards of computer graphics. Display screens are smaller, line quality and contrast is often poor, many interactive techniques are ruled out, and the response provided by the time-shared system is often slow and is compounded by transmission delays. This step towards mediocrity is in distinct contrast to the trends in other branches of computer technology, where standards have continued to rise. It is probably fair to those who have given us the low-cost terminal system to say that they have tried to reproduce the quality of earlier graphics systems at an economic price, but have failed. They have instead created a new branch of computer graphics, namely low-cost graphics, with its own standards.

The designers of satellite systems have been less fortunate, for their systems have remained too costly for use except in research and in the design of expensive products like airplanes and automobile body patterns. Those who have tried to solve the problems of data communication have generally been beaten either by the complexity of the problem or by deficiencies in the time-shared computer's operating system. Because of lack of attention to the provision of languages, these systems have been too difficult for any but the expert programmer to use.

17.4   SINGLE-USER GRAPHICS SYSTEMS

We have seen that there are many problems in building an effective time-shared graphics system, and that some of these problems have no immediate solution. How, then, can we produce a system that is really effective? The answer is quite simple: the central processor and terminal can be combined to form a stand-alone, single-user graphics system. This system then contains all the task scheduling and transformation software, the display file and the user's program and data base.

There is relatively little disagreement these days with the notion that such an approach can lead to graphics systems that are simpler, easier to use and more responsive than time-shared systems. Anyone who remains unconvinced of this should look at the impressive array of advances that have been made in computer graphics using stand-alone graphics systems. These include Sutherland's SKETCHPAD [277] and Roberts' hidden-line algorithm [234], both programmed on TX-2 when it was a single-user machine; the Ledeen character recognizer and the Harvard three-dimensional display [273], both developed on a PDP-1; the GRAIL System [77, 78], developed at the RAND Corporation on an IBM System/360; and Armit's *Multipatch* [8, 9], written for an 8K

PDP-7. Had it been necessary to develop any of these projects under the restrictions, complexities and lack of response that characterize most time-shared graphics systems, it is unlikely that they would have made much progress.

There are arguments against single-user computer graphics, and the strongest is the issue of cost. All the single-user systems mentioned above have been large, expensive installations, except Armit's PDP-7 which sufficed largely because of Armit's ingenuity and programming skill. Since these systems were installed, however, there has been a precipitous drop in computer prices which is still continuing at the time of writing. This has completely altered the economics of computer graphics. It is possible now to justify the use of a single-user system by means of exactly the same argument that was previously used to justify satellites — we can add a substantial processor to the terminal without greatly increasing its cost.

This situation is somewhat paradoxical. According to our earlier discussion of time-shared systems, it must be possible to provide processing power more cheaply from a shared resource, such as a time-shared system, than from a processor dedicated to the terminal user. However, this is true only in an ideal environment. In reality we have transmission delays to contend with; and we have software problems.

The problem of providing software, and operating systems in particular, has been one of the great weaknesses of time-sharing. It has generally taken two years or more from the introduction of time-sharing hardware to the existence of a reliable, well-equipped software system. This has meant that in order to be sure of reliable service it has been necessary to use machines that were several years old, in machine architecture if not in actual construction. This lag between hardware and software implementation has always been particularly long in the case of time-shared graphics systems, and will probably remain that way for some time to come. In the meantime, small machines are a cheaper source of computing power than time-shared systems.

After one has explored the economic aspect of single-user versus time-shared systems, there remains one further persuasive argument. The user of a time-shared system must always be concerned with the amount of processor time he is using and what it will cost him. He is liable to restrict his activity in many situations where additional interaction would get his job done more quickly. This is illogical, for the main reason for using graphics equipment is to enhance ones ability to interact with the computer. The need to conserve CPU cycles vanishes when a single-user system is used.

Compared with the array of complex issues facing the designer of a time-shared graphics system, the problems of designing a single-user system are minor. All of the components of such a system have in fact been described in earlier chapters of this book. The next section proposes in outline a system design that combines these components in an optimum fashion.

17.5   THE DESIGN OF A SINGLE-USER GRAPHICS SYSTEM

The system described here is not intended to cater to all possible graphics applications: such a system cannot at the time of writing be built, except at a price that would put it out of reach of most of its potential users. What is proposed here is a system capable of satisfying the needs of a very large proportion of today's graphics users. Furthermore, it could potentially be built so cheaply that many who do not now contemplate the use of computer graphics could afford to use it.

17.5.1   DESIGN CRITERIA AND STRATEGIES

The three main design criteria are versatility, low cost and ease of use. The basic strategies employed to satisfy these criteria are as follows:

1. *Low cost:* The system is designed to be implemented on a small computer, equipped with a relatively small high-speed memory, a backing store, a line-drawing display and input devices including a keyboard and tablet. The hardware configuration of the system is shown in Figure 17-10.
2. *Versatility:* The use of a local dedicated computer rather than a remote time-shared system enables the system to provide a good response. This response is enhanced by equipping the processor with floating-point hardware, and can be further improved if, as suggested in Section 17.5.3.4, a separate processor is used to perform transformations. The use of a paged associative data structure enables large data files to be constructed very easily without the need for excessive fast memory.

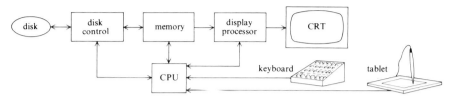

FIGURE 17-10

3. *Ease of use:* The system is designed to be operated and programmed by means of a single, high-level language. This language allows complex pictures to be defined by means of *display procedures*, as described in Chapter 8, and includes features for command language definition.

17.5.2   SYSTEM ORGANIZATION

The organization of the system software is shown in Figure 17-11. Essentially it is the system of Figure 17-1, simplified by the use of display procedures and extended by providing paged associative data structures.

The reader will perceive that the design of each of the system components has been covered by one of the earlier chapters in this book. The following description does not repeat what has previously been discussed, but presents the overall design of each component, with references to the relevant passages in earlier chapters.

17.5.3   DETAILED DESIGN

17.5.3.1   Programming language

Since ease of use is a major design criterion, the choice of programming language is of prime importance. The language chosen here is an extension of Wirth's EULER [310, 311], to which we have referred in Section 16.4. This language demands a fairly unconventional machine structure, for it is fully recursive and block structured, and requires type-checking to be done at run time. In most of the small machines currently available this implies the use of an *interpreter*, rather than compilation of machine code. Some, however, permit the use of *microprogramming* to modify the machine architecture to suit the language.

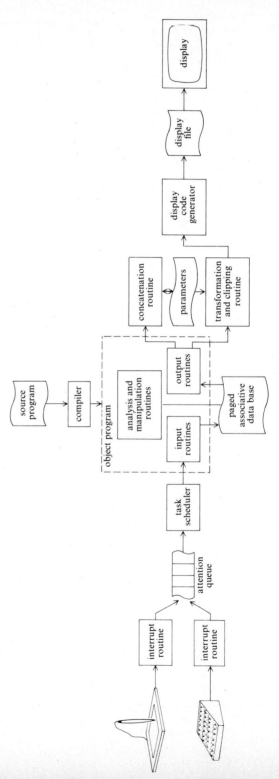

FIGURE 17-11

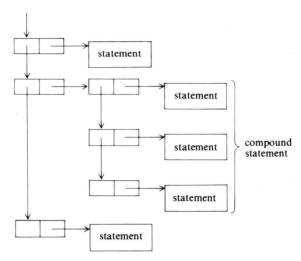

FIGURE 17-12

True interpretation of source statements is undesirable in the case of a language like EULER: instead we compile into a compact interpretive code. It is desirable, however, that this compilation be done *incrementally*, i.e. in a fashion that permits single statements to be modified without complete program recompilation and that allows the direct execution of statements. Incremental compilation is difficult to achieve with a block-structured language like EULER, but can be done by storing the compiled code in a tree-structured form as shown in Figure 17-12. During the debugging phase the source code for each statement is stored alongside its compiled equivalent.

The graphical output facilities of the language are essentially those described in the sections of Chapters 8 and 15 on display procedures. Complex pictures are defined in the form of procedures which may be called with various transformations applied to them:

DRAW RESISTOR AT (100,200) SCALE 0.75

It is possible, however, to create simple pictures by using just the graphical primitives in the language. The language makes use of the hit-detection technique described in Chapter 11, in which the picture is regenerated to test for proximity of the stylus to any point, line or character.

Input functions are provided to allow data to be read from the keyboard and stylus. These functions are supplemented by a state-diagram facility for defining the command language, similar to that of the DIAL language described in Section 15.4.3. The combination of input functions with the DURING and ON statements of DIAL is particularly convenient. For example, the following statement will store the pen position in P when the pen is pressed down, using the input function PENXY:

ON PENDOWN DO P ← PENXY

The data structure facilities are similar to those of LEAP, mentioned in Chapter 16 and described in some detail in Appendix V. However, some modifications are necessary to incorporate these facilities into a language free of type declarations. SAIL's simpler form of the FOREACH statement, for example, avoids the need for defined local variables:

FOREACH X SUCH THAT NEXT·X≡Q DO . . .

A. C. Kay [136] has proposed a complete implementation of LEAP structures in a language based on EULER.

17.5.3.2 Input handling

Inputs from the keyboard and tablet are passed to the program by means of attentions, as described in Chapter 10. These attentions can be checked by means of the ON statements in the language, as illustrated in the example above.

17.5.3.3 Graphical output

Graphical output is performed as described in the sections of Chapters 8 and 15 that relate to display procedures. Graphical primitives pass their parameters directly to one of two transformation and clipping routines, depending on whether rotation is in effect. The transformed, clipped information is then compiled into display code and is added to the display file. Transformations specified in display procedure calls are passed to the concatenation routine.

The display file itself is segmented into frames, each of which can be regenerated or deleted without modifying the rest of the display file. Blocks of free storage for use in constructing the display file are provided by the system's free storage allocation routines.

17.5.3.4 System configurations

The system is constructed in a modular fashion. This permits it to be configured in a variety of ways besides the one shown in Figures 17-10 and 17-11. Two of the possible alternative arrangements are shown in Figures 17-13 and 17-14.

Figure 17-13 shows the use of two processors to enhance the system's performance. One processor is responsible for program interpretation, the other for picture transformation and display file generation. The two processors should ideally share the same memory, since the rate of transfer of information between the program's output procedures and the transformation routine is potentially very high.

In Figure 17-14 we see a system at the opposite extreme, that uses the minimum of memory and processing power, and that offers a very basic graphics capability. The transformation system is reduced to a single clipping routine, and the display file is avoided by the use of a plasma panel or equivalent CRT display. Other configurations can be designed, whose capabilities lie between this one and the original one of Figure 17-10. For example, we can use a refresh display without transformation software, or with windowing but without rotation. Each such addition to the system demands additional fast memory.

17.5.3.5 Networks

No mention has been made during this description of the subject of *file handling*. A file system is vitally important, however, both to enable users of the system to preserve their programs and data, and to enable them to share their work with others and to take part in group projects. A partial solution to this problem can be achieved by equipping the system with a removable disk system for file storage. A file system of this sort will necessarily be a restricted one, however: a large hardware and software investment is involved in building a full-scale file system.

The most promising approach to this problem appears to be the work that is currently under way on developing shared file systems [88]. These systems are effectively small, special-purpose time-shared systems

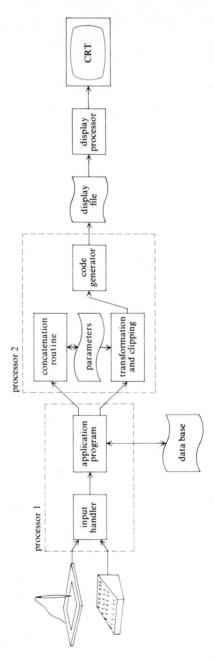

FIGURE 17-13

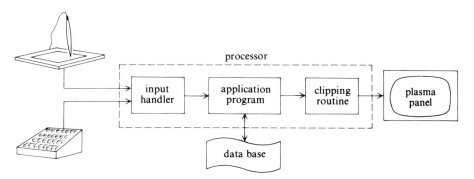

FIGURE 17-14

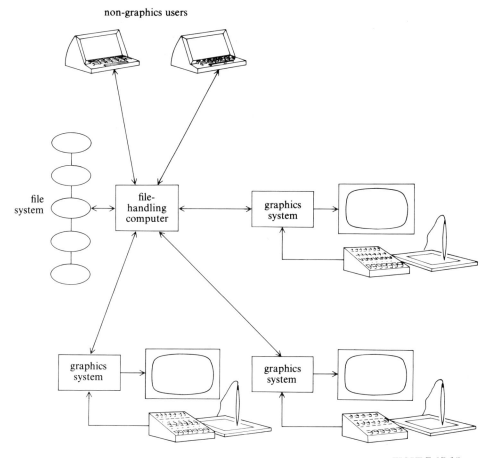

FIGURE 17-15

whose only function is to provide very powerful file-handling facilities to a large number of remote users. A system such as this could provide services to a number of graphics users by attaching their computers to a *network* of the kind shown in Figure 17-15. Provided high-speed transmission could be provided between the file system and the graphics computer, the need for file-handling in the latter could be avoided altogether.

Computer networks offer other advantages besides access to large file systems. They can provide the benefits of a large user community even more effectively than can a single time-shared computer; and they can give the users of small computers access to machines with much greater computing power. Such large machines will not normally provide rapid response, but they will enable large-scale computations to be performed on a remote-entry basis. These advantages have been demonstrated by the ARPA Network [236], a network of high-speed transmission lines and specially designed message processors, connecting research centers scattered widely throughout the United States. Thus by connecting his computer to a network, the single user of a graphics system such as we have discussed could potentially gain all the advantages of access to large file systems and powerful computers, and of membership of a large user community.

17.6   CONCLUSION

We have concluded the final chapter of this book with a description of a feasible low-cost graphics system. We believe that this system represents the most effective use of the techniques described in the earlier chapters. Within a year or two, graphics technology may well progress to the point where even simpler, more powerful systems can be designed and built.

It is clear that great advances can still be made in building low-cost transformation processors, and that these processors can be built not only into displays, but also into computers so as to help them to transform pictures. Hopefully the next few years will also see the development of high-quality, high-performance, inexpensive alternatives to the cathode ray tube. We believe that, even if hardware technology should change drastically, line-drawing computer graphics systems will continue to be built according to the principles we have described.

The most exciting area of computer graphics research at present is not in line-drawing techniques, however, but in the generation of shaded pictures of three-dimensional objects. The technology of this branch of computer graphics is still at an early stage of development, and needs a great deal of effort to be devoted to raising the performance of display hardware and reducing its cost. There has been virtually no work done on the development of programming techniques and languages for this style of computer graphics.

As this research proceeds, we would hope to see increasing use of line-drawing systems in a wide variety of applications. These applications have existed for years, but have been neglected because of the cost and complexity of interactive computer graphics. Cost is no longer the problem that it was; and we hope we have demonstrated in this book the feasibility of building simple graphics systems. The way appears open for computer graphics to fulfil the promise that it first showed to us ten years ago.

BIBLIOGRAPHY

This bibliography is intended to serve two purposes: it contains entries for all references made in the text of this book, and it contains additional entries which refer to a spectrum of articles and papers about computer graphics. Because the literature pertaining to computer graphics is immense, the bibliography is rather selective, and hence represents a biased view of the field.

In order to provide some guidance to the reader interested in pursuing the graphics technology, the bibliography is cross-referenced by subject headings. The paragraphs below attempt to organize the relevant papers into groups of historical interest, of interest due to technically productive ideas, or of only passing interest.

B.1 INTRODUCTION AND META-GRAPHICS

The flavor of computer graphics is perhaps best represented in an article by Sutherland [275] and two by Licklider [162, 164]. Other papers by these two are inspirational [278, 160, 163], or report on developments in the graphics field [276, 161]. Other survey articles of general interest are [54, 295, 120, 56, 181, 76].

A role of graphics in larger social and technological systems is one of the hopes of graphics technology. The papers of Licklider (particularly [163]) hint at the potential of the role. An old article by Bush [38] is particularly interesting in the light of more recent developments of graphics. Other noteworthy papers are [79] and [52].

Several books and conference proceedings have been devoted entirely to computer graphics, and contain good collections of papers: [258, 87, 212, 213].

Films that show interactive computer graphics systems in operation are [188, 189, 222, 269, 14, 146]. Films made with the aid of computer animation systems are [51, 14, 294, 20, 259, 75].

B.2   HARDWARE AND DISPLAY SYSTEMS

The technology of constructing display hardware is described in [65]. This reference describes digital and analog control electronics, phosphor characteristics, manufacturing methods, etc. Other introductions to CRT's are [62] and [257]. Descriptions of some of the newer types of display can be found in the literature: Plasma Panel [22, 117, 263, 214, 304, 34]; Direct View Storage Tube [270]; Silicon target tube [217, 218]; Video Systems [293, 250, 239, 208]; Liquid Crystal displays [59].

A great number of different kinds of display terminals is currently marketed. The *Computer Display Review* [139] gives characteristics of all of these, although often the particularly good or poor features of the display are not readily apparent from the descriptions. Other surveys [158, 184] evaluate display equipment current at the time.

The design of display processors is not adequately documented. Interesting processor designs are [84, 302, 70]. Of historical interest are [17] and [71], which describe one of the first display processor designs. An important general paper on the subject, which introduces the 'Wheel of Reincarnation,' is [193].

Special hardware techniques have been developed to aid common operations in computer graphics: three-dimensional display [84, 273, 111, 297, 114, 225]; stereoscopic viewing [153, 211, 84, 273]; curve generation [67, 24, 231, 84, 273].

The use of raster-scan displays and phosphor characteristics has been thoroughly investigated by television manufacturers. Among the useful developments are: [169, 290, 16, 82, 170, 183, 252]. See also Section B.10.

Other articles on display equipment of various kinds are [121, 228, 299, 291, 106, 109, 112, 179].

B.3 INPUT HARDWARE AND TECHNIQUES

Hardware used for input includes tablet devices [33, 64, 187, 288, 292, 255], the SRI mouse [81], and many others. For descriptions of interfaces of tablets to large time-sharing systems, see [60] and [101]. Devices which record three-dimensional input information are described in [235] and [273].

Descriptions of input techniques are spread throughout the literature (see Sections B.5 and B.7). Of special note are the character recognition methods: a survey of both on-line and off-line methods with a good bibliography appears in [191]; specific systems of note are [107, 286, 23, 21, 60].

A facility for remembering input interactions and selectively re-using them is described in [289]. The light handle technique is described in [199]. See also [271] and [277] for input techniques.

B.4 OPERATING SYSTEMS AND SATELLITES

Relatively few papers have described the problem of servicing displays from a large time-sharing or batch system. Good systems include [205, 282, 293, 215]. Other papers are [26] and [138].

Systems have also been built for small machines to provide interactive services [119]. The small machine may then be connected to a larger system where extended computations are performed. Graphic-1 [207] and Graphic-2 [44, 206] are prime examples of these satellite systems. Other such systems are described in [228, 58, 314, 316, 291, 223]. A study of the design of such a system is [93].

B.5 LANGUAGES

References for specific programming languages are difficult to provide. In some cases, a manufacturer's reference manual is a more informative document than a journal article. A collection of many good papers on

programming languages is [240]. Languages of interest are ALGOL-60
[72, 194], BASIC [260], JOSS [15, 261], APL [126], EULER [311,
303, 310], LISP [306, 178, 287], PL/I [262, 125].

Many languages have been developed exclusively for use in graphics
environments; still others have been augmented to provide adequate
service for displays. Kulsrud's system [151] and the EULER-G
language for the PDP-10 [203, 204] are noteworthy; DIAL [201]
provides state-diagram and display-procedure techniques but is a less
general programming language than EULER-G. The LEAP language
[91, 248, 247] has also been adapted for the PDP-10 as SAIL [283].
GRAIL [77, 78] is an important example of an entirely graphical
language. The Graphic-2 language GRIN-2 is described in [44]. The
AMBIT/G language is described in [43, 45, 249]. Other papers are
[291, 281, 123, 53, 209, 251, 315]. Papers relating to design and
construction of languages are [268] and [90].

Descriptions of graphical command languages may be found in [202,
8, 32]. Interesting techniques for defining command languages are
described in [8, 200, 201, 289]; other papers on this subject are [230]
and [58].

B.6   DATA STRUCTURES

The literature on data structures is vast, and we present here only
articles of special interest to designers of graphics systems. An
introduction is [279]. The field is surveyed well in [309] and [105].
The description of the Sketchpad data structure [277] is a good
introduction to important considerations in graphics. The LEAP data
structures are described in [248, 91, 89]. CORAL, a ring structure, is
described in [281] and [232]. Other papers of interest are [268, 284,
42, 155, 296, 190, 307, 58].

B.7   COMPUTER PROGRAMS USING GRAPHICS EXTENSIVELY

There are a sizeable number of papers describing graphics systems or
large computer programs which make intelligent use of graphics
techniques. Some of these programs were developed with graphical
manipulation as the end goal: Sketchpad [277] and Sketchpad III
[131]. Others were developed with specific applications in mind. For
example, [280, 198, 226, 43] describe graphical systems for specifying
computer programs.

Computer-Aided Design is another application of graphics. A complete description of a cost-effective operational CAD system is given in [216]. A general discussion of CAD appears in [54]. Papers relating to the Multipatch system are [8] and [9]; those relating to the AED system at MIT are [244, 32, 291, 241, 243, 242]. Other CAD systems are [31, 140, 19, 202]. This list by no means exhausts the spectrum of CAD efforts.

Computer Animation is another broad field of computer graphics programs. Surveys of animation techniques are [143] and [5]. An animation system that emphasizes interaction is described in [12, 11, 13, 14]. Knowlton's system is one of the earliest and most productive [142, 20, 146, 144]. Educational films have been one of the most popular outputs of computer animation [259, 75, 253, 122]. Computer animation is now being introduced into television production [118, 51]. Whitney, an artist, has found computer animation an aid in his movie production [46]. Other animation systems are [57, 285, 37, 36].

Systems for mathematical modeling and simulation are another class of program that make extensive use of graphics. A survey of such systems is presented in [265]. Interesting systems include [141, 159, 23, 172, 171]. Others are [152, 219, 266, 314].

The Center for Augmenting Human Intellect has developed an interactive system that manipulates text in useful ways [79, 80].

B.8   ALGORITHMS FOR COMPUTER GRAPHICS

Many of the techniques developed for computer graphics systems are interesting as algorithmic solutions to various numerical and symbolic computational problems.

Hidden-line elimination is one of the oldest problems in computer graphics. Roberts' paper [234] is interesting for historical and technical reasons — the algorithm he developed inspired great activity in this area. Warnock devised an elegant solution [300]. Other algorithms are [165, 174, 173, 99, 100, 6].

Interest in hidden-surface elimination replaced that in hidden-line elimination when half-tone displays became popular. The first display with hidden surfaces removed was developed by General Electric for NASA [246, 245]. The Warnock algorithm was the first to make elimination reasonably cheap [300]. Further activity at the University of Utah led to the Watkins algorithm [301], which has also been implemented in hardware. This algorithm is based on earlier work at Utah [318, 238, 237]. Mahl extended the algorithm to handle quadric surfaces [168], a problem first considered in [305], and subsequently in [317]. The University of Illinois has also developed a hidden-surface algorithm [28, 29], which was extended to show shadows formed by an arbitrarily-placed light source [137, 30]. Another approach has been taken by Newell [197] in which the sorting aspects of hidden-surface elimination are particularly apparent. Yet another hidden-surface algorithm is used by MAGI in movie animation [102].

Incremental algorithms for computer graphics are used extensively. Many of these are built into hardware for line generation, hidden-surface elimination, etc. The flavor of these methods is found in [47, 48, 49].

The clipping algorithm and variations are described in [267] and [47].

Floyd's paper on non-deterministic algorithms, examples of which occur in the Warnock and Watkins hidden-surface algorithms, is [92].

B.9   HALF-TONE TECHNIQUES

Specific computer methods have been developed for producing continuous-tone displays. Warnock describes some *ad hoc* methods for determining intensity values for shading [300]. Gouraud developed interpolation procedures for smoothing polyhedral surface displays [104]. Mahl produced displays of quadric surfaces directly [168].

The details of image presentation on raster-scan displays are contained in papers in Sections B.2 and B.10. Other articles are [83, 74, 208].

B.10   OPTICS, LIGHT, AND THE EYE

There is extensive literature on psychopictorics, photometry, photography, optics, and visual processes which has some bearing on the human perception of computer displays. This information is particularly applicable when subtle images are desired (color, shadows, continuous-tone shading) or when various visual cues are used (stereoscopy, perspective).

Much of the literature is concerned with effects in conventional photography. The books [182] and [195] are excellent surveys of photography. Other relevant articles are [185, 134, 132, 116, 4]. Reproduction of colors is discussed in [319, 150, 113, 166]. Tone calculations for television-like displays are discussed in [133] and [252].

The eye and its visual processes are described in [132] and [66]. The Mach band effect is described in [224]; stereo cues in [135].

A reference on classical optics is [256].

B.11   CURVES AND SURFACES: DESCRIPTION AND DISPLAY

Many techniques for displaying curves in two- and three-dimensions and surfaces in three-dimensions have been developed. However, we have chosen not to include a detailed description of these methods in the body of this book because the field is still underdeveloped: convenient mechanisms for modifying curves, for changing three-dimensional shapes, etc. are not yet widely available. This shortcoming is, to a great extent, a result of the inadequacy of current mathematical representations for curves and surfaces. When a user joins two curves, he may desire that the joint be made 'smooth,' or 'fair.' These desires must be translated into mathematical constraints on the shapes of the curves. In the process of satisfying the constraints, we may be forced to deform other parts of the curves already specified. This is clearly undesirable, except in free-form sketching.

The search for representations of curves and surfaces is driven by a few very important goals: (1) the representation of an object must be quite terse so as not to require a large memory, (2) the representation must yield a convenient *generator* for a display of that curve or surface, (3) the objects must be suitable for easy editing (joining, deforming, etc.), (4) the representation must facilitate other computations related to the objects: cross-section, area, volume, curvature, etc. In addition to finding an adequate representation, work is required to develop an adequate command system (or vocabulary) for describing changes to curves and surfaces. This system should respond quickly to a user's wishes; it may depend upon development of special graphic input devices to aid the interaction.

A survey of curve and surface techniques is given by Forrest in [94].

Several different mathematical representations for curves are used: splines [1, 3], rational cubic polynomials [2, 47, 157, 49, 96, 130], Bezier polynomials [95, 104], and difference equations for conic sections [48, 47]. Hardware has been developed to aid in rapid generation of some curves [231, 24, 84, 67].

The prime work in surface description was done by Coons [55]. He defines a surface as a collection of *patches*, joined at their boundaries. Each patch has a fairly terse description of its shape (64 numbers), and the mechanism for generating a display of the patch is quite straightforward. Further work on Coons patches is described in [156, 157, 94, 8]. Another class of surfaces is sections of quadric surfaces [233, 305, 168, 317].

Other papers pertaining to curves and surfaces are [104, 167, 148, 63].

B.12   MATHEMATICS

The mathematical concepts used throughout this book are described in many standard mathematics texts. An introduction to matrix techniques can be found in [10]. More detailed treatments of analysis techniques are found in [35, 98, 220].

Homogeneous coordinate systems are described fully in [176] and [175], although the treatment is not particularly applicable to graphics (Reference [175] depends on [176]). A good introduction for graphics use is [2]. Roberts lists most of the useful constructs in [233].

Numerical methods for computers are treated in many texts on numerical analysis. References [221, 97, 147, 220] are only a few.

Standard geometry texts describe projective geometries of the type used for perspective display of three-dimensional objects. One such text is [86].

Abbreviations used in the bibliography listing:

ACM	Association for Computing Machinery
JACM	Journal of the Association for Computing Machinery
CACM	Communications of the Association for Computing Machinery
AFIPS	American Federation of Information-Processing Societies
IFIPS	International Federation of Information-Processing Societies
SJCC	Spring Joint Computer Conference
FJCC	Fall Joint Computer Conference
IEEE	Institute for Electrical and Electronic Engineers

1   Ahuja, D. V.
'An Algorithm for Generating Spline-like Curves,' *IBM Systems Journal*, 7, 3/4, 206, 1968.

2   Ahuja, D. V.; Coons, S. A.
'Geometry for Construction and Display,' *IBM Systems Journal*, 7, 3/4, 188, 1968.

3   Akima, H.
'A New Method of Interpolation and Smooth Curve Fitting Based on Local Procedures,' *JACM*, 17, 4, 589, October 1970.

4   Akin, R. H.; Hood, J. M.
'Photometry,' in *Display Systems Engineering*, Luxenberg, H. R., Kuehn, R. L., eds., McGraw-Hill, 1968.

5   Anderson, S. E.
'Computer Animation: A Survey,' *Journal of Micrographics*, 5, 1, 13, September 1971.

6   Appel, A.
'Some Techniques for Shading Machine-Renderings of Solids,' *SJCC 1968*, Thompson Books, Washington, D. C., 37.

7   Appel, A.
'The Notion of Quantitative Invisibility and the Machine Rendering of Solids,' Proceedings 22nd National Conference, ACM, Thompson Books, Washington, D. C., 387, 1967.

8   Armit, A. P.
'Computer Systems for Interactive Design of Three-Dimensional Shapes,' PhD Thesis, University of Cambridge, November 1970.

9   Armit, A. P.
'Multipatch and Multiobject Design Systems,' Proceedings Royal Society, London, A 321, 235, 1971.

10   Ayres, F.
Theory and Problems of Matrices, McGraw-Hill, New York, 1967.

11   Baecker, R. M.
'From the Animated Student to the Animated Computer to the Animated Film to the Animated Student .....,' Proceedings Purdue 1971 Symposium on Applications of Computers to Electrical Engineering Education, Purdue University, 106, April 1971.

12   Baecker, R. M.
'Interactive Computer-Mediated Animation,' MIT Project MAC, TR-61, April 1969.

13   Baecker, R. M.
'Picture-Driven Animation,' *SJCC 1969*, AFIPS Press, Montvale, N. J., 273.

14   Baecker, R. M.; Smith, L.; Martin, E. (film)
GENESYS: An Interactive Computer-Mediated Animation System, available from Digital Computers Group, MIT Lincoln Laboratory, Lexington, Mass. 02173.

15   Baker, C. L.
'JOSS: Introduction to a Helpful Assistant,' Memorandum RM-5058-PR, RAND Corporation, Santa Monica, California, July 1966.

16   Baldwin, M. W. Jr.
'The Subjective Sharpness of Simulated Television Images,' *Bell System Technical Journal*, **19**, 563, 1940.

17   Ball, N. A.; Foster, H. Q.; Long, W. H.; Sutherland, I. E.; Wigington, R. L.
'A Shared Memory Computer Display System,' *IEEE Transactions on Electronic Computers*, EC-15, 5, 751, October 1966.

18   Barron, D. W.; Buxton, J. N.; Hartley, D. F.; Nixon, E.; Strachey, C.
'The Main Features of CPL,' *Computer Journal*, **6**, 134, 1963.

19   Baskin, H. B.; Morse, S. P.
'A Multilevel Modeling Structure for 'Interactive Graphic Design,' *IBM Systems Journal*, **7**, 3/4, 218, 1968.

20   Bell Telephone Laboratories (film)
      Incredible Machine (1969), available from Film Library, Bell
      Telephone Laboratories, Murray Hill, New Jersey, 07974.

21   Bernstein, M. I.; Williams, T. G.
      'A Two-Dimensional Programming System,' Proceedings 1968
      IFIP Congress, Morrell, A. J. H., ed., North Holland Pub. Co.,
      586, 1969.

22   Bitzer, D. L.; Slottow, H. G.
      'The Plasma Panel — a Digitally Addressable Display with
      Inherent Memory,' *FJCC 1966,* Spartan Books, Washington,
      D. C., 541.

23   Blackwell, F. W.; Anderson, R. H.
      'An On-Line Symbolic Mathematics System Using Hand-Printed
      Two-Dimensional Notation,' RAND Report RM-6018-PR,
      January 1970.

24   Blatt, H.
      'Conic Display Generator Using Multiplying Digital-Analog
      Converters,' *FJCC 1967,* Thompson Books, Washington, D. C.,
      177.

25   Bobrow, D. G.; Burchfiel, J. D.; Murphy, D. L.; Tomlinson, R. S.
      'TENEX, A Paged Time Sharing System for the PDP-10,' *CACM,*
      15, 3, 135, March 1972.

26   Bond, A. H.; Rightnour, J.; Coles, L. S.
      'An Interactive Graphical Display Monitor in a Batch-Processing
      Environment with Remote Entry,' *CACM,* 12, 11, 595,
      November 1969.

27   Booth, D. F.; Burtnyk, N.
      'Simulation of Three-Dimensional Object on a Two-Dimensional
      Computer Display,' *Bulletin Information Processing Society of
      Canada,* 1968.

28   Bouknight, W. J.
      'A Procedure for Generation of Three-dimensional Half-toned
      Computer Graphics Representations,' *CACM,* 13, 9, 527,
      September 1970.

29   Bouknight, W. J.
'An improved procedure for generation of half-tone computer graphics representations,' University of Illinois, Coordinated Science Laboratory, R-432, September 1969.

30   Bouknight, W. J.; Kelley, K. C.
'An Algorithm for Producing Half-Tone Computer Graphics Presentations with Shadows and Movable Light Sources,' *SJCC 1970*, AFIPS Press, Montvale, N. J., 1.

31   Bracchi, G.; Somalvico, M.
'An Interactive Software System for Computer Aided Design: An Application to Circuit Project,' *CACM*, 13, 9, 537, September 1970.

32   Brackett, J. W.; Hammer, M.; Thornhill, D. E.
'Case Study in Interactive Graphics Programming: A Circuit Drawing and Editing Program for Use with a Storage-Tube Display Terminal,' MIT Project MAC, TR-63, October 1969.

33   Brenner, A. E.; de Bruyne, P.
'A Sonic Pen: A Digital Stylus System,' *IEEE*, EC-19, 6, 546, June 1970.

34   Brown, F. H.; Zayac, M. T.
'A Multi-Color Plasma Panel Display,' Owens-Illinois, 1971.

35   Browne, E. T.
Introduction to Theory of Determinants and Matrices, University of North Carolina, Chapel Hill, 1958.

36   Burtnyk, N.; Wein, M.
'A Computer Animation System for the Animator,' Proceedings 1971 UAIDE Annual Meeting, Stromberg Datagraphix.

37   Burtnyk, N.; Wein, M.
'Computer-Generated Key-Frame Animation,' *Journal of Society of Motion Picture and Television Engineers*, 80, 3, 149, March 1971.

38   Bush, V.
'As We May Think,' *Atlantic Monthly*, July 1945.

39   Calvert, T. W.
'Projections of Multidimensional Data for Use in Man-Computer Graphics,' *FJCC 1968*, Thompson Books, Washington, D. C., 227.

40   Carr, C. S.; Luther, D. A.; Erdmann, S.
'The Tree-Meta Compiler-Compiler System,' University of Utah Computer Science Technical Report RADC-TR-69-83, March 1969.

41   Chasen, S. H.
'The Introduction of Man Computer Graphics into the Aerospace Industry,' *FJCC 1965*, Spartan Books, Washington, D. C., 883.

42   Childs, D. L.
'Description of a Set-Theoretic Data Structure,' *FJCC 1968*, Thompson Books, Washington, D. C., 557.

43   Christensen, C.
'An Example of the Manipulation of Directed Graphs in the AMBIT/G Programming Language,' in *Interactive Systems for Experimental and Applied Mathematics*, Klerer, M., Reinfelds, J., eds., Academic Press, 1968.

44   Christensen, C.; Pinson, E. N.
'Multi-Function Graphics for a Large Computer System,' *FJCC 1967*, Thompson Books, Washington, D. C., 697.

45   Christensen, C.; Wolfberg, M. S.; Fischer, M. J.
'A Report on AMBIT/G,' Applied Data Research, CA-7102-2611,-2612,-2613,-2614, February 1971.

46   Citron, J.; Whitney, J. H.
'CAMP — Computer Assisted Movie Production,' *FJCC 1968*, Thompson Books, Washington, D. C., 1290.

47   Cohen, D.
'Incremental Methods for Computer Graphics,' ESD-TR-69-193, Harvard University, April 1969.

48   Cohen, D.
'On Linear Difference Curves,' Harvard University, 1969. Also in Computer Display Review [139].

49   Cohen, D.; Lee, T. M. P.
'Fast Drawing of Curves for Computer Display,' *SJCC 1969*, AFIPS Press, Montvale, N. J., 297.

50   Comba, P. G.
'A Procedure for Detecting Intersections of Three Dimensional Objects,' *JACM*, **15**, 3, 354, July 1968.

51   Computer Image Corporation (film)
Caesar (1971), available from Computer Image Corporation, 260 South Beverly Drive, Beverly Hills, California, 90212.

52   Computers and Automation
'Computer Graphics for Society,' *Computers and Automation*, **19**, 10, 28 and 11, 30, 1970.

53   Conn, A. P.
'GRIND: A Language and Translator for Computer Graphics,' Dartmouth College, AFOSR-69-2989 TR, June 1969.

54   Coons, S. A.
'Computer Graphics and Innovative Engineering Design,' *Datamation*, 32, May 1966.

55   Coons, S. A.
'Surfaces for Computer Aided Design of Space Forms,' Massachusetts Institute of Technology, MIT Project MAC, TR-41, June 1967.

56   Coons, S. A.
'The Uses of Computers in Technology,' *Scientific American*, September 1966.

57   Cornwell, B.
      'Computer Generated Simulation Films,' *Information Display*, 8,
      1, 21, January 1971.

58   Cotton, I. W.; Greatorex, F. S. Jr.
      'Data Structures and Techniques for Remote Computer
      Graphics,' *FJCC 1968*, Thompson Books, Washington, D. C.,
      533.

59   Creagh, L. T.; Kmetz, A. R.; Reynolds, R. A.
      'Liquid Crystal Displays,' *1971 IEEE International Convention
      Digest*, 630.

60   Curry, J. E.
      'A Tablet Input Facility for an Interactive Graphics System,'
      Proceedings International Joint Conference on Artificial
      Intelligence, Walker, D. E., Norton, L. M., eds., 33, May 1969.

61   Curry, J. E.
      'Tablet Handling in an Interactive Graphics Environment,'
      Computer Display Review, Keydata Corp., Watertown, Mass.

62   Czech, J.
      The Cathode Ray Tube Oscilloscope, Interscience, New York,
      1957.

63   Danielsson, P. E.
      'Incremental Curve Generation,' *IEEE Transactions*, C-19, 783,
      September 1970.

64   Davis, M. R.; Ellis, T. O.
      'The Rand Tablet: A Man-Machine Graphical Communication
      Device,' *FJCC 1964*, Spartan Books, Baltimore, Md., 325.

65   Davis, S.
      Computer Data Displays, Prentice-Hall, Englewood Cliffs, 1969.

66   Davson, H.
      'Visual Optics and the Optical Space Sense,' in *The Eye*, Davson,
      H., ed., Academic Press, New York, 231, 1962.

67   Dertouzos, M. L.; Graham, H. L.
      'A Parametric Graphical Display Technique for on-line use,'
      FJCC 1966, Spartan Books, Washington, D. C., 201.

68   Desens, R. B.
      'Computer Processing for Display of Three-Dimensional
      Structures,' Naval Postgraduate School, CFSTI AD-706010,
      October 1969.

69   Deutsch, L. P.; Lampson, B. W.
      'An Online Editor,' *CACM*, **10**, 12, 793, December 1967.

70   Digital Equipment Corporation
      'DEC 338 Programmed Buffered Display,' Digital Equipment
      Corporation, Maynard, Mass., 1966.

71   Digital Equipment Corporation
      'Type 340 Precision Incremental CRT Display,' Digital
      Equipment Corporation, Maynard, Mass., 1965.

72   Dijkstra, E. W.
      A Primer of ALGOL 60 Programming, Academic Press, London,
      1962.

73   Duda, R. O.; Hart, P. E.
      'Experiments in the Recognition of Hand-Printed Text: Part II—
      Context Analysis,' *FJCC 1968*, Thompson Books, Washington,
      D. C., 1139.

74   Eastman Kodak
      'Halftone Methods for the Graphic Arts,' Data Book Q-3,
      Eastman Kodak Company, Rochester, N. Y., 1968.

75   Educational Development Corporation (film)
      *Computer animation samplers: "Movies from Computers — an
      Interim Report" 1969, and others,* available from Film Library,
      Educational Development Corporation, 39 Chapel St., Newton,
      Mass. 02160.

76   Ellis, T. O.; Heafner, J. F.; Sibley, W. L.
      'Interactive Man-Machine Communications,' *Instrumentation and Control*, 44, 1, 92.

77   Ellis, T. O.; Heafner, J. F.; Sibley, W. L.
      'The GRAIL Language and Operations,' RAND Report RM-6001-ARPA, September 1969.

78   Ellis, T. O.; Heafner, J. F.; Sibley, W. L.
      'The GRAIL project: An Experiment in Man-Machine Communications,' RAND Report RM-5999-ARPA, September 1969.

79   Englebart, D. C.; English, W. K.
      'A Research Center for Augmenting Human Intellect,' *FJCC 1968*, Thompson Books, Washington, D. C., 395.

80   Englebart, D. C.; *et al.*
      'Computer-Augmented Management-System Research and Development of Augmentation Facility,' Stanford Research Institute, RADC-TR-70-82, Final Report, April 1970.

81   English, W. K.; Englebart, D. C.; Berman, M. L.
      'Display-Selection Techniques for Text Manipulation,' *IEEE Transactions on Human Factors*, HFE-8, 1, 5, 1967.

82   Engstrom, E. W.
      'A Study of Television Image Characteristics: Part I,' *Proceedings of the IRE*, 21, 1631, 1933.

83   Erdahl, A. C.
      'Displaying Computer-Generated Half-tone Pictures in Real Time,' University of Utah Computer Science Technical Report 4-14.

84   Evans and Sutherland Computer Corporation
      'Line Drawing System Model 1: System Reference Manual,' Salt Lake City, Utah, 1971.

85   Everett, R. R.
'The Whirlwind I Computer,' *Review of Electronic Digital Computers*, Joint AIEE-IRE Conference, 70, February 1952.

86   Eves, H.
A Survey of Geometry, Allyn and Bacon, Boston, 1965.

87   Faiman, M.; Nievergelt, J.; eds.
Pertinent Concepts in Computer Graphics, Proceedings of Second University of Illinois Conference on Computer Graphics, University of Illinois Press, 1969.

88   Farber, D. J.; Larson, K. C.
'The System Architecture of the Distributed Computer System — an informal description,' University of California, Irvine, Technical Report 11, 1971.

89   Feldman, J. A.
'Aspects of Associative Processing,' MIT Lincoln Laboratory, 1965-13, April 1965.

90   Feldman, J. A.; Gries, D.
'Translator Writing Systems,' *CACM*, 11, 2, 77, February 1968.

91   Feldman, J. A.; Rovner, P. D.
'An Algol-based Associative Language,' *CACM*, 12, 8, 439, August 1969.

92   Floyd, R. W.
'Nondeterministic Algorithms,' *JACM,* 14, 4, 636, October 1967.

93   Foley, J. D.
'An Approach to the Optimum Design of Computer Graphics Systems,' *CACM*, 14, 6, 380, June 1971.

94   Forrest, A. R.
'Curves and Surfaces for Computer Aided Design,' University of Cambridge, PhD Thesis, July 1968.

95   Forrest, A. R.
'Interpolation and Approximation by Bézier Polynomials,'
University of Cambridge, Computer Laboratory CAD Document
45, October 1970.

96   Forrest, A. R.
'The Twisted Cubic Curve,' University of Cambridge, Computer
Laboratory CAD Document 50.

97   Forsythe, G. E.; Moler, C. B.
Computer Solution of Linear Algebraic Systems, Prentice-Hall,
Englewood Cliffs, 1967.

98   Franklin, J. N.
Matrix Theory, Prentice-Hall, Englewood Cliffs, 1968.

99   Freeman, H.; Loutrel, P. P.
'An Algorithm for the Solution of the Two-Dimensional
Hidden-Line Problem,' *IEEE Transactions*, EC-16, 6, 784,
December 1967.

100   Galimberti, R.; Montanari, U.
'An Algorithm for Hidden-Line Elimination,' *CACM*, 12, 4, 206,
April 1969.

101   Gallenson, L.
'A Graphics Tablet Display for Use Under Timesharing,' *FJCC
1967*, Thompson Books, Washington, D. C., 689.

102   Goldstein, R. A.
'The System for Computer Animation by 3-D Objects,'
Proceedings 1971 UAIDE Annual Meeting, Stromberg Data-
graphix.

103   Goldstein, R. A.; Nagel, R.
'3-D Visual Simulation,' *Simulation*, 16, 1, 25.

104   Gouraud, H.
'Computer Display of Curved Surfaces,' University of Utah,
UTEC-CSc-71-113, June 1971. Abridged version in *IEEE
Transactions* C-20, 623, June 1971.

105   Gray, J. C.
'Compound Data Structures for Computer Aided Design: A
Survey,' Proceedings ACM 20th National Conference, Thompson
Books, 355, 1967.

106   Griffin, J.
'Design Considerations for a Low Cost Graphic Computer
Terminal: Hardware and Software Compromises,' International
Conference on Remote Data Processing, 52, March 1969.

107   Groner, G. F.
'Real-Time Recognition of Hand Printed Text,' *FJCC 1966*,
Spartan Books, Washington, D. C., 591.

108   Groner, G. F.; Clark, R. L.; Berman, R. A.; DeLand, E. C.
'BIOMOD: An Interactive Graphics System for Modeling,' *FJCC
1971*, AFIPS Press, Montvale, N. J., 369.

109   Grover, D. J.
'Low Cost Graphic Display with Serial Access Core,' *Computer
Bulletin*, 15, 1, 33, January 1971.

110   Guedj, R. A.
'GRACE, A Sophisticated Graphic Display System,' 19th
Avionics AGARD Conference on Computers and Display
Systems, NATO, June 1970.

111   Hagan, T. G.; Nixon, R. J.; Schaeffer, L. J.
'The Adage Graphics Terminal,' *FJCC 1968*, Thompson Books,
Washington, D. C., p. 747.

112   Hambury, J. N.; Ironside, J.; Barney, G. C.
'An Economical Display System,' *Computer Bulletin*, 13, 9, 314,
September 1969.

113   Hardy, A. C.; Wurzburg, F. L. Jr.
'The Theory of Three-Color Reproduction,' *Journal of the
Optical Society of America*, 27, 227, 1937.

114   Hempstead, C. F.
'Motion Perception Using Oscilloscope Display,' *Computer Display Review*, Keydata Corp., Watertown, Mass.

115   Hendricks, W. A.
The Mathematical Theory of Sampling, Scarecrow Press, New Brunswick, N. J., 1956.

116   Higgins, G. C.; Jones, L. A.
'The Nature and Evaluation of the Sharpness of Photographic Images,' *Journal of the Society of Motion Picture and Television Engineers*, 58, 277, 1952.

117   Hoehn, H. J.; Martel, R. A.
'A 60 Line per Inch Plasma Display Panel,' *IEEE Transactions* ED-18, 9, 659, September 1971.

118   Honey, F. J.
'Computer Animated Episodes by Single Axis Rotations,' Proceedings UAIDE 1971 Annual Meeting, Stromberg Datagraphix. Also in Purdue Symposium on Applications of Computers to Electrical Engineering Education, Purdue University, 114, April 1971.

119   Hornbuckle, G. D.
'A Multiprogramming Monitor for Small Machines,' *CACM*, 10, 5, 273, May 1967.

120   Hornbuckle, G. D.
'The Computer Graphics/User Interface,' *IEEE Transactions on Human Factors*, HFE-8, 1, 17, March 1967.

121   Hostovsky, R.
'Design of a Display Processing Unit in a Multi-Terminal Environment,' University of Illinois Report 343, July 1969.

122   Huggins, W. H.; Entwisle, D. R.
'Computer Animation for the Academic Community,' *SJCC 1969*, AFIPS Press, Montvale, N. J., 623.

123   Hurwitz, A.; Citron, J. P.; Yeaton, J. B.
'GRAF — Graphical Extensions to FORTRAN,' *SJCC 1967*, Thompson Books, Washington, D. C., 553.

124   IMLAC Corporation
'IMLAC PDS-1 Users Manual,' IMLAC Corporation, Waltham, Mass., 1969.

125   International Business Machines Corp.
'PL/I F Programmer's Guide,' Form C28-6594-4, International Business Machines.

126   Iverson, K.
A Programming Language, Wiley, New York, 1962.

127   Jacks, E. L.
'A Laboratory for the Study of Graphical Man-machine Communication,' *FJCC 1964*, Spartan Books, Baltimore, Md., 343.

128   JEDEC Electron Tube Council
'Optical Characteristics of Cathode Ray Tube Screens,' JEDEC Publication 16A, EIA, Washington, D. C., January 1966.

129   Johnson, C. I.
'Principles of Interactive Systems,' *IBM Systems Journal*, 7, 3/4, 147, 1968.

130   Johnson, T. E.
'Arbitrarily Shaped Space Curves for CAD,' MIT 1966 Summer Session Course.

131   Johnson, T. E.
'SKETCHPAD III: A Computer Program for Drawing in 3-Dimensions,' MIT Electronic Systems Laboratory, ESL-TM-173, June 1963. Also in *SJCC 1963*, Spartan Books, Baltimore, Md., 347.

132   Jones, L. A.
'Psychophysics and Photography,' *Journal of the Optical Society of America*, 34, 66, 1944.

133   Jones, L. A.
'Recent Developments in the Theory and Practice of Tone Reproduction,' *Photographic Journal*, **89B**, 126, 1949.

134   Jones, L. A.
'The Psychological Evaluation of the Quality of Photographic Reproduction,' *Journal of Photographic Society of America*, **17**, 751, 1951.

135   Julesz, B.; Spivak, G. J.
'Stereopsis Based on Vernier Acuity Cues Alone,' *Science*, **157**, 563, 1967.

136   Kay, A. C.
'FLEX — A Flexible Extendable Language,' Computer Science Technical Report 4-7, University of Utah, June 1968.

137   Kelley, K. C.
'A Computer Graphics Program for the Generation of Half-tone Images with Shadows,' University of Illinois, Coordinated Science Laboratory, R-444, November 1969.

138   Kennedy, J. R.
'A System for Time-sharing Graphic Consoles,' *FJCC 1966*, Spartan Books, Washington, D. C., 211.

139   Keydata Corporation
Computer Display Review, Keydata Corporation, Watertown, Massachusetts, yearly.

140   Kilgour, A. C.
'Computer Graphics Applied to Computer Aided Design,' *Computer Bulletin*, **15**, 7, 18, January 1971.

141   Knott, G. D.; Reece, D. K.
'Modelab: A Civilized Curve-Fitting System,' Proceedings, ONLINE 72, Uxbridge, England, September 1972.

142   Knowlton, K. C.
'A Computer Technique for Producing Animated Movies,' *SJCC 1964*, Spartan Books, Baltimore, Md., 67.

143   Knowlton, K. C.
'Computer-Animated Movies,' in *Emerging Concepts in Computer Graphics*, Secrest, D., Nievergelt, J., eds., W. A. Benjamin, New York, 343, 1968.

144   Knowlton, K. C.
'EXPLOR — A Generator of Images from Explicit Patterns, Local Operations, and Randomness,' Proceedings 1970 UAIDE Annual Meeting, Stromberg Datagraphix, 544.

145   Knowlton, K. C.
'Programmer's Description of L-6,' *CACM*, 9, 8, 616, August 1966.

146   Knowlton, K. C. (film)
A Computer Technique for the Production of Animated Movies (1967), available from Technical Information Library, Bell Telephone Laboratories, Murray Hill, New Jersey, 07974.

147   Knuth, D. E.
The Art of Computer Programming, Addison-Wesley, Reading, Mass., 1968.

148   Kubert, B. R.
'PROCS: Perspective Representation of Curves and Surfaces,' Aerospace Corporation, San Bernardino Operations, April 1969.

149   Kubert, B.; Szabo, J.; Giulieri, S.
'The Perspective Representation of Functions of Two Variables,' *JACM*, 15, 2, 193, April 1968.

150   Kuehn, R. L.; Luxenberg, H. R.
'Visual Experience and Colorimetry,' in *Display Systems Engineering*, Luxenberg, H. R., Kuehn, R. L., eds., McGraw-Hill, 1968.

151   Kulsrud, H. E.
'A General Purpose Graphic Language,' *CACM*, 11, 4, 247, April 1968.

152   Lafata, P.; Rosen, J. B.
'An Interactive Display for Approximation by Linear Programming,' *CACM*, **13**, 11, 651, November 1970.

153   Land, R. I.; Sutherland, I. E.
'Real-time, Color, Stereo, Computer Displays,' *Applied Optics*, **8**, 3, 721.

154   Lang, C. A.
'The PDP-Titan Link,' Cambridge University Mathematical Laboratory Technical Report, November 1966.

155   Lang, C. A.; Gray, J. C.
'ASP — a Ring-Implemented Associative Structure Package,' *CACM*, **11**, 8, 550, August 1968.

156   Lee, T. M. P.
'A Class of Surfaces for Computer Display,' *SJCC 1969*, AFIPS Press, Montvale, N. J., 309.

157   Lee, T. M. P.
'Three Dimensional Curves and Surfaces for Rapid Computer Display,' ESD-TR-69-189, Harvard University, April 1969.

158   Lewin, M. H.
'An Introduction to Computer Graphic Terminals,' *Proceedings IEEE*, 1544, September 1967.

159   Lewis, H. R.
'SHAPESHIFTER: An Interactive Program for Experimenting with Complex-Plane Transformations,' ACM National Conference, 717, 1968.

160   Licklider, J. C. R.
'A Picture is Worth a Thousand Words — and It Costs . . .,' *SJCC 1969*, AFIPS Press, Montvale, N. J., 617.

161   Licklider, J. C. R.
'Man-Computer Communication,' in *Annual Review of Information Science and Technology*, 3, 201, Cuadra, C. A.; ed., Encyclopedia Britannica, Chicago, 1968.

162 Licklider, J. C. R.
'Man-Computer Partnership,' *International Journal of Science and Technology*, May 1965.

163 Licklider, J. C. R.
'Man-Computer Symbiosis,' *Transactions IRE*, PGHFE, HFE-1, 4, 1960.

164 Licklider, J. C. R.; Clark, W. E.
'On-Line Man-Computer Communication,' *SJCC 1962*, National Press, Palo Alto, Calif., 113.

165 Loutrel, P. P.
'A Solution to the Hidden-Line Problem for Computer-Drawn Polyhedra,' New York University, Department of Electrical Engineering Report 400-167, September 1967. Also *IEEE Transactions on Computers* EC-19, 3, 205, March 1970.

166 MacAdam, D. L.
'Quality of Color Reproduction,' *Journal of Society of Motion Picture and Television Engineers*, 56, 487, 1951.

167 MacCallum, K. J.
'Surfaces for Interactive Graphical Design,' *Computer Journal*, 13, 4, 352, November 1970.

168 Mahl, R.
'Visible Surface Algorithms for Quadric Patches,' University of Utah, UTEC-CSc-70-111, December 1970. Also in *IEEE Transactions* C-21, 1, January 1972.

169 Maloff, I. G.
'Gamma and Range in Television,' *RCA Review*, 3, 409, 1939.

170 Martin, S. T.; Headrick, L. B.
'Light Output and Secondary Emission Characteristics of Luminescent Materials,' *Journal of Applied Physics*, 10, 116, 1939.

171 Martin, W. A.
'Computer Input/Output of Mathematical Expressions,' Second Symposium on Symbolic and Algebraic Manipulation, ACM, 78, March 1971.

172 Martin, W. A.; Fateman, R. J.
'The MACSIMA System,' Second Symposium on Symbolic and Algebraic Manipulation, ACM, 59, March 1971.

173 Matsushita, Y.
'A Solution to the Hidden-line Problem,' Department of Computer Science, University of Illinois, Document 335, ILLIAC IV, 1969.

174 Matsushita, Y.
'Hidden-line Elimination for a Rotating Object,' *CACM*, 15, 4, 245, April 1972.

175 Maxwell, E. A.
General Homogeneous Coordinates in Space of Three Dimensions, Cambridge University Press, Cambridge, 1951.

176 Maxwell, E. A.
Methods of Plane Projective Geometry based on the use of General Homogeneous Coordinates, Cambridge University Press, Cambridge, 1946.

177 McCallister, S.; Sutherland, I. E.
'Final Report on the Area Warnock Hidden-Line Algorithm,' Evans and Sutherland Computer Corp., Salt Lake City, February 1970.

178 McCarthy, J.; *et al.*
'LISP 1.5 Programmer's Manual,' MIT, Computation Center and Research Laboratory of Electronics, 1965.

179 McDonald, H. S.; Ninke, W. H.; Weller, D. R.
'A Direct-View CRT Console for Remote Computing,' Digest of Technical Papers, 1967 International Solid State Circuits Conference, 68.

180 McQuillin, R. J.
'DECAL-BBN Programming Manual,' DECUS, Maynard, Mass., 1963.

181 Meadow, C. T.
Man-Machine Communication, Wiley, New York, 1970.

182 Mees, C. E. K.
The Theory of the Photographic Process, MacMillan, New York, 1942.

183 Mertz, P.; Gray, F.
'A Theory of Scanning and its Relation to the Characteristics of the Transmitted Signal in Telephotography and Television,' *Bell Systems Technical Journal*, 13, 465, 1934.

184 Michael, G. A.; Cralle, R. K.
'A Survey of Graphic Data Processing Equipment for Computers,' in *Computer Oriented Circuit Design*, Kuo, F. F.; Magnuson, W. G., eds, Prentice-Hall, 1969.

185 Miller, C. W.
Principles of Photographic Reproduction, MacMillan, New York, 1942.

186 Miller, R. B.
'Response Time in Man-Computer Conversational Transactions,' *FJCC 1968*, Thompson Books, Washington, D. C., 267.

187 Miller, S. W.
'Display Requirements for Future Man-Machine Systems,' *IEEE Transactions on Electronic Devices* ED-18, 9, 616, September 1971.

188 MIT Lincoln Laboratory (film)
SKETCHPAD, available from: Digital Computers Group, MIT Lincoln Laboratory, Lexington, Mass. 02173.

189 MIT Lincoln Laboratory (film)
The Interactive Circuit Mask Design Program, available from: Digital Computers Group, MIT Lincoln Laboratory, Lexington, Mass. 02173.

190   Morris, R.
      'Scatter Storage Techniques,' *CACM*, 11, 1, 38, January 1968.

191   Munson, J. H.
      'Experiments in the Recognition of Hand-Printed Text: Part I —
      Character Recognition,' *FJCC 1968*, Thompson Books, Washing-
      ton, D. C., 1125.

192   Myer, T. H.; Barnaby, J. R.
      TENEX Executive Language, Bolt Beranek and Newman,
      Cambridge, Mass., January 1971.

193   Myer, T. H.; Sutherland, I. E.
      'On the Design of Display Processors,' *CACM* 11, 6, 410, June
      1968.

194   Naur, P.; ed.
      'Revised Report on the Algorithmic Language ALGOL 60,'
      International Federation of Information Processing, 1962. Also
      in *CACM*, 6, 1, 1, 1963.

195   Neblette, C. B.
      Photography, Its Materials and Processes, Van Nostrand, New
      York, 1962.

196   Newell, A.; ed.
      Information Processing Language V Manual, Prentice-Hall, New
      York, 1964.

197   Newell, M. E.; Newell, R. G.; Sancha, T. L.
      'A New Approach to the Shaded Picture Problem,' Proceedings
      ACM National Conference, 1972.

198   Newman, W. M.
      'A Graphical Language for Display Programming,' Specialist
      Session of International Computer Graphics Symposium, Brunel
      University, Uxbridge, August 1968.

199   Newman, W. M.
      'A Graphical Technique for Numerical Input,' *Computer Journal*,
      11, 1, 63, May 1968.

200   Newman, W. M.
'A System for Interactive Graphical Programming,' *SJCC 1968*, Thompson Books, Washington, D. C., 47.

201   Newman, W. M.
'An Experimental Display Programming Language for the PDP-10 Computer,' University of Utah, UTEC-CSc-70-104, July 1970.

202   Newman, W. M.
'An Experimental Program for Architectural Design,' *Computer Journal*, 9, 1, 21, May 1966.

203   Newman, W. M.
'Display Procedures,' *CACM*, 14, 10, 651, October 1971.

204   Newman, W. M.; Gouraud, H.; Oestreicher, D. R.
'A Programmer's Guide to PDP-10 Euler,' University of Utah, UTEC-CSc-70-105, June 1970.

205   NIH PDP-10 Users Manual
PDP-10 Display Systems Division of Computer Research and Technology, National Institutes of Health, Bethesda, Md., October 1972.

206   Ninke, W. H.
'A Satellite Display Console System for a Multi-access Central Computer,' Proceedings 1968 IFIP Congress, Morrell, A. J. H., ed., North Holland Pub. Co., 962, 1969.

207   Ninke, W. H.
'Graphic 1 — A Remote Graphical Display Console System,' *FJCC 1965*, Spartan Books, Washington, D. C., 839.

208   Noll, A. M.
'Scanned-Display Computer Graphics,' *CACM*, 14, 3, 143, March 1971.

209   Notley, M. G.
'A Graphical Picture Drawing Language,' *Computer Bulletin*, 14, 3, 68, March 1970.

210 Ophir, D.; Shepherd, B. J.; Spinrad, R. J.
'Three-Dimensional Computer Display,' *CACM*, 12, 6, 309, June 1969.

211 Ortony, A.
'A System for Stereo Viewing,' *Computer Journal*, 14, 2, 140, May 1971.

212 Parslow, R. D.; Green, R. E.; eds.
Advanced Computer Graphics: Economics, Techniques and Applications, Second International Computer Graphics Symposium, September 1970, Plenum Press, 1971.

213 Parslow, R. D.; Prowse, R. W.; Green, R. E.; eds.
Computer Graphics: Techniques and Applications, First International Computer Graphics Symposium, Brunel University, Uxbridge, July 1968, Plenum Press, 1969.

214 Petty, W. D.; Slottow, H. G.
'Multiple States and Variable Intensity in the Plasma Display Panel,' *IEEE Transactions*, ED-18, 9, 654, September 1971.

215 Poole, D. W.; Moorer, J. A.
'Stanford Display Service,' Artificial Intelligence Project, Stanford University.

216 Prince, M. D.
Interactive Graphics for Computer-Aided Design, Addison-Wesley, Reading, Mass., 1971.

217 Princeton Electronic Products
'LITHOCON (TM) Electrical Storage Tube,' Princeton Electronic Products, New Brunswick, N. J., 1970.

218 Princeton Electronic Products
'PEP 801 Computer Graphic Terminal,' Princeton Electronic Products, New Brunswick, N. J., 1971.

219 Priver, A. S.
'An Interactive Graphic System for Curve Fitting and Editing,' RAND Report P-3766, September 1969.

220   Protter, M. H.; Morrey, C. B. Jr.
      Modern Mathematical Analysis, Addison-Wesley, Reading, Mass.,
      1964.

221   Ralston, A.; Wilf, H. S.; eds.
      Mathematical Methods for Digital Computers, Wiley, New York,
      1960 & 1967.

222   RAND Corporation (film)
      The GRAIL System, available from: J. Heafner, RAND
      Corporation, 1700 Main St., Santa Monica, California, 90406.

223   Rapkin, M. D.; Abu-Gheida, O. M.
      'Stand-alone/Remote Graphic System,' *FJCC 1968*, Thompson
      Books, Washington, D. C., 731.

224   Ratliff, F.
      'Mach Bands: Quantitative Studies on Neural Networks in the
      Retina,' Holden-Day, San Francisco, 1965.

225   Rawson, E. G.
      'Vibrating Varifocal Mirrors for 3-D Imaging,' *IEEE Spectrum*, 6,
      9, 37, September 1969.

226   Richardson, F. K.
      'Graphical Specification of Computation,' Department of
      Computer Science Technical Report 257, University of Illinois,
      April 1968.

227   Richardson, F. K.; Oestreicher, D. R.
      'Computer Assisted Integrated Circuit Photomask Layout,' in
      Pertinent Concepts in Computer Graphics, Faiman, M.,
      Nievergelt, J., eds., University of Illinois Press, 1969.

228   Rippy, D. E.; Humphries, D. E.
      'MAGIC — A Machine for Automatic Graphics Interface to a
      Computer,' *FJCC 1965*, Spartan Books, Washington, D. C., 819.

229   Robbins, M. F.; Beyer, J. D.
      'An Interactive Computer System Using Graphical Flowchart
      Input,' *CACM*, 13, 2, 115, February 1970.

230   Roberts, L. G.
'A Graphical Service System with Variable Syntax,' *CACM*, 9, 3, 173, March 1966.

231   Roberts, L. G.
'Conic Display Generator Using Multiplying Digital-Analog Converters,' *IEEE Transactions on Electronic Computers*, EC-16, 3, 369, June 1967.

232   Roberts, L. G.
'Graphical Communication and Control Languages,' Proceedings Information Systems Sciences Second Congress, Spartan Books, Washington, D. C., 211, 1964. Also in Computer Display Review.

233   Roberts, L. G.
'Homogeneous Matrix Representation and Manipulation of *N*-Dimensional Constructs,' MIT Lincoln Laboratory, MS 1405, May 1965. Also in Computer Display Review [139].

234   Roberts, L. G.
'Machine Perception of Three Dimensional Solids,' MIT Lincoln Laboratory, TR 315, May 1963. Also in *Optical and Electro-Optical Information Processing*, Tipper *et al*, ed., MIT Press, 159.

235   Roberts, L. G.
'The Lincoln Wand,' *FJCC 1966*, Spartan Books, Washington, D. C., 223.

236   Roberts, L. G.; Wessler, B. D.
'Computer Network Development to Achieve Resource Sharing,' *SJCC 1970*, AFIPS Press, Montvale, N. J., 543.

237   Romney, G. W.
'Computer Assisted Assembly and Rendering of Solids,' Department of Computer Science, University of Utah, TR 4-20, 1970.

238   Romney, G. W.; Watkins, G. S.; Evans, D. C.
'Real Time Display of Computer Generated Half-Tone

Perspective Pictures,' Proceedings 1968 IFIP Congress, Morrell, A. J. H., ed., North Holland Pub. Co., 973, 1969.

239   Rose, G. A.
'Computer Graphics Communication Systems,' Proceedings 1968 IFIP Congress, Morrell, A. J. H., ed., North Holland Pub. Co., 211, 1969.

240   Rosen, S.; ed.
Programming Systems and Languages, McGraw-Hill, New York, 1967.

241   Ross, D. T.
'A Generalized Technique for Symbol Manipulation and Numerical Calculation,' *CACM*, 4, 3, 147, March 1961.

242   Ross, D. T.
'The AED Approach to Generalized Computer-Aided Design,' Proceedings ACM National Conference, 1967, Thompson Books, Washington, D. C., 367.

243   Ross, D. T.
'The AED Approach to Generalized Computer-Aided Design,' 1967.

244   Ross, D. T.; Rodriguez, J. E.
'Theoretical Foundations for the Computer-Aided Design System,' *SJCC 1963*, Spartan Books, Baltimore, Md., 305.

245   Rougelot, R. S.
'The General Electric Computer Color TV Display,' in *Pertinent Concepts in Computer Graphics*, Faiman M., Nievergelt, J., eds., University of Illinois Press, 1969.

246   Rougelot, R. S.; Shoemaker, R.
'General-Electric Real-Time Display,' NASA Report: NAS 9-3916.

247   Rovner, P. D.
'LEAP Users Manual,' Lincoln Laboratory Technical Memorandum 23L-0009, December 1968.

248 Rovner, P. D.; Feldman, J. A.
'The LEAP Language and Data Structure,' Proceedings 1968 IFIP Congress, Morrell, A. J. H., ed., North Holland Pub. Co., Amsterdam, 579, 1969.

249 Rovner, P. D.; Henderson, D. A. Jr.
'On the Implementation of AMBIT/G: A Graphical Programming Language,' Proceedings International Joint Conference on Artificial Intelligence, May 1969, Walker, D. E., Norton, L. M., eds., 9.

250 Ruder, D.
'Data Disc Television Display System,' Proceedings 1968 UAIDE Annual Meeting, Stromberg Datagraphix, 338.

251 Rully, A. D.
'A Subroutine Package for FORTRAN,' *IBM Systems Journal*, 7, 3/4, 248, 1968.

252 Schade, O. H.
'Image Gradation, Graininess and Sharpness in Television and Motion Picture Systems,' *Journal of Society of Motion Picture and Television Engineers*, 56, 137, 1951.

253 Schwartz, J. L.
'The Computer-Generated Film Facility of the Education Research Center,' Education Research Center, MIT, April 1970.

254 Schwartz, J. L.; Taylor, E. F.
'Computer Displays in the Teaching of Physics,' *FJCC 1968*, Thompson Books, Washington, D. C., 1285.

255 Science Accessories Corporation
'Graf/Pen Sonic Digitizer,' Science Accessories Corporation, Southport, Conn., 1970.

256 Sears, F. W.
Optics, Addison-Wesley, Cambridge, Mass., 1949.

257 Seats, P.
'The Cathode Ray Tube — A Review of Current Technology and

Future Trends,' *IEEE Transactions*, ED-18, 9, 679, September 1971.

258   Secrest, T.; Nievergelt, J.; eds.
Emerging Concepts in Computer Graphics, 1967 University of Illinois Conference on Computer Graphics, W A Benjamin, N. Y., 1968.

259   Senses Bureau (film)
Patchwork 71, a Sampler of Computer Animation in Chemistry (1971), available from Prof. Kent Wilson, The Senses Bureau, Department of Chemistry, University of California, San Diego, La Jolla, California, 92037.

260   Sharpe, W. F.; Jacob, N. L.
An Introduction to Computer Programming Using the BASIC Language, Free Press, New York, 1970.

261   Shaw, J. C.
'JOSS: A Designer's View of an Experimental On-line Computing System,' *FJCC 1964*, Spartan Books, Baltimore, Md., 455.

262   Sibley, R. A.
'A New Programming Language, PL/I,' Proceedings 20th National Conference, Association for Computing Machinery, 543, 1965.

263   Slottow, H. G.
'The Plasma Display Panel — Principles and Prospects,' 1970 IEEE Conference on Display Devices, 57.

264   Smith, A. F.
'Method for Computer Visualization,' MIT Electronic Systems Laboratory, AMC 8436-TM-2, September 1960.

265   Smith, L. B.
'A Survey of Interactive Graphical Systems for Mathematics,' *Computing Surveys*, 2, 4, 261, December 1970.

266   Smith, L. B.
'Use of Interactive Graphics to Solve Numerical Problems,' *CACM*, 13, 10, 625, October 1970.

267   Sproull, R. F.; Sutherland, I. E.
       'A Clipping Divider,' *FJCC 1968*, Thompson Books, Washington,
       D. C., 765.

268   Standish, T. A.
       'A Data Definition Facility for Programming Languages,'
       Computer Science Department, Carnegie-Mellon University,
       1967.

269   Stanford Research Institute (film)
       The Augmented Human Intellect Project, available from
       Stanford Research Institute, 300 Ravenswood Ave., Menlo Park,
       California.

270   Stotz, R.
       'A New Display Terminal,' *Computer Design Magazine*, April
       1968.

271   Stotz, R.
       'Man-Machine Console Facilities for Computer Aided Design,'
       SJCC 1963, Spartan Books, Baltimore, Md., 323.

272   Stotz, R.
       'Specialized Computer Equipment for Generation of
       Three-Dimensional Curvilinear Figures,' MIT Electronic Systems
       Laboratory, ESL-TM-167, January 1963.

273   Sutherland, I. E.
       'A Head-Mounted Three Dimensional Display,' *FJCC 1968*,
       Thompson Books, Washington, D. C., p. 757.

274   Sutherland, I. E.
       'Applied Mathematics 252 Course Notes,' Harvard University,
       Spring 1967.

275   Sutherland, I. E.
       'Computer Displays,' *Scientific American*, June 1970.

276   Sutherland, I. E.
       'Computer Inputs and Outputs,' *Scientific American*, September
       1966.

277 Sutherland, I. E.
'SKETCHPAD: A Man-Machine Graphical Communication System,' MIT Lincoln Laboratory TR 296, May 1965. Abridged version in *SJCC 1963*, Spartan Books, Baltimore, Md., 329.

278 Sutherland, I. E.
'Ten Unsolved Problems in Computer Graphics,' *Datamation*, 12, 5, 22, May 1966.

279 Sutherland, W. R.
'Introduction to Data Structures,' MIT Lincoln Laboratory, August 1968.

280 Sutherland, W. R.
'On-Line Graphical Specification of Computer Procedures,' MIT Lincoln Laboratory, TR 405, May 1966.

281 Sutherland, W. R.
'The CORAL Language and Data Structure,' *Computer Display Review*, Keydata Corp., Watertown, Mass.

282 Sutherland, W. R.; Forgie, J. W.; Morello, M. V.
'Graphics in Time-Sharing: A Summary of the TX-2 Experience,' *SJCC 1969*, AFIPS Press, Montvale, N. J., 629.

283 Swinehart, D. C.; Sproull, R. F.
'SAIL Manual,' SAILON No. 57.2, Artificial Intelligence Project, Stanford University, 1971.

284 Symonds, A. J.
'Auxiliary-storage Associative Data Structure for PL/I,' *IBM Systems Journal*, 7, 3/4, 229, 1968.

285 Talbot, P. A.; Carr, J. W.; Coulter, R. R.; Hwang, R. C.
'Animator: An On-line Two-dimensional Film Animation System,' *CACM*, 14, 4, 251, April 1971.

286 Teitelman, W.
'Real Time Recognition of Hand-Drawn Characters,' *FJCC 1964*, Spartan Books, Baltimore, Md., 559.

287   Teitelman, W.; Bobrow, D. G.; Hartley, A. K.; Murphy, D. L.
BBN-LISP: TENEX Reference Manual, Bolt Beranek and Newman Inc., Cambridge, Mass., July 1971.

288   Teixeira, J. F.; Sallen, R. P.
'The Sylvania Tablet: A New Approach to Graphic Data Input,' *SJCC 1968*, Thompson Books, Washington, D. C., 315.

289   Thomas, E.
'The Storing and Reuse of Real-Time Graphical Inputs,' Masters Thésis, MIT, June 1969.

290   Thompson, F. T.
'Television Line Structure Suppression,' *Journal of Society of Motion Picture and Television Engineers*, 66, 602, 1957.

291   Thornhill, D. E.; Stotz, R. H.; Ross, D. T.; Ward, J. E.
'An Integrated Hardware-Software System for Computer Graphics in Time-Sharing,' MIT Project MAC, TR-56, December 1968.

292   Turner, J. A.; Ritchie, G. J.
'Linear Current Division in Resistive Areas: its application to computer graphics,' *SJCC 1970*, AFIPS Press, Montvale, N. J., 613.

293   Uncapher, K. W.
'The RAND Video Graphic System: An Approach to a General User-Computer Graphic Communication System,' RAND Report R-753-ARPA, April 1971.

294   University of Toronto, L. Mezei (film)
Art From Computers (1971), Available from Ontario Communications Authority, 1670 Bayview Avenue, Toronto, Ontario, Canada.

295   Van Dam, A.
'Computer Driven Displays and their Use in Man/Machine Interaction,' in *Advances in Computers* 7, Alt, F. Z.; Rubinoff, M., eds., Academic Press, 1966.

296   Van Dam, A.; Evans, D. C.
      'A Compact Data Structure for Storing, Retrieving and
      Manipulating Line Drawings,' *SJCC 1967*, Thompson Books,
      Washington, D. C., 601.

297   Vector General Inc.
      'Graphics Display System Reference Manual,' Vector General,
      Canoga Park, Calif., January 1971.

298   Walton, J. S.; Risen, W. M. Jr.
      'Computer Animation: On-line Dynamics Display in Real Time,'
      Journal of Chemical Education, 46, 6, 334.

299   Ward, J. E.
      'Systems Engineering Problems in Computer-Driven CRT
      Displays for Man-Machine Communication,' *IEEE Transactions
      on Systems Science and Cybernetics*, SSC-3, 1, 47, June 1967.

300   Warnock, J. E.
      'A Hidden-Surface Algorithm for Computer Generated Half-tone
      Pictures,' TR 4-15, Computer Science Department, University of
      Utah, 1969.

301   Watkins, G. S.
      'A Real-Time Visible Surface Algorithm,' Computer Science
      Department, University of Utah, UTECH-CSc-70-101, June
      1970.

302   Watson, R. W.; Myer, T. H.; Sutherland, I. E.; Vosbury, M. K.
      'A Display Processor Design,' *FJCC 1969*, AFIPS Press,
      Montvale, N. J., 209.

303   Weber, H.
      'A Microprogrammed Implementation of EULER on IBM
      System/360 Model 30,' *CACM*, 10, 9, 549, September 1967.

304   Weber, L. F.
      'Optical Write-In for the Plasma Display Panel,' *IEEE
      Transactions*, ED-18, 9, 664, September 1971.

305   Weiss, R. A.
'Be Vision, a Package of IBM 7090 Fortran Programs to Draw Orthographic Views of Combinations of Planes and Quadric Surfaces,' *JACM*, **13**, 2, 194, April 1966.

306   Weissman, C.
LISP 1.5 Primer, Dickenson, Belmont, Calif., 1967.

307   Weizenbaum, J.
'Symmetric List Processor,' *CACM*, **6**, 9, 524, September 1963.

308   Williams, F. C.; Kilburn, T.
'A Storage System for Use with Binary-Digital Computing Machines,' *Proceedings IEE*, Part 3, **96**, 81, March 1949.

309   Williams, R.
'A Survey of Data Structures for Computer Graphics Systems,' *Computing Surveys*, **3**, 1, 1, March 1971.

310   Wirth, N.
'A Generalization of ALGOL,' *CACM*, **6**, 9, 547, September 1963.

311   Wirth, N.; Weber, H.
'EULER: A Generalization of ALGOL and its Formal Definition,' Part I: *CACM*, **9**, 1, 13, January 1966; Part II: *CACM*, **9**, 2, 89, February 1966.

312   Wiseman, N. E.
'A Note on Compiling Display File From a Data Structure,' *Computer Journal*, **11**, 2, 141, August 1968.

313   Wiseman, N. E.; Lemke, H. U.; Hiles, J. O.
'PIXIE: A New Approach to Graphical Man-machine Communication,' Proceedings 1969 CAD Conference, Southampton, IEE Conference Publication 51, 463.

314   Wolfberg, M. S.
'An Interactive Graph Theory System,' Moore School of

Electrical Engineering Report 69-25, University of Pennsylvania CFSTI AD-688931, June 1969.

315   Woodsford, P. A.
'GINO: Graphic Input/Output,' University of Cambridge Computer Aided Design Group, June 1969.

316   Woodsford, P. A.
'The Design and Implementation of the GINO 3D Graphics Software Package,' *Software — Practice and Experience*, 1, 4, 335, October 1971.

317   Woon, P.
'On the Computer Drawing of Solid Objects Bounded by Quadric Surfaces,' New York University, Report TR-403-3, June 1969.

318   Wylie, C.; Romney, G. W.; Evans, D. C.; Erdahl, A. C.
'Halftone Perspective Drawings by Computer,' *FJCC 1967*, Thompson Books, Washington, D. C., 49.

319   Yule, J. A.
Principles of Color Reproduction, Wiley, New York, 1967.

AI.1 · MATRICES

The matrix notation for coordinate transformations is used throughout this book. This section is a summary of some elementary mathematical operations on vectors and matrices. Appendix II contains a discussion of these operations as applied to two-dimensional and three-dimensional geometry.

A matrix is an array of elements:

$$
A = \begin{bmatrix}
a_{11} & a_{12} & a_{13} & \cdots & a_{1n} \\
a_{21} & a_{22} & a_{23} & \cdots & a_{2n} \\
\cdot & \cdot & \cdot & \cdots & \\
\cdot & \cdot & \cdot & \cdots & \\
a_{m1} & a_{m2} & a_{m3} & \cdots & a_{mn}
\end{bmatrix}
$$

We shall denote a matrix by an italic upper-case letter, e.g. A; its individual elements are denoted a_{ij}, where i is the row number and j is the column number of the location of the scalar element. The range of row numbers is from 1 to m; column numbers range from 1 to n. We shall indicate the number of rows and columns of A with the notation:

$$A_{[m\ n]}$$

Two degenerate cases of matrices occur with $m = 1$ or $n = 1$:

$$\mathbf{b} = [\ b_{11}\ b_{12}\ \ldots\ b_{1n}\ ]$$

$$\mathbf{c} = \begin{bmatrix} c_{11} \\ c_{21} \\ . \\ . \\ c_{m\ 1} \end{bmatrix}$$

The term *vector* is applied to both of these matrices; vectors are denoted by lower-case bold letters. Although $\mathbf{b}$ is properly called a row vector and $\mathbf{c}$ a column vector, we shall often adopt a simple notation that uses only one subscript:

$$\mathbf{v} = [\ v_1\ \ v_2\ \ v_3\ \ .\ \ .\ \ .\ \ v_1\ ]$$

The number of elements in $\mathbf{v}$ is indicated by $\mathbf{v}_{[l]}$.

A further degenerate case occurs when both m and n are 1:

$$A = [\ a_{11}\ ]$$

This construct is *not* equivalent to a scalar with numeric value equal to a_{11}.

A matrix can be viewed as a collection of vectors: $A_{[3\ 4]}$ is composed of 3 row vectors, each of length 4. Alternatively, we can imagine A to be composed of 4 column vectors, each with three elements. Suppose

$$\mathbf{u} = [\ u_1\ \ u_2\ \ .\ \ .\ \ .\ \ u_l\ ]$$
$$\mathbf{v} = [\ v_1\ \ v_2\ \ .\ \ .\ \ .\ \ v_l\ ]$$
$$\mathbf{w} = [\ w_1\ \ w_2\ \ .\ \ .\ \ .\ \ w_l\ ]$$

Then the notation:

$$A = \begin{bmatrix} \mathbf{u} \\ \mathbf{v} \\ \mathbf{w} \end{bmatrix}$$

is shorthand for the full notation:

$$A = \begin{bmatrix} u_1 & u_2 & .\ .\ . & u_l \\ v_1 & v_2 & .\ .\ . & v_l \\ w_1 & w_2 & .\ .\ . & w_l \end{bmatrix}$$

The transpose A^T of a matrix $A_{[m\ n]}$ is an n x m matrix:

$$\underset{1 \leqslant i \leqslant m}{\forall} \quad \underset{1 \leqslant j \leqslant n}{\forall} \quad a_{ji}^{T} = a_{ij}$$

Arithmetic operations on matrices and vectors are defined in terms of arithmetic operations on the *elements* of the matrices or vectors. For example, two matrices $A_{[m\ n]}$ and $B_{[p\ q]}$ are equal (notation: $A = B$) if and only if $m = p$ and $n = q$ and

$$\underset{1 \leqslant i \leqslant m}{\forall} \quad \underset{1 \leqslant j \leqslant n}{\forall} \quad a_{ij} = b_{ij}$$

The equality is defined on the arithmetic system of which the elements a_{ij} and b_{ij} are part.

Two matrices or vectors can be added, provided they each have the same number of rows and columns:

$$C_{[m\ n]} = A_{[m\ n]} + B_{[m\ n]}$$

where

$$\underset{1 \leqslant i \leqslant m}{\forall} \quad \underset{1 \leqslant j \leqslant n}{\forall} \quad c_{ij} = a_{ij} + b_{ij}$$

Again, the operation '+' is defined on the system of elements.

A scalar s multiplied by a matrix A is a new matrix C of the same dimensions as A; the multiplication is performed on each element of A to yield an element of C:

$$C_{[m\ n]} = sA_{[m\ n]}$$

$$\underset{1 \leqslant i \leqslant m}{\forall} \quad \underset{1 \leqslant j \leqslant n}{\forall} \quad c_{ij} = sa_{ij}$$

The inner product of two vectors, sometimes called the dot product, is only defined on vectors of the same dimensions. The inner product of $v_{[l]}$ and $w_{[l]}$ is a scalar number:

$$\sum_{i=1}^{l} v_i w_i$$

or, as often seen:

$$\mathbf{v} \cdot \mathbf{w} = \begin{bmatrix} v_1 & v_2 & . & . & v_l \end{bmatrix} \begin{bmatrix} w_1 \\ w_2 \\ . \\ . \\ w_l \end{bmatrix} = v_1 w_1 + v_2 w_2 + \ .\ .\ \ v_l w_l$$

The product of two matrices is defined as a generalization of the inner product. The product $C_{[l\ n]}$ of two matrices $A_{[l\ m]}$ and $B_{[m\ n]}$ is computed as follows:

$$\underset{1 \leqslant i \leqslant l}{\forall} \quad \underset{1 \leqslant j \leqslant n}{\forall} \quad c_{ij} = \mathbf{A}_{i*} \ . \ \mathbf{B}_{*j} \quad c_{ij} = A_{i*} \ . \ B_{*j}$$

We may write out the inner product:

$$c_{ij} = \sum_{k=1}^{m} a_{ik} b_{kj}$$

Notice the restriction that the number of columns of A must equal the number of rows of B. Two matrices which meet this restriction are called *conformal*. Notice also that matrix multiplication is not commutative, i.e. the product $B\ A$ gives (assuming $l = n$):

$$c_{ij} = \sum_{k=1}^{n} b_{ik} a_{kj}$$

Inspection of the definition of matrix multiplication reveals one special class of matrices I, the identity matrices, which, when multiplied by a matrix A conformal to I, yields A. This matrix class is:

$$I = \begin{bmatrix} 1 & 0 & 0 & 0 & \cdots \\ 0 & 1 & 0 & 0 & \cdots \\ 0 & 0 & 1 & 0 & \cdots \\ & \cdot & \cdot & & \\ & \cdot & \cdot & & \end{bmatrix}$$

We can show:

$$A I = I A = A$$

We can define the inverse of A, A^{-1}, with respect to the identity:

$$A A^{-1} = A^{-1} A = I$$

In order to compute the elements of A^{-1}, we need to introduce some new notation.

The determinant of a matrix of scalar elements is a scalar number computed from the elements of the matrix. We define the determinant of the 1 x 1 matrix Z:

$$Z = [z_{11}]$$

as the scalar z_{11}. The notation det Z is used to denote the value of the determinant of Z. We proceed to define the determinant of an n x n matrix A as follows ($n > 1$): Let A_{ij} denote the $(n-1)$ by $(n-1)$ matrix derived from A by deleting row i and column j from A. Then we have:

$$\det A = \sum_{i=1}^{n} a_{ij}(-1)^{i+j} \det A_{ij}$$

for some $1 \leqslant j \leqslant n$.

A term of the summation above:

$$c_{ij} = (-1)^{i+j} \det A_{ij}$$

is called the *cofactor* of the element a_{ij} of A. Thus

$$\det A = \sum_{i=1}^{n} a_{ij}c_{ij}$$

We are now prepared to define the inverse A^{-1} of the $n \times n$ matrix A:

$$a_{ij}^{-1} = \frac{(-1)^{i+j} \det A_{ji}}{\det A}$$

(Notice the order of subscripts of A_{ji}). In other words, if matrix C is the matrix of cofactors of A:

$$c_{ij} = (-1)^{i+j} \det A_{ij}$$

then

$$A^{-1} = \left(\frac{1}{\det A}\right) C^{T}$$

Notice that the elements of A^{-1} are undefined if $\det A = 0$. In this case, A is called *singular*. In general, inverting matrices with computers is not as easy as described above, because as $\det A$ gets very small, various roundoff errors occur. Furthermore, the alternating signs in the computation of $\det A$ cause numerical problems. Most matrices used for two-dimensional or three-dimensional transformations are very well-behaved; no special numerical techniques are required to invert them. Forsythe and Moler [97] catalog various procedures for computing inverses of near-singular matrices.

AI.2   VECTORS

A vector is a directed line segment. The vector from point A to point B is denoted by **AB**. We often think of points as determined by coordinates in a Cartesian coordinate system. If A is at (X_a, Y_a, Z_a) and B at (X_b, Y_b, Z_b), then we can represent **AB** by the triple $[(X_b - X_a)\ (Y_b - Y_a)\ (Z_b - Z_a)]$. The origin of the coordinate system plays a special role; we equate the vector $\mathbf{v} = [X\ Y\ Z]$ with the vector **OV**, where V is the point (X, Y, Z).

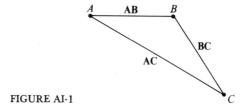

FIGURE AI-1

Vectors **AB** and **BC** add to give **AC,** as shown in Figure AI-1. The vector sum of $w = u + v$ is defined as a vector of scalar sums:

$$w = [\; u_1 + v_1 \quad u_2 + v_2 \quad . \; . \quad u_1 + v_l \;]$$

A scalar s multiplies a vector **v:**

$$s\,v = [\; sv_1 \quad sv_2 \quad . \; . \quad sv_l \;]$$

where the scalar multiplications obey normal conventions for real numbers.

A collection of vectors $v_1, v_2, \ldots v_n$ is linearly independent if:

$$\alpha_1 v_1 + \alpha_2 v_2 + \ldots \alpha_n v_n = 0$$

only when all the α_i are zero.

The vectors $v_1, v_2, \ldots v_n$ *span* the vector space if and only if every vector **m** in the space can be expressed as a linear combination of the **v_i.** For example, the vectors

$$\mathbf{i} = [\; 1 \quad 0 \quad 0 \;] \quad \mathbf{j} = [\; 0 \quad 1 \quad 0 \;] \quad \mathbf{k} = [\; 0 \quad 0 \quad 1 \;]$$

span the three-dimensional space of reals because every vector **m** can be represented as:

$$\mathbf{m} = [\; a \quad b \quad c \;] = a\mathbf{i} + b\mathbf{j} + c\mathbf{k}$$

Furthermore, if the v_i are linearly independent and span the vector space they are called a *basis* of the vector space (Prove: Any n independent n-component vectors are a basis for the n-dimensional vector space).

Two vectors are said to be orthogonal if and only if their inner product is zero. A basis is said to be an orthogonal basis if every vector of the basis is orthogonal to every other vector of the basis (example: i, j, k above).

A common use of three-component vectors is for representation of three-dimensional Cartesian space. The space is usually defined in terms of the orthogonal basis [1 0 0], [0 1 0], and [0 0 1]. Another notation for this basis is the set of unit vectors along the three orthogonal axis directions X, Y and Z.

The magnitude or length of a vector is denoted by $|v|$ and is computed by

$$|v| = \sqrt{v_1{}^2 + v_2{}^2 + \ldots v_l{}^2}$$

The inner product of two vectors is:

$$\mathbf{v \cdot w} = |v| \, |w| \cos \theta$$
$$= v_1 w_1 + v_2 w_2 + \ldots + v_l w_l$$

where θ is the angle between the two vectors (this angle has intuitive meaning only in two- and three-dimensional spaces).

One special operation on three-dimensional vectors is called the cross product:

$$\mathbf{v \times w} = [\, (w_3 v_2 - v_3 w_2)(v_3 w_1 - w_3 v_1)(w_2 v_1 - w_1 v_2) \,]$$

A helpful mnemonic for this is gained by writing:

$$\begin{bmatrix} v_1 & w_1 & i \\ v_2 & w_2 & j \\ v_3 & w_3 & k \end{bmatrix}$$

The first column is the vector **v**, the second **w**, and the third is a shorthand for the Cartesian axis vectors

$$i = [1 0 0] \quad j = [0 1 0] \quad k = [0 0 1]$$

The evaluation of the determinant of the matrix above gives the cross product.

$$(w_3 v_2 - w_2 v_3)i + (w_1 v_3 - w_3 v_1)j + (w_2 v_1 - w_1 v_2)k$$

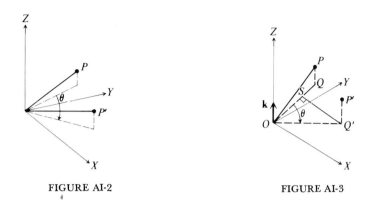

FIGURE AI-2   FIGURE AI-3

Notice that

$$v \times w = - w \times v$$

The cross product of two vectors **v** and **w** yields a new *vector*. This vector is orthogonal to **v** and **w**, as can be seen by taking the inner product:

$$v \cdot (v \times w) = 0$$

which implies that the angle between **v** and $(v \times w)$ is $90°$ or $270°$. The magnitude of the cross product vector is related to the angle between the two vectors:

$$|v \times w| = |v| \, |w| \sin \theta$$

As an example of these operations, consider deriving the matrix transformation for three-dimensional vectors which rotates a point through an angle of θ about the Z axis, as shown in Figure AI-2. Point P is transformed into P' (see Figure AI-3). Define **k** as the unit vector in the Z direction. We have:

$$\mathbf{OP'} = \mathbf{OQ'} + \mathbf{Q'P'} = \mathbf{OQ'} + \mathbf{QP} = \mathbf{OS} + \mathbf{SQ'} + \mathbf{QP}$$

We will compute the three terms of this sum:

1. Determine **OS**. First compute its magnitude:

$$|\mathbf{OS}| = |\mathbf{OQ'}| \cos \theta = |\mathbf{OQ}| \cos \theta$$

The direction of **OS** is the same as that of **OQ**:

$$\mathbf{OS} = \mathbf{OQ} \cos \theta$$

2. Determine **SQ′**. First compute its magnitude:

$$|\mathbf{SQ'}| = |\mathbf{OQ'}| \sin \theta = |\mathbf{OQ}| \sin \theta$$

The direction is perpendicular to **k** and to **OQ**:

$$\mathbf{SQ'} = (\mathbf{OQ} \times \mathbf{k}) \sin \theta$$

3. Determine **Q′P**, which is the same as **QP**. Its magnitude is simply **OP** · **k** and its direction is parallel to **k**:

$$\mathbf{QP} = (\mathbf{OP} \cdot \mathbf{k}) \, \mathbf{k}$$

Hence:

$$\mathbf{OP'} = \mathbf{OQ} \cos \theta + (\mathbf{OQ} \times \mathbf{k}) \sin \theta + (\mathbf{OP} \cdot \mathbf{k}) \, \mathbf{k}$$

Now

$$\mathbf{OQ} = \mathbf{OP} - (\mathbf{OP} \cdot \mathbf{k}) \, \mathbf{k}$$

So

$$\mathbf{OP'} = \mathbf{OP} \cos \theta + (\mathbf{OP} \times \mathbf{k}) \sin \theta - (\mathbf{k} \times \mathbf{k} \, (\mathbf{OP} \cdot \mathbf{k}) \sin \theta) + (\mathbf{OP} \cdot \mathbf{k})(1 - \cos \theta) \, \mathbf{k}$$

The third term is zero because **k** x **k** is 0. Hence

$$\mathbf{OP'} = \mathbf{OP} \cos \theta + (\mathbf{OP} \times \mathbf{k}) \sin \theta + (\mathbf{OP} \cdot \mathbf{k})(1 - \cos \theta) \, \mathbf{k}$$

Notice that **OP′** is a function of (1) **OP**, (2) the angle of rotation θ, and (3) a unit vector **k** along the axis of rotation. **k** may in fact represent *any* rotation axis.

We can carry this one step further and derive the 3 × 3 matrix which is the transformation of the vector **OP** into **OP′**:

$$\mathbf{OP'} = \mathbf{OP} \, R \quad \text{or} \quad [\, x' \ y' \ z' \,] = [\, x \ y \ z \,] \, R$$

We will assume the axis of rotation **k** to be [0 0 1] (aligned with the Z axis). Thus we have:

$$\mathbf{OP}\cos\theta = [\, x\ y\ z\,]\begin{bmatrix} \cos\theta & 0 & 0 \\ 0 & \cos\theta & 0 \\ 0 & 0 & \cos\theta \end{bmatrix}$$

$$\mathbf{OP} \times \mathbf{k} = [\, x\ y\ z\,]\begin{bmatrix} 0 & -1 & 0 \\ 1 & 0 & 0 \\ 0 & 0 & 0 \end{bmatrix}$$

$$(\mathbf{OP} \times \mathbf{k})\sin\theta = [\, x\ y\ z\,]\begin{bmatrix} 0 & -\sin\theta & 0 \\ \sin\theta & 0 & 0 \\ 0 & 0 & 0 \end{bmatrix}$$

We have

$$(\mathbf{OP} \cdot \mathbf{k}) = [\, x\ y\ z\,]\begin{bmatrix} 0 \\ 0 \\ 1 \end{bmatrix} = z$$

$$(\mathbf{OP} \cdot \mathbf{k})(1 - \cos\theta)\mathbf{k} = [\, x\ y\ z\,]\begin{bmatrix} 0 & 0 & 0 \\ 0 & 0 & 0 \\ 0 & 0 & 1 - \cos\theta \end{bmatrix}$$

Substituting into the result for **OP'**:

OP' = **OP** $\cos\theta$ + (**OP** × **k**) $\sin\theta$ + **k**(**OP** · **k**)(1 − $\cos\theta$)

$$= [\, x\ y\ z\,]\left(\begin{bmatrix} \cos\theta & 0 & 0 \\ 0 & \cos\theta & 0 \\ 0 & 0 & \cos\theta \end{bmatrix} + \begin{bmatrix} 0 & -\sin\theta & 0 \\ \sin\theta & 0 & 0 \\ 0 & 0 & 0 \end{bmatrix} \right.$$

$$\left. + \begin{bmatrix} 0 & 0 & 0 \\ 0 & 0 & 0 \\ 0 & 0 & 1 - \cos\theta \end{bmatrix} \right) = [\, x\ y\ z\,]\begin{bmatrix} \cos\theta & -\sin\theta & 0 \\ \sin\theta & \cos\theta & 0 \\ 0 & 0 & 1 \end{bmatrix}$$

c.f. Equation 12-4.

HOMOGENEOUS COORDINATE TECHNIQUES

The homogeneous coordinate representations of points, lines, planes, and surfaces presented in this section are quite useful for describing and manipulating graphical objects. We will discuss only the mathematical aspects of such representations; the mechanics of storing and retrieving object representations in some data structure and of recording relations among objects are ignored.

The term *homogeneous* is applied to the representations described here because the representation for a class of objects involves no explicit constants. For example the equation of a two-dimensional line is $Y = mX + b$. The homogeneous equation for the same line is $mWX - WY + bW = 0$, an equation with three variables. This equation is a representation of the line in a three-space.

Homogeneous representation was developed as a geometer's tool for proving theorems of projective geometry. A problem in n-space has a corresponding problem in an $(n+1)$-space. Results in the $(n+1)$-space are often more easily obtained than those in the n-space. The proof in $(n+1)$-space is then related to the n-space problem by projection of the

$(n+1)$-space problem into n-space. For example, points 'at infinity' in the n-space are in no way exceptional in the $(n+1)$-space.

This section follows closely a paper by Roberts [233]. A more formal development of homogeneous coordinate techniques can be found in Maxwell [176, 175]. Homogeneous representations are particularly useful in describing curves and surfaces. A good survey of these techniques is given by [94].

AII.1   HOMOGENEOUS COORDINATES

The homogeneous representation of an object in n-space is an object in $(n+1)$-space. The mapping from n-space to $(n+1)$-space is one-to-many, i.e. there is an infinity of equivalent representations of the n-space object in $(n+1)$-space. The inverse mapping exists, and is usually called *projection*; there is a many-to-one mapping from $(n+1)$-space to n-space.

Alternatively, a vector in the $(n+1)$ homogeneous space can be viewed as an n-space vector with the addition of one more coordinate to the vector, a scale factor.

The homogeneous representation of the two-dimensional point $[\, x \; y \,]$ is in general $[\, wx \; wy \; w \,]$ where w is any non-zero scalar which is sometimes called the *scale factor*. The homogeneous vector is three-dimensional and can be manipulated as such. The mapping from a homogeneous point $[\, a \; b \; c \,]$ back to its two-dimensional image is simply $[\, a/c \; b/c \,]$; we divide by the scale factor c.

An alternate view of the two-dimensional image of $[\, a \; b \; c \,]$ is that it is a projection on the plane $c = 1$, as shown in Figure AII-1.

The transformation matrices developed in Chapter 6 are in fact transformations of homogeneous vectors. The addition of the '1' to the $[\, x \; y \,]$ vector simply creates a homogeneous vector with $w = 1$. The transformations given in Chapter 6 are chosen so that their application to a homogeneous vector (three-dimensional vector) produces a required effect on the two-dimensional point represented by that vector.

Three-dimensional objects are treated analogously: the homogeneous representation of $[\, x \; y \; z \,]$ is $[\, wx \; wy \; wz \; w \,]$ for any $w \neq 0$. A homogeneous point $[\, a \; b \; c \; d \,]$ has a three-dimensional image $[\, a/d \; b/d \; c/d \,]$. Similarly, the transformations given in Chapter 12 can be used to transform homogeneous representations of three-dimensional points.

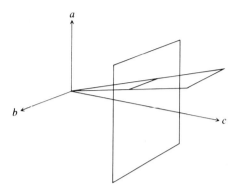

FIGURE AII-1

found in Maxwell [176, 175]. Homogeneous representations are
   We observe that multiplying a homogeneous vector by a non-zero
scalar constant does not alter its projection in n-space. We shall define
n-space equality with the symbol $\doteq$. Thus, even though two vectors are
not =, they may be $\doteq$ if one is a scalar multiple of the other. Example:
the homogeneous points [2 1 0 2] and [4 2 0 4] are $\doteq$ but not =;
both project to the three-space point [1 0.5 0].
   If the point (x, y, z) is to be transformed by a matrix M, we must
choose a value of w to form the vector [wx wy wz w] in order to
evaluate the product:

$$[\, w'x' \;\; w'y' \;\; w'z' \;\; w' \,] = [\, wx \;\; wy \;\; wz \;\; w \,] \, M$$

From a mathematical point of view, the choice of w is not important
for transformations which perform translation, rotation, scaling, or
perspective. In practice, the choice of w may be important. Clearly
$w = 0$ causes a degenerate condition — this is one of the features of the
homogeneous representation. If the calculation of matrix products is
performed with fixed-point computer hardware, the familiar problems
of overflow and truncation affect the accuracy of the result. Suppose
we can represent only integers $-2^{12} \leqslant x \leqslant 2^{12} - 1$. The point $x = 0.25$,
$y = 0.1$, $z = 10$ cannot be represented if we choose $w = 1$; instead we
may choose $w = 20$:

$$[\, wx \;\; wy \;\; wz \;\; w \,] = [\, 5 \;\; 2 \;\; 200 \;\; 20 \,]$$

If we carry this to extremes, and make w reasonably large, we could
overflow the maximum allowable integer, 4095. However, a
homogeneous representation allows us to change w whenever we need

in order to achieve maximum significance without overflow. For instance, the computation:

$$[\,5 \quad 2 \quad 200 \quad 20\,]\begin{bmatrix} 20 & 0 & 0 & 0 \\ 20 & 0 & 0 & 0 \\ 20 & 0 & 0 & 0 \\ 1 & 0 & 0 & 1 \end{bmatrix} = [\,4160 \quad 0 \quad 0 \quad 20\,]$$

produces an overflow. We could, however, scale each multiplication by, say, a factor of 1/2, and get:

$$[\,5 \quad 2 \quad 200 \quad 20\,]\begin{bmatrix} 20 & 0 & 0 & 0 \\ 20 & 0 & 0 & 0 \\ 20 & 0 & 0 & 0 \\ 1 & 0 & 0 & 1 \end{bmatrix} = [\,2080 \quad 0 \quad 0 \quad 10\,]$$

which represents the same n-space point.

AII.2 NOTATION

We shall require a uniform notation for matrices, vectors and scalars throughout the description of manipulation techniques.

Matrices: Represented by italic upper-case letters, e.g. A.
  A^{-1} is the inverse of A.
  A^T is the transpose of A.

Vectors: We shall distinguish row vectors and column vectors.
  Row vectors: **p,r,v**
  Column vectors: γ, λ
  The transpose of a row vector, $\mathbf{p}^T$, is a column vector.
  The transpose of a column vector, γ^T, is a row vector.

Scalars: Other lower-case letters will represent scalars. We shall make
  three conventions:
  1. a_{ij} are elements of matrix A.
  2. s, t are parametric variables
  3. x, y, z, w are specific elements in a vector

In general, primes $(',\,'')$ will be used freely to indicate *transformed* objects, e.g. γ' is a column vector, distinct from γ, but related to γ for descriptive purposes.

We shall occasionally represent homogeneous vectors as [wx wy w]. The strings 'wx' and 'wy' are diphthongs — they represent one number. The notation is used to suggest that the *ordinary* (two-space) point represented by this homogeneous vector is [x y].

AII.3   TWO-DIMENSIONAL POINTS AND LINES

1. A point in two-space is a three-element row vector:

$$\mathbf{v} = [\ wx\ \ wy\ \ w\ ]$$

This vector is a homogeneous representation of the point [x y]. We will assume that [x y] is represented in a Cartesian coordinate system; several metric properties below depend on this.

The two-dimensional coordinate points of the homogeneous point [a b c] are:

$$x = a/c \qquad y = b/c$$

Any scalar multiple of **v** (e.g. sv) represents the same two-dimensional point as **v**.

2. A line is represented by a column vector:

$$\gamma = \begin{bmatrix} a \\ b \\ c \end{bmatrix}$$

3. The condition that a point **v** is on a line γ is:

$$\mathbf{v} \cdot \gamma = 0$$

This is an inner product, and is equivalent to the scalar equation:

$$a\ (wx) + b\ (wy) + c\ (w) = 0$$

If $\mathbf{v} \cdot \gamma$ is not zero, then **v** does not lie on the line γ. The sign of $\mathbf{v} \cdot \gamma$ is positive if **v** lies on one side of γ, negative if it lies on the other side.

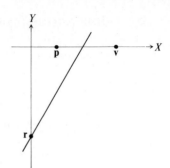

FIGURE AII-2

Example:

$$\mathbf{v} = [\,1 \quad 0 \quad 1\,]$$
$$\mathbf{p} = [\,1 \quad 0 \quad 4\,] \qquad \gamma = \begin{bmatrix} 2 \\ -1 \\ -1 \end{bmatrix}$$
$$\mathbf{r} = [\,0 \quad -1 \quad 1\,]$$

Then $\mathbf{v} \cdot \gamma = 1$, $\mathbf{p} \cdot \gamma = -2$, and $\mathbf{r} \cdot \gamma = 0$. If we draw a two-space picture of these points and line, as shown in Figure AII-2, then the perpendicular distance from a point $\mathbf{v}$ to a line γ is determined by $\mathbf{v} \cdot \gamma$ but must be normalized:

$$\text{distance} = (\mathbf{v} \cdot \gamma)\,\frac{1}{w}\,\frac{1}{\sqrt{a^2 + b^2}} \qquad \text{where} \quad \begin{aligned} \mathbf{v} &= [\,wx \; wy \; w\,] \\ \gamma^T &= [\,a \; b \; c\,] \end{aligned}$$

4. The line γ between two points $\mathbf{p}$ and $\mathbf{v}$ is given by:

$$\mathbf{v} = [\,v_1 \; v_2 \; v_3\,] \qquad \mathbf{p} = [\,p_1 \; p_2 \; p_3\,]$$

$$\gamma = \begin{bmatrix} p_3 v_2 - p_2 v_3 \\ p_1 v_3 - p_3 v_1 \\ p_2 v_1 - p_1 v_2 \end{bmatrix}$$

or $\gamma = \mathbf{v} \times \mathbf{p}$ (cross product).

We can easily verify that both $\mathbf{p}$ and $\mathbf{v}$ are on the line γ, i.e. $\mathbf{p} \cdot \gamma = 0$ and $\mathbf{v} \cdot \gamma = 0$.

5. The point **v** at the intersection of lines γ and λ is computed as follows:

$$\gamma = \begin{bmatrix} a \\ b \\ c \end{bmatrix} \qquad \lambda = \begin{bmatrix} d \\ e \\ f \end{bmatrix}$$

$$\mathbf{v} = [\ (fb - ec)\ (cd - af)\ (ea - db)\ ]$$
or $\mathbf{v} = \gamma \times \lambda$ (cross product).

Notice that the point $\mathbf{v}' = \lambda \times \gamma = -\mathbf{v}$ represents the same two-dimensional point as **v**. We can verify that $\mathbf{v} \cdot \gamma = 0$ and $\mathbf{v} \cdot \lambda = 0$, i.e. **v** lies on both γ and λ.

6. A transformation H of the three-space is a 3 x 3 matrix. This transformation matrix is of the same form as the transformations described in Chapter 6.

1. A point **v** is transformed into a point $\mathbf{v}'$: $\mathbf{v}' = \mathbf{v}\,H$
2. A line γ is transformed into a line γ': $\gamma' = H^{-1}\,\gamma$

If we define a line γ by the line equation $\mathbf{v} \cdot \gamma = 0$, we notice that a transformation of this line preserves the form of the line equation. Suppose a point **v** is on the line γ. The line γ transforms into $\gamma' = H^{-1}\,\gamma$; the point **v** into $\mathbf{v}' = \mathbf{v}\,H$. The new point and line are still related by the line equation:

$$\mathbf{v}' \cdot \gamma' = 0$$
$$\mathbf{v}\,H\,H^{-1}\,\gamma = 0$$

7. We will demonstrate a transformation T on $(n+1)$-space homogeneous vectors, which translates points in the space so that **v** is translated to the origin of the n-space, i.e. $\mathbf{v}\,T = [\ 0\ 0\ v_3\ ]$.

$$\mathbf{v} = [\ v_1\ v_2\ v_3\ ]$$

$$T = \begin{bmatrix} 1 & 0 & 0 \\ 0 & 1 & 0 \\ -v_1/v_3 & -v_2/v_3 & 1 \end{bmatrix}$$

We can verify that $\mathbf{v}T = [\, 0\ 0\ v_3\,]$. This transformation is similar to the translation transformation given in Chapter 6.

8. The condition that two lines λ and γ are perpendicular is:

$$\left(\gamma^T \begin{bmatrix} 1 & 0 & 0 \\ 0 & 1 & 0 \\ 0 & 0 & 0 \end{bmatrix}\right) \cdot \lambda = 0$$

9. The condition that two lines λ and γ are parallel is:

$$\begin{bmatrix} 1 & 0 & 0 \\ 0 & 1 & 0 \\ 0 & 0 & 0 \end{bmatrix} \lambda \doteq \begin{bmatrix} 1 & 0 & 0 \\ 0 & 1 & 0 \\ 0 & 0 & 0 \end{bmatrix} \gamma$$

10. The line λ which is normal to line γ and passes through point $\mathbf{v}$ is computed by:

    1. Prepare the translation matrix T from $\mathbf{v}$.
    2. $\lambda = T\,K\,\gamma$ where

$$K = \begin{bmatrix} 0 & 1 & 0 \\ -1 & 0 & 0 \\ 0 & 0 & 0 \end{bmatrix}$$

Example: if $\gamma^T = [\, a\ b\ c\,]$, then $\lambda^T = [\, bv_3\ -av_3\ (-bv_1 + av_2)\,]$.

11. The line which is parallel to line γ and passes through point $\mathbf{v}$ is λ:

    1. Prepare T from $\mathbf{v}$.
    2. $\lambda = T\,L\,\gamma$

$$L = \begin{bmatrix} 1 & 0 & 0 \\ 0 & 1 & 0 \\ 0 & 0 & 0 \end{bmatrix}$$

AII.4   GENERAL REMARKS

We can illustrate a technique used to derive items 4, 5, 7, 10 and 11. Consider 4: we wish to find γ such that $\mathbf{p} \cdot \gamma = 0$ and $\mathbf{v} \cdot \gamma = 0$ both hold, i.e.

$$[\, p_1\ p_2\ p_3\,] \cdot \gamma = 0$$
$$[\, v_1\ v_2\ v_3\,] \cdot \gamma = 0$$

There is one more degree of freedom left unspecified because of the third homogeneous coordinate — remember that any scalar multiple of a line vector is a line vector which represents the same two-dimensional line. We will therefore be free to choose any value for c:

$$[\; 0 \quad 0 \quad 1 \;] \cdot \gamma = c$$

Then

$$\begin{bmatrix} p_1 & p_2 & p_3 \\ v_1 & v_2 & v_3 \\ 0 & 0 & 1 \end{bmatrix} \gamma = \begin{bmatrix} 0 \\ 0 \\ c \end{bmatrix}$$

Or, using matrix notation:

$$Q\,\gamma = \begin{bmatrix} 0 \\ 0 \\ c \end{bmatrix}$$

Computing the inverse of Q, we get:

$$\gamma = Q^{-1} \begin{bmatrix} 0 \\ 0 \\ c \end{bmatrix}$$

If Q has a non-zero determinant, we can compute the inverse Q^{-1},

$$Q^{-1} = \frac{1}{p_1 v_2 - p_2 v_1} \begin{bmatrix} v_2 & -p_2 & (p_2 v_3 - p_3 v_2) \\ -v_1 & p_1 & (p_3 v_1 - p_1 v_3) \\ 0 & 0 & (p_1 v_2 - p_2 v_1) \end{bmatrix}$$

which gives

$$\gamma = \frac{c}{p_1 v_2 - p_2 v_1} \begin{bmatrix} p_2 v_3 - p_3 v_2 \\ p_3 v_1 - p_1 v_3 \\ p_1 v_2 - p_2 v_1 \end{bmatrix}$$

If we let c be $(p_1 v_2 - p_2 v_1)$ then we have precisely the results of 4. If the determinant $(p_1 v_2 - p_2 v_1) = 0$, then Q^{-1} does not exist, i.e. the original points $\mathbf{p}$ and $\mathbf{v}$ are the *same point* in two dimensions.

As a second example, we shall find a line λ which is normal to another line γ and passes through the point v (item 10). We require that $\lambda \cdot v = 0$ and (from 8)

$$\left(\gamma^T \begin{bmatrix} 1 & 0 & 0 \\ 0 & 1 & 0 \\ 0 & 0 & 0 \end{bmatrix} \right) \lambda = 0$$

These can be rewritten as:

$$[\, v_1 \; v_2 \; v_3 \,]\, \lambda = 0$$

$$[\, a \;\; b \;\; 0 \,]\, \lambda = 0$$

We also require a third condition. This arises because there are infinitely many λ's which are equivalent descriptions of the line. So we will arbitrarily set

$$[\, 0 \;\; 0 \;\; 1 \,]\, \lambda = d$$

The three equations may now be written as one matrix equation:

$$\begin{bmatrix} v_1 & v_2 & v_3 \\ a & b & 0 \\ 0 & 0 & 1 \end{bmatrix} \lambda = \begin{bmatrix} 0 \\ 0 \\ d \end{bmatrix}$$

$$\lambda = \frac{1}{v_1 b - v_2 a} \begin{bmatrix} b & -v_2 & -bv_3 \\ -a & v_1 & v_3 a \\ 0 & 0 & v_1 b - v_2 a \end{bmatrix} \begin{bmatrix} 0 \\ 0 \\ d \end{bmatrix}$$

$$= \frac{d}{v_1 b - v_2 a} \begin{bmatrix} -bv_3 \\ v_3 a \\ v_1 b - v_2 a \end{bmatrix}$$

Again, setting $d = -bv_1 + av_2$, we get the result of 10. However, suppose $-bv_1 + av_2 = 0$; then the inverse of the matrix above does not exist. In this case, we should have made the requirement

$$[\, 0 \;\; 1 \;\; 0 \,]\, \lambda = d$$

instead, and then the matrix would be invertible. We can show that

$$\lambda = \begin{bmatrix} bv_3 \\ -av_3 \\ av_2 - bv_1 \end{bmatrix}$$

is always a solution.

AII.5   THREE-DIMENSIONAL POINTS, LINES AND PLANES

1. A point in three-space is a four-vector:

$$\mathbf{v} = [\ wx \quad wy \quad wz \quad w\ ]$$

which is simply an extension of the two-dimensional notation. The three-dimensional point represented by a homogeneous point $[\ a \ b \ c \ d\ ]$ is simply the point $[\ a/d \ b/d \ c/d\ ]$. Any scalar multiple of the homogeneous representation for a point represents the same three-dimensional point.

2. A line can be represented parametrically as a function of the free parameter t:

$$\mathbf{v} = [\ t \ \ 1\ ]\, L$$

The matrix L is 2 x 4. Any value of t will yield a point on the line. Lines may also be represented as the intersections of planes, but this representation is not suitable for most applications.

Example: Find the parametric representation of the line through $[\ 1 \ 0 \ 1 \ 1\ ]$ and $[\ 0 \ 1 \ 1 \ 1\ ]$. We must choose values of t at these two points; we choose 0 and 1.

$$[\ t \ \ 1\ ]\, L = [\ wx \quad wy \quad wz \quad w\ ]$$
$$[\ 0 \ \ 1\ ]\, L = [\ 1 \ 0 \ 1 \ 1\ ]$$
$$[\ 1 \ \ 1\ ]\, L = [\ 0 \ 1 \ 1 \ 1\ ]$$

This clearly yields the equation

$$\begin{bmatrix} 0 & 1 \\ 1 & 1 \end{bmatrix} L = \begin{bmatrix} 1 & 0 & 1 & 1 \\ 0 & 1 & 1 & 1 \end{bmatrix}$$

which is solved by finding the inverse of the left-hand 2 x 2 matrix:

$$\begin{bmatrix} -1 & 1 \\ 1 & 0 \end{bmatrix}\begin{bmatrix} 0 & 1 \\ 1 & 1 \end{bmatrix} L = \begin{bmatrix} -1 & 1 \\ 1 & 0 \end{bmatrix}\begin{bmatrix} 1 & 0 & 1 & 1 \\ 0 & 1 & 1 & 1 \end{bmatrix}$$

$$L = \begin{bmatrix} -1 & 1 & 0 & 0 \\ 1 & 0 & 1 & 1 \end{bmatrix}$$

Any scalar multiple of L, sL, yields the same line in three dimensions.

3. A plane is represented by a column vector:

$$\gamma = \begin{bmatrix} a \\ b \\ c \\ d \end{bmatrix}$$

The plane equation (condition that a point **v** be on the plane γ) is:

$$\mathbf{v} \cdot \gamma = 0$$

Actually, **v**·γ is a measure of the distance from **v** to the plane γ; it is positive if **v** lies on one side of the plane and negative if it lies on the other (This is the central idea of Roberts' volume representation). The actual perpendicular distance from **v** to γ is:

$$(\mathbf{v} \cdot \gamma) \frac{1}{w} \frac{1}{\sqrt{a^2 + b^2 + c^2}}$$

where

$$w = \mathbf{v} \cdot \begin{bmatrix} 0 \\ 0 \\ 0 \\ 1 \end{bmatrix}$$

Any non-zero scalar multiple of a plane vector is a vector which represents the same three-dimensional plane. Notice, however, that if the scalar multiplier is less than 0, **v**·γ changes sign.

4. Three planes γ_1, γ_2, and γ_3 intersect in one point **v** such that

$$\mathbf{v} \cdot \gamma_1 = 0 \qquad \mathbf{v} \cdot \gamma_2 = 0 \qquad \mathbf{v} \cdot \gamma_3 = 0$$

Rewriting these three equations, and adding the fourth (scale factor) equation:

$$\mathbf{v} \begin{bmatrix} \gamma_1 \end{bmatrix} \begin{bmatrix} \gamma_2 \end{bmatrix} \begin{bmatrix} \gamma_3 \end{bmatrix} \begin{bmatrix} 0 \\ 0 \\ 0 \\ 1 \end{bmatrix} = \begin{bmatrix} 0 & 0 & 0 & d \end{bmatrix}$$

We solve the equation $\mathbf{v}\,Q = [\,0\ \ 0\ \ 0\ \ d\,]$ by finding the inverse of Q, Q^{-1}:

$$\mathbf{v}\,Q\,Q^{-1} = [\,0\ \ 0\ \ 0\ \ d\,]\,Q^{-1}$$
$$\mathbf{v} = [\,0\ \ 0\ \ 0\ \ d\,]\,Q^{-1}$$

The vector $\mathbf{v}$ is thus the bottom row of the inverse of the 4 x 4 matrix. If the matrix has no inverse, then the three planes do not intersect in one point.

5. Three points $\mathbf{p}, \mathbf{r}$ and $\mathbf{v}$ determine a plane γ unless all are colinear.

$$\mathbf{p}\cdot\gamma = 0 \qquad \mathbf{r}\cdot\gamma = 0 \qquad \mathbf{v}\cdot\gamma = 0$$

$$\begin{bmatrix} \boxed{\mathbf{p}} \\ \boxed{\mathbf{r}} \\ \boxed{\mathbf{v}} \\ 0 \ \ 0 \ \ 0 \ \ 1 \end{bmatrix} \gamma = \begin{bmatrix} 0 \\ 0 \\ 0 \\ d \end{bmatrix} \quad \text{or} \quad Q\gamma = \begin{bmatrix} 0 \\ 0 \\ 0 \\ d \end{bmatrix}$$

The left-hand matrix will have an inverse if and only if $\mathbf{p}$, $\mathbf{r}$ and $\mathbf{v}$ are Not colinear. Then

$$\gamma = Q^{-1} \begin{bmatrix} 0 \\ 0 \\ 0 \\ d \end{bmatrix}$$

where d can be any non-zero number, say $\det Q$.

6. Transformations of the $(n+1)$ homogeneous space are performed with a 4 x 4 matrix H. This transformation matrix is of the same form as the transformations introduced in Chapter 12.

1. Points transform as $\mathbf{v}' = \mathbf{v}\,H$
2. Planes transform as $\gamma' = H^{-1}\,\gamma$
3. Parametric lines transform as do points: $L' = L\,H$

7. The translation transformation T is simply an extended form of the two-dimensional form.

$$v = [\, v_1 \quad v_2 \quad v_3 \quad v_4 \,]$$

$$T = \begin{bmatrix} 1 & 0 & 0 & 0 \\ 0 & 1 & 0 & 0 \\ 0 & 0 & 1 & 0 \\ -v_1/v_4 & -v_2/v_4 & -v_3/v_4 & 1 \end{bmatrix}$$

8. The plane γ is parallel to the plane λ through a point $\mathbf{v}$:

1. Prepare T from $\mathbf{v}$ as in item 7.
2. $\gamma = T J \lambda$, where

$$J = \begin{bmatrix} 1 & 0 & 0 & 0 \\ 0 & 1 & 0 & 0 \\ 0 & 0 & 1 & 0 \\ 0 & 0 & 0 & 0 \end{bmatrix}$$

To show that these planes are parallel, consider a point $\mathbf{p}$ on λ:

$$\mathbf{p} \cdot \lambda = 0$$

The distance from $\mathbf{p}$ to γ is

$$(\mathbf{p} \cdot \gamma) \, \frac{1}{w} \, \frac{1}{\sqrt{a^2 + b^2 + c^2}} \quad \text{where } w = \mathbf{p} \begin{bmatrix} 0 \\ 0 \\ 0 \\ 1 \end{bmatrix} \quad \text{and } \gamma = \begin{bmatrix} a \\ b \\ c \\ d \end{bmatrix}$$

The second factor of the normalization is a property of λ and is constant. The first we shall set to 1, and change the scale factor (fourth coordinate) of $\mathbf{p}$ if necessary. The conditions then become:

$[\, x \;\; y \;\; z \;\; 1 \,] \, \lambda = 0$
$[\, x \;\; y \;\; z \;\; 1 \,] \, \gamma = \text{constant}$

$$\begin{aligned}
[\, x \; y \; z \; 1 \,] \, \gamma &= [\, x \; y \; z \; 1 \,] \, T J \lambda \\
&= [\, (x - v_1/v_4) \, (y - v_2/v_4) \, (z - v_3/v_4) \; 0 \,] \, \lambda \\
&= (\, [\, x \; y \; z \; 1 \,] + 1/v_4 \, [\, -v_1 \; -v_2 \; -v_3 \; -v_4 \,] \,) \, \lambda \\
&= [\, x \; y \; z \; 1 \,] \, \lambda + 1/v_4 \, [\, -v_1 \; -v_2 \; -v_3 \; -v_4 \,] \, \lambda \\
&= 1/v_4 \, [\, -v_1 \; -v_2 \; -v_3 \; -v_4 \,] \, \lambda
\end{aligned}$$

which is constant (independent of x, y and z).

A SMALL-MACHINE INSTRUCTION SET

This Appendix describes the instruction set used in some of the chapters to illustrate programming techniques. The instruction set is similar to those of a number of small machines used extensively with graphical displays. Readers will note a distinct similarity with the IMLAC PDS-1 and the DEC family of 18-bit computers.

The instruction set is based on a simple single-accumulator machine organization. There are no index registers, but indirect addressing is permitted. Instructions fall into three categories: addressable, non-addressable, and input-output. A typical addressable instruction is written as follows:

LAC P

meaning, 'load the accumulator with the contents of location P.' Indirection is applied by means of the I symbol:

DAC I Q

meaning, 'deposit the contents of the accumulator in the location addressed by the contents of location Q.' Labels are indicated by a symbol at the left-hand margin, followed by a colon:

LBL: LAC Q

The following instructions are used in this book (the reader can find the complete instruction set in reference [124]):

Addressable:

LAC A Load accumulator with contents of A
DAC A Deposit contents of accumulator in A
ADD A Add to accumulator the contents of A
LAW A Load accumulator with address of A, i.e. 'load immediate'
ISZ A Increment contents of A, skip if result is zero (accumulator not affected)
JMP A Jump to address A
JMS A Subroutine jump: store incremented program counter in A, jump to $A+1$

Non-Addressable:

CLA   Clear accumulator
SZA   Skip on zero accumulator
SNA   Skip on non-zero accumulator

Input-Output:

ION   Turn interrupts on
IOF   Turn interrupts off
DXL   Load display X-register
DYL   Load display Y-register
DIP   Intensify point
DXI   Load display X-register and intensify
DYI   Load display Y-register and intensify
KCF   Clear keyboard flag

KSF	Skip on keyboard flag set
KSN	Skip on keyboard flag clear
KRB	Read keyboard buffer contents into accumulator
BCF	Clear button flag
BSF	Skip on button flag set
BSN	Skip on button flag clear
BRN	Read button number into accumulator

THE SAIL LANGUAGE

The SAIL programming language is based on ALGOL, and was developed at Stanford University for the PDP-10. Its general structure and conventions are those of ALGOL-60, but additional features are included in SAIL: functions for manipulating arbitrary-length text strings, an interface to the PDP-10 input/output facilities, and data-structure facilities called LEAP (see also Appendix V).

A syntax of SAIL is presented below, together with brief descriptions of the effect of the various constructs. A more complete reference guide for SAIL is found in [283].

The notation for the syntax description was developed by Floyd, and employs some standard conventions. All bold-faced characters stand for themselves. An italic identifier, perhaps with prime symbols ('), stands for a class of symbol strings: for example I stands for all legal identifiers, which is the class which includes A, B, . . . Z, AA, AB, . . . A9, BA, . . . B9, . . . Z9, AAA, etc. All italic characters are *meta-symbols;* they are used for notational purposes only, and are not part of the SAIL syntax. Additional meta-symbols are defined below.

The symbol | means 'or;' if A is defined as $B \mid C$, this means that a string is an A if it is a B or if it is a C. B and C are called *alternatives:* either one is an A.

The notation $A°$, or equivalently, $\langle A \rangle°$, means any number (including zero) of inscriptions, one after the other, each of which is an A. For example, $\langle A \mid B \rangle°$ means A or B or AA or AB or BA or BB or AAA, or Λ, where Λ means no inscription at all.

The notation A^+ means any number (but at least one) of inscriptions, one after another, each of which is an A. It abbreviates $AA°$.

The notation $[\![A]\!]$ means an optional occurrence of A; it abbreviates $\langle A \mid \Lambda \rangle$.

The notation $A\overset{+}{}B$ means A or ABA or $ABABA$, etc.; it abbreviates $A \langle B A \rangle°$.

Brackets $\langle \rangle$ are used simply as parentheses to show the scope of the above operators.

A special notation is used for expressions that can have one of several types: τ-expressions. A τ-expression is either an Algebraic expression (AE), a Boolean expression (BE), an Item expression (IE), or a Set expression (SE). For example, the definition of a τ-expression below is really a short notation for four definitions, one for AE, one for BE, one for SE, and one for IE.

SAIL Algebraic Grammar

Class of Strings	Symbol	Definition	Explanation
letters	λ	**A**|**B**|**C**...|**Z**|**a**|**b**...|**z**| # |!|\$	
digits	δ	0|1|2...|9	
symbols	σ	all ASCII characters except "	
string constant	Σ	$" \langle \sigma \mid "" \rangle ° "$	String constants are formed by enclosing the string in double-quotes: "This is a string". A double-quote is included in a string constant as " " .
identifier	I	$\lambda \langle \lambda \mid \delta \rangle °$	Identifiers start with a letter. Each subsequent character may be a letter or digit. Identifiers may be of arbitrary length.
variable	V	$I \mid I \overline{[AE^+,]}$	A SAIL variable is denoted by a single identifier, or by an array-element specification, used to address individual elements in arrays. Examples are $S[1,2]$, $t[j]$. The subscript may be an arbitrary arithmetic expression (see below).
constant	C	$\delta^+ [. \delta°] [@ [+ \mid -] \delta^+] \mid . \delta^+ [@ [+ \mid -] \delta^+] \mid ' \delta^+$	These forms are used to define numeric constants. A constant is assumed to be an integer unless it has a period or exponent (number following @) in it. The last form (number preceded by apostrophe) denotes an octal constant.
	$\mid \Sigma \mid$ **NULL**		These forms are string constants. NULL is a string of length zero; it has no characters in it.
	$\mid$ **TRUE** $\mid$ **FALSE**		These constants are provided for convenience. Each is an integer: TRUE is −1, FALSE is 0.
function value	F	$I [[\overline{(A^+,)}]]$	A function call is specified by the identifier of the function, followed by an optional list of arguments. Examples are $CVS(123)$ and $WAIT$.

argument A $\tau E \mid V$

An argument to a function or procedure is either an expression or a variable. There are two mechanisms for passing arguments to functions and procedures: by VALUE and by REFERENCE. The exact form of each argument to a function or procedure is specified in the declaration of the procedure. If an argument is passed by VALUE, its value will be available to the procedure. If it is passed by REFERENCE, the procedure is given the address of the argument; the procedure can thus modify the contents of the argument by using this address as a reference to the argument.

expression" AE'' ⟨+|−|ABS|LNOT⟩° ⟨V|C|F|(BE)|(AE)⟩↑ ⟨*|/|DIV|%|MOD|LSH|ROT|&⟩ ⟨+|−|LOR|XOR|EQV|LAND⟩

This is the basic form for assembling simple arithmetic and string expressions. The meanings of the various operators are described in a table below. The familiar operations of addition (+), subtraction (−), division (/) are provided, along with others for special purposes, including string concatenation (&). Operands are formed from variables, constants, function calls, or parenthesized expressions.

expression' AE' AE'' | AE'' [AE TO AE] | AE'' [AE FOR AE]

We further expand the facilities of expressions by including operators which extract substrings from string expressions. AE'' must be a string for these operators to be valid.

boolean expr BE' [NOT] [AE' ⟨ < | ≤ | = | ≠ | > | ≥ ⟩] AE' AND OR

A boolean expression is composed using the operators NOT, AND and OR. The operands are either comparison specifications (less than, equality, etc), or expressions (these are TRUE if non-zero, FALSE if zero). The symbols ≤, ≠ and ≥ have equivalent reserved words LEQ, NEQ and GEQ.

τ-expression τE $\tau E'$ | IF BE THEN τE ELSE τE | CASE AE OF $(\overline{\tau E^{+}, })$ | $\langle V \leftarrow \rangle^{+} \tau E$

Finally, we permit conditional expressions and selection expressions. Examples are: IF J=0 THEN 12 ELSE K/2, CASE $(J−1)$ OF (1,3,2,3). The last form permits assignments imbedded in expressions, e.g, $B+(j \leftarrow k \uparrow 2)$.

statement S $V \leftarrow \tau E$

This is the assignment statement. The expression is evaluated, and then the value of the variable V is replaced with that of the expression.

   $| V \leftrightarrow V$

The swap operator causes the contents of the two variables to be swapped. The operation is equivalent to:

```
temp ← v1;
v1 ← v2;
```

The operator $\leftrightarrow$ has the equivalent reserved word **SWAP**.

$| I : S$

Label I is defined to refer to the following statement.

$| \langle$ **GO** $[\![$ **TO** $]\!]$ $|$ **GOTO** $\rangle I$

This is the transfer statement, which causes the computer to execute the statement labeled with I next. Example: GO *last*, GOTO *FIRST*.

$| I [\![(\overline{A^+},)]\!]$

This is a procedure call, with an optional list of arguments. The procedure whose name is I is executed, and then the next statement after the procedure call statement is executed.

$| \wedge$

This is the empty statement. It is included as a notational convenience.

$| \Sigma S$

A string constant given before a statement is a comment.

$| \beta | \Delta | R$

A statement may be a block, or *compound statement*, consisting of other statements. Additionally, macro definitions and resource requirements may be given as statements.

$|$ **RETURN** $[\![(\tau E)]\!]$

This statement is used to exit from a procedure or function. The optional expression specifies the value which a function should return to its caller. In any case, the execution of the procedure or function is terminated.

$|$ **DONE** $|$ **NEXT**

These statements are only meaningful inside iterative statement forms such as FOR . . . , WHILE . . . , and DO . . . The DONE statement causes the iterative loop to be terminated; the statement following the iterative statement is executed next. The NEXT statement causes the control of the iterative loop to generate the next value of the iteration variable, and check its bounds, etc., whatever is specified in the iterative statement. For example, if we use NEXT inside the statement FOR $J \leftarrow 1$ STEP 1 UNTIL 4, when $J = 2$, NEXT will cause the next value of J to be calculated (3). If that value is still a legal value for execution by the loop, then execution will continue at the statement following the NEXT statement. If not (e.g. the new value of J is 5), then the loop is terminated, as if DONE had been executed.

$|$ **IF** BE **THEN** S $|$ **IF** BE **THEN** S **ELSE** S

Conditional execution of statements is controlled with the IF . . . THEN construct: the boolean expression is evaluated. If its value is non-zero (true), then the statement following the THEN is executed. In the second form, IF . . . THEN . . . ELSE, the first statement is executed if the boolean expression value is non-zero (true); the second if the value is zero (false).

| CASE *AE* OF BEGIN $S\overset{\rightarrow}{}$; END

One of a group of statements may be executed depending on the value of the expression. If its value is 0, the first statement is executed; 1, the second statement, etc.

|[NEEDNEXT]| **WHILE** *BE* **DO** *S*

If the boolean expression *BE* evaluates to true (non-zero), then *S* is executed. After execution of *S*, the test is once again evaluated, and *S* executed again if it is true, etc. If *BE* is ever evaluated to false (zero), then the statement following the WHILE statement is executed. The NEEDNEXT specification conditions this loop to be compiled so that the NEXT statement will operate correctly inside the loop.

| **DO** *S* **UNTIL** *BE*

This statement is similar to the WHILE statement, except that the expression *BE* is evaluated *after* executing *S* rather than before.

|[NEEDNEXT]| **FOR** $V \leftarrow \tau E$ |[**STEP** *AE* ⟨ **UNTIL** *AE* | **WHILE** *BE* ⟩]|$\overset{\rightarrow}{}$, **DO** *S*

This is the most common iterative statement: a variable assumes a range of values; a statement *S* is executed once for each of these values. The FOR.. STEP.. UNTIL form is similar to:

$$V \leftarrow E1;$$

L: IF $(V - E3) * \text{SIGN}(E2) \leq 0$ THEN BEGIN

$$S;$$
$$V \leftarrow V + E2;$$
$$\text{GO TO } L$$
$$\text{END};$$

where *E1*, *E2*, and *E3* are the three expressions in the FOR.. STEP.. UNTIL statement and SIGN is a function whose value is +1 if the argument is positive, and −1 if the argument is negative.

| **START!CODE** $\overline{\langle \text{assembly-instruction} \rangle}\overset{\rightarrow}{}$; **END**

This statement allows the programmer to insert PDP-10 machine instructions in his SAIL program.

β   **BEGIN** |[Σ]| ⟨*D*⟩$^{\circ}$ $\overline{S}\overset{\rightarrow}{}$; **END** |[Σ]|

block   A block is a collection of statements, together with optional declarations. The optional string constants following the BEGIN and END are used to name the block. The compiler will check to make sure that names of matching BEGINs and ENDs match.

declaration   D $[\![\mu]\!] \tau \, T^+$, | LABEL T^+,

This is a simple declaration for a collection of variables. An example is INTEGER I,J,K. The declared variables may be referenced anywhere within the block in which they are declared, or within any blocks nested inside the block in which they are declared. If, at any deeper level, a variable of the same name is declared, then the new declaration has effect only inside its block and subblocks. This phenomenon is called *block-structured scope of variables*. The LABEL declaration is used to declare names of labels needed in the current block.

| $[\![$ PRELOAD!WITH $\overline{AE^+}$; $]\!] \, [\![\mu \, u \, \tau$ ARRAY T^+, $[\, AE : AE^+ \,]$

This form of declaration allocates ARRAYs for variables. The expression pairs are evaluated, and become the lower and upper bounds for the array subscripts. If the declaration occurs in any but the outer block of the program, the array is allocated dynamically; when the block containing the declaration is exited, the array is deleted. The PRELOAD!WITH optionally specifies a list of expressions which is used to initialize the contents of the array. The first expression in the list is the value of the first element of the array, the second the value of the second, etc.

| $[\![$ INTERNAL $]\!]$ $[\![$ RECURSIVE $]\!]$ $[\![\tau]\!]$ PROCEDURE H ; S

This declaration defines functions and procedures. The portion H is called the procedure head; the statement S the procedure body. Usually the procedure body is a block, and can thus contain many, many statements. Technically, however, all these statements are merely the declaration of the procedure. The procedure is declared RECURSIVE if it is to be used recursively; SAIL compiles faster procedure-entry instructions for non-recursive procedures. If a procedure has a type, it is often called a function. If the declaration INTERNAL is used, then the procedure name is made available to other programs.

| $\langle$ FORTRAN | FORWARD | EXTERNAL $\rangle$ $[\![\tau]\!]$ PROCEDURE H

This form of procedure declaration has no body. If the declaration is EXTERNAL or FORTRAN, the body of the procedure is assumed to lie in some other program which will be retrieved when this one is loaded (e.g. library function). The FORTRAN declaration is used to declare a procedure whose definition and body will appear later in the program. The FORWARD declaration allows statements which call the procedure to be compiled before the actual procedure is.

| Δ | R

Macro definitions and resource requests are also legal declarations.

simple type	τ	**INTEGER** | **REAL** | **BOOLEAN** | **STRING**
modifier	μ	**INTERNAL** | **EXTERNAL** | **OWN** | **SAFE**

These modifiers specify that the name being declared should be made available to other programs (INTERNAL), that the object being declared is in some other program, where it is declared INTERNAL (EXTERNAL), that it should be allocated statically (OWN – only meaningful for arrays), or that no subscript bounds checking instructions need be compiled for this array (SAFE).

procedure heading	H	$I [\![\, (\overline{Q^{+};}) \,]\!]$

The procedure heading specifies the procedure name (I), and optionally the argument list for the procedure.

procedure formal	Q	$[\![$ **VALUE** | **REFERENCE** $]\!] \, \tau \, [\![$ **PROCEDURE** $]\!] \, \overline{I^{+},} \mid [\![$ **SAFE** $]\!] \, \tau \, \textbf{ARRAY} \, \overline{I^{+},}$

The VALUE and REFERENCE attributes determine how the arguments are to be passed to the procedure (see discussion of arguments, above).

macro definition	Δ	$\textbf{DEFINE} \, \overline{I \, [\![\, (\overline{I^{+},}) \,]\!] = \Sigma} \, ,$

This declaration is used to define the macro of name I, with an optional parameter-list. Every subsequent occurrence of the identifier I will cause the input scanner to scan the macro body (the string constant Σ) instead. The parameter list specifies dummy variables which are substituted when the macro is expanded. Example: DEFINE G(X)="X←INCHWL". An invocation of the macro might look like G(STR1), which is expanded to STR1←INCHWL.

resource request	R	**REQUIRE** $C \langle$ **SYSTEM!PDL** | **STRING!PDL** | **STRING!SPACE** | **ARRAY!PDL** | **NEW!ITEMS** | **PNAMES** $\rangle$ | **REQUIRE** $\Sigma \langle$ **LOAD!MODULE** | **LIBRARY** $\rangle$

This declaration is used to pass information to load-time or execution-time processes. The LOAD!MODULE and LIBRARY specifications permit other programs and libraries to be loaded automatically with this one. The !PDL names are used to alter default push-down list sizes; example: REQUIRE 1000 SYSTEM!PDL. The NEW!ITEMS and PNAMES options are used for the LEAP facilities.

program		$[\![\, \textbf{ENTRY} \, \overline{I^{+},} \, ; \,]\!] \, \beta$

This class defines a SAIL program. Usually, it is simply a block. If, however, the program is part of a library and has specific entry points, those entry points are specified before the program block.

LEAP Augmentations to the Algebraic Grammar

If the name of the class of strings being defined is starred (*), then the definition cites more alternatives to the same definition in the algebraic grammar.

variable*	V	DATUM (V) ‖ [$\overline{AE}^{+}$,] ‖

Each item has a DATUM associated with it. This datum is treated like any other variable in the SAIL system. In particular, if the DATUM is an array, then we must specify a subscript list for accessing a particular element of the array.

statement*	S	PUT IE IN V ∣ REMOVE IE FROM V

The PUT and REMOVE statements are used for adding and deleting item instances from SETs. The variable V is the set descriptor, and is altered to define the altered set.

∣ MAKE P ∣ ERASE P

These statements add and delete associations from the 'associative store.' The specification P is usually a *triple*: MAKE $A \oplus B \equiv C$.

∣ DELETE (IE)

The DELETE statement informs the data-structure routines that an item (IE) is no longer needed. The item number may be reused later, however, if NEW is called.

∣ ‖ NEEDNEXT ‖ FOREACH $\overline{I}^{+}$, SUCH THAT X DO S

This is the FOREACH statement, which searches the associative store for data which matches a particular context specification X. The identifier list specifies a group of ITEMVARs which are *bound* during the course of the search. That is, the ITEMVARs are given ITEM values which satisfy the context specification. The statement S is executed once for each group of values (and sometimes more than once).

context	X	⟨ $\overline{P \mid I \text{ IN } SE \mid (BE)}$ ⟩ AND

The context specification is used to describe precisely the pattern of items to be retrieved by a FOREACH statement. Clauses are composed with AND: all clauses must be true for a particular group of items to be acceptable to the context. Each clause may be a specification of a triple to find in the associative store, an item to find in a set, or a boolean expression to be evaluated. There are some complicated restrictions on the exact nature of these clauses. An example of a legal context is:

FOREACH X SUCH THAT $A \oplus B \equiv X$ AND X IN FATHERS AND (DATUM(X)>AGE) DO ...

boolean expr* BE' $SE \langle < | \leqslant | = | \neq | > | \geqslant \rangle SE \,|\, IE \text{ IN } SE$

These are additional boolean expressions for comparing item expressions and sets. For example, a set A is less than a set B if it is a proper subset of B. The last form evaluates TRUE if the item IE is a member of the set SE.

item expression IE' $I \,|\, V \,|\, F \,|\, \textbf{ANY}$

An item expression evaluates to a description of an item, an item *number*. Usually, this originates in a variable (called an ITEMVAR), or as an ITEM declared to the program. A function may also yield an item value. The use of ANY is restricted: it is intended to be used with the FOREACH statement to identify 'don't care' places in the context specification.

$| \textbf{NEW} [\![(\langle AE \,|\, BE \,|\, SE \,|\, I \rangle)]\!]$

The NEW function requests a fresh item descriptor from the data-structure routines. In effect, a new item is created and added to the system. The optional argument to NEW is used to specify the initial DATUM of the item. If the argument is an identifier of type ARRAY, then a copy of that array becomes the initial DATUM. Otherwise, the value of the expression argument becomes the initial DATUM.

$| [P] \,|\, \langle \textbf{FIRST} \,|\, \textbf{SECOND} \,|\, \textbf{THIRD} \rangle (IE)$

This form of item expression identifies a *bracketed triple*. Its value is the item which is associated with the triple. For example, if we MAKE $A \oplus B \equiv [E \oplus F \equiv G]$, this involves making the association $E \oplus F \equiv G$, creating a new item (say W), associating the item with the made triple, and then making $A \oplus B \equiv W$. The FIRST, SECOND and THIRD functions are used to find the three component parts of a bracketed triple item such as W. In the example, FIRST (W) is E.

set expression SE' $\langle \overrightarrow{\{IE,\}} \,|\, \textbf{PHI} \,|\, (N) \,|\, (SE) \,|\, V \,|\, F \rangle - \cap \cup$

derived set N $IE \langle ' \,|\, \oplus \rangle IE$

triple P $N \equiv IE$

The derived set is formed by searching the associative store, e.g. $A \oplus B = X$ is the set of all items X such that $A \oplus B = X$. A set expression is composed using the operators of union, intersection, and subtraction. The operands are derived sets, sets returned as values of funtions, the empty set PHI, and literal sets (specified by listing the items which are elements, e.g. $\{A, B, C\}$).

declaration* D $[\![\tau]\!] \textbf{ITEM} \overrightarrow{I,}$

This is a standard definition for item constants. Each generates a fixed item number. Whenever a reference to the item is discovered within the scope of the declaration, the item number is substituted. The item number is not reclaimed when the block in which the item is declared is exited: item presence is independent of block structure. The type of an item is declared so that the DATUM operator will operate correctly. If the DATUM is itself an array, then we need an alternate form of the declaration:

| [μ] τ **ARRAY ITEM** $\overline{[\,AE : AE^{\dagger}\,,\,]}$

    The type of array is specified, as well as the bounds. When the block in which this declaration occurs is entered, an array of appropriate size is created and remembered as the DATUM of the item.

| [μ] [τ | τ **ARRAY**] **ITEMVAR** $\overline{I}^{\dagger}$,

    This declaration defines a variable which can hold an item number, i.e. an instance of the item. The value of the variable is the item number last stored into it. ITEMs are like constants; ITEMVARs like variables. The *type* of the ITEMVAR is used to determine how a DATUM operator will be interpreted. If the type is INTEGER, then the DATUM will be assumed to be of type integer. The ARRAY ITEMVAR form is used to specify that the DATUM is an array and will require subscript specification.

| [μ] [τ | τ **ARRAY**] **ITEMVAR** $\overline{I}^{\dagger}$, $[\,AE : AE^{\dagger}\,,\,]$

    This declaration creates an ARRAY of ITEMVARs. Again, the type of the ITEMVAR is needed for interpretation by the DATUM operator. If the DATUM of each item in the ITEMVAR ARRAY is itself an integer array, then we have the somewhat confusing declaration: INTEGER ARRAY ITEMVAR ARRAY.

| [[**INTERNAL**] | [**RECURSIVE**] | [τ] [**ARRAY**] **ITEMVAR PROCEDURE** H ; S
| (**FORWARD** | **EXTERNAL**) [τ] [**ARRAY**] **ITEMVAR PROCEDURE** H

    Functions may also return item numbers as values. This declaration specifies the type of the DATUM of the item returned.

| [**VALUE** | **REFERENCE**] [**SAFE**] [τ | τ **ARRAY**] **ITEMVAR** [**ARRAY**] $\overline{I}^{\dagger}$,

    This includes the various kinds of ITEMVARs as possible arguments to procedures.

procedure formal* Q

simple type* τ **SET**

    This final addition is that SETs are in every way a standard data type. Declarations involving SETs are thus not different from those involving INTEGERs.

SAIL OPERATORS

The various operators imbedded in the syntactic description above can be specified more precisely. We shall define the domains for the various SAIL data types, the 'automatic' conversions between domains, and finally the specifications for the individual operators.

The domains are:

S	Strings: 7-bit character strings of variable length
I	Integers: $-3.435 \times 10^{10} < I < 3.435 \times 10^{10}$
R	Reals: $-1.701 \times 10^{38} < R < 1.701 \times 10^{38}$; smallest number: 1.469×10^{-38}
Item	Item descriptors: maximum of 4096 items
Set	Sets: variable-length collections of items
B	Booleans: $(0, -1)$

A (algebraic) $S \cup I \cup R \cup B$
N (numeric) $I \cup R \cup B$

In addition, we shall define the domain V to be a reference to any SAIL variable.

The following are implicit conversion rules between domains:

$I \Rightarrow R$	Convert the integer to floating-point representation. No errors are possible.
$R \Rightarrow I$	Truncate the real number so that $I = \lfloor$ ABS $(R) \rfloor *$ SIGN(R). Errors may result if the magnitude of the real number cannot be represented in fixed-point format.
$S \Rightarrow I$	A string is converted to an integer: I is the binary code for the first ASCII character of S. If S is the null string, I is 0.
$I \Rightarrow S$	S becomes a one-character string. The ASCII code of the character is I MOD 128.
$I \Rightarrow B$	If I is non-zero, B is TRUE, else FALSE.
$B \Rightarrow I$	If B is TRUE, I is -1, else 0.

An ordering can be imposed on the domains for the purposes of some of the description below. It will then make sense to speak of the *maximum* of two domains, as defined by the ordering. The ordering is:

$$S \subset I \subset R$$
$$B \subset I$$

Operators

Application	Kinds of Arguments and Results (conversion to these types may occur, given above conversion rules)	Domains
$e_1 + e_2$	$A + A \Rightarrow N$	$d_1 + d_2 \Rightarrow \max(d_1, d_2, I)$
$e_1 - e_2$	$A - A \Rightarrow N$	$d_1 - d_2 \Rightarrow \max(d_1, d_2, I)$
$e_1 * e_2$	$A * A \Rightarrow N$	$d_1 * d_2 \Rightarrow \max(d_1, d_2, I)$
e_1 / e_2	$R / R \Rightarrow R$	$R / R \Rightarrow R$
		This operation is a floating-point divide.
$e_1 \% e_2$	$I \% I \Rightarrow I$	$I \% I \Rightarrow I$
		This operation is an integer divide.
$e_1 \uparrow e_2$	$A \uparrow A \Rightarrow N$	$d_1 \uparrow d_2 \Rightarrow \max(d_1, d_2, I)$
		This is exponentiation.
$-e_1$	$-A \Rightarrow N$	$-d_1 \Rightarrow \max(d_1, I)$
$e_1 \text{ MOD } e_2$	$I \text{ MOD } I \Rightarrow I$	$I \text{ MOD } I \Rightarrow I$
		If the result of the MOD operator is e_3, then $e_1 - e_3$ is a multiple of e_2, $\text{ABS}(e_2) < \text{ABS}(e_3)$
$\text{ABS } e_1$	$\text{ABS } A \Rightarrow N$	$\text{ABS } d_1 \Rightarrow \max(d_1, I)$
		This is the absolute-value operator.
$e_1 \text{ LOR } e_2$	$A \text{ LOR } A \Rightarrow N$	$d_1 \text{ LOR } d_2 \Rightarrow \max(d_1, I)$
		The operator or's the bits of e_1 and e_2.
$e_1 \text{ LAND } e_2$	$A \text{ LAND } A \Rightarrow N$	$d_1 \text{ LAND } d_2 \Rightarrow \max(d_1, I)$
		LAND and's the bits of e_1 and e_2.
$e_1 \text{ XOR } e_2$	$A \text{ XOR } A \Rightarrow N$	$d_1 \text{ XOR } d_2 \Rightarrow \max(d_1, I)$
		XOR computes the exclusive-or of the bits of e_1 and e_2.
$e_1 \text{ EQV } e_2$	$A \text{ EQV } A \Rightarrow N$	$d_1 \text{ EQV } d_2 \Rightarrow \max(d_1, I)$
		EQV computes the equivalence of the bits of e_1 and e_2.
$\text{LNOT } e_1$	$\text{LNOT } A \Rightarrow N$	$\text{LNOT } d_1 \Rightarrow \max(d_1, I)$
		The value is the complement of the bits of e_1.
$e_1 \text{ LSH } e_2$	$A \text{ LSH } I \Rightarrow N$	$d_1 \text{ LSH } I \Rightarrow d_1$
		The bits of e_1 are shifted left by e_2 positions ($e_2 < 0$ implies right shift)
$e_1 \text{ ROT } e_2$	$A \text{ ROT } I \Rightarrow N$	$d_1 \text{ ROT } I \Rightarrow d_1$
		The bits of e_1 are rotated left e_2 positions ($e_2 < 0$ implies right rotate)

$e_1 = e_2$

$e_1 \neq e_2$

$\begin{cases} A = A \Rightarrow B \\ \text{Set} = \text{Set} \Rightarrow B \\ \text{Item} = \text{Item} \Rightarrow B \end{cases}$

The 'equal' compare is performed on a type $= \max (d_1, d_2, I)$.
Sets are equal if they each have exactly the same members.
Instances of items are equal if they have the same item number.

$e_1 < e_2$
$e_1 \leqslant e_2$
$e_1 > e_2$
$e_1 \geqslant e_2$

$\begin{cases} A < A \Rightarrow B \\ \text{Set} < \text{Set} \Rightarrow B \end{cases}$

Compare done with type $\max (d_1, d_2, I)$
The four tests are equivalent to the mathematical notions of: $\subset \subseteq \supset \supseteq$

$e_1 \ \& \ e_2$ $S \ \& \ S \Rightarrow S$

String concatenation. The resultant string is $e_1 e_2$.

$e_1 \ [\ e_2 \ \text{TO} \ e_3 \ ]$ $S \ [\ N \ \text{TO} \ N \ ] \Rightarrow S$

Extract a substring of e_1, starting at character e_2 (numbering begins at 1) and continuing through character e_3.
As a convenience, the character ∞, if used in expressions e_2 or e_3, means 'LENGTH(e_1).'
INF is a reserved word equivalent to ∞.

$e_1 \ [\ e_2 \ \text{FOR} \ e_3 \ ]$ $S \ [\ N \ \text{FOR} \ N \ ] \Rightarrow S$

Equivalent to $e_1 \ [\ e_2 \ \text{TO} \ e_2 + e_3 \ ]$

$e_1 \ \text{IN} \ e_2$ Item IN Set $\Rightarrow B$

Evaluates true if the item is in the set.

IF e_1 THEN e_2 ELSE e_3 IF B THEN A ELSE $A \Rightarrow A$

IF d_1 THEN d_2 ELSE $d_3 \Rightarrow d_2$
If d_1 is TRUE, then e_2 is evaluated, otherwise e_3

CASE e_0 OF $(e_1, e_2 .. e_n)$ CASE N OF $(A, A..A)$ $\Rightarrow A$

CASE d_0 OF $(d_1, d_2 .. d_n) \Rightarrow d_1$
The value $i = e_0 + 1$ selects e_i for evaluation.

FUNCTIONS

Name and form   *Meaning*

LENGTH $(S) \Rightarrow I$ Number of characters in the string S.

LENGTH (Set) $\Rightarrow I$ Number of items in the set.

EQU $(S, S) \Rightarrow I$ The two strings are compared, character by character. If they are equal, -1 is returned, else 0.

COP (Set) $\Rightarrow$ Item   Value of function is one of elements of set.

LOP (Set) $\Rightarrow$ Item   Same as COP, except selected item is removed from the set.

LOP $(S) \Rightarrow I$ I gets the ASCII character code for the first character of S; the character is also removed from S. If S was NULL, I is 0.

RAN $(R) \Rightarrow R$	Pseudo random number generator.
SQRT $(R) \Rightarrow R$	Square root.
LOG $(R) \Rightarrow R$	Natural logarithm.
LOG10 $(R) \Rightarrow R$	Logarithm to base 10.
EXP $(R) \Rightarrow R$	Exponentiate e by argument.
ALOG $(R) \Rightarrow R$	Antilogarithm.
SIN $(R) \Rightarrow R$	Sine function; argument in radians.
COS $(R) \Rightarrow R$	Cosine function; argument in radians.
SIND $(R) \Rightarrow R$	SIN; argument in degrees.
COSD $(R) \Rightarrow R$	COS; argument in degrees.
TAN $(R) \Rightarrow R$	Tangent function; argument in radians.
ATAN $(R) \Rightarrow R$	Arctangent function.
ASIN $(R) \Rightarrow R$	Arcsine function; result in radians.
ACOS $(R) \Rightarrow R$	Arccosine function; result in radians.
SINH $(R) \Rightarrow R$	Hyperbolic sine.
COSH $(R) \Rightarrow R$	Hyperbolic cosine.
TANH $(R) \Rightarrow R$	Hyperbolic tangent.

CVS $(I) \Rightarrow S$	Return a string which is a decimal notation for integer I.
CVD $(S) \Rightarrow I$	Return the number for which S is a decimal print-string. Initial spaces are discarded; − and + are legal prefixes.
CVOS $(I) \Rightarrow S$	Return a string which is an octal notation for I.
CVO $(S) \Rightarrow I$	Return the number for which S is the octal print-string. Initial spaces are discarded; − and + are legal prefixes.
CVF $(R) \Rightarrow S$	Generate free-form string notation for the real R.
CVE $(R) \Rightarrow S$	Generate E-format string notaton for R, e.g. 1.34@3.
CVG $(R) \Rightarrow S$	Generate appropriate string notation for R, minimizing use of scientific notation.
CVI $(I) \Rightarrow$ Item	Return item descriptor whose item number is I.
CVN (Item) $\Rightarrow I$	Return item number of Item.
CVIS (Item, $V) \Rightarrow S$	This function retrieves the 'print-name' of the Item. Only items declared to the compiler with the ITEM declaration have print-names. If no print-name can be found, V is set to −1, else 0.
CVSI $(S, V) \Rightarrow$ Item	This function looks up the string in the table of item print-names and returns the item number. If no such item can be found, V is set to −1, else 0.

CVSTR $(I) \Rightarrow S$ I is assumed to be 5 packed ASCII characters; S is a 5-character string with those characters.

CVASC $(S) \Rightarrow I$ The first five characters of S are packed into I.

CVXSTR $(I) \Rightarrow S$ I is assumed to be SIXBIT; S is a 6-character ASCII string which represents the same characters.

CVSIX $(S) \Rightarrow I$ The first 6 characters of S are converted to SIXBIT and packed in I.

ILDB $(V) \Rightarrow I$ Argument is assumed to be a byte pointer. It is incremented to point to the next byte following the one it is presently pointed at, and the new byte is returned.

LDB $(I) \Rightarrow I$ Same as ILDB, except pointer not incremented.

POINT $(I_1, V, I_2) \Rightarrow I$ Creates a byte pointer. The pointer will point to a byte of V; the byte will be I_1 bits long, and begin at bit I_2 (0 is leftmost bit).

PROCEDURES (STATEMENTS)

IDPB (I,V) Increment the byte ponter V, and deposit the integer I in the byte pointed to by V.

DPB (I,V) Deposit the value of I in the byte pointed to by the byte-pointer V.

IBP (V) Increment the byte pointer V.

ARRBLT (V_1, V_2, I) Transfer the binary word at V_2 to V_1, the one at $V_2 + 1$ to $V_1 + 1$, etc., for a total of I words.

SETFORMAT (I_1, I_2) This sets format information for the functions CVS, CVOS, CVE, CVF and CVG. I_1 specifies the minimum width for strings created by these functions. I_2 is the number of digits to include following the decimal point.

INPUT/OUTPUT FUNCTIONS AND PROCEDURES

OUTSTR (S) Types the string S on the user teletype.

INCHWL $\Rightarrow S$ Waits for a *line* to be typed in, and returns all characters in the line, with the exception of the 'carraige-return' and 'line-feed' characters.

INCHRW $\Rightarrow I$ Waits for a single character to by typed in, and returns the 7-bit ASCII code for that character.

OPEN $(I_1,S,I_2,I_3,I_4,I_5,V_1,V_2)$ Establishes a connection number I_1 to a device named by S. Connection operates in mode I_2; I_3 input buffers are allocated; I_4 output buffers; I_5 is the maximum number of characters read in in one input request; V_1 is a descriptor for the break indicator; V_2 for end-of-file indicator.

LOOKUP (I,S,V) The file named S is attached to connection number I for reading. V is set non-zero if the attachment fails, e.g. there is no such file on the device OPENed for connection I.

ENTER (I,S,V) The file named S is attached to connection I for writing. V is set non-zero if the file cannot be written.

CLOSE (I) Terminate file attachment on connection I.

RELEASE (I) Terminate connection I.

INPUT $(I_1,I_2) \Rightarrow S$ Input request on connection I_1, using a 'break table' numbered I_2. The input file is assumed to be ASCII characters. This input request may involve waiting until enough input characters are available, e.g. a line is typed in at a teletype.

OUT (I,S) Write out string S on connection I.

WORDIN $(I) \Rightarrow A$ Read a 36-bit binary number from connection I.

WORDOUT (I,A) Write a 36-bit binary word A on connection I.

ARRYIN (I_1,V,I_2) Read I_2 binary words from connection I_1. Deposit them in core memory sequentially, starting at location V.

ARRYOUT (I_1,V,I_2) Write I_2 binary words on connection I_1. Words are fetched from core starting at V.

SETBREAK (I,S_1,S_2,S_3) Set up a 'break table' numbered I. The characters in S_2 will be omitted from the input stream when doing an INPUT request. If the character "I" is in S_3, then the characters of S_1 are the 'break characters;' if "X" is in S_3, then all ASCII characters except those in S_1 are the 'break characters.' A break character terminates an input request. If "S" is in S_3, then discard the break character when it is read; if "A" is in S_3, then append the break character to the end of the input string; if "R" is in S_3, retain the break character so that it may be returned as part of the next input request.

THE LEAP DATA STRUCTURES

AV.1   THE LEAP ASSOCIATIVE DATA STRUCTURE

The following is only a brief description of LEAP structures, in which certain features have been omitted for the sake of simplicity. Those interested in studying LEAP in more detail should consult the various published references [91, 248, 247].

LEAP is an extension of Algol 60. It was implemented first on the TX-2 computer at MIT Lincoln Laboratory, and later at Stanford University's Artificial Intelligence Project where it was called SAIL (see Appendix IV and [283]). The structures in SAIL are, however, somewhat different from those described here.

AV.1.1   ITEMS

All data structure systems allow items of information to be added to the structure. Sometimes they are called *elements*, sometimes *cells*, and there are of course many other names for them. In list and

ID   datum

ID	datum
1	---
2	---
3	---
	≡
173	10

FIGURE AV-1

ring-structures these items are stored in memory provided by the free-storage system, and are associated with other items by means of pointers. In LEAP, items are all stored in a single *table*, as shown in Figure AV-1. Each one is referred to by its address in this table, known as its ID. In the same way that data may be stored into elements of a ring-structure, we may associate a *datum* with each item in the table. LEAP allows us to build *associations* between items, and to group items in *sets*. These structures refer to items only by their ID's, which may therefore be thought of as *internal names*.

An item is created by means of the *new* operator. This operator finds a vacant space in the table, and assigns it to the new item; the address in the table becomes the item's ID. We can define the datum of a new item by including it in parentheses:

  new(10)

Figure AV-1 shows the state of the table as it might be after processing this operator. The new item has been assigned 173 as ID.

AV.1.2   SETS

Sets are implemented in LEAP as linked lists, each element containing an ID. Figure AV-2 shows a typical set. As you can see, the set is ordered by ascending ID's, so as to speed up set operations.

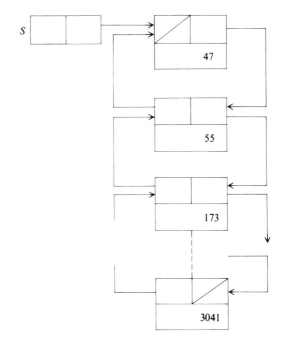

S

47

55

173

3041

FIGURE AV-2

LEAP permits a number of operations to be carried out on sets. They include the following (*S1, S2, S3* are sets; *x, y* are items):

$S1 \leftarrow \phi$ make *S1* an empty set
$S2 \leftarrow [x,y]$ make *S2* a set containing *x,y*
$S3 \leftarrow S1 \cup S2$ make *S3* union of *S1* and *S2*
$S3 \leftarrow S1 \cap S2$ make *S3* intersection of *S1* and *S2*
put *x* **in** *S1*
remove *x* **from** *S2*
x **in** *S1*   test for members (result *true* or *false*)
$S1 \subset S2$ test for subset (result *true* or *false*)
$S2 = S3$ test for identical (result *true* or *false*)

For example, the following program reads the name and sex of 20 children and creates two sets containing the girls and boys. A single set is then created of all children. Notice the use of an *itemvar* (item variable) to store the ID of the newly created item.

```
begin set boys, girls, children;
    itemvar x;
    string name, sex;
    integer i;
    boys←girls←φ;
    for i←1 step 1 until 20 do
        begin read(name); x←new(name);
            read(sex);
            if sex="male" then put x in boys
                else put x in girls
        end;
    children←boys ∪ girls
end
```

AV.1.3   SCANNING SETS

LEAP includes the *foreach* statement for scanning sets:

```
foreach x in boys do
    if datum (x)="jones" then put x in joneses;
```

Here *x* is treated as a *local* variable which in turn holds the ID of each item in the set. The result of the above statement is to create a set 'joneses' containing all the boys called 'jones.'

AV.1.4   ASSOCIATIONS

The main purpose of the LEAP data structure is to allow *associations* to be formed from items, and to permit various retrieval operations to be carried out on these associations. Associations have the form:

$$a \cdot o \equiv v$$

where *a, o* and *v* are items. The meaning of this association is clarified if we call *a* the *attribute*, *o* the *object* and *v* the *value* of the association. Examples of associations are:

$$father \cdot john \equiv pete$$
$$son \cdot john \equiv tom$$
$$color \cdot box \equiv red$$

Notice, however, that each of the three elements of an association must be the name of an *item* or an *itemvar*. It is not possible to use numerical values as follows:

> *age · tom ≡ 17*

Instead, we must create an item whose datum is 17:

> *age · tom ≡* **new**(17)

LEAP keeps a record of all associations created during execution. These are normally the result of a *make* statement:

> **make** *father · john ≡ pete;*
> **make** *son · john ≡ tom;*
> **make** *age · tom ≡* **new(***17)***;**
> **make** *father · tom ≡ john;*

The simplest way of visualizing this file of associations is as a table with three columns, each row defining an association, as shown in Figure AV-3a. Figure AV-3b shows the actual values that might be stored in the association table, and the corresponding item table.

Associations which have been created with the **make** statement can be removed from the association file with the **erase** statement:

> **erase** *father · john ≡ pete*

This removes the entry in the association table, but leaves all three items still in the item table. An item can be removed altogether with:

> **delete** *pete*

The **foreach** statement can be used on associations, and is in this form one of the most powerful means of data retrieval. For example:

> **foreach** *father · x ≡ y* **do make** *son · y ≡ x;*

Here both *x* and *y* are local variables. The **foreach** statement finds all the associations with attribute 'father,' and makes a new 'son' association with object and value transposed. If the association already exists, then it is not duplicated. Thus the effect of this statement is to add only one further association, *son · pete ≡ john,* leaving the association table as shown in Figure AV-4.

Notice that the **foreach** statement must know which variables are *locals* and which represent real items. For example, if *y* were an item or

attribute	object	value
father	john	pete
son	john	tom
age	tom	(17)
father	tom	john

datum

1	——	father
2	——	john
3	——	pete
4	——	son
5	——	tom
6	——	age
7	17	—

a	*o*	*v*
1	2	3
4	2	5
6	5	7
1	5	2

(a)   (b)

FIGURE AV-3

itemvar, the example above would simply find all the sons x of y. For this reason, *local* variables must be declared as such:

        local $x,y;$

The following example finds all the books on philosophy with less than 500 pages, puts them in a set and prints their names and authors:

        begin set *shortlist;*
          local $x,y,z;$
          shortlist←φ;
          foreach *subject* · $x \equiv philosophy$ **and** *pages* · $x \equiv y$
             and datum $(y) < 500$ **do put** x **in** *shortlist;*
          foreach x **in** *shortlist* **and** *title*· $x \equiv y$ **and** *author*· $x \equiv z$ **do**
             begin *print* (**datum** (y));
               print (**datum** (z));
             end
        end

a	o	v
1	2	3
4	2	5
6	5	7
1	5	2
4	3	2

FIGURE AV-4

AV.2   IMPLEMENTATION

When the **foreach** statement is applied to associations, every association in the table that has the appropriate attribute, object or value must be found and the rest of the statement applied to it. This is likely to be a lengthy operation. If we could be certain that associations would always be accessed by attribute, we could build lists of associations with the same attribute, and then scan these lists. Scanning by attribute, however, is not the only way in which the data file will be accessed. The following is a list of the seven different types of access that may be made:

Form name	Form	Example	Interpretation
$F0$	$a \cdot o \equiv v$	$son \cdot John \equiv Pete$	true if association exists otherwise false
$F1$	$a \cdot o \equiv ?$	$son \cdot John \equiv x$	sons of John
$F2$	$a \cdot ? \equiv v$	$son \cdot x \equiv Pete$	father of Pete
$F3$	$? \cdot o \equiv v$	$x \cdot John \equiv Pete$	relationship of Pete to John
$F4$	$a \cdot ? \equiv ?$	$son \cdot x \equiv Z$	all father-son pairs
$F5$	$? \cdot ? \equiv v$	$x \cdot z \equiv Pete$	all associations with Pete as value
$F6$	$? \cdot o \equiv ?$	$x \cdot John \equiv Z$	all associations of which John is object.

We see firstly that there is symmetry in a, o and v about the forms of request; and that there is some need to be able to locate associations according to their content. The LEAP data structure does this by (a) storing associations three separate ways according to their attribute, object and value, and (b) using a *hash-code* derived from the ID's of these three items to locate the association. The way this is done is shown in Figures AV-6 to AV-8.

— use-list —
headers
addressable
double
single
— double —
addressable
double
single
— double —
single
— double —

FIGURE AV-5

Associations are stored in three areas, called the *A-page*, the *O-page* and the *V-page*. The reason for calling them 'pages' will soon become clear. At the head of each page several words are devoted to *use-list headers;* the rest of the page is divided into double and single cells as Figure AV-5 depicts. The position on the page at which an association is stored is determined by hash-coding: on the *A*-page, for example, the position is found by hashing together the ID's of the attribute and object. In the example of Figures AV-6 to AV-8 the hashing function is simply an exclusive-or of the two ID's. The association is then stored in the corresponding *addressable double* as shown.

Not all of the information in the association is stored in the addressable double. On the *A*-page, for example, only the object ID is stored in the double, and a pointer leads to a list of value ID's. The double itself is placed on a *use-list* containing all the associations with the same attribute. The same scheme is used on all three pages, rotating cyclicly through attribute, object and value.

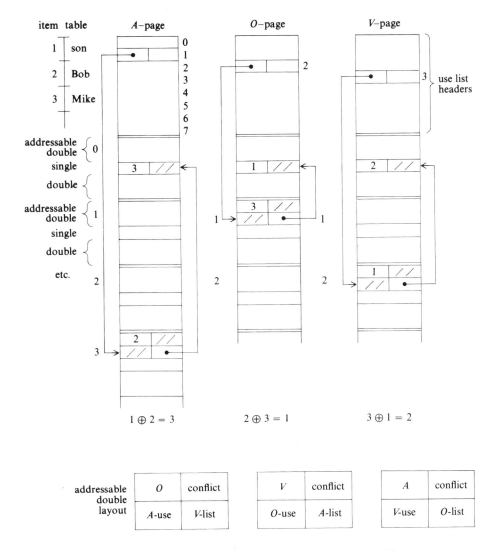

state of structure after   *make* son · Bob ≡ Mike

FIGURE AV-6

Figure AV-6 shows the three pages after only one association has been made. At this point each page is accommodating the association partly in the double cell addressed by hashing, and partly in the first available single cell. In Figure AV-7 a second association has been added. Since this has the same attribute as the first, both share the same

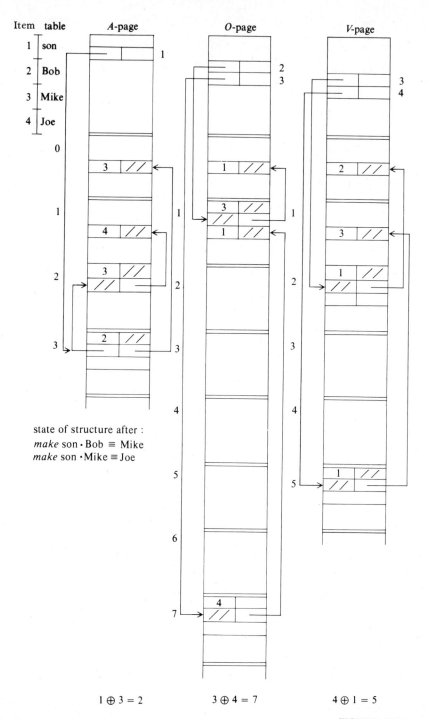

state of structure after :
make son · Bob ≡ Mike
make son · Mike ≡ Joe

$1 \oplus 3 = 2$ $3 \oplus 4 = 7$ $4 \oplus 1 = 5$

FIGURE AV-7

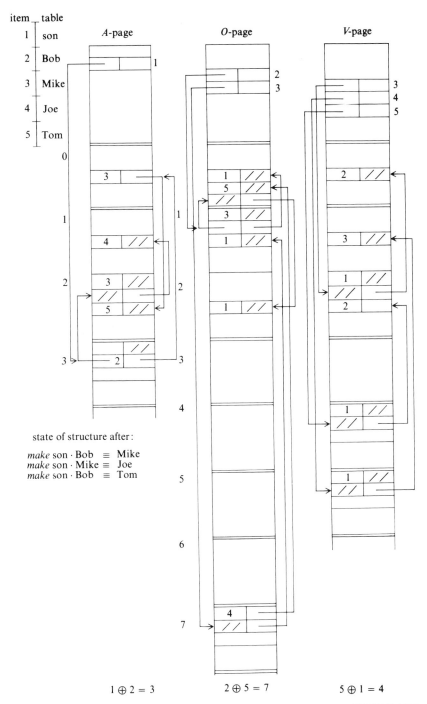

item — table
1 | son
2 | Bob
3 | Mike
4 | Joe
5 | Tom

state of structure after:

make son · Bob ≡ Mike
make son · Mike ≡ Joe
make son · Bob ≡ Tom

$1 \oplus 2 = 3$ $2 \oplus 5 = 7$ $5 \oplus 1 = 4$

FIGURE AV-8

use-list on the A-page. In every other respect, this association is stored in the same fashion as the first.

The third association introduces two complications, *multiple values* and *hashing conflict*. The attribute and object are the same as in the first association, so they obviously hash to the same spot on the A-page; the value is added to the value-list starting from this point. On the O-page the object and value hash to an address already occupied by an association with a different object-value pair, so the *conflict* pointer is used to point to a double cell in which the association is stored. In this manner any number of associations may be added to the structure, until there are no single or double cells left.

The pages illustrated allow only eight use-lists per page, and therefore can refer only to ID's in the range 0 to 7. Further pages are therefore allocated to cope with larger ID's: for example, an association with ID's 31, 27, and 55 would be stored on the fourth A-page, the third O-page and the sixth V-page.

Retrieval from this structure is carried out by choosing the page according to the items whose ID's are known. Let us consider two of the seven forms of association:

$$F1: \quad a \cdot o \equiv ? \qquad \text{e.g. } son \cdot bob \equiv x$$
$$F4: \quad a \cdot ? \equiv ? \qquad \text{e.g. } son \cdot x \equiv z$$

The first is 'solved' by choosing the A-page corresponding to the upper bits of the attribute ID. Then the lower bits of the attribute ID are hashed with the object ID to give the association's address. The result is the list of values of this association.

The second is 'solved' with the aid of the same A-page, by traversing the appropriate A-use-list. The correct use-list is indicated by the lower bits of the attribute ID. The result is the set of objects found in the associations on this use-list, together with the values of each association.

The other retrieval forms are resolved by one or other of these techniques, cyclically permuting A, O and V. In brief, the methods are as follows:

$F0: \quad a \cdot o \equiv v$ choose A-page, hash a and o, look for v in value list;
$F1: \quad a \cdot o \equiv ?$ choose A-page, hash a and o, get value list;
$F2: \quad a \cdot ? \equiv v$ choose V-page, hash v and a, get object-list;
$F3: \quad ? \cdot o \equiv v$ choose O-page, hash o and v, get attribute-list;

F4: $a \cdot ? \equiv ?$ choose A-page, scan A-use-list, return each object and each value in value list;

F5: $? \cdot ? \equiv v$ choose V-page, scan V-use-list, return each attribute and each object in object list;

F6: $? \cdot o \equiv ?$ choose O-page, scan O-use-list, return each value and each attribute in attribute list.

In each of these, associations must be checked for conflicts, and if necessary the conflict list must be traversed to find the right association.

AV.3   CONCLUSION

One obvious and desirable feature of this data structure technique is the retrieval mechanism. Except in the case of conflicts, the number of accesses to the data structure is proportional to the number of associations which satisfy the retrieval request. This means that no time is lost in accessing data in which we are not interested. This contrasts sharply with ring-and list-structures, where a complete list may have to be traversed in order to reach a few items of information.

Another good feature of the LEAP structure is the way paging is organized. Since all the associations concerning one attribute are stored on a single page, questions of the type:

foreach *father* $\cdot x \equiv y$ **do** $\cdots$

can be answered by bringing into core only one page. Thus despite the use of disc or drum memory for holding pages, very few accesses to the disc or drum are necessary. Usually four pages are permitted to remain in core at a time, and this allows quite complex **foreach** statements to be executed rapidly.

The penalty for this is a limitation on the number of different associations which have the same attribute, object or value, all of which have to fit on one page. This means that pages must be fairly large, and even so the structure may become 'full' in an inconvenient way. When this happens, the entire structure must be *re-hashed*, using a larger page size: this is a costly but effective way of avoiding the main drawback of the LEAP structures.

THE WARNOCK HIDDEN-LINE ALGORITHM

This appendix describes an implementation of the Warnock algorithm which is described briefly in Chapter 14. Specific Looker and Thinker computations are described, followed by a SAIL program implementation.

AVI.1   THE LOOKER

The task of the Looker is to classify a polygon as either (1) a surrounder of the window, (2) disjoint from the window, or (3) an intersector of the current window. In addition, it may compute some details of any intersection (e.g. 1 vertex, 1 free edge, etc).

The computations all closely resemble *clipping*: a set of lines representing the edges of a polygon is clipped against the window (Notice that this is two-dimensional clipping). If any edge of a polygon intersects the window, then the polygon is an intersector. Further information is available from the clipping operation, such as the screen

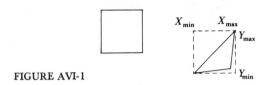

FIGURE AVI-1

coordinates of the clipped edge. Another way to decide whether an edge passes through the window is to substitute the coordinates of the corners of the window into the line equation of the edge. If the signs of the four resulting numbers are the same, then all four corners of the window lie on one side of the line, and the line does not pass through the window.

If no edges of a polygon intersect the window, then the polygon is disjoint from the window or it surrounds the window. The mechanism for distinguishing these two cases requires a fair amount of computation, and it is often convenient to be able to detect disjoint polygons very rapidly. If any of the following conditions are met, the window and the polygon are disjoint:

1. All vertices of the polygon lie to the right of the window.
2. All vertices of the polygon lie to the left of the window.
3. All vertices of the polygon lie below the window.
4. All vertices of the polygon lie above the window.

This check can be performed quickly if, for each polygon, minimum X, maximum X, minimum Y, and maximum Y values of the coordinates of all its vertices are stored. These minimum and maximum values can be viewed as defining a rectangle which surrounds the polygon. Comparison of that rectangle and the window quickly tells whether further computation is required (*cf.* boxing), as can be seen from Figure AVI-1. If this simple check fails, it is still possible that the window and polygon are disjoint, but more computation is required to make the decision.

If the line equations for the edges of the polygon determine that all four corners of the window lie on the interior side of all the edges, then the polygon surrounds the square (This requires that the line equations be formulated appropriately). This condition is sufficient but not necessary for concave polygons (see Figure AVI-2).

The method for determining surroundedness which Warnock uses is to draw a line from part of the window to a point known to be far

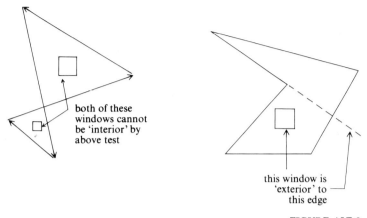

both of these
windows cannot
be 'interior' by
above test

this window is
'exterior' to
this edge

FIGURE AVI-2

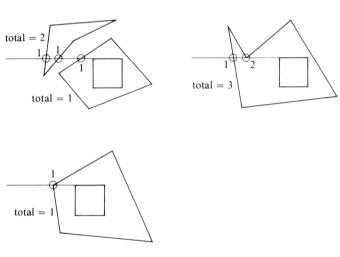

FIGURE AVI-3

outside the polygon. We then count the number of edges of the
polygon which intersect the line. If the number is odd, then the
polygon surrounds the window; if even, the polygon does not surround
the square (disjoint). The only difficulty with this computation occurs
when a vertex of the polygon lies directly on the line. In this case, the
vertices adjacent to the vertex on the line are considered. If these two
vertices are on different sides of the line emanating from the window,
then one intersection is recorded, otherwise two (see Figure AVI-3).

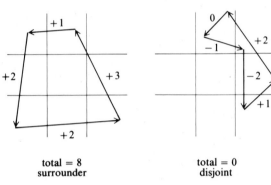

FIGURE AVI-4

FIGURE AVI-5

Another way to determine whether a polygon surrounds the window is to compute the angle about the window through which each edge passes, and to keep a running total of these incremental angles as each edge of the polygon is processed in order. If the resulting total angle is zero, then the polygon is outside the window (disjoint). If the total angle is ±360 degrees, the polygon surrounds the window. If the total angle is ±720 degrees, the polygon surrounds the window twice and must overlap itself. If the resulting angle is not a multiple of 360 degrees, the angle computation has gone astray. The technique can be simplified to consider only 8 regions around the window, as shown in Figure AVI-4. The incremental angle of the directed line segment in Figure AVI-4 is +2. The total cumulative angle determines whether the polygon surrounds the window or is disjoint (see Figure AVI-5).

The incremental angle ($\Delta\alpha$) is calculated as follows:

$$\Delta\alpha = \text{(region number of second endpoint)} -$$
$$\text{(region number of first endpoint)}$$

if $\Delta\alpha > 4$ then $\Delta\alpha \leftarrow \Delta\alpha - 8$;
if $\Delta\alpha < -4$ then $\Delta\alpha \leftarrow \Delta\alpha + 8$;

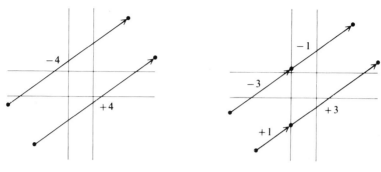

One tricky case arises when the incremental angle is ±4, as shown in Figure AVI-6. Although these two lines have endpoints in the same regions, they have different incremental angles. The computation of the correct angle can be made by intersecting the line with one of the window boundaries, and then calculating the incremental angle of each part of the two line fragments formed.

This simplified angle measurement can be performed as a side effect of applying a clipping procedure to the edges of the polygon. The clipping operation will yield, for each edge (1) whether it intersects the window at all, (2) if not, the value of the incremental angle traced by the edge. If this information is computed for all edges, the polygon can easily be determined to be (1) a surrounder, (2) a disjoint polygon or (3) an intersector of the window.

AVI.1.1   DEPTH CALCULATIONS

The Looker and Thinker occasionally need to compute the depth (Z_s value) of a polygon at given screen coordinates X_s, Y_s. This computation is performed in the screen coordinate system, and is equivalent to intersecting a ray from the eye through the screen at point X_s, Y_s with the plane of the polygon.

The computation is aided by storing, for each polygon, the equation of the plane of the polygon in screen coordinates:

$$a\, X_s + b\, Y_s + c\, Z_s + d = 0$$

The value of Z_s at any screen position (X_s, Y_s) can then be quickly computed.

AVI.2   THE THINKER

The range of Thinkers suitable for the Warnock algorithm is almost boundless. Two interesting Thinkers which handle penetrating planes are given below. They use the following symbolic notation: S is the number of surrounders of the window; I is the number of intersectors of a window, less those whose *planes* are behind the plane of some surrounder.

The Thinkers are:

1. Never Display by Computation. The Thinker must distinguish only two cases (just as in Figure 14-18):

   1. $I \neq 0$ or Penetrate $\neq 0 \Rightarrow$ Fail
   2. Penetrate $= 0$ and $I = 0 \Rightarrow$ Success; window empty

2. Display by Computation if only one intersector polygon lies in front of a (possibly non-existent) surrounder. The Thinker distinguishes three cases:

   1. $I > 1$ or Penetrate $\neq 0 \Rightarrow$ Fail
   2. Penetrate $= 0$ and $I = 0 \Rightarrow$ Success; window empty
   3. $I = 1 \Rightarrow$ Success; clip each edge of the intersector against the window and display.

   Case 3 yields success only if the intersector polygon does not penetrate the plane of a critical surrounder (hider); otherwise, the decision must be to fail.

EXERCISES

1. Suggest various mechanisms for retaining the ancestral information. Examine the methods in the light of the uses the algorithm makes of this data: storing when a polygon is examined, retrieving as each window is processed, and saving/restoring information as the recursive controller processes different windows. How does the efficiency of the ancestral data structure interfere with the ordering of the polygon list by Z_{min}?

2. If we restrict the class of surfaces so that no polygons can penetrate each other, what simplifications can be made in the algorithm, excluding those mentioned in Chapter 14?

3. One version of the Warnock algorithm restricts the class of polygons to triangles. If polygons of more than 3 sides are required, they are created from collections of triangles. The motivation for this procedure is that the algorithm will be much more efficient. Give an algorithm for decomposing a collection of polyhedra into a representation consisting only of triangles. Can the Warnock algorithm be made to operate more efficiently on triangles than on arbitrary polygonal faces? What are the drawbacks of this technique? How, if at all, does the subdivision of polygons into triangular regions affect the final line-drawing? What if we are generating a shaded picture?

4. Where does the Warnock algorithm spend its time?

```
BEGIN "WARNOCK ALGORITHM"

COMMENT
* * * * * * * * * * * * * * * * * * * * * * * * * * * * * * * * * * * * * * * * * * * * * * * * * * * * * * * * * *
*                                                                                                                 *
*                              D A T A   S T R U C T U R E                                                        *
*                                                                                                                 *
* * * * * * * * * * * * * * * * * * * * * * * * * * * * * * * * * * * * * * * * * * * * * * * * * * * * * * * * * *

THERE ARE THREE KINDS OF OBJECTS IN THE SYSTEM: POINTS, EDGES, AND POLYGONS.  DATA ABOUT THESE
OBJECTS ARE RETAINED IN ARRAYS.  FOR EXAMPLE, A 'POINT' HAS THREE COORDINATES, HENCE THREE ARRAYS
ARE DECLARED, INDEXED BY THE 'POINT NUMBER', ONE ARRAY FOR EACH OF THE THREE COORDINATES.

POINTS:   EACH POINT IS REPRESENTED BY ITS X,Y AND Z COORDINATE IN THE SCREEN COORDINATE SYSTEM.
          THESE VALUES ARE STORED IN THE ARRAYS XS, YS AND ZS.

EDGES:    EACH EDGE IS REPRESENTED BY THE 'POINT NUMBERS' OF THE TWO ENDPOINTS OF THE EDGE.  IN
          ADDITION A POINTER IS KEPT TO POINT TO THE 'NEXT' EDGE ON THE POLYGON.  THE THREE ARRAYS ARE
          THUS: ED!1, ED!2, AND ED!LINK.

POLYGONS: EACH POLYGON IS REPRESENTED BY A LIST OF EDGES.  THIS LIST IS THREADED THROUGH THE ED!LINK
          CELL OF EACH EDGE, AND A POINTER TO THIS LIST IS RETAINED FOR EACH POLYGON (POLY!EDGE).
          OTHER DATA ALSO PERTAIN TO POLYGONS: THE FOUR COEFFICIENTS OF THE PLANE EQUATION (POLY!A,
          POLY!B, POLY!C, POLY!D).  THE ZS VALUE OF THE VERTEX WHICH LIES CLOSEST TO THE EYE
          (POLY!ZMIN), AND TWO LISTS: POLY!LINK WHICH LINKS ALL POLYGONS ON A LINKED LIST, AND
          POLY!LIST, WHICH IS USED BY THE LOOKER AND THINKER TO REMEMBER STATUS OF POLYGONS EXAMINED.

THE ARRAY 'HISTORY' IS USED TO KEEP TRACK OF ANCESTRAL RELATIONS.  THE ARRAY IS INDEXED BY LEVEL
NUMBER (DEPTH OF RECURSION OF THE MAIN SUBROUTINE) AND BY THE POLYGON NUMBER IN QUESTION.  THE ENTRY
IN THE ARRAY IS EITHER:

              -1  ...  NO ANCESTRAL INFORMATION, MUST TEST THE POLYGON
               8  ...  THE POLYGON IS A SURROUNDER AT THIS LEVEL
               0  ...  THE POLYGON IS DISJOINT AT THIS LEVEL

EACH LINE OF THE PROGRAM CONCERNED WITH ANCESTRY IS PRECEDED WITH THE CHARACTERS ##.  IF THESE LINES
ARE REMOVED, THE PROGRAM WILL STILL GENERATE THE SAME FINAL PICTURE, BUT THE COMPUTATION TIME
REQUIRED WILL BE GREATER.  THIS PARTICULAR IMPLEMENTATION OF THE ANCESTRAL INFORMATION IS VERY
INEFFICIENT, AND IS CHOSEN FOR MAXIMUM CLARITY.  A BETTER IMPLEMENTATION IS GIVEN IN WARNOCK'S
PAPER.


DEFINE POLYMAX = "16", EDGEMAX = "63", POINTMAX = "31", ## = "", SAFER = "SAFE" ;

SAFER REAL ARRAY XS, YS, ZS [1:POINTMAX];
SAFER INTEGER ARRAY ED!1, ED!2, ED!LINK [1:EDGEMAX];
SAFER REAL ARRAY POLY!A, POLY!B, POLY!C, POLY!D, POLY!ZMIN [1:POLYMAX];
SAFER INTEGER ARRAY POLY!EDGE, POLY!LINK, POLY!LIST [1:POLYMAX];

## SAFER INTEGER ARRAY HISTORY [1:12, 1:POLYMAX];
## INTEGER LEVEL;
```

```
REAL WLX,WRX,WBY,WTY,ZMIN,ZMINMAX,Z1,Z2,Z3,Z4,NX,NY,NZ,PX,PY,PZ,
     XX1,XX2,YY1,YY2,ZMIN1,ZMIN2,ZMIN3,ZMIN4,ZMAX1,ZMAX2,ZMAX3,ZMAX4;

INTEGER P,SURROUNDERS,INTERSECTORS,POLYPTR,HIDER,PENETRATE,
        NEXTEDGE,DELTATHETA,THETA,HOLD,OLDP,J;


COMMENT
* * * * * * * * * * * * * * * * * * * * * * * * * * * * * * * * * * * * * * * * * * * * * * * * * * *

                M I S C E L L A N E O U S    P R O C E D U R E S

* * * * * * * * * * * * * * * * * * * * * * * * * * * * * * * * * * * * * * * * * * * * * * * * * * *
;

INTEGER PROCEDURE GET!NEXT!EDGE;         "PROCEDURE TO LOAD THE VALUES OF NX,NY,NZ AND PX,PY,PZ
BEGIN INTEGER I;                          WITH COORDINATES OF THE ENDPOINTS OF THE NEXT EDGE
                                          OF THE CURRENT POLYGON.
                                          RETURNS 0 IF NO MORE EDGES.
     IF NEXTEDGE = 0 THEN RETURN (0);     RETURNS -1 IF IT HAS FOUND ANOTHER EDGE."
                                          "NO MORE EDGES"

     I ← ED!1[NEXTEDGE];                  "GET INDEX TO POINT NUMBER"
     PX ← XS[I]; PY ← YS[I]; PZ ← ZS[I];  "FILL UP PX,PY,PZ"

     I ← ED!2[NEXTEDGE];                  "SAME FOR THE OTHER ENDPOINT"
     NX ← XS[I]; NY ← YS[I]; NZ ← ZS[I];

     NEXTEDGE ← ED!LINK [NEXTEDGE];       "PREPARE FOR NEXT CALL"
     RETURN (-1)

END;

REAL PROCEDURE GETZ (INTEGER P; REAL X,Y);   "RETURN THE DEPTH OF THE POLYGON P AT SCREEN
BEGIN;                                        COORDINATES X,Y"

     RETURN ((-POLY!A[P]*X-POLY!B[P]*Y-POLY!D[P])/POLY!C[P])

END;
```

```
COMMENT
* * * * * * * * * * * * * * * * * * * * * * * * * * * * * * * * * * * * * * * * * * * * * * *

          C L I P P I N G   R O U T I N E S

* * * * * * * * * * * * * * * * * * * * * * * * * * * * * * * * * * * * * * * * * * * * * * *

THIS IS A VARIATION ON THE CLIPPING PROCEDURE GIVEN IN SECTION 12.3.3.  THE  SUBROUTINE  'PUSH'  HAS
BEEN USED TO CONSERVE SPACE.  THE FUNCTION 'ANGLE' IS USED TO COMPUTE THE NUMBER OF THE QUADRANT
(0-7) IN WHICH AND ENDPOINT LIES.
;

INTEGER PROCEDURE WCODE (REAL X,Y);
RETURN ( (IF X < WLX THEN '1 ELSE 0)+
         (IF X > WRX THEN '10 ELSE 0)+
         (IF Y < WBY THEN '100 ELSE 0)+
         (IF Y > WTY THEN '1000 ELSE 0));

INTEGER PROCEDURE CLIP;
BEGIN INTEGER C1,C2;

    PROCEDURE PUSH (INTEGER AL; REAL BT);     "PUSH POINT 1 TOWARD POINT 2 --
       BEGIN                                   IF AL = 0 PUSH AGAINST AN X BOUNDARY, ELSE Y
                                               BT =  THE BOUNDARY"

       IF AL = 0 THEN BEGIN
                 YY1 ← (YY2-YY1)*(BT-XX1)/(XX2-XX1)+YY1;
                 XX1 ← BT
       END ELSE BEGIN
                 XX1 ← (XX2-XX1)*(BT-YY1)/(YY2-YY1)+XX1;
                 YY1 ← BT
       END;  WCODE (XX1,YY1);         "RECOMPUTE CODE FOR THIS POINT"
       C1 ← "PUSH";
       END "PUSH";

    INTEGER PROCEDURE ANGLE (REAL X,Y);     "COMPUTE 'ANGLE' FOR X,Y"
    BEGIN
          IF X < WLX THEN BEGIN
                 IF Y > WTY THEN RETURN (3);
                 IF Y < WBY THEN RETURN (5);
                 RETURN (4)
          END;
          IF X > WRX THEN BEGIN
                 IF Y > WTY THEN RETURN (1);
                 IF Y < WBY THEN RETURN (7);
                 RETURN (0)
          END;
          IF Y > WTY THEN RETURN (2);
          IF Y < WBY THEN RETURN (6)

    END;
```

```
DELTATHETA ← 0;

C1 ← WCODE (XX1, YY1 ← NX, YY1 ← NY);
C2 ← WCODE (XX2, YY2 ← PX, YY2 ← PY);

WHILE NOT (C1 = C2 = 0) DO BEGIN "CLIP"
    IF C1 LAND C2 THEN BEGIN INTEGER A1,A2,A3;
                                        "THE LINE IS BEING REJECTED.  WE MUST COMPUTE
                                         THE 'ANGLE' SUBTENDED BY THE LINE.  THE
                                         WE DO THIS BY CONSIDERING XX1,YY1, THE
                                         COORDINATES OF SOME INTERMEDIATE POINT."
        A1 ← ANGLE(NX,NY); A2 ← ANGLE(XX1,YY1); A3 ← ANGLE(PX,PY);
        IF ABS(A1 ← A1-A2) > 3 THEN IF A1 < 0 THEN A1 ← A1+8 ELSE A1 ← A1-8;
        IF ABS(A2 ← A2-A3) > 3 THEN IF A2 < 0 THEN A2 ← A2+8 ELSE A2 ← A2-8;
        DELTATHETA ← A1+A2;
        RETURN (0);                     "RETURN 0 IF LINE DOES NOT INTERSECT WINDOW"

    END;

    IF C1 = 0 THEN BEGIN C1 SWAP C2;
                         XX1 SWAP XX2;
                         YY1 SWAP YY2
                   END;

        IF C1 LAND '1 THEN PUSH (0,WLX) ELSE
        IF C1 LAND '10 THEN PUSH (0,WRX) ELSE
        IF C1 LAND '100 THEN PUSH (1,WBY) ELSE
        IF C1 LAND '1000 THEN PUSH (1,WTY) ELSE

    END "CLIP";
    RETURN (-1);                        "RETURN -1 IF THE LINE INTERSECTS THE WINDOW"
END "CLIP";


COMMENT
* * * * * * * * * * * * * * * * * * * * * * * * * * * * * * * * * * * * * * * * * * * * * * * * * *
* * * * * * * * * * * * * * * * * * * * * * * * * * * * * * * * * * * * * * * * * * * * * * * * * *

                            D I S P L A Y   P R O C E D U R E S

* * * * * * * * * * * * * * * * * * * * * * * * * * * * * * * * * * * * * * * * * * * * * * * * * *
* * * * * * * * * * * * * * * * * * * * * * * * * * * * * * * * * * * * * * * * * * * * * * * * * *
;

EXTERNAL  PROCEDURE  BEGIN!FRAME;
EXTERNAL  PROCEDURE  END!FRAME;
EXTERNAL  PROCEDURE  GEN!DOT (INTEGER X,Y);
EXTERNAL  PROCEDURE  GEN!LINE (INTEGER X,Y,X1,Y1);

REQUIRE "DIS" LOAD!MODULE;
```

```
PROCEDURE DISPLAY!START;
BEGIN      BEGIN!FRAME;                              "CALL THIS SUBROUTINE TO START A DISPLAY FRAME"

END;
PROCEDURE DISPLAY!END;
BEGIN      END!FRAME;                                "CALL THIS SUBROUTINE TO END A DISPLAY FRAME
                                                      AND TO PUT IN UP ON THE SCREEN"

END;

PROCEDURE SHOWDOT (INTEGER X,Y);
BEGIN      GEN!DOT (X,Y);                            "GENERATE AN INTENSIFIED DOT AT X,Y"

END;
PROCEDURE SHOWLINE (INTEGER X,Y,X1,Y1);
BEGIN      GEN!LINE (X,Y,X1,Y1);                     "GENERATE A LINE FROM X,Y TO X1,Y1"

END;


COMMENT
************************************************************************************************
               R E A D - I N   D A T A   S T R U C T U R E
************************************************************************************************

PROCEDURE TO FILL UP DATA STRUCTURE FROM A FILE WITH COORDINATE INFORMATION, ETC. IN IT THE DETAILS
OF THIS PROCEDURE ARE NOT IMPORTANT, AND ARE LISTED HERE JUST SO THAT WE CAN   BE    SURE    THE    PROGRAM
WORKS.
;

PROCEDURE READFILE;
BEGIN INTEGER POINTNUM,EDGENUM,POLYNUM,I,J,K,L; REAL R;
      DEFINE G(X) = "ARRYIN(1,R,1); X ← R;";

      INTEGER PROCEDURE FINDEDGE;              "GET EDGE INDEX"
      BEGIN INTEGER M; G(M);
            IF ED!LINK[M] = -1 THEN RETURN (M);
            EDGENUM ← EDGENUM+1;
            ED!1[EDGENUM] ← ED!1[M];
            ED!2[EDGENUM] ← ED!2[M];
            RETURN (EDGENUM)

      END;
```

```
OUTSTR ("FILE NAME:");
OPEN (1,"DSK",'13,2,0,200,L,L);
LOOKUP (1,INCHWL,L);

G (POINTNUM);                                   "READ NUMBER OF POINTS IN FILE"
G (EDGENUM);                                    "NUMBER OF EDGES"
G (POLYNUM);                                    "NUMBER OF POLYGONS"

IF POINTNUM > POINTMAX OR EDGENUM > EDGEMAX OR POLYNUM > POLYMAX THEN
    OUTSTR ("TOO MUCH DATA"&'15&'12)
ELSE BEGIN

FOR I ← 1 STEP 1 UNTIL POINTNUM DO BEGIN
    G(XS[I]); G(YS[I]); G(ZS[I])
END;

FOR I ← 1 STEP 1 UNTIL EDGENUM DO BEGIN
    G(ED!1[I]); G(ED!2[I]); ED!LINK[I] ← -1
END;

POLYPTR ← 0;                        "INITIALIZE POINTER TO ALL OF POLYGONS"
FOR I ← 1 STEP 1 UNTIL POLYNUM DO BEGIN
    POLY!LINK[I] ← POLYPTR; POLYPTR ← I; "LINK ON LIST OF POLYGONS"
    G (J);                          "READ AND DISCARD SHADING VALUE"
    G (J);                          "READ NUMBER OF EDGES IN THIS POLYGON"
    POLY!EDGE[I] ← K ← FINDEDGE;    "INDEX OF FIRST EDGE"
    WHILE J NEQ 1 DO BEGIN
        K ← ED!LINK[K] ← FINDEDGE;  "LINK EDGES TOGETHER"
        J ← J-1
    END;
    ED!LINK[K] ← 0;                 "TERMINATE LIST"
                                    "NOW RUN DOWN LIST OF EDGES,
                                     MAKING SURE THEY ARE IN CORRECT ORDER"
    K ← POLY!EDGE[I];               "HEAD OF LIST"
    J ← ED!2[K];                    "GET ONE OF THE POINTS"
    IF J NEQ ED!1[ED!LINK[K]] AND J NEQ ED!2[ED!LINK[K]] THEN ED!1[K] SWAP ED!2[K];
    WHILE K DO BEGIN
        J ← ED!LINK[K];             "NEXT EDGE"
        IF J AND ED!2[K] NEQ ED!1[J] THEN ED!1[J] SWAP ED!2[J];
        K ← J
    END

END

END
END
```

```
END;
```

```
COMMENT
**************************************************************************
**************************************************************************

               I N I T I A L I Z A T I O N   O F   P O L Y G O N S

**************************************************************************
* *

PROCEDURE INITPOLYGONS;
BEGIN REAL X1,X2,X3,Y1,Y2,Y3,Z1,Z2,Z3;
      INTEGER CHANGE,OLDP,J;

                                        "PROCEDURE TO INITIALIZE POLYGON INFORMATION:
                                        (1) COMPUTE PLANE COEFFICIENTS OF EACH POLYGON
                                        (2) COMPUTE ZMIN FOR EACH POLYGON
                                        (3) SORT POLYGON LIST BY ZMIN VALUES"

OLDP ← 0;
P ← POLYPTR;
WHILE P DO BEGIN "EACH POLYGON"
    NEXTEDGE ← POLY!EDGE[P];
    GET!NEXT!EDGE;                      "INITIALIZE GET!NEXT!EDGE ROUTINE"
    X1 ← PX; Y1 ← PY; Z1 ← PZ;          "SAVE COORDINATES OF ONE POINT"
    GET!NEXT!EDGE;                      "NOW GET TWO MORE POINTS"

                                        "WE NOW HAVE COORDINATES OF THREE POINTS:
                                              X1    Y1    Z1
                                              PX    PY    PZ
                                              NX    NY    NZ

                                        WE WILL USE THESE POINTS TO COMPUTE THE PLANE
                                        COEFFICIENTS.  THIS COMPUTATION ASSUMES THAT THE
                                        3 POINTS ARE NOT COLINEAR."

    X3 ← NX-X1; Y3 ← NY-Y1; Z3 ← NZ-Z1;
    X2 ← PX-X1; Y2 ← PY-Y1; Z2 ← PZ-Z1;

    POLY!A[P] ← Y3*Z2 - Y2*Z3;
    POLY!B[P] ← X2*Z3 - X3*Z2;
    POLY!C[P] ← X3*Y2 - X2*Y3;

    POLY!D[P] ← -(POLY!A[P]*X1+POLY!B[P]*Y1+POLY!C[P]*Z1);
```

```
                                        "NOW COMPUTE ZMIN FOR THIS POLYGON"
ZMIN ← 0;
NEXTEDGE ← POLY!EDGE[P];
WHILE GET!NEXT!EDGE DO IF ZMIN > PZ THEN ZMIN ← PZ;   "GREATER THAN LARGEST POSSIBLE SCREEN COORDINATE"
POLY!ZMIN[P] ← ZMIN;                                  "NOW SAVE RESULTS"

IF POLY!C[P] = 0 THEN BEGIN        "CANNOT POSSIBLY SEE THIS POLYGON"
                                   "THE Z COEFFICIENT IS ZERO, WHICH MEANS THE
                                    POLYGON IS EDGE-ON TO THE VIEWER.
                                    DELETE THIS POLYGON FROM THE LIST OF POLYGONS"
    IF OLDP = 0 THEN POLYPTR ← P ELSE POLY!LINK[OLDP] ← POLY!LINK[P]
END ELSE OLDP ← P;
P ← POLY!LINK[P];              "LOOK AT NEXT POLYGON"

END "EACH POLYGON";

DO BEGIN "SORT"                "A BUBBLE SORT"
    CHANGE ← FALSE;
    OLDP ← 0; P ← POLYPTR;

    WHILE P DO BEGIN
        J ← POLY!LINK[P];          "GET INDEX TO NEXT POLYGON IN LIST"
        IF J NEQ 0 AND POLY!ZMIN[P] > POLY!ZMIN[J] THEN BEGIN
                                   "INTERCHANGE P & J IN THE LIST"
            IF OLDP = 0 THEN POLYPTR ← J ELSE POLY!LINK[OLDP] ← J;
            POLY!LINK[P] ← POLY!LINK[J];
            POLY!LINK[J] ← P;
            CHANGE ← TRUE;
            OLDP ← J;              "PREVIOUS CELL"
        END ELSE BEGIN
            OLDP ← P;
            P ← POLY!LINK[P]
        END
    END
END "SORT" UNTIL NOT CHANGE;

LEVEL ← 1;                                "INITIALIZE LEVEL"
FOR P ← 1 STEP 1 UNTIL POLYMAX DO HISTORY[1,P] ← -1;  "INITIALIZE HISTORY TO LOOK AT EVERY POLYGON"

##
##
END;
```

M A I N   R E C U R S I V E   P R O C E D U R E

COMMENT
* *

THIS IS THE MAIN PROCEDURE. IT EMBODIES THE LOOKER, THE THINKER, AND MOST OF THE CONTROLLER.
ARGUMENTS TO THE PROCEDURE SPECIFY THE LOCATION AND SIZE OF THE WINDOW UNDER CONSIDERATION. IF THE
WINDOW MUST BE SUBDIVIDED, THIS PROCEDURE CALLS ITSELF RECURSIVELY.

```
RECURSIVE PROCEDURE WARNOCK (INTEGER LEFT,BOTTOM,SIZE);
                              "FIRST, INITIALIZE THE THE WINDOW LIMITS FOR THE
                               CLIP ROUTINE.  THE TOP AND RIGHT EDGES OF THE
                               WINDOW SHOULD BE JUST LESS THAN THE BOTTOM AND
                               LEFT EDGES OF THE WINDOWS ADJACENT TO THIS ONE."
BEGIN

      DEFINE EPSILON = ".00001";

      WLX ← LEFT; WRX ← WLX+SIZE-EPSILON;
      WBY ← BOTTOM; WTY ← WBY+SIZE-EPSILON;

##    FOR P ← 1 STEP 1 UNTIL POLYMAX DO HISTORY[LEVEL+1,P] ← HISTORY[LEVEL,P];
##                                     "PROMOTE HISTORY ONE LEVEL FARTHER DOWN"

                                        "INITIALIZE THINKER LISTS"
      SURROUNDERS ← INTERSECTORS ← 0;
      ZMINMAX ← 0;                      "LARGER THAN LARGEST ZS COORDINATE"

      P ← POLYPTR;                      "START LOOKING DOWN THE POLYGON LIST"
      WHILE P DO BEGIN "LOOKER"
           IF POLY!ZMIN[P] > ZMINMAX THEN DONE;   "DO NOT LOOK FARTHER"
           THETA ← HISTORY[LEVEL,P];              "GET THIS POLYGON'S STUFF"
##         IF THETA = -1 THEN BEGIN "MUST EXAMINE"
           THETA ← 0;              "INITIALIZE CUMULATIVE ANGLE AROUND WINDOW"
           NEXTEDGE ← POLY!EDGE[P];  "INITIALZE GET!NEXT!EDGE ROUTINE"

           WHILE GET!NEXT!EDGE DO BEGIN "LOOP FOR ALL EDGES"
                IF CLIP THEN BEGIN "EDGE PASSES THROUGH THIS WINDOW"
                     POLY!LIST[P] ← INTERSECTORS;
##                   INTERSECTORS ← P;     "PUT ON INTERSECTORS LISTS"
                     THETA ← -1;      "THE POLYGON INTERSECTS THE WINDOW"
                     DONE;            "NO USE CLIPPING OTHER EDGES"

                END ELSE THETA ← THETA+DELTATHETA;  "UPDATE ANGLE"
           END "LOOP FOR ALL EDGES"
           END "MUST EXAMINE";
           HISTORY[LEVEL+1,P] ← THETA;    "REMEMBER FOR NEXT LEVEL"
##         IF ABS(THETA) = 8 THEN BEGIN "FOUND SURROUNDER"
           POLY!LIST[P] ← SURROUNDERS;
           SURROUNDERS ← P;
```

```
        Z1 ← GETZ (P,WLX,WBY);     "GET DEPTHS AT CORNERS OF WINDOW"
        Z2 ← GETZ (P,WLX,WTY);
        Z3 ← GETZ (P,WRX,WBY);
        Z4 ← GETZ (P,WRX,WTY);

                                   "NOW COMPUTE THE MAXIMUM OF THESE"

        IF Z2 > Z1 THEN Z1 ← Z2;
        IF Z3 > Z1 THEN Z1 ← Z3;
        IF Z4 > Z1 THEN Z1 ← Z4;

        ZMINMAX ← Z1;              "AND STORE IN ZMINMAX"

    END "FOUND SURROUNDER";
    P ← POLY!LINK[P]
END "LOOKER";

BEGIN "THINKER"
```

```
"NOW WE CAN BE A SMART THINKER OR A NOT-SO-SMART THINKER;
BOTH THINKERS HANDLE PENETRATING PLANES CORRECTLY.
FIRST, WE FIND ONE CRITICAL SURROUNDER OF THE WINDOW.  IF
TWO SURROUNDERS PENETRATE, WE GO TO FAIL, SINCE ...
THEN, EACH INTERSECTOR IS COMPARED TO THE CRITICAL SURROUNDER :
   1. THE INTERSECTOR IS HIDDEN BY THE SURROUNDER --
        REMOVE INTERSECTOR FROM LIST
   2. THE INTERSECTOR IS COMPLETELY IN FRONT OF SURROUNDER --
        LEAVE IN LIST
   3. OTHERWISE, INTERSECTOR MUST PENETRATE SURROUNDER; FAIL

WHEN THIS PROCESS IS FINISHED, WE EXAMINE THE INTERSECTOR LIST:
SMARTER THINKER:
   IF # OF POLYGONS IN INTERSECTOR LIST = 0,   DO NOTHING
                                        = 1,   DISPLAY VISIBLE
                                                PORTION OF POLYGON
                                        > 1,   FAIL

NOT-SO-SMART THINKER:
   IF # OF POLYGONS IN INTERSECTOR LIST = 0,   DO NOTHING
                                        > 0,   FAIL

WE WILL SHOW THE SMART THINKER"
```

```
ZMIN1 ← ZMIN2 ← ZMIN3 ← ZMIN4 ← 0;        "INITIALIZE DEPTHS OF HIDER"
HIDER ← PENETRATE ← 0;

WHILE SURROUNDERS DO BEGIN                 "GET DEPTHS OF SURROUNDER AT CORNERS OF WINDOW"

    Z1 ← GETZ (SURROUNDERS,WLX,WBY);
    Z2 ← GETZ (SURROUNDERS,WLX,WTY);
    Z3 ← GETZ (SURROUNDERS,WRX,WBY);
    Z4 ← GETZ (SURROUNDERS,WRX,WTY);

                                          "NOW SEE IF THE DEPTHS OF THIS SURROUNDER ARE CLOSER
                                           TO THE EYE THAN ANY OTHER SURROUNDERS"

    IF Z1 < ZMIN1 AND Z2 < ZMIN2 AND Z3 < ZMIN3 AND Z4 < ZMIN4 THEN
        BEGIN "NEW HIDER WHICH IS CLOSER THAN PREVIOUS ONES"
            HIDER ← SURROUNDERS;
            ZMIN1 ← ZMAX1 ← Z1;
            ZMIN2 ← ZMAX2 ← Z2;
            ZMIN3 ← ZMAX3 ← Z3;
            ZMIN4 ← ZMAX4 ← Z4
        END ELSE
    IF Z1 > ZMAX1 AND Z2 > ZMAX2 AND Z3 > ZMAX3 AND Z4 > ZMAX4 THEN
        BEGIN "NEW POLYGON IS DEEPER THAN THE PRESENT HIDER -- DO NOTHING"
        END ELSE
        BEGIN "POLYGONS PENETRATE"
                                          "COMPUTE MINIMUM AND MAXIMUM DEPTHS OF
                                           THE PENETRATING PLANES"
            PENETRATE ← TRUE;
            IF Z1 < ZMIN1 THEN ZMIN1 ← Z1;
            IF Z2 < ZMIN2 THEN ZMIN2 ← Z2;
            IF Z3 < ZMIN3 THEN ZMIN3 ← Z3;
            IF Z4 < ZMIN4 THEN ZMIN4 ← Z4;

            IF Z1 > ZMAX1 THEN ZMAX1 ← Z1;
            IF Z2 > ZMAX2 THEN ZMAX2 ← Z2;
            IF Z3 > ZMAX3 THEN ZMAX3 ← Z3;
            IF Z4 > ZMAX4 THEN ZMAX4 ← Z4
        END;

    SURROUNDERS ← POLY!LIST[SURROUNDERS];   "LOOK AT NEXT ONE"

END;
```

```
IF NOT PENETRATE THEN BEGIN "NO SURROUNDERS PENETRATED"

                "NOW REMOVE FROM INTERSECTORS LIST ANY POLYGONS
                 HIDDEN BY THE HIDER POLYGON"

OLDP ← 0; P ← INTERSECTORS;

WHILE P AND HIDER DO BEGIN
    Z1 ← GETZ (P,WLX,WBY);
    Z2 ← GETZ (P,WLX,WTY);
    Z3 ← GETZ (P,WRX,WBY);
    Z4 ← GETZ (P,WRX,WTY);

    IF Z1 > ZMAX1 AND Z2 > ZMAX2 AND Z3 > ZMAX3 AND Z4 > ZMAX4 THEN
        BEGIN "COMPLETELY HIDDEN -- REMOVE FROM LIST"
            J ← POLY!LIST[P];   "NEXT ENTRY ON LIST"
            IF OLDP = 0 THEN INTERSECTORS ← J ELSE POLY!LIST[OLDP] ← J
    END ELSE BEGIN "ONLY NEEDED BECAUSE SMART THINKER"
        OLDP ← P;            "SAVE FOR NEXT TIME THROUGH"

        IF Z1 < ZMIN1 AND Z2 < ZMIN2 AND Z3 < ZMIN3 AND Z4 < ZMIN4 THEN

        BEGIN "INTERSECTOR COMPLETELY IN FRONT OF SURROUNDER -- DO NOTHING"
        END ELSE
        BEGIN "INTERSECTOR PENETRATES SURROUNDER(S)"
            PENETRATE ← TRUE;   "FLAG THAT PENETRATION OCCURRED"
            DONE;               "NO USE LOOKING AT MORE INTERSECTORS"

        END

    END;
    P ← POLY!LIST[P]

END;
```

```
IF NOT PENETRATE THEN BEGIN "NO INTERSECTORS PENETRATE SURROUNDER(S)"

                                "NOW LOOK AT INTERSECTORS REMAINING IN THE LIST AND
                                DECIDE WHAT TO DO:
                                1 IF NO INTERSECTORS OR ALL HAVE BEEN REMOVED
                                FROM THE INTERSECTOR LIST BECAUSE THEY ARE
                                HIDDEN BY SURROUNDERS, WE CAN RETURN -- THE
                                SCREEN IS BLANK IN THIS AREA"

        IF INTERSECTORS = 0 THEN RETURN;

                                "2. IF THERE IS JUST ONE POLYGON WHICH INTERSECTS
                                THE WINDOW, THEN WE MAY DISPLAY ANY
                                PORTIONS OF EDGES WHICH INTERSECT THE
                                WINDOW. NOTICE THAT THERE MAY ALSO
                                HAVE BEEN A SURROUNDER, BUT WHICH IS DEEPER
                                THAN THE INTERSECTOR."

        IF POLY!LIST[INTERSECTORS] = 0 THEN BEGIN "JUST 1 POLYGON"
            NEXTEDGE ← POLY!EDGE[INTERSECTORS];
            WHILE GET!NEXT!EDGE DO
                IF CLIP THEN SHOWLINE (XX1,YY1,XX2,YY2);

            RETURN;                           "SUCCESSFULLY PROCESSED WINDOW"

        END "NO INTERSECTORS PENETRATE SURROUNDER(S)"
        END "NO SURROUNDERS PENETRATED"
        END "THINKER";

                                "COME HERE IF PROCESSING OF THIS WINDOW
                                HAS 'FAILED' "

        IF SIZE < 2 THEN SHOWDOT (LEFT,BOTTOM) ELSE

            BEGIN                "SUBDIVIDE THE WINDOW, AND CALL RECURSIVELY"

            SIZE ← SIZE % 2;
            LEVEL ← LEVEL+1;
            WARNOCK (LEFT,BOTTOM,SIZE);
            WARNOCK (LEFT+SIZE,BOTTOM,SIZE);
            WARNOCK (LEFT,BOTTOM+SIZE,SIZE);
            WARNOCK (LEFT+SIZE,BOTTOM+SIZE,SIZE);
            LEVEL ← LEVEL-1;

            END
END "WARNOCK";

DISPLAY!START;                   "HERE BEGINS MAIN EXECUTION"
READFILE;                        "INITIALIZE THE DISPLAY"
INITPOLYGONS;                    "READ IN A DATA STRUCTURE"
                                 "INITIALIZE POLYGON INFORMATION"

WARNOCK (0,0,1024);              "CALL THE RECURSIVE PROCEDURE"

DISPLAY!END;                     "FINISHED GENERATING THE DISPLAY -- SHOW IT"

END
```

APPENDIX VII

THE WATKINS HIDDEN-SURFACE ALGORITHM

This appendix gives details of an implementation of the Watkins hidden-surface algorithm which is outlined briefly in Chapter 14. A detailed description is given, followed by a SAIL program for the algorithm.

Three separate parts of the algorithm will be described in turn: (1) the data structure for a scene, (2) the processing at the beginning of each scan-line, and (3) the hidden-surface computations within each scan-line.

AVII.1 DATA STRUCTURE

The scene description is in terms of planar polygons, described by their edges. Each edge is described by its endpoints (see Figure AVII-1). The coordinates of the vertices are recorded in screen coordinates, and all are assumed to lie within the bounds of the screen. Each edge contains pointers to the two polygons which the edge separates. In some cases, the edge is part of only one polygon, as shown in Figure AVII-2.

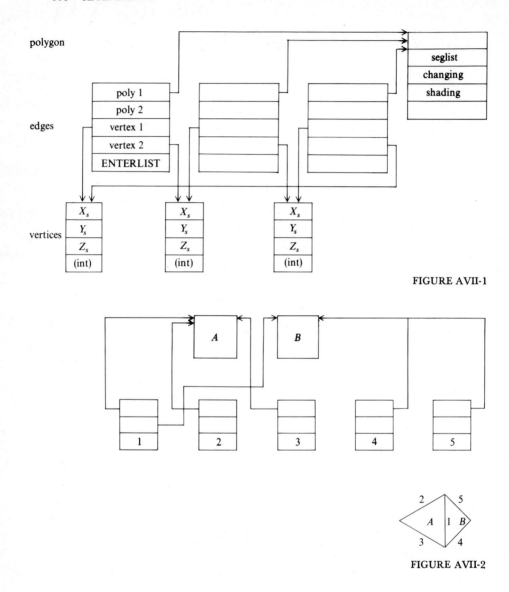

FIGURE AVII-1

FIGURE AVII-2

Visible segments of the polygon are shaded in one of two ways: one intensity level may be stored in the *SHADING* entry of the polygon block and used for the entire polygon, or the Gouraud shading algorithm may be used, in which case an intensity is stored with each endpoint description.

The *ENTERLIST* field of an edge description is used to create a list of edges which enter (begin) on each scan-line (see Figure AVII-3).

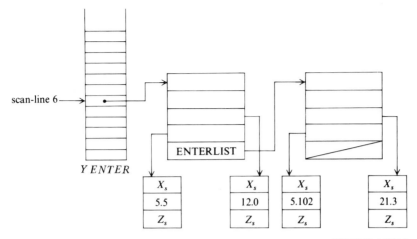

scan-line 6 →

Y ENTER

ENTERLIST

X_s		X_s	X_s		X_s
5.5		12.0	5.102		21.3
Z_s		Z_s	Z_s		Z_s

FIGURE AVII-3

Notice that the value of Y_s is stored to high precision. In the figure, the scan line at $Y_s = 6$ is clearly the first scan on which an edge that begins at $Y_s = 5.102$ will be encountered.

As the algorithm starts to process a scan-line, the *YENTER* entry for that scan-line is used to find edges which must be added to the current list of segments. If an edge separates two polygons, then segments for each of the polygons may be generated when the edge enters.

Segments are described by relevant information for both edges of the segment, as shown in Figure AVII-4. At any given scan-line, the values of Xleft, Zleft, Xright, and Zright determine the position of the segment. The values of DXleft, DZleft, DXright, and DZright are increments which are added to Xleft, Zleft, Xright and Zright before processing the next scan-line. Thus Xleft, Zleft, etc. are simple linear functions of Y_s. The values for $Shad$left, $Shad$right, $DShad$left, and $DShad$right are optional; they are needed to implement the Gouraud continuous shading algorithm.

The Yleft and Yright fields are negative counts of the number of scan-lines which must be processed before the edge terminates, or exits from the picture (see Figure AVII-5).

Segments are linked together in the *XSORT* list, sorted in order of increasing value of Xleft.

The *POLYGON* field of the segment block points to the polygon of which this segment is part; the *POLYSEGMENT* field is a linked list of all segments for a particular polygon, sorted by increasing value of

FIGURE AVII-4

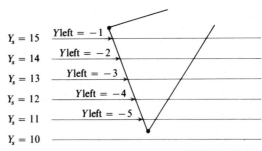

FIGURE AVII-5

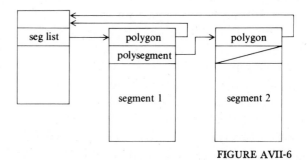

FIGURE AVII-6

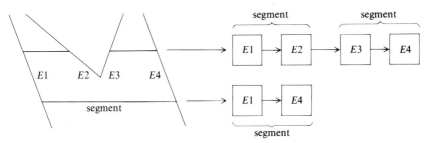

FIGURE AVII-7

Xleft (see Figure AVII-6). Segment descriptions are not part of the original scene description; they are created from the edge descriptions recorded in YENTER as each scan-line begins.

AVII.2   PROCESSING AT THE BEGINNING OF EACH SCAN-LINE

1. Update the values of Xleft, Zleft, Xright and Zright for each segment currently in the *XSORT* list. The *XSORT* list links all segments which were considered on the previous scan-line. Also add 1 to Yleft and Yright. If any part of a segment does not appear on this scan-line (i.e. Yleft = 0 or Yright = 0 after incrementing), then mark the polygon of which it is a part as *CHANGING*. In fact, the *CHANGING* field of the polygon descriptor is used to link a list through all changing polygons. These polygons have edges entering or exiting on this scan-line.

2. Process all entering edges listed in *YENTER* for this scan-line. The processing involves (1) creating new segment blocks if necessary and (2) inserting the new edge correctly in the list of segments for each polygon (*POLYSEGMENT*) affected by the new edge.

   One way to visualize the segment list for a polygon is as a list of *edges*, sorted by their X_s locations. The segment block happens to contain *pairs* of these edges, as shown in Figure AVII-7. The mechanism of inserting new edges (and deleting old ones — ones with Yleft = 0 or Yright = 0) is very easy to implement if edges are recorded individually, and not paired together as segments. However, the segment representation is extremely convenient for later processing, and so it is retained.

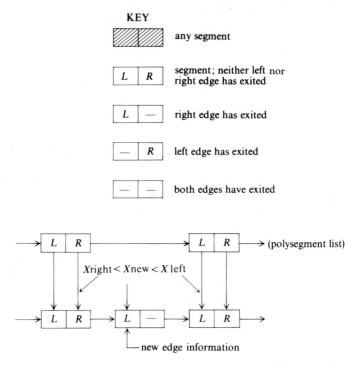

FIGURE AVII-8

We shall describe a scheme for inserting new edges which is inefficient of memory but which is easily explained. It amounts to interpreting the segment list for a polygon as the edge list described above. If a new edge falls between (in the X_s coordinate) the left and right edges of an existing segment, that segment is split. Later on, we will compact this list. The operations are:

(a) Insert the edge between existing segments in the *POLYSEGMENT* list, as shown in Figure AVII-8.
(b) Split a segment, as shown in Figure AVII-9.

There is one subtlety to the '<' comparison used in the tests of the X_s location of an edge: if two edges have precisely identical X_s values, then the DX values for the edges (DXleft or DXright) are compared instead. In this fashion, two edges which enter at precisely the same point (as many do) will create correct segment descriptions. For example, edges $E2$ and $E3$ both commence on the scan-line shown in Figure AVII-10.

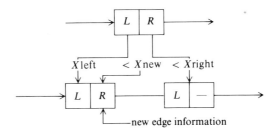

FIGURE AVII-9

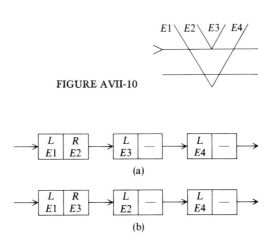

FIGURE AVII-10

FIGURE AVII-11

Figure AVII-11a shows segments correctly created, and Figure AVII-11b shows segments incorrectly ordered (because $X_{E2} = X_{E3}$).

Any polygon which has an entering edge is put in the *CHANGING* list.

3. Process changing polygons. If an edge of a polygon enters or exits on this scan-line, the polygon has been marked as changing by either step 1 or 2. The segment list for such a polygon may need to be fixed up because holes are left in the segment list by incomplete segments of the form:

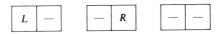

Figure AVII-12 shows the transformations made on the list.

(a) Delete completely exited segment:

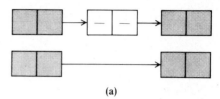

(a)

(b) Fill in a blank right edge:

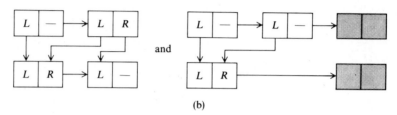

(b)

(c) Fill in a blank left edge:

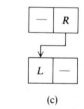

(c)

FIGURE AVII-12

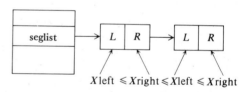

FIGURE AVII-13

The transformations are applied to the list of segments attached to a polygon from left to right, and have the effect of deleting all partial segments. When finished, we should have an integral number of whole segments; the edges should be in strictly left-to-right order (X_s coordinate) as shown in Figure AVII-13.

4. Sort all segments by Xleft, creating a new *XSORT* list. This list will include segments retained from the previous scan-line and those which are new on this scan-line.

The four steps 1 to 4 can, to some extent, be distributed throughout the algorithm. For instance, if no edges enter or exit on a scan-line, only steps 1 and 4 are required. These both involve scanning the *XSORT* list of all segments; the steps can be combined to save the overhead of looking at each segment block.

AVII.3   PROCESSING A SCAN-LINE

A scan-line is divided into *spans*, and the hidden-surface problem is solved for each span. There are two fundamental parts of the processing: the Looker and the Thinker. These are very similar in function to the Looker and Thinker of the Warnock algorithm. The Looker is presented with each segment which lies wholly or partly within the span being processed; it remembers enough information for the Thinker to decide which of the four cases outlined in Section 14.4.1 pertains for this span. The Thinker is activated after all candidate segments have been processed by the Looker; it decides whether a simple case (1 to 3 of Section 14.4.1) pertains, and if so generates display information for this span. If however, the Looker and Thinker detect a complicated case, the Thinker *fails*, causing the span to be subdivided.

Just as in the Warnock algorithm, an overall Controller is responsible for calling the Looker and Thinker, subdividing the span, etc. The bookkeeping for segments is fairly complicated, and is also handled by the Controller (Figure AVII-14). The *XSORT* list is the main source of segments to pass to the Looker. However, we must be careful to remember each segment we process in the span in one of two lists:

SEGOUT: The right edge of the segment is in this span, i.e. no span to the right of this one will need to know about this segment.
SEGACT: The right edge of this segment extends to the right of the right limit of this span. Thus, this segment should also be considered when processing subsequent spans on this scan-line.

If the processing of the span succeeds, subdivision is not necesary, the segments listed in *SEGOUT* need not be considered again on this scan-line, and the segments in *SEGACT* are retained for processing in

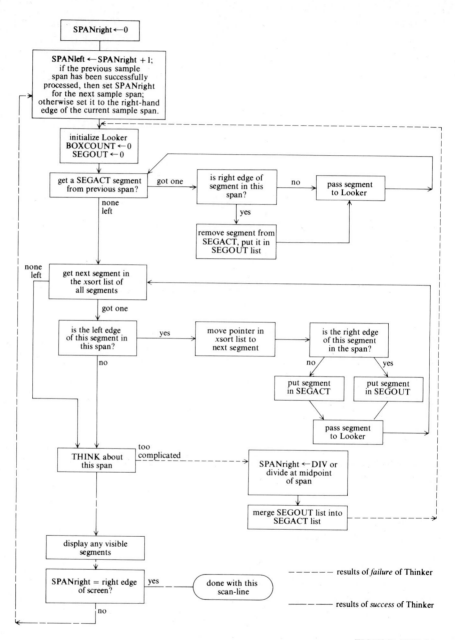

FIGURE AVII-14

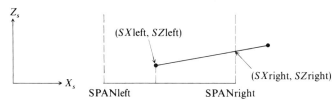

FIGURE AVII-15

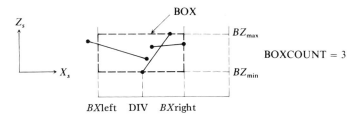

FIGURE AVII-16

the next span. If the span is subdivided, however, *all* segments considered in the original span must also be looked at in the subspans — the *SEGOUT* list is merged into the *SEGACT* list in this case.

AVII.4   THE LOOKER

The Looker accumulates information about relationships among segments in a span. It first computes coordinate values for the left-most and right-most parts of the segment inside the sample span (see Figure AVII-15). If *SPAN*left = *SX*left and *SPAN*right = *SX*right, then the segment is a *spanner*. If not, the leftmost endpoint inside the span is computed and stored in *DIV* (this is a possible point for subdivision of the sample span).

The segment is then compared with others that have already been passed to the Looker for this span. We keep track of a *box* which surrounds, in X_s and Z_s, all segments which have been Looked at (see Figure AVII-16). A count of the number of segments in the box is kept in *BOXCOUNT*. The variable *BOXTYPE* is also associated with the box.

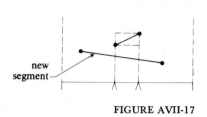

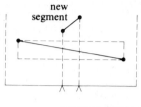

FIGURE AVII-17   FIGURE AVII-18

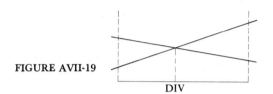

FIGURE AVII-19

DIV

The processing of the new segment depends on the old value of
BOXCOUNT (initialized to zero at the beginning of each span).

1. *BOXCOUNT* = 0. Nothing was in the box. Remember the computed
    values *SX*left, *SZ*left, *SX*right and *SZ*right as the extremities of the
    box. Set *BOXCOUNT* to 1.

2. *BOXCOUNT* = 1. Several cases are detected (in order):

    (a) The new segment hides the segment in the box, as shown in
    Figure AVII-17. This condition can be readily detected by (1)
    establishing that the left and right ends of the new segment extend
    beyond those of the segment in the box and (2) comparing Z_s values
    of the segments at the points indicated by $\wedge$. In this case, discard the
    segment currently in the box and remember (as in case 1) the values
    of the new segment as the extremities of the box.

    (b) The segment in the box hides the new segment (see Figure
    AVII-18). This condition is detected as in 2(a). In this case, no
    further processing is done; the new segment is ignored.

    (c) Both segments are *spanners* (see Figure AVII-19). Because
    neither 2(a) nor 2(b) pertains, the segments must intersect inside the
    span. The point of intersection is computed and stored in *DIV*.
    BOXTYPE is set to 1 to indicate that such an intersection has been

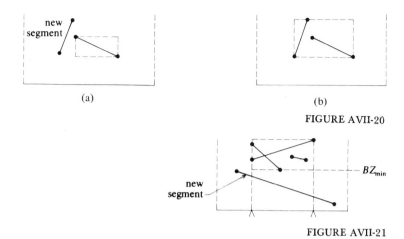

FIGURE AVII-20

FIGURE AVII-21

computed. In addition, pointers to the two segments are retained to aid display generation. $BOXCOUNT$ is set to 2, and the extremities of the box are enlarged if necessary to surround both segments.

(d) A complicated case is shown in Figure AVII-20a. $BOXTYPE$ is set to 0, $BOXCOUNT$ to $BOXCOUNT + 1$, and the extremities of the box are enlarged to surround both segments, as shown in Figure AVII-20b.

3. $BOXCOUNT > 1$. Two cases are detected (in order):

(a) The new segment hides the entire box, as shown in Figure AVII-21. This condition is detected by (1) establishing that the left and right ends of the new segment extend to or beyond the limits of the box, and (2) comparing the Z_s depth of the segment to BZ_{min} at the points indicated by $\wedge$. In this case, discard the current box and remember (as in 1) the values of the new segment as the extremities of the box. Set $BOXCOUNT$ to 1.

(b) A complicated case is shown in Figure AVII-22. We proceed as in 2(d).

There is one subtlety to the computation of the aspect of segments to spans. Figure AVII-14 shows that the operation of moving to the next span to the right involves:

$$SPAN\text{left} \leftarrow SPAN\text{right} + 1$$

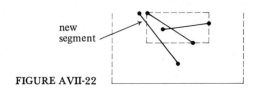

FIGURE AVII-22

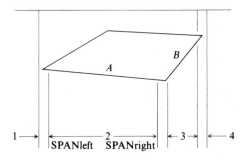

FIGURE AVII-23

This is crucial to the smooth operation of the algorithm, and avoids troublesome determinations of where a vertex (junction of two segments) lies. Figure AVII-23 shows a view in the X_s-Z_s plane of the segments created by a perspective view of a cube.

The conditions that a segment lie in a span are:

$$X\text{left} \leqslant SPAN\text{right}$$

and

$$X\text{right} \geqslant SPAN\text{left}$$

This convention means that segment A lies in span 2; segment B does not. However, segment B lies in span 3, but segment A does not.

AVII.5   THE THINKER

The Thinker uses the results of the Looker to generate intensity information if a simple case is detected, or to announce failure if the Looker terminated with a complicated case.

1. Nothing is visible in the span ($BOXCOUNT = 0$). Nothing need be displayed.

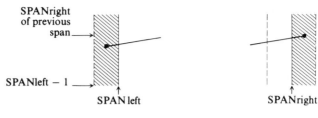

SPANright
of previous
span

SPANleft − 1

SPAN left

SPANright

2. Only one segment is visible in the span ($BOXCOUNT = 1$). The region of the span from the left edge of the box to the right edge of the box is shaded according to the shading information recorded with the polygon, of which the segment in the box is part.
3. Simple intersection ($BOXTYPE = 1$). The calculated point of intersection divides the span in two parts, each of which is shaded appropriately for the segment that is visible.
4. Complicated case ($BOXCOUNT > 1$ and $BOXTYPE = 0$). The Thinker announces failure in this case. If an endpoint was detected in the box (DIV), the Controller divides the span at that point (i.e. $SPANright \leftarrow \lfloor DIV \rfloor$. Otherwise, $SPANright \leftarrow \lfloor (SPANright + SPANleft)/2 \rfloor$ (The operation $\lfloor \ \rfloor$ stands for 'truncated integer part of').

AVII.6   SAMPLE POINTS

The details given above are sufficient to build a hidden-surface elimination program. It can be speeded up considerably by taking advantage of scan-line coherence. We record a list of $SPANright$ values or *sample points* which will divide the scan-line into spans, each of which will require no further subdivisions in order to process.

Successful subdivisions on one scan-line are remembered as sample points. More specifically, we remember the *edges* of segments which provoked the successful subdivision (subdivisions usually occur at segment edges). Such edges always lie just beyond the span, as shown in Figure AVII-24. The conditions for such an edge are:

$$\lfloor X \rfloor = SPANleft^{-1} \quad or \quad \lfloor X \rfloor = SPANright$$

When such a candidate sample point is detected, the X_s value *on the next scan-line* is computed using the incremental DX value. This is then

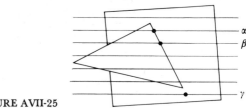

FIGURE AVII-25

recorded as a sample point, provided that the subdivision turns out to yield a simple case for the Thinker. The Thinker and the Looker thus cooperate in determining sample points.

An *implied edge* is usually a sample point as well. Implied edges are edges formed by the intersection of two planar polygons. The Looker handles these cases specially. Unfortunately, we cannot directly determine where the implied edge will appear on the *next* scan-line. However, after the edge positions have been computed for two consecutive scan-lines, we can extrapolate for all others (see Figure AVII-25). The intersections for α, β determine the direction of the implied edge. A dummy segment block is created, put in the *XSORT* list, and used to keep track of where the implied edge lies. It is never passed to the Looker.

How does the implied edge terminate? On line γ, the point shown is a sample point because it lies on the extrapolated implied edge. However, the Thinker discards this point as a sample point because the same segment is visible to the left of the point and to the right of the point; hence it is not a required sample point. The implied edge segment block is now discarded.

EXERCISES

1. Why must *SEGACT* segments be passed to the Looker before segments coming from the *XSORT* list? (Hint: consider the case shown in Figure AVII-26. What effect does the order of passing the segments 1, 2, 3 to the Looker have on the outcome?)

2. Streamline the process of inserting new segments and deleting old ones at the beginning of a scan-line.

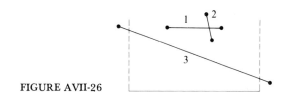

FIGURE AVII-26

3. Suggest modifications to the display output section which would permit continuous shading to be performed on surface patches (Section 14.5.2).

4. Where does the Watkins algorithm spend its time?

5. For many scenes, the algorithm can be speeded up by almost a factor of 2 if all surfaces obscured by other surfaces *on the same body* are not processed, i.e. if we have a *convex* polyhedron, we can use Roberts' observation that a surface with a normal which points away from the eye cannot possibly be visible. How should the algorithm be changed to incorporate this idea? How is the decision about normals made? Does it depend on a data structure which associates polygons together into polyhedra (which the Watkins algorithm described above does not)? Can this decision be left to a preprocessor, which then only passes to the Watkins algorithm information about those polygons which are potentially visible?

6. Suggest a method for using the Watkins algorithm to make wire-frame line-drawings (e.g. Figure 12-3).

```
BEGIN "WATKINS ALGORITHM"

COMMENT
* * * * * * * * * * * * * * * * * * * * * * * * * * * * * * * * * * * * * * * * * * *

                    D A T A   S T R U C T U R E S   &   S T O R A G E

* * * * * * * * * * * * * * * * * * * * * * * * * * * * * * * * * * * * * * * * * * *

THE NAMES FOR DATA STRUCTURE ELEMENTS ARE ALL AS DESCRIBED IN THE BODY OF THE APPENDIX.

THE SYMBOL ## IS USED TO FLAG ALL LINES WHICH CONCERN SAMPLE-POINT COLLECTION AND USE.    IF THESE
LINES ARE REMOVED (AND ONE LINE MUST BE INSERTED -- SEE COMMENTS IN TEXT), THE PROGRAM WILL STILL
FUNCTION CORRECTLY, BUT WILL REQUIRE SOMEWHAT MORE PROCESSING TIME (E.G. 20% FOR THE DRAWING OF
FIGURE 14-8).

THIS PARTICULAR PROGRAM DOES NOT INCLUDE THE EXTENSIONS NECESSARY TO USE THE GOURAUD LINEAR
INTERPOLATION TECHNIQUES.    THEY CAN BE ADDED IN A STRAIGHTFORWARD FASHION.    THE PROGRAM IS CLUTTERED
ENOUGH WITHOUT THE SLIGHT ADDITIONAL COMPLEXITY.
;
COMMENT DEFINE THE SIZE OF THE SCREEN;
        DEFINE XRESOLUTION = "512",YRESOLUTION = "512";

COMMENT DEFINE THE MAXIMUM NUMBER OF SEGMENTS, VERTICES, EDGES, AND POLYGONS;
        DEFINE MAXSEG = "60",MAXPOINT = "40",MAXEDGE = "50",MAXPOLY = "50";

COMMENT DEFINE MACROS FOR FLAGGING SAMPLE-POINT LOGIC, ETC.;
        DEFINE ## = "",SAFER = "SAFER";

COMMENT POLYGON DATA BLOCKS;
        SAFER INTEGER ARRAY CHANGING,SEGMENTLIST,SHAD[1:MAXPOLY];

COMMENT EDGE DATA BLOCKS;
        SAFER INTEGER ARRAY P1,P2,V1,V2,ENTERLIST[1:MAXEDGE];

COMMENT VERTEX DATA BLOCKS;
        SAFER REAL ARRAY XS,YS,ZS[1:MAXPOINT];

COMMENT SEGMENT DATA BLOCKS;
        SAFER INTEGER ARRAY POLYGON,POLYSEGMENT,XSORTLEFT,XSORTRIGHT,ACTIVE[1:MAXSEG];
        SAFER INTEGER ARRAY YLEFT,YRIGHT[1:MAXSEG];
        SAFER REAL ARRAY XLEFT,DXLEFT,ZLEFT,DZLEFT,
                         XRIGHT,DXRIGHT,ZRIGHT,DZRIGHT[1:MAXSEG];

COMMENT MISCELLANEOUS VARIABLES;
        INTEGER SEG,SEG1,PTR,PREVIOUS,NEXT,IMPLST,IMPLST2,POLYCHANGELIST,
                FREELIST,EDGELIST,I,J,K,SEGFST,Y1,Y2,VV1,VV2,
                DELY,P,SEGCNT,LASTSEGMENT,SEGSAM,Y,YFIRST,YLAST,TE1,TE2,CHANGE,
                SEGACT,IX,SEGLO,SEGOUT,CURSEG;

        REAL REALDELY,XFIRST,XSLOPE,ZFIRST,ZSLOPE,SHADFIRST,SHADSLOPE,SPANLEFT,SPANRIGHT;

        SAFER INTEGER ARRAY VISPOS,VISSEG[1:MAXSEG];

        SAFER INTEGER ARRAY YENTER [1:YRESOLUTION];
```

```
COMMENT
* * * * * * * * * * * * * * * * * * * * * * * * * * * * * * * * * * * * * * * * * * * * * * * * * * * * * * * * * * * * * * * * *

                    D I S P L A Y   O U T P U T

* * * * * * * * * * * * * * * * * * * * * * * * * * * * * * * * * * * * * * * * * * * * * * * * * * * * * * * * * * * * * * * * *
;

EXTERNAL PROCEDURE BEGIN!FRAME;
EXTERNAL PROCEDURE END!FRAME;
EXTERNAL PROCEDURE GEN!RASTER (INTEGER Y,XBEG,XEND,INTBEG,INTEND);

REQUIRE "DIS" LOAD!MODULE;

PROCEDURE SHOWINIT;
BEGIN    BEGIN!FRAME;

END;                          "CALL THIS SUBROUTINE TO START A DISPLAY FRAME"

PROCEDURE SHOWCLOSE;
BEGIN    END!FRAME;           "CALL THIS PROCEDURE TO END THE FRAME AND PUT
                               IT UP ON THE SCREEN"

END;

PROCEDURE SHOW;
BEGIN INTEGER I,X,SEG,POLYG,SAMP;
      SAMP ← 0;
      IF SEGCNT > 1 THEN BEGIN

      FOR I ← 1 STEP 1 UNTIL SEGCNT DO BEGIN
          SEG ← VISSEG[I];
          X ← VISPOS[I];

          IF SEG THEN BEGIN POLYG ← POLYGON[SEG];
          GEN!RASTER (Y,SAMP,X,SHAD[POLYG],SHAD[POLYG]);   "THIS PUTS OUT A PART OF SCAN-LINE Y,
                                                            BETWEEN SAMP AND X (HORIZONTAL MEASURE).   THE
                                                            SHADING IS LINEARLY INTERPOLATED BETWEEN
                                                            THE TWO INTENSITIES GIVEN FOR THE BEGINNING
                                                            AND ENDING INTENSITIES."

          END;

              SAMP ← X

          END
          END

END;
```

```
COMMENT
*************************************************************************
*                                                                       *
*            M I S C E L L A N E O U S    P R O C E D U R E S           *
*                                                                       *
*************************************************************************
;

INTEGER PROCEDURE GETBLOCK;              "GET A BLOCK FROM FREE STORAGE AND
BEGIN INTEGER I;                          INITIALIZE YLEFT AND YRIGHT ENTRIES TO 0"

    IF (I ← FREELIST) = 0 THEN OUTSTR("NO MORE FREE STORAGE");
    YLEFT[I] ← YRIGHT[I] ← 0;
    FREELIST ← ACTIVE[I];
    RETURN(I);

END;

PROCEDURE RETBLOCK (INTEGER I);          "RETURN A SEGMENT BLOCK TO FREE STORAGE"
BEGIN;   ACTIVE[I] ← FREELIST;
         FREELIST ← I

END;

PROCEDURE PUTINXSORT (INTEGER SEG);      "PUT THE SEGMENT AT THE HEAD OF THE XSORT LIST"
BEGIN;   IF SEGFST THEN XSORTLEFT[SEGFST] ← SEG;
         XSORTLEFT[SEG] ← 0;
         XSORTRIGHT[SEG] ← SEGFST;
         SEGFST ← SEG

END;

PROCEDURE REMOVEFROMXSORT (INTEGER SEG);    "REMOVE A SEGMENT FROM THE XSORT LIST"
BEGIN INTEGER I;
      IF SEGFST = SEG THEN SEGFST ← XSORTRIGHT[SEG];

      IF (I ← XSORTRIGHT[SEG]) THEN XSORTLEFT[I] ← XSORTLEFT[SEG];
      IF (I ← XSORTLEFT[SEG]) THEN XSORTRIGHT[I] ← XSORTRIGHT[SEG]

END;
```

```
COMMENT
* * * * * * * * * * * * * * * * * * * * * * * * * * * * * * * * * * * * * * * * * * * * * * * * * *

THE          LOOKER

* * * * * * * * * * * * * * * * * * * * * * * * * * * * * * * * * * * * * * * * * * * * * * * * * *
THE LOOKER IS A SUBROUTINE WHICH EXAMINES THE SEGMENT INDEXED BY 'SEG', AND ADDS IT TO THE PRESENT
BOX, ETC.  THE FLOW-CHART FOR THE LOOKER IS CONTAINED IN THE BODY OF THE APPENDIX.

VARIABLES USED BY THE LOOKER:

       BXLEFT,BXRIGHT      --- LEFT AND RIGHT EDGES OF BOX.
       BZMIN,BZMAX         --- NEAR AND FAR EDGES OF THE BOX.
       BZLEFT,BZRIGHT      --- WHEN ONLY ONE SEGMENT IS IN THE BOX, THESE CONTAIN THE ZS
                               COORDINATES OF THE LEFT AND RIGHT ENDS OF THAT SEGMENT.
       BOXCOUNT            --- COUNT OF NUMBER OF SEGMENTS IN THE BOX
       BOXTYPE             --- 1 IF WE HAVE COMPUTED THE INTERSECTION OF TWO PENETRATING SEGMENTS
                               (IMPLIED EDGE) ELSE 0
       DIV                 --- THE PLACE TO SUBDIVIDE THE SPAN IF NEEDED.
       BFULL               --- TRUE IF THE ONE SEGMENT IN THE BOX IS A SPANNER.
       BSEG1               --- THE INDEX OF THE FIRST SEGMENT IN THE BOX.
       BSEG2               --- THE INDEX OF THE SECOND SEGMENT IN THE BOX (THIS IS KEPT BECAUSE OF IMPLIED EDGES)

       SXLEFT,SXRIGHT      --- XS COORDINATES OF LEFT AND RIGHT ENDS OF THE SEGMENT BEING EXAMINED.
       SZLEFT,SZRIGHT      --- SAME FOR ZS COORDINATES.

       SFULL               --- TRUE IF SEGMENT BEING LOOKED AT IS A SPANNER.


REAL BXLEFT,BXRIGHT,BZLEFT,BZRIGHT,BZMIN,BZMAX,SXLEFT,SXRIGHT,SZLEFT,SZRIGHT,DIV,SDIV;

INTEGER BOXCOUNT,BOXTYPE,BFULL,SFULL,BSEG1,BSEG2;

COMMENT
SEVERAL SUBROUTINES ARE CREATED FOR USE BY THE LOOKER:

LOADBOX  --- TAKES THE PRESENT SEGMENT, AND 'LOADS' IT INTO THE BOX.  THE EXTREMITIES OF THE
             SEGMENT ARE REMEMBERED AS THE EXTREMITIES OF THE BOX.

XPANDBOX --- THE PRESENT SEGMENT IS 'ADDED' TO THE BOX.  IF NECESSARY, THE EXTREMITIES OF THE
             BOX ARE EXPANDED TO ENCLOSE THE NEW SEGMENT.

BZINT    --- IF ONLY ONE SEGMENT IS IN THE BOX, WE MAY HAVE A DESIRE TO COMPUTE THE 'DEPTH' OF THAT SEGMENT
             AT SEVERAL POINTS. THE BZINT FUNCTION DOES THIS, GIVEN AN XS COORDINATE AS ARGUMENT.

ZINT     --- THIS FUNCTION COMPUTES THE DEPTH OF THE SEGMENT BEING LOOKED AT, GIVEN AN XS COORDINATE AS ARGUMENT.
```

```
PROCEDURE LOADBOX;
BEGIN ;  BOXCOUNT ← 1;                              "LOAD UP THE BOX WITH THE CURRENT SEGMENT"
         BOXTYPE ← 0;                               "THERE IS ONE SEGMENT IN THE BOX"

         BXLEFT ← SXLEFT;                           "RECORD EXTREMITIES OF BOX"
         BXRIGHT ← SXRIGHT;
         BZLEFT ← SZLEFT;
         BZRIGHT ← SZRIGHT;
         BSEG1 ← SEG;                               "REMEMBER INDEX OF SEGMENT IN THE BOX"

         BZMIN ← BZLEFT;                            "COMPUTE NEAR AND FAR EDGES OF BOX"
         BZMAX ← BZRIGHT;
         IF BZMIN > BZMAX THEN BZMIN SWAP BZMAX;

         DIV ← SDIV;                                "REMEMBER DIVISION POINT"
         BFULL ← SFULL;                             "AND WHETHER THE SEGMENT SPANS THE SPAN"
END;

PROCEDURE XPANDBOX;
BEGIN ;                                             "EXPAND THE BOX TO INCLUDE THE LATEST SEGMENT"

         BSEG2 ← BSEG1; BSEG1 ← SEG;                "REMEMBER NEW SEGMENT INDEX"
         BOXTYPE ← 0;
         BOXCOUNT ← BOXCOUNT+1;                     "COUNT NUMBER OF SEGMENTS IN BOX"

         IF SDIV < DIV THEN DIV ← SDIV;             "REMEMBER LEFTMOST DIVISION POINT"

         IF SXLEFT < BXLEFT THEN BXLEFT ← SXLEFT;   "NOW EXPAND THE LEFT,RIGHT,FAR, AND NEAR EDGES OF
         IF SXRIGHT > BXRIGHT THEN BXRIGHT ← SXRIGHT;    THE BOX IF NECESSARY TO FIT THE NEW SEGMENT"

         IF SZLEFT < BZMIN THEN BZMIN ← SZLEFT;
         IF SZRIGHT < BZMIN THEN BZMIN ← SZRIGHT;
         IF SZLEFT > BZMAX THEN BZMAX ← SZLEFT;
         IF SZRIGHT > BZMAX THEN BZMAX ← SZRIGHT
END;

REAL PROCEDURE BZINT (REAL X);
RETURN (IF BXRIGHT = BXLEFT THEN BZLEFT ELSE
        BZLEFT+(BZRIGHT-BZLEFT)*(X-BXLEFT)/(BXRIGHT-BXLEFT));

REAL PROCEDURE ZINT (REAL X);
RETURN (IF SXRIGHT = SXLEFT THEN SZLEFT ELSE
        SZLEFT+(SZRIGHT-SZLEFT)*(X-SXLEFT)/(SXRIGHT-SXLEFT));
```

```
PROCEDURE LOOKER;
BEGIN   ;                        "NOW PROCESS A SEGMENT WITH RESPECT TO THE CURRENT BOX"
                                 "1. COMPUTE THE EXTREMITIES OF THE SEGMENT INSIDE THE SPAN"

    SXLEFT ← XLEFT[SEG]; SZLEFT ← ZLEFT[SEG];    "PICK UP VALUES FROM SEGMENT DESCRIPTOR"
    SXRIGHT ← XRIGHT[SEG]; SZRIGHT ← ZRIGHT[SEG];

    SFULL ← TRUE;

    IF SXLEFT > SPANLEFT THEN SFULL ← FALSE ELSE BEGIN
        SZLEFT ← ZINT(SPANLEFT);
        SXLEFT ← SPANLEFT
        END;

    IF SXRIGHT < SPANRIGHT THEN SFULL ← FALSE ELSE BEGIN
        SZRIGHT ← ZINT(SPANRIGHT);
        SXRIGHT ← SPANRIGHT
        END;

                                 "NOW COMPUTE THE LEFT-MOST ENDPOINT OF THE SEGMENT INSIDE
                                 THE SPAN. THIS IS USED TO SUBDIVIDE THE SPAN IF NECESSARY"

    SDIV ← IF SXLEFT LEQ SPANLEFT THEN SXRIGHT ELSE SXLEFT;

                                 "2. LOOK AT PRESENT VALUE OF BOXCOUNT TO DECIDE WHAT TO DO"

    IF BOXCOUNT = 0 THEN BEGIN   "BOXCOUNT = 0"
        LOADBOX
    END ELSE
    IF BOXCOUNT = 1 THEN BEGIN   "BOXCOUNT = 1"

                                 "IF THE BOX CONTAINS A SEGMENT WHICH
                                 HIDES THIS ONE, REJECT THIS ONE"

        IF BXLEFT LEQ SXLEFT AND BXRIGHT GEQ SXRIGHT
            AND BZINT(SXLEFT) LEQ SZLEFT AND BZINT(SXRIGHT) LEQ SZRIGHT THEN RETURN;

                                 "IF THIS IS A SEGMENT WHICH HIDES
                                 THE BOX, THEN MAKE THIS THE BOX"

        IF SXLEFT LEQ BXLEFT AND SXRIGHT GEQ BXRIGHT
            AND ZINT(BXLEFT) LEQ BZLEFT AND ZINT(BXRIGHT) LEQ BZRIGHT THEN LOADBOX ELSE

                                 "IF BOTH ARE FULL, WE CAN INTERSECT
                                 THE SEGMENTS TO FIND THE IMPLIED EDGE."
        IF SFULL AND BFULL THEN BEGIN "INTERSECT" REAL TEMP;
            TEMP ← BXLEFT + (BXRIGHT-BXLEFT)*(SZLEFT-BZLEFT)/
                            (BZRIGHT-BZLEFT-SZRIGHT+SZLEFT);
            XPANDBOX;            "NOW INCREASE BOX SIZE"
            BOXTYPE ← 1;         "SAY THAT IT IS A COMPUTED INTERSECTION"
            DIV ← TEMP;          "RECORD POSITION OF IMPLIED EDGE"

            IF BZLEFT < SZLEFT THEN BSEG1 SWAP BSEG2;
                                 "BSEG1 IS ALWAYS VISIBLE AT THE LEFT"

            END "INTERSECT" ELSE
        BEGIN "TOO COMPLICATED"
            XPANDBOX
        END

    END "BOXCOUNT = 1" ELSE
```

```
IF BOXCOUNT > 1 THEN BEGIN "BOXCOUNT > 1";
    "IF MORE THAN ONE ELEMENT ALREADY THEN EITHER:
        1. THIS SEGMENT HIDES THE WHOLE BOX, IN WHICH CASE BOX ← THIS SEGMENT
        2. IF THE BOX HIDES THE SEGMENT, RETURN — DO NOTHING
        3. THE BOX INTERSECTS THIS SEGMENT — INCLUDE IN BOX";

    IF SXLEFT LEQ BXLEFT AND SXRIGHT GEQ BXRIGHT
        AND SZLEFT LEQ BZMIN AND SZRIGHT LEQ BZMIN THEN LOADBOX

    ELSE IF BXLEFT LEQ SXLEFT AND BXRIGHT GEQ SXRIGHT AND
            BZMAX LEQ SZLEFT AND BZMAX LEQ SZRIGHT THEN RETURN

    ELSE XPANDBOX

    END "BOXCOUNT > 1";

END "LOOKER";
```

COMMENT
✳ ✳

T H E   T H I N K E R

✳ ✳

THE THINKER SUBROUTINE DECIDES WHETHER THE PRESENT SAMPLE SPAN (SPANLEFT TO SPANRIGHT) CONTAINS
SEGMENTS WHICH ARE SIMPLE ENOUGH TO DISPLAY, BASED ON INFORMATION COMPUTED BY THE LOOKER. THE
SUBROUTINE RETURNS TRUE IF THE SITUATION WAS SIMPLE AND AS A SIDE-EFFECT, IT HAS CALLED FOR ENOUGH
INFORMATION ABOUT THE VISIBLE SEGMENTS TO BE SAVED THAT A DISPLAY CAN BE GENERATED FOR THIS
SCAN-LINE.

THE THINKER USES A SUBROUTINE, STOREPIC, TO RECORD DISPLAY DATA IN AN ARRAY. STOREPIC TAKES TWO
ARGUMENTS, THE XS POSITION AT WHICH THE SEGMENT STARTS, AND THE INDEX OF THE THE VISIBLE SEGMENT.
IF THIS INDEX IS 0, THEN THIS SECTION OF THE SCAN-LINE IS BLANK. STOREPIC RECORDS A COLLECTION OF
PAIRS:

```
X1 ... SEGMENT NUMBER
X2 ... SEGMENT NUMBER
X3 ... SEGMENT NUMBER
```

THESE ARE USED, AT THE END OF THE SCAN-LINE, TO CREATE SHADING COMMANDS FOR THIS SCAN-LINE.

THE RECORDSAMPLE ROUTINE IS CONCERNED WITH THE COLLECTION OF SAMPLE POINTS FOR THE TRAVERSE OF THE
NEXT SCAN-LINE. A SAMPLE POINT IS RETAINED IF A SPAN EDGE CORRESPONDS TO THE EDGE OF THE VISIBLE
SEGMENT. SAMPLE POINTS ARE RECORDED IN A LIST. SAMFST POINTS TO THE FIRST ENTRY IN THE LIST, SAMLST
TO THE LAST. SAMLINK IS AN ARRAY OF PONTERS. SAMX IS THE X-VALUE OF THE SAMPLE POINT.

RECORDSAMPLE TAKES THREE ARGUMENTS, A 'LEFT' FLAG, AND A 'RIGHT' FLAG. IF THE 'LEFT'
FLAG IS 1, THE LEFT EDGE OF THE SEGMENT WILL BE CONSIDERED AS A CANDIDATE FOR A SAMPLE POINT. IT
MUST IN ADDITION LIE BETWEEN SPANLEFT-1 AND SPANLEFT. IF THE 'RIGHT' FLAG IS 1, THE RIGHT EDGE IS
CONSIDERED AS A CANDIDATE. IT MUST ALSO LIE BETWEEN SPANRIGHT AND SPANRIGHT+1. THE VARIABLE
LASTSAMP IS USED TO BE SURE WE DO NOT INCLUDE AS A 'LEFT' SAMPLE THE SAME POINT WE INCLUDED AS A
'RIGHT' SAMPLE ON THE PREVIOUS SPAN.

```
## SAFER INTEGER ARRAY SAMLINK[1:MAXSEG*2];
## SAFER INTEGER ARRAY SAMX   [1:MAXSEG*2];

## INTEGER SAMFST,SAMLST,SAMPLE,SAMFRE,IMPLIEDLEFT;
## REAL LASTUSED,LASTSAMP;

## PROCEDURE PUTSAMPLE (REAL X);            "PUT A SAMPLE IN THE SAMPLE LIST FOR NEXT SCAN-LINE"
## BEGIN ;
##   I ← SAMFRE;                            "GET A FREE SAMPLE BLOCK"
##   SAMFRE ← SAMLINK[I];                   "AND FIX UP FREE-STORAGE"
##   IF SAMLST THEN SAMLINK[SAMLST] ← I ELSE SAMFST ← I;  "MAKE CHAIN"
##   SAMLST ← I;                            "LAST SAMPLE TO BE RECORDED"
##   SAMX[I] ← X;                           "RECORD X POSITION OF SAMPLE POINT"
## END;

## PROCEDURE RECORDSAMPLE (INTEGER SEG,LEFT,RIGHT);   "PERHAPS RECORD A SAMPLE POINT IN THE SAMPLE LIST"
## BEGIN ;

##   IF LEFT AND IMPLIEDLEFT AND XLEFT[SEG] LEQ SPANLEFT AND SEG = POLYSEGMENT[IMPLIEDLEFT] MOD 10000 THEN BEGIN
##                                             "THE SEGMENT IS PART OF AN IMPLIED EDGE
##                                              WHICH IS THE LEFT SAMPLE POINT--
##                                              RETAIN THE IMPLIED EDGE AS A SAMPLE POINT"

##     PUTSAMPLE (XLEFT[IMPLIEDLEFT]+DXLEFT[IMPLIEDLEFT]);
##     IMPLIEDLEFT ← 0;                        "THE IMPLIED EDGE SEEMS TO HAVE FURNISHED A GOOD SAMPLE"

##   END;

##   IF LEFT AND YLEFT[SEG] < -1 AND (LEFT = -1 OR SPANLEFT-1 < XLEFT[SEG] LEQ SPANLEFT) THEN BEGIN  "LEFT EDGE"
##     IF SAMLST = 0 OR LASTSAMP NEQ SPANLEFT-1 OR LEFT = -1 THEN BEGIN
##       PUTSAMPLE (XLEFT[SEG]+DXLEFT[SEG]);
##       LASTSAMP ← SPANLEFT-1

##     END

##   END;

##   IF RIGHT AND YRIGHT[SEG] < -1 AND SPANRIGHT LEQ XRIGHT[SEG] < SPANRIGHT+1 THEN BEGIN  "RIGHT EDGE"
##     PUTSAMPLE(XRIGHT[SEG]+DXRIGHT[SEG]);
##     LASTSAMP ← SPANRIGHT

##   END

## END;
```

```
PROCEDURE STOREPIC (REAL X; INTEGER SEGMENT);
BEGIN;
                                "FIRST CHECK TO SEE IF WE ARE JUST ADDING MORE TO THE
                                 LAST SEGMENT RECORDED AS VISIBLE"

    IF SEGCNT = 0 OR SEGMENT NEQ LASTSEGMENT THEN BEGIN
            SEGCNT ← SEGCNT+1;         "THIS INDEXES XI..POLY PAIRS"
            LASTSEGMENT ← SEGMENT;     "REMEMBER WHO IS VISIBLE"
    END;

    VISPOS[SEGCNT] ← X;               "RECORD THE X POSITION OF THE START OF THE SEGMENT"
    VISSEG[SEGCNT] ← LASTSEGMENT;     "AND RECORD THE SEGMENT INDEX"

END;

BOOLEAN PROCEDURE THINKER;
BEGIN;

    IF BOXCOUNT = 0 THEN BEGIN "NOTHING VISIBLE"
            STOREPIC (SPANRIGHT,0);   "GENERATE DISPLAY OF 'BLANK'"
            RETURN (TRUE);            "DISPLAY GENERATED; DO NOT SUBDIVIDE"
    END;
    IF BOXCOUNT = 1 THEN BEGIN "ONLY 1 SEGMENT -- DISPLAY DIRECTLY"
                                      "FIRST CHECK TO SEE IF BLANK TO LEFT OF BOX"
            IF BXLEFT NEQ SPANLEFT THEN STOREPIC (BXLEFT,0);
                                      "NOW SHOW THE VISIBLE SEGMENT"
            STOREPIC (BXRIGHT,BSEG1);
                                      "AND CHECK TO SEE IF BLANK TO RIGHT OF BOX"
            IF BXRIGHT NEQ SPANRIGHT THEN STOREPIC (SPANRIGHT,0);

##          RECORDSAMPLE (BSEG1,1,1); "RECORD BOTH EDGES OF SEGMENT IF APPLICABLE"
            RETURN (TRUE);            "DISPLAY GENERATED"
    END;
    IF BOXTYPE = 1 THEN BEGIN "INTERSECTING PLANES CASE"
                                      "THE PLANES INTERSECT AT DIV
                                       --FIRST OUTPUT THIS SEGMENT, THEN MAKE AN IMPLIED
                                       EDGE IF NEEDED, THEN OUTPUT SECOND SEGMENT."

                                      "FIRST SEGMENT"
##          STOREPIC (DIV,BSEG1);
##          RECORDSAMPLE (BSEG1,1,0); "CONSIDER LEFT EDGE AS SAMPLE"

##                                    "NOW LOOK IN LIST OF IMPLIED EDGES LEFT OVER FROM LAST
##                                     TIME.  IF WE FIND IT, WE NOW HAVE ENOUGH INFORMATION
##                                     TO DEAD-RECKON THE EDGE.  FILL IN THAT INFORMATION"

##          SEGSAM ← BSEG1*10000+BSEG2;
##          SEG ← IMPLST;             "LOOK FOR THIS PAIR OF SEGMENTS"
##          PREVIOUS ← 0;             "LOOK IN IMPLIED LIST"
##          WHILE SEG DO BEGIN
##                  IF SEGSAM = POLYSEGMENT[SEG] THEN DONE;  "FOUND IT"
##                  PREVIOUS ← SEG;
##                  SEG ← XSORTRIGHT[SEG];   "LOOK FARTHER DOWN LIST"
            END;
```

```
##  IF SEG THEN BEGIN "FOUND A PREVIOUS ONE"
##                                      "NOW TAKE IT OUT OF IMPLIED EDGE LIST"
##      IF PREVIOUS THEN XSORTRIGHT[PREVIOUS] ← XSORTRIGHT[SEG] ELSE
##          IMPLST ← XSORTRIGHT[SEG];
##
##      DXLEFT[SEG] ← DIV-XLEFT[SEG];      "NOW FILL IN THE DXLEFT PART OF THE SEGMENT BLOCK"
##      XLEFT[SEG] ← DIV;                  "WHERE WE ARE NOW"
##
##      IF 1 LEQ XLEFT[SEG]+DXLEFT[SEG] LEQ XRESOLUTION THEN
##      BEGIN "IMPLIED EDGE WILL BE WITHIN BOUNDS ON NEXT SCAN-LINE"
##          PUTINXSORT(SEG);
##          RECORDSAMPLE (SEG,-1,0);       "PUT IN SAMPLE LIST WITHOUT FAIL"
##      END ELSE RETBLOCK (SEG)
##  END "FOUND A PREVIOUS ONE" ELSE
##  BEGIN "DETECTED NEW IMPLIED EDGE"
##      J ← GETBLOCK;
##
##      POLYSEGMENT[J] ← SEGSAM;      "REMEMBER THE TWO SEGMENTS WHICH CAUSED THE IMPLIED EDGE"
##                                   "NOW FIND THE EARLIEST THAT EITHER SEGMENT WILL EXIT"
##
##      I ← YLEFT[BSEG1];
##      IF I ∨ YRIGHT[BSEG1] THEN I ← YRIGHT[BSEG1];
##      IF I ∨ YLEFT[BSEG2] THEN I ← YLEFT[BSEG2];
##      IF I ∨ YRIGHT[BSEG2] THEN I ← YRIGHT[BSEG2];
##
##      YLEFT[J] ← I;                "IMPLIED EDGE DEFINITELY ENDS HERE"
##      POLYGON[J] ← 0;              "INDICATION THAT THIS IS AN IMPLIED EDGE"
##      XLEFT[J] ← DIV;              "X LOCATION OF IMPLIED EDGE"
##      XSORTRIGHT[J] ← IMPLST2;     "PUT ON NEW IMPLIED EDGE LIST"
##      IMPLST2 ← J
##  END "DETECTED NEW IMPLIED EDGE";
##
##  STOREPIC (SPANRIGHT,BSEG2);      "RECORD OTHER VISIBLE PIECE"
##  RECORDSAMPLE (BSEG2,0,1);        "CONSIDER THE RIGHT EDGE"
    RETURN (TRUE);                   "WE HAVE PROCESSED THE SPAN"

    END "INTERSECTING PLANES CASE";

    IF SPANLEFT = SPANRIGHT THEN BEGIN "MUST NOT SUBDIVIDE FURTHER"
        "THERE IS STILL COMPLEXITY INSIDE THIS SPAN,
        BUT FURTHER SUBDIVISIONS ARE USELESS BECAUSE
        THE RESOLUTION OF THE CRT WILL NOT BE ABLE
        TO DISPLAY THE OUTPUT.   THE EFFECT OF
        FAILING TO SUBDIVIDE HERE IS SIMPLY THAT
        THE SEGMENT VISIBLE TO THE LEFT OF THIS TINY
        SPAN WILL ALSO BE VISIBLE IN THIS SPAN"

        RETURN (TRUE)

    END;

    RETURN (FALSE);                  "UNABLE TO MAKE A DECISION -- MUST SUBDIVIDE"

    END;
```

```
COMMENT
* * * * * * * * * * * * * * * * * * * * * * * * * * * * * * * * * * * * * * * * * * * * * * * * * *

                          C O N T R O L L E R

* * * * * * * * * * * * * * * * * * * * * * * * * * * * * * * * * * * * * * * * * * * * * * * * * *
;

PROCEDURE HIDDEN;
BEGIN "ELIMINATE"                         "FIRST INITIALIZE SEGMENT FREE STORAGE LISTS"

      FOR I ← 1 STEP 1 UNTIL MAXSEG-1 DO ACTIVE[I] ← I+1;
      FREELIST ← 1;

 ##   FOR I ← 1 STEP 1 UNTIL MAXSEG*2-1 DO SAMLINK[I] ← I+1;
 ##   SAMFRE ← 1;

BEGIN "HIDDEN-LINE INITIALIZATION"        "NO IMPLIED EDGES AT THE START"
 ##   IMPLST ← IMPLST2 ← 0;

      SEGFST ← 0;                         "XSORT LIST IS INITIALLY NULL"

      PTR ← EDGELIST;                     "LOOK AT EVERY EDGE IN THE LIST"
      WHILE PTR DO BEGIN
            NEXT ← ENTERLIST[PTR];        "THIS IS THE NEXT EDGE TO LOOK AT"
                                          "PREPARE TO SORT THE EDGE INTO THE YENTER LISTS"
                                          DO NOT INCLUDE THE EDGE IF NEITHER POLYGON IT
                                          BOUNDS IS VISIBLE (SHAD = 0)"

            IF (P1[PTR] AND SHAD[P1[PTR]]) OR (P2[PTR] AND SHAD[P2[PTR]]) THEN
               BEGIN "SORT INTO YENTER"
                     J ← V1[PTR]; K ← V2[PTR];   "ENDPOINTS OF EDGE"
                     IF YS[J] > YS[K] THEN BEGIN "REARRANGE SO THAT VERTEX 1 IS ALWAYS LOWER"
                         V1[PTR] SWAP V2[PTR];
                         J ← K
                     END;
                     I ← YS[J] + .999999999 ;   "COMPUTE FIRST SCAN LINE ON WHICH IT IS VISIBLE"
                     IF 1 LEQ I LEQ YRESOLUTION THEN BEGIN
                         ENTERLIST[PTR] ← YENTER[I];
                         YENTER[I] ← PTR;   "CHAIN ON LIST"
                     END ELSE OUTSTR ("EDGE OUT OF BOUNDS")
               END "SORT INTO YENTER";

            PTR ← NEXT
      END;

      SHOWINIT;                           "NOW INITIALIZE THE DISPLAY-GENERATING CODE"

END "HIDDEN-LINE INITIALIZATION";
```

```
FOR Y ← 1 STEP 1 UNTIL YRESOLUTION DO BEGIN "DISPLAY GENERATION"

BEGIN "PROCESSING BEFORE STEPPING ACROSS SCAN-LINE"

        POLYCHANGELIST ← -1;              "NO CHANGING POLYGONS AT THE START"

                                          "1. UPDATE XLEFT,XRIGHT,ZLEFT,ZRIGHT FOR
                                              ALL SEGMENTS IN XSORT LIST.
                                              ALSO ADD 1 TO YLEFT, YRIGHT. IF EITHER
                                              OF THESE BECOMES = 0, MARK THE POLYGON AS CHANGING"

SEG ← SEGFST;                             "XSORT LIST"
WHILE SEG DO BEGIN
        XLEFT[SEG] ← XLEFT[SEG]+DXLEFT[SEG];
        XRIGHT[SEG] ← XRIGHT[SEG]+DXRIGHT[SEG];
        ZLEFT[SEG] ← ZLEFT[SEG]+DZLEFT[SEG];
        ZRIGHT[SEG] ← ZRIGHT[SEG]+DZRIGHT[SEG];

        Y1 ← YLEFT[SEG] ← YLEFT[SEG]+1;
        Y2 ← YRIGHT[SEG] ← YRIGHT[SEG]+1;

        IF Y1 = 0 OR Y2 = 0 THEN BEGIN    "MARK THE POLYGON AS CHANGING"
                PTR ← POLYGON[SEG];       "INDEX OF POLYGON"
                IF PTR = 0 THEN BEGIN     "IMPLIED EDGE ENDED"
                        REMOVEFROMXSORT(SEG);
                        RETBLOCK (SEG)
                        END ELSE
                IF NOT CHANGING[PTR] THEN BEGIN
                        CHANGING[PTR] ← POLYCHANGELIST;
                        POLYCHANGELIST ← PTR
                        END
                END;
        SEG ← XSORTRIGHT[SEG];            "LOOK AT NEXT ON XSORT LIST"

        END;
```

```
"2. INSERT NEW SEGMENTS INTO THE SYSTEM.  THEY MUST
 BE INSERTED INTO THE POLYSEGMENT LISTS. FOR EACH
 POLYGON AND INTO THE XSORT LIST.  BE CAREFUL
 ABOUT THE ORDERING OF THE POLYSEGMENT LIST."

"GET POINTER TO LIST OF ENTERING EDGES"

"GET ENDPOINTS OF EDGE"
"AND GET INTEGER PARTS OF Y VALUES"
"NEGATIVE NUMBER OF SCAN-LINES TO GO"
"DELTA Y WITH FULL SIGNIFICANCE"

"COMPUTE THE COEFFICIENTS OF THE LINEAR DIFFERENCE
 EQUATIONS FOR THIS EDGE."

"CORRECT FOR PARTIAL LINE"

"LOOK AT BOTH POLYGONS BORDERING THIS EDGE"

"NOW MARK THIS POLYGON AS CHANGING"


PTR ← YENTER[Y];
WHILE PTR DO BEGIN "ENTERING EDGES"

VV1 ← V1[PTR]; VV2 ← V2[PTR];
YFIRST ← YS[VV1]; YLAST ← YS[VV2];
DELY ← YFIRST - YLAST;
REALDELY ← YS[VV2]-YS[VV1];

IF DELY < 0 THEN BEGIN "MAKE SEGMENTS FOR THIS EDGE"

XSLOPE ← (XS[VV2]-XS[VV1])/REALDELY;
  XFIRST ← XS[VV1]+XSLOPE*(Y-YS[VV1]);
ZSLOPE ← (ZS[VV2]-ZS[VV1])/REALDELY;
  ZFIRST ← ZS[VV1]+ZSLOPE*(Y-YS[VV1]);

FOR P ← P1[PTR],P2[PTR] DO BEGIN "LOOK AT BOTH POLYGONS
IF P THEN BEGIN "A REAL POLYGON"

   IF NOT CHANGING[P] THEN BEGIN
        CHANGING[P] ← POLYCHANGELIST;
        POLYCHANGELIST ← P

    END;
```

```
"LOOK AT ALL SEGMENTS OF THIS POLYGON. WE
 WANT TO INSERT THE NEW EDGE IN THE CORRECT
 LEFT-RIGHT SPOT"

SEG ← SEGMENTLIST[P];
PREVIOUS ← 0; J ← 3;
WHILE SEG DO BEGIN "LOOK AT SEGMENTS"
        "FOR EACH SEGMENT, THE NEW EDGE IS EITHER
        1. TO THE LEFT OF A VALID SEGMENT:
            GO AHEAD AND INSERT THE SEGMENT HERE
        2. SPLITTING A VALID SEGMENT:
            SPLIT OLD SEGMENT, INSERT NEW ONE
        3. TO THE RIGHT OF A VALID SEGMENT:
            GO ON LOOKING FARTHER DOWN THE LIST

        THERE ARE FOUR CONDITIONS WE WILL COMPUTE:
        1. XS OF NEW EDGE < XS OF LEFT EDGE OF SEGMENT
        2. XS OF NEW EDGE < XS OF RIGHT EDGE OF SEGMENT
        3. LEFT EDGE OF SEGMENT VALID (YEND1 < 0)
        4. RIGHT EDGE OF SEGMENT VALID (YEND2 < 0)"

TE1 ← (XFIRST < XLEFT[SEG]) OR (XFIRST = XLEFT[SEG] AND XSLOPE < DXLEFT[SEG]);
TE2 ← (XFIRST < XRIGHT[SEG]) OR (XFIRST = XRIGHT[SEG] AND XSLOPE < DXRIGHT[SEG]);
Y1 ← (YLEFT[SEG] < 0); Y2 ← (YRIGHT[SEG] < 0);

I ← -(TE1*8)-(TE2*4)-(Y1*2)-(Y2);

        "NOW, BASED ON THE NUMBER FORMED FROM THE CONDITIONS,
        DECIDE WHAT TO DO"

J ← CASE I OF (3,3,3,3,3,1,3,2,3,3,1,0,3,1,1,1);

IF J NEQ 3 THEN DONE;   "DONE; OTHERWISE LOOK FARTHER DOWN LIST"

    PREVIOUS ← SEG;
    SEG ← POLYSEGMENT[SEG]
END "LOOK AT SEGMENTS";
```

568

```
IF J = 1 OR J = 3 THEN BEGIN  "INSERT NEW SEGMENT BETWEEN 'PREVIOUS' AND 'SEG'"
        SEG1 ← GETBLOCK;                    "GET A NEW BLOCK"
        POLYGON[SEG1] ← P;                  "RECORD POLYGON NUMBER"
        XLEFT[SEG1] ← XFIRST;
        DXLEFT[SEG1] ← XSLOPE;
        ZLEFT[SEG1] ← ZFIRST;
        DZLEFT[SEG1] ← ZSLOPE;
        YLEFT[SEG1] ← DELY;
        PUTINXSORT(SEG1);                   "PUTS SEGMENT IN THE XSORT LIST"
        IF PREVIOUS THEN POLYSEGMENT[PREVIOUS] ← SEG1 ELSE SEGMENTLIST[P] ← SEG1;
        POLYSEGMENT[SEG1] ← SEG

END ELSE
BEGIN  "SPLIT THE SEGMENT"
        SEG1 ← GETBLOCK;                    "GET A NEW ONE"
        POLYGON[SEG1] ← P;                  "RECORD POLYGON NUMBER"
        XLEFT[SEG1] ← XLEFT[SEG];           "COPY LEFT PARTS"
        DXLEFT[SEG1] ← DXLEFT[SEG];
        ZLEFT[SEG1] ← ZLEFT[SEG];
        DZLEFT[SEG1] ← DZLEFT[SEG];
        YLEFT[SEG1] ← YLEFT[SEG];
        YLEFT[SEG1] ← 0;                    "NO LONGER VALID EDGE"

        XRIGHT[SEG1] ← XFIRST;
        DXRIGHT[SEG1] ← XSLOPE;
        ZRIGHT[SEG1] ← ZFIRST;
        DZRIGHT[SEG1] ← ZSLOPE;
        YRIGHT[SEG1] ← DELY;
        PUTINXSORT (SEG1);
        IF PREVIOUS THEN POLYSEGMENT[PREVIOUS] ← SEG; PREVIOUS ← SEG1
        POLYSEGMENT[SEG1] ← SEG; PREVIOUS ← SEG1

END  "SPLIT THE SEGMENT"
END  "A REAL POLYGON"
END  "LOOK AT BOTH POLYGONS BORDERING THIS EDGE"
END  "MAKE SEGMENTS FOR THIS EDGE";

PTR ← ENTERLIST[PTR];                       "GET NEXT EDGE TO ENTER ON THIS SCAN-LINE"
END "ENTERING EDGES";
```

```
"NOW USE THE VALUE OF J COMPUTED IN THE
 LOOP TO DECIDE HOW TO FIX UP THE LIST"
```

```
"NUMBER OF SCAN-LINES TO GO"
```

```
"NOW INCLUDE NEW EDGE"
```

```
                                   "3.  COMPACT THE SEGMENTLIST'S OF EVERY CHANGING POLYGON"

WHILE POLYCHANGELIST NEQ -1 DO BEGIN "PROCESS A CHANGING POLYGON"
      P ← POLYCHANGELIST;  POLYCHANGELIST ← CHANGING[P];
      CHANGING[P] ← 0;                "THIS POLYGON NO LONGER CHANGING"

      PREVIOUS ← 0;
      SEG ← SEGMENTLIST[P];           "GET LIST OF SEGMENTS FOR THIS POLYGON"
      WHILE SEG DO BEGIN "TRANSFORM THE LIST"
            Y1 ← YLEFT[SEG];  Y2 ← YRIGHT[SEG];
            IF Y1 < 0 AND Y2 < 0 THEN BEGIN "SCAN FARTHER"
                  PREVIOUS ← SEG;
                  SEG ← POLYSEGMENT[SEG]

            END ELSE
            IF Y1 = 0 AND Y2 = 0 THEN BEGIN "REMOVE THIS SEGMENT"
                  I ← POLYSEGMENT[SEG];
                  IF PREVIOUS THEN POLYSEGMENT[PREVIOUS] ← I ELSE SEGMENTLIST[P] ← I;
                  REMOVEFROMXSORT (SEG);   "TAKE OUT OF XSORT LIST"
                  RETBLOCK (SEG);          "AND RETURN TO FREE STORAGE"
                  SEG ← I;                 "NOW LOOK AT NEXT ONE"

            END ELSE
            IF Y1 = 0 AND Y2 < 0 THEN BEGIN "MOVE RIGHT TO LEFT"
                  YLEFT[SEG] ← YRIGHT[SEG];  YRIGHT[SEG] ← 0;
                  XLEFT[SEG] ← XRIGHT[SEG];
                  DXLEFT[SEG] ← DXRIGHT[SEG];
                  ZLEFT[SEG] ← ZRIGHT[SEG];
                  DZLEFT[SEG] ← DZRIGHT[SEG]

            END ELSE
            BEGIN "RIGHT SIDE IS EMPTY -- LOOK AT NEXT SEGMENT"
                  NEXT ← POLYSEGMENT[SEG];
                  IF NEXT = 0 THEN OUTSTR("NEXT ERROR");
                  IF YLEFT[NEXT] < 0 THEN BEGIN "MOVE NEXT'S LEFT TO MY RIGHT"
                        YRIGHT[SEG] ← YLEFT[NEXT];  YLEFT[NEXT] ← 0;
                        XRIGHT[SEG] ← XLEFT[NEXT];
                        DXRIGHT[SEG] ← DXLEFT[NEXT];
                        ZRIGHT[SEG] ← ZLEFT[NEXT];
                        DZRIGHT[SEG] ← DZLEFT[NEXT]

                  END ELSE
                  IF YRIGHT[NEXT] < 0 THEN BEGIN "MOVE NEXT'S RIGHT TO MY RIGHT"
                        YRIGHT[SEG] ← YRIGHT[NEXT];  YRIGHT[NEXT] ← 0;
                        XRIGHT[SEG] ← XRIGHT[NEXT];
                        DXRIGHT[SEG] ← DXRIGHT[NEXT];
                        ZRIGHT[SEG] ← ZRIGHT[NEXT];
                        DZRIGHT[SEG] ← DZRIGHT[NEXT]

                  END ELSE
                  BEGIN "DELETE 'NEXT' ENTIRELY"
                        POLYSEGMENT[SEG] ← POLYSEGMENT[NEXT];
                        REMOVEFROMXSORT (NEXT);
                        RETBLOCK (NEXT)

                  END
            END "RIGHT SIDE IS EMPTY -- LOOK AT NEXT SEGMENT"
      END "TRANSFORM THE LIST"
END "PROCESS A CHANGING POLYGON";
```

```
DO BEGIN "SORT THE XSORT LIST"                "4. RESORT THE XSORT LIST"
    CHANGE ← FALSE;
    SEG ← SEGFST;
    WHILE SEG DO BEGIN "RAMBLE DOWN LIST"
        I ← XSORTRIGHT[SEG];          "NEXT SEGMENT TO RIGHT"
        IF I = 0 THEN DONE;
        IF XLEFT[SEG] > XLEFT[I] THEN BEGIN "SWAP"
            CHANGE ← TRUE;
            IF (K ← XSORTLEFT[SEG]) THEN XSORTRIGHT[K] ← I;
            XSORTLEFT[I] ← K;
            XSORTLEFT[SEG] ← I;
            IF (K ← XSORTRIGHT[I]) THEN XSORTLEFT[K] ← SEG;
            XSORTRIGHT[SEG] ← K;
            XSORTRIGHT[I] ← SEG;
            IF SEGFST = SEG THEN SEGFST ← I
            END "SWAP" ELSE SEG ← XSORTRIGHT[SEG]
        END "RAMBLE DOWN LIST"
END "SORT THE XSORT LIST" UNTIL NOT CHANGE


END "PROCESSING BEFORE STEPPING ACROSS SCAN-LINE";


    SEGACT ← 0;                                "NO ACTIVE SEGMENTS YET"
    SEGCNT ← 0;                                "NO OUTPUT DISPLAY SEGMENTS YET"

#                                              "ANY IMPLIED EDGES NOT INCLUDED IN XSORT
####                                            LIST DURING THE PREVIOUS SCAN-LINE SHOULD BE DELETED"
######  WHILE IMPLST DO BEGIN IMPLST ← XSORTRIGHT[J ← IMPLST];
#####           RETBLOCK (J)
#####           END;

#####   IMPLST ← IMPLST2;                      "IMPLIED EDGES GENERATED ON PREVIOUS
#####                                           SCAN-LINE WILL BE IN IMPLST"
#####   IMPLST2 ← 0;

        CURSEG ← SEGFST;                       "POINTER INTO XSORT LIST"

        SPANRIGHT ← 0;                         "START AT VERY LEFT OF SCREEN"

##      SAMPLE ← SAMFST;                       "SAMPLE LIST IN WHICH TO LOOK THIS TIME"
###     SAMLST ← 0;                            "AND INITIALIZE THE LIST FOR NEXT SCAN LINE"
##      LASTUSED ← 0;                          "LAST SAMPLE POINT EXTRACTED FROM LIST"
```

```
DO BEGIN "SAMPLE ACROSS THE SCAN LINE"

        SPANLEFT ← SPANRIGHT+1;

##                                      "IF WE DO NOT USE SCAN-LINE COHERERNCE SPEEDUPS, THEN THE
                                         STATEMENT 'SPANRIGHT ← XRESOLUTION;' SHOULD GO HERE"

##      IF SPANLEFT > LASTUSED THEN BEGIN "MOVED TO RIGHT OF LAST SAMPLE SPAN"
##      IF SAMPLE THEN BEGIN "MORE SAMPLES LEFT"
##          SPANRIGHT ← SAMX[SAMPLE]; "THIS IS THE NEW RIGHT SAMPLE POINT"
##          IX ← SAMPLE; SAMPLE ← SAMLINK[SAMPLE]; "GET NEXT SAMPLE FOR NEXT TIME"
##          SAMLINK[IX] ← SAMFRE; SAMFRE ← IX; "RETURN SAMPLE BLOCK TO FREE LIST"
##          LASTUSED ← SPANRIGHT; "AND RECORD LAST SAMPLE TAKEN"
##      END ELSE SPANRIGHT ← XRESOLUTION
##      END ELSE SPANRIGHT ← LASTUSED;

##      IMPLIEDLEFT ← 0;                "LEFT EDGE IS NOT AN IMPLIED EDGE"

WHILE TRUE DO BEGIN "SUBDIVIDE SAMPLE SPACE"

        BOXCOUNT ← 0;                   "INITIALIZE THE LOOKER"
        SEGOUT ← 0;                     "LIST OF SEGMENTS WHICH EXIT ON THIS SAMPLE SPAN"
        PREVIOUS ← 0;
        SEG ← SEGACT;                   "FIRST LOOK AT ALL ACTIVE SEGMENTS"

        WHILE SEG DO BEGIN "ACTIVE SEGMENTS"

            NEXT ← ACTIVE[SEG];         "CDR DOWN ACTIVE SEGMENT LIST"
            IF XRIGHT[SEG] < SPANRIGHT+1 THEN BEGIN "IT ENDS IN THIS SPAN"

                IF PREVIOUS THEN ACTIVE[PREVIOUS] ← NEXT ELSE SEGACT ← NEXT;
                ACTIVE[SEG] ← SEGOUT; "PUT IN SEGOUT LIST"
                IF SEGOUT = 0 THEN SEGLO ← SEG; "REMEMBER END OF SEGOUT LIST"
                SEGOUT ← SEG;

                                        "NOW CALL THE LOOKER FOR THIS SEGMENT"
            END "IT ENDS IN THIS SPAN" ELSE BEGIN
                IF XRIGHT[SEG] GEQ SPANLEFT THEN LOOKER;
                IF XLEFT[SEG] LEQ SPANRIGHT THEN LOOKER;
                PREVIOUS ← SEG

            END;
            SEG ← NEXT
        END "ACTIVE SEGMENTS";
```

```
WHILE CURSEG DO BEGIN "XSORT SEGMENTS"

    SEG ← CURSEG;
    IF XLEFT[SEG] > SPANRIGHT THEN DONE;
                                "DONE WITH XSORTED SEGMENTS BECAUSE THIS
                                 NEXT SEGMENT IS TO THE RIGHT OF OUR SAMPLE SPAN.
                                 IT WILL BE LOOKED AT WHEN THIS SPAN HAS BEEN
                                 SUCCESSFULLY PROCESSED, AND WE MOVE THE
                                 SAMPLE SPAN TO THE RIGHT"

    CURSEG ← XSORTRIGHT[CURSEG];

    IF POLYGON[SEG] = 0 THEN BEGIN "IMPLIED EDGE BLOCK"
        IF 1 LEQ XLEFT[SEG] LEQ XRESOLUTION AND POLYSEGMENT[SEG]%10000 = LASTSEGMENT THEN
        BEGIN "OK TO KEEP IMPLIED EDGE"
                                "THE IMPLIED EDGE IS STILL WITHIN X-BOUNDS OF THE SCREEN, AND
                                 THE SEGMENT VISIBLE TO THE LEFT OF THIS SAMPLE IS THE ONE
                                 WHICH IS THE LEFT-PARTNER OF THE IMPLIED EDGE"
            IMPLIEDLEFT ← SEG; "MERELY FLAG THAT THIS SPAN BOUNDED BY AN IMPLIED EDGE"
        END ELSE BEGIN "THROW OUT IMPLIED EDGE"
            REMOVEFROMXSORT(SEG);
            RETBLOCK (SEG);
        END

    END "IMPLIED EDGE BLOCK" ELSE
    BEGIN "REAL EDGE BLOCK"
                                "CHECK TO SEE IF POLYGON HAS FOLDED ON ITSELF OR REALLY
                                 ISN'T VISIBLE YET (A SINGLE POINT)"

        IF XLEFT[SEG]+1 < XRIGHT[SEG] THEN BEGIN "LOOKS GOOD"
        IF XRIGHT[SEG] < SPANRIGHT+1 THEN BEGIN "EXITS THIS SPAN"
            ACTIVE[SEG] ← SEGOUT;
            IF SEGOUT = 0 THEN SEGLO ← SEG;
            SEGOUT ← SEG; "PUT IN SEGOUT LIST"
        END ELSE BEGIN
            ACTIVE[SEG] ← SEGACT;
            SEGACT ← SEG; "PUT IN ACTIVE SEGMENT LIST"
        END;
        LOOKER; "CALL THE LOOKER ON THIS SEGMENT"
        END "LOOKS GOOD"
    END "REAL EDGE BLOCK";
END "XSORT SEGMENTS";
```

##############

```
                                        "COME HERE AFTER THE LOOKER HAS PROCESSED ALL SEGMENTS
                                        WHICH LIE PARTLY OR WHOLLY WITHIN THE CURRENT
                                        SAMPLE SPAN.
                                        NOW CALL THE THINKER FOR THIS SPAN.  IF IT RETURNS
                                        'TRUE', WE ARE DONE WITH THIS SUBDIVISION, OTHERWISE
                                        WE MUST SUBDIVIDE FURTHER."

        IF THINKER THEN DONE;

                                        "APPEND SEGOUT LIST INTO SEGACT LIST"
        IF SEGOUT THEN BEGIN ACTIVE[SEGLO] ← SEGACT; SEGACT ← SEGOUT END;

                                        "NOW DECIDE HOW TO SUBDIVIDE"
                                        "GET INTEGER LOCATION OF DIVISION POINT"
        I ← DIV;
        IF I GEQ SPANRIGHT THEN BEGIN "DIVIDE AT MIDPOINT"
            I ← (SPANLEFT+SPANRIGHT)/2;
            SPANRIGHT ← I
        END ELSE SPANRIGHT ← I;

    END "SUBDIVIDE SAMPLE SPACE";

##  IF IMPLIEDLEFT THEN BEGIN ;       "AN IMPLIED EDGE IS THE LEFT SAMPLE POINT, BUT
##                                     THE EDGE DISAPPEARED ON THIS SCAN LINE"
##      REMOVEFROMXSORT(IMPLIEDLEFT);
##      RETBLOCK(IMPLIEDLEFT)
##  END

    END "SAMPLE ACROSS THE SCAN LINE" UNTIL SPANRIGHT = XRESOLUTION;

##                                     "TERMINATE THE SAMPLE LIST FOR THIS LAST SCAN-LINE"
##  IF SAMLST THEN SAMLINK[SAMLST] ← 0 ELSE SAMFST ← 0;

    SHOW;                              "SHOW WHATEVER VISIBLE SEGMENTS GENERATED"

END "DISPLAY GENERATION";

SHOWCLOSE;                             "ALL DONE GENERATING DISPLAY FRAME"

END "ELIMINATE";
```

```
COMMENT
* * * * * * * * * * * * * * * * * * * * * * * * * * * * * * * * * * * * * * * * * * * * * * * *
*                                                                                           *
*              R E A D   I N   D A T A   S T R U C T U R E                                   *
*                                                                                           *
* * * * * * * * * * * * * * * * * * * * * * * * * * * * * * * * * * * * * * * * * * * * * * * *


PROCEDURE READINSCENE;
BEGIN INTEGER POINTNUM,EDGENUM,POLYNUM,I,J,K,L; REAL R;
    DEFINE G(X) = "ARRYIN(1,R,1); X ← R;";

    "PROCEDURE TO FILL UP DATA STRUCTURE FROM A FILE
     WITH COORDINATE INFORMATION, ETC. IN IT. THE DETAILS
     OF THIS PROCEDURE ARE NOT IMPORTANT, AND ARE LISTED HERE
     JUST SO THAT WE CAN BE SURE THE PROGRAM WORKS."

    OUTSTR ("FILE NAME:");
    OPEN (1,"DSK",'13,2,0,200,L,L);
    LOOKUP (1,INCHWL,L);

    G (POINTNUM);        "READ NUMBER OF POINTS IN FILE"
    G (EDGENUM);         "NUMBER OF EDGES"
    G (POLYNUM);         "NUMBER OF POLYGONS"

    IF POINTNUM > MAXPOINT OR EDGENUM > MAXEDGE OR POLYNUM > MAXPOLY THEN
        OUTSTR ("TOO MUCH DATA"&'15&'12)   "INPUT WAS FOR 1024X1024 SCREEN SIZE"
    ELSE BEGIN

    FOR I ← 1 STEP 1 UNTIL POINTNUM DO BEGIN
        G(XS[I]); G(YS[I]); G(ZS[I]);
        XS[I] ← XS[I]/2; YS[I] ← YS[I]/2;
    END;

    EDGELIST ← EDGENUM;
    FOR I ← 1 STEP 1 UNTIL EDGENUM DO BEGIN    "CHAIN LIST OF EDGES"
        ENTERLIST[I] ← I-1;                    "GET THE TWO POINT INDICES"
        G(V1[I]); G(V2[I]);
    END;

    FOR I ← 1 STEP 1 UNTIL POLYNUM DO BEGIN    "GET SHADING INTENSITY FOR THIS POLYGON"
        G(SHAD[I]);                            "GET NUMBER OF EDGES FOR THIS POLYGON"
        G(J);
        WHILE J DO BEGIN                       "GET AN EDGE NUMBER"
            G(K);
            IF P1[K] = 0 THEN P1[K] ← I ELSE P2[K] ← I;
            J ← J-1;
        END

    END
    END
    RELEASE (1)
END "READINSCENE";


READINSCENE;      "EXECUTE THE PROGRAM!"
HIDDEN;           "READ DATA STRUCTURE"
END;              "GENERATE PICTURE"
```

THE LEDEEN CHARACTER RECOGNIZER

The Ledeen character recognizer is concerned with processing strokes drawn by the user on a tablet, and deciding what character is represented by the strokes. The correspondence between characters and stroke-sets is made during *training* — the user draws the strokes representing a character, and has an opportunity to tell the recognizer what character was represented with the strokes. The recognizer augments the memory of stroke-sets to include the new information.

The recognizer itself is only concerned with characterizing stroke-sets. Other tasks, such as servicing interrupts from the tablet device, inking the screen to show the strokes drawn, etc. are left to other parts of the graphics system.

The input, then, to the character recognizer is a set of strokes; each stroke is a list of x, y points detected by the tablet. Usually, the graphics system which accumulated the stroke set establishes some conventions for the user's convenience. For example, how are we to know when the user has finished drawing the last stroke for this character? One adequate method is to wait for 1/2 second. If the user starts drawing again within that period, then he has another stroke for the character; otherwise the stroke set is complete, and is ready to be analyzed by the character recognizer.

We shall use a concrete example to describe the recognizer: the character 'D' has been drawn with two strokes: first a downward vertical stroke and then the curved stroke. Each stroke read in is put through the following computations:

1. Compute the minimum and maximum x and y coordinates visited by the stroke. This amounts to drawing a box around the stroke and recording the coordinates of the edges of the box. We will denote the numbers derived as *xmin, xmax, ymin,* and *ymax.*

2. Compute the center of the stroke: $xcenter \leftarrow (xmin + xmax)/2$, $ycenter \leftarrow (ymin + ymax)/2$. We then check quickly to see whether the stroke was a dot, a horizontal line, or a vertical line. The check for a dot is simply: is $(xmax - xmin) + (ymax - ymin) < \epsilon$, where ϵ is a parameter (say 8 units on a 1024 x 1024 tablet). The check for a vertical or horizontal line is basically a check on the aspect ratio of the box surrounding the stroke. For example, the stroke is considered horizontal if $(ymax - ymin) * aspect < (xmax - xmin)$, where *aspect* is a parameter (say 3). If the stroke is classified as a dot or horizontal or vertical, go directly to step 4. The first stroke of the example 'D' will be classified as a vertical stroke.

3. We now have the task of assigning a set of *properties* to each stroke. The stroke will be characterized by this property set, and recognition of characters will be performed by comparing property sets. The box which surrounds the stroke is divided into nine regions. Each region has a quadruple associated with it:

(1,1,0,0)	(0,1,0,0)	(0,0,0,0)
(1,1,0,1)	(0,1,0,1)	(0,0,0,1)
(1,1,1,1)	(0,1,1,1)	(0,0,1,1)

Thus, every point on the stroke has associated with it one of the 4-vectors. Furthermore, as the points in the stroke are looked at successively, we get a sequence of vectors. These are then reduced to a property as follows: create from the sequence a new one, in which the first element of the sequence is 8 times the vector for the first point on the stroke, and the subseqent elements show only *changes* in the original sequence. For example, if the sequence for the second stroke of the 'D' is:

(1,1,0,0) (1,1,0,0) (0,1,0,0) (0,1,0,0) (0,1,0,0) (0,0,0,0)
(0,0,0,0) (0,0,0,1) (0,0,0,1) (0,0,0,1) (0,0,1,1) (0,0,1,1)
(0,0,1,1) (0,1,1,1) (0,1,1,1) (0,1,1,1) (1,1,1,1) (1,1,1,1)

then the new sequence is:

(8,8,0,0) (0,0,0,0) (1,0,0,0) (0,0,0,0) (0,0,0,0) (0,1,0,0)
(0,0,0,0) (0,0,0,1) (0,0,0,0) (0,0,0,0) (0,0,1,0) (0,0,0,0)
(0,0,0,0) (0,1,0,0) (0,0,0,0) (0,0,0,0) (1,0,0,0) (0,0,0,0)

Notice that the computation of each vector of the sequence (for all but the first) is simply an exclusive-or of two adjacent vectors of the original sequence.

The *property vector* of this stroke is defined as the arithmetic sum of the vectors of this new set. The property vector thus records where the stroke started and how many times each internal boundary (2 vertical and 2 horizontal) of the box shown above was crossed. For example, the sum of the sequence above is: $(10,10,1,1)$. This vector represents four separate properties, P_1, P_2, P_3, and P_4. Thus the value of P_1 is 10, P_2 is 10, P_3 is 1, and P_4 is 1.

4. We are now in possession of four properties pertaining to each stroke drawn in. In the case of dots and horizontal or vertical lines, the properties are:

	P_1	P_2	P_3	P_4
Dot	0	8	0	8
Horizontal	9	9	0	8
Vertical	0	8	1	1

The reason for making dots, verticals and horizontals special cases is that normalization of these strokes to fit in the box described above would make the algorithm very sensitive to slightly wavy vertical or horizontal lines. The first stroke of the 'D' example is vertical, and is therefore assigned the property set (0,8,1,1). The property set for the second stroke is (10,10,1,1) as computed in step 3. We now assemble the properties of the two strokes, as follows:

Property	Stroke 1	Stroke 2	Centers
P_1	0	10	9
P_2	8	10	8
P_3	1	1	0
P_4	1	1	8

The last column is a set of properties based on the *centers* of each of the strokes, and is computed as follows: define a new box, similar to the one above, but which surrounds the whole character, not just one of the strokes. (This box is simply the smallest rectangle which includes all the boxes created for the individual strokes). Then, the center point of each stroke will have a property vector as defined by this box, and we can form a sequence of these vectors for the first, second, third, etc. stroke drawn in. The stroke centers for the example character 'D' have the following sequence:

$$(1,1,0,1) \ (0,1,0,1)$$

The sequence becomes a property sequence by multiplying the first vector by 8 and recording subsequent changes:

$$(8,8,0,8) \ (1,0,0,0)$$

The properties for this sequence are then the sums of the properties of the individual elements of the sequence: P_1 is 9, P_2 is 8, P_3 is 0, and P_4 is 8.

We now change our representation slightly, and choose to say that the character is represented by the sequence of numbers developed for each property (i.e. read across in the property/stroke table above). The sequence developed for P_1 above is simply 0,10,9; the sequence for P_2 is 8,10,8; etc. Each sequence has as many elements as the number of strokes, plus one.

5. Armed with the four property sequences, we interrogate the information we have saved about characters. For each property, we keep a list of sequences which have been computed for that property at some time. For example, P_1's list might look like:

    1,1,1
    1,0
    8,8
    1,1,0
    . . .

and so on. When the user is training the recognizer, this list is augmented whenever a new sequence for P_1 is found.

These sequences are associated with character codes simply by listing, for each sequence, a set of pairs (*character, weight*). The *character* entry is a code for the character represented, and the *weight* is a weighting factor used when making final decisions about which character was drawn in.

Suppose that the data structure had at least the following entries:

P_1 sequence: 0,10,9 ⇒ (D,3)
P_2 sequence: 8,10,8 ⇒ (D,3)
P_3 sequence: 1,1,0 ⇒ (A,4) (B,3) (D,3) (H,5)
P_4 sequence: 1,1,8 ⇒ (B,3) (D,3)

Given the four property sequences computed in step 4, we make a list of *candidates* as follows: the P_1 sequence is found in the list of recorded sequences, and each character and its weight are added to the candidate list. The other property sequences are also found; the candidates are listed and their weights summed. In addition a frequency count is kept, i.e. the number of times this character was retrieved from the above data structure (in other words, the number of terms in the sum):

    D   3+3+3+3=12   4
    A   4   1
    B   3+3=6   2
    H   5   1

The final decision about which character was drawn is made by examining the candidate list. The winning character is the one with the highest weight; the frequency count is used only to break ties.

The procedure for *training* the recognizer builds the data structure of property sequences, character codes, and weights. Below is the data structure actually built during a brief training session. The characters trained are A, B, C, D, E, F, G, H, I, U, V. Notice that U and V are not distinguishable. Notice also that in most cases, the sequences have very few candidates. Thus, the recognizer is very often quite sure about its decision about a character, simply because there may be only one candidate. In the structure below, sequences are always 9-vectors. That is, the property sequences are padded with trailing zeroes to make a 9-vector. For example, the P_4 sequence 1, 1, 8 from the example above becomes 1, 1, 8, 0, 0, 0, 0, 0, 0.

PROPERTY: 1

0	0	0	0	0	0	0	0	0	— (I,3)	
9	1	0	9	2	0	0	0	0	— (A,1)	
9	1	9	2	0	0	0	0	0	— (A,3)	
0	1	9	2	0	0	0	0	0	— (A,1)	
0	12	9	0	0	0	0	0	0	— (B,3)	
2	0	0	0	0	0	0	0	0	— (C,4)	(G,3)
0	10	9	0	0	0	0	0	0	— (D,3)	
2	9	1	0	0	0	0	0	0	— (E,3)	
2	0	9	1	0	0	0	0	0	— (E,1)	
1	9	0	0	0	0	0	0	0	— (F,2)	(J,3)
0	0	9	0	10	0	0	0	0	— (H,2)	
0	0	9	9	0	0	0	0	0	— (H,3)	
1	9	9	0	0	0	0	0	0	— (J,1)	
9	0	0	0	0	0	0	0	0	— (U,3)	(V,4)

PROPERTY: 2

0	0	0	0	0	0	0	0	0	—
9	1	8	9	1	0	0	0	0	— (A,1)
9	1	9	1	0	0	0	0	0	— (A,3)
8	1	9	1	0	0	0	0	0	— (A,1)
8	12	8	0	0	0	0	0	0	— (B,3)
2	0	0	0	0	0	0	0	0	— (C,4)
8	10	8	0	0	0	0	0	0	— (D,3)

8	0	0	0	0	0	0	0	0	−	(I,3)	
2	9	8	0	0	0	0	0	0	−	(E,3)	
2	8	9	10	0	0	0	0	0	−	(E,1)	
1	9	8	0	0	0	0	0	0	−	(F,2)	(J,3)
3	0	0	0	0	0	0	0	0	−	(G,3)	
8	8	9	8	10	0	0	0	0	−	(H,2)	
8	8	9	10	0	0	0	0	0	−	(H,3)	
1	9	9	0	0	0	0	0	0	−	(J,1)	
9	0	0	0	0	0	0	0	0	−	(U,3)	(V,4)

PROPERTY: 3

0	0	0	0	0	0	0	0	0	−				
1	1	0	0	2	0	0	0	0	−	(A,1)			
1	1	0	0	0	0	0	0	0	−	(A,4)	(B,3)	(D,3)	(H,5)
1	0	0	0	0	0	0	0	0	−	(C,4)	(I,3)	(E,3)	(F,2)	(J,1)
1	0	0	2	0	0	0	0	0	−	(E,1)			
2	0	0	0	0	0	0	0	0	−	(G,3)	(J,3)	(U,3)	(V,4)

PROPERTY: 4

0	0	0	0	0	0	0	0	0	−		
1	1	8	8	8	0	0	0	0	−	(A,1)	(H,2)
1	1	8	8	0	0	0	0	0	−	(A,4)	(H,3)
1	1	8	0	0	0	0	0	0	−	(B,3)	(D,3)
1	0	0	0	0	0	0	0	0	−	(C,4)	(I,3)	(G,3)
1	8	8	0	0	0	0	0	0	−	(E,3)	(F,2)
1	8	8	8	0	0	0	0	0	−	(E,1)	
1	8	9	0	0	0	0	0	0	−	(J,4)	
2	0	0	0	0	0	0	0	0	−	(U,3)	(V,4)

The training program is a fine example of an interactive graphics program. The user should be able to control the program with one input device, the tablet stylus. He draws several strokes; as he does so, the inking technique is used to show the strokes on the CRT screen. When the stroke-set is complete, the recognizer is called to try to recognize the character using whatever data structure has already been built. The program may then display to the user the results of the recognition: if no candidate characters were found, the recognizer declares it does not 'know' the character; if the final decision was close, the recognizer may say it 'thinks' it has made a correct recognition and display the character; if the final decision is overwhelming, it may be 'sure' of the identity of the character.

In any case, the user may wish to cause information about the character he just drew to be added to the data structure. If the recognizer correctly identified the character, he may use the 'yes' light-button to increase the weights associated with the recognition of the character from the stroke-set. If the recognizer failed to identify the character, the user may reply with the 'no' light-button which causes a menu of all possible characters to appear; he uses the stylus to point to the correct character. If the user decides that he does not want to change the data structure for this character, he can use the 'abort' light-button to ignore this character. This process is repeated until the recognizer achieves an acceptable identification rate. Then the data structure can be output, as in the list above, so that the training need not be repeated.

This particular training scheme only *increases* the weights associated with a property set. If a character is correctly recognized and the 'yes' response given, then four weights are increased, one for each of the four property sequences recorded for the character.

EXERCISES

1. Draw each letter of the alphabet as some stroke sequence and determine the properties for each letter. Which ones will be hard to distinguish? Can you specify drawing conventions which make all characters distinguishable (e.g. draw V with 2 strokes)? Can you suggest modifications to the algorithm which would distinguish all characters without resorting to inconvenient drawing conventions?

Although there is extensive literature devoted to display hardware, it offers few aids in selecting and testing a display system. This appendix attempts to provide some useful hints. A good overall strategy is to devote some time to pondering and designing critical software pieces of the display system before making a purchase decision. For example, if the instruction set of a display processor is deficient, it will preclude building structured display files which may be crucial to the application.

AIX.1 TYPE OF DISPLAY

A great variety of graphics systems is available. The majority may be organized, for purposes of performance evaluation, into classes according to the type of display device used:

1. Random Access CRT's
2. Direct View Storage Tubes, full-screen erase only

3. Silicon target tubes with selective erase
4. Raster-scan devices

The first decision is: how much information is to be displayed? Class 1 devices have fixed limits before refreshing produces flicker; the limit of classes 2 to 4 is the spatial resolution of the screen. The second question is: how often are display updates made and of what kind? Updates generally involve *erasing* old information and *posting* new. Class 1 devices permit high-speed updating at any time during a refresh cycle; the updates will appear during the next cycle. Erasing is extremely rapid. Interactive techniques like dragging, tracking, inking, etc. are quite easily implemented. The cost of erasure for classes 2 to 4 is very high (see Section 17.3.2). To give an example of an acute case, consider using a display to show lines of text, which 'scroll' up as new text is added at the bottom. With a class 1 display and an adequate display processor, scrolling is merely a matter of rearranging a few pointers. However, for class 2 to 4 devices, scrolling requires rewriting *every* text line on the screen in a new place.

AIX.2   SCREEN CHARACTERISTICS

The choice of screen size, phosphor type, and brightness should be determined according to the application for the display. These factors will affect viewing comfort, eye fatigue, and sharpness of the display image.

The brightness and contrast of the image are important for comfortable viewing. Brightness is governed by beam current, phosphor efficiency, and refresh rate. Typically, a brightness of 4 foot-Lamberts is adequate.

Contrast ratio is the ratio of the brightness of an illuminated spot to that of a dark spot (see Figure AIX-1). Reflected light and luminescence due to stray electrons contribute to illumination of a 'dark' spot. The stray electron problem occurs predominantly in DVST's: some flood electrons penetrate the charged grid even if it is negatively charged. A typical contrast ratio for a DVST is 4. Conventional CRT's have typical contrast ratios of 25. Reflected light is the largest contributing factor on these screens, because glass will reflect about 4% of incident illumination. The contrast ratio can be improved by reducing incident light (darkening the room) or by

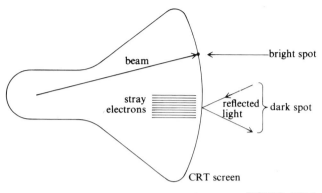

FIGURE AIX-1

reducing the reflection coefficient. One surprisingly good way of increasing contrast is to place a neutral-density filter in front of the CRT screen: reflected light will be attenuated twice, that generated by phosphor luminescence only once.

The speed of the phosphor should be matched to the application. If the phosphor is slow (400 ms decay time), moving displays will leave unpleasant after-images. Slow phosphors, however, permit longer refresh cycles, and hence more complicated flicker-free pictures. The use of certain kinds of fast phosphors may lead to eye fatigue — the eye responds to certain repetition frequencies.

The color of the phosphor may be important on aesthetic grounds. In addition, if the display is to be used in conjunction with color filters to produce high-quality color pictures, the color spectrum of the phosphor must have adequate power in all the filter frequencies.

AIX.3   RESOLUTION, PRECISON, AND REPEATABILITY

Every CRT display has two analog control systems whose performance affects the display: the deflection system and the beam current control system. The performance of these systems is measured partially by values for resolution, precision, and repeatability:

Resolution is a measure of the number of separately addressable positions on the coordinate grid. If a 10 inch display has 1023 addressable points along each axis, then the resolution of the deflection system is 1023/10 or 102.3 points per inch.

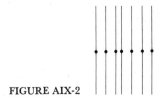

FIGURE AIX-2

Precision (or accuracy) is a measure of the linearity of addressable grid points. Ideally, a point at a certain address x should be $x*10/1023$ inches from the $x = 0$ line (for a 10 inch display, coordinates 0 to 1023). Precision is a measure of the distance from this ideal location to the actual location of a dot displayed at x. If the grid is uneven, we might see the pattern of Figure AIX-2.

Repeatability is a measure of the stability of the deflection system. We address the point (a,b) at intervals of minutes, hours, or days, and measure precisely the physical location of the dot on the CRT face. The repeatability is the maximum distance between any two measurements. Repeatability is a particular problem in class 3 displays, because the beam motions which are used for selective erasure must strike the screen at precisely the same spot as the beam motions that originally created the display, perhaps some minutes earlier.

A good display will have a resolution of 100 points/inch, a precision of 0.02 inch, and a repeatability of 0.02 inch. An excellent display will have a resolution of 400 points/inch, a precision of 0.007 inch, and a repeatability of 0.01 inch.

The *useful* resolution of a display is not the resolution of the deflection system. The size of a spot on the screen may be larger than the distance between grid points, in which case the spot size limits the resolution. The relation between spot size and deflection resolution is critical, and is described following a discussion of spot size measurements.

Quoted spot-size measurements are often unrealistically small. The illumination as a function of distance when a beam hits a phosphor-coated screen is shown in Figure AIX-3. Manufacturers usually use a 'shrinking raster' method to measure spot size. This method is roughly equivalent to the Rayleigh resolution criterion: the illumination from two spots, separated by a distance δ, as shown in Figure AIX-4, must sum in such a way that an interior local minimum occurs, as shown in Figure AIX-5. This condition corresponds roughly to $\delta = \Delta_1$ in Figure AIX-3, i.e. the 60% point on the illumination curve.

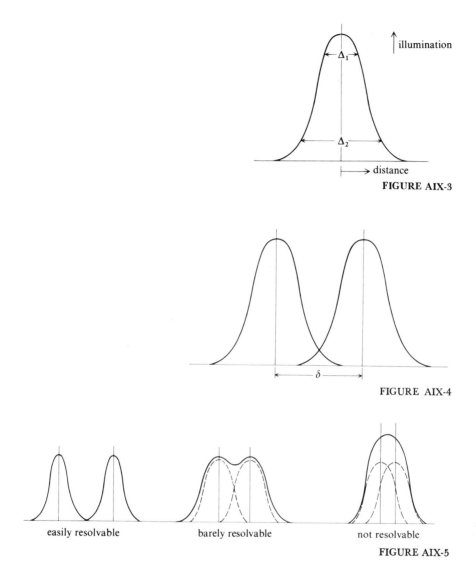

FIGURE AIX-3

FIGURE AIX-4

easily resolvable   barely resolvable   not resolvable

FIGURE AIX-5

However, if a vector is drawn with spots like this, the *subjective* width of the line is closer to $\delta = \Delta_2$. The subjective spot size Δ_2 is roughly twice the size of the spot size as measured with a shrinking raster (See Davis [65] for further discussion of CRT resolution measurements).

The situation is further complicated because reducing brightness reduces spot size. Manufacturers can arrange to cite almost any spot size merely by making measurements when the spot intensity is below a

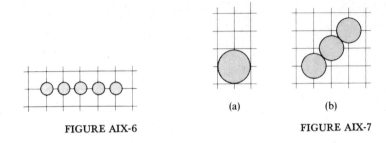

FIGURE AIX-6   (a)   (b)

                               FIGURE AIX-7

useable level. To be meaningful, the spot size should be measured when the contrast ratio is 25 or greater.

The relation between spot size and the resolution of the deflection system is important: the spot size should be about 1.4 times the grid spacing. If the spot size is smaller than the grid spacing, a line cannot be formed by a series of dots (see Figure AIX-6). If the spot size is much larger than 1.4 times the grid spacing, the resolution of the display will be limited to the spot size, as shown in Figure AIX-7a. If the *subjective* spot size is $\sqrt{2}$ times the grid spacing, then adjacent spots are observed as one line (see Figure AIX-7b). This relation is mandatory for displays that use digital vector generation.

The beam control circuitry is responsible for adjusting the brightness, or intensity, of the screen luminescence. Some displays may provide only 8 discrete intensities, some up to 1024. If continuous shading methods are to be used (see Section 14.5), at least 64 intensities are needed. The intensity settings should be adjusted so that emitted light energy varies logarithmically with the digital setting, thus permitting a wide dynamic range of intensities to be displayed. Control of beam current alone is often insufficient to produce a wide range of light energics, in which case the drawing rate (dwell time) must be slowed in order to achieve large energies emitted from a single point. In fact, a display with only 1 intensity level can be used to produce excellent shaded pictures by repeatedly intensifying a dot n times to generate an intensity n.

AIX.4   SPEED

The speed with which conventional CRT displays can paint dots and lines limits the complexity of the image that can be drawn. The rate of drawing depends on (1) the speed of the deflection system, including

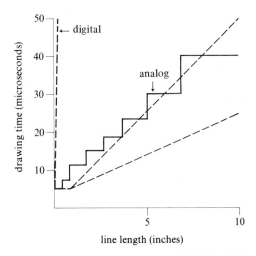

drawing time (microseconds)

line length (inches)

digital-to-analog conversion and amplifier settling times, (2) the speed of the vector generator (or other processing) in the display hardware, and (3) the speed with which display commands can be delivered from the main computer.

The type of deflection system, electrostatic or electromagnetic, is the largest determinant of deflection speed. Electrostatic systems are very fast (3 microsecond full-screen motion), but tend to have other bad effects (see focus distortion, below) and to be costly. Magnetic deflection systems usually require 30 microseconds for a full-screen beam motion. Smaller motions take smaller times (see Section 3.4). When a manufacturer states a settling time, care should be taken to ascertain the precision to which the deflection system has settled after that time, and the size of motion used to make the settling time measurement.

Speeds of vector generators differ greatly. In general, analog generators are faster but more expensive than digital generators. Figure AIX-8 shows the relation between drawing time and line length for several hypothetical vector generators. The line-generation times include delays introduced by the deflection system. A judgement of adequate speed depends on the application: a display which can draw fewer than 200 5-inch lines in a 30 millisecond refresh cycle is inadequate for most purposes.

The time required to deliver a command from the computer to the display hardware may have to be added to the time required to draw each line. Some displays overlap fetching a command with drawing the vector for the previous command, or with deflection settling times. One system even uses pipeline methods to attain high speeds [84].

AIX.5   SPECIAL FACILITIES

Displays often offer a variety of special options: character generators, transformation hardware, special input devices, etc. Very often the special-purpose hardware is well-suited to one particular task, but may offer limited or no flexibility to experiment with that task.

Character generators are very often essential in a display system. If the display is to be used as an alphanumeric terminal, 30 lines of 80 to 100 characters is minimum reasonable capacity; the total capacity of the screen should not be below 2000 characters. The character set should be large enough for the application: lower case characters are always a good idea; special symbols (e.g. Greek letters, mathematical symbols) may also be needed. Programmable character sets are an excellent way to maximize the flexibility of a character generator. The final observation about character generation is that characters should be legible, should not appear to swim on the display, and should be aesthetically pleasing. There are two main kinds of character generators, those which use a dot matrix and those which draw a collection of lines or strokes to form a character. Stroke character generators are usually fast, but legibility may depend on careful adjustment of analog circuitry. Dot matrix generators draw legible characters at medium speeds, but large characters plotted with dots are often ugly.

Transformation hardware is offered by some manufacturers to aid in scaling, rotating, clipping, scissoring, and generating perspective: the hardware is used as a pre-processor for every line or dot presented to the display. Alternatively, the transformations may be performed with software before delivering data to the display. The cost of the special hardware is justified only if high speed is required. Many displays have discrete scaling ability (enlargement factors of 1, 2, 4, or 8) which is virtually useless except for character size control. Rotation ability is implemented either with analog circuits (multiplying digital-to-analog converters) or with digital elements. The digital method usually has more resolution and precision than the analog, and the numerical results of the computation can be returned to the computer for further computation, if desired. Clipping is a more versatile method of eliminating off-screen objects than scissoring because vector-generation time is not devoted to off-screen objects and, more importantly, because the windowing transformation allows clipping against an arbitrary window and displaying in an arbitrary viewport.

Some displays provide aids to generating depth cues in images of three-dimensional scenes. The effectiveness of each kind of cue may depend on the application. The kinetic depth effect requires rotation hardware for three-dimensional data. Stereoscopy can be implemented inexpensively with optical aids [153]. Intensity modulation for showing depth is itself quite inexpensive, but is usually installed only on expensive high-performance displays. Perspective generation requires implementing the division by depth in digital or analog hardware. Some displays rely on the kinetic depth effect and intensity modulation to provide depth cues, and omit the perspective division.

Various special features can be built into vector generators: dashed lines, curved lines, etc. These often do not precisely meet the needs of an application. For example, a triangle generated with dashed lines might be as shown in Figure AIX-9.

Curve drawing hardware should be examined with particular care. It will always be limited to a certain class of curves, so complex curves must be constructed from simple ones. If the mathematical formulation of the curves is inconvenient for the application, the curve generator may be useless.

Special input devices are always offered with display hardware: light pens, tables, mice, function buttons, etc. Unfortunately, the principle of separation of input and output functions is often violated by these devices: a cursor will always appear on the screen in a position corresponding to the stylus position. The input data and the output effect must be separable. Stylus device interfaces often lack flexibility: two kinds of inputs are required, attentions when the pen switch opens or closes or when the pen is moved a certain distance, and direct readings of coordinates on demand from the main computer. Light pens are not recommended because they are very difficult to program and to use.

AIX.6   DISPLAY PROCESSORS

One of the most crucial aspects of a display's performance is its ability to allow simple display file compilation. This depends on the design of the display processor instruction set, on the way in which the main computer controls the display processor, and on the way in which the display addresses main memory. Required readings on this subject are [193, 302, 84].

AIX.6.1   INSTRUCTION SET

1. It is a good idea to design a display file compiler for the particular display processor under consideration. This effort may uncover deficiencies in the instruction set that affect double-buffering, creation of segmented display files, etc. It will give some idea of the size of display files required for typical images.

2. All instructions should be fixed-length, consisting of an op-code, possible modifiers, and a data field. The data field may contain immediate data for use by the processor, or may specify the address of the data. Conditional and looping instructions in the display processor offer a generality that is hard to use with display file compiler techniques.

3. The interpretation of an instruction bit-pattern should be unique. Thus the effect of an instruction should not depend on instructions executed previously. This is essential for debugging display files.

4. The instruction set must include adequate instructions for constructing a segmented display file, the simplest of which is the jump instruction. This observation does not apply to display channels, for these cause the main computer to be interrupted at the end of each segment; software is then used to decide which segment is to be displayed next.

5. The instruction set should optionally include subroutine handling instructions for tracing a structured display file or graphical data structure. The best subroutine mechanism is the one that uses a push-down stack for saving the state of the display registers. Again, displays connected to the computer via channels do not have addressable instructions; the main computer can be used to interpret subroutine calls, to maintain a stack, etc.

AIX.6.2   CONTROL BY THE COMPUTER

1. The host computer must be able to start the display processor at a particular spot, to stop it instantaneously, and to read into the computer enough information to later restart the display in exactly the same state. This is essential if the main computer occasionally intervenes during image refreshing in order to perform other chores such as tracking the light-pen or displaying output messages on the screen.

2. We should consider what attention conditions inside the display processor will interrupt the host computer, whether some essential attentions fail to cause interrupts, and whether there is sufficient information available to the computer to take correct action when each interrupt is generated.

3. We should consider whether the display is capable of fitting easily into the environment provided by the operating system of the main computer. Problems often encountered in time-sharing systems are: ensuring that a memory space for the display file is never swapped or paged, providing attention information to the user with low overhead (tablet points may be reported as often as every 250 microseconds), giving the display user high priority for processing input attentions which require rapid updates to the display. For examples of two very different interfaces to time-sharing systems, see [215] and [205].

4. Correct interface design permits diagnostic programs run in the main computer to detect many display processor malfunctions. This may necessitate an 'execute a single display instruction' command to the display processor.

AIX.6.3   ADDRESSING

1. The addressing mechanism used by a program which creates a display file should probably also be used by the display processor when executing the display file. If the operating system uses paging or bounds-relocation registers, so should the display.

2. Writing into memory by the display should be protected with hardware against destroying sensitive parts of the operating system or

user program. If a stack is used to save all return addresses and internal status, then this protection is simply a limit to the size of the stack.

3. If one display processor serves several users by driving several CRT's, the display processor must facilitate cycling among the several display files. If one display file is extremely long or has illegal instructions in it, the other displays should be unaffected. The ability to serve multiple users requires that the entire state of the display processor can be saved and later restored when it is time to resume a user's display file.

4. Displays that have buffer memory separate from the main computer memory belong to the category of remote terminals, because the display and the application program cannot reference a common graphical data structure or structured display file.

AIX.7   PERFORMANCE TESTS

The analog control circuitry and beam-control structures of a CRT may introduce distortions into the image being displayed. Below is a list of the more important distortions, of the evaluations of some causes of each, and of tests which will demonstrate the amount of distortion. Display hardware has adjustments for some of these distortions, and it is very instructive to ask for a demonstration of the alignment process to show (1) the range of adjustment available to cure a particular distortion, (2) the adjustment process itself, its documentation, its simplicity or complexity, (3) whether the various adjustments interact so severely that problems cannot be cured without creating others, and (4) whether the alignment procedure always yields an acceptable result.

AIX.7.1   PIN-CUSHION AND BARREL DISTORTION

This distortion is most pronounced in CRT's with conventional electrostatic deflection systems. The asymmetry of the deflection plates is the chief cause of the distortion. The distortion can be measured by drawing a large square on the screen, and determining the amount of curvature of the lines displayed (see Figure AIX-10).

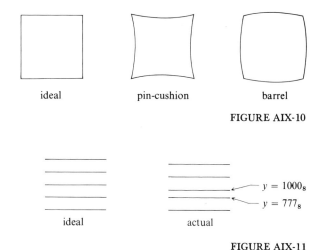

ideal   pin-cushion   barrel

FIGURE AIX-10

$y = 1000_8$

$y = 777_8$

ideal   actual

FIGURE AIX-11

AIX.7.2   FOCUS DISTORTION

The spot size may grow as the beam is deflected to off-axis points. This problem is usually severe in electrostatic deflection CRT's. Accurate testing requires the ability to measure spot size, but if the problem is pronounced, the larger off-axis spot sizes will be clearly visible.

AIX.7.3   LINEARITY

Most digital-to-analog converters require careful design to insure that the spacing between successive grid locations is constant. This can be tested by displaying a set of closely-spaced parallel lines, and observing the evenness (see Figure AIX-11). The non-linearities appear when high-order bits of the deflection coordinate change. For example, the spacing between $y = 777$ (octal) and $y = 1000$ may be different from that between $y = 1000$ and $y = 1001$.

AIX.7.4   DEFLECTION NOISE

Noise is often introduced into deflection signals by the 60 Hz power line. This is a particular problem of magnetic deflection systems because magnetic fields generated by power supply transformers and fan motors may affect the beam position. A test for 60 Hz noise

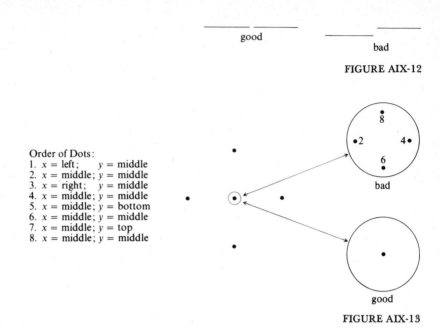

Order of Dots:
1. $x = $ left; $y = $ middle
2. $x = $ middle; $y = $ middle
3. $x = $ right; $y = $ middle
4. $x = $ middle; $y = $ middle
5. $x = $ middle; $y = $ bottom
6. $x = $ middle; $y = $ middle
7. $x = $ middle; $y = $ top
8. $x = $ middle; $y = $ middle

good

bad

FIGURE AIX-12

bad

good

FIGURE AIX-13

involves creating a display file with approximately 16.4 millisecond refresh cycle time. Presence of noise will cause the display to 'swim.' Another test uses the following pattern: a horizontal line is displayed, followed by invisible vectors which consume α milliseconds, then another horizontal line calculated to meet the first one is displayed (see Figure AIX-12). The time period α is varied over ranges of 4 to 16 milliseconds. The point of this test is to display the first line when the 60 Hz power voltage is maximally positive, and the second when it is maximally negative.

AIX.7.5   HYSTERESIS

Hysteresis is a distortion introduced by residual magnetic fields in the deflection yokes and metal surrounding the CRT. If the magnetic deflection current remains high for a period of time, and then returns to zero, the pieces of the yoke may become partially magnetized, and thus continue to deflect the beam slightly. A test for this effect consists of a pattern which plots dots at high deflection, perhaps arranging to

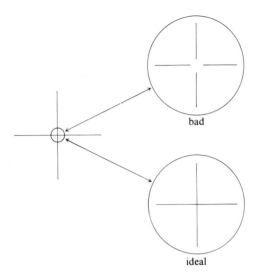

FIGURE AIX-14

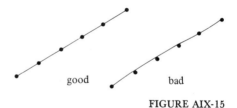

FIGURE AIX-15

leave the high deflection in effect for some time, followed by dots at the center of the screen (see Figure AIX-13).

Another version of this test is to draw lines between points 1 & 2, 3 & 4, 5 & 6, and 7 & 8, as shown in Figure AIX-14.

AIX.7.6   LINE STRAIGHTNESS

Analog vector generators often have difficulty generating precisely straight lines. Two tests will show the amount of non-linearity. Generate a pseudo-random line, and a sequence of dots computed to lie on the line (see Figure AIX-15). This test should be performed for lines of many lengths and orientations. In addition, we can generate three lines known to intersect, as in Figure AIX-16.

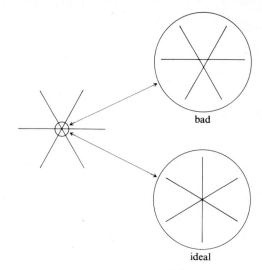

bad

ideal

FIGURE AIX-16

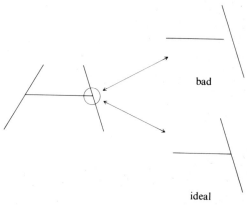

bad

ideal

FIGURE AIX-17

AIX.7.7   LINE ENDPOINT ACCURACY

It is vitally important that line endpoint positions are accurate. Analog vector generators must be designed so that beam current is turned on and off at the proper endpoints of the line. If the timing is incorrect, or if deflection lags vary, the line will not begin or end at its proper endpoints. To test for this, we can generate pseudo-random H patterns as shown in Figure AIX-17. It is important to try this test for lines of many lengths.

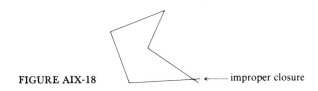

FIGURE AIX-18 ←—————improper closure

AIX.7.8   LINE BRIGHTNESS

Appropriate intensity correction is required for all vector generators. If this correction is not adequate, lines of different lengths or slopes may have different brightnesses. One test is to fill the screen with pseudo-random lines, and observe the result. A better one is to generate a rubber-band line and observe intensity variations as the line's length and direction change.

AIX.7.9   CLOSURE OF RELATIVE VECTORS

Cumulative errors in relative vector generation can be detected by drawing a closed polygon using only relative vectoring. The display may show an open polygon (see Figure AIX-18). This unpleasantness was prominent in early analog vector generators, and stimulated improvements such as feedback which are part of most modern displays.

INDEX